THINGS CHINESE

Things Chinese

J. Dyer Ball
With an introduction by
H.J. Lethbridge

HONG KONG
OXFORD UNIVERSITY PRESS
OXFORD NEW YORK TOKYO

Oxford University Press

Oxford London New York Toronto
Kuala Lumpur Singapore Hong Kong Tokyo
Delhi Bombay Calcutta Madras Karachi
Nairobi Dar es Salaam Cape Town
Melbourne Auckland

and associated companies in
Beirut Berlin Ibadan Mexico City Nicosia

First published by Sampson Low, London, 1892
Fifth edition published by Kelly and Walsh, Limited, Shanghai 1925
This edition reprinted, with permission and with the addition of an introduction, by Oxford University Press, 1982
Second impression 1984

ISBN 0 19 581525 4

Cover design by Colin Tillyer
Printed in Hong Kong by Nordica Printing Co
Published by Oxford University Press, Warwick House, Hong Kong

INTRODUCTION

ANY visitor to Hong Kong will be struck by the co-existence within the Colony of the old and the new, the traditional and the modern, once he moves outside the central business district of Hong Kong Island, where the great banks and hotels are located, or outside Tsim Sha Tsui, Kowloon, a vast commercial emporium. The distinctive features of 'Chinese' Hong Kong will become visibly, vividly clear in the New Territories or on the islands, such as Lantau, Lamma or Cheung Chau. He will then discover elements of traditional China in the small fishing villages and village communities that abound there, though in diminishing numbers. It is there, especially, that the visitor will be able to observe rituals and ceremonies that are rooted in the past, for Taoist, Buddhist and Confucian beliefs and practices have not been eradicated, only modified, by the march of modernization. But even in the urbanized areas a discerning visitor will still discover temples, for example, and other types of traditional Chinese architecture. The Man Mo Temple in Hollywood Road, a road well-known to the seeker after Chinese antiques and gewgaws, remains inviolate, a symbol of the older Hong Kong and its social order. The city has not been entirely remade by the local speculator and developer.

Dyer Ball's *Things Chinese* is an excellent reference book for anyone curious about the Chinese past and Chinese civilization. There is much of great interest in the book. A reading of the entries under 'Adoption', 'Ancestor-worship', 'Betrothal', 'Birth', 'Divorce', 'Marriage', 'Mourning' and the 'Status of Women' should provide the reader with a sound knowledge of the traditional patterns of Chinese marriage and the family and allow him to assess the changes that have occurred in that institution in modern times. A dip almost anywhere would be rewarding, for there are long articles on such subjects as agriculture and architecture, on the geography, history and government of China. Even the pastimes of the Chinese are not neglected: Dyer Ball's interest in the humble and commonplace, in the Chinese workaday world, makes this a worthwhile book in an age where social and economic history have become a dominating interest for the historian and the common reader. It is one of the best books of its type.

A number of reference books on China have appeared over the years: few have survived. One of the better known is probably Samuel Couling's *Encyclopaedia Sinica*, published in Shanghai in 1917. Samuel Couling (1859-1922) spent 25 years as a missionary in Shantung, North China. He spoke several Chinese dialects fluently, and as editor and proprietor of *The New China Review* was regarded as a sinologue of sound repute. Colonel Valentine Rodolphe Burkhardt (1884-1967), the author of *Chinese Creeds and Customs*, issued in three volumes (1953-8), also has his admirers, especially in Hong Kong where he spent his last years in residence at Stanley. Like Couling, Burkhardt worked for many years in China (1923-39) and garnered not only much homely but also much recondite information about the Chinese.

James Dyer Ball, the compiler of *Things Chinese, or Notes Connected With China*, a dictionary or encyclopaedia of Chinese culture, society and history, is in many ways superior to both. Dyer Ball (he is usually referred to as such) also had a firm grasp of many Chinese dialects — Cantonese and Hakka in particular — and an extensive knowledge of the anthropology and sociology of China, a society he had observed first as a youth in Canton and later from over 35 years of service with the Hong Kong Government. *Things Chinese* is a fine book, stuffed full of strange and exotic facts, as well as much practical and useful information. It is a pleasure to introduce the work to a new generation of readers.

Dyer Ball was born in Canton in December 1847, the son of the Reverend Dyer Ball, a Protestant missionary doctor in that city, which was the site of much evangelical activity at that time. He was educated at home, in Canton, and then at King's College, London, where the study of Chinese had already taken root, and at University College, Liverpool. It is not clear why he returned to the Far East so soon after completing his education in England but it was probably for family reasons, since his parents were still resident in South China and engaged in missionary work. He married in 1885 a young woman from (as one would expect) his own social and religious milieu — Gertrude Jane, the second daughter of the Reverend Samuel Joseph Smith, a China missionary. They — Dyer Ball and his wife — had two sons and a daughter, all born in Hong Kong.

His first occupation was that of master at the Government Central School, Hong Kong. This establishment had been opened in 1861 as a non-religious (secular) school for Chinese boys. In 1866 it was thrown open to pupils of all races. Then, in 1878, he was appointed Acting Assistant Interpreter in the Supreme Court because of his mastery of Cantonese and other local dialects. He was lucky to have been given a post in the Hong Kong Civil Service. This came about from the decision taken in 1875 by Sir Richard MacDonnell, the Governor, to stop the recruitment of Cadet Officers (administrative officers as we would now term them) directly from England. Sir Richard was worried about the government's finances and wished to retrench spending. By raising the pay of the lower government clerkships, he hoped to attract talented local Europeans into the Hong Kong Civil Service, and thus save money. Dyer Ball was one of the few to be recruited in this anomalous way. The Colonial Office in London disallowed the Governor's innovation and later the Cadet Scheme, which had been established in 1861, was re-introduced.

Dyer Ball remained in the Hong Kong Civil Service for over 35 years, retiring in January 1909. He moved slowly, grade by grade, up the ladder of preferment until he became Registrar-General and Protector of the Chinese (after 1913 called the Secretary for Chinese Affairs), an acting appointment. It should be noted that the position of Registrar-General was normally given to a person with special knowledge of the Chinese and of their languages. Dyer Ball was admirably suited for this role. It is likely that if he had been a Cadet Officer, he would have achieved it sooner.

There have been a great number of British civil servants who have taken to the craft of writing or editorship — Edmund Gosse (British Museum Library), Austin Dobson (Board of Trade), Humbert Wolfe (Ministry of Labour), Harold Nicolson (Foreign Office), Edward Marsh (Colonial Office), to name but a few — and many in the Colonial Service, such as Leonard Woolf, Frank Swettenham, Victor Purcell and Arthur Grimble. Before 1939, the British and Colonial Civil Services did not make unconscionable demands on members of the administrative grade; hours were gentlemanly and amateurism not frowned upon. A love of literature, writing or scholarship did not debar an official from a successful career. Dyer Ball, it is clear, was one. Over the years he wrote a large number of books; some were slight, but many detailed and scholarly such as *Things Chinese* (1892) and *The Chinese at Home; or, The Man of Tong and His Land* (1911). Among his publications is even a book on Chinese food — *The English-Chinese Cookery Book. Containing 200 Receipts in English and Chinese.*

The 1906-7 edition of *Who's Who in the Far East* (a Hong Kong venture), a kind of *Debrett* for the Old China Hand, informs us that Dyer Ball and his family lived at 'Fernside, Mount Kellett, Peak.' The Peak District was then the abode of all senior officials; its elevation symbolized the separation of the European official from the *hoi polloi* who dwelt below; it was, moreover, an area reserved exclusively for the white population (the one exception was the millionaire Sir Robert Ho Tung, an Eurasian). We have no account of how Dyer Ball spent his leisure hours — perambulating with walking-stick and spaniel, a quiet game of tennis, a little croquet, chess in the evening? But it seems obvious he was a bookman at heart, a scholar who doubtless spent most evenings in study or reading, and his Sundays at church. The sheer amount of information contained in *Things Chinese* implies that this must have been so, for the range of topics touched upon is impressive; the book is clearly a product of wide reading. No clubman, bon viveur or *flâneur* could have accomplished so much.

The first edition was issued by Sampson Low of London and dated 1892. There were further editions in 1893, 1900 and 1903; the fifth, revised by E. Chalmers Werner, appeared in 1925, six years after Dyer Ball's death at North Finchley, London. The book's publishing history is confused and need detain us briefly. It appears to have been printed in Shanghai on the presses of Kelly and Walsh, the celebrated Shanghai publishing firm, and the foreign editions given a new title page, or superscribed with the imprint of a London or New York publisher. This device was commonly used by Kelly and Walsh to market their books abroad.

Each edition tended to grow in bulk, from 497 pages in the first, to 816 in the fourth, declining, after Werner's emendations and excisions, to 766 in the fifth. There were always some subtractions and rewriting, but far more additions and expansions as Dyer Ball attempted to keep the text up-to-date and to incorporate fresh material gleaned from a growing number of books on China; this was especially so after 1900, for the Boxer Uprising and the subsequent siege of the Legations at Peking put China firmly in the news and aroused much Western interest in that far-distant and, to foreigners, exotic country. Had not Napoleon exclaimed: 'When China rises, the world will tremble!'

Things Chinese quickly established itself as a reliable standard reference work, and it was praised by sinologues in Europe and America as a basically sound work for the common reader and the student of China. Dyer Ball was a gifted amateur; but he was also a careful and scholarly writer and recognized as such by Henri Cordier, the distinguished bibliographer and editor of *T'oung Pao*, the leading sinological journal of the day. After Dyer Ball's death, in 1919, it was Cordier who wrote the *nécrologie* for that journal.

E.T.C. Werner (1864-1954), British Consul at Foochow, retired on pension from the Consular Service in 1915 but remained in Peking. He was a dedicated Sinophile. He continued to devote himself to research into Chinese civilization, but now as a full-time scholar. He was the first foreigner to be elected a member of the Chinese Government's Historiographic Bureau in Peking, and in 1922 was elected president of the Peking Historical Association. He had already spent over 20 years in completing Part 9 of Herbert Spencer's *Descriptive Sociology*. Part 9, which dealt with Chinese society, compiled and abstracted by Werner, appeared in 1910. This volume is rarely consulted today. It suffers from being based too uncritically on Spencer's abstract schema of evolutionary sociology, which postulated that social development is similar to organic development and that the laws of change may be deduced and confirmed empirically. Werner also published a number of less contentious books on China, notably *Myths and Legends of China* (1922), a volume in a popular series on folklore issued by Harrap, and a *Dictionary of Chinese Mythology* (1932), brought out by the enterprising Kelly and Walsh.

The certainties of yesterday tend to become the prejudices of tomorrow: *idées reçues*, rejected by the enlightened. There is a passage in Werner's *Autumn Leaves* (1928), his autobiography, which reads very oddly today although it was conventional wisdom at the time:

> There can be no doubt, to my mind, that in all sexual matters, 'East is East, and West is West' and should never meet. I observed this rule scrupulously throughout my long residence in China, but cannot honestly say that it was observed by all foreign residents, nor even by all members of the Consular Service, in that country. Even if temporary only, such a union cannot but be degrading. To the thinking man, it is unthinkable. If permanent, and the union is 'blessed' with children, biology proves that the offspring of parents of widely different races inherit the worst characteristics of both sides — though

> there is a certain amount of precociousness, it is soon followed by deterioration. Any right-minded man would loathe to have, for example, Chinese, Tibetan, or Korean children or grand-children, all his life to see his own features in theirs, and yet unable to alter the ugly fact.

'Biology', needless to say, does not support any of Werner's assertions about the dread consequences of miscegenation. He had been too deeply influenced by the tide of Social Darwinism and Eugenics which flowed so strongly in the late nineteenth century, the high tide of British imperialism. If we turn to Dyer Ball, we shall also discover a number of assumptions or sentiments that most of us would now reject as false or otiose.

The reader will soon be struck by Dyer Ball's admiration for missionary work and by his conviction that Christianity had the God-given power to regenerate China, so that this ancient but ramshackle civilization could take its place among the comity of nations. It is also clear he believed that a modernized China would contain a strong Christian component among its future leadership. In his preface to the fourth edition (1903), he claims: 'This ever-increasing element of Christianity, under whose fostering care nearly all the material progress the country has ever made in recent years has had its inception, is not to be despised nor overlooked in prognostications of the future.' We should not be too surprised by these pious statements, although the march of Chinese history has shown them to be false, for they were shared by many of his contemporaries. Dyer Ball was, after all, the child of a missionary household. His obituary in *The Hong Kong Telegraph* (March 6,1919) states that he always 'took a great interest in religious work among the Chinese.' He was also a member of the Committee of the Anti-Opium Society, a body strongly supported by the missionary interest in China. In Hong Kong he was a most active member of the Union Church and collaborated in writing its history. Inevitably, *Things Chinese* reflects strong religious views.

Professor Raymond Dawson's *The Chinese Chameleon* (1967) is subtitled 'An analysis of European conceptions of Chinese civilization.' Some of the interest in *Things Chinese* must reside in the light it throws on European views of China and the Chinese at the turn of the century. The entry under 'Topsyturvydom' is particularly revealing, and fascinating. Dyer Ball observes:

> It is the unexpected that one must expect, especially in this land of topsyturvydom. The Chinese are not only remote from us with regard to position on the globe, but they are our opposites in almost every action and thought. It never does to judge how a Chinese would act under certain circumstances from what we ourselves would do if placed in similar conditions: the chances are that he would do the very actions we would never think of performing; think the very thoughts that would never occur to us; and say what no foreigner would ever think of uttering.

He then lists a large number of 'contrarieties'; yet his tone is neither derisive nor condescending. A Chinese, he continues, 'turns his names backforwards, as we do in our directories: the surnames first and the other names afterwards; and in the same way he transposes (according to our ideas) his titles of respect and relationship . . .' The phrase 'according to our ideas' implies that there are no fixed rules for social behaviour: social systems are simply different social systems, and each may work as well as any other (although a little better, perhaps, if there is the leaven of Christianity). Further entries on 'Abatement', 'Bathing', and the 'Chinese People' all reveal attitudes of interest to the social historian.

Dyer Ball retired on pension from the Hong Kong Civil Service on January 25, 1909. Soon afterwards he left for England and spent his retirement in a small house in North Finchley, then a quiet residential suburb like Balham or Holloway (where the Grossmiths' Mr Pooter lived) in South London. There were many chapels in North Finchley and large Nonconformist congregations. One feels Dyer Ball was very much at home among these chapel-going Sabbatarians. He died at home on February 22, 1919, a victim of the great influenza epidemic that afflicted Britain after the First World War. One son remained behind in Hong Kong as Clerk of Councils in the Colonial Secretary's Office, the third generation of Dyer Balls to live and work in the Far East. E.T.C. Werner, who admired *Things Chinese* and proposed that a fifth edition should be published, stayed on in Peking until the Japanese occupied the city. He was interned during the war but released in 1945 and returned to Peking. He left China finally in 1949 when the Communists achieved power. The country no longer had any attraction for him and he had no family left in China. His wife had died before the outbreak of war and his adopted Chinese daughter had been murdered at the age of 20 in Peking.

BIBLIOGRAPHY

Ball, James Dyer, *The Chinese at Home; or, The Man of Tong and His Land* (London: Religious Truth Society, 1911).

Burkhardt, V.R., *Chinese Creeds and Customs* (Hong Kong: South China Morning Post, 3 vols., 1953–8).

Couling, Samuel, *Encyclopaedia Sinica* (Shanghai: Kelly and Walsh, 1917).

Dawson, Raymond, *The Chinese Chameleon* (London: Oxford University Press, 1967).

Eitel, E.J., *Europe in China: The History of Hong Kong* (Hong Kong: Kelly and Walsh, 1895).

Endacott, G.B., *A History of Hong Kong* (London: Oxford University Press, 1958).

Furse, Sir Ralph, *Aucuparius: Recollections of a Recruiting Officer* (London: Oxford University Press, 1962).

Symonds, Richard, *The British and Their Successors* (London: Faber & Faber, 1966).

Werner, E.T.C., *Autumn Leaves: An Autobiography* (Shanghai: Kelly and Walsh, 1928).

THINGS CHINESE;

OR, NOTES CONNECTED WITH CHINA.

BY

J. DYER BALL, M.R.A.S.,

M.N.C.Br.R.A.S., H.M.CIVIL SERVICE, HONGKONG.,
AUTHOR OF 'CANTONESE MADE EASY,' 'HOW TO SPEAK CANTONESE,'
'HOW TO WRITE CHINESE,' 'HAKKA MADE EASY,'
AND OTHER WORKS.

FIFTH EDITION. REVISED BY

E. CHALMERS WERNER,

H.B.M. CONSUL, FOOCHOW (retired),
AUTHOR OF 'DESCRIPTIVE SOCIOLOGY—CHINESE,' 'CHINA OF THE
CHINESE,' 'MYTHS AND LEGENDS OF CHINA,'
ETC.

KELLY & WALSH, LIMITED,
SHANGHAI, HONGKONG AND SINGAPORE.
1925.

PRINTED IN SHANGHAI, CHINA, AT THE PRESS OF KELLY & WALSH, LTD.

PREFACE TO THE FIFTH EDITION.

"THINGS," of course, was intended by the author to include the people, their ideas and actions, and the results of those ideas and actions, and of their interactions. But I feel sure that it was not his intention to compile an encyclopædia (which to be complete would require several stout volumes),—he, in fact, modestly calls his work "Notes connected with China,"—but to write, in non-technical language, a popular reference book. For this type of book the author's system of comparatively few main headings supplemented by a copious index seems the best.

It is now twenty-two years since the issue of the fourth edition. During that period many changes have taken place in China, the most momentous being the substitution of the republican for the monarchical form of government. That change has necessitated putting most of the statements relating to what was then the present in the past tense. Beyond that, and subjecting each section to a thorough revision, I have not altered the character of the work, the only structural change being the addition in brackets, where necessary, of the northern pronunciation of Chinese words after the Cantonese pronunciation adopted by the author; thus, I hope, making the work more widely useful.

EDWARD CHALMERS WERNER.

Peking, *June*, 1925.

PREFACE TO THE FOURTH EDITION.

NEARLY forty years spent in China have given the author many opportunities of observing and studying the Chinese in almost every aspect of their life and character, and, while indebted to other writers as well, he has largely availed himself of these personal observations and experiences in the production of this book.

The first appearance of Mr. Basil Hall Chamberlain's 'Things Japanese' gave rise to the idea of 'Things Chinese,' until now, in the words of that author in the Preface to his Fourth Edition of 'Things Japanese' (for edition after edition of it and 'Things Chinese' have been issued nearly *pari passu*), 'In the unlikely event of anyone instituting a minute comparison between this edition and its predecessor, he would find minor alterations innumerable—here a line erased, there a paragraph added, or again a figure changed, a statement qualified, a description or a list brought up to date, even a score (or two or more) of completely new articles inserted. But take it altogether, the book remains the same as heretofore.' So the same may be said of this Fourth Edition of 'Things Chinese.' A word here, a line there, now a clause, then a term struck out, a phrase deleted, or sentence altered—all have had their share in making it necessary to put the word 'revised' on the title-page. As regards the companion word, 'enlarged,' the additional headings consist mostly of short articles, occasionally only a few lines, or a sentence, or a paragraph; but though mostly short, this defect, if it be one, has, the author hopes, been atoned for by their number.

Two paragraphs from Mr. J. B. Coughtrie's pen are included under the heading of Art, and several emendations in the same article are due to his critial acumen and artistic taste. The advice of Mr. Charles Ford, F.L.S., was sought on several points connected with the short article on Botany. The author has also pleasure in acknowledging, as regards this edition, the kindness of Dr. J. C. Thomson in reading over the articles on Acupuncture, Beri-beri, Doctors, Leprosy, Mosquitoes, Plague, and Vaccination, as well as for some suggestions made by him; and to any others—English or Chinese—from whom a suggestion may have been received, or a fact gleaned, the author desires to express his best thanks.

Since this book first issued from the press, China has indeed been the theatre in which the leading European Powers have passed rapidly over a corner of the stage; and in the minds of many residents in the Far East the question is whether all this military display has resulted in any good commensurate with the efforts put forth. Not that the raising of the dastardly siege of the Legations and the invasion of North China was not necessary, but whether more lasting good to China, and more stability in the relationships between the foreign residents in that land and the Chinese themselves, should not have resulted from it.

The grim tragedy enacted by the massacres and war, what has seemed the farce in which many of the blood-stained instigators and perpetrators enjoy a peace with honour, followed by the usual comedy of an indemnity or compensation for losses, drawn from the pockets of those (the Westerners, in the shape of tariff charges) to whom it is eventually to be paid—for thus it has ever been with China of late: the expenses of our punitive wars have been recouped to us from the purses of our own merchants; or, if a new departure has been made on this occasion, wrung from the unwilling hands, and filched from the purses of a populace distant in many cases from the seat of outrages, and who are entirely innocent of them. Filched, we say, because much of the money ostensibly taken for the purposes of the indemnities is diverted to the bottomless money-bags of the greedy and avaricious officials, who are only too glad, under the pretext of buying off the 'foreign devil,' to have the grand opportunity of making their own fortunes rapidly, while all the opprobrium is shunted off on to the shoulders of the outside barbarian—all these things would seem to hold out little hope of a betterment of things in the future.

And yet the war—for war it was against the *de facto* government of China, notwithstanding all the diplomatic attempts to deny it—brought out more than one good trait in China's best men; and more good still might have been educed out of the evil, or in spite of the evil, could the opportunities only have been seized to strengthen further those who have the good of their misgoverned country really at heart. Amidst all, and perhaps in consequence of, the crushing defeats inflicted on the progressive party by the reactionists, many a foreign writer is apt to forget the latent power for good and progress still inherent in the 'new party'; and though some of the ancient 'things Chinese'—the corruption, overweening pride, and self-sufficiency, etc., of the 'old party'—may not be swept away for many a long year, yet still this new force which has arisen of late years, with its new-born and fresh-inspired patriotism (a growth of only some three or four years), is bound to increase as knowledge increases, and as knowledge increases, its power will make itself felt in increasing proportions.

It is a mistake to look only on this mighty empire—which is beginning to bestir itself and respond to Western influences—with the official goggles of Peking, and prophesy jeremiads of woe alone. Strife and commotions, upheavals and rebellions, will, doubtless, agitate and agitate in the future as they have done in the past; but with further enlightenment and years, the elements of good will gain more power, and tell in the long run.

Let us consider that a hundred years ago there was not a Protestant Christian in China, and that now there are a hundred thousand, and that the great mass of these have been enrolled during the last fifty years. If they progress during the next century in the ever-multiplying numbers of a geometrical progression, as they have done in the past, before long, this new section of the body politic will necessarily make itself felt in the counsels of China. This ever-increasing element of Christianity, under whose fostering care nearly all the material progress the country has ever made in recent years has had its inception, is not to be despised nor overlooked in prognostications of the future. It is a factor that, as it increases in strength—which no one who has watched its progress can doubt it is bound to do—will demand, along with the moderate section of the progressives, a voice, their adherents will occupy foremost positions in time, and have their share in the government of the country.

The evolutionary forces are at work: Western nations are surrounding the ancient centre of the Far East, and conditioned by its new environments, the foremost men are yearning for progress towards a higher plane of existence for their native country and themselves. These aspirations of the best of her sons are not those of hordes of Huns led by an all-world conqueror. True progress does not always consist in the conquering of other nations, nor in holocausts of human victims offered to the God of War. The Chinese as a nation have been a peace-loving people.

The little white stone of Western progress and Christianity has been cast into the well-nigh stagnant pool of Chinese thought, and it has sunk deep into its very heart, unseen to a great extent in its progress; but its influence is making itself visible on the surface in ever increasing ripples, which are extending far and wide, and have not yet reached their limit. The point of impact of this disturbing element seems but small, compared with the vast mass of old-world traditions and modes of thought, and the influence, at first sight, may be considered to be but superficial, hastened only to waste its efforts on the sandy shore of the arid desert of Chinese literature (as some have described it), which apparently bounds all Chinese mental effort and movement; but, though hidden to a great extent from those who only look on the surface, it is making itself felt at the heart of the nation, and will continue to do so, more and more, as it sinks deeper and deeper into the centre of the vital existence of the country. In other words, let us not take a pessimistic view of everything connected with China, for the influences that are at work are greater than many would think; and though the visible outcome is but comparatively small at present (as compared with the hoary mass to be moved), yet they are bound to extend in the future, and to exert even more influence in time to come, and to achieve more in the days of to-morrow—in that land where the to-morrows are so long of coming—than it has ever done in the yesterdays of the long ago.

J. DYER BALL.

October 1903.

THINGS CHINESE

ABACUS.—The abacus, the counting-board or calculating-frame, is as much a necessity in a merchant's office, or shroff's counting-room, as his account-books; without the abacus he would be at a complete loss to make up his accounts, and his books would therefore be unnecessary. Except with those who, within recent years, have come under the influence of Western education (*see* EDUCATION), arithmetic forms no part of a school-boy's work.

Not even the simplest knowledge of arithmetic will ever be learned by him as a lesson, unless he is destined for a mercantile life, or to be a tradesman, or hawker, etc.; even then he learns only just as much as it is absolutely necessary for him to know and that as a part of his business training. What little idea of figures he does possess, he picks up when bargaining for food or toys, or when staking a few cash for sweetmeats at the wayside stall. The ordinary Celestial is content to get through life with as scanty a 'knowledge of addition, subtraction, multiplication, and division as would serve an English youngster of six or eight years of age.' A very little goes a long way with him, but nearly every man can finger the abacus to a greater or lesser extent; and those who have much to do with accounts get very dexterous in the use of it, going through the calculations most rapidly. We once had the curiosity to time a Chinese accountant from a native shipping office when turning different items expressed in taels and their decimals—items of four, five, and six figures—into dollars and cents, and we found he worked these sums out in from ten to fifteen seconds.

The *modus operandi* is as follows:—Putting his abacus down on the table before him, and his books a trifle more to the left, the accountant commences his calculations, using the thumb and forefinger of his right hand to flick the little balls up or down as he requires, only using his other three fingers, when, his sum done, he sweeps the upper balls to the top of the board, and the lower ones down to the bottom—the positions they occupy when not in actual use. The principle is simply that of the framework of wires with coloured beads used in England for teaching children to count. With the Chinese, however, the counting-board is an oblong tray with bars running from top to bottom, and a transverse partition running from one side to the other, dividing the board into two unequal divisions. On each bar are seven balls, two in the upper division and five in the lower; each of those below stands for one, each of those above, for five; so, if one is to be represented, one of the lower ones is pushed up against the cross-bar, or if two, two are placed in the same position, and so on till four, after which all the lower balls are pushed back again, and one of the upper ones is brought down to the middle partition to stand for five. If six is to be represented, one of the lower balls is pushed up to the cross-bar, on the other side of which is the upper ball, for five and one make six. The other lower balls are added one after the other to represent seven, eight, and nine respectively, while for ten, one on the next bar to the left is used, the calculation going on in the same way as before. The operator fixing then on one of the upright bars as representing units, the next bar to the left stands for tens, the next one for hundreds, the next for thousands, and so on, while in the opposite direction, to the right hand, the decimals—tenths, hundredths, thousandths, and so on, are represented on the consecutive bars.

The great defect of the abacus is, that it simply represents the process of calculation as it proceeds, for, as can readily be understood, each step in the calculation calls new combinations of balls into play, and has the effect of obliterating the previous step; so that, if a mistake has been made, the whole process has to be gone over again. The abacus is simply used, therefore, to record the results of the mental calculations as they proceed. The processes by which these results are produced are not shown, and, while each new operation is being recorded on the board, it naturally follows that—the balls which have been used for the last answer being taken as the reckoning goes on to show the new answer—as each computation is gradually, or quickly, set down as it goes on, as it proceeds, *pari passu,* the preceding answer is as gradually, or as quickly, as the case may be, effaced.

The Chinese merchants or traders so habituate themselves to the use of the abacus that they become quite dependent on it, and it is amusing to see the utter helplessness they often display in trying to add two simple numbers together without an abacus.

The abacus is derived from an old system of counting by tallies; it is variously stated to have come into use in the third, twelfth, and fourteenth centuries A.D.

When, at daylight, the shutters are taken down from the

shop-fronts in Canton, the shopman ensures, as he thinks, good luck for the day by shaking the balls of the abacus to and fro; at first slowly, but gradually increasing in speed until finally a continuous sharp clicking sound is produced.

References,—Vissière, *Recherches sur l'origine de l'abaque chinois*; Schlegel, *T'oung Pao*, 1893, pp. 96-9; Lacouperie, *Numismatic Chronicle*, vol. iii, 3rd series, pp. 297-340; *Journal of the Peking Oriental Society*, ii, 161-9; 'How to use the Chinese Abacus,' *New China Review*, iii, 127-30.

ABATEMENT.—Nearly every Chinese tradesman, or merchant, states the price of his goods with a view to an abatement being made. The only exceptions amongst purely native establishments are tea, cake, and druggists' shops, for at such places there is no need to haggle. Exception must also be made in favour of the shops dealing almost exclusively with Europeans, where many are beginning to conform to foreign customs and have a fixed price.

A Chinese will take as much as he can get, but as a general rule it is quite safe to suppose that he is asking a quarter or a third more than he expects to receive; consequently offer him half of what he asks, then, while he gradually falls in his price, as gradually rise in the offer made to him until neutral ground is reached, when split the difference and he will probably be glad to take what you give him. But this must all be done with a perfect nonchalance; no eagerness to obtain the object must be shown; no words of praise must fall from your lips; any little defects in it must be pointed out:—'It is naught, it is naught, saith the buyer: but when he is gone his way then he boasteth.'

When in doubt as to the value of anything, a very good plan is to go about beating down the price in several different shops. A pretty shrewd guess may then be made as to what is a fair value for the article; for when a shopman sees a customer on the point of leaving his shop, he will come down to nearly, if not quite, as low a figure as he is prepared to accept.

A Chinaman dearly loves a bargain, and he finds a positive pleasure in chaffering over the price, which the foreigner (to whom time is money) can scarcely appreciate. Looked at from a Western standpoint, it is simply appalling to think of the hours, days, weeks, months, and years, which must be wasted in the aggregate in China over the carrying out of this Eastern trait of character.

There is an amusing skit, translated by Giles in his 'Historic China and other Sketches,' which is an admirable parody on the language of the market and the shop, and holds up this custom of the Chinese to ridicule. It is styled 'The Country of Gentlemen,' and represents an ideal state of society where the tables are turned—the buyer cracking up the goods he is purchasing, and offering, and insisting on the seller taking, a higher price than is demanded for them, while the latter depreciates his wares, asking far too little for them, the two haggling over the price at great length—as in the every-day world in China—the only difference being that buyer and seller have changed places.

ABORIGINAL TRIBES.—The present race of Chinese is supposed to have come into the country some four or five thousand years ago. They were not the first occupiers of the soil, however, and it has been only very gradually that they have succeeded in driving out the aborigines, for large tracts of country in the south and south-west of the eighteen provinces are still possessed by the former inhabitants, who hold their own against the Chinese, and are reported in some parts even to have thousands of the latter as slaves in their inaccessible fastnesses, thus retaliating on their aggressors, who some centuries since exposed them to the same treatment.

These tribes were gradually herded into the furthest corner of the Chinese empire, and are packed closest in the province remotest from the central power in the north, Yünnan (where they comprise two-thirds of the population) containing 15 or 16 main tribes, Kueichou 6 or 7, Kuangtung, Kuangsi, and Ssŭch'uan 3 each. Besides those in Honan, Hunan and on the Tibeto-Ssŭch'uanese border there are also isolated tribes in other provinces, such as the Jung in Fukien (which may in some cases be regarded as remnants left behind as the general migration moved southward).

The general divisions according to language are (*pace* Bourne) into Lolo, Shan, and Miao-tzŭ, or (*pace* Davies) into Mon-Khmer, Shan, and Tibeto-Burman. These include numerous tribes and sub-tribes.

The provinces in which these representatives of former races are found, are Kueichou, Ssŭch'uan, Yünnan, Kuangtung, Kuangsi, Hunan, Honan, and the island of Hainan.

In Ssŭch'uan a considerable portion of the west and south-west of the province is sparsely inhabited by some forty or fifty native tribes and sub-tribes, of whom little is known: some are very warlike, and constant depredations are committed by them. They have their own chiefs, languages, customs and manners. The late Mr. Colborne Baber, of the Consular Service, obtained a specimen of the written language of the Lolos—one of these tribes. It is a most peculiar sort of caligraphy, and presents no point of resemblance to the Chinese language or any other that one is familiar with.

'Between the province of Ssŭch'uan and Tibet are found a

number of tribes who are little known to the outside world. These are the great Rong with their five states, the wild Goloks, the sleek Sifan, the cross-bred Bolotsze, the thieving Hehshui people, the warlike Nosu or Lolos, and the sturdy Ch'ing. The last named are found just inside China proper. They dwell mostly in the districts of Wenchuan, Weichow, Lifan, Mongchou, and Southern Songpan. They are a pastoral, farming folk, the remnant of a once great nation whose numbers have been slowly lessened by conquest and absorption, until now they do not probably exceed a quarter of a million. Chinese historians say they are part of the San-Miao, the aborigines of China. Though in some places they have still their own chiefs, they are all under Chinese jurisdiction.'

In Kueichou they appear to be scattered all over the province; and the same may be said of Yünnan, where about two-thirds of the 'inhabitants consist of various tribes of Lo-lo, Li-su, Mu-su, Man-tzŭ, and Miao-tzŭ.' In Kuangtung they are located in the north-west of the province, and in Kuangsi in the north-east.

In the island of Hainan, the aboriginal Le, or Loi, tribes have maintained their independence against the Chinese for nearly two thousand years, having been driven from the coast into the mountains in the interior. They are divided into civilized and uncivilized Les, and are physically strong and well developed. They have the art of writing, which is described by the Chinese as 'like the wriggling of worms.' There is so great a difference in some of the languages spoken by the different tribes, that they converse with each other in Chinese. The women are tattooed and wear skirts. There are also some of the Miao-tzŭ amongst them; these Miao-tzŭ being found largely in other parts of China.

In Formosa (subject to Japan since 1896), out of a total area of 13,893 sq. miles the aboriginal tribes occupy 7,146 sq. miles (the eastern and larger part of the island). Besides the Peipohuans (*see* below) there are nine aboriginal tribes, numbering in all about 122,000 individuals. The various tribes differ in physical characters, dialects, habits, etc., and are hostile toward each other. The Taiyal, the most powerful in the island, tattoo their faces, are of a fierce nature, and head-hunters. The other eight tribes are in a somewhat more advanced condition. Most of them, except perhaps the Bunun and Tsarisen, are peaceful people, engaged in hunting, fishing, agriculture, or cattle-breeding. Except the Yami, they are not of low intelligence. The women are fully clothed, the men usually naked from the middle of the thigh downward.

It will thus be seen that the aborigines occupy large districts in many parts of the country, especially in the mountainous and hilly regions of some of the provinces. As has been already said, in some portions of the country they retain their former possessions, but from other tracts they have been driven to upland fastnesses, as the ancient Britons were forced to retire to Wales.

To show the number and extent of these remnants of a former race and civilization in China, it may be pointed out that in the provinces of Hunan, Kueichou, Kuangsi, Yünnan, and Ssŭch'uan, the aboriginal tribes—Miau-tzŭ and others—occupy an area of country equal to that of France, and are some millions in number, representing numerous tribes and sub-tribes; as many as one hundred and eighty being mentioned, though perhaps not so many are in existence now. They are supposed to have come through Burma into China. As is the case with most of these aboriginal inhabitants of China, the dress of the women is more distinctive than that of the men.

Out of the 11,000,000 inhabitants of the province of Yünnan, two-thirds are 'cultivated savages,' *i.e.* Lo-lo, Li-su, Mu-su, Man-tzŭ, and Miao-tzŭ.

In the Lín-cháú [Leichou] prefecture of the Kuangtung province and the south of the Hunan province are to be found the Iu tribes, who were brought in the twelfth century from the Kuangsi province, and settled on the mountains. Their hair is worn long, they are short in stature, and have scanty beards. They, as well as other aboriginal tribes, wear cloths bound round their legs from the knee to the ankle. No foreigner is allowed by the Chinese to penetrate into their haunts, which are now restricted in extent from what they were originally, for the more civilized Chinese have confined them within recent times to the high and inaccessible mountains. They have no written language, and their speech is quite distinct from the Chinese. Their number is perhaps 50,000.

It has been suggested that the Japanese are descendants of the Man or Miau tribes, who crossed over from the south of China to their future island home. At the time of their emigration they were the only inhabitants of the south of China.

So little is known about many of these communities of primitive man scattered here and there throughout China, their mountain homes are so inaccessible, the accounts of their curious customs, simplicity, origin, and peculiarly written languages—when they have any,—the harsh and cruel treatment they have received from the Chinese, their patriotic stand for hearth and home against these invaders: these, and many other reasons, combine to make them objects of interest to the man of science, the traveller, the philanthropist, and the missionary.

The names of the more important tribes, with a few notes as to their chief peculiarities, are given below. The tribes in Formosa are included, though politically they are not now under Chinese rule.

A-ka. A Woni (*q.v.*) dog-eating tribe.

A-si. *See* Zi.

Ami. A tribe occupying the middle eastern coast district of Formosa, and numbering (in 1911) 31,576.

Atayal. *See* Taiyal.

Bunun. A head-hunting tribe occupying a large central district in southern Formosa, east of the Ami, and numbering (in 1911) 15,807.

Chung Chia. In Yünnan, Kueichou, Kuangsi, and Kuangtung. Said to have come from Kiangsi. Number between six and seven millions. Are ruled by local tribesmen, with appeal to Chinese courts. Worship no deities, but recognize a Good and Evil Being. No legends of creation or deluge. Funeral rites differ from those of the Chinese. No written language. Speech monosyllabic. Men's costume similar to Chinese, but women wear tight coats and long skirts, and do not bind their feet; they do three-fourths of the work of the tribe. Do not dance, but are fond of singing. *See* also Shan.

Hei Miao. Black Miao (*see* Miao Chia). Wear dark-coloured clothes. In S.E. Kueichou. Originally from Kiangsi. The most intelligent and self-reliant of the Miao tribes.

Hua Miao. The Flowery Miao (*see* Miao Chia). The women wear parti-coloured clothes. Morally the worst of the Miao tribes.

Hsi-fan. Western Barbarians. Inhabit the regions on the border of China and Tibet. All except the most easterly are Tibetans in religion and customs, but in some districts they have a cult of their own. Their language is connected with the Lolo speech. Physically they are shorter and darker than the Tibetans.

I-chia. *See* Lo-lo.

Iu. A tribe which came from Kuangsi in the twelfth century A.D. and settled in the mountainous districts of Hunan and the Leichou peninsula of Kuangtung. Short in stature. Wear hair long. Number about 50,000. Speech distinct from Chinese. No written language.

Ka-tu. *See* Wo-ni.

Kachin. A hill-tribe of Burma, extending into W. Yünnan.

Ko-lao, or Liao. The oldest non-Chinese tribe now found in Kueichou; nearly extinct. Demonism prevalent. Language different from any other in the province. Men dress like Chinese, but women have peculiar costume of their own, wear hair in topknot, and do not bind their feet.

La. The Shan name of tribes akin to the Wa. Found in K'êngma and neighbouring Chinese states.

La-shi. A mixture of Chinese and Ma-su blood. *See* Mo-so.

Lao-lao. *See* Lo-lo.

Li-chia. *See* Mo-so.

Li-mu. *See* Loi.

Li-so. The Chinese name of a thinly scattered tribe in

Yünnan in the Salwin basin. Call themselves Li-su. Hunt with cross-bows. In north, live in primitive savagery; in south, influenced by Chinese customs.

Liao. *See* Ko-lao.

Liao-liao. *See* Lo-lo.

Lo-hei. The Chinese name for the La-hu, a hill-tribe living in S. Yünnan between the Mekong and the Salwin. They are probably a hybrid race of Lo-lo and Wa. Speak a Lo-lo dialect. Very warlike. Weapons, cross-bow and poisoned arrows.

Lo-lo, Lao-lao, or Liao-liao. The Chinese name for the most widely spread native race of W. China, being found from W. Ssŭch'uan to Kueichou, and forming the bulk of the population in Yünnan. They occupy a territory of 11,000 sq. miles. The native name is No-su or Nei-su, but they prefer to call themselves I-chia. The Chinese also call them Man-tzŭ and Man-chia. In Ssŭch'uan they are tall, with comparatively fair complexions, and often regular features. They have a written language of about 3,000 words, said to be only used for religious purposes. A characteristic feature of their dress is a grey felt cloak, fastened round the neck and reaching below the knees, worn both by men and women.

Loi (Li-mu, etc.). About 15 to 20 tribes living in the interior of Hainan. In the interior mountainous country are known as 'Wild Lois.' These are surrounded by a belt of 'Tame Lois,' and the latter again by a coast belt of Chinese, with whom they trade on market days. They may have sprung from the Siamese. Some are found in the Leichou peninsula in Kuangtung. In stature and complexion they resemble the Malays. They have no idols and no written language. Their costume varies: the men usually wear their hair in a topknot; the women wear theirs hanging down the back and tied. The men wear a short coat and two pieces of cloth hung from the waist. The women are tattooed, and wear short coats and short petticoats. Bone and silver ornaments, large brass earrings, and heavy bead collars are worn.

Ma-lu. *See* Ma-ru.

Ma-ru. Call themselves Lawng. Shan name Ma-lu. Other names La-lang and Lang. A dog-eating tribe living in W. Yünnan. Not numerous. An extension of the tribe found on the E. branch of the Irawadi.

Man-chia. *See* Lo-lo.

Man-tzŭ. *See* Lo-lo.

Mhong. *See* Miao-chia.

Miao-chia or Miao-tzŭ. The Chinese name for the numerous eighty-three (or more) tribes calling themselves Mhong, whose headquarters are in Kueichou (their original home), but who are also found in S. Yünnan, Ssŭch'uan, and Hunan. They are simple, inferior in morals to the Chinese, given to drink, and fond of music and dancing. They are ruled by a headman responsible to the Chinese magistrates. The Chinese say 'they require peculiar treatment to be managed.' They have legends of creation and deluge; great fear of demons; but no idols; and sacrifice to the dead. The tribes differ in dialect, dress, etc. In Kueichou they are the serfs or tenants of the Lo-los. The men and women wear dark blue turbans; the women embroidered clothes and short, white kilted skirts. The men wear a white feather stuck in their hair. Weapons: cross-bow and poisoned arrows.

Min-chia. The Chinese name for a mixed race who call themselves Pe-tso, settled in Yünnan, but said to have come originally from Nanking. No written language. Speech probably belongs to Mon-Khmer group.

Mo-sha. *See* Mo-so.

Mo-so, Mo-sha, Mo-ti, or Li-chia. A tribe living in Li-kiang and Ho-king prefectures in Yünnan. They call themselves Na-shi or La-shi. Said to have come originally from Mongolia *via* S.W. Tibet. Their language resembles that of the Lo-lo (to whom, however, they deny that they are related). Ancestor-worship and Tibetan Buddhism. Cremation. Men wear Chinese dress with green stone earnings; women, pleated skirts and hair in topknot.

Mo-ti. *See* Mo-so.

Na-shi. *See* Mo-so.

Nei-su. *See* Lo-lo.

No-su. *See* Lo-lo.

Pai-i. *See* Shan.

Paiwan. A tribe occupying a large district in the southernmost part of Formosa. In 1911 they numbered 21,093.

Peipohuan. A semi-civilized race living among the Chinese population of Formosa.

Pi-o. *See* Wo-ni.

Piyuma. This tribe occupies a small district on the S.E. coast of Formosa. In 1911 they numbered 6,522.

P'u-man. The Chinese name for a scattered tribe living in S. and S.W. Yünnan (said to be the name given by the Chinese to the Yao). Supposed by some to be a Shan race; placed in the Wa-Palaung group.

Pu-tu. *See* Wo-ni.

Saisett. The smallest of the Formosan tribes, with a population of 757 (1911), occupying an inland district on the N.W. frontier of the Taiyal territory.

Shan. The Burmese name for a race found in Burma, Siam, and China. They call themselves Tai (T'ai in Siam). The Chinese name is Pai-i, or in Kueichou, Chung-chia (or Chung Chia). Found in Yünnan, Kueichou, Kuangsi, Kuangtung, and on Ssŭch'uan borders. They inhabit the hot valleys, the Chinese keeping to the hills. Some of them in Yünnan are of the Buddhist religion. The style of their monasteries and their language vary E. and W. of the Salwin. They have two distinct forms of writing, one for religious and the other for ordinary purposes. The men dress like the Chinese, but the women's costume varies in different localities.

Tai (T'ai). *See* Shan.

Tai-loi. The Shan name for hill-tribes in Yünnan, akin to the Wa and La tribes, but Buddhist. The women wear striped coloured skirts and coats ornamented with shells.

Taiyal. The most powerful tribe in Formosa, occupying an enormous territory in the northern part, with an extensive coast-line on the E. In 1911 they numbered 28,242. They tattoo their faces, are head-hunters, and very fierce by nature.

Tsarisen. A fierce tribe, occupying an inland district of S. Formosa. The population in 1911 was 13,995.

Tsuou. A peaceful tribe living in the most central district of Formosa, west of the Bunun. Population (1911), 2,322.

Vonuum. *See* Bunun.

Wa. The Shan name for a head-hunting tribe, the greater portion of which is in Burma, but extends into Yünnan in the district between the Salwin and Mekong. They are probably the same as the La. They wear few or no clothes.

Wo-ni. The Chinese name for those hill-tribes in S. Yünnan who speak Lo-lo dialects, but who are inferior to that race in physique and appearance. Amongst them are the Pu-tu, Pi-o, and Ka-tu.

Yami. A tribe of low intelligence occupying a small island called Botel-Tobago about 40 miles to the E. of South Cape, the southern extremity of Formosa. In 1911 they numbered 1,667.

Yao. A race inhabiting Kuangsi (as headquarters), Kuangtung, Yünnan, and perhaps also Hunan. Said to be newcomers to Yünnan, and to have preceded the Miao and Lo-lo in Kueichou. Chinese tradition says they were cave-dwellers. They now live entirely on the hills. Their language is similar to that of the Miao.

Ya-ch'io Miao. A Miao tribe said to have come from Tongking. They offer annual sacrifices to heaven and earth. The women wear dark blue and white clothes.

Zi, or A-si. Probably Ma-rus or La-shis who have been conquered by the Lepai Kachins, from whom they are indistinguishable except for the retention of their own language. They extend in scattered communities along the Burmo-Chinese frontier.

References.—Arnold, *The Peoples of Formosa;* Baber, *Travels and Researches in Western China*; Bureau of Aboriginal Affairs, Taihokou, *Report on the Control of the Aborigines in Formosa; China Review*, xiv, 121; *Aborigines of Formosa*, xx; *Loi Aborigines of Hainan*, xi, 42; *Notes on Hainan and its Aborigines; New China Review*, ii, 311-2; *Chinese and Japanese Repository*, Oct. 1883; Clark, *Kueichou and Yünnan Provinces;* Clarke, *Among the Tribes in South-west China;* Davies, *Yünnan; East of Asia*, vol. iii; *The Lois;* Henry, *Lingnam;* Hosie, *Three Years in Western China;* Johnston, *From Peking to Mandalay;* d'Ollone, *Les derniers Barbares;* d'Orleans, *Du Tonkin aux Indes;* Pottinger, *Upper Burma Gazetteer;* Rockhill, *The Land of the Lamas;* Sainson, *Histoire particulière de Nan-Tchao;* Scott, *Gazetteer of Upper Burma; T'oung-pao*, 1911; *Essai de Dictionnaire Lo-lo Français*, 1908; *Les Mo-sos*, 1909; *Quelques Peuplades Lo-lo;* Vial, *Les Lolos.* A very interesting work is extant in manuscript in Chinese, profusely illustrated with coloured pictures showing the costumes, etc.

ACADEMY. *See* IMPERIAL ACADEMY

ACUPUNCTURE.—Acupuncture is one of the nine branches of practice recognised in medical science among the Chinese, and is of most ancient origin, having been in use from time immemorial. If we are to believe tradition, the Emperor Hwang-tí was the originator of it. In the sixth century B.C., Pien Ts'iao [Pien Ch'iao (*i.e.*, Ch'in Yüeh-jên)] was skilled in its application; and there is extant to this day a work [*Huang Ti su wên*], written in the third or fourth century B.C., which treats of it. Some six hundred or more years ago, *i.e.*, during the time of the Sung dynasty, it may be said to have been ' reduced to a science; for one of two copper figures of the human body, made in 1027 A.D. by order of the then ruling Emperor, with markings to illustrate its principles, still exists.' There are 367 of these markings, every square inch on the surface having its own name 'and being assigned some relationship, purely imaginary, with the internal parts.' Acupuncture is extensively treated of in the medical works of the Chinese, and is a very common remedy. Many directions are given as to the manner of its use, and the user is cautioned against wounding the arteries, for which purpose he should known the position of the blood-vessels. 'The operator has a manikin full of holes, and by close study of this he learns where to drive his needle,' the latter being inserted 'in parts of the body which may be pierced without fatal results.' As many as eight needles may be seen protruding from the flesh of the stomach. 'Sometimes heat is applied to the outer end of the needle, and this is called hot acupuncture;' but it 'is never heated before insertion.' It is also used in connection with cauterizing, as a means of dispelling evil spirits. In some cases the needle has been known to break in the body of the patient, and has had to remain there till extracted by the skill of the Western practitioner.

The needle used looks 'very much like a sewing-machine needle, but is longer and coarser than that. Some of the Chinese doctors have needles two feet long, and are supposed by ardent admirers to be able to drive these instruments entirely through the patient's body; but the great size of the needles is in reality intended to represent the greatness of the owner's skill and reputation. The needles used are of nine forms as follows:—The arrow-headed, blunt, puncturing, spear-pointed, ensiform, round, capillary, long, and great. The point of insertion, the depth, and the direction are all important . . . and the method is usually to drive them through the distended skin by a blow from a light mallet. They are frequently made red-hot, and occasionally are left in the flesh for days together.'

It is considered to be a universal panacea. It was carried over 'from China to Japan before the dawn of history'; scarification and acupuncture being the peculiar forte of these two nations. Dr. Lockhart says that acupuncture 'is very dexterously performed by the Chinese. It is largely resorted to for rheumatism, deep-seated pains of all kinds, sprains, swelling of the joints, etc.' It was introduced into Europe from China by a Dutch surgeon named Ten-Rhyne in the seventeenth century.

References.—Rémusat, *Nouveaux Mélanges Asiatiques*, i, 358-80; Lockhart, *Medical Missionary in China; China Medical Missionary Journal*, Dec. 1892; *Journal of the Peking Oriental Society*, i, 146-7.

ADOPTION.—It is a matter of the first importance that a man should have a son to offer sacrifices at the Ancestral Hall and to worship at his tomb. The cry with a Chinese is not 'Give me children, or else I die,' but 'Give me a son, or I cannot die in peace,' and, failing a son of his own, he adopts one. It is impossible, with our ideas on the subject, to understand what a matter of prime importance this is with a Chinese. To show how it enters into the very essence of family life in China, we quote from the learned and interesting brochure by Parker on 'Comparative Chinese Family Law,' as follows:—

'The Chinese adoption of agnates is . . . not a matter of choice . . . , but of compulsion. The brother, when living, may demand a nephew, and, when dead, a nephew is given to him unasked. It is not only in his interest, but in that of the whole family, that the succession should be continued. So unfortunate are those considered who have no heirs, that in each town there is a public *lararium* dedicated to orbate persons deceased, and the officials sacrifice periodically to their *manes*.'

'Again, there is absolutely no distinction between such adopted son and a natural-born son. He cannot be disinherited, at least for any reason not equally applicable to a natural son; he mourns for his adoptive father as a natural son would mourn, and for his natural father as a nephew.' Once adopted, he cannot be adopted by another. 'It is a family arrangement, and needs no magisterial authority.' What seems a curious feature in it, to our ideas, is, that 'it may be made without the knowledge of the deceased adopter, whether he is married or not (provided he is over sixteen years of age[1]) and even after his death.'

But this curious feature is explained when we remember that the adoption does not take place for the individual adopter in China, but for the benefit of the family—the family being the unit of society, and the individual nothing but a fractional part of it (the family).

'In treating of adoption in China, it is important to distinguish between the adoption of persons bearing the same surname and those bearing a different surname. If a Chinese has no son, he adopts, if possible, a nephew, who is the son of his brothers. If there are no nephews, then he adopts the grandson of one of his uncles, or the great-grandson of one of his granduncles. In order words, he endeavours to obtain a pure agnate. If there are no agnates of a suitable generation, or if there are agnates of a suitable generation, but not of a suitable age, he next looks to the children of his sisters, or the grandchildren of his aunts. It is generally only when neither agnates nor cognates of suitable age and generation are accessible that he adopts a perfect stranger, and, even then, he endeavours to find one of the same surname. . . . Adoption of an agnate is generally effected during the lifetime of the adopter, who is considered entitled to choose any nephew (except the eldest son of the next brother), before an assembly of agnates, and an entry is made in the genealogical register of the family. A rich man, of course, in practice, finds it easier to obtain the object of his choice than a poor one, and the handsome son of a rich brother is similarly less easy to secure as an heir than the plain

[1] A Chinese is of age at sixteen.

son of a poor brother. . . . Each elder brother can continue to adopt the sons of his younger brethren until he finds an heir who will live; and elder brothers are in duty bound to give a son in posthumous adoption to a younger brother who has died childless. . . . An adopted agnate or cognate takes his place before natural sons subsequently born to the same father. An adopted stranger is liable . . . to exclusion by the agnates of his deceased adoptive father.'

About five per cent. of Chinese families, it is considered, adopt children; seventy per cent. of them being males. In some provinces and districts strangers are frequently adopted, and in Amoy the traders have a peculiar custom of adopting a son to act for them as a commercial agent abroad. In adopting strangers, the child is generally purchased from parents too poor to keep their own offspring, while sometimes kidnappers make a profit by the sale of the poor innocent victims they have inveigled into their toils.

Thus adoption may be distinguished as legal or perfect (*ssŭ chi*: adoption of a brother's son, uncle's grandson, etc.); simple (*kuo fang*: adoption of son or daughter of same stock, but incapable of becoming heir); benevolent (*ch'i yang* or *shou yang*: adoption of ditto, but not of the same stock); and the simulated form mentioned below.

There is a secondary species of what might be termed pseudo-adoption. As true adoption amongst the Chinese is generally due to a certain amount of superstition connected with ancestral worship, so the spurious adoption, as a rule, is even more dependent upon the superstitious beliefs of this credulous people. There are different varieties of this, the parties to one kind being sometimes called godparents and godchildren by Europeans.

The custom has its foundation in the superstition that it is possible to cheat the malignant spirits to whose evil machinations are due the death or illness of children. If the parents, then, are afraid that they will not be able to bring up a child, or that, falling short of that, disease may attack it, or ill-luck fall to its lot, they hit upon the expedient—sometimes suggested by the fortune-teller—of this semi-adoption. Presents are made by the child's parents to the so-called adopter, and return presents are received. The adoptive parent takes a considerable interest in his or her adopted child, presents and visits being made by both sides on the respective birthdays of the primarily interested parties, and at feasts, etc.; but, beyond this, there are no definite duties incumbent on the so-called godparent. The child still remains in its natural parents' house, and, in the event of its parents dying, the so-called godparent is not bound to take the child into his, or her, keeping, even if left destitute. On the other hand, the child, if its so-called godparent dies, is bound to wear mourning, not deep, as in the case of its own parents, but only half-mourning. It is supposed that the spirits will be deceived into the belief that the child has really been adopted into the new family, and the disease, death, disaster, or ill-luck, that would otherwise ensue, are effectually prevented, while at the same time the boy's or girl's family retain their child, and, if an eldest son, will have an heir to sacrifice to them after death.

Sometimes this spurious adoption takes place between families that are friendly, merely with the object of drawing them nearer to each other, but it is oftener the result of the superstitious belief already mentioned.

This superstition gives rise to other varieties of false adoption, such as giving a child in adoption to a banyan tree, a bamboo, a bridge, an idol, or a stone lion in front of a temple. (These stone lions are objects of worship by barren women in the hopes of obtaining offspring.) The bamboo is preferred to other trees, as it is a prince amongst trees (the Chinese do not know the bamboo as a grass), and is so useful. In all these cases it is believed that the spirits inhabiting these several objects—their guardian deities—will take the child under their protection and insure it immunity from the 'ills that flesh is heir to.' On a small piece of red paper is written: 'Given in adoption,' then follows the word 'male' or 'female,' and the surname and name of the child. This is pasted upon the object which is selected, and three incense sticks, joss paper, wine, pork, chicken, and cooked rice are offered; offerings are also made at the end of the year for protection rendered, as well as at the New Year, and in the case of idols, on their birthdays. The piece of red paper once put up is not renewed, as the spirit is thus supposed to be sufficiently informed by the one notice. The mother of the child, or sometimes a 'praying woman,' as she is called, performs the ceremony, offering up a prayer, informing the spirit that the child is placed under its protection. These proceedings are sometimes undertaken at the instigation of the fortune-teller.

When an idol is selected, it is generally that of some favourite god, or goddess, such as Kwún Yam [Kuan Yin], The Goddess of Mercy, or Kwán Taí [Kuan Ti], The God of War, or T'ín Hau [T'ien Hou], The Goddess of Heaven, or Man Ch'öng [Wên Ch'ang], The God of Literature, or even the Tutelary Spirit (Lares) of the Bridge, or the Tutelary Spirits placed at the two entrances to a village, but not those of the house. In the case of a god being selected, part of his name (*i.e.*, one of the characters forming his title or designation) is combined with that of the child, forming a new name for the latter, which is, however, only used by the parents. The god selected is worshipped on his birthday, and styled 'the adopted father.'

Were no other proof available of the slight esteem in which girls are held by the Chinese, it would be shown by the difference in the estimated percentage of those of each sex who are the subjects of this false adoption; for in the extreme south of China it is believed that 50 per cent. of boys are thus subjected to adoption, and only 10 per cent. of girls.

References.—The Penal Code (*Ta Ch'ing lü li*), Sect. LXXVIII; Parker, *Comparative Chinese Family Law;* Hoang, *Le Mariage Chinois; China Review,* Vol. xiv; *Journal N.C.B.R.A.S.,* Vol. xxvii.

AGAR-AGAR.—Amongst curious objects mentioned in books on China appears agar-agar, edible seaweed.

It is 'the Malay name for a species of marine alga, the *Fucus saccharinus* of botanists; growing on the rocky shores of many of the Malayan islands, and forming a considerable article of export to China. . . . It is esculent when boiled to a jelly, and is also used by the Chinese as a vegetable glue.' 'Of late years it has been largely adopted in the European cuisine as a substitute for isinglass with which to make jellies, etc., though wanting somewhat in delicacy and taste. The principal place of production is Pulo Pangkor Laut (Dindings) opposite Perak.' The Chinese, who call it Shek fá ts'oí [*hai ts'ai, hai tsao, hai yao,* or *k'un pu*], also use it as a medicine.

AGRICULTURE.—'The glory of the farmer is that, in the division of labours, it is his part to create. All trade rests at last on his primitive activity.' Thus Emerson begins his 'Essay on Farming,' and it might have been written by a Chinese; for it is with a feeling of this nature that the Chinese have classed the tillers of the ground as next to the scholar, and before the merchant and the artisan: these being the four estates into which the people are divided by them. 'From the earliest dawn of legendary history, agriculture has been regarded' by the Chinese 'as a high and ennobling calling.' This all, of course, from a theoretical point of view—on paper, in books, documents, proclamations, precepts, and exhortations—while in actual everyday life, the boor (in the original meaning of the word), *i.e.,* the rustic, clownish countryman, sinks to a subordinate position as compared with that of the relatively more cultivated town resident, the wealthy citizen and merchant, who elbow the farmer from the van, and relegate him to an inferior position; the official, being the apotheosis of the scholar, takes, of course, the first position. Yet, notwithstanding this, a high idealistic position for the cultivator of the soil is fostered by not a few of the institutions and habits peculiar to the Chinese. As an instance of this, there is the example which was set by each Chinese Emperor of ploughing in the Temple of Agriculture in Peking at the Spring Equinox every year, thus inaugurating the commencement of the farming season. The Emperor took the field, not as a warrior, but as a farmer, and, as an example to his subjects, he walked behind the plough, and thus dignified the toil of his meanest field-labourer, or rather the public ennobling of agriculture in this manner added dignity to the office of this great ruler of mankind. The viceroys or governors of the different provinces perform the same ceremony annually. The following short account of the performance of these acts by Li Hung-chang in Canton in 1900, when Viceroy of the Two Kuang provinces, will give some idea of what was done on such occasions:—

'On the 9th ultimo, between 8 and 9 a.m., H.E. the Viceroy Li Hung-chang and all the principal Chinese officials went in court dress by chair to the Temple of Shên Nung beyond the East Gate, and worshipped the patron saint of agriculture, and the spirits of land and grain, after which they proceeded on to a bamboo stage, lined with flags on two sides, and seated themselves. Then came an old man leading an ox to the front of the stage, followed by two husbandmen carrying a pair of hoes and two sets of harrows, and twelve boys representing the signs of the Zodiac. The Provincial Governor, the Tartar General, the Judge, and the Magistrates descended from the stage, and assisted at the ceremony of tilling and harrowing by handling the hoes and harrows, and scattering seeds, while the twelve boys sang songs to the accompaniment of music. The ceremony of agriculture is performed once a year by the officials three days after the tomb festival.'

A modified form of this ceremony is now performed by the President of the Republic.

An object lesson is thus given to the people throughout the country and a 'deep sense of the importance of agriculture to the public welfare' typified. Important it is in a threefold sense:—Firstly, because of its regular supply both of food and labour to the people; secondly, the needs of the Government are met by moderate taxes, although, unfortunately, owing to faulty administration and probably to the rapacity of the officials, they are frequently increased to six times the nominal assessment; thirdly, an agricultural population, it has been found, is governed with greater ease than a purely mercantile or warlike community.

Not only did the Son of Heaven show an example to the meanest agricultural labourer by guiding the plough with his royal hands; but the Chinese Government still poses as a benefactor of the humble farmer, and to a great extent carries into benevolent action the fostering of this most important branch of labour. With this end in view, the taxes imposed are in relative value to the productiveness of the soil under cultivation; the reclamation of fields on the river banks or the sea-shore is easily effected, 'the terms not being onerous'; and waste land, whether on the hill-sides or level ground (if poverty of soil requires a lengthened time for the recouping of the industrious farmer for capital expended), is untaxed until ample time has elapsed for his labours to prove remunerative with an assessment superimposed, five harvests being allowed to the farmer who thus 'reclaims from a state of nature.' And yet with all this encouragement to tillage many tracts of country still lie waste, some of it the most fertile in the country; partly because the people have not the skill and capital to drain and render it productive, partly because they have not sufficient prospect of remuneration to encourage them to make the necessary outlay, and sometimes from the outrages of local banditti making it unsafe to live in secluded districts.

If we are to believe the Chinese accounts, agriculture was the invention of Shin [Shên]-nung, the Divine Husbandman, for he it is who is credited not only with the invention but also with the introduction of husbandry amongst the Chinese. This mythical or semi-mythical monarch reigned 2838–2698 B.C.

Professor Rein commences his magnificent work on 'The Industries of Japan,' as follows:—

> 'In contrast with the nomadic races of Central Asia, the inhabitants of the monsoon region have for thousands of years been tied to the soil. They are intensely devoted to agriculture, especially in China and Japan. Little opportunity is left in these countries for cattle raising; and since meadows and pastures are wanting, milk, butter, and cheese—the principal food of the nomadic Mongolian peoples—were unknown to the Chinese and Japanese. Eggs, and the products of fishing and the chase, play a far more important *rôle* than the flesh of domestic animals. . . . Since sheep were but seldom found in China . . . wool was formerly of small consideration in the matter of clothing. Hemp and cotton goods, and silk among the rich, especially in the winter, are the stuffs with which the population is clothed.'

As would naturally be expected, the diverse climatic conditions of such a vast country—extending from the plains of Manchuria to the mephitic vales of Yünnan, and from the sea-coast provinces to the high mountains and great table-lands of Tibet—result in various and dissimilar products from the different regions embraced under the name of China; but diverse as these products are, the large proportion of them are cultivated for food purposes. Cotton, hemp, indigo, and mulberry for silk are almost the only important plants which are grown that are not alimentary. The basin of the Yangtzŭ forms the great cotton region; 'hemp is largely cultivated north of the Mei-ling, and it also grows in Fuh-kien'; the southern provinces produce in large quantities the rice which forms the staple of food for millions of Chinese; while the northern, colder regions are more suited to the maturing of millet and corn. Again, the tea plant is unknown in the northern provinces, the sunshine and the moist temperature to be found between the twenty-third and thirty-fifth degrees of latitude suiting it better; the sugar-cane is only to be seen growing in the south and south-eastern parts of China; and the poppy is unfortunately fast extending its area of cultivation through different provinces—east, west, north, and south, and actually constituting a third of the whole cultivation of the province of Yünnan; though restricted (temporarily at least) by the anti-opium measures introduced at the beginning of the twentieth century (*see* OPIUM).

The memorable sentence of Arthur Young's, so often quoted in the West in favour of small farms and peasant proprietors—'Give a man the secure possession of a rock, and he will turn it into a garden,' is equally applicable to the Chinese farmer.

The never-tiring industry of the Chinese is fully exemplified in the unremitting toil of the farmer: in the sweat of his brow does he earn his daily bread; 'week in, week out, from morn till night,' is he to be found—now with his primitive plough upturning the soil, now with unsavoury concoctions of manure assisting the growth of the plant, (for Chinese manuring is applied more to the growing plant itself than to the soil); now with the assistance of his son working the tread-mill waterwheel to fill his artificial water-channels, or with quick step, or half trot, wending his way with water buckets (gigantic watering-pots) between his rows of vegetables, and supplying artificial rain to his crops. Nor do his ingenious contrivances for irrigation stop here; for natural brooklets are deflected from their wanton course and trained here and there down the hill-sides, reviving the thirsty terraced fields as they go, artificial channels being formed, first large, then smaller ones, leading to every little plot—tiny rills carrying moisture to every bit of parched ground; large wheels with buckets fixed to them turn slowly and raise some hundreds of tons of water each day from the streams, which, while giving the motion to these wheels, are thus assisting in each revolution to rob themselves of their watery treasures; well-sweeps (the *shădŭf* of Egypt) ladle out the contents of pools constructed for the gathering of rain-water; and even a pail or shallow vessel, with ropes attached to each side, is used to scoop up the precious fluid from the running brook, a man standing on each bank and with a swinging motion skimming the vessel just enough under the surface to take up sufficient water, when it is raised and with a jerking motion emptied, this all being done with remarkable rapidity and smoothness of motion. Thus a perfect network of minute streamlets and water-courses penetrate to each lilliputian field, to be turned off or on at the will of the Chinese farmer, who, when the ground has had enough moisture, closes the little aqueduct with a lump of mud. Man's labour is thus utilised and supplemented in various ways by different contrivances; even the cattle are sometimes employed to turn the waterwheel, and, as we have seen, the stream itself is yoked into the same service. All this obtains in the southern provinces.

'In the north of the country, where wheat, millet, and other grains are largely grown, the rain supply in summer and the snow in winter furnish all the moisture which the farmers require in ordinary years.'

Few, if any, carts are to be seen in the farmyard in the southern or eastern provinces of China; man is essentially the beast of burden, aided, of course, by woman, though in some districts, women are not employed in field-labour at all.

The convenient carrying-pole with a bucket, or pail, or basket, or bamboo loop, as the exigencies of the case may require, suspended from each end, serves all purposes of porterage, and is amply sufficient for conveying root-crops, grass, water, manure, and anything else that may require to be transported short or long distances. To such an extent does man perform labour, which is relegated to the horse or ox in other lands, that the Chinese farmer may even be seen carrying his plough off from, or on to, the field, though the water-buffalo is yoked to it when it is used to scrape the soil; the same animal pulls the harrow in its course over the surface of the ground or as it stirs up the miry bottom of the semi-aquatic rice-field. These uncouth, unwieldy-looking animals are driven to and from their work, as well as guided in it, by boys, and it is interesting to see the complete control which these tiny youths have over these huge, ungainly, and stupid-looking beasts.

Primitive, indeed, as well as ingenious, are the tools of the Chinese farmer: content he has been to follow in the wake of the first inventive genius amongst his progenitors, who used the ubiquitous bamboo, spraying out its end as a rake, or who, sticking a piece of iron on a pointed stick, was satisfied with the achievement, and yoked his bullock to this rudimentary plough—a coulter serving to turn over only a few inches of soil; for the agricultural implements of the Chinese are few in number as well as of simple construction. In all probability, if not invented by the redoubtable Shin [Shên]-nung himself, these tools of the farmer have been in use for centuries with no alteration or improvement effected in them. One writer thus describes the Chinese plough and harrow:—

'The plough is made of wood, except the iron-edged share, which lies flat and penetrates the soil about five inches. The whole invention is so simple and rude that one would think the inventor of it was a labourer, who, tired of the toil of spading, called the ox to his aid and tied his shovel to a rail;—fastening the animal at one end and guiding the other, he was so pleased with the relief, that he never thought of improving it much further than to sharpen the spade to a coulter and bend the rail to a beam and handle. The harrow is a heavy stick armed with a single row of stout wooden teeth, and furnished with a framework to guide it; or a triangular machine, with rows of iron teeth, on which the driver rides to sink it in the ooze.'

These two instruments are employed in rice cultivation. A broad hoe is used in the dry fields and soft lands, the impetus of the blow being increased by the weight of its large wooden blade edged with iron, or by a blade made entirely of iron. The spade is but sparingly had recourse to, as compared with its constant employment in Western lands. As the seed is not sown broadcast, the farmer is able with busy hoe to loosen the soil and keep his fields beautifully clear of weeds. No machinery, except such as has already been named, is found in the farm-yard. Besides the above there are mattocks, rakes made of bamboo, bill-hooks which do duty for scythes, pruning knives, and sickles. Flails are used on thrashing floors (made of chunam and containing a few square feet each) for thrashing rice, peas, mustard, turnips, and other seeds from the stalks, or unshod oxen are employed for the same purpose. Winnowing machines are also used, which, it is said, have been copied in the West. A small wheel, hand-turned and within the machine, separates the chaff from the grain by creating a strong wind, which meets the grain as it falls from the hopper into which it is fed, and blows the light husks away from the heavier seeds.

The Chinese farmer, as a general rule, is more a peasant proprietor, or, if not that, a peasant farmer rather than a farmer in our sense of the term, though here and there large farms are to be met with on the frontier provinces and up north. So minute are the sub-divisions, that at times a ridge or two of potatoes, or vegetables, in a field will belong to one person and the rest of the field will be parcelled out in equally small portions. In this connection, the following extract from a report on Agriculture in China, published by the Department of Agriculture at Washington, will be of interest:—

'Thus in Kwong Tung [Kuangtung] . . . one-sixth of an acre will support one person, and the proprietor of two acres of good land, having a family of five, can live without work on the produce of his little property. Seven acres constitute wealth, as it is reckoned in China, and few landowners have a hundred acres.' Emigration 'and infanticide . . . alone prevent such overcrowding as would render existence on the land impossible for the population as a whole. In the north, where the soil is less fertile, the holdings are larger, and the standard of comfort among the people is higher. In Manchuria, farms of 500 acres are not uncommon, and there are some much larger estates; but the great farms are cultivated in common by families, some of which consist of two hundred members. Even in the north, it is said that a family of six or seven persons can live on three acres of land, and that five acres constitute comfort, or what is so considered among people satisfied with the bare necessities of existence.'

The authority for the statement as to the Kwong-tung [Kuangtung] province seems to be an account by Miss Fielde of farming matters in the Swatow district, and this same authoress also says:—

'At this rate of production and consumption, the arable land in the State of New York, with a reduction of one-half its returns on account of its more northern latitude, would support the total population of the United States at the present time; and the occupied arable land of the United States, with its producing power diminished, on account of climate, to one-half that of land at Swatow, would feed a population equal to that of the whole world, or over 1,400,000,000.'

Another author says:—

'The Chinese are rather market gardeners than farmers, if regard be had to the small size of their grounds. They are ignorant, too, of many of those operations whereby soils naturally unfruitful are made fertile, and the natural fertility sustained at the cheapest rate by proper manuring and rotation of crops; but they make up for the disadvantages of poor implements by hard work.'

The hill-sides are often terraced for rice, and places which would otherwise only be waste land are utilised for the production of this useful cereal as well as other plants; but it is erroneous to suppose that the whole of China is a vast garden, or that every hill is cut into a succession of steps from base to summit. Rice, being the staple of food in the South, is largely cultivated, the fields lying under water for a considerable portion of the year on that account. Little footpaths, only wide enough for one pedestrian at a time, divide these rice-fields from one another. The flat low grounds formed from the alluvial deposits of rivers are a favourite and suitable situation for such fields, large retaining banks protecting the chess-board mass of fields from the incursions of the river. Another footpath (wider than those in the centre of the fields) runs along the tops of these banks, and the sloping sides are utilised for the cultivation of fruit-trees, such as plantains, lychees, whampees, etc. Two or three crops of rice are produced in one year, as well as a crop or two of fish, which latter, introduced in a young stage into the enclosed water lying on the fields, are grown to a size fit for food in a short time. In some country districts, pea-nuts, sugar-cane, and native tobacco are cultivated. A numerous variety of vegetables is also to be seen. These are mostly of a poorer quality than European vegetables, and are often of a kind unknown to the Western world. Much of Chinese agriculture consists in rearing them. The sweet potato, the yam, taro, beans, cucumbers, pumpkins, squashes, water-melons, vegetable marrows, brinjals, etc., all engage the attention of the Chinese agriculturist, and provide him and many of his fellow-countrymen a relish to take with their plain-boiled rice; a small modicum of salt, or fresh fish, or meat sometimes, giving a little additional savouriness to their daily fare. For on such frugal diet, or on even a scantier one, do the Chinese farmers and millions of the labouring classes perform their daily tasks.

The cultivation of the soil is marked by extreme care and attention to details.' The fields are clean and well kept. The labourer is at his task from early morn till dewy eve, or at all events till the hour for the evening meal. Nothing is wasted; nothing lost in China. 'Fertilising materials are collected from all conceivable sources . . . and thus the productiveness of the soil is maintained, while its condition is kept up to the mark by the most laborious industry.' Continuous manuring while the plants are growing (supplied in a liquid form) would seem to obviate the necessity for a constant rotation of crops in the eyes of the Chinese; for they are adepts at manuring, and keep up the character of the soil in this way, though a rotation of crops is also said to be always practised in some parts of China. The night-soil of the cities—nay, of every little hamlet even, and the contents of the primitive wayside urinals, are carefully husbaned and utilised, to the disgust of the olfactory nerves of those unaccustomed to such an ancient mode. Pots and pans and crocks and broken sherds are placed at every convenient, as well as every inconvenient, spot for the collection of this liquid manure, at times regardless of all Western ideas of decency. This is deluged with water and poured on the growing plants with a ladle from buckets in the morning and evening hours. Other materials are gathered for the same purpose, the motto in China being to waste nothing, and nothing almost seems to come amiss: mud from the rivers, canals, and tanks—a splendid fertiliser in a country like this, where the rivers act as main sewers and dust-bins, and their tributaries feed the main channels with sufficient material pilfered from the crumbling banks to form rich alluvial deposits—the sweepings from the streets, hair from the barbers' shops, the refuse paper, etc., from fire-crackers after being exploded, lime and plaster with years of wood soot impregnating it, gathered from kitchens and old buildings, soot itself, old bones, the refuse of fish and animals, castings from animals and fowls—all are eagerly gathered from every spot and made use of; and so also is vegetable rubbish which is charred under turf, 'the residue is a rich black earth, which is laid upon the seeds themselves when planted; the refuse left after expressing the oil from groundnuts, beans, vegetables, tallow, tea, and cabbage seeds, etc., is likewise mixed with earth and made into cakes, to be sold to farmers.'

Captain Gill, though considering that Chinese agriculture had been overestimated, yet says that in one respect it is 'peculiar, namely in the care which is taken with ground once under cultivation to see that nothing is lost.' The economy of the minute is exemplified in farming in China as in most other callings in that great land, so made up of the savings of what would be despised as trifles in other lands of smaller size.

Agriculture in China is a *petit culture.*

To one accustomed to fields laid down in grass and clover, it is curious to notice the absence of these features so common amongst us; what might be pasture or meadow lands, such as the bottom of valleys and flat land, are used for rice and other crops.

The spring and summer in the South are characterised by a relatively high temperature, light winds, dampness, and frequent rain alternating with dry spells, but the early winter is the dry season in which for several months clear skies prevail, accompanied by a cold temperature which increases as the winter progresses and the new year comes in, till in January, February, and March, the temperature is keen, and is rendered intensely disagreeable by the dampness which is apt to be present to a considerable extent in the shape of rain, mists, and fogs. The typhoons which bring torrents of rain in their train are often frequent visitants in the summer months when the south-west monsoon is blowing, the north-east monsoon being the winter wind. Vegetation and agriculture, of course, depend largely upon these climatic conditions, the copious rains, bright sunshine, and mountain mists, all have their share in producing the rapid growth of the plant; but Nature tends her own products with a careful hand, for fogs and mists, followed by April showers, commence the irrigation of the land, parched and dried with the moistureless year-end; these lighter showers are succeeded, as the hardened earth is gradually moistened, and better able to drink in the heaven-sent floods, by heavier thunder-storms and drenching rains, to be again succeeded by the torrential downpours, following in the wake of the dreaded cyclonic typhoon. No frosts of any appreciable influence, as a rule, occur in the neighbourhood of Hongkong and Canton; but the case is different further north in higher latitudes.

The cost and difficulty of transport no doubt exert a deterrent effect on the development of Chinese agriculture, though this is being lessened in some parts by the introduction of Western methods of distribution.

The Chinese farm-house is not, as a general rule in the South, to be found in the centre of the ground which the farmer has under cultivation, but at some distance, perhaps, from the fields, forming with all the other farm-houses of the neighbourhood a little hamlet or village, from which the men issue at early dawn to proceed to the scene of their labours, and to which they return when their work is over. This economises space and affords more security to the denizens of the little communities from the attacks of robbers, though it is a wonder what temptation can exist for attacks from such, when the farmers are so little removed themselves from the abject depths of poverty. The small holdings and farms are sometimes rendered still more fractional in size with the death of each proprietor, as on his demise his possessions are often divided amongst his family, such being the general outcome of the law of succession. Disputes as to the inheritance of land give rise to many feuds and crimes. Such family quarrels often form the principal incident on which the stories in many a Chinse novelette hinge.

'To find a parallel to the agricultural condition of the country, we must look to our Colonial Empire, where settlers apply for uninhabited lands, and receive the rights over them in exchange for small annual payments. This is the principle on which lands have been appropriated in times past, and still are leased out to farmers. As a rule, the land so let is taken up by a clan, the members of which cultivate it much on the principle of the village communities. . . . Ten families constitute, as a rule, a village holding, each family farming about ten acres. To such a community is allotted a common village plot, which is cultivated by each family in turn, and from which the tribute grain is collected and paid. The surplus, if any, is divided between the families. Towards the end of the year a meeting is held, at which a division of the profits is made on one condition. Any farmer who is unable to produce the receipt for the income-tax on his farm ceases to be entitled to any benefit arising from the village plot.'

The following appreciative notice of Chinese farming is from the pen of Mrs. Hales, late of Amoy:—

'It is doubtless true, as asserted, that irrigation, as practised in Japan and China to-day, is crude and unsystematic, but it would be a mistake to assume that we have nothing to learn from those countries in these matters. People who have depended for centuries upon artificial methods of watering a large part of their artificial lands ought to have gained some valuable experience, and it is our business to profit by studying what they have accomplished. It may freely be admitted that the methods of the Chinese and Japanese are not modern, and that they fail to avail themselves of many of the contrivances by which people in the Western world would carry on agricultural pursuits; but, at the same time, we must not shut our eyes to the fact that the Chinese accomplish results which make the intensive farming of the French seem slipshod efforts when a comparison is made. Recent investigators of the subject have expressed the opinion that if the same degree of skill were applied to make the soil of England produce farm products that is expended upon the land of China, Great Britain would be independent of foreign nations for its food supplies, and could support a larger population than the census now shows. Or a still more forcible comparison is made by pointing out that if China had made no better use of her soil than the most skilful European peoples had made of theirs, the empire would not be able to support one-half its present population.'

Under the Republic, with its Ministry of Agriculture and Commerce, many Western methods of agriculture and rearing are being introduced, training schools established, and experiments of various kinds made.

References.—Williams, *Middle Kingdom*, ii, 1-14; Douglas, *Society in China*, pp. 120-36; Fielde, *A Corner of Cathay; Journal N.C.B.R.A.S.*, Vol. xxiii; Hongkong daily papers, April 24th and 25th, 1893 (an account of the Emperor ploughing); *Reports of the U.S. Dept. of Agriculture;* King, *Farmers of Forty Centuries*. *See also* BUFFALO; LAND TENURE; SILK; TEA; and RICE.

ALCHEMY. *See* TAOISM.

ALMANAC. *See* CALENDAR and TIME.

Things Chinese

ALMONDS.—The Chinese are fond of almonds. One of the chief native restaurants in Hongkong is known by the name of the 'Almond Blossom.' Almonds are used in cakes, etc., and in the preparation of what is known as 'almond tea,' sold in the streets at night, and considered good for coughs, etc. The almond is not a product of China. The Chinese confound apricot and peach kernels with the almond, and they 'are found promiscuously supplied under the common term *hung yun* [*hsing-jên, hêng-jên, or hang-jên*].'

References.—Smith (F. P.), *Contributions towards the Materia Medica and Natural History of China.*

AMUSEMENTS.—The Chinese, though a hard-working and industrious people, are not behind other nations in their love of amusements, and enter with great zest and gusto into the enjoyment of them, most heartily assisting, in the French sense of the term, at shows, processions, etc. It needs but a saunter through the crowded and busy streets of a Chinese city to see that, though there is much bustle and unceasing toil, there is, on the other hand, an unfailing provision for the relaxation of the tired workers and the delectation of the younger members of society. Theatres are crowded, though the performances last for long weary hours, if not days. The various birthdays of the gods, or religious festivals, are hailed with delight, for then the streets are matted over and hung with puppets, gorgeously dressed in mediæval costume, representing historical scenes; while glittering chandeliers, ablaze with light, shed a bright radiance on the erewhile gloomy streets, and transform them into a dazzling vision of light. All these illuminated streets converge to one centre, where, in front of the temple in honour of whose god the exhibition is being held, a grand temporary structure, towering in height above all the other surrounding buildings, is erected, gorgeous with painted scenes in many-coloured hues, brilliant with clusters of crystal lights, and all the magnificence of ceremonial, gaudy show, and paraphernalia of heathen worship. Here all the grandeur is centred, radiating out through all the surrounding streets, and here it is that the crowd is at its thickest—a compact mass, open-mouthed, gazing to their hearts' content, enjoying to the full all the entrancing sights, the celestial music of clashing cymbals, twanging guitars, harsh flageolets, and shrill flutes.

The annual Regattas of the Dragon Boat Feast give an outing to many a child and lady, who attired in their holiday best, line the banks of the rivers, and watch the narrow snake-like boats dashing up and down in impromptu races and spurts with their rivals from neighbouring villages. (*See* DRAGON BOATS).

Another great outing is that on the day for 'Ascending on High'; many, who can afford the time, go to the summit of some high mountain, or lofty hill, in remembrance of the deliverance of a family in olden times from destruction by a similar action. (*See* ASCENDING ON HIGH).

The Full Moon Festival is kept gaily, when indigestible moon-cakes are seen at all the confectioners' stalls and shops. Every boat hangs out one or more tasteful paper lanterns, which, suspended from bamboo poles, make a general illumination over the dark waters of the deep and murky river, and, overhead, the full-orbed moon in harvest splendour shines down from the clear sky on a scene of tropical, Oriental beauty. The faint glimmer of the tiny craft is eclipsed anon by boats, all ablaze with one glow of light from innumerable lamps. These larger vessels slowly float down the stream in the distance.

Visits to flower-gardens give a variety to the monotony of everyday life, and even the sombre worship at the tombs, after the prescribed ceremonials are through, is transformed into pleasant picnics and happy family re-unions.

Besides these outdoor entertainments, there are different games of cards, dominoes, chess, etc., the two former being almost invariably associated with gambling. (*See* PO-TSZ). Numerous other games are played, whose whole end and object is gambling pure and simple, amongst which may be noted games with dice, encounters of fighting crickets, and quail matches. The *jeunesse dorée* of a literary or artistic taste also amuse themselves and while away the passing hour by wine parties, at which capping of verses takes place. Their leisure moments are sometimes beguiled by making pen-and-ink sketches on fans, or inscriptions on the same articles of necessity for a warm climate, or by the composition of antithetical sentences, which are inscribed on scrolls and presented as souvenirs to friends.

Western athletic games and sports are now largely practised by the Chinese, especially by the scholars attached to the universities, colleges, and schools. Before the overthrow of the monarchy in 1912 outdoor sports were not in vogue with the Chinese. When one saw anything approaching the kind going on there was almost always sure to be some utilitarian object in view, as in archery, which was practised for the military examinations. (*See* ARMY and EXAMINATIONS). The gymnastic exercises with heavy weights were undertaken with the same object. Very rarely one might see a few young

Celestial swells, paddling together in a canoe, but this was uncommon enough not to be a typical sight.

As to out-door games, the most violent in which adults engaged was shuttlecock. (*See* SHUTTLECOCK). A more sedentary pastime is that of flying kites in which grown-up men and youngsters indulged (*see* KITES). Very ingenious were the different forms and shapes of kites made, and some, like birds, were so well manipulated, when in the air, as to deceive one at first sight.

The sports and games referred to in the last two paragraphs have, however, by no means been ousted by the newer forms. They were in temporary abeyance during the first few years of the Republic, owing to fear of punishment by the authorities, but have since re-appeared in all parts of the country.

Blind singing girls perambulate the streets at night, ready to accompany their song with the guitar (p'éí-p'á) [*p'i-p'a*], itinerant ballad-singers of the other sex can be hired by the day. Story-tellers are pretty sure to get a good crowd round them while interesting episodes in Chinese history are recounted to their listeners. In any open space, or lining the broader streets, are peep-shows, the more crude native production being replaced in many cases, during the last twenty or thirty years, by stereoscopic views. Jugglers, and Punch and Judy shows, performing monkeys, as well as gymnasts, are always certain of a circle of admiring spectators.

The ladies join in a few of these amusements, as has already been pointed out, but until recently were debarred from the great majority of those which could not be enjoyed in the privacy of their dwellings. They killed time by playing cards and dominoes, occasionally going to the theatre, gossiping, and visiting—when they were quickly carried in closed chairs through the narrow streets, invisible to every one, and every one and everything nearly invisible to them. It is only in recent years that they have acquired in most cases complete freedom, visit places of amusement with their relatives and friends, and join in outdoor sports, such as tennis and bicycling, as well as in modern indoor games.

As to children's toys and sports, though one writer in an English periodical very sapiently (?) remarks that there are no toys in China, yet it needs but a few steps in a Chinese city to show the absurdity of the statement. Besides taking their share in the enjoyments of their elders, they have more especially for their benefit, tops, paper lanterns in the shape of fish, iron marbles, toy cannon and weapons, and a thousand and one different games and toys with which the ingenuity of the caterers for their amusement fills the toyshops, and covers the stalls at the street corners.

References.—Williams, *Middle Kingdom*, Vol. i; *N. & Q. on C. & J.*, iii, 88; Parker, *John Chinaman;* Headland, *Chinese Boy and Girl;* Gray, *China*, Vol. i; Medhurst, *Foreigner in Far Cathay;* Davis, *Chinese*, Vol. i; Doolittle, *Chinese;* Tchêng-ki-tong, *Chinese Painted by Themselves;* Moule, *New China and Old; Nineteeth Century*, March, 1906; *Journ, N.C.B.R.A.S., N.S.*, iii, 107; *Cycle*, June, 1870; *China Review*, Vols. vii, ix, xiii, etc.

AMAH.—A nurse. In north China called *ma-ma*. The Indian *ayah*.

AMBER.—In Chinese *hu-po*. First mentioned in the first century A.D. In powdered form used in Chinese medicines. Originally imported from Kashmir and Burma, and later from Persia. There are numerous imitations made from sheep's horn, copal, shellac, colophony, and glass.

Referencc.—Laufer, *Historical Jottings on Amber in Asia.*

ANALECTS.—The *Lun yü, Digested Conversations*, or *Discussed Sayings*, of Confucius and his disciples. It is the first of the Four Books (*q.v.*). It dates from the beginning of the fifth or end of the fourth century B.C. Is supposed to have been compiled by the grand-disciples of the sage. There are numerous translations (Legge, Zottoli, Soothill, Couvreur, etc.).

ANCESTOR-WORSHIP.—True to their practice of retaining customs and habits for centuries and milleniums, the Chinese nation has not given up this most ancient form of worship; and the original worship of ancestors, like the older formation of rocks on the earth's surface, is strong as the everlasting hills, and, though overlaid by other cults, as the primary rocks are by other strata, is still at the foundation; nearly all the other methods of worship being later additions and accretions. The worshipping of ancestors thus underlies most of their religion, and many of their everyday acts and deeds. 'Social customs, judicial decisions, appointments to the office of prime minister, and even the succession to the throne are influenced by it.' A magistrate, for instance, will pass a much lighter sentence on a criminal if he is the eldest or only son, in the case one or both of his parents have recently died, than he otherwise would, for fear of preventing him sacrificing to the dead. An Emperor on accession to the throne must be younger than his predecessor, in order to worship him. Ancestor-worship has been defined as including 'not only the direct worship of the dead, but also whatever is done directly or indirectly for their comfort; also all that is done to avert the calamities which the spirits of the departed are supposed to be able to inflict upon the living, as a punishment for inattention to their necessities.' Under such a description as this, the actions which it gives rise to will be found to permeate nearly every phase of Chinese life:—concubinage, adoption, house-building (both of private dwellings and clubs), the institution of hospitals, the laying out of streets, modes of revenge, and methods of capital punishment, all are partly due to the same cause. The consuming desire to have sons, and the despising of daughters centre in this, and many of their superstitions and beliefs take their motive force from it. This worship is the only one that is entitled to the name of the National Religion of China, as the dead are the objects of worship of poor and rich, young and old, throughout the length and breadth of this immense country. The Chinese are willing to relinquish every other form of worship and religion, but this is so interwoven into the texture and fabric of their everyday life, and has such a firm hold on them, that scarcely anything, short of the miraculous, forces them to give it up, with such tenacity of purpose do they cling to it. The Roman Catholics, with more wordly wisdom than piety, allowed their converts at one time to retain this worship—though not now; the Protestant missionaries find it the most formidable obstacle to the introduction of Christianity; the Mohammedans in China do not allow it; and it is one of the strongholds of opposition to all Western progress and science.

Believing that the spirits in the next world stand in need of the same comforts and necessities as the inhabitants of this world, they hold it is consequently the bounden duty of friends and relatives of the deceased to forward these to them; but with that curious trait of the Chinese mind which believes in large promises, but small fulfilments—in great show and little reality—the articles sent into the spirit world for the use of their departed relatives, instead of being (as they formerly were) the veritable articles used in this stage of existence, are, like so many things Chinese, shams. For houses, boats, clothes, sedan-chairs, bills of exchange, mock-silver dollars, and every conceivable object of use in this mundane sphere of existence, paper and bamboo models are substituted. Expense, of course, is not spared in the production of these objects, but still it will readily be understood that articles made of such flimsy materials cannot be worth a tenth, or a hundredth, or even sometimes a thousandth part of the genuine article. These are forwarded into the next world by being burned. They proceed even further, for they send supplies to the beggar spirits, who may have been neglected by living relatives, or who may have no relatives living, and to the spirits of those who have died at sea, in war, of starvation, or abroad. 'They believe that nearly all the ills to which flesh is heir, such as sickness, calamity, and death are inflicted by these unfortunate and demoniacal spirits.'

The usual, if not universal, belief with the Chinese, is that a man possesses three souls. After death one goes into the Ancestral Tablet prepared for it, where it receives the worship of the man's descendants at proper and stated times; at such times also, worship is paid at the grave to another soul; while the third goes into the nether world to receive the rewards or punishments of the deeds done in this, finally to return to the upper world again as a god, a man, a beast, a bird, or a reptile, according to his merits. This third soul can also be worshipped at the City Temple, the god of which is the ruler of departed spirits, and has an *entourage* of officials, lictors, and attendants, like the Governor of a Chinese City. Bribery and corruption reign rampant there amongst the spirits, just as in the venal world of China.

The Ancestral Tablet is generally a plain, oblong piece of hard wood, split nearly the whole way up, and stuck into a small transverse block of wood. On one of the inner surfaces and on the front outer surface, are written the name and age of the deceased with other particulars. Incense is burnt night and morning before the tablet, and the near relatives prostrate themselves before it for forty-nine days.

The following is the story of the origin of the custom:—

'The custom of erecting a tablet to the dead is said to have originated during the Chau dynasty (B.C. 350) when one Káí Tsz-chúí, attendant on the sovereign of Tsin, cut out a piece of his thigh and caused it to be dressed for His Majesty, who was fainting with hunger. Káí Tsz-chúí, not being able to continue his march from the pain he suffered, concealed himself in a wood. This prince on his arrival at the state of Tsi sent soldiers to take care of him, but they, being unable to discover him, set fire to the wood, where he was burnt to death. The prince, on discovering the corpse, erected a tablet to his manes, which he begged to accompany him home, and there caused incense to be offered to him daily.

The tablets used by the boat people in Canton are smaller, and differ in other respects also from those used on shore. Immediately after death, plain ones are in vogue amongst the floating population, but after three years or so they are ornamented and painted. A very curious custom also prevails amongst this *tán-ká* [*tan-chia*] people in connection with this matter. Images are made of deceased members of the family, and, what is still more curious, there are images of the children who have died—curious, because children are not ancestors, and the Chinese do not erect tablets to anyone under twenty years of age who has not been married. The boys are usually represented in these cases as riding on lions or white horses, and the girls on white storks.

The Man-tzŭ Aborigines, in Western Ssŭch'uan, take an unburnt piece of wood from the funeral pyre; on the smooth surface they picture a rude likeness of the head of the family who has been there cremated, and place this in the house as the Ancestral Tablet.

'It is computed that the public worship of ancestors cost the Empire £6,000,000 annually; and the private worship £24,000,000.' The latter amount has probably not yet depreciated to any considerable extent.

When a Chinese directs in his will that a certain portion of his estate is to be reserved for the carrying out of ceremonies at his grave, in accordance with the principles of ancestor-worship, English Courts of Law, in the cases that have come before them, have decided that such a bequest is void, as tending to a perpetuity; for money cannot be bound up for an indefinite period, which is not intended for a charitable purpose. (*See* cases of Yip Cheng Neo *v.* Ong Cheng Neo, L. R. 6 P. C., Appeals 381; also Hoare *v.* Osborne, L. R. 1 Eq. 585. The latest decision is, 'In the matter of the estate of Tso Wing Yung (*Judgt.*),' reported in *China Mail* of 6th May 1891).'

'Ancestral land is land that has been originally set apart for ancestral worship, and is increased by purchase from time to time in the name of the deceased ancestor, in whose name also the Government taxes are paid. The rent of ancestral lands is devoted to the upkeep of the ancestral temple, to the education of the members of the clan, to the worship of ancestors, to the relief of poor members of the clan, to the marriage expenses of those who require assistance, and to the funeral expenses of those whose relatives are poor. Such land is always held in the name of the ancestor who bequeathed the property, the land being nearly always leased to members of the clan, who cultivate it and pay a yearly rent. Sometimes the different branches of a clan cultivate the land in rotation, the branch in occupation of the land being held responsible for the payment of the expenses incurred on account of the objects for which the land was originally transmitted. Clan land cannot be alienated without the consent of the representatives and elders of the whole clan. The rent roll is kept by a committee of the clan.'

References.—Yates (M. T.), *An Essay on Ancestral Worship* (dealing with it generally) and *The Attitude of Christianity toward Ancestral Worship* (dealing with it historically); De Groot, *Religious System of China*, Vols. iv to vi.

ANTIQUITIES.—There are far fewer antiquities in this venerable land of such a hoary age than at first would be supposed. Some inscriptions are to be found here or there on boulders; but these are mostly of a modern date, according to Chinese ideas.

The houses and temples are built of such perishable materials, and the climate, typhoons, and insect life all militate against their preservation for more than two or three centuries, without extensive repairs which often constitute a virtual rebuilding. A stone dwelling of ancient times has been discovered in the North; and were an archæological society in existence and conditions of life in China somewhat different from what they are at present, more of such remains of antiquity might be unearthed.

The old stone drums of the Chow dynasty are amongst some of the most venerable relics of antiquity handed down to the present time. Finds of ancient coins buried in the earth or as heirlooms, passed on from generation to generation, reward every now and then the enthusiastic numismatist, as well as curios of one sort or another, the general collector; but on the whole, barring such instances, the study of antiquities in China is disappointing.

'Bricks and tiles of the Ch'in and Han dynasties have always been highly prized and considered as relics. In the neighbourhood of a small hamlet, a little west of Kiang-ying, a rare discovery was made of this kind of bricks, manufactured centuries ago, at an ancient grave. Exposure to the weather had somehow caused a part of the mound to slide down and thus lay bare the inner casement of the tomb built up of this kind of bricks. There are over two thousand bricks in all. In size they are a little larger than the ordinary bricks, but on the four corners of each there are impressions of old coins. Besides the bricks a vase was also unearthed. As to the date of these relics only experts and antiquarians can determine.'

See also PRIMITIVE MAN and PORCELAIN.

APPLES.—The apple and pear tree 'grew wild in Europe and Asia in prehistoric times.' The apple-tree now grows in North China, the climate in the South is too hot for it. There are two kinds: a larger (*p'ing-kuo*)—soft and insipid—and a smaller (*sha-kuo*), a kind of crab-apple; but neither is the genuine *malus* of the West. Large quantities of good-sized apples of the Western species are now imported from Japan and other countries.

ARCHITECTURE.—The Chinese have made but small advance in architecture: they have not proceeded beyond the first steps of architectural construction. The first principle which they have acted upon appears to be that of raising two side-walls to support the beams of the roof. The length of these beams, in buildings of any size, necessitates the adoption of rows of pillars to support them. To obviate the too great multiplicity of these pillars, what has been described as 'a very pretty system of "king" and "queen" posts has been contrived, by which the pressure of several beams is transmitted to a single pillar.' These are often beautifully carved, and there is much scope for variety. Tradescant Lay, from whom we have already quoted, further says:—

'A lack of science and of conception is seen, . . . but fancy seems to have free license to gambol at pleasure, and what the architect wants in developing a scheme, he makes up by a redundancy of imagination.' Williams says:—'In lighter edifices, in pavilions, rest-houses, kiosks, and arbours, there is, however, a degree of taste and adaptation that is unusual in other buildings, and quite in keeping with their fondness for tinsel and gilding rather than solidity and grandeur.' Another sinologist says:— 'Their ornamentation is often beautiful. But, even in their ornamentation, the Chinese rarely, if ever, exhibit congruity of detail. The details are often perfect, but they are seldom in such full harmony with other details as to present to the spectator the pleasing aspect of a harmonious work of art.'

Their construction is bad; very little regard is paid to outline, except in pagodas, roofs of temples, and bridges, but the ornamentation is the pleasantest feature, on which the greatest care is bestowed.

The impressions produced by the first sight of Canton are thus described by an old resident in China. Before reaching China, accounts had been received of the destruction by fire of a Chinese theatre, and the deaths of thousands of natives. Arrived in front of the city, a remembrance of the frightful catastrophe led the newcomer to suppose that the torn-down look of the houses and sheds was the result of the destructive element; the idea never occurring that the usual habitations of the citizens of an enormous city like this were such as these. The magnificent churches and cathedrals, the stately edifices, the superb mansions, are all wanting in a Chinese city; instead of the broad streets, spacious avenues, and large squares—congeries of narrow lanes, a maze of alleys (scarcely one entitled to the name of a street, according to our acceptation of the term); and the few open spaces in front of the temples—not worthy to be dignified with the title of squares. Lining both sides of the way, if in a family street, the walls are formed of bluish-grey bricks, neatly pointed in mortar with granite foundations, reaching several feet above the surface of the ground. Two or three long steps of granite, extending from wall to wall of the house, lead up to the front, which, with the exception of the door in the centre, presents a blank wall to the passer-by. There are no windows, only a plain, massive, double-leaved door of thick planks fastened by two wooden bolts. These doors are often left open during the day, and the privacy of the inmates ensured by two outer, lighter-constructed doors, also of wood, only reaching a little more than half-way up the doorway. The side-walls of the house project a couple of feet or so, and support the eaves, which are carried out a corresponding distance, and shelter the few feet in front of the entrance. The walls are generally the thickness of the length of a brick, and after eight or ten courses, a course of binders is laid. The door once entered, over the high wooden threshold, one finds one's self under a small introductory roof, which shelters the porter's room, and facing one is a row of large doors, made of boards, in sets of three pairs or so, reaching from wall to wall; beyond these is a small court, open in the centre to the sky, where some green glazed pots of ornamental flowers, or plants, are standing on similar flower-stands. The whole house is now before one, the separate apartments being under different roofs, the foremost being the reception hall; for a Chinese residence is a collection of small buildings, except amongst the poorest classes.

A ground floor is all that many houses can boast of, and this is generally tiled with red flooring-tiles, a foot square and an inch in thickness. Marble tiles are occasionally laid on the ground, but they are not highly polished. If there are first floors, they are usually under one or more of the inner roofs.

In some of the houses (more especially in the hongs and godowns fronting the river in Canton) there are as many as six, eight, ten, or twelve separate roofs, one behind another, all in a row, with courtyards between each, and covered passages on each side of these open spaces; the latter serve the double purpose of giving light and ventilation, taking the place of windows, which are mostly confined to the interior of the houses, where they open on the courtyard.

The tent, it has very generally been thought, has furnished the model for the construction of the roof in kiosks and other buildings; but one or two writers have lately dissented from this opinion.

Ceilings are but seldom seen in the poorer Chinese houses, nor are the walls plastered or papered. In the houses of the richer classes a *p'êng* of bamboo or wooden laths, covered with paper, forms the ceiling, and the walls are either whitewashed or pasted over with plain or patterned paper, usually white. The roof-tiles are laid in alternate rows of roll and pantile (or small semi-cylindrical, and broad, slightly concave ones), the traces, it has been pointed out, of early, split-bamboo roofing, and not of the tent structure. In good roofs, a second layer of these is put on above the other, or even a third on the top of all.

The habitations of the poor are often the merest hovels, and many workmen, as well as the poorest classes, live in matsheds, the framework of which is made of bamboo, and the walls and roofs of oblongs formed of bamboo leaves fastened together. These matsheds, built of the 'attap,' as it is called by the Malays, are very convenient, since they are easily and quickly put up without a single nail, the bamboo poles being tied together with long strings of split rattan, and even more easily taken down when done with, for the fastenings are cut instead of being untied. They are largely used as temporary structures for religious festivals and for many other objects, one of the most curious being the construction of one over a house in the course of erection to protect it, and the workmen, from the heavy tropical rains.

Along the banks of the rivers, over the mud-flats, are found many of the poorest sheds and shanties, of a non descript character—old boats often forming the foundation, and the superstructure made of anything and everything, reminding one of Mr. Peggotty's famous ark, as described in '*David Copperfield.*'

The houses of the better classes have much ornamentation about them. Stucco-work, representing human figures, birds, animals, and flowers, is often found over the front of a house, as on a frieze, and below the projecting roof; or the same kind of decoration is found on inner walls, and affords a pleasant relief to the plain monotony of the otherwise bare, brick walls. In Swatow, the whole front wall is often adorned by six or seven large medallion-like pictures which lend a brightness to the otherwise plain surface. In fact, ordinary buildings are more highly ornamented up the coast than is the case further south. Variety is also given by the octagonal, circular, and pear-shaped doorways, which pierce the walls in the suites of apartments, and in gardens, and rockeries of the superior class of houses; a quaint picturesqueness is added to the general effect by the geometrical patterns of the combination of door and window in one, the rows of which serve as screens or partitions between the different rooms, as well as by the fixed open-work partitions of like construction. Carvings of fruit and gaudy paint-work also add their bizarre attractiveness to the *toute ensemble.*

The roofs of shops are built like those of private houses, the shape being that of a V turned upside down; but instead of sheltering themselves behind a plain, brick wall, as in the case of the dwelling-houses, they are quite open to the street, and often have an upper storey supported in the front by a broad breastsummer. The whole shop is open to the street, and is closed up at night by shutter-doors. (In Swatow the shutters over the counter are transverse and not upright; they fold up from the counter and down from the roof, meeting in the space in the centre.) A granite counter occupies a portion of the space in front, and a hardwood counter runs at right angles to it back into the shop. Behind the shop proper is the counting-room. The signboards, though not strictly speaking an architectural feature of the buildings themselves, add much, by the brilliancy of their reds and greens and gilding, to the picturesqueness of the business streets, and relieve the sameness which would otherwise result from the want of architectural decoration. The largest ones are ten—or even more—feet in length, and are suspended at each side of the shop front; some are set in stone bases, others hang over the entrances or in the shop itself. The view which meets the eye on glancing down a street full of shops with its scores or hundreds of many-coloured signboards is quite kaleidoscopic, as the glare of the tropical sun flashes on their variegated hues; while in the softer shades of the covered-over streets (in Central and Southern China cities) they serve to lighten up the semi-religious gloom.

In the construction of the temples and public buildings where space is not so restricted, the main structures—two or three in number—stand isolated, with stone-paved paths and steps leading up to terraces of the same material on which they are built, venerable trees shading the otherwise open spaces. The dwellings of the abbots and monks, or the subsidiary buildings, are at the sides or behind, with numerous corridors leading to the apartments or suites of rooms. Most of what has been written above applies to Canton and its neighbourhood, for of the inhabitants of the various provinces (sometimes even of districts) of China, it may be said with truth, to a greater or lesser extent, '*hi omnes lingua, institutiso, . . . inter se differunt,*' and their dwellings, though in the main constructed on the same general outlines, have peculiarities of their own in different parts of the country; for instance in Amoy, many of the houses have an upward curve at each end of the top of the roof, quite foreign to those in the extreme south of China.

'There is nothing more incomprehensible to a foreigner than an official residence, with its gates, folding doors, halls, side-rooms, balconies, carved and frescoed pillars, lattices, and matted ceilings. . . . The frescoes are gaudy, and represent every conceivable subject, from genii walking among clouds to a moth upon a peach. The roof is a tangled mass of Asiatic glory. The Ssŭch'uanese houses excel in their exterior decorations; the ridges, gateways, and corners, are beautifully trimmed with broken bits of blue and white porcelain, which, at a distance, have a most pleasing effect. . . . The houses, except in the large cities, are flimsy affairs, with walls of pounded earth, and roofs thatched with straw.'

The principal material for house construction in Swatow and its neighbourhood is earth, or river sand, or decomposed granite, mixed with lime in the proportion of seven parts of the former to three of the latter. This is rammed in between boards, hardens, and appears to be most durable.

The roof has been considered the chief feature of Chinese architecture; and there is no doubt that a great amount of decorative art is expended on the massive roofs of the larger and finer temples and public buildings. 'The lightness and grace of the curve of these heavy roofs is worthy of all praise;' they are sometimes constructed double, or in such a manner as to give the appearance of two roofs. The object of 'this is to lend an air of greater richness and dignity.' The roof, it will thus be seen, does not occupy, in public buildings and temples, the subsidiary position that such a part of the structure takes in the West: it is the most striking object in this class of buildings, and with the numerous varnished timbers and posts, the green-glazed tiles and glazed dragons, pearls, etc., and unhidden by plastered ceilings, it looks most picturesque. On the other hand, the roofs of private dwellings are simply for use. The importance of the roof to the Chinese is shown by the curious practice, often seen, of putting up the ridge-pole before the rest of the house is built. It is then supported on a framework of poles, a promise of the building that is to rise to its height in the future.

It would naturally be expected that such an ancient land as China would be full of old ruins. Such is, however, not the case; even the Great Wall has been reconstructed once or twice. There are some structures still standing that have stood for more than a thousand years; but to find older ones than this, it is necessary to excavate the mounds—the tombs of ancient cities—where a few stone buildings may be found: one, built seventeen centuries ago, was recently discovered. Cave and rock dwellings are also to be seen in some parts. The great majority of buildings are modern, in the sense that that word has when applied to anything in China; for many things that are classed under that category would be considered to be mediæval or ancient in the West. The reason for this paucity of relics of antiquity is not far to seek: much of the material employed is not fitted to withstand the ravages of ages, and, when it is, the flimsy style of construction does not ensure that durability which it might otherwise hope to attain; added to which the humidity of the climate, and the insidious attacks of insects, all militate against handing down to posterity the works of its forefathers. A very curious feature in Chinese building-construction is that so little stone has been employed. The streets are paved with it; the city walls are partially built of it; the foundations of houses are constructed of it; so are the end-counters in shops, as well as some of the outer columns in temples; but otherwise it is a rare thing to find it entirely used in the building of any structure, except commemorative arches and bridges. 'The Chinese have been acquainted with the arch from very early times, though they make comparatively little use of it.' Many elegant bridges have been constructed in different parts of the empire, some of great length.

Commemorative arches, as these peculiar quaint portals may be styled, were generally put up by imperial command or permission, to commemorate the virtuous and brave. They are now erected less frequently than formerly. They consist of a large centre and two smaller side gateways, the material employed in the south of China being generally granite, and, in the West, soft, grey sandstone. There is a considerable amount of ornamentation about them, usually in the way of carving, etc.; 'in the west of China the flowers and figures carved in relief are of marble, delicately fitted and highly polished.' In the streets over which they are erected, they at all times form a pleasant contrast to the otherwise common lack of architectural adornment. They are embellished with inscriptions, setting forth the virtues of the individuals whose deeds are immortalised by their erection. The pagoda is one of the most graceful specimens of Chinese architecture. (*See* PAGODAS).

The cupola or dome is almost entirely unknown. Mohammedan architecture deserves some mention, and it is possible that the superiority of the Ming architecture may be traced to it.

References.—Chambers, *Designs of Chinese Buildings; Transactions of Royal Institute of British Architects*, 1874; Fergusson, *History of Indian and Eastern Architecture; Journ. N.C.B.R.A.S.*, N.S., Vol. xxiv; Paléologue, *L'Art Chinois;* Williams, *Travels in N. China* (cave dwellings); Williams, *Middle Kingdom*, Vol. ii; Bushell, *Chinese Art;* and most text-books on China.

ARMS.—To find a counterpart to the arms which the Chinese have used in the past, and which are still not obsolete amongst them, one must turn to some of the weapons employed by us in the West in the times, for instance, of the Tudors, the Stuarts, and the Commonwealth; for the antiquated spears, pikes, and halberds, like those of mediæval Europe, are still modern instruments of warfare amongst this ancient people, and, though fast being superseded, they have not yet been entirely laid aside.

Of spears, there are a number of varieties; among which may be noticed one similar to the partisan of the time of James I, called a *kik* [*chi*]; another is like the pike of the time of Cromwell, called a *t'iú* [*ch'iu*]; and yet another, somewhat like a voulge or boulge, of the time of Henry VII.

Of halberds, there are several different kinds, known as *t'ín fá fú* [*t'ien hua fu*]; some of which resemble the halberds of the times of Henry VIII, Charles II, and the double-axed halberd of the period of Charles I; while another variety, known as the *pún yüt fú* [*pan yüeh fu*], from the crescent on one side, resembles one of the time of Henry VII; another, also called a *kik*, is like one used during the reign of William III.

All these halberds and spears, with the exception of the voulge and the pike, are also ancient weapons amongst the Chinese. A trident, a formidable weapon, is also amongst the arms of the Chinese.

Swords and daggers are thus distinguished in China: a sword (*kím*) [*chien*] is two-edged; a dagger (*tò*) [*to*] has only one edge. Further, swords are always single, while daggers may be single or in pairs; in the latter case, one side of each dagger is flat, so that the two many lie close together and fit into one scabbard or sheath; thus occasionally a Chinese dagger would, by us, be termed a sword. The common Chinese sword is like that of the Roman soldier, but probably a little longer. At one time the Chinese officers carried swords, while the men were armed with daggers. A second kind of sword, but coming under the category of daggers, has a flat belly, or blade, which tapers away to a sharp point. The sword would seem to be guardless, having a transverse bar simply, the hand, grasping the short hilt above it, being entirely unprotected, while in the flat-bellied sword mentioned above, and in many daggers, a guard runs from the bar at the hilt, forming a semi-circle with the rest of the handle; this cross piece being only on the edge side.

Bows and arrows also form part of the equipment of those soldiers who are not armed with Western weapons of precision, though it is said that in modern times they are more for show at examinations than for use in battle. The bows are made of horn and bamboo. Cross-bows have also been employed by the Chinese in warfare.

Dr. Williams thus describes the matchlock and cannon:—

'The matchlock is of wrought iron and plain bore; it has a

longer barrel than the musket, so long that a rest is sometimes attached to the stock for greater ease in firing; the match is a cord of hemp or coir, and the pan must be uncovered with the hand before it can be fired, which necessarily interferes with, and almost prevents, its use in wet or windy weather. The cannon are cast, and, although not of very uniform calibre from the mode of manufacture, are serviceable for salutes.'

The cannon in use before recent years were all muzzle-loaders, some on the city walls in Canton being more than two hundred years old. Of late, breech-loaders and rifles of modern European construction have been coming into use, as portions of the Chinese army are being provided with them (*See* ARMY): but many of the Chinese mandarins are wedded to their old style, and when reverses occurred in the war with Japan in 1894, believing that they were due to the use by their own soldiers of rifles and modern arms, they proceeded to cast thousands of gingals, so as to provide their army with them and ensure victory. Gingals, or jingals, are long tapering guns, six to fourteen feet in length, borne on the shoulders of two men and fired by a third. They have a stand, or tripod, the whole outfit reminding one of a telescope. By means of a single support, they are set in the bulwarks of boats, when employed in naval warfare, or for the protection of peaceful merchantmen, and being less liable to burst than cannon, they formed until recently the most effective gun the Chinese possessed.

Two-men jingals 'are a little over ten Chinese feet long, and are of large bore. When ready to be fired, the front-rank man grasps hold of the middle of the barrel as it rests in the hollow of his right shoulder, while the rear man takes aim and draws the trigger. Formerly the flash-pan was used, but with the introduction of percussion caps, the jingals have been fitted with nipples. These weapons are claimed to have conquered China, being introduced by the Manchus when they invaded the empire of the Ming dynasty, and with jingals, Chinese Turkestan was conquered by the Emperor Ch'ien-lung's armies in the seventeenth century. The ordinary charge for a jingal of this sort is a good handful of gunpowder, with a two-and-a-half ounce bullet. Sometimes on the battlefield, the jingals are loaded with an extra allowance of gunpowder, and three bullets—often four—are rammed in to create as much destruction as possible.'

Another weapon of attack used in naval warfare, and especially by pirates, is what is known amongst English-speaking people as the stink-pot:—

'This unsavoury name conveys a wrong impression, as the article so described bears but little resemblance, in shape or material, to its namesake used some centuries ago by pirates on the Atlantic side. The proper name for them is "hand-bomb," or "hand-grenade." They are simply earthen pots, large enough to contain from two to three pounds of powder; the opening at the top is very small, and after they are filled with gunpowder, the lids are cemented on with chunam, which renders the whole air-tight and impervious to dampness. Around the pot, and on the lid of it, a lot of slow match is attached. The man who throws the "hand-bomb," stands on the yard of the foresail, at the foremast head, in the same way as a leadsman does with a hand lead when taking soundings. At the right moment he lets it go, so that it will fall amongst the men on the opposing vessel. The concussion, when it strikes, causes it to break, when the powder comes into contact with the burning match and explodes. Junks defend themselves against these "hand-bombs" by spreading a fishing-net or something similar, tightly drawn about seven feet above the deck. When the "hand-bombs" strike the net, its elasticity causes them to rebound, and fall overboard before they explode. The only smell observable in the explosion of these "hand-bombs" is that of ordinary gunpowder. The powder used contains more charcoal and less saltpetre than ordinary powder, hence it explodes with less force and rapidity. The special virtue of these "hand-bombs" in defence and attack, is that in exploding, they throw the pieces of the pot about with great force, the hot fragments inflicting severe wounds and burns on anyone within range. They are a mild kind of bombshell, being much slower in operation and less deadly in effect than the ordinary shell. The deadly smell supposed to be connected with them is all a fiction.'

Since Western military methods were introduced (A.D. 1901 onward) most of the modern types of weapons have been adopted by the Chinese.

References.—Werner, *Descriptive Sociology—Chinese.*

ARMY.—The military elements, which may be grouped together under the general term of the Chinese army, are various in number and different in composition. It has been well said that—

'The enormous and complicated military power of the Chinese Empire is of a nature to defy any detailed description on a brief scale. The ramifications of the various systems relating to its origin, constitution, and control, have no cohesion with each other. Each province of the Empire has a separate force at the disposal of its Governor.'

Under the Manchu *régime* (A.D. 1644-1912) the three main, but quite distinct, divisions were:—

(1) The eight banners, comprising 'all living Manchus and descendants of the Mongolian and Chinese soldiery of the conquest.' (A.D. 1644). These furnished guards for the palace and garrisons in various chief cities and other places.

They are described as having been 'untrained, ill-disciplined, and cowardly.'

(2) The Chinese provincial army of the 'Green Standard,' comprising the land and marine forces. The former numbered 400,000 or 500,000 and is 'an effete organisation discharging the duties of sedentary garrisons, and local constabulary.'

Orders were issued in 1898 by the Central Government at Peking to disband this force and use the funds thus saved for soldiers trained in European methods; but these commands were disobeyed by the Viceroys.

(3) The braves or irregulars, enlisted or disbanded as required, and used for actual warfare. No approximate guess can be made of their numbers.

Of late years a fourth division should be added, in which should be classed those trained on European lines, some 10,000 in number. After the Japanese War, thirty-five German instructors, under Captain Reitzenstein, were engaged to drill these troops.

As a consequence of the war with Japan in 1894 and the Boxer rebellion in 1900, the above system was proved to be inefficient. Nominally, the troops in the Eighteen Provinces numbered about 650,000, but, owing to peculation, the actual number was probably less than half that for which pay was drawn by the provincial authorities.

Reform having been shown, by bitter experience, to be indispensable, in the year 1901 the military forces were reorganized in three divisions: campaign, reserve, and police corps. Each division was to comprise twelve infantry battalions, one cavalry regiment, three battalions of artillery, and one company of engineers. The new *lu chün* land forces were also organized, and in 1903 and 1906 six Divisions enrolled. To carry out further reforms and developments, the Ministry of War (*Lu Chün Pu*) was established, with the object of creating thirty-six Divisions within ten years,—a programme hindered by subsequent political upheavals. At the end of the Monarchical period there were said to be 800,000 men under arms. In August, 1913, the strength of the regular army was 500,000.

Latterly, the Chinese army has not consisted so much of one body as of several armies under the command of the various rival military governors, who practically rule the country in defiance of the civil authorities.

The tendency has been to imitate in large part the Japanese military system, which in turn was copied from the German.

There are several arsenals in different parts of the country, capable of manufacturing large- and small-arm ammunition, smokeless powder, etc.

On the coast, at the different treaty ports, as well as at some other places, for example, at the Bogue, fortifications after the Western style have been constructed, and breech-loading guns, of modern make, have been provided.

References.—Mayers, *Chinese Government; Chinese Repository,* vol. xx; *Mémoires sur les Chinois,* Tom. vii; Dyer Ball, *Things Chinese,* (4th edit.) and Mesny, *Chinese Miscellany,* Vol. i (for accounts of the pre-Republican Chinese army); *China Year Book* (for statistics of modern army).

ART.—Chinese ideas of painting differ widely from those obtaining in Western countries: the laws of perspective, and light and shade, are almost unknown, though the former is occasionally honoured with a slight recognition. Height usually represents distance in a Chinese painting, that is to say, distant objects are put at the top of the picture, and nearer ones below them, while little difference is made in the size. As regards light and shade, no shading is put into many Chinese landscapes, though M. Paléologue states that native artists have sometimes attained to the expression of the most artistic and delicate effects of light and shade, instancing the grand landscape school of the T'ang dynasty as producing perfect works under this class. The arrangement of objects and the grouping of persons in natural attitudes, would appear not to be taught, according to our ideas on the subject. Symmetry is the object aimed at; the subsidiary parts are treated with as much care as the principal; the smallest details are elaborated with as much minuteness as the most important. Figures are nearly always represented full-faced; and the heads are often stuck on at a forward angle of forty-five degrees to the rest of the body; this being the scholar's habitual attitude and one indicative of much study. What the Chinese delineator considers of prime importance is the representation of the status occupied by the subject: as his rank in the official service, or grade in the literary corps, or social position. The presentation of a living, feeling soul, revealed in its index, the face, sinks into utter insignificance in comparison with the exposition of the external advantages of rank and fortune, or of the tattered rags of the old beggar fluttering in the breeze. Rough outline sketches, in ink, of figures and landscapes are much admired. In these, impossible mountains, chaotic masses of rock, flowers, trees, and boats, are depicted in such a manner as to call forth but little enthusiasm from the Western observer.

'As draughtsmen, their *forte* lies in taking the portrait of some single portion of Nature's handiwork. Many of these they have analysed with great care, and so well studied as to hit off a likeness with a very few strokes of the pencil. . . . There is a peculiarity among the Chinese which has risen from the command they have over the pencil—they hold it in nearly a perpendicular direction to the paper, and are therefore able, from the delicacy of its point, to draw lines of the greatest fineness, and, at the same time, from the elastic nature of the hairs, to make them of any breadth they please. The broad strokes for the eyelash and the beard are alike executed by a single effort of the pencil.'

It has been pointed out that the exigencies of Chinese writing demand an education of the eye and hand, analogous to that required in designing. The handling of the hair brush—the Chinese pen—every day gives a facility and readiness of touch and expression.

The Chinese artist has learned a lesson which has only within the last few years been understood by us in our natural history museums—he copies all the parts of a bird in detail, and then, it has been aptly said:—

'He studies the attitudes, and the peculiar passions of which attitudes are the signs, and thus represents birds as they are in real life, . . . though they may be rudely executed in some of their details. Nor is this fidelity confined to birds alone, neither is it a new advance in their art, as we find it recorded of Ts'ao Fuh-hing [Fu-hsing], a famous painter of the third century A.D., that, having painted a screen for the Sovereign, he added the representation of a fly so perfect to nature that the Emperor raised his hand to brush the fly off.'

A cat has been seen to go up to examine a bird which was drawn standing on a spray in a most natural manner. These stories point out one of the most striking characteristics of certain Chinese painting—its graphic character—and remind us of Apelles's horse which the living horses neighed to, as well as the other famous story of a horse trying to eat a sheaf of corn on the canvas. With equally minute care they faithfully copy flowers, bamboos, and trees, noting carefully the minute ramifications of branches, as well as the action of each particular kind of wind on the objects painted; while, however, all these points are being attended to with a patience worthy of the highest commendation, as it produces a sort of fidelity to nature, yet at the same time 'the whole perchance is vastly deficient in correspondence and proportion.' This entering into the mysteries of nature and the reproduction of some of them with an approach almost to photographic fidelity, scarcely to be expected from them, judging by some of the other productions of their pencils, is of interest and use to the botanical student, since the illustrations in such a native work, for instance, as the great Materia Medica, the *Pên ts'ao*, give a far better idea from their, in many instances, great truthfulness, than the mere letter-press would convey to the foreign student. Their attempts at depicting animal life result in rude, uncouth forms, but the conventionality of the attitudes of the human figure frequently lends a charm which does not attach to many of their products. The proportion and grouping together of the component parts of a picture are defined by a conventional canon, to the rigid adherence of which is due much of the unreality so conspicuous in their attempts at portraying the human passions, and they have remained at the same imperfect development of this branch of their art for many centuries (this stage has been compared to that of Italian painting in the time of Giotto and Simone Memmi); added to which is their entire ignorance of anatomy, the result of this ignorance being often a caricature of the human body. At the same time all praise must be given to the delicacy of their colouring, which, without any scientific laws to guide them, they seem intuitively to know how to apply. They are very fond of their works of art, and the mansions of the wealthy are hung with scrolls, depicting landscapes and sprays of flowers, with birds, and insect life, etc. Even the poorer classes adorn their humbler dwellings with cheaper specimens of pictorial art, and scarcely a boat of any pretensions on the Canton River but is ornamented with a few pictures, while the sellers of sketches in black and white find a ready sale for their wares in the streets.

It is necessary, however, to remember that our commendation is awarded to purely native art, the bastard productions of those daubers who seem to thrive in Hongkong and some of the Treaty Ports being altogether beneath contempt.

The Chinese, in some localities, are clever at fresco or encaustic painting, which they employ upon their temples and better-class houses in the form of panels and friezes both internally and externally (See ARCHITECTURE). Never, so far as we can learn, have they made any use of oil as a medium for their pigments; 'but it must, of course, be remembered that the latter addition to be painter's resources was equally unknown in Europe down to the fifteenth century.'

The native pigments are very primitive, and their cakes, or sticks, of water-colour are on a par with the very cheapest toy outfits of an English juvenile. Their Chinese ink, however, is admirable and superior to any other in the world. Their pencils and brushes, also, leave little to be desired, being exactly adapted to their manner of work. It would be impossible, however, for an English watercolourist to produce his effects with such tools, and it would be idle to expect the Celestial to make any advance in art as it is practised in Western countries until he throws over his conservatism and adopts the paper, colours, and brushes of modern Europe.

Religion, nature, history, and literature, have all inspired the Chinese artist with a more or less varying degree of success.

If implicit credence were to be given to the accounts of the Chinese themselves, painting was first practised B.C. 2600, but the art in China has quite a venerable enough antiquity without ascribing to it such a hoary one. Mural decoration appears to have been the first application of it, and the Chinese Emperors frequently had the walls of their palaces so adorned. In the third century before the Christian era, paintings were made on bamboo and silk, whether pen and ink sketches, or in colour, it is difficult to say; but a great impetus was given to the art when, in the first century of our era, paper was invented.

'The first painter of whose labours we possess any definite record,' belongs to the third century of the Christian era, 'over six hundred years after the period of Zeuxis,' though Dr. Anderson, from whom we quote, informs us, that 'a passing allusion to a portrait is found in the works of Confucius.' The same authority says that the Chinese must have attained to some proficiency in the art of drawing before the Buddhist era: 'it is probable that the higher development of painting in China was due to the influence exercised by specimens of Indian and Greek art introduced with the Buddhist religion.' At the head of the list of Chinese painters stands then the name of Ts'ao Fuh-hing [Fu hsing] (the memory of those who preceded him having been lost), a retainer of the Emperor Wú Sun K'üan [Ch'üan, *i.e.*, Ta Ti] (A.D. 229-251). He was 'famous for Buddhist pictures and sketches of Dragons,' and he is the hero of the marvellous story of the fly. Another story is that of a dragon which was painted by him and preserved until the Sung dynasty, when it produced rain in a time of drought. The second artist whose name has been preserved is that of Chang Sang-yíú [Sêng-yu]. He painted Buddhist pictures for the 'devout monarch Wú Tí' (A.D. 502–50). Anderson thus writes concerning him:—

'It is doubtful whether any of his works are now in existence, but his style has been handed down by followers, amongst whom are numbered many famous masters of the brush.' Another wonderful dragon story is narrated of him. It 'credits him with the delineation of a dragon of such miraculous semblance to "nature" that with the final touches the pictured monster became suddenly inspired with life, and in the midst of sable clouds and deafening peals of thunder, burst through the walls to vanish into space.'

The second epoch commences sometime after the introduction of Buddhism into China. This religion exerted a beneficent effect on the stagnant state of ancient art with the new vistas it opened out, and the new fields for fresh achievements. Buddhism was vigorous in those days, and Buddhist monasteries were multiplied to such an enormous extent, that in A.D. 845 there were more than four millions of them. They were schools of literature and art, and many paintings were executed on long rolls of silk illustrative of the life and death of the founder of Buddhism and Buddhistic subjects.

Other schools arose which also devoted themselves to religious, as well as other kinds of art. Between A.D. 265 and 618, Chinese authors mention about five hundred painters of celebrity, in addition to those of the religious school. Besides the subjects belonging more especially to the latter, the delineation of the human face, of the animal creation, and of landscape, engaged the attention of the artist. One example alone may be mentioned as an instance of the high position which art held at that period: one of the members of Wu Tí's (A.D. 502–50) Privy Council was appointed to adorn the Imperial Temples with paintings.

The third epoch of Chinese art commences with the T'ang dynasty (A.D. 618–907) and ends with that of the Sung. At the beginning of this period, Chinese painting divides itself into the northern and southern schools, so named from the respective parts of the country in which those belonging to them resided, the chief distinction between the two being that the southern was less trammelled by the canons of art to which the northern school rigidly adhered. They, however, represented tendencies rather than what is usually understood by the word "schools." To the former belonged Ouan Mo-kie [Wang Mo-chieh], described as one of the most original artists of China. Like many of China's artists, he was not painter alone, but poet and musician too, for the beauties of the landscapes, which were his special forte, were not only interpreted by his brush, but sung by his muse as well. He reduced his methods to writing, and for two centuries afterwards, viz., the eighth and ninth, they led the artistic world to go direct to Nature as their mistress and model. 'The most brilliant painter of this epoch is Aú To-huan.' Mountains with pagodas, convents and Buddhistic scenes were what he delighted to paint.

In the seventh century, we find two brothers, famous painters, named Yen Lí-teh [Li tê] and Yen Lí-pun [Li-pên], 'the latter of whom is especially remembered for a series of historical portrait-studies of ancient paragons of loyalty and learning.'

Wú Tao-tsz [Wu Tao-tzŭ, or Wu Tao-yüan] is the name which merits most attention in the eighth century. He attracted the notice of the Emperor Ming Huang [Hsüan Tsung, A.D. 713–56], 'with whom he remained in high favour till his death. His style is said to have been formed upon that of Chang Sang-yíú [Shêng-yu], whose spirit was believed to have reappeared upon earth in the person of his follower.' His chief renown was won in religious art, 'but his landscapes were remarkable for picturesque feeling and strength of design, and of his lifelike portraitures of animals.'

Also worthy of mention, though not of such renown, are the names of Wang Wei, a landscape painter holding high rank in court (A.D. 713–42), and Han Kan, a protégé of the last, remembered chiefly for his painting of horses. Among other names, famous during the T'ang dynasty as painters, may be mentioned Lí Tsien [Chien] and his son Lí Chung-ho, 'noted for drawings of figures and horses;' Yuën [Yüan] Ying, 'best known for his minutely drawn representations of insect life;' Kiang [Chiang] Tao-yin and Li Chêng [Ch'êng], landscape painters.

'The artistic appreciation of natural scenery existed in China many centuries before landscape played a higher part in the European picture than that of an accessory.'

During the ninth and tenth centuries, the painting, in all their various movements, of animals and flowers, occupied the attention of all the artists, but at the same time the Buddhist school still pursued its course and produced works of great merit. In the tenth century, two artists of the first rank deserve mention—King [Ching] Hao and Hoang Tsuan [Huang Ch'üan]. There are two specimens of the latter's style in the British Museum in London.

The fourth epoch is that of the Sung dynasty, and is marked by a rejuvenescence of literature and art after the troubled periods which immediately preceded it; but owing to the disfavour into which Buddhism fell, the religious school of art also lapsed into a state of decadence in the twelfth and thirteenth centuries, though a few artists of great ability are still to be found in this branch. The Sung dynasty 'was rich in famous artists.' We many call attention to Muh Ki [Muh Ch'i], Liang Chí [K'ai], Kwoh Hi [Kuo Hsi], the Emperor Hwei [Hui] Tsung, Lí Lung-yen [Li Lung-mien, or Li Kung-lin], Ma Yuën [Yüan], Hia Kwei [Hsia Kuei], Yuh Kien [Yü Chin], Hwui [Hui] Su, and Mih Yuën-chang [Mi Yüan-chang]. 'Ngan Hwui [Hui], who lived in the thirteenth century, is usually associated with the great painters of the Sung dynasty.' The school of landscape artists, started on the right track under the former epoch, rose to the 'highest point of art.' The beauties of springtime with its joyous bursting of bud, leaf, and flower; the sweets of summer; the sadder traits of autumn, and the snow-clad beauties of winter, all engaged their brushes. Amongst the masters of this style may be mentioned the two Lí Cheng [Ch'êng], one the chief of the northern school, and the other belonging to the southern; the former was followed by numerous artists during the eleventh, twelfth, and part of the thirteenth centuries, but unfortunately, in the devotion to their master, they began to copy the style of the man rather than to follow him in his sincere admiration of Nature herself. In conjunction with 'a new tendency,' which 'manifested itself, each school, each studio,' took as a speciality the production of a certain 'picturesque detail, and ceased to see landscape in its whole.' As examples of this tendency may be instanced the two brothers, Ma Yuën [Yüan] and Ma K'on [K'un], who confined themselves to 'pines, cypresses, cedars, and steep rocks'; another only cared to reproduce 'the effects of snow'; others confined their attention to the feathery bamboo with its stiff stems, tender green leaves, and the graceful curves of the topmost boughs; another speciality was 'clusters of flowers in the spaces between glazed tiles on a roof,'—surely a singular taste; 'bullfinches, bamboos, and rocks' are named as the objects on which Lí Ti exercised his brush; snow-laden pines and clumps of trees were what another artist loved to reproduce; while 'plum-trees and flowers' were what Chong [Chung] Jên singled out as worthy of his skill; other painters had the good sense not to confine themselves to one speciality. Some wonderful productions of birds, lifelike and natural, were painted during this period.

The fifth epoch is that of the Yuan [Yüan], or Mongol dynasty. The Mongol conquest of China stirred up the comparatively stagnant pool of Chinese native life, and introduced a stream of vivifying influence from the more Western nations. Other styles of art were introduced to the Chinese, who had for some centuries seen but little from outer lands to inspire their genius, or spur on their adaptive efforts. These influences from abroad, more felt in other branches of art, did not make such an impression on painting as one might suppose, though some traces of such influence are to be found. Coupled with this, there was also a renaissance of Buddhism, which the tide of Mongol rule brought in with it, and which made itself felt in the artistic world, as well as elsewhere. The divisions, which we have noted in the Sung period, still continued. The characteristic of the painters under the Yüan dynasty is 'the taste for bright and brilliant colours.' A tiger and cubs, executed by one of the artists of this dynasty, is to be seen in the British Museum.

The sixth epoch is that of the Ming dynasty (A.D. 1368–1644). Painting benefited in the first years of this dynasty by the improvements in technical art which took place, though again not to such an extent as in some of the other branches of art, and it, during this period, began to decline from about the middle of the dynasty. Consequently, it is convenient to divide this epoch into two portions, lasting respectively from A.D. 1368 to 1488, and from 1488 to 1643. The style of this first period of Ming dynasty art may be characterised as without much originality, but with other characteristics of first importance: a style of art 'without great eminence, but without decay.'

> 'There were, however, as late as the fifteenth and sixteenth centuries, many painters of great merit; but the best of these, including Lin Liang and Lü Ki [Chi], were avowed imitators of the older masters. The one exception to the general decay in later centuries was a style which, so far as we are aware, numbered only two important followers — Ch'êng Chung-fu [Chung-ch'i] and Lí-kin Kü-sze [Li-yin Chin-shih]. . . . These artists, seeking better results in the painting of portraits, than had been found attainable by pursuing the caligraphic ideal, ventured to represent the outlines and shadows of the face as they saw them.'

In the second period of this epoch 'begins the decline of Chinese painting.' The causes of this decadence are to be found centuries previously, when, for a study at first hand, was substituted a servile imitation of some master-hand, whose inspiration was derived from the faithful communion with Nature herself, which his disciples neglected. That snare of the Chinese in so many branches of their learning and knowledge, the blind following of set rules and canons, again showed itself in their reproduction of the phases and aspects of Nature in her revelations to man, for instead of lifting up their eyes and seeing the fields ripe for a harvest, ready for those who would reap it, they contented themselves with the achievements of the past, and let the golden opportunities slip.

The difference between these two periods (the first and second halves of the Ming dynasty) is marked, and the beginning of a new style is seen, which prevailed in the seventeenth and eighteenth centuries.

The seventh epoch is that of the Ch'ing (Manchu) dynasty, and under it the decadence, foreshadowed and commenced in the preceding dynasty, becomes an accomplished fact. The absence of inspiration is seen, and for it is substituted the use of certain illustrated works, which serve as dictionaries for the aspirant to fame from which the painter copies the different figures or objects, already prepared for his use in all possible situations of ordinary Chinese life; he has degenerated into a copyist, for it only remains for him to group them. Under the third Emperor, Yung Ching [Chêng] (A.D. 1723–36), there was a tendency toward improvement, but the bounds of tradition were not burst: it stopped short of a renovation of the whole art. The Jesuit missionaries at Peking attempted to introduce the principles of Western art as applied to painting, but, though they executed numerous works, the Chinese were not far enough advanced in Western notions to adopt such a complete reversal of all their preconceived ideas and canons of art. In the South, George Chinnery, an English artist, who painted many scenes of Chinese life, exerted, in the first half of the present century, some influence on the painters patronised by the foreign residents of Canton and Macao; and the copying by these of foreign portraits has doubtless modified their modes of expression and improved their style to some extent, but the body of Chinese painters has not been affected thereby. The painting of nude figures has always been regarded by the Chinese as an offence against propriety, and generally is still so regarded in spite of its introduction in native schools modelled on Western systems.

In conclusion, to sum up the whole matter, we perhaps cannot do better than supplement the quotations we have already made from Anderson by another one:—

'There is, perhaps, no section of art that has been so completely misapprehended in Europe as the pictorial art of China. For us the Chinese painter, past or present, is but a copyist who imitates with laborious and indiscriminating exactness whatever is laid before him, rejoices in the display of as many and as brilliant colours as his subject and remuneration will permit, and is original only in the creation of monstrosities. Nothing could be more contrary to fact than this impression, if we omit from consideration the work executed for the foreign market—work which every educated Chinese would disown. The old masters of the Middle Kingdom, who, as a body, united grandeur of conception with immense power of execution, cared little for elaboration of detail, and, except in Buddhist pictures, sought their best effects in the simplicity of black and white, or in the most subdued of chromatic harmonies. Their art was defective, but not more so than that of Europe down to the end of the thirteenth century. Technically, they did not go beyond the use of water colours, but in range and quality of pigments, as in mechanical command of pencil, they had no reason to fear comparison with their contemporaries. They had caught only a glimpse of the laws of chiaroscuro and perspective, but the want of science was counterpoised by more essential elements of artistic excellence.

'In motives they lacked neither variety nor elevation. As landscape painters they anticipated their European brethren by over a score of generations, and created transcripts of scenery that for breadth, atmosphere, and picturesque beauty can scarcely be surpassed. In their studies of the human figure, although their work was often rich in vigour and expression, they certainly fell immeasurably below the Greeks; but to counterbalance this defect, no other artists, except those of Japan, have ever infused into the delineations of bird life one tithe of the vitality and action to be seen in the Chinese portraitures of the crow, the sparrow, the crane, and a hundred other varieties of the feathered race. In flowers the Chinese were less successful, owing to the absence of true chiaroscuro, but they were able to evolve a better picture out of a single spray of blossom than many a Western painter from all the treasures of a conservatory.

'If we endeavour to compare the pictorial art of China with that of Europe, we must carry ourselves back to the days when the former was in its greatness. Of the art that preceded the T'ang dynasty we can say nothing. Like that of Polygnotus, Zeuxis, and Apelles it is now represented only by traditions, which, if less precise in the former than in the latter case, are not less laudatory; but it may be asserted that nothing produced by the painters of Europe between the seventh and thirteenth centuries of the Christian era approaches within any measurable distance of the great Chinese masters who gave lustre to the T'ang, Sung, and Yuën [Yüan] dynasties, nor—to draw a little nearer to modern times—is there anything in the religious art of Cimabue that would not appear tame and graceless by the side of the Buddhistic compositions of Wú Tao-tsz [tzŭ], Lí Lung-yen and Ngan Hwui [Hui]. Down to the end of the Southern Empire in 1279 A.D., the Chinese were at the head of the world in the art of painting, as in many things besides, and their nearest rivals were their own pupils, the Japanese.... Japanese culture has lent many elements of poetry and grace to the parent art [*i.e.*, in Japan itself, not in China], in the Shi-jo school it added something in touch; and chiefly through the Yamato and U Kiyo-yé schools it contributed numberless original features in motive; but in strength the palm must still rest with the Middle Kingdom, and China may claim as its own every main artistic principle that guided the brushes of Kanaoka, Meichō, and Motonobu. It is, indeed, often difficult for any but an expert to distinguish a work of the earliest

Japanese leaders of the "Chinese school" from a Chinese picture, and many a design that adorns the modern porcelain and lacquer of Japan is to be traced almost line for line to a Chinese original of eight or nine centuries ago. . . . In the last hundred years, while the Chinese have been content to rest upon the achievements of their forefathers . . . the energy of their quondam pupils has brought Japan before the world as the sole heir to almost all that is most beautiful in the art of the great Turanian race.'

References.—Chavannes and Petrucci, *Ars Asiatica;* Petrucci, *Les Grandes Artistes: Les Peintres Chinois; Encyclopédie de la Peinture Chinoise;* Paléologue, *L'Art Chinois;* Hirth, *Scraps from a Collector's Notebook;* Hirth, *Chinese Painters;* Fenellosa, *Epochs of Chinese and Japanese Art;* Bushell, *Chinese Art;* Strehlneek, *Chinese Pictorial Art;* Binyon, *Paintings in the Far East;* Giles, *An Introduction to the History of Chinese Pictorial Art;* Waley, *Chinese Painting;* Sei-ichi-take, *Three Essays on Oriental Painting;* Anderson, *The Pictorial Arts of Japan;* Wu Hsing-fu, *Chinese Paintings.*

ASCENDING ON HIGH.—In the Han dynasty one Hêng Ching received a warning from the magician Fei Ch'ang-fang that a dreadful catastrophe would happen to him and his family. To avert it he escaped to the heights; and in commemoration of this event, on the ninth day of the ninth moon, many Chinese take a holiday, or an excursion of a few hours, to some neighbouring hill or mountain, where some of them fly paper kites.

This Ch'ung Yöng [Chung Yang] festival is looked upon more as a partial holiday than as a feast in the strict sense of the term. Many Chinese, though perhaps not five per cent of the whole population, avail themselves of this opportunity for a little relaxation from business; those who do so being such as are blessed with leisure, or who desire an outing, or who are specially superstitious; though, on the whole, few make it a day of worship.

This half-feast, half-holiday brings itself more prominently into the notice of the foreign resident in Hongkong than is the case with some of the other semi-religious observances of the Chinese. The Peak tramway, providing a convenient mode of reaching a summit, is largely availed of, to the wonderment of the English traveller, who is at a loss to understand why such an exodus of natives from the town is taking place. About 3000 usually take advantage of this convenient mode of ascent, though on a wet day the number may be reduced to one-half of that, trams running continuously throughout the day for their accommodation. Dressed in their gala-day best, with silks and satins galore, and with happy faces, family groups may be seen wandering along the mountain roads, while troops of friends and acquaintances may be noticed chatting their loudest and enjoying the treat of a whiff of fresh air after months of confinement in narrow streets and close shops. Up at the Peak itself, the base of the flag-staff is black with human beings, who, from the distance, look like ants on a lump of sugar; and on the road, slowly meandering their zigzag course up the hill, are clusters of pedestrians; other black specks on the path are home-bound wanderers wearily wending their downward course, though many patronise the tram again and besiege the empty cars, like excursionists in England, the disappointed ones, who have to wait for the next trip, nearly blocking the station.

ASIATIC SOCIETY (China Branch of).—*See* CHINA BRANCH OF THE ROYAL ASIATIC SOCIETY and NORTH CHINA BRANCH OF THE ROYAL ASIATIC SOCIETY.

ASTROLOGY.—According to Chinese ideas, the sun, moon, planets and stars cause climatic changes, which influence the people's moral conduct, destinies, etc. Astrology, however, did not reach so scientific, or quasi-scientific, a stage as that attained by the European systems. It was based on certain sections of the early classical writings, with the addition of the *yin* and *yang* cosmology and its subsequent developments. In practice, the theory was applied to the ascertaining of " lucky " or " unlucky " days, etc., for the settlement of doubts or guiding of actions. One of the commonest inscriptions (carved or written on a red-painted board, or written on red paper and posted up on a wall) is, ' May a lucky star auspiciously shine (on us).' The Chinese almanacs contain detailed particulars of the beneficent or malevolent influence supposed to be exerted by the planets or stars on the destinies of mortals.

AUDIENCE.—During the Monarchical Period the audience by the Chinese sovereign of foreign ambassadors, envoys, etc., was one of the burning questions of the day in the Far East. The following appeared in the London *Times* some years since:—

' Perhaps, in course of time, they [the Chinese] will begin to see the absurdity of shutting up their Emperor from the foreign ministers accredited to him. There may have been good and substantial reasons, from the Chinese point of view, in refusing to present foreigners to the Empress Dowager when she acted as Regent; but there is no reason whatever—even a Chinese reason—for persisting in keeping the Emperor and the foreign ministers apart. In the last century the Emperor of the present dynasty received foreigners, and condescended to be instructed by them. The present Emperor receives his own ministers in audience every day, and is not treated as a semi-divine being, on whose face ordinary mortals may not look, as the Mikado of Japan was in former times. There is no reason in principle or Chinese practice why the sovereign should not receive the ministers at his Court, and, not to speak of earlier Emperors, there is the precedent of T'ung Chi [Chih], his predecessor, who granted an audience to the *Corps Diplomatique*. It is the absence of reason about the business, the obstinate persistence in withholding this usual mark of mutual respect, that renders it so irritating.'

To get some idea of what the Chinese standpoint of view was, it must be remembered that through ages past it has been the theory—a theory well sustained by practice, and where practice failed to support, it, well bolstered up by Chinese historians—that China was the Suzerain State, and all other kingdoms its vassals, who, if they did not pay tribute, were in a state of rebellion, and should present this open and visible sign of fealty. All presents from other sovereigns were styled 'tribute'; and to such a length was this carried, that when China was divided by two reigning houses, and when the so-called vassal kingdom was in reality the leading state in China, and the so-called Imperial family ruled over but a small moiety of the Empire, yet all presents from the more powerful state were classed as tribute in history, while those from the Emperor, which, as given to a more influential state by a weaker and inferior one, were in reality more entitled to the name of tribute, were classed as presents. It must further be remembered that China has been the leading nation of Eastern Asia for many centuries past, while the rest of the world was comparatively unknown; all surrounding nations have been their inferiors, who have looked up to the Middle Kingdom as the centre from which their letters, literature, knowledge, art, and science have all originated and emanated. It was on all these causes, and for all these reasons, that the preposterous claim of the Chinese was founded and maintained.

The receiving of all their envoys and ambassadors at the Courts of Europe, to which they have been accredited for a quarter of a century, was not sufficient, in face of these antiquated views, to move them from their position; for, judged from the same standpoint, it was only to be expected that China's envoys should be received with every mark of respect and honour —nay more, their theories would naturally lead them to expect that they should be received with that homage accorded to them by their neighbours, such, for instance, as by Corea in past times—a homage rendered to them as representatives of the Son of Heaven—a homage given by virtue of the claim of the latter to universal sovereignty.

Whatever may have been the private opinion of the handful of enlightened officials, the belief held by the majority of them, namely, the theory enunciated above, had to be upheld at every cost; for such beliefs die hard in China. And if the pressure of foreign opinion rendered necessary some show of alteration, plausible excuses were put forward, or subterfuges resorted to; and eventually we find the representatives of the most powerful nations on the earth received twice—long ago once, and again in 1891, after years of a refusal to grant it—in an Audience Hall, especially reserved for the audience of tributary nations, with only a statement on the last occasion, that such should not be the case again. The Emperor, by a decree of the 12th December, 1890, expressed his intention of fixing a day every year for the reception with honour of all the Foreign Ministers resident in Peking. After the general reception, mentioned above, the Austrian-Hungarian Minister was received in another out-building, which was also associated with humiliation.

Count Cassini, the Russian Minister, insisted, in 1892, on presenting his credentials personally to the Emperor, a bold stand, and the only one which carried the day with Chinese officials.

The Chinese seemed indisposed, to put it mildly, to receive Foreign Ambassadors in the Imperial Palace; out-buildings were made to do duty for these functions. The point, of course, was that until the Chinese Emperor received Foreign Ambassadors on exactly the same footing that our Sovereign receives the Chinese accredited to the Court of St. James, and until every disposition to shirk this proper mode of dealing with the Audience Question was gone, it would still remain unsettled. The humiliating ceremony of 'kow-tow' [*k'ou-t'ou*] was not demanded at the last receptions given prior to a complete change in the system, for the very good reason, doubtless, that the Chinese were well aware it would not be performed. And as a straw showing a slight change in the current of the stupid pride and arrogance of the past, it was pleasing to see that the Czarewitch, on his visit in 1891 to the high officials in Canton, had an Imperial-yellow sedan-chair provided for him—an honour never previously granted to a European, and an honour only reserved in China for the reigning family.

As indicative of some of the first signs of this change, for the better, were to be noticed the fact that the late British Minister to Peking (Mr. O'Conor) presented his credentials in person to the Emperor in the Chêng Kuang-tien and not in the 'Hall of Tributary Nations.' The Austrian Ambassador had previously also been received in a proper manner, and the other representatives of their respective countries were afterwards accorded receptions more befitting the nations whose interests they had in hand than had been the case for many years past.

'The Russian and French Ministers refused audience except within the Palace walls; when China was being defeated by Japan then the right was conceded of audience within the Palace Wall to all the nations. The Hall selected for it was the Wên Wa [Hua] Tien.' They feared the Japanese would attack Peking (the Chinese dreaded two of the Powers in the event of the attack on Peking and the overthrow or weakening of the dynasty) and they wished to conciliate the Great Western Powers; and by granting this important but inevitable concession, to secure their mediatorial influences in suspending or averting the threatened descent on the capital and in the bringing about of peace.'

On the defeat of China by Japan, the Foreign Ministers were received in audience in the Wên Hua Tien within the Palace (No. 12, 1894). This was the first occasion on which audience was granted in a proper place and in a proper manner.

In this connection, the two following newspaper cuttings from periodicals published in 1898 are interesting:—

'The Chinese authorities have been much perplexed over the question of Prince Henry's suitable reception by the Emperor, and after considerable hesitation, it has been decided that for the first time in Chinese history, His August Majesty will stand to receive his guest. The officials are as yet in much too great trepidation to discuss the details of the return visit.'

'Prince Henry of Prussia has paid his state visit to the Emperor of China in Peking. He was admitted to an audience at the Summer Palace on terms of equality never before granted.'

In 1899 (and repeatedly since), the Empress Dowager gave audience to the foreign ladies from the legations in Peking.

As a result of the 'Boxer' war of 1900, the Ministers of Great Britain, Germany, France, Russia, Japan and Portugal were received in 1902 in audience in the Hall where the Emperor received his own officials every morning. Thus at last the Audience Question was set at rest.

References.—China Review, Vol. iii; *Amer. Hist. Review,* Vol. ii; Gundry, *China Past and Present.*

AWETO.—The aweto has well been termed the strangest insect in the world; for, were the fact not well vouched for by scientists, it would be incredible that a caterpillar should blossom out into a plant. The vegetable fungus which takes root in the neck of the caterpillar grows upward even to the height of six or eight inches and downward in the body of the buried aweto until vegetable matter has supplanted all the animal tissues within the outer skin of the insect—the form of the latter being perfectly retained; this accomplished, it dies, or (shall we say?) they die; for both plant and animal die, becoming dry and hard and of a brown colour. This odd combination then looks like a wooden caterpillar with a big horn sticking out of its neck. The Chinese have in their Materia Medica what would appear to be exactly the same creature as the above. It is produced, if our Chinese authority is reliable, in Sz-chüan [Ssŭch'uan], as well as in New Zealand. It is known as the *toong ch'oong hah ts'o*, [*tung ch'ung hsia ts'ao*], 'winter-worm summer-grass,' or more commonly as the *toong ch'oong ts'o*, 'winter-worm grass.' It is considered to be a tonic, and is boiled with pork for that purpose; the soup thus produced, and the aweto itself, being taken. There is an inferior kind which is said to come from Japan, but is stated to be of no use.

BAMBOO.—China would not be the China we know, were the bamboo wanting. Existence would well-nigh seem impossible to the Chinese without it—'a universal provider' for a nation's endless wants. What iron is to the English, such is the useful bamboo to the Chinese. Not by any means that the use of iron is unknown in China, far from it; it is largely used for many purposes; but bamboo is even more extensively employed, not only for the purposes that iron is ill fitted for, but also for many for which that metal is well adapted. Pages might be filled with a mere list given of the uses to which it is put. Bamboo has been called the universal material. There are few things which cannot be made of it. The question is not what it is used for, but what it is not used for; and, after a lengthened residence in China with the discovery every now and then of some fresh article made of bamboo, the answer, with but little reservation, would appear to be that it is used for nearly everything. To the Chinese it is, perhaps, the most valuable product of their land. They excel in manufacturing it into different articles. The last thing that one would suppose it to be fit for is food: the hard silicious culms look anything but tempting to an epicure. It is, however, not these in their hardened mature state, but the fresh young sprouts as they come out of the ground that, cooked till tender, form a fine vegetable, or, otherwise treated, make a pickle, or comfit. The graceful slender stems—strong, but light—serve an infinitude of purposes: the framework of matsheds is almost entirely constructed of them, whether they be the gigantic temporary structures erected for religious festivals which tower above all the other buildings (See AMUSEMENTS); or the more modest dwellings of the poorer classes; or the complicated network of scaffolding round the rising house or the building under repair.

Their long tubular structure adapts them admirably for water-pipes when the thick septum at each joint has been broken through. The street-coolie, or the chair-coolie, would be badly off without the bamboo: it provides carrying-poles for the first, whilst the whole framework of the sedan-chair, and the shafts are often of this material. The boatman's pole for his boat, the ribs for the sailor's mat-sail, and the sampan woman's awning for her small craft, are all constructed of the bamboo. Could the bamboo age that now reigns in China be suddenly abolished by some magician's enchantment, the whole of the fairies that ever peopled fairyland would find their hands more than full to provide substitutes for all the household articles, the agricultural implements, the toys for the children, and the innumerable objects of everyday use which are made of this ubiquitous plant. The roots make the divining blocks lying on every temple altar, while the divining sticks that keep them company are slender slips of bamboo contained in a bamboo vase; the mats for the worshippers to kneel on are made of its dried leaves; the incense sticks have a thin slip of bamboo, round the upper part of which adhere the fragrant spices brought from Araby the Blest and the Sandal-wood Islands (Sandwich Islands). We can scarcely keep our eyes off bamboo in China whether in-doors or out. Rain-hats, or sun-hats, large sized and small (the large ones having the spread of an umbrella, of which the handle is the man or woman who uses it, or when a youngster claps one on his head, we have a walking mushroom, so over-shadowed is he by his gigantic head-gear), the policeman's or soldier's conical small hat, constructed to ward off strokes and parry blows—these are all made of bamboo. The native umbrella, handle and ribs and spring, is ingeniously constructed of it as well, while oiled paper serves in the place of silk or cotton. The Robinson Crusoe-like raincoat of the extreme South is made of leaves—a garment of leaves—of this gigantic grass sewn together. The old man's staff, the blind beggar's stick, the sewing woman's pole to which to fasten her seam, the washerwoman's clothes-lines, are bamboo. The rake of the farmer, the foot-rule of the carpenter and tailor, the measures of the rice-shops, and many chop-sticks are made of it. Rags are too precious in China to be wasted on the manufacture of paper, for when the decent garment begins to show the wear and tear of the merchant prince, it descends in the social scale, serving in turn the shopman and coolie, and finally, when all respectability is gone out of it, forms a covering for the wretched beggar, if any ability to cover remains in it at all. In lieu of rags, the bamboo, soaked for a length of time and reduced to pulp, then dried and made into sheets, furnishes paper for the student's class-book, the merchant's account-books, and the author's scribbling paper. The latter writes with a pen, the handle of which is a fine bamboo tube; the vase for holding his pens is of the same material. Chairs, tables, stools, couches, ornaments, stands, images, lantern-handles, canes, instruments of torture, handles of spears, cages for birds, hen-coops, musical instruments (such as flutes, fifes, fiddles, etc.), pillows, dutch-wives, ladders, lattice-work, bars of doors and windows, primitive-looking lamps and lanterns, nutmeg-graters, pepper-dusters, floats, watering-wheels, rafts, bridges, watch-towers, tobacco and opium-pipes, ropes, window-blinds, curtains, brooms, brushes, baskets of every kind, cricket-traps, snares to catch game, combs, tallies for checking cargo, summonses for secret society meetings, the framework and handles of fans, are all of this cane; but we must stop, or we should have to make an inventory of much that is in common use by John Chinaman, and which he would sadly want were he deprived of his bamboo. It even supplies him with medicine in the shape of tabasheer, a silicious concretion found inside the stems; while the green outer surface of the young bamboo is scraped off and used as a cooling drink (being boiled with water) for fever, in combination with other medicines, or alone. The green buds (of the leaves) are also employed in the same way and for the same purpose. Order was and still largely is maintained throughout the whole country by it, and a sprig of it is borne in the van of the funeral procession.

'The numerous plants which common parlance lumps together under the general name of "bamboo" really form three distinct genera, known to Botanists as *Bambusa, Arundinaria,* and *Phyllostachys*, and each including many species.'

'Throughout life the Chinaman is almost dependent upon it for support, nor does it leave him until it carries him to his last resting place on the hill-side, and even then in company with the cypress, juniper, and pine it waves over and marks his tomb.'

Wallace would scarcely regard the bamboo as a tropical plant, while Rein calls the monsoon district the old home of many kinds, where the largest and most beautiful are cultivated, and whence some varieties—the hardiest doubtless—have crossed the tropic of Cancer and colonised both in Japan and China far beyond. The idea that such regions are too raw and cold for such delicate plants is fallacious. The bamboo is hardier than its slender stalks, tender green leaves, and graceful swaying masses of feathery tufts would at first glance lead one to suppose, for it holds its own and, if properly protected, will winter through snows amidst the cold of Mid-China. In early times it grew extensively in N. China, which had then a moister soil than now. Chambers's 'Encyclopædia' informs us that a few species of bamboo are found in the Himalayas at an altitude of 12,000 feet.

The bamboo is one of the most rapidly growing plants in existence—six feet or more in a single night is a record performance in plant growth, while at the other end of the scale is the slow growing tree, taking a year to accomplish the same height.

Among the curiosities of the bamboo world are the purple bamboo, the tortoise-marked bamboo, the Sampan wood bamboo (bright red when young), the purple or black bamboo the golden bamboo, the solid bamboo (which 'is not a species, not even a variety, but merely a sport'), the square bamboo, the Dragon's beard (scarcely a foot high, with needle-like stems, while at the other extreme is the bamboo the stem of which is nearly 1½ ft. in diameter), striped bamboos, forked bamboos, and the bamboo of filial obedience, which last a Chinese author thus describes:—It 'has long and slender stems, forming a large clump. In the summer its sprouts come from the inside and produce coolness, which they transmit to the parent bamboo . In the winter they come up outside and afford protection to the parent plant by covering it up. This is why it is called " loving filial-affection." ' It is natural that such a filial-hearted plant (hollow-hearted though it is) as the bamboo appears to be, should respond to filial piety in the human species, and one variety of this estimable member of the vegetable kingdom bears in Japan the name of one of the twenty-four paragons of Chinese filial piety, who for his sick mother, longing for soup made from bamboo shoots in winter, wept so copiously in a bamboo plantation that his tears, like the warm rains of spring, softened the hard wintry ground and caused the tender shoots to burst forth, in reward of his pious affection. The ingenious Japanese has produced artificial varieties of the bamboo, such as the 'Hundred Leaved Bamboos,' and bamboos with crooked stems. These are the result of removing the sheaths and cutting the stems.

There are many varieties of the bamboo; some twenty or more in the south of China; one Chinese writer describes sixty varieties. They are of different sizes and colours—green, yellow, and black—with large and small leaves, from the tiny dwarf bamboo which, when full grown, is only large enough to form a low hedge, and is glorified with the name of the

'Goddess of Mercy Bamboo,' up to the larger sizes, whose feathery sprays rise to a height of fifty or even sometimes seventy feet. It is a most graceful object, touching with rare beauty every few yards of the Chinese landscape, and has inspired many a poet and artist. If the bamboo is kind to the Chinaman, he returns it with interest, as some of his best work is bestowed upon it, and it forms the *motif* in numerous works of art. What would many a hideous carving be but for its 'saving grace'; the artist would be lost but for its lines of beauty, while its tawny yellow or bright green stems and waving top plumes of duller green, the whole object, 'so delicate in tint and shape, soft of hue, . . . indefinite in outline, . . . like wonderful grey-green lace against the opalescent sky,' appeals not only to the most æsthetic side of the Celestial's nature, but also to that of the matter-of-fact Western traveller.

Baden Powell says:—

'I always think bamboos in a landscape add just that finish which a spray of maidenhair gives to a bouquet.'

In two recent years, has the bamboo flowered in Hongkong, though ordinarily one may live many years in China without noticing it. A spray of it in flower looks somewhat like a head of oats, but much smaller.

'The flowering of the bamboo is considered to be a very rare occurrence. Once in eighteen, twenty, and even twenty-five years does it flower, and still less seldom does it produce seed.' 'Externally the seed resembles a pear in shape, and is of a deep olive-green colour, gradually changing to a dark or rifle-green. On opening the seed longitudinally, a thick coat of coriaceous matter is found covering the germinal centre. It has a strong vegetable smell.'

Of late the bamboo has been introduced as an ornamental plant into gardens in England, with great success. In a garden in the Midlands, some fifty species flourished exceedingly well, though not attaining the size they do where the climate was more favourable for their growth. It was previously unknown out of doors in England, though well known on the Mediterranean. Rein tells us in his magnificent work, 'The Industries of Japan,' that *Bambusa arundinacea* was introduced into hot-houses in England in 1730, and until 1813 was the only kind there.

References.—Henry, *Ling Nam;* Williams, *Middle Kingdom,* i. 358-60; Shaw, *Chinese Timber and Forest Trees.*

BAMBOO BOOKS.—*See* LITERATURE.

BANKS AND BANK-NOTES.—There are no chartered banks in China, but private banks are very common. Their number 'is large in proportion to the business of a town,' their capital, in many cases, also being small, amounting to a few thousand taels. The native banks do not appear to have hit upon the device of cheques; a foreign bank in Hongkong, the National Bank of China, having been the first to introduce these convenient orders for money to the Chinese in their own language in that colony. Since then the system has been largely adopted by native banks. The native banks, however, generally 'issue circular letters of credit to travel through the Empire, and the system of remittance by drafts is as complete as in Europe; the rates charged are high, however.' Promissory notes are largely availed of by the native banks and their customers in their dealings with each other. A very curious feature in these transactions is that the interest is often not stated in the note itself, but is written on the envelope in which the note is enclosed, though in the ordinary promissory note it is inserted in the note. Native banks are classified as (1) Official Banks, dealing with the government revenue; (2) Exchange (*Hui-p'iao*) Banks, dealing in mercantile transactions; (3) Ordinary Banks; (4) Provincial Banks, having official status, but with shareholders; (5) Banks whose business is modelled on foreign methods, but with Chinese capital.

As cash, the common copper mite and for long only known coin amongst the Chinese, is heavy and difficult to transport in any quantities, it was only natural that, keen merchants as they are, the Chinese should have early invented bank-notes. 'The date seems to have been about A.D. 800.' The earliest specimen known to exist in any country was purchased in 1890 by the British Museum, where it may be now seen under a glass case in the King's Library. The label to it states that it was issued 300 years earlier than the establishment (at Stockholm) of the first European bank which sent out notes. This wonderful note is about the size of a piece of foolscap paper and is almost blackish in colour. It was issued during the reign of Hung Wú, A.D. 1368–99. Each money shop has its own device, though the general features are the same: an ornamental border surrounds the oblong paper, and since the Chinese printing is in columns, the greatest length is from top to bottom, and not from side to side as in the English bank-note; the name of the bank or shop issuing it is put in large characters, transversely, as a heading; below this are several rows of characters, the centre one often being somewhat to this effect—'On production of this note pay——cash,' the other columns containing necessary particulars, such as the number of the note, the date, etc.; besides which, some moral sentences very often form an adornment.

'The check on over-issue of notes lies in the control exercised by the clearing-house of every city, where the standing of each bank is known by its operations. The circulation of the notes is limited in some cases to the street or neighbourhood wherein the establishment is situated; often the payee has a claim on the payer of a bill for a full day if it be found to be counterfeit or worthless—a custom which involves a good deal of scribbling on the back . . . to certify the names. Proportionally few counterfeit notes are met with, owing more to the limited range of the notes, making it easy to ask the bank, which recognises its own paper. . . . Their face value ranges from one to a hundred *tiao*, or strings of cash, but their worth depends on the exchange between silver and cash, and as this fluctuates daily, the notes soon find their way home.

A *tiao* is 1000 cash, but the denominations of the notes vary, ranging in value from 100 cash to 1000 cash and $1. Great inconvenience is sometimes caused by the failure of the firms which have issued this paper money.

These bank-notes are not used in the extreme south of China, though they are very common at Foochow and in the North.

The issue of these notes at the present day is due entirely to private enterprise, but the Government have acted as bankers more than once in this one respect. Marco Polo, the celebrated Venetian traveller, was in China at such a time and, speaking of Kublai Khan's purchases, he thus describes them:—

'So he buys such a quantity of those precious things every year that his treasure is endless, while, all the while the money he pays away costs him nothing at all. If any of those pieces of paper are spoilt, the owner carries them to the mint, and by paying three per cent. on the value he gets new pieces in exchange.'

The total issue during Kublai Khan's reign of thirty-four years, amounted, it is estimated, to the sum of $624,135,500. This, however, was carried too far by the subsequent Mongol Emperors, and added fuel to the flame of discontent felt by the Chinese against their foreign rulers, yet the new Chinese dynasty (the Ming) which succeeded to the throne, was obliged at first to issue notes for nearly a hundred years. The Manchu dynasty has also had recourse to them during the great T'ai-p'ing rebellion, but their circulation did not extend beyond the metropolis.

The following extract refers to Chinese banking in 1894:—

'A remarkable impression has been just created in Shanghai by the renewed proof of the strength of the Chinese Banks. It was they who lent the Japanese banks Taels 4,000,000 to tide over a cotton account and it is generally believed that within very few years they will be financing many foreign concerns. This phenomenon of the rise of Chinese banking is an ironical commentary on the Consortium, which was mainly designed because it was believed that China was bankrupt.'

References.—Williams, *Middle Kingdom*, ii. 85, 86; *Wesleyan Methodist Magazine*, July, 1896 (for woodcut of a Chinese bank-note); Holcombe, *The Real Chinaman*, pp. 343-6; Wagel, *Finance in China; Currency and Banking;* Edkins, *Banking and Prices in China;* Richard, *Comprehensive Geography*, pp. 316-20; *Chinese Economic Bulletin*, No. 173.

BANNERS, THE EIGHT.—*See* ARMY.

BANYAN.—The *ficus indica.* A species of fig-tree, found in India and S. China, remarkable for its vast rooting branches. These develop pendulous roots, which soon become new stems, the tree in this manner spreading over a great surface. The wood of the banyan is of no value, but the tree furnishes lac and caoutchouc, and the bark and milky juice are used as medicine.

BASKETS.—Baskets are made largely of bamboo. There are numerous kinds used for domestic purposes or for the market or in daily toil, and different parts of the country have them of different shapes and sizes. The plain material is sometimes used; at other times it is varnished over; while again some baskets are gaudily painted in glaring colours.

BATHING.—The Chinese, as a people, are not addicted very much to bathing. As a general rule, with multitudes of them, a wash of the face and hands with hot water once a day or so constitutes the sum total of their ablutions. This is called 'wiping the face and hands,' and how perfunctorily it is performed the water-marks on dirty ears and necks is sign enough. Others, however, amongst them are very cleanly; especially is this the case sometimes with one's chair-coolies, who, after their day's labours, have buckets of hot water and wash themselves all over. In the neighbourhood of Foochow, there are sulphurous springs to which, Tseng Ki-tong tells us, the well-to-do people repair in summer to bathe. In all cities there are numerous bathing establishments. The baths in these are usually distinguished as *kuan t'ang*, "official rooms," and *k'o p'ên*, "guest baths," the prices being, on the average, forty and twenty copper cents respectively. In these two classes each bath is in a separate cubicle. For the poor there are baths used in common, at a charge of ten copper cents per person.

BATS.—Bats are emblematical of happiness; and constantly appear in paintings, carvings, and decorative designs. The "Five Bats" represent the "Five Happinesses," the characters for "bat" and "happiness" having the same sound.

Large specimens are allowed in great number to congregate in and haunt some official buildings. A superstition prevails in the South that the hair will fall off the head of those who touch them.

Dr. Porter Smith says of bats:—

'This animal is very common in China, being a frequent visitor of foreign houses, in quest of mosquitoes, which it devours most satisfactorily. As it is supposed to feed upon the stalactites which are frequently met with in the caves it is wont to hybernate in, its medical properties are rated at considerable value by the Chinese. From its asserted extreme longevity and its excellent sight, this curious creature is credited by the Chinese with the power of conveying these desirable qualities to those who consume the disgusting preparations made from all parts of its body.'

References.—Dobson, *Asiatic Chiroptera*, London, 1876; *Journal N.C.B.R.A.S., N.S.*, 1916; *Proceedings Zoological Society*, 1870, p. 615; 1898, p. 769; Doré, *Rec. sur les Sup. en Chine*, p. 475, etc.

BÊCHE DE MER.—Called in Malay, *tripang:* in Portuguese, *bicho-de-mar* = sea-worm; it is known by the name of sea-cucumber in England, its appearance and shape being like that vegetable; but it is, however, a dirty brown. It is found in the seas of the Malay Peninsula and Archipelago.

And 'in the upper part of the Gulf of Siam, and is so abundant on the northern coast of Australia that the people of Celebes, receiving advances from the resident Chinese, have been long in the habit of making annual voyages thither in quest of it. Gutted, dried in the sun, and smoked, it is considered cured, and fit for its only market, that of China, to which many hundred tons are yearly sent for the consumption of the epicures of that country. The fishery of the *tripang* is to China, what that of the sardine, tunny, and anchory is to Europe. It is, for the most part, caught by hand, for it has little power of locomotion, but in deep water it sometimes dives.' 'The *tripang*, or sea-slug, is of several varieties. The greater portion is caught in shallow water, where it can be picked up off the bank without diving.'

'They lie apparently motionless on sandy ground. Out of water, they die immediately and become a shimy mass. They must, therefore, be cut up at once, the digestive canal being taken out, and then they are dipped in boiling water and dried in the air.'

These banks on the Aroe Islands of pearls and *tripang* are often several miles in width, intersected by deep channels. The Chinese know this esculent holothuria by the name of *hoi shum* [*hai shên*], or 'sea ginseng.' Its culinary preparation is as follows:—It is soaked for a couple of nights, and becomes soft, when it is washed, and then steamed with water and pigeon or duck. Instead of simple water, that in which pork bones have been boiled is sometimes used. It has a sweet taste.

BED.—The Chinese bed commonly consists of two thickish boards laid side by side on two trestles, with a woven mat instead of mattress; blankets and cotton wadded coverlets being used for warmth in winter. Large wooden bedsteads of slighter construction and of more framework style than among us are also used. In the North, with the severe winters experienced there, the people sleep on *k'angs*, which are built of bricks, and hollow inside for fires; in fact, the northern Chinese sleep on brick stoves. Residence in the Far East affords a perpetual commentary on the customs mentioned in the Bible; and it is no uncommon sight in China to see a man take up his bed and walk, *i.e.*, he rolls up his blankets, earthen-ware, leather, or wooden pillow, and coverlet all inside his mat, and shoulders it, or carries it under his arm, and thus takes his bed with him and goes where he likes.

Much pity has been wasted and much useless indignation expended respectively on Chinese servants, and 'old China hands,' who have taken these domestics with them when on a visit to their native lands, and knew the absurdity of providing their amahs, or 'boys,' with the unappreciated and useless luxury of iron bedsteads and spring mattresses. The Chinese understand the anatomical advantage of sleeping on an unresilient bed.

BEES.—Bees in China are more easily handled than those in England, so much so that it has been thought they did not sting at all, or had no sting; but this is wrong, for they can and do sting. They are smaller than the English bees. Wild bees are also found. The natives smoke them and thus capture them, wrapping them up in a cloth, and take them home to rear. The hives are curious-looking objects: some are like hour-glasses about two feet long, while others are not so willow-waisted, but more cylindrical in shape; both sorts are fastened high up horizontally aganist walls of buildings, or over the front-door. The entrances to the hour-glass ones are at the ends, and to the cylindrical ones at the side in the middle. These apertures, of which there are several, are very small, being only large enough for the tiny insects to push through one at a time.

Honey is used by the Chinese, but is often adulterated: it is eaten as an article of diet, but is more often taken medicinally.

BELLS.—All temples have bells hung in them, some several centuries old, as can be seen from the inscriptions on them. They are beaten as part of the religious ceremony. The bell has no clapper; but is struck with a piece of wood, a round, smooth surface generally being prepared on the surface of the bell for that purpose. Foreign visitors to Chinese temples often strike the large, sonorous bell, hung up at the side of the idol's shrine. It might be as well if they followed the good advice to 'touch not . . . handle not' in this respect, and remember what would be thought if a 'heathen Chinee' visited one of our churches and took liberties with the different objects in them as his fancies prompted him.

Bells are one of the Chinese antiques found on sale in curio shops.

Bells formed ancient musical instruments, singly, or in numbers suspended in frames.

Bells are not used in domestic life as amongst us; there being in most cases no door-bells to houses, visitors have to hammer and bang at the doors with stick, umbrella, or hand, and shout themselves hoarse till heard. Nor are bells used for summoning servants, nor employed in factories, boats, or ships.

On the old-style doors, however, the brass tabs tapped against the spherical plates to which they are attached serve the same purpose. Modern electric bells are now also largely in use.

BERI-BERI.—Beri-Beri, a Malay name for a common disease in the East, known as *kakke* in Japan, which has hitherto been an obscure, mysterious complaint, baffling the doctors by its different phases, and claiming as its victims many of the inhabitants of the Malay and Eastern Archipelagoes, India, China, and Japan, and other countries. In China it is found only on the coast and along the banks of the great rivers. But it is now better known, as facts in connection with it have been carefully studied, so that in doctor's parlance it is authoritatively described as:—

'A specific form of multiple peripheral neuritis, occurring endemically, or as an epidemic, in most tropical and sub-tropical climates, and also, under certain artificial conditions, in more temperate latitudes. The mortality is considerable, sometimes very high, death being usually dependent on heart paresis.' Dr. Manson further says of it:—'My idea about the matter is . . . that beri-beri is a germ disease; that the germ resides in the soil, in the houses and surroundings of beri-beri spots; there it distils a poison which, on being absorbed by man, produces neuritis much in the same way that alcohol does. . . . And this toxin, being inhaled or swallowed by man, produces in him a specific neuritis, and he can carry this germ inside him from one place to another. 'So far as I have been able to interpret them, this is the only hypothesis which fits in with all the facts of the case.'

Among the many different things that beri-beri has hitherto been ascribed to, are damaged grain, damaged fish, rain, wind, heat, cold, rheumatism, and malaria. Beri-beri is fostered by damp, by great heat, and most often attacks those who sleep on or near the ground. Overcrowding is favourable to it, consequently it frequently breaks out amongst prisoners in gaols, children in schools, miners in camps, labourers in plantations, soldiers in armies, and the crews of ships. Large cities and villages, as well as jungle lands are all subject to it.

The disease takes one or the other of two forms, the dropsical ("wet"), and the atrophic ("dry"). One patient will appear dropsical and another emaciated and reduced to a skeleton, and the same patient will present these different aspects at different periods of the disease. A man who has every appearance of being very ill will recover, while another who looks as if he had very little the matter with him will rapidly develop dangerous heart symptoms and suddenly die out of hand.

As one of the marked features of the disease is an inability to use the legs properly, 'ankle-drops' being also one of the symptoms, and hence the Chinese term it *kök hay* [*chiao ch'i*], or 'feet humour,' or *wan* 'numbness.'

References.—Manson, *Tropical Diseases;* Pekelharing, *Beri-beri* (trans. by Cantlie) ; Jeffery and Maxwell, *Diseases of China.*

BETEL-NUT.—Betel-nuts (*ping-lang*) are produced in great quantities in Hainan. An inferior kind is imported from Singapore for use in adulteration.

'The fruit of the Areca palm, a tall, graceful tree, sometimes reaching a height of 60 ft. The nuts are surrounded by a yellow, tough fibre, enclosed in a thickish green rind. To prepare them for use, the entire fruit is split, and the halves dried in the sun. When dry, the nut is separated from its envelope and is sold for chewing with *sirih* leaf and lime. Its use communicates a blood-red colour to the lips and gums, and the same hue to the saliva which the natives eject.'

The taste is astringent.

The sirih, or betel-vine, is a leaf used to chew with the betel-nut and lime. The plant is cultivated in China, for the leaf. A dab of the prepared lime is smudged on to the leaf and the betel-nut is then wrapped up in it, put in the mouth and chewed. (It is now largely supplanted by tobacco and opium smoking.) From this circumstance the leaf gets its name, *pun long laú* [*ping lang lao*], 'betel-nut wrapper,' *i.e.* the sirih leaf (*Piper betle or Chaveca betel*). It is used medicinally, both for outward application, when the leaf is rubbed on, and taken internally in cases of accident.

Reference.—*Notes and Queries on China and Japan,* Sept., 1868.

BETROTHAL.—Betrothals are generally negotiated—for

they are matters of business and not of sentiment—by the go-betweens, who are mostly women, and who make it their business to find out a suitable *parti*. They are commissioned by the parents, the parties themselves having, as a general rule, no voice in the matter, often being of too tender an age to understand what it means. Unborn infants are even sometimes informally betrothed, *i.e.*, the parents agree that the children when born, if of opposite sexes, shall in future life be husband and wife; this is carried so far that married couples occasionally promise that if they ever have children of different sexes they shall be given in marriage to one another; but the usual age for betrothals in many parts of the country is ten, twelve, or even older.

The go-betweens are generally women of the status of elderly servants who have the free *entrée* into the houses of those desirous of contracting matrimonial alliances, in the same manner that an ordinary broker would—in fact they are marriage brokers. Sometimes they are specially sent for by the parties desirous of their services, and at other times they visit families unsolicited, on account of information received. These go-betweens have a hand in the matter from beginning to end, and are responsible for the proper conduct of the whole affair; they are not employed only to bring the families contracting marriage together. The first ceremonials consist in the go-between being commissioned by the young man's family to obtain from the girl's family her name and the moment of her birth; this is done that the horoscope of the two may be examined by a fortune-teller in order to ascertain whether the proposed alliance will be a happy one. These particulars are written on paper, and should the fortune-teller give a favourable reply to the inquiries, the second ceremonial takes place, that of sending the go-between back with an offer of marriage. The assent in writing is asked for, and forms the third ceremonial. Fourthly, presents are sent to the girl's parents. Fifthly, the go-between requests them to choose a lucky day for the wedding. The preliminaries are concluded by the bridegroom going in a procession to bring the bride home. The Chinese speak of three convenants and six ceremonies, which may be stated to be as follows:—

The three convenants are:—

The Contract of Marriage,

The Receipt of Betrothal Money,

The Deed of the Delivery of the Bride.

The six ceremonies are:—

The Small Presents,
The Inquiry for the Name of the Bride,
The Payment of the Betrothal Money,
The Request to fix the Day,
The Sending of a Goose,
The Fetching of the Bride.

Betrothal presents are called *ch'á lai* [*ch'a li*], tea presents, or ceremonials. They consist of a present of tea, cakes, betel-nuts, and money, given by the future husband's family to the family of his future wife. The go-between takes, or accompanies, these presents (to the girl's family) which are carried in *hòp* [*ho*], or round flat boxes made of wood. A few dollars are also put into the boxes. With concubines, money alone is most generally given. The Chinese have a phrase, *shik yan ch'á laí* [*shih yen ch'a li*], which means that these ceremonial presents have been accepted and eaten, and consequently that the daughter is betrothed. If there are no presents, there is no betrothal.

Betrothals are strictly binding; and it would seem that on the woman's side they cannot be broken without the consent of the man, accompanied by a money salve. No misconduct, however flagrant, on the side of the youth at least, is held to be a release from the covenant.

'From the time of engagement until marriage, a young lady is required to maintain the strictest seclusion. Whenever friends call upon her parents she is expected to retire to the inner apartments, and in all her actions and words guard her conduct with careful solicitude. She must use a closed sedan whenever she visits her relations, and in her intercourse with her brothers and the domestics in the household maintain great reserve. Instead of having any opportunity to form those friendships and acquaintances with her own sex, which among ourselves become a source of so much pleasure at the time, and advantage in after life, the Chinese maiden is confined to the circle of her relations and her immediate neighbours. She has few of the pleasing rememberances and associations that are usually connected with school-day life, nor has she often the ability or opportunity to correspond by letter with girls of her own age. Seclusion at this time of life, and the custom of crippling the feet, combine to confine women in the house almost as much as the strictest laws against their appearing abroad; for in girlhood, as they know only a few persons, except relatives, and can make very few acquaintances after marriage, their circle of friends contracts rather than enlarges as life goes on. This privacy impels girls to learn as much of the world as they can, and among the rich their curiosity is gratified through maid-servants, match-makers, peddlers, visitors, and others. Curiosity also stimulates young ladies to learn something of the character and appearance of their intended husbands, but the rules of society are too strict for young persons to endeavour to form a personal attachment, though it is not [absolutely] impossible for them to have a look at each other if they wish.'

These strict rules have been somewhat relaxed during the last decade, though they are still closely observed by the more conservative families and generally in places distant from progressive centres.

There are no relations between the betrothed parties. The two are as utter strangers to each other as any other man or woman, if not more so: no courting; no moonlight rambles; no gradually getting better acquainted with each other and thereby getting better fitted to live together. It is simply a business transaction in almost all cases, the active parties in which are the parents, while the most interested parties are simply passive. The children are supposed never to meet or speak to each other, and it would be unpardonably bad taste were the parents representing the one side ever to discuss the subject with those of the other side. Under these circumstances there are, of course, no engagement rings, nor for that matter is a wedding ring worn by Chinese ladies when married.

What has been stated above is in regard to the betrothal of a chief or legitimate wife. With concubines, or secondary wives, it is quite different. In their case a go-between may be employed or not. In such a betrothal, all that generally takes place in Canton is for the woman to pour out a cup of tea for her future husband to drink, and a parcel of money, wrapped up, of course, in red paper and containing two, or three, or ten dollars or so, is placed on the tray for her; but in other places there may not be so much ceremony about it as that. The bargain money may even be paid right into her own hands, but this is only the case with very low people, as it is not thought the right thing for either party to have direct dealings with one another.

References.—Möllendorff, *Family Law;* Parker, *Comp. Chinese Family Law; Chinese Customs;* Gray, *China;* Doolittle, *Social Life;* Williams, *Middle Kingdom;* De Groot, *Religious System;* d'Hérisson, *Études; China Review,* viii, etc.; *Journ. N.C.B.R.A.S., N.S.,* xxvii, etc.

BIBLIOGRAPHY.—Möllendorff's *Manual of Chinese Bibliography* is a most valuable work of reference with regard to European books, essays, and articles on China down to the year 1876: it contains 4639 titles. There is also the encyclopædic work of M. Henri Cordier, *Bibliotheca Sinica: Dictionnaire Bibliographique des Ouvrages Relatifs à l'Empire Chinois,* in two large volumes of 1396 pages, with a supplement issued in three parts (1893–5); it is a perfect storehouse of information on books relating to China. A new and revised edition in four volumes was issued in 1904–8. The *Chinese Repository*, xviii, 402, 657, published a list of 402 works. The *China Review*, published in Hongkong once every two months during the years 1872 to 1901 (twenty-five volumes), contained a list of books and magazine articles on China, under the heading of 'Collectanea Bibliographica.' As to native works, Wylie's *Notes on Chinese Literature* is invaluable: it treats of 1745 Chinese books. For an account of the immense compendiums of former works, made by authority of different Emperors, one should refer to Mayers's *Bibliography of the Chinese Imperial Collection of Literature*, published in the *China Review*, vol. vi. pp. 223–86.

BIRDS' NEST SOUP.—Birds' nest soup is even more of a luxury in China, than turtle soup is in England. An old resident in China thus writes of it:—

'Perhaps the costliest dainty of the Chinese cuisine, and is as much prized by Chinese gourmands as turtle is in England. It is not nasty, but it is, to a European palate, exceedingly insipid; it is a white, soft, slippery substance, not unlike a badly made junket, or flummery, and the taste for it is certainly an acquired one.'

The nests from which the soup is prepared are not like an ordinary nest made up of sticks and twigs, hay and grass, but are of a gelatinous substance, secreted by the bird itself for the purpose, or, as it has been wittily put, the bird makes them 'all out of its own head.' Darwin puts it in plain English:— 'The Chinese make soup of dried saliva'; in scientific language, they are described as being produced from the 'inspissated mucus from the salivary glands.'

Birds' Nests of this kind have been described as:—

'Externally resembling ill-concocted fibrous isinglass, and of a white colour, inclining to red; their thickness is little more than that of a silver spoon, and their weight from a quarter to half an ounce. When dry, they are brittle and wrinkled; the size is rather larger than a goose-egg; the dry, white, and clean the most valuable.'

'These nests are constructed in caves on the sea-shore, the swiftlet, which makes them, being a native of Malaya and Ceylon. Gomanti are the largest birds' nest caves in the world . . . from which there is an out-turn of over $15,000 worth yearly.' The nests are gathered at considerable risk, and the best quality commands a high price, ranging from three to thirty dollars a pound, while the inferior grades are mixed more or less with twigs, etc. The Chinese consider it strengthening and stimulating, and it forms the first dish at all grand dinners. Here is a receipt for preparing *Potage aux Nids d'Hirondelles*, translated from the Chinese:—

'Take clean white birds' nest shreds, or birds' nests, and soak thoroughly. Pick out all feathers. Boil in soup or water till tender, and of the colour of jadestone. Place pigeons' eggs below, and add some ham shreds on top. Boil again slowly with little fluid. If required sweet, then boil in clear water till tender, add sugar-candy, and then eat. This is a most clear and pure article, and thick (or oily) substances should not be added. It should be boiled for a long time; for, if not boiled till tender, it will cause diarrhœa.'

BIRTH (CUSTOMS CONNECTED WITH).—There are quite a number of superstitions connected with the birth of children. As an instance of them it may be noted that certain coins are worn by women before the event, as they are thought to ensure an easy delivery. Midwives are nearly always in attendance; they are utterly ignorant women, and sad are the tales that many a foreign doctor could tell of the wretched plight Chinese women have been reduced to under their unskilful treatment, or want of treatment. They are engaged a month beforehand, except in very poor cases.

Shortly before birth, when the birth-pangs come on, the mother-in-law and midwife worship all the household gods (all the gods that may be in the house) and the ancestral tablets, but there is no going to the Temple or Ancestral Hall for the purpose. These acts of worship consist in burning incense before the objects of adoration, and extempore prayer (there being no form of prayer for the purpose) for a quick and happy delivery, and for the welfare of child and mother; the woman herself does not offer any prayer.

Many people have a charm ready procured from a temple, and some, on the birth of the child, at once fasten it to the body or round the neck, or a piece of cypress is tied to the body, either alone or in addition. A piece of raw ginger is hung up at the street door to keep off evil spirits and strangers, as it is feared the advent of the latter may cause the death of the child, the supposition being that the stranger's birthday will, or may, clash with that of the child; and it is for the same reason that the characters which represent the hour and date of birth of bride and bridegroom are handed to a fortune-teller, so that he may find out whether they do or not. If they do, the bride or bridegroom might die. To return to the new-born infant—a piece of fern (or *cyclas revoluta*, probably) is hung up by a red cord, in order to avert evil consequences and keep off bad spirits. This is also suspended at the street door on other occasions as well, but the use of the ginger, we have mentioned already, is confined to the birth of a child.

One of our informants tells us that, from his experience, the new-born infant is washed with warm water at once (whether this is due to foreign influence or not we cannot say), while from other sources we learn that such an idea is scouted. No dainty little baby garments are ready for the stranger, worked with the expectant love of the mother, or given by friends in anticipation of the interesting event, but his tender little limbs and body are wrapped up in swaddling bands, which consist of old warm clothes both of men and women—a little bundle of old clothes, awkward and ungainly for the tiny mite inside it. After this, the new-born babe may probably not be washed again thoroughly (if he has ever yet been subjected to such an operation) for the first month, for fear the child should get cold; he, or she, may be wiped over with a cloth; but after that time, the luxury of an occasional wash, such as it is, may be indulged in. A special kind of fine little cake, sweet and delicate in taste, is sometimes the only food the little stranger is regaled with for the first few days. For the first month, the mother must have ginger and vinegar with everything she takes. She eschews her ordinary food—chicken boiled with ginger and vinegar, or (if too poor to afford the fowl, cheap enough though it be in China), ducks' eggs boiled with the same condiments, and pig's feet boiled with the same articles form her diet: and these she eats twice or thrice a day. Such a dietary is considered to be tonic, and after the month is up, she returns to her ordinary food.

And now comes a most important event—the shaving of the child's head. A lucky day is selected for it. It must not be after the thirtieth day, but it may be before or on the day itself, *i.e.*, the shaving takes place on the completion of the month (the month, of course, has sometimes 29 days and sometimes 30 days) if that should prove to be a lucky day; if not, an earlier day is selected, never a later one. After the shaving is over (on the same day—never before the operation), the ancestors first are worshipped and then the household gods, thanks being offered to them for the addition to the family, and prayers for the prolongation of the life newly bestowed. Either the Temple or Ancestral Hall, or both, are often also visited for the same purpose by those who are making a great fuss over the event. Offerings are, of course, made. The mother-in-law, or some relative, goes to perform these religious acts, and not the father or mother: it is very rarely, if ever, that the mother goes on these occasions. The child, however, dressed in its best, is carried in the arms when this worship takes place. On the first occasion when a child is shaved, which necessary operation from a Chinese standpoint takes place, as we have already seen, when the baby is either a month or nearly a month old, eggs, dyed red, are sent round to relatives, friends and acquaintances. The number to be sent is not fixed by custom, nor is it necessary for any written communication to accompany them; a verbal message that they are from so-and-so is sufficient. The recipients are expected to give a present to the child on its being a month old, when a feast is held, to which they are invited. These red eggs are sent, in the South of China, irrespective of the sex; in the North, only a boy is entitled to them, and of the boys of a family, only the first born.

The Chinese have almost as great a love for dinners as the English, and it is only natural that a feast should take place when the child is a month old; this is called *köng ts'ò* [*chiang ts'u*], ginger and vinegar. Cards of invitation are issued to this *köng chök* [*chiang ch'ih*], or ginger dinner, to which the guests are both friends and relatives. Unless the family is poor, the male friends go to a restaurant for their feast; if poor, and there are only two or three relatives, it may be given in the house. The women's repast, on the other hand, is spread in the house.

If, however, there are many friends and relatives, two feasts are held: the first is for the relatives, and is at the house, even if they are males; the second is for friends, and is at a restaurant. In such cases the relatives are invited on the day of the shaving, even if it takes place before the month is up; the invitations are sent out the day before, or to those at a distance, earlier; and the friends also, whether invited at the same, or another time, may also be asked as well before the month is up. The feast may be held at another time than the shaving date, either for relatives, or friends, or both; the chief thing seems to be to celebrate the event by a feast. Two dishes are on the tables: the one containing the pickled ginger which gives the name to the entertainment, and the other red eggs dyed with *yín chí* [*yen chih*], Chinese rouge, or with foreign dye-stuffs. The invited guests make presents of gold and silver jewellery, or articles of clothing, to the infant, accompanied with *laí-shí* [*li hsi*] (cash or silver folded within red paper); the latter is given if nothing else is, more presents, of course, being given to a boy than to a girl.

The swaddling bands being discarded, the little manikin (or the 'little wifie' to a lesser extent) comes out gorgeous in scarlet and red—bright with colours; amulets and charms adorn him and safeguard him from evil spirits and demons: a tiny mirror flashes, perchance, from the front of his forehead, to dismay the ugly devils by a sight of their hideousness; a row of gilt deities benignly encircle his brow, to guard him; silver locks and chains bind him, so that no harm may befall him: many and wonderful are the means used to protect him by these and other mysterious and occult expedients and devices from all injury, while common-sense rules of health and cleanliness are unknown and ignored. The tribute paid by childhood, from the very moment of birth and onwards, to the insanitary conditions that surround it must be enormous, not only in the immediate sacrifice of life, but in the way of sowing seeds of future disease and weakness. It is wonderful that so many children escape with a fair amount of health to carry on the increasing round of human life and toil in this populous land of China. Out of every 1,000 Chinese children born in Hongkong only 72 live beyond twelve months or so.

BIRTHDAYS.—As a general rule it may be said that the principle of topsy-turvydom comes into play in the difference in observing birthdays in China and England: here in China the 'grown-up's' birthdays are kept and the child's almost entirely ignored, while with us, in our own lands, the contrary is more commonly the case. A mother, however, in the Shun Tak district of the Canton Province will give a steamed fresh fowl's, or a fresh or salt duck's, egg to her child on its birthday, to eat, the idea being that as the yolk of these eggs is what the Chinese call red, in their loose way of designating colours in their common speech, so the child's heart may be red or *sum hoong* [*hsin hung*], as it is termed; and this is equivalent to the phrase *fát fun* [*fa fên*], which means zealous, or enthusiastic, or diligent. Some parents, and sometimes others as well, in the same district will give a present of new clothes or toys, etc., on a birthday.

But the great day in a child's life is when it is a month old. The first anniversary of the birthday is kept also in Canton, and presents are also given by the parents, and sometimes by friends. These presents, however, only consist of eatables; though, at times, different articles are placed before the child on that day, such as books and pens, an abacus, or different tools, and what the child picks up shows, it is believed, that in after life he will follow the profession, calling, or trade which uses the articles selected.

No notice is taken of the birthday when a youth or maiden attains his or her full age, *shing ting* [*shêng ting*], as it is called, which is at the early age of sixteen in China. Few males marry before this age, but girls often marry earlier, even at fourteen, which is really thirteen according to our mode of reckoning. The Chinese generally reckon by the years, or parts of years, in which anyone has lived: thus a child born on the last day of the year is two years old on the next day; and as each New Year arrives, all the inhabitants of this populous empire add a year to their lives. We might therefore almost say that New Year's Day serves as a birthday to all the 400,000,000 people of China, and consequently it is not worth keeping. If one desires to know accurately the exact age of any Chinese, it is necessary to enquire the year, month, and day in which he was born.

After a man is married, his birthday assumes more importance, and his father-in-law or mother-in-law sends him presents of eatables or clothing; whether his own father or mother do so or not is left to their own fancy.

With the Chinese it is not considered the proper thing for those nearly related to make presents; the utmost extent to which it is thought well to go in this respect is to say, for example, to a near relative, 'Do you like this? If you do, I'll give it to you.' There is a saying, *Chee-ts'un mò mun* [*chih ch'in wu mên*], *i.e.*, 'There is no ceremony between those most nearly related.' The presentation of gifts partakes according to their ideas of the ceremonious.

All the sons and daughters have to prostrate themselves on the ground (the *kowtow*) before their parents on their birthdays, and this is universally done, except perhaps by the very lowest dregs of society. This is the practice on New Year's Day as well. On the birthdays it is called *pie show* [*pai shou*]; and on these birthdays, in the Shun Tak district, it is the custom of the children to put their cash together and buy sweetmeats, such as sugared kam-kwats, dried sweet persimmons, sugared citrons, etc., etc., boil them in water, and present this water to the parents to drink. Sometimes clothes, etc., are given; but this latter is not a fixed custom—custom is inexorable in China.

When grown-up, the children give a wine-party to their parents on their birthdays, inviting relatives on both sides of the family to it. Fowls and vegetables are cooked—in fact, a feast is prepared.

The birthdays when a man attains the age of 21, 31, and so on to 91, are considered of more importance than the others. This is owing to a man's life being dominated by the mysterious and mystical *yöng* [*yang*] principle, by which the first years in the decades are considered as of importance as entering on the first of the new decade. This prevails throughout China. With women, though, in other parts of China it is the same, and in the Kwongtung [Kuangtung] province this is also the case to a great extent; yet others have a local custom of keeping the even tens of their ages as important birthdays, such as 20, 30, and so on. This is on account of the equally mysterious and mystic *yum* [*yin*] principle, pertaining to women, inclining to these even years. The principle of these two, the *yum* and *yöng*, pertaining to the even and the odd, is laid down in that abstruse classic, the *Yik King* [*I ching*], or Book of Changes.

It will be noticed from the above that the first thing the Chinese give on birthdays is food, the second in importance is clothing.

The birthdays of many gods are kept, and are called *tahn* [*tan*]. The idols are worshipped by their votaries on these anniversaries, either in the people's own houses or in the temples of the gods, and offerings of food, etc., are presented to them. The worshippers say the spirits thus worshipped take the spiritual portion or ethereal essence of the eatables, and they, the worshippers, then feast on the remains, which to human eye and taste are in precisely the same condition as they were before being offered. All the absurdities this gives rise to are clearly perceived by the Chinese, who say *p'ung shun loh shik* [*fêng shên lao shih*], which means using the excuse of worshipping the gods to get food for themselves. There is another similar saying, *sow ching ng tsong meeoo* [*sao ching ê tsung miao*], which refers to subscriptions being obtained to repair temples and then the money being diverted to the bellies of those who have collected it. One could almost fancy these swindlers saying that the spiritual essences of the silver satisfied the gods, while they took, like those who offered food, the substantial portion themselves.

BOATS.—Leaves floating on the water first suggested the idea of boats to the Chinese, so some native writers inform us; other accounts ascribe their origin to the sight of drift-wood, or to a natural development from the more primitive raft. Whether or not fallen leaves were the first hints of future possibilities, the boats of China might almost be compared to the leaves of the forest in number, and their varieties are about as great as that of the foliage of China. Boats large and small, long and short, broad and narrow, boats for hawkers, for fishing, for pleasure—boats ready for any and everything; boats for smuggling, for pirates, for honest tradesmen, for lepers, for beggars, for everyone; boats for passage, for ferries, for bridges, for marriages, for feastings, for theatres, or rather for theatrical troupes and their properties. Is there anything that boats are not provided for in China?

Boats

It has been said there are more boats in China than in all the rest of the world put together. The extensive sea-board, and the innumerable rivers and streams are a sufficient reason for this multiplicity of craft of one kind or another.

If we credit what the natives themselves say, boats were first built in the third century before the Christian era.

'One account ascribes the invention to Ho Sín Kwú [Ho Hsien Ku], a pious woman, who became one of the eight Taoist genii. Her first craft was a mere raft, without means of propulsion. But one day when she was washing clothes in the river, she took a hint from a fish that was rowing with its fins and steering with its tail, and she then put oars and a rudder upon her boat.'

In mediæval times the Chinese not only held their own, but took the lead in adventurous voyages to distant shores (See CHINESE ABROAD), which awaken the surprise and admiration of those who have investigated the subject; but gradually these voyages have been discontinued; and even in modern times, they have shrunk into short passages between different seaports on the coast of China and closely adjacent countries, the voyages in native craft to the Straits Settlements and neighbouring lands and islands being but few, while the long trips to India, and other distant lands, in the large old junks carrying from three to ten and twelve sails (the present sea-going junks seldom have more than three or four sails) and a crew of 250 or more men, mentioned by the mediæval travellers, Friar Jordanus, Ibn Batuta, and Marco Polo, are now entirely a thing of the past. The old must die out before the new, and the modern steamship is running, in fact has run, the heavy lumbering junk off many of its old established sea-routes; even a beginning has been made in inland waters in the same direction, and eventually the picturesque clumsy old craft is bound to disappear in the world's march of progress, which even now influences distant Cathay. Notwithstanding their uncouth shape and clumsy-looking sails, they undoubtedly are picturesque objects, and look as if they had been begun in some antediluvian age and never finished off. Their *bizarre* hulls, high sterns further augmented by the gingerbread work, the divergent rake of their masts, their large nut-brown matting sails, topped sometimes with a gay red pennant, all lend a distinct charm and piquant flavour of their own to the junk, and make it of a kind not to be found elsewhere in the world. They offer very effective objects for the painter's brush: whether as brown sails speckled on the sun-lit sea; or whether the diverse style of their build with their queer-shaped hulls are more carefully studied; or whether, all tattered and torn, the ragged sail of the weather-beaten craft on its return voyage suggests a conflict with stormy winds, while a more forlorn appearance still is apparent when, dismantled, they are undergoing repairs, or when heeled over on the sand for breaming, or when cast high and dry on the beach, or stranded on the rocks, with their bare poles of masts and gaping sterns, out of which stick their queer-shaped enormous rudders. Still more picturesque was the sight of a squadron of war-junks, with brightly painted hulls and many-coloured banners, of all shapes and sizes, and streaming pennants like the old mediæval galleys of Europe, lying ready to start on an expedition to subdue the rebellious subjects of His Imperial Majesty the Emperor of China.

Scores of books might be written on the many-featured sides of life to be found on boats in China: their history from earliest times to the present; their shapes and sizes and builds and rigs, from the curious Hakka boats, with their nine or a dozen sails spread fan-like on an improvised framework of bamboo poles, down to the tiny fisher's canoe.

What interesting chapters could be indited anent thousand and millions of human beings, whose whole lives are spent on the rivers and canals which flow past, or cut through, so many Chinese cities—inhabiting dwellings without foundations (and for which the occupants pay no ground-rent), as the flowing stream supports them in more senses than one; the strange and varied experiences to be found in travelling by boat will still afford material for many a volume of novel adventure in the future as they have in the past; the origin of some of the boat populations, their curious customs, habits and superstitions—these all have been but lightly touched upon as yet, and present an interesting field to be worked by the ethnologist, the comparative mythologist, and the lover of folklore.

The following extracts from consular reports, by Mr. Byron Brenan, are interesting as showing how an attempt has been made to copy the paddle-wheel in one species of boat in Canton, and how steam-launches were (toward the end of the nineteenth century) making their way into use:—

'The evolution of the Chinese passenger-boat is proceeding cautiously. Twenty years ago sails and sweeps were the powers used; then came stern-wheel boats worked by manpower, these are still extensively used. . . The next stage was a towboat lashed alongside a passenger-boat, and the next, it may be hoped, will be the amalgamation of the tug and the tow.

'The stern-wheel passenger-boats are a striking feature on the busy river at Canton. They are long, low, box-looking craft, the largest being of about 100 tons measurement. The inside of the box is divided into compartments in which the passengers lie down or squat, for there is not head room. The roof is flat, and on this sit a crowd of passengers sheltered from the weather by stiff bamboo mats. At the stern is the compartment where the men work. The largest kind of boat has twenty-four men. The machinery on a large boat consists of four shafts laid across the boat at a distance of 3 feet from each other. At each of these shafts six men work a sort of tread mill; they hold on to a cross-bar above with their hands, while their feet work the three wooden pedals which are fixed on three iron arms radiating from the centre; there is thus an angle of 120 degrees between two pedals. The pedals along the shafts are so dispersed that the six men do not keep step. As No. 1 puts his foot on one pedal, No. 2 is already half-way through his step, and so on. These series of tread mills are connected with the stern paddle-wheel by means of cranks, so that one revolution of the tread mill makes one revolution of the stern-wheel. The stern-wheel is 8 feet in diameter and has 8 floats, and when the men are working easily it makes 16 to 18 revolutions a minute, and the speed attained is 3½ to 4 miles an hour. On a long journey the men rest in turn, three working to one resting, and in this way the boat is kept going during the whole of the day.

'The number of native-owned steam-launches running between Canton and the numerous towns of the Delta is constantly increasing. Besides their use by officials, and in the customs, likin, and salt preventive services, they are constantly employed to tow passenger-boats; but, in this case, only to and from fixed stations. The launches engaged in towing are taxed, and ply under severe pains and penalties. However, since the opening of the West River in 1897, steam traffic on the Canton waterways has been placed under the control of the Imperial Maritime Customs.'

At Swatow and other places in China, such as between Soochow, Hangchow, and Shanghai, steam-launches are plying as passenger-boats, and it is hoped that, as time goes on, they will be increased, as notwithstanding the multiplicity of boats and the magnificent rivers in many parts, intercommunication is slow. The use of the steam-launch has increased very much; they are to be found on the P'oyang Lake and in other parts of Central China, and there is scarcely now a navigable stream in connection with the Canton River, at all events in the Delta, which is not traversed daily by steam-boats. 'For every ten persons who travelled ten years ago there are a hundred to-day' (1901).

There are several Chinese companies running large launches between Hankow and Changsha, which carry passengers and tow other boats.

In 1900 there were eighteen launches running from Amoy inland to distances of sixty, twenty-six, thirteen, and ten miles, carrying some 600,000 passengers, an increase of 10% on 1899, though the fares had been doubled.

The traffic represented by steam-launches at Wuchow, under the Chinese flag, amounted in tons to 24,138 in 1900. At Samshui, launches have also increased in numbers.

In the neighbourhood of Canton, steam-launches made 132,972 trips in inland waters in 1900, ' or a daily average of about as many trips as there are days in the year.'

Reference.—Werner, *Descriptive Sociology.*

BOOK OF CHANGES, BOOK OF HISTORY, BOOK OF POETRY.—*See* LITERATURE.

BOOKS ON CHINA.—The books written on China are numerous, and are constantly being added to (See BIBLIOGRAPHY). Nearly every one who has taken any marked interest in the country or people has written about one or both; more especially is this the case in times of disturbance or other events attracting public attention, as the siege of the legations in Peking and the military operations in the North in 1900, which awaken special interest in China. Missionaries, merchants, military and naval men, scholars, professors, teachers, interpreters, consuls and vice-consuls, ambassadors and diplomats, statesmen, travellers and globe-trotters, literary men, reviewers, novelists and poets, as well as the Chinese themselves, have all contributed their quota to instruct Europe and America as to things Chinese; and the views presented from such varied standpoints are naturally diverse. The books produced range through all branches of the subject: the languages and peoples, the history, geography, natural history, government, customs and manners, books, arts and industries, religions, politics and commerce—all come in for their full share of attention.

We do not propose to give a complete list of the best books on China, but the perusal or study of the following ten will give a very good idea of this interesting people as they were under the Empire:

(1) Williams' *Middle Kingdom.*—To those who wish to get a general idea of the Empire, and all that concerns it and its people, there is not a better book. It is a perfect repository of information for the general reader, and the last edition will doubtless maintain its position as a text-book on the subject for many years to come.

(2) Gray's *China.*—A book in two volumes, profusely illustrated by Chinese drawings and giving much information, not in the style of a text-book, but in the form of a personal narrative of what the author himself saw during his long residence in China.

(3) Giles's *Historic China, and other Sketches.*—An octavo volume of 400 pages, containing short sketches of the different historical periods, and essays, all written in a light and pleasant sytle, and containing much information.

(4) Doolittle's *Social Life of the Chinese.*—A book full of all the curious superstitions, strange ceremonies, and customs of the Chinese, more particularly those pertaining to Foochow.

(5) Henry's *Ling-nam.*—A pleasant, brightly-written book of travels in the Canton province, with descriptions of its beautiful scenery, fine rivers, and thickly populated districts.

(6) Miss Gordon Cumming's *Wanderings in China,* is light, pleasant reading, and gives the general reader a good idea of the coast ports.

(7) Williamson's *Journeys in North China,* contains an immense amount of reliable information, principally about that portion of China.

(8) Douglas's *Society in China* is even better than his former work, *China,* which we recommended in a former edition as being well fitted to give a good general idea of China and its people, within compact limits.

(9) *Journal of the North China Branch of the Royal Asiatic Society.* (See NORTH CHINA BRANCH OF THE ROYAL ASIATIC SOCIETY.)

(10) Legge's *Chinese Classics* contain the bible of the Chinese nation, which every school-boy was taught to learn by heart, and on which the government of the whole empire and the fabric of Chinese society was based until nearly the end of the Monarchical Period.

The above books might be increased to ten times ten easily enough; nor, by placing these first, do we intend to imply that many of the others would not equally claim to be mentioned with them. With such an *embarras de richesses* it is difficult to know where to begin. Of books of travel, we may instance *Old Highways in China,* by Mrs. Williamson, as a light and readable book, containing a good deal about the women and children. Another book interesting to young people is *Children in Blue and What They Do,* by Miss Codrington. *The Real Chinaman,* by Holcombe, is a very readable book. To those who want to know the why and wherefore of things Chinese, there are Couling's *Encyclopaedia Sinica,* Richard's *Comprehensive Geography,* and Werner's *Descriptive Sociology—Chinese* (the first work to present the phenomena of the Chinese civilization—its morphology, physiology, and development in a complete and scientific manner).

Quite a literature is springing up on Western China; Mrs. Bryson's *Child Life in China* treats of Hankow and the neigh-

bourhood of the Yang-tzŭ, so does Cornaby's *A String of Chinese Peach Stones*, in the way of tales and folklore, finally ending in a story of the rebellion of rebellions in modern times in China, the great T'ai P'ing Rebellion; Baber's *Travels and Researches in Western China*, published as a supplemental paper of the Royal Geographical Society, vol. i, pt. i, 1882; Hosie's *Travels in Western China; Three Years in Western China; On the Trail of the Opium Poppy;* and Hart's *Western China*—these are all most interesting books and well worthy of perusal. In this connection there is also Little's *Yang-tsz Gorges* and his more recent work, *Mount Omi and Beyond: A Record of Travel on the Thibetan Border*. Mrs. Little's *Intimate China: Chinese as I Have Seen Them*, and her *The Land of the Blue Gown* should also be mentioned.

Richthofen's splendid work, *China*, contains besides a general description of the country, valuable sections on the geology, palæontology, etc., and much useful information by a traveller 'of great scientific ability,' whose explorations have been described as 'at once the most extensive and the most scientific of our age.' It is written in German.

Peking is treated of in *Peking, Histoire et Description avec 524 Gravures anciennes et nouvelles, reproduites ou exécutés par des Artistes chinois d'apres les plus précieux documents*,' by Favier; Marache's *Pékin et ses Habitants*; Bretschneider's *Recherches Archéologiques et Historiques sur Pékin et ses Environs*; and Bitchurin's *Description of Peking*. Later works are Gamble's *Peking, A Sociological Survey*, and Bredon's *Peking*.

Concerning Canton, one may read Gray's *Walks in the City of Canton*, which, besides giving much information, is also useful as a guide-book. Mention should also be made of the Rev. Hilderic Friend's *The Willow Pattern*, written by one who lived amongst the people, and took the greatest interest in all their habits and customs; it is consequently a very truthful picture of Chinese life, told in the guise of a tale.

Macao has been treated of in a book, now rare and out of print, viz.:—Lungstedt's *Macao and China*, over the production of which the author spent much labour and research. There is also a German book lately published on this interesting old European settlement in the Far East, viz., *Macao: Der Erste Stützpunkt Europäischen Handels in China*, by Kutschera.

Swatow customs, people, and folk-lore, are treated of in a trio of books by Miss Fielde, entitled *Pagoda Shadows, A Corner of Cathay, and Chinese Night's Entertainment.*

Moule's *New China and Old* has something to say of Ningpo, Hangchow, and Shanghai; besides treating of Chinese subjects in general.

Besides numerous magazine articles, the large island of Hainan has been admirably treated in a new book in French, *L'Empire de Chine. . . Haï-nan et la côte continentale voisine,* by Madrole. Here may be mentioned a recent work, styled *European Settlements in the Far East,* which not only deals with all the Treaty Ports in China, but of the similar spots in the adjacent countries as well. A few books deal with separate provinces, such as Mayer's *Kwong Tung,* Armstrong's *Shán Tung,* and Davies's *Yünnan.*

The transition from these to a lighter class of reminiscences of olden days, may be made by the reading of an old resident's recollections of earlier days, under the names of *Bits of Old China,* and *The Fan-kwai in Canton.*

A vast amount of learning, erudition, and research are shown in many of the periodicals published on China, especially in the *China Review, Transactions of the N.C. Br. of the R.A.S.,* already mentioned, the *Chinese Repository,* and *New China Review.* The second of these (now called *Journal, etc.*), is the only one now issued. Any one who will take the trouble to make himself acquainted with most of the Articles and Notes contained in these three periodicals, to say nothing of *Notes and Queries on China and Japan, The Chinese Journal and Missionary Recorder,* and *Journal of the Peking Oriental Society,* will find that there is scarcely a subject connected with China that has not been most learnedly discussed in those pages.

Here may also be mentioned a number of interesting *brochures* issued from the Jesuit press at Shanghai, under the general name of *Variétés Sinologiques.*

To those who are fond of the marvellous, treated in a sober manner, let us recommend *Mythical Monsters,* by Gould; to those who wish a light story-book on the same subject, there is Giles's *Strange Stories from a Chinese Studio,* Dennys's *The Folklore of China*; and Wieger's *Folklore Chinois Moderne.* The only monograph on Chinese mythology is Werner's *Myths and Legends of China* (1922).

From myths to worship is an easy transition, and here we have a whole host of books, especially if under this category we include books dealing with the philosophical systems. *The Dragon, Image, and Demon; or, the Three Religions,* by du Bose, will give an idea of the multiplicity of objects of worship: it deals primarily with the neighbourhood of Soochow, though much is applicable to all parts of China. Edkins's *Religion in China,* and his *Chinese Buddhism,* Legge's *The Religions of China,* and Beal's *Buddhistic Literature in China,* treat fully of these subjects. Also to be noticed as worthy of the highest commendation is De Groot's *Religious System of China,* Parker's *China and Religion* and his *Studies in Chinese Religion*; Soothill's *The Three Religions of China*; Granet's *La Religion des Chinois*; and Clennell's *The Historical Development of Religion in China.* To those who are content with comparatively short essays, there is Douglas's *Confucianism and Taouism,* containing two admirable monographs on these two religions, or philosophies. Then there are the works of Faber, noted for sound scholarship; *The Mind of Mencius; or Political Economy, founded upon Moral Philosophy,* and *A Systematic Digest of the Doctrines of Confucius,* besides his other works in both German and English. And the Bible of the Taoists, the *Tao Teh King,* translated by Chalmers; there are besides two translations of the Taoist philosopher, by Balfour and Giles respectively, and Legge's translation in the *Sacred Books of the East* Series. Other valuable translations of classical works are Steele's *I li,* Bruce's *Chu Hsi and His Masters,* and his *The Philosophy of Human Nature.* Among useful treatises also are Suzuki's *History of Chinese Philosophy* and Tucci's *Storia della Filosofia Cinese Antica.*

There are numbers of volumes containing short papers, or essays, among which we may mention the admirable *Hanlin Papers; or, Essays on the Intellectual Life of the Chinese,* in two series, by Martin; Balfour's *Leaves from my Chinese Scrapbook*; and Medhurst's *The Foreigner in Far Cathay;* among these also might be classed the interesting work, *Chinese Characteristics,* by Smith, and his later work, *Village Life in China: A Study in Sociology.* Watters's *Essays on Chinese Literature* is a valuable work. His *Stories of Everyday Life in China* contains interesting narratives collected from native sources. The gift to see ourselves as others see us will be granted by a perusal of *Those Foreign Devils: a Celestial on England and Englishmen,* translated by Wilkinson, *As the Chinese See Us,* by Selby and *John Chinaman,* by Parker.

For the historical student there are Boulger's *History of China,* and his *Short History*; Ross's *History of the Manchus,* and his *Corea,* which necessarily deal largely with China. There is also Hirth's learned *brochure, China and the Roman Orient: Researches into their Ancient and Mediæval Relations as represented in old Chinese Records*; Wieger's *Textes Historiques*; Cordier's *Histoire Générale de la Chine*; *Li Ung Bing's Outlines of Chinese History*; and Chavannes' vast work *Les Mémoires Historiques de Sz-Ma Ch'ien*; Parker's *A Thousand Years of the Tartars*; *China: Her History, Diplomacy and Commerce from the Earliest Times to the Present Day; Ancient China Simplified;* and *China Past and Present*; Macgowan's *History of China* and his *Pictures of Southern China*; Mrs. Bishop's *Korea and Her Neighbours*; and Giles's *Biographical Dictionary.* The terrible siege of the foreign legations in Peking produced a number of books; among these *The Siege in Peking: China Against the World,* by an Eye-witness, will be found most interesting and well written.

Dealing with the Government of China are Mayers's *Chinese Government,* and *List of the Higher Metropolitan and Provincial Authorities of China,* compiled by the Chinese Secretaries, H.B.M. Legation, Peking.

On legal matters may be instanced Staunton's *Penal Code* and Alabaster's *Notes and Commentaries on the Chinese Criminal Law.*

Those who are interested in the part that different European nations have played in the Far East, and in the political outlook in that part of the world, will doubtless find the following books to their taste, viz.:—*Problems of the Far East,* by Curzon; *The Problem in China and British Policy, China in Decay,* and *Russia in Asia: A Record and Study,* 1558-1899, by Krausse. One of the most interesting of this class of books is *The Englishman in China during the Victorian Era, as illustrated in the career of Sir Rutherford Alcock,* by Michie.

A pleasant taste of Chinese literature may be obtained from Giles's *Gems of Chinese Literature,* being gleanings from all times and periods, his *A History of Chinese Literature,* and Martin's *Lore of Cathay.*

Those fond of poetry will find it treated of in Davis's *Poetry of the Chinese;* and Giles's *Chinese Poetry in English Verse;* Waley's *Chinese Poems*; and those delighting in rhymes will find Stent's *Entombed Alive, and other Songs and Ballads from the Chinese,* a lively book to beguile a pleasant half-hour; *Pidgin-English Sing-song,* by Leland, is amusing. Two most interesting illustrated books by Headland are *Chinese Mother Goose Rhymes,* and *The Chinese Boy and Girl.*

In drama, there are Stanton's *The Chinese Drama* and Johnston's *The Chinese Drama.*

Freemasons and those interested in secret societies will find Schlegel's *Thian Thi Hwui,* of great interest. A small book has also been lately published, Stanton's *Triad Society. A Collection of Chinese Proverbs* by Scarborough, and Smith's *Chinese*

Proverbs, will suit another class of readers. The translation of the *Ch'êng Yü K'ao, A Manual of Chinese Quotations*, by Lockhart, is another work of value.

Philologists have their tastes provided for in Edkins's *China's Place in Philology*, and *The Languages of China before the Chinese*, by Lacouperie.

The collector of china has had some aids provided in Hirth's *Ancient Porcelain: A Study in Chinese Mediæval Industry and Trade*, ond Bushell's *Chinese Porcelain before the Present Dynasty*. It is a pity that the illustrations of this last work could not have been reproduced; but his larger book is splendidly got up and illustrated. Another book is *Chinese Porcelain*, by Gulland. Large works on porcelain are Hobson's *The Wares of the Ming Dynasty*, and Hobson and Hetherington's *The Art of the Chinese Potter*. Numismatists will find their tastes catered for in Lockhart's *The Currency of the Farther East, from the Earliest Times up to the Present Day*.

Collections of photographs with more or less of letterpress, may be instanced as another class of books on China, amongst which we may notice *Chinese Pictures: Notes on Photographs*, by Mrs. Bishop.

A very large and constantly increasing number of books in French (besides those already mentioned) have been issued from the press, dealing with China, and ranging from the learned works of Julien to the light literature by Tcheng Ki Tong. The other principal languages of Europe have all been requisitioned to describe this people and their country, such as German, Italian, Spanish, Portuguese, Russian, and even Latin.

There is also a literature growing up dealing with China and the Chinese from the Missionary standpoint. One of these is Gibson's *Mission Problems and Mission Methods in South China* (Swatow). Also in this connection may be mentioned a number of biographies of eminent missionaries.

But we have already occupied more than enough space in this rapid survey of books treating of China and the Chinese, and have necessarily left many works unnoticed. The number produced has increased enormously within the last few years, and will probably continue to do so with the ever-growing number of foreign residents. We cannot, however, close without a passing reference to Marco Polo, the celebrated Venetian traveller of the Middle Ages, the pioneer of the army, which, with ever-increasing numbers, has visited the ere-while Kingdom of the 'Grand Khan,' Kublai Khan; but the present itinerants, unlike their great predecessor, who resided for years in the country, are content to 'do' China in a few days or months, and then hasten to instruct the ignorant world in books and pamphlets, which, often amidst interesting and sprightly narratives of stirring events, contain a mass of crude and undigested second-hand information of the people they scarcely know, and of the country they have skimmed through, 'or rather passed by,' so rapidly. Generally, the best books are those written by scholars who came to China in their teens or early twenties, who have made their life-careers of thirty or more years in China, have collected and digested their own facts, and speak, read, and write the Chinese language. They are in the best position to understand and appreciate a people and a literature otherwise not easily understood or appreciated.

References.—Cordier, *Bibliotheca Sinica;* Möllendorff, *Manual of Chinese Bibliography*; and the valuable catalogues issued by Kelly & Walsh, Shanghai, etc., Probsthain & Co., Luzac & Co., and Kegan Paul, Trench, Trübner & Co., London.

BOOKS FOR LEARNING CHINESE.—Beginners are often at a loss to know what books to get to learn the different so-called dialects, or rather spoken languages of China; and we often have enquiries made on this subject. We therefore give some directions as to the books to procure:—

AMOY.—For a phrase-book, Macgowan's *Manual of the Amoy Dialect,* and for Dictionaries, English-Amoy: his *English-Chinese Dictionary in the Amoy Dialect.* For Amoy-English Dictionary, *Chinese-English Dictionary of the Vernacular or Spoken Language of Amoy, with the principal variations of the Chang Chew and Chin Chew Dialects,* by Douglas. Besides these books, there is a large assortment—the largest in the country—of Romanised Colloquial books prepared by the missionaries.

CANTONESE.—For learning the language, Dyer Ball's *Cantonese Made Easy; The Cantonese Made Easy Vocabulary, How to Speak Cantonese, Readings in Cantonese Colloquial,* by the same author. The two varieties of Dictionaries required, are Eitel's *Cantonese-English Dictionary;* and Chalmers's *English-Cantonese Dictionary.* For the acquisition of a few phrases there is a small book specially prepared, freed as much as possible from all difficulties: *An English and Cantonese Pocket Vocabulary,* also by Dyer Ball.

FOOCHOW.—Maclay's *Manual of the Foochow Dialect,* and Maclay and Baldwin's *Chinese-English Dictionary.*

HAINAN.—The Gospels in Romanised Colloquial.

HAKKA.—Dyer Ball's *Easy Sentences in the Hakka Dialect, with a Vocabulary*; this is prepared simply for those who wish to acquire a mere smattering of Hakka; for others there has also been prepared by the same author, *Hakka Made Easy.* There are also the Romanised Colloquial books prepared by the German Missionaries, as well as the New Testament, and part of the Old, in Character Colloquial.

MANDARIN (PEKINGESE).—Wade's *Tzŭ-Êrh-Chi* (Colloquial Series). Giles's *Chinese without a Teacher, Hundred Best Characters,* and *Second Hundred Best Characters,* and Kranz's *Four Thousand Characters.* Edkins's *Mandarin Grammar*; Mateer's *Mandarin Lessons.* There is also one by a Japanese, Goh—the *Kuan Hua Chih Nan*; and a translation by Hopkins, *The Guide to Kuan Hua.* This book has been translated into Cantonese by May. Baller's *Mandarin Primer; An Idiom a Lesson*; Morgan's *The Chinese Speaker*; *New Terms and Expressions*; and Mrs. Mateer's *Handbook of New Terms* are works of great value. *Dictionaries.*—Stent's *A Chinese and English Vocabulary in the Pekingese Dialect* and Williams's *Syllabic Dictionary of the Chinese Language;* Giles's *Chinese-English Dictionary*; Soothill's *The Student's Four Thousand Tzŭ*; Hemmeling's *English-Chinese Dictionary*; and the *Standard English-Chinese Dictionary* published by the Commercial Press, Shanghai, are standard works.

NINGPO.—Morrison's *Anglo-Chinese Vocabulary of the Ningpo Dialect;* and many Romanised books.

SHANGHAI.—Edkins's *Grammar of the Shanghai Dialect*; and his vocabulary in English-Chinese.

SOOCHOW.—Lyon's *Introductory Lessons in the Soochow Dialect.*

SWATOW.—The simplest is Giles's *Hand-book of the Swatow Vernacular Dialect, with a Vocabulary.* A very good phrase-book is Lim's *Hand-book of the Swatow.* For an English-Chinese Vocabulary, *English-Chinese Vocabulary of the Vernacular or Spoken Language of Swatow,* by Duffus. The only Chinese-English Dictionary is Miss Fielde's, but unfortunately the English spelling of the Chinese words is not the same as in the other books. For a combination of phrase-book and grammar, there is *Primary Lessons in Swatow Grammar* (Colloquial), by Ashmore.

TAI-CHOW.—Book of Psalms.

To read Chinese.—A good knowledge of the Colloquial should precede all attempts to learn the Book Language, except for scholars in America or Europe, who simply learn Chinese as they would Latin, Greek, Hebrew, Sanscrit, or any other language for which they have no colloquial need.

Dyer Ball's *Readings in Cantonese Colloquial,* leads from pure and simple colloquial by easy stages to a semi-mixed style of colloquial and book language.

A very good book is Williams's *Easy Lessons in Chinese.* Another aid to beginners will be found in the *Chinese Chrestomathy*, an old book, which, with all its faults, is an excellent one in many respects.

An admirable way to learn the Book Language is to follow the plan of Chinese school-boys by going through the school-books, commencing with such as the Third, Fourth, and Fifth Character Classics, reading aloud after the teacher so often that whole pages of the books can be repeated off by heart. A translation of the two first-named by Giles is to be had: and Eitel has also more lately published translations of them. Some knowledge might be acquired of the *Four Books* and *Five Classics*,—the *Four Books*, at all events; if there is time for it, learned in the same manner as the simple school-books, mentioned above. Legge's *Chinese Classics* should be used here. Those published with Chinese text, English translation, and notes, etc., are five volumes in number. The *Li-Ki*, without the Chinese text, is published in the same series in two volumes, and the *Yik King* in one volume. Wade's *Tzŭ Êrh Chi, Documentary Series* and Hirth's *Text Book of Documentary Chinese* are now somewhat out of date for modern official correspondence. Besides these two compendiums there is the *Text Book of Documentary Chinese*, by Hare, which contains many Chinese documents, such as petitions, bills, agreements, memorials, letters, etc., etc., with English tables of contents. Hirth's *Notes on the Documentary Style* is also a very useful book. After going through the whole, or a portion of the books mentioned above, the learner will know pretty well what is best adapted for his requirements should he intend to proceed further. Sydenstricker's *Construction and Idiom of Chinese Sentences*, and Morgan's *A Guide to Wên Li Styles* are works of great value for the student. We might also mention Bullock's *Progressive Exercises in the Chinese Written Language*, for those who cannot obtain a native teacher.

Writing.—To learn how to form the Character in the correct way, there is Dyer Ball's *How to Write Chinese.*

BOTANY.—There is still a great deal for botanists to do in China, in the way of collecting, examining, and making known to the world the result of their labours, for there are yet vast regions unexplored.

'The Chinese flora is extremely rich. Forests, in the European sense, are rare; but evergreens, flowering shrubs, and especially resinous plants, are found in great variety. Proceeding southwards, the transition is very gradual from the Manchurian to the tropical flora of Indo-China. Hence in some of the central districts there is a remarkable intermingling of species belonging to different zones, the bamboo flourishing by the side of the oak, while wheat and maize crops are interspersed with paddy-fields, sugar, and cotton planations. In general the cultivated species are everywhere encroaching on the wild flora.'

We quote the above from Keane's *Asia*, edited by Temple.

Owing to the monsoons, there is 'a more regular distribution of the rainfall,' and a rainy season in spring; the result is an 'extremely regular succession of seasons, which . . . is favourable to a careful garden-like agriculture.' In the North, wheat and millet are cultivated, while in the South, rice, sugar-cane, mulberries, the tea-plant, and oranges are grown. Cotton and indigo are also produced in China.

One of the most marked differences, noticeable to the new arrival in China, especially in the South, is the absence of meadows and pasture-lands. 'Hongkong, in its more sheltered valleys and ravines, presents an extraordinary varied flora,' closely connected with that of Sikkim, Assam, Khasia, and North-East India, 'and will probably hereafter prove to be connected with it by a gradual transition across South China.' Many other species are more tropical, like those of the Indian Archipelago, Malayan Peninsula, and even Ceylon and Africa. 'Northwards of Hongkong the vegetation appears to change much more rapidly. Very few of the species known to range across from the Himalayas to Japan are believed to come much further south than Amoy, where, with a difference of latitude of only two degrees, the tropical features of the Hongkong flora have (as far as we know) almost entirely disappeared.' It is quite wonderful what a 'very large total amount of species are crowded upon so small an island' as this little colony of Hongkong. There are over 1,000 species, and 550 genera of phanerogamic plants described in Bentham's *Flora Hongkongensis.* Since this was published, about 240 additional species have been discovered in Hongkong, bringing the total number of indigenous plants in this island up to about the same number as is known in the whole of the British Islands.

In a work (originally published in separate parts in the Linnæan Society's Journal) entitled *Index Floræ Sinensis*, there are some 12,000 or more species, representing the whole number of plants at present known to exist in China. The number is being constantly added to by zealous botanists in different parts of the country, as many as a thousand, or even more, having been discovered in six years.

We give a list of some of the genera most numerous in species:—

Clematis, 31.
Anemone, 16.
Ranunculus, 15.
Nasturtium, 9.
Stellaria, 16.
Camellia, 14 or more.
Ilex, 20.
Euonymus, 19.
Vitis, 24.
Acer, 15.
Crotalaria, 14.
Indigofera, 14.
Astragalus, 21.
Desmodium, 25.
Prunus, 21.
Spiræa, 19.
Rubus, 41.
Potentilla, 26.
Rosa, 17.
Pyrus, 14.
Saxifraga, 20.
Sedum, 28.
Eugenia, 14.
Viburnum, 27.
Lonicera, 34.
Hedyotis, 21.
Vernonia, 12.
Aster, 31.
Artemisia, 22.
Senecio, 35.
Saussurea, 28.
Lactuca, 21.
Rhododendron, 65.
Primula, 43.
Lysimachia, 35.
Ardisia, 18.
Symplocos, 18.
Jasminum, 15.
Ligustrum, 14.
Cynanchum, 24.
Gentiana, 57.
Ipomæa, 26.
Solanum, 13.
Veronica, 14.
Pedicularis, 94.
Plectranthus, 18.
Scutellaria, 17.
Amarantus, 9.
Chenopodium, 9.
Polygonum, 63.
Rumex, 11.
Aristolochia, 10.
Piper, 9.
Chloranthus, 11.
Machilus, 16.
Litsea, 23.
Lindera, 20.
Wikstrœmia, 13.
Elæagnus, 12.
Loranthus, 14.
Euphorbia, 23.
Phyllanthus, 11.
Glochidion, 10.
Mallotus, 13.
Ficus, 42.
Pilea, 20.
Elatostema, 9.
Boehmeria, 11.
Betula, 10.
Quercus, 58.
Castanopsis, 13.
Salix, 31.

Some of the orders numerous in species are:—

Ranunculacæa, 107.
Leguminosæ, 301.
Saxifragaceæ, 70.
Umbelliferæ, 56.
Caprifoliaceæ, 78.
Rubiaceæ, 106.
Compositæ, 325.
Ericaceæ, 79.
Primulaceæ, 97.
Oleaceæ, 52.
Asclepiadeæ, 59.
Gentianacæ, 81.
Convolvulaceæ, 49.
Scrophularineæ, 200.
Acanthaceæ, 51.
Verbenaceæ, 56.
Labiatæ, 136.
Polygonaceæ, 80.
Laurineæ, 73.
Euphorbiaceæ, 131.
Urticaceæ, 120.
Cupuliferæ, 101.

Besides these, there are many species of Solanaceæ, Amaryllideæ, Liliaceæ, Aroideæ, Orchideæ, Labiatæ, and Coniferæ. Many gramineous and alliaceous plants are cultivated for food; but volumes might be written on China's extensive economic botany. We cannot pass from Chinese plants without a notice of the bamboo in its many varieties, useful for food, for dress, for furniture, for boat-and ship-building, for the erection of houses, and for almost everything that man needs or human ingenuity can apply it to. (See BAMBOO.) Worthy also of mention are the fan palms of the South of China, from which so many of these articles of necessity in a warm climate are manufactured (See FANS) not only for home consumption, but for extensive exportation to America and other countries. The pea-nut (See PEA-NUT) and the plant from which the cool grass-cloth is manufactured are largely cultivated.

Chinese botany, if the thing is worthy of such a scientific name, is quite unscientific in its methods. Some of the illustrations in botanical works are so truthful that, if the genera are known, they afford a means of ready identification; but no pains are taken to represent specially the seed-vessels and flowers, so that it is well-nigh impossible to tell what species a plant so depicted belongs to, unless it is already known. The plants are not divided according to their orders, genera, or species, but the classification is more of this style:—

Five divisions of the Vegetable Kingdom, viz.—Herbs, Grains, Vegetables, Fruits, and Trees. These are again subdivided into families, though the plants grouped under a family are very dissimilar. The same word is used for the lowest division, and at times might signify a genus, a species, or even a variety. Herbs are divided into nine families: 'Hill-plants, odoriferous, noxious, scandent, or climbing, aquatic, stony and mossy plants, and plants not used in medicine.' This will give some idea of the mode of classification, for we cannot follow them through the other four grand divisions.

References.—Bretschneider, *Botanicon Sinicum;* Bentham, *Flora Hongkongensis,* and Supplement; Forbes and Hemsley, *Index Floræ Sinensis: An Enumeration of all the Plants known from China Proper, Formosa, Hainan, Corea, the Luchu Archipelago, and the Island of Hongkong, together with their Distribution and Synonymy.*

BRONZE.—The Chinese appear to have possessed the art of both making and ornamenting bronze-work from a high antiquity. The Nine Tripods mentioned in the *Shu ching* are ascribed to the Hsia dynasty (2205–1766 B.C.) At the time of the Shang dynasty (1766–1401 B.C.) the work bore evidence of having arrived at an advanced stage. It was intimately connected with their ancient beliefs, for bronze vases and other vessels were in use in those most primitive of cults, which have still full sway over the Chinese mind: the worship of Nature in its visible manifestations of heaven and earth, the stars, winds, streams, and mountains, formed the official religion of the Chinese, and was confined, as a State religion, to the governing classes; it was supplemented in the case of individuals and families by the worship of ancestors. Unfortunately the rigid cast of the Chinese worship of antiquity and of set forms, has so bound them down to a faithful copy of all that has been done by their predecessors, that these bronze vessels are copied to the most minute particular at the present day, and have been for a score or more centuries. The artistic mind was thus hampered and confined to a reproduction of what have been considered the masterpieces of antiquity; play of individual taste and fancy has been restricted and shut up within its own country, with but little, if any, inspiration from external sources; Chinese art thus remained till the first century A.D., when a new influence exerted a beneficial effect on it.

But before passing on to a consideration of the influence of Buddhism, it is interesting to notice the presence of a decorative design, which in the West has been styled 'the Greek,' on account of its being found in Greek and Etruscan art. The questions naturally present themselves as to whether: (1st.) This design has been copied by the Chinese from the Greeks; and the answer is that this seems improbable. (2nd.) Whether the design has been arrived at independently by both nations; and the answer is that this is not improbable, for the design of the Chinese seems slightly different from that of the Greeks, and it has been suggested that it has arisen from the representation of the two pervading principles of Nature, the *Yin* and the *Yang*. (3rd.) Whether the design is of such remote antiquity that it may have been carried from some cradle of the human race, and thus been common originally to both; it would appear, in our present state of knowledge, that this question must be left unanswered.

At first, animal forms were the original models for the Chinese in their sacrificial vessels, but they were not confined to the representation of animals, for vases of curious and antique forms are found, and libation vessels like a reversed casque mounted on three feet. Ancient bronze work was made for other purposes besides the two already named, being used by the Emperor for bestowal as presents.

Buddhism, which we have already referred to, introduced in its train objects of virtu and art for the native Chinese to copy; and it served as an incentive in presenting a broader field for the Chinese art-worker to roam over, less fettered than the narrow limits confined him to. Many of the treasures of art, which owe their origin to its inspiration, have doubtless perished in the iconoclastic persecutions which this religion has met more than once since its establishment in China; for the human figure now formed a subject for the Chinese artist, and gods and goddesses innumerable were depicted, and it is here that the best samples of Chinese art are to be found, the finest specimens being produced about A.D. 1426, and from A.D. 1621 to 1643, reaching their higest excellence under the reign of K'ang Hsi, A.D. 1662.

Taoist idols and symbols have had their share in providing objects of art for the Chinese bronze-worker. Arabian, or Persian art, has also, in the time of the Mongol rulers of China, exerted some influence on Chinese bronze art, by giving it certain beauties of form which it had not previously possessed, as well as new decorative and ornamental designs; and in this connection one must mention the bronze astronomical instruments in Peking, made for the Observatory there, during the time of Kublai Khan. Some of these were taken to Berlin by the Germans in 1900, but were returned in accordance with the provisions of the Treaty of Verseilles. We can only refer *en passant* to the incrustations of gold, or the beautiful ornamentation 'with delicate scrolls and flowers in niello work of silver or gold wire, inserted into grooves cut in the metal' on bronze work, which greatly enhances its beauty; nor can we do more than call attention to the damaskeen work, probably introduced from India, as well as the gilded bronze, due to Buddhist influence on Chinese art.

References.—Paléologue, *L'Art Chinois;* Bushell, *Chinese Art;* Strehlneek, *Chinese Pictorial Art; Journ. N.C.B.R.A.S., N.S.,* Vol. xlvii.

BUDDHISM.—China presents the unique spectacle of three powerful so-called religions, holding sway concurrently over the teeming millions of its inhabitants; and though strong opposition has been shown to the younger members of this trinity of religions by the older one—Confucianism—yet there is now an outward peace. Each of them is a complement of the other, and attempts to meet a different want in human nature: Confucianism appeals to morality and conduct; Taoism is materialistic; and Buddhism, metaphysical. Two only are indigenous (though Taoism may have been influenced by Indian ideas): Buddhism is foreign, introduced in A.D. 67 (the year the expedition said to have been sent by Ming Ti to India returned to China, but the records differ as to the exact date), for the Emperor dreamt of a gigantic image of gold, and sent to India in search of the new religion; but some believe it was known in China before that, even as early as 217 B.C. The first centuries of its arrival were marked by the translation into Chinese of numerous Buddhistic works; and there was considerable progress in making proselytes, for in the fourth century nine-tenths of the inhabitants of China were Buddhists. It is impossible to give an estimate of the number at the present day, as every Chinese, who is not a Mohammedan or Christian, is a Buddhist, as well as a Taoist and a Confucianist, often at one and the same time. The eclectic nature of the Chinese, and the mutual adaptation of the systems—a give and take—to one another, in the course of centuries of combined occupation of the Chinese religious mind, have rendered the outcome more of an amalgamation, or rather a mechanical combination of the three; for their partnership is not of that intimate character that it can be compared to a chemical union, where the different elements combine to produce a new substance. All three are likewise established faiths in China: their sages and divinities are admitted into the state pantheon and honoured by state patronage. One is tempted to illustrate this combination of the three, so intimately are they sometimes blended together, as a tripartite union of body, soul, and spirit: Confucianism, with its ever-present essence, permeating the whole body politic and social system, forming the soul; but here the comparison must stop, for it cannot, with any approach to truth, be carried further, except to say that there are two other members of this partnership.

Buddhism is divided into two great branches, the Northern and Southern. The Buddhism of China, Nepal, Tibet, Mongolia, Corea, Japan, and Cochin China belong to the Northern; that of Ceylon, Burma, and Siam to the Southern. There are several points of difference between them: the sacred books among the Northern Buddhists are either in Sanscrit, or translated from it; while among the Southern, Pali is the sacred language. The Northern Buddhists have the story of the Western Paradise, perhaps evolved from the human mind as the result of longings for some tangible residence of future bliss (but more probably due to migration from a Western ancestral home), which the doctrine of Nirvana does not satisfy with its absorption into a passionless state. In this 'pure land of the West,' the saints are 'exempt from suffering, death, and sexual distinction,' surrounded by the most beautiful scenery, and 'live for æons in a state of absolute bliss.' The Goddess of Mercy, who takes very much the same place as the Virgin Mary among Roman Catholics, belongs to this division of Buddhism. 'In the Southern branch the Hindoo traditions in respect to cosmogony and mythology are adhered to more rigidly; while in the Northern branch a completely new and far more extensive universe, with divinities to correspond,' is believed in.

Though these three, especially Taoism and Buddhism, are so blended and mixed together, the latter obtrudes itself more on the view than the other two. Its temples, as well as its priests, are more numerous. It is very interesting to notice the various phases which this wide-spread form of religion has developed in different lands. In China, it is polytheistic, and has borrowed and adopted deities from Taoism. In fact, Buddhism has adapted itself to circumstances, and finding certain beliefs prevalent among the Chinese, instead of combating them, has taken them under its wing, and thus gained by accretion, not only beliefs, but numbers.

Nor does Buddhism seem only to have borrowed from Taoism, and in this connection the following extract from a paper by Professor Max Müller in the *Fortnightly Review* for July, 1896, may be interesting:—

'Huc and Gabet, while travelling in Tibet felt startled at the coincidences between their own ecclesiastical ritual and that of the Buddhist priesthood in Tibet. They pointed out, among other things, the crosier, the mitre, the dalmatic, the cope, the service with two choirs, the psalmody, exorcism, the use of censers held by five chains which shut and open by themselves, blessings given by the Lamas in extending their right hand over the heads of the faithful, the use of beads for saying prayers, the celibacy of the priesthood, spiritual retreats, worship of saints, fastings, processions, litanies, holy water—enough it would seem to startle Roman Catholic missionaries. They ascribed them to the devil who wished to scandalise pious Roman Catholics who might visit Tibet. . . . . We cannot escape from the conclusion that this large number of coincidences proves an actual historical communication between Roman Catholic and Buddhist priests. And such a channel through which these old Roman Catholic customs could have reached Tibet can be shown to have existed. It is an historical fact that Christian missionaries, chiefly Nestorians, were very active in China from the middle of the seventh to the end of the eighth century. Their presence and activity in China during these centuries are attested not only by the famous monument of Hsian-fu, but likewise by various Chinese historians, and we have no reason to doubt their testimony. The Nestorian Christians had monasteries and schools in different towns of China and were patronised by the Government. We know that one of the monks in the monastery at Hsian-fu was at work under the same roof with a well-known Buddhist monk from Cabul, trying to translate a Buddhist Sanscrit text into Chinese. The prosperity of the Nestorian missions in China lasted till the year 841, when the Emperor Wû-tung [Wu Tsung] issued his edicts for the suppression of all Buddhist and likewise of all Christian monasteries. While Buddhism recovered after a time, Christianity seems to have been rooted out, and when Marco

Polo visited Hsian-fu, he tells us that the people were all idolaters.'

Referring to many of the ethics of Buddhism being identical with the precepts in the Holy Scriptures, it has been pointed out that it is erroneous to suppose that Christianity has borrowed them from the Buddhists, as they were freely taught by Moses and the Prophets centuries before Buddha existed:—

. 'The ethics of Buddhism were evidently derived from those notions with whom the inhabitants of India had commercial and other relations, including the Jewish, which was in its greatest prosperity 500 years before Buddha was said to have existed. . . . Evidence has been given by Strabo and other ancient writers to [of] the great commercial intercourse existing, in the tenth century B.C. between India, Persia, Parthia, Media, and the countries south of the Euxine, as well as the ancient traffic by sea which recent research had shown to have existed . . . carried on from India round Ceylon and up the Red Sea, the ships being mostly manned by those intrepid mariners, the Phœnicians.'

On the other hand, Roman, Catholicism seems to have borrowed a little from Buddhism, Buddha himself having been made a saint.

The Buddhism of the first few centuries of the Christian era in China was a vigorous immigrant, fresh and lusty with life; eager to attempt great things in its new chosen home, with strength and vigour, prepared to spread its principles; and ready to endure the fiery baptisms of persecution through which it had later on to pass. A very different thing to the emasculated descendant that now occupies the land with its drones of priests, and its temples; in which scarce a worthy disciple of the learned patriarchs of ancient days is to be found. Received, with open arms, persecuted (first in A.D. 420), patronised, smiled upon, tolerated, it, with the last phase of its existence, has reached not the halcyon days of peace and rest, but its final stage, foreshadowing its decay from rottenness and corruption, for it has long passed its meridian. It was at the zenith of its power in the tenth and twelfth centuries, not only being popular, but exerting great literary influence. It excites but little enthusiasm at the present day in China; its priests are ignorant, low, and immoral; addicted to opium; despised by the people; held up to contempt and ridicule; and occasionally even the gibe and joke of the populace. The nuns likewise hold a very low position in the public estimation. The belief in the transmigration of souls; the desire for the merit of good works in charity bestowed on priests, and gifts to the large monasteries, so frequent throughout the length and breadth of the land; as well as the superstitious beliefs in charms and masses for the dead; faith in the worship of the Goddess of Mercy, and a trust in the efficacy of other gods:—all these may be looked upon as the strong supports of Buddhism in China at the present day; but the scoff of the infidel, and the sneer of the atheist is slowly undermining some parts of this religious structure; and a better religion and a purer, which will stand true to its colours, will have more chance of success in future than Buddhism has had in the past. 'The Light of Asia' is setting in obscure darkness, while the first glimmering rays of 'The Light of the World' are chasing that darkness away, and 'The Sun of Righteousness' is arising 'with healing in His wings.' With the establishment of the Republic and religious liberty, Buddhism, however, received a new lease of life, which has been fostered by the propagation of Japanese Shintoism and other forms of Buddhism.

References.—David's *Buddhism,* gives the best account for the general reader of Buddhism, as a religion. Eitel's *Three Lectures on Buddhism* give in a popular form, and in a few pages, an account of Chinese Buddhism, which is more lengthily treated of in Edkins's *Chinese Buddhism;* Beal's *Buddhism in China* is interesting and smaller than the last. Edkins's *Religion in China* contains much on Buddhism. Beal's *Buddhist Literature in China* treats of works translated into Chinese. Eitel's *Handbook for the Student of Chinese Buddhism* is a dictionary of the Sanscrit terms used in Chinese, their translations into the latter, with an account of their meanings, other useful works are: Hackmann, *Buddhism as a Religion;* Parker, *Studies in Chinese Religion; China and Religion;* Elliot, *Buddhism;* Johnston, *Buddhist China;* De Groot, *Le Code de Mahayana en Chine;* and Waddell, *The Buddhism of Thibet.*

BUFFALO (WATER BUFFALO).—This animal is called by the Chinese the water-ox, or cow; by naturalists, *Bos bubalus.* Crauford and Dr. Dennys thus describe it:—

'The same useful, powerful, ugly, sluggish, and unwieldy animal which exists in all the warm countries of Asia, and which was introduced into Greece, Egypt and Southern India in the Middle Ages. It is only, however, within ten or twelve degrees of the equator that it is found of great size, strength and vigour. . . . The flesh of this semi-aquatic animal is coarse. . . . The wound inflicted by an enraged buffalo is fearful. The victim is generally gored in the thigh, the femoral artery being ripped open.'

The buffalo is a dangerous animal for Europeans to approach, as it has a repugnance to strangers, but with its friends is thoroughly docile, and in perfect control of the little boys who have the task of driving them to and from the fields, and of guiding them when pulling the harrow and plough, often riding on their backs. So common is this sight that the metaphor of a lad astride a buffalo's back, blowing the flute, frequently enters into Chinese descriptions of rural life, and the buffalo with the herd-boy thus engaged appears in paintings and is used for decorative designs, etc.

The buffalo can scarcely be said to be covered with hair, a few straggling ones being all that Nature has vouchsafed to it; one author describing it as having 'a hairless hide.' Through this scanty pretence of a covering the light black colour of the skin shows without any concealment. Each horn is nearly semi-circular, and bends downward, while the head is turned back so as almost to bring the nose horizontal. This peculiar carriage of the head enables the animal to submerge nearly the whole of the body and head under the surface of the water in the pools and ponds in which they delight to lie, to cool themselves or to get rid of the gnats. It is very curious to see a herd of them thus immersed with only the tips of their noses showing. The habits of this animal make it cheap to keep him in good condition, while he can do more work than the ox. The milk of the buffalo-cow in the South of China is richer than that of the cow in that part of the world.

CALENDAR.—See TIME.

CAMPHOR.—This useful drug is the product of the camphor tree, a species of laurel, which grows abundantly in Fukien, and Kuangtung, and is met with as a timber-tree in Kiangsi, Hupei, and other provinces to some extent. The tree attains a large size, is of much use, and gives employment to many carpenters, shipwrights and boat-builders, the wood being valuable for the manufacture of trunks and chests-of-drawers. The odour of the wood is pleasant, and when fresh and strong of some utility in keeping away moths and insects from clothing, the wood itself not being subject to the attack of white ants, etc. Vessels are constructed partially or wholly of it as well.

The drug is employed medicinally by the Chinese, and another use they make of it is for thinning lacquer; but the Chinese are not careful in the preparation of the former, and the result is very impure. Williams describes the process as follows:—

> 'The gum is procured from the branches, roots, leaves, and chips by soaking them in water until the liquor becomes saturated; a gentle heat is then applied to this solution, and the sublimed camphor received in inverted cones, made of rice-straw, from which it is detached in impure grains, resembling unrefined sugar in colour.'

Dr. Porter Smith tells us:—'It is met with in granular lumps or grains, of the colour of dirty snow, and having a strong terebinthinate odour, and a warm, bitter, aromatic taste, with an aftertaste somewhat cooling. It is not so strong as the English drug, but it is more volatile. Very good camphor is brought from Tsiuen-chau fu [Ch'üan-chou Fu] in Fuh-kien [Fukien].'

Rein says:—'Japanese camphor is much purer and more valuable, and therefore commands a higher price than Chinese.'

More than one variety of camphor is procurable in the Chinese drug shops; the common dirty stuff, sold at a cheap rate, being of little use. The better qualities are either from abroad, or have had more care taken in the preparation. 'A variety called icicle-flakes is procured from a different species of tree, is said to come from Chang-chau [chou] fu, in Fuh-kien, and the tree yielding it . . . is described as growing in Canton province.'

Since the loss of the Island of Formosa, the Chinese production of camphor is confined to that of the mainland. In a British Consulate Report from Foochow occurs the following passage:—

'Camphor trees grow in this neighbourhood, and I cannot but think that if the Chinese were sufficiently long-sighted to take proper care of the existing trees, and to plant young ones, a considerable trade in camphor might be fostered. Heretofore Formosa has been a camphor-producing country. Now that this has been transferred to Japanese rule, the Chinese, unless they take measures to prevent it, will lose the camphor trade entirely.'

The industry in Fukien, because of the cutting down of the camphor trees, is now practically extinct. Some attempts have been made to develop it in other provinces, but so far with limited success, chiefly owing to want of capital.

The Japanese in 1899 made camphor a Government monopoly, in Formosa. The Chinese had retained it as a State monopoly until 1868, when rights were granted to private concerns.

Camphor has risen enormously in value lately. It has been erroneously thought that this was due to the extended use of it in the manufacture of smokeless powder; but it was only employed experimentally at first for that purpose, which could not have affected the market value. It is, however, extensively used in the manufacture of celluloid.

'Cabinets made of camphor-wood are much esteemed, not only for the fine grain and silky sheen of the wood, but for its efficacy against the attacks of insects. The camphor-laurel ranks among the stateliest of trees, frequently attaining to an enormous height and girth.'

'The total yearly consumption of camphor is estimated at about 5,000,000 catties, of which 4½ million catties are produced in Formosa and in the interior of Japan, thus nearly the whole supply of the world being the Japanese product. It is stated that there are camphor trees in South China, but the yield is very poor as compared with Japan.'

'The Chinese yield has never exceeded 220,000 lbs.'

Care should be taken in the damp climate of the South of China that camphor-wood chests-of-drawers and boxes are well-seasoned before use.

CANNIBALISM.—It is but rarely that cannibalism as such, is practised in China, though a horrible practice of eating the gall, and sometimes taking the blood of criminals, who have paid the penalty for their crimes with their forfeited lives, is common enough, the idea being that the courage of the victim will enter into the individual who thus consumes the seat of courage, the gall. If such a practice can be called cannibalism, then it may be said in general terms that it is almost wholly confined to this species of semi-cannibalism. It would, however, be burking the truth entirely to overlook the intermittent occurrence at rare intervals of cases in which the whole body has been devoured by savage men, infuriated by the passion of war, and the bodies of decapitated criminals are sometimes eaten. Such cases are, however, uncommon. An atrocious instance of its perpetration is narrated in the *China Mail* of the 31st August, 1895, which, summarised, was as follows:—Disputed water-rights, a prolific source of trouble between Chinese villages, caused an internecine war between two of them, Pien Ch'êng and Tang Ch'êng, seven miles from Ty Sami in the Kwong-tung [Kuangtung] province. Reprisals followed the cutting of a sea embankment which let in the water and destroyed the rice crops of one village, a small war lasted for a month, different villages were involved in the struggle, and a large number of deaths ensued. Three prisoners on one side and four on the other were taken alive, killed and eaten—'every eatable portion was consumed, most of it being given to the children of the respective villages. . . . Though not unprecedented in that district, such an act of cannibalism is unusual.' Were justice available at the courts of law, such village fights would not occur; and it is further a forcible illustration of the evil results of the officials leaving the villagers to manage their own affairs. Of course, when matters get to such a pass, the mandarins step in. Again the Hongkong *Daily Press* of 22nd January, 1896, contains the following:—

'There is probably not a foreigner in Formosa but knows of the custom of eating portions of the bodies of savages by the Chinese, and who is not aware of the markets in settlements of Formosa, containing the human flesh of the savage for sale. During the savage outbreak of 1891, so great was the loss of life that savage flesh was brought in and sold like pork in the open market.'

Another curious feature of Chinese life is shown in the custom of filial children cutting out a portion of their own living flesh and cooking it for their sick parents, who are to partake of it, not knowing the source whence it comes. Such cases are by no means rare, and generally meet with the applause of the people, the encomium of the mandarin, and the approval of the government.

It will thus be seen that, horrible as it may seem, such a thing as cannibalism is not entirely unknown in China.

CAPITAL CITIES.—The country now included in China has been the *venue* of so many different States in ancient times, due to the vicissitudes incident to conquest and war, as well as to other causes, that various cities have been the capital of the empire at different periods of its existence.

Hangchow is one of the most famous of these. Marco Polo waxes eloquent in his praise of it: 'The noble and magnificent city of Kin-sai, a name that signifies "the celestial city," and which it merits from its pre-eminence to all others in the world, in point of grandeur and beauty, as well as from its abundant delights, which might lead an inhabitant to imagine himself in paradise.' All writers agree in praising its situation, and the beauty of the surroundings, as well as the richness of the city, though they do not go into the ecstasies of the mediæval Italian. Hangchow (then called Lin-an) was the metropoolis during the latter part of the Sung dynasty (A.D. 1129–1280), when the northern part of the empire was in the hands of the Kin Tartars.

The ancient capital of Shang-tu, rendered famous by Coleridge's exquisite poem, 'In Xanadu did Kublai Khan,' is now in ruins.

The chief city of Shantung is Chi-nan-fu [now hsien], once the capital of the ancient state of Tsi (1100-234 B.C.).

K'ai-fung-fu, or Pien Liang, had the honour of being the metropolis from A.D. 960 to 1129.

The After Hans had their capital at the chief city (Ch'êng-tu) of Sz-chuan [Ssŭch'uan], where their rule extended over the West of China.

Si-ngan-fu [Hsi-an Fu] 'has been the capital of the empire for more years than any other city.'

Nanking, *i.e.*, the Southern capital, has been the metropolis of China several times, once from A.D. 317 to 582. It was here that the seat of government was established in the former part of the Ming dynasty, A.D. 1368–1403, though Hung Wu, the founder of that dynasty, intended Hwui-chow to be the capital. The famous porcelain tower was at Nanking, and here it was too that the T'ai P'ing rebels made their headquarters for many years. The Southern Mandarin was the Court language of China, owing to Nanking being the capital, until displaced by the Northern.

Peking is the Northern capital, and has been so for many centuries, but it was not the capital of the whole of China until the time of Kublai in A.D. 1264. On the fall of the Mongol dynasty, the centre of government was transferred to Nanking until A.D. 1416, when Peking again became the metropolis, and has remained so ever since. It is owing to Peking being the capital that the Northern Mandarin is spoken in Peking, and is the Court language of China, otherwise it would be an insignificant dialect.

The capitals of the early patriarchs Yao and Shun were at what are now P'ing-yang Fu and P'u-chou Fu (both in Shansi), respectively. The following table gives the names of the capitals from the earliest to the present times:—

Dynasty, etc.	*Ancient Name.*	*Modern Name.*
Hsia	Yang-hsia	T'ai-k'ang Fu (Honan).
Shang	Po	Shang-ch'iu Fu (Honan).
	Hao	Ch'ang-an Fu (Shensi).
Chow	”	” ”
	Lo-i	Lo-yang Fu (Honan).
Ch'in	Hsien-yang	Hsien-yang Fu (Shensi).
Han (Western)	Ch'ang-an	Ch'ang-an Fu (Shensi).
” (Eastern)	Lo-yang	Lo-yang Fu (Honan).
” (Minor)	Ch'éng-tu	Ch'êng-tu Fu (Ssŭch'uan).
Chin (Western)	Lo-yang	Lo-yang Fu (Honan).
” (Eastern)	Chien-k'ang	Chiang-ning Fu (Kiangsu).
Sung (House of Liu)	” ”	” ”
Ch'i (Southern)	” ”	” ”

Liang (Southern)	Chien-k'ang	Chiang-ning Fu (Kiangsu).
Ch'ên (Southern)	" "	" "
Sui	Ch'ang-an	Ch'ang-an Fu (Shensi).
T'ang	" "	" "
Liang (Posterior)	Lo-yang	Lo-yang Fu (Honan).
T'ang (Posterior)	" "	" "
Chin (Posterior)	Pien-liang	K'ai-fêng Fu (Honan).
Han (Posterior)	" "	" "
Chow (Posterior)	" "	" "
Sung	" "	" "
" (Southern)	Lin-an	Hang-chow Fu (Chêkiang).
Yüan	Yen	Shun-t'ien Fu (Chihli).
Ming	Ying-t'ien	Chiang-ning Fu (Kiangsu).
	Pei-p'ing	Shun-t'ien Fu (Chihli).
Ch'ing	Shun-t'ien	" "
Min Kuo	" "	" "

References.—Notes and Queries on China and Japan, i. 60. *China Mail* 3rd September, 1892.

CARVING.—Carving seems to be an art just designed for the patient persevering toil of a Chinaman; for no labour is too great to bestow on the most minute undertaking, and, in a country where time enters so little into the essence of life, days and months are lavishly spent on what would be thought elsewhere to be unremunerative work.

Over the fronts of certain shops, such as eating-houses, it is common to have a broad piece of woodwork highly decorated with carvings of figures, houses, flowers, richly gilded, all in *alto-relievo;* and in private dwellings there is some carving to be found on the large doors or screens which serve as partitions. There is also an amount of it to be found in certain boats, especially on the so-called flower-boats, which have a screen of carved woodwork, rising to considerable proportions, over the entrances of the large ones.

Bamboo vases for holding pens are a common article for the decorative artist to exercise his skill on.

Carving

Wood, bamboo, stone, ivory, and seeds, all form fit subjects for the untiring industry of the Chinese; but all this carving in wood, bamboo, and olive seeds, is according to Western ideas, often rendered grotesque in the extreme by a rigid adherence to the canons of Chinese art; for perspective is ignored, and the harmony of proportion between the different objects is lost sight of.

Religion causes the production of countless numbers of carved images, in wood and stone, in all attitudes and positions, decked out in all the different insignia of office, or armed with weapons. The best specimen, perhaps, of all this motley group is the God of Literature, represented as standing on one foot on a monster's head, while one arm is stretched to its utmost extent, the hand holding a Chinese pen: there is a certain amount of abandonment and freedom from the stiff conventionality of the sedate or hideous images which do duty as Chinese idols, the flowing drapery and slender form of this personification of Literature having lent themselves readily to the artistic eye of the carver, who has not failed to take advantage of them. Specimens of the Eight Genii are also sometimes found, as well as other carvings of the same class as that last mentioned, in which the natural twistings of the roots or fibres have been utilised, with skilful touches here and there to heighten the effect, or supplement what Nature has left undone.

Boles of trees are also sometimes made use of as curios, while stands for ornaments and vases, under the skilful manipulation of a workman, blessed with a certain play of fancy, become as curious objects of art as the carved stone vessels they support. Chinese ebony, or black-wood, as it is likewise called, is largely used for the above purposes, and is carved into the imitation of lotus leaves, seed-vessels, and many other objects. The white-wood carved work of Ningpo is much admired; frames for pictures, little models of boats, carts, figures of men and animals, and many other objects are produced in it.

The carving in ivory and sandal-wood is perhaps better known in the West, as large quantities of it are made for exportation. The concentric balls of ivory have attracted much interest and speculation; there is, however, no trickery in their production, but, like most things of the kind among the Chinese, they are the result of patient toil, the balls being carved *in situ* one within the other: the outside ball is first carved, and, through the holes thus made, instruments are introduced, and gradually the outside crust, as it were, forming the outermost ball, is detached from the remaining interior mass, while, by the same means, the surface of this interior mass is carved. This process is repeated with every successive ball until a globular mass of intricate hollow balls is the result of the ingenuity of the Chinese artist-workman.

The carved soap-stone ware of Foochow is well known among the foreign residents in China: models of pagodas, shoes, Chinese graves, plates, memorial arches, and many other things, are produced in it. The hard seeds of the olive and peach are elaborately carved in the South into models of boats and other objects. Wood-carving is of very ancient origin in China, though the influence of Buddhism in the second century gave an artistic life to what had before not been raised much above a mechanical art. No signatures or dates are borne on Chinese carvings; it is therefore difficult, if not impossible, to assign a date to them.

Reference.—Paléologue, *L'Art Chinois*,

CHESS.—Chess is an ancient game in China, and is said to have been invented by the first emperor of the Chow dynasty, Wu Wang, 1120 B.C.; though it is questioned whether the invention is not to be referred to a date some four hundred years later. Chess is mentioned in the Chinese classics, but the game in olden times appears to have been somewhat different from the present one, which came into general use after the Sung dynasty.

Chess has always been looked upon as a minic war fare, and the likeness is more marked in Chinese chess, for there are the general, the secretaries, the elephants, horses, chariots, cannon, and soldiers; the two armies are also divided by a river. The similarities between the game as played in the West and China are obvious; but the resemblances between that played in China and in other Eastern countries are of such a nature as to point to a closer relationship. There are sixty-four squares, as on the English board, with sixteen pieces on each side; but here the general points of resemblance cease, for there is a river running through the middle of the board, and the squares are uniform in colour, the pieces not being placed on them but on the intersections of the lines; nor are they placed in two rows of eight each, but the first row contains nine pieces, consisting of the principal ones, while a line of five soldiers is deployed in front, near the river, and these are supported by two cannon a little to their rear. The knight, in the English tour of the board, can only have sixty-four moves, and in the course of that number has touched every square on the board; but were the Chinese equivalent of the knight, viz., the horse, to go on such a round, he would have nearly half as many moves again, for the intersections of the lines, being the resting-places for the pieces, increase the number of such positions to a total of ninety. The general and his two secretaries are confined to four squares, which, unlike the other squares on the board, are crossed by diagonal lines; along these lines, and on them alone, the secretaries move, but only across one square at a time; the general also only moves one square at a time, in a straight line, but not diagonally. Though these pieces are confined to the four squares, they have, on account of their positions being placed at the intersections of lines, more than four places that they can occupy; the general has nine points he can rest on, and the secretaries five. The elephants, which flank the secretaries on each side, are also restricted in their movements, being confined to their own side of the board, not being allowed to cross the river, but they have more freedom of motion within such limits, being permitted to move diagonally through two squares, both back and forward. The horses, which are the next pieces, have the curious combination of movement peculiar to the knight in the Western game, viz.:—a straight motion followed or preceded by a diagonal one, but, unlike the English game, the Chinese equivalent of the knight, can only move one point forward, sideways or backward, and one diagonally, nor can the horse jump over any other piece. The chariots take the place of the castles in the English game, occupying the same position on the board, having the same moves, and they are the most powerful of all the pieces; from the restricted moves of the general (=king), castling is impossible. The cannoniers have the same power of movement as the chariots, but, curiously enough, take, only when a piece intervenes, leaping, like an English knight, over the obstruction. The five soldiers move like the English pawns, only forward in the first brunt of battle; they gain increased power of motion on crossing the river into the enemy's territory, when they move sideways as well; there is, however, no merit in their reaching the extreme end of the board, for they can never move back, and there is no changing them for a higher piece.

The chessmen are called red and black, but the black ones are the natural colour of the wood—white. They are not carved to represent what they stand for, but have the names cut into the top of the wood, being otherwise exactly like English draughtsmen. The carved ivory chessmen, made by the Chinese workers in ivory are simply meant for the foreign market.

The longitudinal lines are numbered, but not the transverse, and by the use of the names of the chessmen, and of the expressions forward, backward, and sideways, a game can easily be played from the book, or a game recorded as it is played.

In taking pieces, the captured one is removed, and the capturing one is placed on the point the captured occupied, except in the case of the cannonier. The object, as in the English game, is to checkmate. The general, though confined to headquarters, *i.e.*, the four squares already named, is in check if no piece intervenes between him and the opposite general on the same straight line. He cannot be captured, and, like the English king, cannot move into check.

The limited power of movement of a number of the pieces, as well as the want of a queen, due naturally to the low estimation that woman is held in, in the East, restrict, it is said, the combinations in Chinese chess more than in the Western game. Notwithstanding all, the Chinese game 'has its own elements of skill.' The equilibrium of power is not so greatly displaced as at first sight might appear, because, of the sixteen chessmen, eleven are principal pieces, and only five soldiers, though, with the exception of the chariots, the power of each chessman is less than in the Western game.

Literary men and women often play chess, and it is quite a common subject of Chinese paintings; but it is not the pastime of the common people to the great extent it appears to be in Japan.

Different sorts of chess have been played at different times in China; and there is still another game in vogue, perhaps of even earlier origin than the common chess, which is called *waí-k'éí* [*wei-ch'i*], or 'blockade chess.' There are 324 squares, or 361 positions on the board, and 300 pieces, which are black and white, and stand, as in the common chess, on the crossings of the lines. We have not space for a full account of this game, but will content ourselves with saying that the pieces are placed by each player alternately on the board, and the object is to surround the opponent's men and their crossings, 'or neutralise their power over those near them.'

There is also 'a three-handed game played upon a three-legged board. . . . The "chess of the Three Kingdoms."'

References.—Journ, N.C.B.R.A.S., N.S. Vols. iii; vi; xxiii; *Journ. R.A.S.*, 1885; Giles, *Historic China and Other Sketches;* Wilkinson, *Manual of Chinese Chess.*

CHILDREN.—China is alive with children. The whole land is swarming with them, and not the land alone, but the water also. The small boats in Canton, that partly take the place of cabs and carriages in the West, will not only have representatives of a past generation (typified by an ancient grandam almost too antiquated to wield an oar), of the present generation by the buxom mother, but also of the future generation, represented by half a dozen boys and girls of all ages and sizes, from the little pickaninny (who is carried pick-a-back by a sister not much bigger than himself) to the eldest sister, who, being fifteen, is engaged, and at the transition stage between girlhood and womanhood. A walk on shore will bring one, at every village and hamlet, into a swarm of youngsters, almost as numerous as the swarms of gnats and mosquitoes over one's head. The wonder is where they come from, and where and how they live. Clothing does not cost much; for a number of old rags for swaddling bands is all that is provided for the new arrival at first, and then in the country-side, in summer at all events, a single jacket is enough, or in many cases the nut-brown skin of the little ones is considered sufficient. Clothing is added with additional years, being delayed longer in the case of boys than in that of girls.

Childhood does not appear so charming to our Western eyes when surrounded by all the squalor and dirt incident to Chinese village and city life; but, amidst all their filth and wretchedness, children will still be children the wide world over, and they have, even among the seemingly stolid Chinese, the faculty of calling forth the better feelings so often found latent. Their prattle delights the fond father, whose pride beams through every line of his countenance, and their quaint and winning ways, and touches of nature, are visible even under the disadvantges of almond eyes and shaven crowns.

The relative position of the two sexes, at their start in life, in clearly shown by the following well-known quotation from the Classics:—

'Sons shall be his,—on couches lulled to rest.
  The little ones, enrobed, with sceptres play;
Their infant cries are loud as stern behest;
  Their knees the vermeil covers shall display.
As king hereafter one shall be addressed;
  The rest, as princes, in our states shall sway.
And daughters also to him shall be born.
  They shall be placed upon the ground to sleep;
Their playthings, tiles; their dress, the simplest worn;
  Their part alike from good and ill to keep.
And ne'er their parents' hearts to cause to mourn;
  To cook the food, and spirit-malt to steep.'

For a month a Chinese baby is nameless; then, emerging from the state of being a mere unit in babydom, it has a feast given in its honour; a tentative name is bestowed on it, or rather, in the expressive phraseology of the Chinese, it has its name 'altered' from that of 'Baby,' or 'Love,' to something more distinctive; and its head is shaved,—a most wise provision in a country where parasites are accepted as an infliction of Providence to teach patience. Severity is held up as a proper treatment for children; natural affection, however, often carries the day, so that there is, as the outcome, a constant conflict between the two principles, such as the Persians represent as existent between the principles of good and evil; neither, in the case under question, being, however, an unmitigated good or an unqualified evil. If the child cries, as a rule everything it wants is given to it. At other times, the parents give way to violent fits of temper in their efforts to bring the child to obedience, when it is beaten with great cruelty, on the head, or anywhere, with sticks of firewood, or anything that comes handy, and, like a typhoon, these violent outbursts upset everything.

Notwithstanding all these trials, as well as the theory that play is a waste of time, the Chinese child has a fair amount of enjoyment, which it fully appreciates, and makes good use of. Marriages galore, and funerals, with bands of music; processions and feasts; toys, primitive in construction and cheap in material to be sure—and what child does not know how to enjoy toys?—are all specially provided for his delectation, and how he enters into the spirit of everything with true zest needs only to be seen to be understood.

New Year's time is the most glorious of all for little John Chinaman. In all his fine toggery he trudges along at his father's side to pay his New Year's calls, his little brain busy at work calculating how many cash he will get in presents from his father's acquaintances, while the old gentleman himself is thinking of the good bargains that this year will bring. 'Kung-héí, fát ts'oí [*kung hsi fa ts'ai*],' here they are, the little man bowing and scraping and shaking his chubby little fingers in exact imitation of his elders. A veritable chip of the old block, he takes his pleasures gravely, but, the visits over, he evidently enjoys the fun to the full, as with lighted joss-stick, as assiduously as a *chiffonnier,* he carefully turns over the mass of smoking paper fragments, the remnants of the long string of crackers his big brother has just let off, to be rewarded by half a dozen which have missed fire.

But before many years the boy's free childhood is over and his education is begun; his name is again 'altered' to a new one, though at the same time he keeps his childhood's name, or 'milk name,' as it is expressed sometimes, through life. (See BIRTHDAYS.)

Reference.—Headland, *The Chinese Boy and Girl.*

CHINA.—The origin of the name by which this country is known to the nations of the West is not certain. If we are to take the evidence of some ancient Indian books, such as the laws of Manu, the name China was in use in the twelfth century B.C. It has also been supposed to be derived from the family of Tsin [*Ch'in*], but this would give a later origin to it. The chief of this family obtained eventually, after having made history for some centuries, sway over the whole of China, and even long anterior to that period, the kingdom subject to this sept, being situated at the north-west portals of China, might have had its name given by strangers to the rest of the land.

Cathay is a designation of a much later date, being derived from the Ki-tah, or Khitan (hence Khitai, Khata, or Cathay), who ruled the North of China in the tenth century. This name was used for nearly a thousand years by the inhabitants of Central Asia, and from them it spread to other nations. The Russians still call China, Khitai. It is interesting and curious to notice the pairs of names which have been applied to China, those that used them being often ignorant that they were one and the same country: one being 'the name of the great nation in the Far East as known by land,' and learned from overland travellers, the other its name as known by sea, and learned from navigators. We cannot do more here than just name them in couples,—Seres, Sinæ; Khitai, Machin; Cathay, China. None of these names are used by the natives themselves. The 'Celestial Empire' has some Chinese excuse for its origin; *T'in Chow* [*T'ien Ch'ao*], which Williams translates as 'Heavenly Dynasty,' being used to a slight extent in the sense of the 'Kingdom which the dynasty appointed by Heaven rules over,' but not being a term of general application among the common people. The latter use several names: *Chung Kwok* [*Kuo*], 'The Middle Kingdom' or 'China'—and it is possible to obtain native maps of the world with China not only in the middle, but monopolising nearly the whole of the map, while England and other countries are represented as small inlands or single cities lying round its borders. *Chung Kwok* 'can be traced back to more than a thousand years before Christ. In those far-off days it was used to denote the province of Honan, which is almost the centre of China. As the reigning family became more and more powerful, they gave the name to the whole country.' Another common name is *T'ong Shán* [*T'ang Shan*), 'The Hills (or Country) of T'ong'; the T'ong (T'ang) dynasty, being one of the most celebrated in ancient history, the name in all probability took its rise then. From the same source the usual name in vogue, in the South of China, for the people, is *T'ong yan* [*T'ang jên*], 'the men of T'ong,' while in the North it is *Hán jin* [*Han jên*], 'the men of Hán,' Hán again being the name of another ancient dynasty.

The following names also appear for the people and country in literature, viz., *Laí Man* [*Li Min*], or 'the Black-haired Race'; *Chung Wá Kwoh* [*Hua Kuo*], 'The Middle Flowery Kingdom,' [or more correctly, 'The Middle Kingdom': the last two words should be taken together] in contradistinction to *Ngoi Téí* [*Wai Ti*], 'the Outlying Lands.'

An old name for China is *Wá Há* [*Hua Hsia*], 'The Glorious Há'; Há again being an ancient dynasty, while the name *Taí Ts'ing Kwok* [*Ta Ch'ing Kuo*], 'The Great Pure Kingdom,' was used during the Ts'ing [Ch'ing or Manchu] dynasty.

Since the establishment of the Republic the name used is *Min Kuo*, 'Republic' or *Chung Hua Min Kuo*, 'Chinese Republic' (literally, 'Central Flowery Republic' but *Chung Hua* means 'China').

Different religions have also bestowed their appellations on this much-named country; the Buddhist have called it by the Hindoo name of *Chin Tán, or* 'Dawn,' and *Chin Ná;* and the Mohammedans, *Tung T'ò*, or 'Land of the East.' The former, Edkins says, 'may be the China of Ptolemy.' The general concensus of opinion now is that the 'Land of Sinim,' mentioned in the Book of Isaiah, is China. In modern Latin, that used by learned men in modern times, *Lingua sinica* is the Chinese language; and the term sinologue (properly, sinologist) is one applied to scholars of the Chinese language. Again the Seres of the Greeks and Romans are also considered to be the Chinese.

References.—Edkins, *Buddhism;* Williams, *Middle Kingdom;* Gillespie, *Land of Sinim;* Yule, *Travels of Marco Polo*, vol. i., introduction, p. 11. For the arguments in support of the Seres being the Chinese, see Anthon, *Classical Dictionary*, Article 'Seres,' where numerous authorities are quoted. Roman authorities are also given in Andrew's *Latin-English Dictionary*, as well as in Cordier's *Bibliotheca Sinica.*

CHINA BRANCH OF THE ROYAL ASIATIC SOCIETY.— In January, 1847, a Philosophical Society was founded in Hongkong. A few days later its name was changed to the Asiatic Society of China, and in the same year, being admitted as a branch of the Royal Asiatic Society, it became the China Branch of the Royal Asiatic Society. It published six volumes of *Transactions*, the last being issued in 1859. This society is a separate institution from the North China Branch of the Royal Asiatic Society (q.v.).

CHINESE ABROAD.—How well adapted John Chinaman is for going abroad, the following quotation from Sir Walter Medhurst's pen will show:—

'The phases of character in which the Chinese possess the most interest to us Western peoples, are those which so peculiarly fit them for competing in the great labour market of the world. They are good agriculturists, mechanics, labourers, and sailors, and they possess all the intelligence, delicacy of touch, and unwearying patience which are necessary to render them first-rate machinists and manufacturers. They are, moreover, decile, sober, thrifty, industrious, self-denying, enduring, and peace-loving . . . They are equal to any climate, be it hot or frigid: all that is needed is teaching and guiding, combined with capital and enterprise, to convert them into the most efficient workmen to be found on the face of the earth. . . . Wherever the tide of Chinese emigration has set in, there they have proved themselves veritable working bees, and made good their footing, to the exclusion of less quiet, less exacting, less active, or less intelligent artisans and labourers.'

It is not only in recent years that the Chinese have gone abroad: they go now as emigrants, diplomatists, and students but records show that they were as enterprising and daring in their expeditions in former periods as any Western nations were at such times. The use of the mariner's compass enabled the Chinese to put to sea with a confidence they would otherwise not have possessed; for it came in as a *dernier ressort* when fogs obscured the headlands by day, or mists clouded the stars at night. The compass was first used by the geomancers (see FUNG SHUI), who even observed its variation. A simpler kind was employed at sea, as all the surrounding concentric circles, with the names of the zodiacal signs, etc., were unnecessary there; and this compass, so primitive in its construction—and it is interesting to notice that it was originally a floating compass—has been used by the Chinese 'for about eight hundred years.' They took voyages to Japan and Corea—one to the latter country being undertaken three hundred and seventy years before Christopher Columbus launched his frail barques in search of the new world across the Atlantic.

They not only went in their own vessels, but during the T'ang dynasty, in the ninth century, the Chinese merchants at Canton 'were in the habit of chartering foreign—probably Arab—vessels with foreign sailing masters to trade beween Canton and Colombo. . . . They took carrier pigeons with them, and sent back word by them to their charterers.'

Things Chinese

The Mongols, ruling at one time in both China and Persia, carried on intercourse between these two countries by sea—thus semi-circumnavigating Asia—in large fleets, carrying ambassadors and merchandise. Aided by the compass, and taking advantage of the north-east monsoon, they started on their long and hazardous voyage, returning with the favouring gales of the south-east monsoon. Traffic was even kept up to recent years, with the numerous islands to the south-east of Asia in the neighbourhood of the Straits Settlements, Borneo and Celebes, and the same navigation was carried on between the North and South of China till the steamer traffic drove the slow and unwieldy junk from the trade. In olden days, however, not only Java, but India, Ceylon, the Gulf of Persia, and Arabia were all visited by the enterprising and commercial Chinese. 'All this was done before the days of Vasco de Gama, and the credit of the first use of the mariner's compass must be awarded to the Chinese. The Arabs borrowed it from them, and it then passed to the Red Sea and the Mediterranean.'

Marco Polo informs us that the Emperor of China sent ships to the southern part of Africa.

Emigration was, however, prohibited by Chinese law; but in spite of this large numbers of Chinese have left their native country, either temporarily or permanently. To some countries, such as the Straits Settlements, there has, for many years past, been a constant emigration of contract coolie labourers, almost all from two or three of the southern provinces. Schemes for emigration to various other countries have, as a rule, not proved successful.

The strong opposition to the settlement of Chinese in America has drawn special attention to them in that quarter of the globe, but, notwithstanding so much talk about them, the numbers that have gone over are not so large as one would naturally have expected (Chinese workmen first went to America in 1855, when 3,526 coolies went under contract), for in the United States, in 1870, there were only 56,000, in 1880, 105,642 in 1890, 107,475, (total population of the United States in 1924 was 105,710,000). In 1894, 105,312 registered themselves, out of what was stated to be, in round numbers, 110,000. About 8,000 registered in the Pacific States, 6,247 in New York, and 1,784 in Pennsylvania. New York had 1,000 Chinese laundries in 1895. There is a regular Chinese town within the city of San Francisco with a population of more than 30,000, and theatres, opium dens, and gambling dens. The Chinese are found as far north as Alaska. The greater number of them seem to be in the Western States. In

1890, 96,844, or 90.11 per cent., were in the Western portion of the country. The rate of increase since 1870 has been as follows: 1860 to 1870, 80.91 per cent.; 1870 to 1880, 66.88 per cent., 1880 to 1890, 1.91 per cent., or an increase of 2,010. There were said to be less than 100,000 or 120,000 in the States in 1900. Emigration has almost practically stopped, as only certain classes are allowed to enter, such as *bonâ fide* merchants (partners), including shop-keepers, travellers for curiosity, and genuine students, not simply those who wish to acquire a knowledge of English for business purposes, and members of the diplomatic and consular bodies. The wives and families of those resident in the States are allowed to join their husbands and fathers. In 1901, the Chinese had decreased by 17,675, the number being 89,800.

The right of voluntary emigration was recognized by the Treaty of 1868, but there have been uprisings against the massacres of the Chinese in various parts from time to time. In 1892, the Geary Act prohibited their immigration, but generally the situation now is that they are allowed to enter the United States under severe restrictions, including a heavy poll-tax.

'The first immigrant Chinese to land in the United States were two men and one woman who arrived in San Francisco on the *Brig Eagle* in 1848; in the next two years a few laborers who had escaped from Peru and worked their passage as sailors reached San Francisco. Real immigration, however, did not begin until 1852, at the end of which year the Chinese population was at least eighteen thousand.

The first arrivals were not gold hunters, but with the discovery of that precious metal thousands followed who were: by 1860 almost thirty-five thousand were in the country of whom many were in the mines, while many others were engaged as servants, laundrymen, and farm hands. Thousands worked on the construction of the Central Pacific and other railroads.

The number of Chinese within the United States remained almost stationary in the ten years from 1880-1890; in the latter year it reached its zenith when 107,488 were reported. After this it fell rapidly: in 1900, there were 89,863; in 1910, 71,531; and in the census of 1920, there were but 61,639 reported, a decrease during the past ten years of 13.8 per cent.

The great majority of these people are on the Pacific coast, but there are comparatively large colonies of them in the larger eastern cities; more than two-thirds are urban residents. Of the total number in 1910, only 4,675 were females; 14,935 claimed to be native-born; three fifths of this number had arrived in America in or prior to 1890.'

'There were 4,383 Chinese in Canada, in 1881,' and 11,000 in 1900. 'This, however, does not include the large number scattered about in the outlying parts of British Columbia, and in the Yukon mining region, for the Chinese are great placer miners.' 'Despite the poll-tax of $50 Gold per head, which is exacted from every Chinaman entering Canada, . . . 14,000 Chinese immigrants have arrived in Canada since the tax was instituted in 1886, yielding nearly $700,000 to the federal treasury. As domestics, market-gardeners, and laundrymen, they fill so important a place in the life of British Columbia that repeated agitation for increased restrictions upon their entry has as yet failed to produce any effect at Ottawa. . . . A monster petition' was [in July, 1896] 'got up, asking the Dominion Government to increase the poll-tax to $500 (since agreed to)'—and was 'widely signed in the province, reciting that Chinese labour is driving out white labour in the mining, salmon fishery, and other industries.'

The numbers that entered the Dominion have fluctuated in different years: for the fiscal year ending 30th June 1891, it was 2,114; while the next year it was 3,276. They are pretty numerous in British Columbia and Vancouver. Some thirteen years ago there were some 5,000 Chinese in the city of Victoria alone. 'It was with their aid that the Western section of the great Canadian Pacific Railway was constructed, and they have been the pioneers of, or aids to, many valuable industries and enterprises being opened up.'

'The mining of gold and the building of the Canadian Pacific Railroad conjoined to start Chinese immigration into Canada early in the seventh decade of the last century—just at the time that trouble between the white and yellow miners was starting in Australia. In those days immigration was free, no restrictions having been made.

When the legislators noted the numbers of Mongolian laborers flocking to the Pacific ports, they first appointed a royal commission to make enquiries and then as a result of the commissioners' report imposed, in 1886, a tax of fifty dollars a head on Chinese entering the dominion, and restricted them to one for every fifty tons. This affected the Chinese but little; by 1891 they numbered 9,129, and by 1901, 16,792; therefore, beginning on January 1, 1901, the tax was increased to one hundred dollars a head. Surprised when they found that this tax was insufficient, the Canadian Parliament ordered. despite the protests of the Chinese, that on and after January 1, 1904, a five-hundred-dollar tax should be collected. Between June, 1900, and January 1, 1904, more than sixteen thousand Chinese paid the one-hundred-dollar head tax; apparently at this time there were about twenty-eight thousand Chinese in the country.

The five-hundred-dollar tax had an immediate and noticeable effect: during the half year ending June 30, 1904, no Chinese paid the tax; during the year ending June 30, 1905, eight paid; during the following years twenty-two and ninety-one paid, respectively. Then came a remarkable change: in the year ending June 30,1908, 1,482 Chinese entered after paying the five-hundred-dollar tax. In 1908-1909 the figures were 1,411; 1909-1910, 1,614; 1910-1911, 4,515; 1911-1912, 6,083; 1912-1923,

7,078; 1913-1914, 5,274; 1914-1915, 1,155; 1915-1916, 20; 1917-1918, 650; 1918-1919, 4,066; 1919-1920, 363.'

The sudden rise beginning in 1909 and continuing to 1916 is accounted for by the enormous increase in wages resulting from the state-created monopoly. Various causes conspired to reduce the numbers in the later years. For further developments see MacNair, *The Chinese Abroad*, pp. 76-79.

'According to the census of 1911, there were 27,774 Chinese in the Dominion; of these over ten thousand were in British Columbia; Ontario and Quebec ranked next with about four thousand each; the rest were scattered through Manitoba, Nova Scotia, New Brunswick, and Prince Edward Island, in the order named.'

In Trinidad there were, about the year 1883, 4,000 or 5,000 Chinese, but they have decreased to probably about 2,000 or 3,000, [2,200 in 1900]. The total population of Trinidad and Tobago is now 391,000. They used to work in sugar plantations, but are now principally shopkeepers, as well as general merchants, miners and railway builders, etc. There were three Chinese males in Grenada in 1891, out of a population of 53,209 (66,000 in 1924). In the Leeward Islands (total population in 1924, 125,000), by the census of 1891, there were 83 males and 39 females, natives of China, making a total of 122. In Antigua (total population, 33,000) the numbers were 66 and 3, making a total of 69. In Jamaica (total population in 1921, 858,000), in 1891, they had increased to males 373, females 108, total 481, of whom 347 were born in China; thus rising from .02 of the total population in 1881, to .08 in 1891. In 1911 the number was 2,100. The few Chinese (who are all Cantonese) in Curaçao are not permanent settlers, but only temporary sojourners from Trinidad or Venezuela. Most of the Chinese at St. Pierre, in the island of Martinique, lost their lives in the eruption of Mont Pelée in 1902. In 1918, there were about 25 pure-blooded Chinese on the island, and from 300 to 350 mixed with other races.

'Between 1853 and 1867, Chinese immigrants were imported into British Guiana, Trinidad and Jamaica, but the experiment did not prove a success, owing to difficulties which arose with the Government of China in respect of repatriation.'

In British Guiana (total population now 306,000), by the census of 1881, there were 4,393 Chinese, while their estimated number in 1887 was males 2,115, females 1,061, total 3,176; in 1888, 3,074; and in 1891, 2,475. In 1893, there seem to have been about the same number, viz., 3,000, for in the same year the Legislature of British Guiana offered a bounty of $25 a head for 5,000 Chinamen from the United States. They were wanted to work under contract on sugar plantations and in gold mines. It was stated in 1900 that there were 2,900, and that they were decreasing in numbers. By 1911, the number was 2,622 (1,481 males, and 1,141 females). In 1918, there were about 1,500 Chinese (all Cantonese) in Ecuador, including 30 females. They have been increasing at the rate of about 100 a year.

In Surinam, or Dutch Guiana, with a population of 57,000 inhabitants (90,000 in 1924), there is a sprinkling of Chinese.

In Chile (total population in 1922, 3,792,000), in 1885, the Chinese numbered 1,164, in 1903 there were 7,000.

In Peru there were, in 1903, 50,000 Asiatics, chiefly Chinese, viz., 47,000, out of a population of 2,500,000 (now more than 4,000,000). The estimated number (there has been no census since 1876) now is not less than 50,000 or more than 150,000. They are said to be pouring into Brazil and Mexico in large numbers. The first colony of Asiatics in the New World—in modern times, at least—was almost without a doubt, one of Chinese consisting of several hundred tea growers taken from the interior of China to Brazil soon after 1810, through the influence of the Count of Linhares, prime minister of Portugal. The estimate of 20,000 for the number now in Brazil is considered rather too high.

In Mexico, in 1893, there were said to be about 3,000 Chinese, of which number 600 were employed in the mines in the State of Sinaloa. In 1895 there were less than 1,000. The census of 1910 gives 13,203, of whom 85 were women. The total population of Mexico in 1924 was 17,000,000. In Panama there are some 3,500 Chinese, the majority (about 2,500) in and around the city of Panama. All are from Kuangtung.

There are considerable numbers in Guatemala, scattered throughout the country; and a few in Costa Rica, the province of Limon having about 250, all from Kuangtung.

In Cuba and Porto Rico, in 1877, there were 43,811 Chinese. In 1887, there were more than 45,000. By 1903 they had increased to 90,000 in these countries. In 1907 there were only 11,217 in Cuba. In Porto Rico, in 1900, there were 75 Chinese, but in 1910 only 12. In the Virgin Islands, in 1917, there were only 15.

During the period 1847-1874, it has been estimated that between a quarter and a half million laborers were shipped from Amoy, Canton, Hongkong, and Macao—especially from the two places last named—to Cuba, Peru, Chile, and the Sandwich

Islands. In 1864, for example, from Macao there were shipped to Cuba 4,479, and to Peru 6,243; in 1865, 5,207 to Cuba, and 8,417 to Peru. During the same years 2,716 laborers were shipped from Canton by Cuban agents acting under the French flag.

In Hawaii, in 1884, there were 17,939 Chinese; in 1886, 20,000; in 1890, 15,000; in 1896, 21,616; in 1900, 25,767; in 1910, 21,674; in 1924, 23,000 out of a total population in that year of 260,000, 'the pure-bred Hawaiians, who have been declining during the last 100 years, numbering only 31,019 (23,700 in 1920.)' In 1899 the Chinese were estimated 'at 27,000; 6,000 of whom were employed on sugar plantations. Many useless swamps in these islands have been reclaimed by the Chinese and used for the cultivation of rice. 'Until 1886, Chinese labourers were largely employed in the sugar plantations of Hawaii:' after that, Japanese took the places they had filled. As sugar fell in price, the Chinese, being cheaper labourers, were taken on again, and hundreds of them arrived in the Islands for that purpose, until, in 1893, there were 40,000 settled in the Sandwich Islands. Many Chinese hold very good positions, the professions including several Chinese lawyers. The American Exclusion Act against the Chinese now applies to Hawaii.

In Mauritius and its dependencies (to which Chinese emigration began in 1843 or earlier), by the census of 1891, there was a total of 3,151 Chinese, of whom 9 were females, being a decrease in numbers, as the previous census showed a Chinese population of 3,558. In 1911 there were 3,686 in Mauritius, and 350 in Fiji (of whom 29 were females).

In 1890 they were increasing largely in numbers in Kimberley, having established themselves in 75 shops, many of them being employed as masons, carpenters, and painters. In 1906 there were 55,000 working in the Transvaal gold mines. In subsequent years they have immigrated in increasingly large numbers. The shipment had begun in June, 1904. The number of Chinese in South Africa, with the exception of contract labourers, has been small, and most of these have been in the Transvaal.

In the Cape of Good Hope a Chinese exclusion act was passed in 1904; this provided for the total prohibition of Chinese male adults, and for the registration of all resident male adult Chinese. The enforcement of this act reduced the number of Chinese from 1,393 at the beginning, to 711 on January 1, 1917. The census of 1891 gave the Chinese in Cape Colony as 215 males and no females; this number has, however, largely increased since. In November, 1901, the Chinese in Port

Elizabeth, by a round enumeration, were 390, of whom 6 were women.

In India and Ceylon there are some Chinese to be found, and there is said to be unmistakable evidence of their presence in Mysore in ancient times. Quite recently, even further evidence of their work, it is considered, has been discovered, for while sinking a main shaft in the Harnhalli gold mine, a number of mining implements of various kinds were found which had been used by the old miners in their work a thousand or more years ago, and it is supposed that the workings were made by Chinese. The tools are said to be like Chinese ones, and unlike Hindoo ones.

In Burma they are numerous. The whole trade of Burma is in Chinese hands. Sir L. Griffin considers that the future of Burma belongs to the Chinese. A great proportion of the trade of Rangoon is in their hands. 'They are numerous in all the commercial towns up country, such as Mandalay, etc., and have increased very rapidly—none of the indigenous races, such as the Burmese, Taliens, or Karens, have multiplied so greatly. They are wanted in such places where the population is small. They possess the very qualities which the Burmese lack, and are respectable citizens. . . . They are the best of all immigrants in the East.' For centuries past the Western Chinese have had commecial intercourse with Burma, and a few hundreds were 'settled as merchants in Bhamo, Mandalay, Fangyan, and other places,' but the British annexation of the country increased their number: so that in 1903 there were probably 5,000 Yün-nan and Sz-chuan [Ssŭch'uan] men living in Burma, who are in the habit of taking Burmese wives, the sons of these unions going to school in Yün-nan to learn Chinese, and learning Burmese in the land of their birth. From South-Eastern China the immigration has lasted many years, but in small numbers until recently, when British rule afforded greater security. In 1903 there were probably some 35,000 Chinese from the Eastern Coast in Burma, which, with the 5,000 already mentioned as from the West of China, would make not far short of 40,000 Chinese in Burma, there being 10,000 in Mandalay, while there were probably 21,000 in Rangoon, though we have seen it stated that there are 40,000 in the latter city alone. The total population of Burma in 1921 was 13,205,564.

There were about 1,000 Chinese settled in Haiphong about the year 1893, 'where they have monopolised every pursuit requiring skill, perseverance, and commercial acumen.' In 1890, out of a population of 15,000, 5,600 were Chinese.

In the City of Hué, in the capital of the Kingdom of Annam, 800 are Chinese, the total population being estimated at 100,000; and in Tourane, Haiphong, and other ports in Tonkin, the trade is chiefly in the hands of the Chinese.

The population of Cochin-China, in 1889, was 1,864,214 (in 1924, 3,452,250), of which 56,528 were Chinese. In 1900, the number of Chinese had risen to 100,000; in 1910, to 232,000. In Saigon, out of a population of 16,213, there were 7,346 Chinese. In 1903 there were 73,857 Chinese, out of a population of 2,252,034.

In the town of Cholon, four miles from Saigon, there were, in 1889, 14,944 Chinese, out of a population of 37,441.

'The people [of Cambodia] are apathetic and indolent, and have allowed the trade to fall into the hands of the Chinese,' who in 1924, numbered 140,000 out of a total population of 2,000,000.

'Prior to the Franco-Chinese War of 1884 the Chinese people passed back and forth freely in Indo-China; at this time it was estimated that there were twenty-five thousand Chinese in Tonkin, and forty thousand in Cochin China (lower Annam). In 1900, the total Chinese population of this French possession was about one hundred thousand; ten years later computations based on French official reports showed that there were about two hundred and thirty-two thousand in the whole colony. In Cochin China there were in the neighbourhood of one hundred and fifteen thousand Chinese, of whom seventy thousand resided in Saigon and Cholon, and forty-five thousand in the provinces; a considerable share of this is a floating population. . . . Cambodia alone, in 1919, had a Chinese population of one hundred and forty thousand. . . . In 1919, it [Cholon] had almost one hundred thousand Chinese residents.'

There were in 1903 nearly one million and a half of Chinese subjects resident in Siam (the latest estimate being 1,350,000; another figure is 1,400,000). They 'have almost monopolised the local trade,' and the general revenue is farmed out to them. At least 200,000 Chinese from the Island of Hainan alone are believed to be in Siam. The whole population of Siam, estimated at from 6,000,000 to 10,000,000 in 1903, is now variously given as 8,800,000 and 9,250,000. Bankok is 'occupied by a mixed Siamese and Chinese population, estimated at from 400,000 to 500,000 [a later estimate puts it at 350,000]. As in so many other parts of Further India, the Chinese have here almost monopolised the local trade.'

'We point with just pride to the great Chinese trading communities of Hongkong and Singapore, which have grown up under our fostering care. The annual immigration from

South China amounts to over 200,000 per annum, while about three-fourths of that number annually return to their native land. In and around the Straits Settlements we are supposed to have at least 600,000 Chinese, not counting those in Borneo, the Dutch colonies, or the Philippines. If all territory under direct British rule be included, they slightly outnumber the children of the soil.'

'Figures vary as to their number according to whether pure-blooded Chinese are referred to, or those having Chinese blood. They have been estimated to number as high as two and a half to three millions. . . .' Of the total population 'possibly ten per cent. were Chinese; in Bangkok there are about two hundred thousand. To and from this city there is a constant flow of Chinese from the ports of the homeland. . . . A large part of the Chinese population is from Kwangtung, and most of the remainder from Fukien. . . . Those who have observed the life of Siam agree that by their contributions of brain and blood the Chinese have added stamina to the population, and brought the country to its present plane of prosperity.'

For scores of years they have been pouring into Malaysia, and all surrounding islands. An early intercourse between China and these islands is known to have existed. One work ascribes the beginning of this to the fifth century of the Christian era, and this intercourse was afterwards renewed in the tenth century (see also below). When the Portuguese first arrived in this part of the world in the sixteenth century, they found Chinese junks lying at Malacca, and what was evidently a prosperous trade being carried on by the Chinese. From all that can be gathered, they seemed in these early days to have been simply birds of passage. At all events, there is no evidence to show that they settled down amongst their new surroundings and became inhabitants of the land. The following quotation relates to the early years of the twentieth century:—

'The annual influx of Chinese emigrants into the Peninsula cannot be ascertained; but some notion of its amount may be formed from the number which lands in Singapore. This, on an average of years, is about 100,000 (in 1894 it was over 137,000), of whom about one-fourth settle in the island, the majority being sent on to Penang or dispersed among the neighbouring States. The number that return yearly to China from the same port is about 70,000, most of them resorting to it from neighbouring countries for the convenience of a passage.

'The emigrants from China are all from the four maritime provinces of the empire—Kwongtung [Kuangtung], Fokien [Fukien], Chêkiang and Kiangnan. Four-fifths of the whole number come from Amoy and Swatow, and about a tenth part from Canton; the emigrants from the two more northerly provinces forming but a very small fraction. Nearly all the emigrants consist of the labouring classes—fishermen, artisans, and common day-labourers. They usually arrive at their places of destination in great poverty, and are obliged to mortgage their labour to their resident countrymen in consideration of their passage-money.

'From the nature of the emigration, the proportion of males to females is always great. . . . The result, of course, is that the increase of the Chinese population by natural means is very slow.'

This paucity of women is one of the peculiar features of Chinese emigration. Naturally children are also absent, for, if those going to try their fortunes abroad have wives and children, they are left at home, where they are considered to be more the adjuncts of the ancestral abode than the peculiar property of the individual himself, to say nothing of being companions of the father and husband. No doubt the abject poverty of most of the emigrants is also one cause for all home ties being sundered; for none of the middle or upper classes are to be found amongst them.

'In 1795, there were three thousand Chinese in Penang; in 1826, six thousand or more were in Singapore. . . . In 1918, the Chinese in British Malaysia numbered approximately one million: in the Federated Malay States the number was 433,244, while an almost equal number was in the Straits Settlements—432,764. These figures do not include the Chinese scattered in Johore, Kedah, Perlis, Kelantan, and Trengganu, which are under British protection. The Chinese population of Singapore itself varies, but is around two hundred thousand or about two-thirds of the population of the city. There are more Chinese in Singapore than in any other city outside of China.' The efforts of the Chinese have succeeded in producing more than half of the world's tin supply. 'Their energy and enterprise have made the Malay States what they are to-day, and it would be impossible to overstate the obligation which the Malay government and people are under to these hard-working, capable, law-abiding aliens.'

The total population of the Straits Settlements, in 1891, was 512,905; in 1920, 876,160, of whom 50 per cent. were Chinese, and 35 per cent. Malay. Of the Chinese only 18 per cent. were female. The increase of the Chinese, from 1881 to 1891, was 53,662 or 30.7 per cent., while the Malays and other natives only increased 9.5 per cent. There are 4,450 Chinese in every 10,000 of the population. They are Hokkiens (natives of the Fukien province), Teo Chews (natives of the neighbourhood of Swatow), Cantonese, Hakkas (see HAKKAS), or Khehs (as the Hakkas are called in the Amoy or Swatow speech), Hylams (natives of the Island of Hainan), and Straits-born Chinese. The census of 1891 gives the population of Singapore Island as 184,544, and that of 1921 as 418,360, the Chinese being

121,908 and the Malays 35,992. Penang had 87,920 Chinese, and Malacca 18,161. Penang in 1903 had more than 90,000, and Malacca 29,000.

The increase by the census of 1901 amounts to 53,944 or 23.7 per cent., and in every 10,000 of the population there were 4,927 Chinese. This proportion has since increased. The Cantonese have increased in the ten years 20.4 per cent.; the Hokkiens 25.5; the Teo Chiu 1, and the Straits-born Chinese 26.7 per cent. The latter have increased in greater proportion than any of the others, they numbering 44,022 in 1901 as against 34,757 in 1891. During the ten years 1891–1901, the disproportion between the sexes was reduced: in 1891 it was in every 1,000 persons over 15 years of age, male 857, females 143; in 1901 it was 831 and 169 respectively.

'The population of the State [of Johore] is remarkable for containing a larger number of Chinese than of Malays. The exact figures have not been ascertained, but probably come to 200,000, viz.: Malays, 35,000, Chinese, 150,000 [that is three-quarters of the population], and Javanese, 15,000. More than half are to be found within 15 miles of the Singapore Straits. The Chinese are chiefly found as cultivators of gambier and pepper, spread over about this range of country in the extreme southern end of the Peninsula, nearest to Singapore, of which Johore has been described as the "back country." These cultivators go from Singapore, the capitalists for whom they cultivate are Singapore traders, and all their produce and most of their earnings find their way back to Singapore again.'

Hundreds go by almost every steamer from China to the Straits and adjacent countries. More than 100,000 landed in Singapore in a single year; and, not including those in Borneo, the Dutch Colonies and the Philippines, there are a million Chinese in the Straits Settlements and their immediate neighbourhood.

In Negri Sembilan, a group of nine small States, the entire population in 1891 was 41,617 (130,000 in 1924), of whom about 5,511 were Chinese, and amongst them 37 females. It is now stated that over one-third of the population is Chinese. Of them Dr. Dennys says, 'The number of Chinese engaged in tapioca estates and in mines have greatly increased, and, for years to come, there must be a perceptible monthly increase.'

In Sungei Ujong, with a total population in 1891 of 23,000, 18,000 were Chinese. In Jelebu also, the Chinese form a large proportion of the population.

In 1891, the census gave the population of Selangor as 81,592 (294,000 in 1924), of whom 50,884 were Chinese. They, both as traders and miners, form the most important element of the population, and are emigrants from the south of China, being chiefly composed of Hakkas (Khehs) and Cantonese.

'At Larut, and at the chief mining settlements in the interior' of the State of Perak, 'the Chinese form a large part of the population.' In Perak, in 1891, there were 94,345 Chinese, or 44 per cent. of the whole population. The Perak census of 1901 shows a total population of 329,665 (494,000 in 1924), of which there were 150,239 Chinese. In every 10,000 of the population the Chinese numbered 4,557. 'The Chinese have increased enormously in the Federated Malay States of late, but there is still a vast disparity between the sexes; so great in fact that, in the total figures for the States, there are 491,313 males, of all races, to only 185,825 females.' In Perak they have increased 363 per cent. since 1879, and were nearly equal to the Malay population, which, in 1891, was 96,719. They now exceed them. The total population of the State was then 214,254. In Pahang there were, in 1891, 3,241 Chinese, out of a total population of 57,462 (118,700 in 1924).

Notwithstanding all this, the demand for Chinese (and Indian) labour in the Federated Malay States has grown so great that wages have risen sometimes to double or treble the rate paid a few years previous to 1903, and important works, such as roads, railways, and irrigation, have been seriously delayed, and so earnestly is John Chinaman wanted in that part of the world that the Government of those States has actually arranged for direct steam communication with several Chinese ports and provinces 'a subsidy of $5 a head for every Chinese labourer imported by this means, up to a certain number and for a term of years.'

'Chinese furnish nearly all the miners, as well as the oporators [in the Malay Peninsula]. They have succeeded, employing primitive methods, where Europeans have failed, and mining promises to remain in their hands. That accounts for the great increase in the Chinese population, from 163,000 in 1891 to 303,000 in 1901. In Perak and Selangor, the great tin-producing States, the Chinese outnumber the Malay by 78,000. The Malay population has advanced, however, from 230,000 in 1891 to 313,000 in 1901.'

'The Chinese—who, in 1911, out-numbered even the people of the country—by their enterprise, their industry, and their capital, under the guidance and administration of British Residents, made the Federated States what they were till rubber planting introduced a great agricultural industry. The appointment of British Residents to advise the Malay rulers in Perak, Selangor, and Negri Sembilan dates from 1874. During the next thirty years it was Chinese capital and Chinese effort, employed in working the rich alluvial tin deposits of those states, which brought into the country this large Chinese population and enabled the Government to raise from them a revenue more than sufficient to pay the costs of administration and to construct all necessary public works, including thousands of miles of excellent roads and a thousand miles of railway. Until 1900, or even later, the Chinese of the Malay States believed only in tin mining, just as the Mauritius planter believes in sugar. Times have changed, and the wave of rubber planting caught the Chinese, who opened large estates of their own, or invested in locally-formed companies. While the well-to-do became owners, many of the labouring class left the mines for the plantations, where they earned higher wages with less effort. There are a few European owners and managers of tin mines worked with machinery on scientific principles, but with these exceptions mining in Malaya is in the hands of Chinese.

'Though tin mining and rubber growing give employment to the great bulk of the Chinese population, these industrious people are the principal shopkeepers and contractors; while Straits-born and Malay States-born Chinese, educated in the schools of the Colony and the Malay States, fill many subordinate posts in the Government service. As intelligent, hardworking, honest citizens of British Malaya, easy and pleasant to deal with, and loyal to the Government of their birth or adoption, the Chinese have won a deservedly high reputation, and their contribution to the public revenues is far higher than that of any other race.'

Of the total population of Hongkong, estimated in 1920, of 514,000, 501,000 were Chinese. It is thus to all intents and purposes a Chinese city whose excellent rule by a foreign power has brought the economic prosperity for which the place is noted.

'The Chinese, who have been settled in most Bornean towns for generations, conduct all the trading operations,' the natives being 'indolent and wanting in enterprise,' In British N. Borneo, out of a total population in 1924 of about 227,000, 30,000 were Chinese. Sandakan, the capital of British North Borneo, had a population of 7,132 in 1891 (8,000 in 1924), of whom 3,627 were Chinese. There were 20,000 in 1903. In 1911, the number was 26,000. There is room for 5,000,000, and they would be received gladly. In Labuan they number over 1,000, 'are the chief traders, and most of the industries of the Island are in their hands,' the total population being about 6,000, but composed mostly of Malays. The Chinese seem destined to be the future inhabitants of this part of the world; the demand for them is increasing. They land as coolies, but their industry and superior qualities to those of the natives raise them speedily to the position of planters, shopkeepers, and merchants. 'These Chinese are mostly Hakkas, Cantonese, Hainanese, Swatow, and Amoy men.'

In 1920, rough estimates were as follows: North Borneo, 150,000; Brunei, 2,000; Sarawak, 250,000. In Dutch Borneo there are 40,000 Chinese, mostly in the Western Division.

'The Dutch East Indies possess a quarter of a million Chinese inhabitants.'

'The population of Java, in the year 1890 . . . amounted to over 24,000,000 (38,000,000 in Java and Madura in 1924), of whom the Chinese mustered only 242,000. In the islands lying beyond Java, the Chinese are less numerous, numbering about 210,000, and of these 80,000 are settled in Deli and on the East coast of Sumatra. There are 24,000 in Rhio, mostly employed in cultivating the pepper and gambier gardens of the Sultan and other native chiefs. In Banca and Billiton there are 35,000 (52,000 in 1924) engaged in tin-mining. In the western division of Borneo, there are 32,000, who earn a living by mining, cultivation, and trade. In these islands the Chinese (who number in all about 500,000) are found to be not a dangerous but a highly useful element in the population. Without Chinese labour, tobacco growing in Deli and tin-mining in Banca and Billiton would certainly not have reached the development they have now attained. As to the western division of Borneo, where the Chinese (who number about 40,000) were formerly so turbulent and rebellious, their pride has been so thoroughly taken down by military force that during the last forty years the Government has effectually kept them in check. In the outlying islands, the natives are of a harder stamp than the Javanese, and do not allow themselves to be turned to undue profitable account by the Chinese. In Java, this is otherwise, and the Chinese, through their control of the revenue farming system, have a wide field for extortion and "squeezing" among the people. Danger from the Chinese in Java arises not from their number, but from the power thus put into their hands.'

'According to the latest official estimates (1917) there are about seven hundred thousand Chinese resident in the Dutch East Indies, of whom more than three hundred thousand are in Java. The majority of these have arrived during the past half century. Of those in Java over fifty thousand are in the cities of Batavia, Surabaya, and Samarang; sixty thousand or more are in ten other of the larger cities. A partial explanation of this city-dwelling characteristic so noticeable here is that until a few years ago a Dutch law restricted the dwelling places of the Chinese; since the repeal of this law they have scattered somewhat.

The Chinese are settled chiefly in Java, Borneo, Banka and the east coast of Sumatra. In Banka most of them are Hakkas from the district of Ka-ing-chiu in Kwangtung. On this island there were, according to the census of 1917, about fifty-five thousand Chinese, of whom almost twenty thousand were contract laborers in the government tin mines. On the near-by island of Billiton there were fifteen thousand seven hundred and fifty such laborers in privately owned mines. Not all the Chinese in these two islands are contract laborers; many are business men and mine owners. In Sumatra, between 1876-1898, over fifty-six thousand from Swatow entered by government encouragement to work the tobacco fields, Japanese labor having proved quite ineffectual.'

In the Anamba Islands there were, in 1892, it is said, about 1,500 Malays and 600 Chinese.

It is estimated that there are 100,000 Chinese in the Philippine Islands (all the inland trade being carried on by Chinese pedlars), 'of which upwards of 40,000 dwell in the capital and its environs' (but see below). During the year 1892, 5,273 Chinese arrived in Manila in excess of those who left during that year. The number, in 1890, was 8,867 arrivals in excess of departures. There were 51,567 Chinese in Manila in 1901, of whom 349 were women, and it is estimated that at least one-third of the 180,000 inhabitants of Manila are of Chinese descent. The American Exclusion Act now applies to the Philippines.

'It cannot be accurately known what the present number of Chinese in the Philippines is, in as much as complete vital statistics are restricted to Manila. By the census of 1918 there were reported to be 17,856 in that city. There are probably about fifty thousand—though some estimates run as high as seventy thousand—in the archipelago. About eighty-five per cent. are from Fukien, the remainder being mostly from Kwangtung.'

'Few Chinese settled in Japan prior to the nineteenth century.' In 1874-5 there were 'not less than ten thousand.' After the China-Japan War of 1894-5 it was estimated that there might be one thousand Chinese in Yokohama, and twenty-five hundred in the whole country. 'At the end of 1904 their numbers totaled 8,411, while by 1911 they had dropped to 8,145; at the end of 1918, however, they had risen to 12,139.'

The total number of Chinese in Japan, in 1888, was 4,805. In 1890, Yokohama had a Chinese population of 2,625, out of a foreign population of 4,218, and Nagasaki 684, out of a total of 1,004 foreign residents. In 1889, Hakodate had 33 Chinese residents, out of a total of 69 foreigners. Osaka had 135 Chinese, and Kobe 767. In 1903, there were 7,000 Chinese in Japan; in 1910, 8,462. In Kobe 1,767 in 1901; another account gives 1,288 males and 367 females, and in Tokyo, 181. In 1924, the number is given as 3,670. The war with Japan took such of the Chinese population of the Island of Formosa as remained there under the Japanese flag.

'Even at the present time about fifteen hundred of the laborer and merchant classes leave the Foochow district annually for

Formosa.' The number of Chinese and Chinese half-castes has increased rapidly during the past few years. In 1900 the natives totaled 2,802,919; at the end of 1914 the total was 3,307,302, while only three years later the number reported was 3,395,605—a fact which would tend to illustrate and prove the correctness of the assertion . . . that the genius of Chinese colonization is economic rather than political, and that Chinese emigrants prosper under a strong and stable foreign government.'

'The numbers of Chinese in Kwantung have steadily increased in recent years. In 1908, the number reported was 408,378; in 1912 it was 496,696; at the end of 1915 it had risen to 566,401, comprising more than five-sixths of the total population of the leased area.

In Corea there were, a few years previous to 1903, only 100; but immigration has been extensive enough to add very materially to their number, so that there were, in 1890, 1,057 Chinese, in 1894, 1,234, and in 1899, 3,134.

'The number of Chinese in Korea was never considerable and it is said that at one time, in spite of Korea's subordinate position, Chinese were prohibited from going to that country by its rulers.

At the time of the annexation of Korea to the Japanese Empire there were 9,970 Chinese in the country; two years later there were 15,517; at the end of 1916 there were 16,904 reported, of whom about 1,170 were women. The latest available reports estimate the Chinese population at about 19,000, constituting by far the largest alien population of the country. The great majority of these people are from Shantung.'

In Siberia, in 1882, a dozen; they are now 'swarming along the auriferous banks of the Upper Yenisei River,' and (1903) number there 3,500. From the 1st of January, 1893, till the 23rd of April of the same year, when any further arrivals were stopped, 10,260 Chinese coolies entered Vladivostock with passports from Chefoo. The Chinese in Vladivostock numbered 30,000, in 1895, and carry on various businesses in a small way.

'No complete and accurate figures are available. . . . One report refers . . . to the "hundreds of thousands of Chinese in the maritime provinces of Siberia;" another says: "In Vladivostock and vicinity there are about twenty-five thousand Chinese, and in the Pri-Amur District about one hundred thousand." In Nikolsk-Usurisky there are said to be 7,750 Chinese, and in Khabarovsk 6,850. On the left bank of the Amur there are about sixty thousand and many more are settled at the mouth of the Zeya River, and in the Amur province. During the years 1910-12 more than fifty-two thousand Chinese are reported to have arrived by steamer, while about forty-five thousand departed during the same period.' The settlers are almost exclusively Shantung and Shensi men.

The total population of Australia in 1903 was about 4,000,000 (5,247,000 in 1920), out of which there are some 40,000 of Chinese race—about one Chinaman in every hundred of the population. The last estimate reduces the number to between 25,000 or 30,000.

'The first settlers from China seem to have been those who entered Queensland between 1840 and 1859, encouraged by white settlers who needed shepherds; convict labour was insufficient to supply the demand and thus the way was opened for the Mongolians. . . . It was the discovery of gold that led to the influx of Chinese in the sixth decade of the nineteenth century. In 1854, in Victoria, there were 2,341 Chinese; by 1857, there were more than twenty-five thousand in the gold fields of that colony, and by the end of 1859 it was estimated that they numbered at least forty-two thousand. In New South Wales, also, the gold called loudly for miners; in 1856, eighteen hundred Chinese were listed, while five years later their numbers had risen to about thirteen thousand.'

'Since 1888, the number of Chinese in Australia has steadily dropped: the number, including half-castes, in 1891 was 38,077; in 1901, it was 33,165; in 1911, it was 25,772; while at the end of the year 1920, the estimated number was only 21,118, including 848 females. A considerable part of this population is transient. . . . Most of the Chinese in Australia are Cantonese.'

'If it had not been for Chinese industry and Chinese labour and enterprise, many parts of Australia would have remained worthless to the present time, and, after all, the Chinese competes with the European in Australia in comparatively few trades. By the Chinese in Australia the heavy poll-tax is felt to be too restrictive, more especially to Chinese having places of business in two or more of the Australian Colonies [for they are restricted in going from one colony to another], while it is contended that serious hurt is done to the shipping interests on account of the veto practically established against Chinese immigration from Hongkong and adjacent ports. Mr. Way Lee maintains that the plea set up by our Australian cousins that the Chinese work too cheaply is altogether fallacious. No Chinaman, he says, will work for less than £1 per week in Australia; whereas, on the other hand, Japanese labour can be obtained for 30 shillings per month, and Kanaka labour for the astonishing low figure of £6 a year per man. Added to this, each Chinese landing in New South Wales has to pay a poll-tax of £100; in Queensland £30; in Victoria, South Australia, Tasmania, Western Australia, or New Zealand £10; and in some of these Colonies they are not allowed to work in the mines.'

In Western Australia further legislation, we understand, has been taken against the Chinese, who numbered in that Colony, in 1893, 1,378.

In Queensland, in 1890, there were 7,242, of whom 92 were females; the proportion of Chinese to the total estimated population has steadily decreased in numbers for more than five years, for, in 1884, the proportion was 4.16 per cent.; in 1885, 3.75 per cent.; in 1886, 2.87 per cent.; in 1887, 2.50 per cent.; in 1888, 2.13 per cent.; in 1889, 1.89 per cent.; and in 1890, 1.71 per cent. The death-rate of Chinese in Queensland is lower than that of the European races. Two Chinese women were married in 1890 in Queensland, and, considering the animus felt against the Chinese there, it is not surprising to find that they were married to their own countrymen, but of the 24 Chinamen married during the same period, 22 were married to natives of Queensland, and English, Scotch, and Irish women.

'In the period extending from 1866 to 1885, 295 Chinamen married in Victoria alone. Of their brides, only four were from their own country. Of the remainder, 138 were natives of the colony—all, with five exceptions, white women—49 were born in other Australian colonies, 53 in England and Wales, 15 in Scotland, 24 in Ireland, 2 in Germany, and 2 in the United States; while France and Spain had the distinction of each furnishing a lady unconventional enough to ally herself with a swain from the Flowery Land.'

In Victoria, the Chinese are likewise decreasing in numbers. In 1881, they numbered 12,123, while in 1891 the figures were, including half-castes, 9,377, of whom 605 were females. There were said to be 9,000 in Victoria (1900); and now only 6,248.

In South Australia, in 1891, there were 2,734; in 1900, 3.000. They are found in Northern Australia, where, the Earl of Kintore says, they have 'had the greatest share in its development, so far as it has gone'; and it is considered that they are indispensable for its further development. In the Northern Territory of South Australia there were in 1891, 3,392 Chinese, out of a total population of 4,898.

The entire population of New South Wales, by the census of 1891, was 1,132,234 (2,002,631 in 1920), of which the Chinese numbered 14,156. In 1901 it was stated to be over 10,000, of which the women only numbered 677. The first genuine Chinese paper printed in Australia was started in Sydney in 1895 under the title of *The Chinese Australian Herald.*

There were 844 Chinese in Tasmania (total population in 1920, 216,751) in 1881.

There were 4,585 Chinese in New Zealand (total population in 1920, 1,320,000) in 1889, in 1901 about 5,000, but the poll-tax of £10 imposed, in 1881, on every Chinese new arrival, who intended to be a resident, reduced the immigrants from 1,029 in 1881 to 23 in 1882. The figures rose again to 354 in 1887, but they again fell off; and, in most of the Australian Colonies, they have decreased in numbers—the Northern Territory is an exception—owing to the restrictive legislation against them, the other Colonies having followed suit with the poll-tax. Many of them are shop-keepers and general merchants, miners and railway builders, and some of the most solid men in the community. There have been 178 Chinese naturalised in New Zealand during the ten years ending in 1889, and they 'are said to make excellent citizens'; more than 9 per cent. of those naturalised during that time being Chinese, they occupying the fourth place on the list of those naturalised; Germans, Danes, and Swedes taking the lead. Naturalisation is, however, only effective in the Colony in which it is granted.

In New Zealand, 'forty years ago there were about thirty-five hundred of them engaged in alluvial mining; a Chinese was the pioneer in gold dredging, and in this work he and his countrymen contributed to the development of the colony. . . . In dairying, also, the Chinese were pioneers in this country. But the white inhabitants have officially discouraged Chinese immigration and their numbers are limited. . . . In 1881, there were 5,004 Chinese in the islands; three years later the effect of taxation was observable—there were 4,542; in 1896, they had dropped to 3,711, but during the years 1894-95, the number of Chinese arrivals was found to be exceeding the departures. It was decided to impose a poll tax of one hundred pounds and to limit the number that might be carried on any ship to one for every two hundred tons. This was carried into law in 1896 by the Chinese Immigrants Amendment Act; at this time there were 3,711 Chinese in the Dominion. In 1901 there were 2,875 Chinese; in 1906, 2,570; in 1916; 2,147, including 135 half-castes; in April, 1920, the number of registered Chinese aliens was 2,376, including twenty-seven females. . . . A very unusual condition was noted during the year 1920 when the 1,477 arrivals exceeded the departures by a total of 1,097. This aroused considerable alarm in the Dominion, which, like Australia, intends to remain a white man's country.

There were three Chinese in British New Guinea in 1890-1.

It will thus be seen what numbers of them are scattered over the world. Even London has a fluctuating population of them, chiefly sailors and firemen of the steamers trading with China. In 1898, out of 1,204 received into the Strangers' Home for Asiatics in Limehouse, nearly half were Chinese.

'The Chinese in the British Isles are negligible in number and position. In London and in Liverpool there are ever-changing numbers of sailors and laborers. In the latter city there are several Chinese laundries. The Chinese give little trouble to the English and seldom come into prominence. In 1901, there were 387 Chinese, and in 1911, 1,319 were reported for England and Wales; these figures do not, of course, include several thousand sailors who do not establish a domicile in the country.'

The following paragraph refers to the beginning of the twentieth century. The numbers, of course, vary in the course of years.

'There are very few Chinese in England—only 767, all told, according to the last enumeration (but see above). Yet only three counties are wholly without Chinamen—Hereford, Rutland, and Westmoreland. Most of our Orientals live in London or its neighbourhood. There are 302, in all, in London. The South-Eastern counties are favourites with these visitors; Surrey has 45, Kent has 49, Sussex has 36, Hants has 24. There are 17 Chinese in Croydon, 5 in Brighton, 4 in Hastings, 5 in Reading, 3 in Southampton, and 4 in Portsmouth. Middlesex has 45, and Essex 28. In Gloucester there are 22 Chinese, in Lincolnshire 11, in Cheshire 14, in Durham 10, and 51 in Lancashire. But many of them must find life rather lonely. There is only one Chinaman in all Oxfordshire, one in Huntingdon, one in Derbyshire. The other counties have from two to nine. [Hereford, Rutland and Westmoreland have none]. In many of the large towns a solitary Chinaman is often found. Norwich has one, for instance; so have Coventry, Bolton, St. Helens, Blackburn, Preston, and South Shields. Birmingham, Salford, and Hanley have only two each. In all Yorkshire there are only 23. The Chinese seem to like Ireland; there are a total of 112 in that island. But they avoid both Scotland and Wales. There are only 29 Chinese in Scotland and 16 in Monmouthshire and Wales. Most of the Chinese in Great Britain are either Government officials, students, or domestic servants, and the females are to the males as three to four.' The proportion of women to men of Chinese nationality in England is 75 per cent.

'The Chinese colony is quite a separate section of Oriental life in London. There are several shops in Limehouse Causeway owned by Chinese, with Chinese hieroglyphics over their doors, and run in regular Chinese fashion. The very reckoning of change is done by enumerators on the counter, after the old Roman fashion. With some of these shops gambling dens and opium rooms are regularly maintained.'

The *Pall Mall Gazette* suggested, a few years ago, a solution of the modern ever-present 'servant-girl' difficulty to be found in their employment by the harassed English matron, as household servants. It has been said that:—

'Many native labourers in Germany have been displaced by Chinese,' while a Mecklenburg paper is stated to have 'regularly advertised contracts for Chinese labour, the prevalent term of agreement being for ten years, a cash payment of 200 marks being made in advance.' The Germans in East Africa have imported Chinese labour 'for agricultural purposes, as the natives will not work more than is absolutely necessary to earn a bare subsistence'; 240 Chinese coolies having been sent from

Singapore. 'The planters in Portuguese Africa have resolved to engage a large number of Chinese contract labourers for their fields in that country, owing to the great want of labour.'

'In Hamburg there are many Chinese dock-labourers.'

'In German New Guinea, experience has taught . . . that for plantation work no other labourers can compete with the Chinese.' The coolie traffic of Holland with China is nearly 'half a million per annum; while that of England is under 50,000; of Portugal, a few hundreds; of Germany, Hawaii, and the South American Republics, hardly as much.'

Like the Briton, the Chinese are found nearly everywhere; like him, the Chinaman has the faculty of making himself at home abroad; and, like the Briton, he looks forward, after making his pile, to return to his home and spend the remainder of his days in ease and comfort; and again, like the Briton, the countries he blesses by his presence owe in some cases, their salvation, and in others incalculable benefits to him.

References.—The information, where not original, has been culled from as immense variety of sources too numerous to particularize. Interesting information about the Chinese in the Straits Settlements is given in Denny's *Descriptive Dictionary of British Malaya.* The Census Returns of the Straits Settlements and other British Colonies may also be mentioned. Information has also been supplied by the Chinese Government Bureau of Economic Information. MacNair's *The Chinese Abroad* contains the latest information on the whole subject. See also Song Ong Siang, *One Hundred Year's History of the Chinese in Singapore.*

CHINESE PEOPLE, CHARACTERISTICS OF.—With regard to the physical characteristics, the Chinese belong to the Mongolian family, possessing its yellowish skin, lank, coarse, black hair, and almost rudimentary beard and whiskers, and scanty hair-growth on the rest of the body, prominent cheekbones, eyes almost invariably black, lack-lustre in expression, and obliquely sloping towards the nose, there being either no bridge to that organ, or in other cases scarcely any, and broad nostrils; there is also 'a small flap of skin of the upper eyelid overlapping just above the inner' angle of the eye, at least, in South China. The face is round; they have small hands and feet, and long tapering fingers. The ankles of many of the common boat-women are very neat. 'They are well built and proportioned, but short in stature, especially in the South, where a man of six feet in height is such a rarity as to be nicknamed "Giant."' The average height in the North is a few inches above that in the South; and difference exists as to complexion in the different parts of the empire and between different classes, owing to exposure to the sun and the weather, which falls to the lot of some, and which others escape. This is most strikingly manifest in the skin of the Cantonese boatman, which will be browned all over the body, except round his waist, where, being constantly covered by his rolled-up trousers, it is of a considerably lighter hue. The Swatow fisherman is often swarthy almost to blackness, nor is there a mid-region round his loins of a lighter shade, as he works in the garb of old Adam, minus the fig-leaves. The faces of some of the ladies are fairer, shielded as they are from all exposure, than those of many of the inhabitants of the South of Europe. With a dark skin one scarcely expects to find soft texture, but that of even the common women is soft. To a stranger, newly arrived from Western lands, there appears a remarkable sameness in all the people—all are black-haired, blackeyed, with clean-shaven heads and faces, except the elders, who cultivate their scanty beards, and all exemplifying the same general characteristics—they present so much uniformity to one unaccustomed to such a mass of an unknown and distinct type that the question often presents itself:—How do those who are brought into intimate relationships with them distinguish one from the other? And a ready answer presents itself in what seems to the uninitiated, the analogous case of a shepherd knowing each sheep under his care. A few months' residence and familiarity with the new type shows that amidst the general uniformity there are many points of difference, and a slight appreciation of what constitutes Chinese beauty is occasionally awakened. That these crude opinions of Chinese physical sameness are far from the truth, it needs but to instance the similar opinion held by the Chinese as to ourselvees.

In an examination of Chinese for colour-blindness, 1,200 men and women were tested with these results:—Colour-blind, 20; completely green-blind, 14; completely red-blind, 5; and one partially so. The Chinese are often unable to distinguish between green and blue, their language following suit to a great extent, for there is one word which means both green and blue.

Notwithstanding the relatively insanitary conditions of their life, not a few of the Chinese appear to attain a good old age; the hard life and exposure to which most of the labouring classes are subject age many of them, on the other hand, very soon; especially is this the case with the women, who are scarcely passed the bloom of girlhood before coarse features show the strain on their physical powers.

After this general description of the physical characteristics of the Chinese, we give a scientific account of the Ideal Mongolic type compared with the Ideal Caucasic type, for which we are indebted to Keene's *Asia*, edited by Sir R. Temple:—

—	Ideal Mongolic Type.	Ideal Caucasic Type.
Shape of Head . .	Normally brachycephalic, *i.e.*, round horizontally.	Normally dolichocephalic, *i.e.*, long horizontally.
Facial Angle . .	Prognathous, index Nos. 76 to 68.	Orthognathous, index Nos. 82 to 76.
Features	Square, angular, and flattened.	Rounded off and oval.
Cranial Capacity .	1,200 to 1,300 cubic centimetres.	1,300 to 1,400 cubic centimetres.
Cheek-bones . .	High and prominent.	Low and inconspicuous.
Ears	Large and standing out from the head.	Small, well formed, close to the head.
Mouth	Large, with thick lips.	Small, with bright-red, moderately thin lips.
Nose	Broad, flat, short, and somewhat concave.	Long, narrow, high, straight or somewhat convex—tip projecting beyond the nostrils.
Forehead	Low, receding, narrow.	Straight, broad below, fully developed.
Eye	Small, almond-shaped, oblique upwards and outwards, orbits wide apart, iris black.	Large, round, straight; orbits rather close set; iris normally blue or grey, but very variable.
Chin	Very small and receding.	Full and slightly projecting.
Neck	Short and thick set.	Long, slender, and shapely.
Figure	Squat, angular, heavy, muscular, inclining to obesity.	Symmetrical, slim, active, robust.
Hands and Feet .	Disproportionately small.	Medium-sized or large.
Stature	Below the average—5 ft. to 5 ft. 4 in.	Medium or above the average—5 ft. 4 in. to 5 ft. 9 in.
Complexion . . .	Pale-yellowish, tawny or olive, inclining to a leathery-brown and cinnamon — no red or ruddy tinge.	Fair or white, inclining to brown and swarthy — normally with ruddy tinge.
Hair	Dull-black, long, coarse, stiff, and lank, cylindrical in section.	Long, wavy, and normally light brown, but very variable — glossy, jet-black, flaxen, red, etc., elliptical in section.
Beard	Very scanty or absent.	Full, bushy, often very long.
Eyebrows . . .	Straight and scanty.	Arched and full.
Expression . . .	Heavy, inanimate, monotonously uniform.	Bright, intelligent, infinitely varied.
Temperament . .	Dull, taciturn, morose, lethargic, but fitfully vehement.	Energetic, restless, fiery and poetic.

An ethnological study and comparison of the inhabitants of different parts of China would afford much interest and instruction. Shirokogoroff's researches are too long and technical to quote here. Through the kindness of the Hongkong Government we have been allowed to inspect the books in Victoria Gaol, and we find the following was the height of 1000 Chinese male prisoners (the fractions of inches have been omitted):—

4 feet 6 inches = 1	4 „ 9 „ = 1	4 „ 10 „ = 11	4 „ 11 „ = 17	
5 „ 0 „ = 44	5 „ 1 „ = 77	5 „ 2 „ = 112	5 „ 3 „ = 172	

Height	Number	Height	Number
4 feet 6 inches	= 1	5 feet 4 inches	= 178
4 „ 9 „	= 1	5 „ 5 „	= 164
4 „ 10 „	= 11	5 „ 6 „	= 117
4 „ 11 „	= 17	5 „ 7 „	= 62
5 „ 0 „	= 44	5 „ 8 „	= 28
5 „ 1 „	= 77	5 „ 9 „	= 13
5 „ 2 „	= 112	5 „ 10 „	= 2
5 „ 3 „	= 172	5 „ 11 „	= 1

We discarded from our investigations all under the age of 21 by Chinese reckoning, which is a year or two less than by English computation. but maturity is early attained in a hot climate. Neither does the fact that the measurements are those of prisoners on their admission to gaol militate against them being reliable as average statistics for Chinese in this part of China, as the majority, if not all the prisoners, form a very good sample of Southern Chinese. The great proportion of them are artisans and coolies, and are typical of the whole of their class; a few of the better class of Chinese are also to be found amongst them.

The height of 100 female prisoners was as follows:—

Height	Number	Height	Number
4 feet 6 inches	= 1	5 feet 0 inches	= 27
4 „ 7 „	= 5	5 „ 1 „	= 10
4 „ 8 „	= 4	5 „ 2 „	= 13
4 „ 9 „	= 9	5 „ 3 „	= 5
4 „ 10 „	= 11	5 „ 4 „	= 0
4 „ 11 „	= 14	5 „ 5 „	= 1

The average height of the Chinese is said to be 5 feet 4 inches, while the average of the English is 5 feet 8½ inches.

As regards their mental characteristics, much might be, and has been, written; the latter largely tinctured by the mental media through which the various observers viewed their idiosyncrasies.

One of the most marked peculiarities is their wonderful memory in the way of study. Trained for centuries in this particular groove, the result has been that books are easily learned by heart and repeated from beginning to end without mistake. Their patience, perseverance, and industry are deserving of all praise; no task is considered too trivial, no labour too arduous to engage in. Their politeness, peaceableness, and dread of giving offence are often carried to an extreme. Their economy, credulity, lack of sincerity and sympathy are all characteristics on which page after page might be written.

As has been said of the Japanese, so may it be said equally well of the Chinese:—

'His very politeness may compel him to hide a disagreeable truth, or, at the utmost, to express it in very indirect language. His native tongue, with its elaborate impersonal forms of address and even of command, reflects the whole social sentiments of the people. It abounds in . . . negations, in honorifics to the person addressed, in deprecatory phrases concerning self, or self's belongings.'

These assist the fatal want of veracity so noticeable amongst the Chinese, for it must be confessed that the obligations of truth are not so binding with them as with us. This trait of character is constantly exhibited in the courts of justice. They are, however, not worse than most Orientals in this respect; in fact, they are better than many.

Having thus lightly touched upon a few of the characteristics of this wonderful, little understood, much lauded, as well as much decried people, we will ourselves retire to the background and present a symposium of opinions of residents, authors, statesmen, missionaries, travellers, and others.

'It is an abuse of terms, to say that they are a highly moral people. . . . A morality that forgets one-half of the decalogue must be wonderfully deficient, however complete it may be in the other. . . . I think, however, we may affirm . . . that the moral sense is in many particulars highly refined among them. . . . Respect to parents and elders, obedience to law, chastity, kindness, economy, prudence, and self-possession are the never-failing themes for remark and illustration. . . . The happiness and general prosperity of the Chinese are so conspicuous that they merit a short analysis. Let us see then of what elements they are compounded:—

'(1) An habitual readiness to labour. (2) Frugality in the use of wordly goods. (3) Skill competent to enable the people to turn all advantages to the best account. (4) An exact conception of money's worth.'—*Tradescant Lay.*

'In the Chinese character are elements which in due time must lift her [China] out of the terribly backward position into which she has fallen, and raise her to a rank among the foremost of nations. Another ground of hope . . . lies in the matter-of-fact habits of the Chinese, their want of enthusiasm and dislike of change, which are rather favourable than otherwise to their development as a great community.'—*Wells Williams.*

'The mental capacities of the people are of no inferior order. Their administrative powers are remarkable. Sir Frederick Bruce is reported to have said that "Chinese statesmen were equal to any he ever met in any capital in Europe." . . . Certain it is, they hold their own with our British diplomatists. Chinese merchants cope successfully with our own in all departments of trade; in fact, are gaining ground on them. (See Consul Medhurst's "Report on the Trade of Shanghai," *Blue Book* [China], No. 7, 1870.) . . . Their *literati* are equal to any intellectual task Europeans can set before them. . . . The common people are shrewd, painstaking, and indomitable; and the more I have travelled among them the more have I been impressed with their mental promise, docility, and love of order.

. . . The Chinese have always been the imperial race in the Far East. . . . It is true that at present they are in a most deplorable condition. Their old principles of government are disregarded; the maxims of their classics utterly ignored by the generality of their rulers; rapacity and corruptions pervade every department of the State. . . . Absence of truth, and uprightness and honour,—this is a most appalling void, and, unfortunately, it meets one *in all classes and professions of the people.* I do not refer to money matters, for, as a rule, they stand well in this respect. . . . The Chinese are not naturally an anti-progressive people. They are peculiarly amenable to reason, have no caste, and no powerful religious bias. Their history shows that they have adopted every manifest improvement, which has presented itself, for these many centuries. . . . The truth is, the Chinese have all the mental, moral, and religious instincts of our common nature. . . . The fact that they have preceded us in many of the most important discoveries of modern times, such as the compass. . . . printing, the manufacture of paper, silk, porcelain, etc., proves their inventive genius. . . . They are peaceable and civil to strangers.'—*Williamson.*

Here are a few extracts from older writers:—

'Such Europeans as settle in China, and are eye-witnesses of what passes, are not *surprised* to hear that mothers kill or expose several of their children; nor that parents sell their daughters for a trifle, nor that the empire is full of thieves; and the spirit of avarice universal. They are rather surprised that greater crimes are not heard of during seasons of scarcity. If we deduct the *desires* so natural to the unhappy, the innocence of their habits would correspond well enough with their poverty and hard labour.'—*Premare.*

'The Chinese are so *madly* prejudiced in favour of their own country, manners, and maxims, that they cannot imagine anything, not Chinese, to deserve the least regard.'—*Chavagnac.*

'So unwilling are the Chinese to allow themselves to be surpassed, or that any other people possess that of which they cannot boast, that they fancy resemblances where there are none, and, after striving in vain to find them, they still hope that such there are, and that if there should happen to be none, they are of no importance, or surely they would have been there.'—*Milne.*

'The superiority which the Chinese possess over the other nations of Asia is so decided as scarcely to need the institution of an elaborate comparison. . . . It may be considered as one proof of social advancement on the part of the Chinese, that the civil authority is generally superior to the military, and that letters always rank above arms. . . . The Chinese are bad political economists. . . . The advantageous features of their character, as mildness, docility, industry, peaceableness, subordination, and respect for the aged, are accompanied by the vices of specious insincerity, falsehood, with mutual distrust and jealousy. . . . The superior character of the Chinese as *colonists* in regard to intelligence, industry, and general sobriety, must be derived from their education, and from the influence of something good in the national system. . . . The comparatively low estimation in which *mere* wealth is held, is a considerable moral advantage on the side of the Chinese. . . . Poverty is no reproach among them. . . . The peaceful and prudential character of the people may be traced to the influence and authority of age. . . . The Chinese frequently get the better of Europeans in a discussion, by imperturbable coolness and gravity. . . . It is the discipline to which they are subject from earliest childhood, and the habit of controlling their ruder passions, that render crimes of violence so unfrequent among them. . . . Hereditary rank without merit is of little merit to the possessor.'—*Davis.*

'As a direct refusal to any request would betray a want of good breeding, every proposal finds their immediate acquiescence: they promise without hesitation, but generally disappoint by the invention of some slight pretence or plausible objection: they have no proper sense of the obligations of truth.'—*Barrow.*

'The Chinese . . . are in general of a mild and humane disposition, but violent and vindictive when offended."—*Staunton.*

'Genius and originality are regarded as hostile and incompatible elements.'—*Gillespie.*

And again some extracts from later writers:—

'Ingenuity is a gift largely bestowed upon the Chinaman; it is indeed one of his most marked characteristics,—but it is ingenuity of that peculiar kind which works with very slender materials. . . . Almost every Chinaman is, by a kind of natural instinct, good both at cooking and at bargaining.'—*Cobbold.*

'This mysterious race. . . . Hardworking, frugal, and orderly when their secret societies are kept under due control, they are admirable and trustworthy men of business, while as artisans their industry is only exceeded by their skill and versatility.'—*Griffin.*

'The love of antiquity is inborn in the Chinese, they live in the past. . . . To them the past is not a mass of musty records, filled with the suffocating odours of decay, as it appears often to us, but a rich treasure-house fragrant with the aroma of purest wisdom and noblest example. . . . They are exclusive to the extremest degree. . . . Conservatism has been carried to such an extreme that the whole nation has become fossilised. . . . Closely connected with this spirit of exclusiveness is an overweening pride and absurd conceit in their own superiority, and an unreasoning hatred of everything foreign. . . . Taking the people as a whole, their fundamental qualities of industry, stability, and readiness to submit to authority, contain the promise of cheering results in the future.'—*Henry.*

'One of the most remarkable national peculiarities of the Chinese is their extraordinary addiction to letters, the general prevalence of literary habits among the middling and higher orders, and the very honourable pre-eminence which from the most remote period has been universally conceded to that class which is exclusively devoted to literary pursuits. . . . I have left the country with the conviction that the Chinese nation, as a whole, is a much less vicious one than, as a consequence of opinions formed from a limited and unfair field of observation, it has been customary to represent it; further, that the lower orders of the people generally are better conducted, more sober and industrious, and, taken altogether, intellectually superior to the corresponding class of our own countrymen.'—*Rennie.*

'I find here a steady adherence to the traditions of the past, a sober devotion to the calls arising in the various relations of life, an absence of shiftlessness, an honest and, at least, somewhat earnest grappling with the necessities and difficulties which beset men in their humbler stages of progress, a capacity to moralise withal, and an enduring sense of right and wrong. These all form what must be considered an essentially satisfactory basis and groundwork of national character. Among the people there is practical sense; among the gentry, scholarly instincts, the desire for advancement, the disposition to work for it with earnestness and constancy. Amongst the rulers, a sense of dignity, breadth of view, considering their information, and patriotic feeling. Who will say that such a people have not a future more wonderful even than their past.'—*Seward.*

'The moral character of the Chinese is a book written in strange letters, which are more complex and difficult for one of another race, religion, and language to decipher than their own singularly-compounded word-symbols. In the same individual, virtues and vices, apparently incompatible, are placed side by side. Meekness, gentleness, docility, industry, contentment, cheerfulness, obedience to superiors, dutifulness to parents, and reverence for the aged, are in one and the same person, the companions of insincerity, lying, flattery, treachery, cruelty, jealousy, ingratitude, avarice, and distrust of others. The Chinese are a weak and timid people, and in consequence, like all similarly constituted races, they seek a natural refuge in deceit and fraud. But examples of moral inconsistency are by no means confined to the Chinese, and I fear that sometimes too much emphasis is laid on the dark side of their character, . . . as if it had no parallel amongst more enlightened nations. Were a native of the empire, with a view of acquiring a thorough knowledge of the English people, to make himself familiar with the records of our police and other law courts, the transactions that take place in what we call the "commercial world," and the scandals of what we term "society," he would probably give his countrymen at home a very one-sided and depreciatory account of this nation.'—*Gray.*

'I find the Chinese most polite. . . . The only thing no man can accuse the Chinese of is love of change.'—*Mrs. Gray.*

'The earnest simplicity and seriousness with which an amiable and lettered man in China will sit and propound the most preposterous and fantastic theories that ever entered a human brain, and the profound unconsciousness he shows of the nonsense he is talking, affect one very curiously. . . . There are few things in which the Chinese do not claim pre-eminence, and it is this habit of self-complacency which renders them so very much averse to being enlightened on those points on which they habitually are found wanting. The belief in their own infallibility cannot but be a standing obstacle to the progress of the people in all departments where it prevails, and the difficulty of getting a Chinaman to acknowledge that he is beaten in an argument is but another phase of the same phenomenon. It is a sufficient answer, for him, that, however useless or hurtful a given practice may be, it is the "custom" of the country; and the belief that all the customs which have descended from generation to generation are, for that very reason, incapable of improvement, renders him a very hopeless subject to deal with. . . . There are few things more amusing, and at the same time more exasperating, to a European than the utter confusion of thought which characterises the Chinese as a race. . . . There seems a looseness of reasoning; a want of consecutiveness, in the mental process of the Chinese which argues an inherent defect in their constitutions.'—*Balfour.*

'The truth is that a man of good physical and intellectual qualities, regarded merely as an economic factor, is turned out cheaper by the Chinese than by any other race. He is deficient in the higher moral qualities, individual trustworthiness, public-spirit, sense of duty, and active courage—a group of qualities perhaps best rendered in our language by the word manliness; but in the humbler moral qualities of patience, mental and physical, and perseverance in labour, he is unrivalled.'—*Bourne.*

'John Chinaman is a most temperate creature. . . . During the whole course of my many years' residence in the country, I do not remember to have seen a dozen instances of actual drunkenness. . . . They are a sociable people amongst themselves, and . . . their courtesies are of a most laboured and punctilious character. . . . The Chinese are essentially a reading people. . . . The Chinese have not, it is true, that delicate perception of what the claims of truth and good faith demand, which is so highly esteemed among us Westerners, but they know and prize both characteristics, and practical illustrations thereof are constantly observable in their relations one with another, and with foreigners. . . . Honesty . . . is by no means a rare virtue with the Chinese. . . . As regards the question of courage, again it must be admitted that the Chinese possess more of the quality than they have hitherto had credit for. . . . Both kindliness and cruelty, gentleness and ferocity, have each its place in the Chinese character, and the sway which either emotion has upon their minds depends very much upon the associations by which they are for the moment surrounded. When in their own quiet homes, pursuing undisturbed the avocations to which they have been accustomed, there are no more harmless, well-intentioned, and orderly people. They actually appear to maintain order as if by common consent, independent of all surveillance or interference on the part of the executive. But let them be brought into contact with bloodshed and rapine, or let them be roused by oppression or fanaticism, and all that is evil in their disposition will at once assert itself, inciting them to the most fiendish and atrocious acts of which human nature has been found capable. . . . There is no more intelligent and manageable creature than the Chinaman, as long as he is treated with justice and firmness, and his prejudices are, to a reasonable extent, humoured.'—*Medhurst.*

'There exist no more honourable, law-abiding and industrious citizens than the Chinese.'—*Earl of Kintore.*

Here are opinions then as diverse as possible. What more pat than the following:—'The Chinese must be a strange people, from the varying accounts which are given of them by different observers. They are over-estimated in some things and undervalued in others, misunderstood in most.'—What is the truth? We believe it to consist in a true mean. If a man or woman will view this people with a mental calmness, not on the one hand carried away with too great an enthusiasm—a fault easily committed, owing to their wonderful antiquity and many good points in their character—and on the other hand, if prejudice is resolutely banished, their good points will be seen, while their failings will also be noticed.

References.—Smith, *Chinese Characteristics;* Werner, *Descriptive Sociology—Chinese;* Shirokogoroff, *Anthropology of Northern China.*

CHINESE, PROFESSORS OF, ABROAD.—There have been Professorships of Chinese at a few of the leading Universities in England for some years. On Dr. Legge's retirement from Hongkong, a number of his friends and admirers subscribed toward the foundation of a Chair of Chinese at Oxford, with the proviso that he should be the first occupant. This was in 1875 or 1876. He held it for many years, until his death in 1897. The income is about £95 a year. The post was later (1898 or 1899 to 1915) filled by Professor Bullock, and after his death by Professor Soothill.

Prior to this there was a Professorship of Chinese in King's College, London, Mr. Fearon (1847) and then Professor Summers (1853) taking the classes. Professor Douglas and Rev. G. Owen were later occupants of the Chair. A number of years ago Mr. Kidd was Professor of Chinese at University College, London, and later the late Professor Terrien de Lacouperie, and Mr. Geo. Brown (1901).

A Professorship of Chinese was established in 1888 at Cambridge, with Sir Thomas Wade and later (1897) Professor H. A. Giles as Professors, the latter having filled some similar appointment at Aberdeen for a short time previously.

Things Chinese

Professor E. H. Parker has been Reader in Chinese at University College, Liverpool, for many years, and since 1901 has occupied the position of Professor of Chinese at Owen's College, Manchester. This Chair was established tentatively by the Lancashire County Council, by special grant and subscriptions made toward it, in view of the large trade between the county and China.

'The University of London established a special department, called the Department of Practical Chinese, the objects of which are:—

'(1) To provide courses of instruction in modern Chinese, organised with a view to the needs of (*a*) persons engaged, or about to engage, in business in China as clerks, merchants, etc.; (*b*) officers employed, or about to be employed, in the Diplomatic, Consular, Military, and Customs Services in or connected with China; (*c*) civil railway, and mining engineers about to be employed in China, and other classes to whom a knowledge of colloquial Chinese is important.

(2) To encourage study and research in connection with modern Chinese questions and existing Chinese institutions, etc.

'Mr. George Brown, late British Consul at Kiukiang, will be appointed Director of the department, and be directly responsible to the University for its organisation. The course of instruction will be given by Mr. Brown, assisted by one or more native Chinese teachers, and such other persons as it may be desirable to appoint. The University will provide suitable accommodation for the work of the department at the University Buildings, South Kensington.

'The China Association has undertaken to guarantee a sum of £500 a year for five years for the expenses of the department, and to take steps to raise a fund for its permanent endowment.' In 1915 the School of Oriental Studies was established in Finsbury circus as part of the London Institution, and a chair of Chinese endowed.

M. Papov, late Consul-General and First Dragoman of the Russian Mission at Peking, is the Professor of Chinese Language and Literature at the University of St. Petersburg (afterwards Petrograd and Leningrad). Later Professors were Ivanov and Alexiev. There is also an Oriental Institute at Vladivostock.

Public classes for the study of Chinese were started in Lyons in 1900, the Chamber of Commerce of that city and the Government of Indo-China assisting. The Professor was Mr. Courant.

M. Vissière was the Professor at L'Ecole des Langues Orientales in Paris. The Professor in Le Collége de France at Paris from 1893 until his death was M. Chavannes. Mr. Schlegel was Professor of Chinese at Leyden, and, after his death, M. de Groot until his resignation shortly before his death. There are Chairs for Chinese at a dozen European Universities, *e.g.* Berlin, Hamburg, Vienna, etc. One was founded at Hanoi in 1901.

In the United States there are several; the late Dr. S. Wells Williams having filled one at Yale for a number of years; Mr. Fryer, late of Shanghai, occupied a similar position at Berkeley, California; and a donation of $100,000 was made for a Chinese Professorship at Columbia University, New York. Dr. Hirth has filled the Chair since 1902.

CHOP-STICKS.—Lansdell thus describes these useful adjuncts to the Chinese table:—

'Chop-sticks are a pair of cylindrical [square or squarish at the holding part] rods, rather longer [they are really a good deal longer] and not quite so thick as lead pencils, which are held between the thumb and fingers of the right hand and are used as tongs to take the food and carry it to the mouth—an operation by no means easy to the unpractised.'

No knives appear at a Chinese table, the food being already carved and cut up into pieces either large enough for a mouthful, or so well cooked that the chop-sticks can easily separate them, or, again, the chop-sticks lift the small piece of quail or duck to the mouth and a bite is taken off. With rice, the edge of the bowl is put to the under lip, and the chop-sticks shovel it into the mouth, along with the tiny bits of meat and vegetables that have already been picked up by them and placed on the top of the rice. To our Western ideas, every one using their own chop-sticks to dip into the dishes on the table is not pleasant; nor is the use again of the earthenware spoons in the soups and broths so liked by the Chinese, to ladle out from the central dish or big bowl into one's own little bowl, to our taste either. Tiny wire forks are used for the sweetmeats at the table.

Chop-sticks are of ivory, bone, bamboo, etc. The Chinese name, *k'uai tzŭ,* means hasteners, the English form being derived from the Cantonese pronunciation of the word *chi,* quick.

CICADA.—This noisy insect is very common. 'Their strident noise is overpowering, and most annoying to invalids. The bodies measure about 3 inches in length.' They are caught with some species of bird-lime, made of the ashes of the China fir, glutinous cooked rice, and water. This is stuck on to the end of a bamboo pole, which is then pushed up amongst the branches of the trees, and the insect caught by its sticky nature. Chinese boys play with cicadas, holding them in their hands, or tying them to a piece of string.

The cast skin of the cicada (töü shim) [*t'iao chia*] is used as medicine for convulsions, and fever in children. It is boiled in water with a creeper called ngaú t'ang [*kou t'êng*], the hooked creeper (nauclea sinensis, Oliv.), and the rush, which is used as a lamp-wick, and sometimes in serious cases a little bit of sycee, about a mace in weight, is put into the water. These are boiled together for half an hour, and then the water is forced down the child's throat, as, being bitter, the child will not drink it willingly.

The cicada in one stage of his existence passes two years underground. It is only the male which is able to give vent to its passion of love in the curious ear-arresting, noisy, strident, loudly sibilant, and distracting song, though song is a word too suggestive of harmony to be applied to the scissors-grinding cicada. It sounds like the loud forceful emision of the two consonants s and z, viz., sz——sz, and this is continued for half a minute or a minute, and having been raised to a loud crescendo, it ends abruptly with a 'shish-jick,' to be started again after a short interval. The horrors of a sultry summer day are increased to fatigued and exhausted man by the intermittingly continued songs of half a dozen or a dozen cicadas, ensconced in the neighbouring trees. The musical apparatus consists 'of two membranes over air-tubes in' the 'throat, with hollow-sounding cavities behind each, which increase the volume of its notes. . . . Cicadas are neither crickets, locusts, nor grasshoppers.' Their bodies look as if headless, and are blunt. The male lives a short time, leaving the female, who gorges herself on green leaves, and finally lays many eggs on twigs and branches. The larvæ burst from their eggs, and burrow through the tree to the ground, eating as they go, and remain for two years as chrysalides.

CITIES.—Cities were divided into three classes in China: provincial cities, prefectorial, or departmental cities, and district cities, but the prefectorial office was abolished after the Revolution of 1911. The fact of them being capitals and the seats of Government doubtless constitutes them cities. Every city is protected with a wall (or walls), except Hü-i Hien in Anhui, the extent and size being conditioned by its grade, or rank, as above; but some have been demolished, wholly or partially, of late years. The largest cover within their circumference a considerable extent of ground, which is not all thickly covered with houses, but even contains market-gardens, etc., as well as private parks attached to the yamêns, or official residences. In fact, a bird's-eye view of a native city from its walls is often very picturesque, with the fine trees adding grace to the mass of red-tiled, low-lying houses, broken every now and then by a pagoda, or the lofty buildings above the city gates.

The walls round the Tartar and Chinese cities of Peking (taken as one city) are a little over 20 miles in circumference. The city proper in Canton is about 6 miles round. One of the smallest and most recent cities in China is probably that of Kowlung, now in British territory.

Many cities have large suburbs lying outside the walls. Cities have, however, not a monopoly of walls in China, as robbers, and the disturbed state of many parts of the country, cause even villages to be walled and surrounded with moats.

A cathedral is not one of the constituent factors in determining a place to be a city, but every city has one temple to Confucius, at least; and it often happens that a city is not only a district capital, but also that of a department, and sometimes that of a province as well. In such cases there must be a temple for each: so in Canton, which is the capital for two districts, one department and one province, there are consequently no less than four Confucian temples.

Besides this, at all events in a large city, there is a City Temple to the God of the City. There were also examination halls in most cities. Many of these have now been demolished.

CLAN.—This division of the people in China is analogous to that of the Scotch clan in many respects, and is productive of feud and disaster to themselves and others sometimes, as well as of protection at other times to those belonging to the same clan, as a few generations ago was the case among the Highland clans of Scotland. The nucleus round which the clan gathers is the ancestral temple and worship; here are the headquarters for all who are descendants of a remote ancestor. Genealogies are kept, often with the greatest care, in which are noted all the migrations of the family; and so particular are the Chinese with regard to this point, that on the tomb-stones, in some places, are put the numbers of the generations since the family came to that country-side.

In many villages all the inhabitants belong to one clan, just as in the Highlands of Scotland one part of the country will be found almost entirely peopled by one clan alone. As in China the unit of the population or nation is not the individual, but the family, it may be easily understood of what paramount importance the clan is; and it is one of the greatest disgraces possible for a man to be disowned or put out of the clan, even if it be only temporarily. It is worse, of course, to be punished for a generation, and worst of all if the punishment is for ever —that is to say, if his branch of the family is excluded from the clan for ever.

Disputes often take place between members of different clans, and lead to quarrels, reprisals, and fights, into which the whole clan is dragged; and eventually, the soldiery, after perhaps some lives have been lost on both sides, are sent to put a stop to the internecine strife; in fact these petty wars are waged so fiercely, that in some instances they approach the vindictiveness displayed in the Italian vendetta.

It should, however, be observed that the system of clans is more marked in the South of China, and most especially so in the Kwang-tung and Kwang-si provinces.

The secret societies, especially in the Straits Settlements, take their rise in the clan system to a great extent.

References.—Chinese Recorder and Missionary Journal, vol. ix. Nos. 4 and 5; Williams, *Middle Kingdom,* i. 432 *et seq; Chinese Repository,* iv. 411.

CLASSICS.—See LITERATURE.

CLIMATE.—In a land of such vast dimensions, it may readily be understood that the climate varies with each part of the country, and almost any variety of climate may be found in different parts of China. The extremes of cold and heat are not only found in the extremes of the North and South, but in the North are even found together; for China, like the eastern sea-board of the Northern States of America, has a winter in the North approaching an Arctic one for severity, while the summer heat is tropic in its intensity, even greater for a short period than it is in many parts far South.

In some places the atmosphere is saturated with moisture during a large part of the year, while in other regions, except in the rainy season, the air is dry and clear.

The climate at Newchwang is more moderate than at some of the ports further down the coast. It is said that both Chefoo and Japan 'have a much higher average temperature . . . ; the thermometer rarely goes above 88° and the nights are always cool: often chilly.' The climate of Chefoo has been described as 'scarcely different from that of New York, Boston, or Edinburgh.'

The extremes of range in Peking are 120° and 20° below zero Fahrenheit. The rainfall is generally lower than 16 inches in the year, but little snow falls, and it does not remain on the ground more than a few days; the rivers are locked in ice for three months. As the heat increases, sand and dust is blown about with great force, forming dust-storms. September and October are the two most delightful months at Peking.

The summer heat of Wei-hai-wei is thus described:—

'It is a cooler place than Japan, *i.e.*, the ports in Japan where the fleet goes. Our maximum heat this summer has been about 87° in the shade, and this only on one or two days. For a month or so it ranged about 82° in the hottest part of the day, cooler at nights, and now and then a drop of 8° to 10° in the day. And this has been, in that matter, an average summer. On Liükŭngtao, cricket and other games have, during the whole time, been freely indulged in. It is certainly a cooler place to spend August and September in than Chefoo, and in time Wei-hai-wei may take away much of the popularity of that place as a summer resort.'

Of Ningpo it has been said that the winters may be compared to the winters in Paris, and the summers for a short season, to those of Calcutta. The climate is very damp, the ground being marshy, and the extremes are greater than at Shanghai. The range of the thermometer is from 24° to 107°, and a fall or rise of 20° in two hours is not unusual.

In Shanghai the great heat, while it lasts, is very trying, but fortunately it is not of long duration.

The riverine ports are very hot in summer: Kiukiang, lying in a hollow and being screened from the southern (summer) breeze by the Kuling mountains, gets the name of being 'the hottest place in all China'; the heat in the month of August there is dreaded, for there is 'a succession of cloudless and intensely hot and oppressive weather.' At the end of July, 1892, the thermometer was at 102° in the shade. It even reached 104° Fahrenheit on the 13th, 14th, 15th and 18th August, 1900, and 24° on the 9th January of the same year. It is also very hot in Nanking in July and August. These hot dog-days last for about thirty days, but, after they are over, the nights get cooler. As an instance of the degree of heat experienced at such times we may mention that at the end of July, 1892, the thermometer kept pretty regular at 96°. Towards the end of July, 1892, the thermometer, at Hankow, at midnight, registered 97°.

Of the West of China a recent writer says.—

'Rains are frequent, and heavy clouds cover the heavens three-fourths of the year; and, in absence of clouds, a smoky mist veils the earth from the piercing rays of the sun. The climate is equable, and even the summer, although long and severely hot in July and August, is modified by frequent showers. . . . The winters are very mild; while frost is seldom seen, and snow is almost unknown, except upon the mountains. Experience shows the climate to be fairly' healthy, 'and no more trying than that of Central China.'

The climate of Amoy has been described as 'delightful.' But the word 'delightful' must be taken as comparing it with the climate of some other parts of China less fortunately situated. The thermometer ranges from 40° to 96°. For example, during three months in that port in the summer of 1889, the temperature was at 93° for a day or two; the heat was intense, but fortunately it was a dry heat. This dry heat in Amoy is generally moderated by a fresh sea-breeze which springs up nearly every day in the course of the forenoon and dies down in the evening. The heat during the night is very great, until the sea-breeze, rising with the tide, slightly cools the atmosphere.

At Swatow the heat is great in summer, ranging nearly as high as at Amoy. During June, 1892, the thermometer was between 90° and 92½°; but, as in Amoy, sea-breezes spring up and make the heat more bearable, while at Double Island, at the entrance to the estuary on which Swatow is situated, the evenings are cool in summer, though the days are hot.

The heat at the three cities of Hongkong, Canton, and Macao, is of long continuance, but not of so excessive a character as further up the coast, where its duration is shorter. In Canton, the thermometer ranges from about 40° or 50° to 88° or thereabouts, and it rarely rises higher or falls lower. The sea-air moderates the climate at Macao and Hongkong. The rainfall of the latter place is greater than at Macao and Canton, and occasionally attains the extraordinary figure of 30 inches in 24 hours, the annual mean for 21 years being over 86 inches; for 1891 it was very abundant, the total for the twelve months being 117.30. Drought occurs in some seasons, and rain does not fall for months to any appreciable extent. The climate in Hongkong in summer is often of a hot, muggy nature, and while it lasts, harder to bear than a dry heat of even higher temperature. In the mountain-sheltered town, and on the lower levels, the thermometer will rarely rise higher than 88° and 89° though it very occasionally registers, on two or three days, 93° in the hottest part of Queen's Road, while on the Peak levels, free to the sea-breezes, and cooled by the high elevation of from 1,500 to 1,800 feet, the mercury falls from 4° to 10° lower, according to the season of the year, the greatest difference between the two levels being in summer. These higher levels, are, however, subject to mountain mist and fog. Fogs rarely visit Macao. The winter months in these three ports form the most delightful season of all the year, especially is this the case in October, November, and December, and even in January. Clear cool weather, with Italian skies, provides the beau ideal of existence. The Peak climate is said to be even finer than that of Chefoo—one of the sanitaria for foreign residents in the North of China.

The climate of China, especially in the North, is also said to have moderated considerably from what it was some centuries or thousands of years ago. On the other hand, the reckless denudation of the hills of wood and forest, by the inhabitants, has doubtless had a considerable effect in increasing the dryness and parched aspect of everything during certain seasons of the year in China. It has been noticed that, in Hongkong, since extensive tree-planting has been carried on, the summers appear to be somewhat cooler.

The mere range of the thermometer does not form a fair criterion, in this land of the heat, of the way in which the temperature affects the human frame. Humidity and other considerations have to be taken into account.

In the South of China the climate seems adapted, as a rule, for children of foreign parents up to the age of eight or ten, but after that they are inclimed to shoot up like hot-house plants, and require a more bracing air. The climate in China gets the blame of much that should be laid to indiscretions in diet, and careless exposure to the sun, or neglect of a fair share of exercise. If all these points are carefully attended to, a man or woman may, and often does, with of course some exceptions, enjoy very good health. Some constitutions appear unable to stand the climate, while occasionally others thrive better than in their own lands.

The Chinese, as a race, are physically weaker than the English, but this should not all be laid to the account of the climate; insanitary surroundings, ignorance of the laws of health, and other causes also having a share in it. Generally, however, with the greater use of athletics, knowledge of medicine, observance of cleanliness, etc., there has been improvement in recent years.

COCKROACH (*Blatta orientalis*).—'This disgusting insect' is found in large numbers, especially in storerooms and sideboards. It is very destructive, eating holes in coats, trousers, and dresses where a stain of food may have attracted them, and nibbling the edges of shirt-cuffs and collars, so that they soon get ragged, trailing over dishes in the pantry, etc. With books, they are especially annoying, staining the covers of cloth-bound ones as if spots of rain had fallen on them; they are extremely fond of some colours—books bound in red and blue suffer most as a rule, the whole covers being stained with them. (See INSECTS). Some of the big active onces are very vigorous and rapid in their flight about a room at night, and annoying, especially to nervous ladies, though, except for the unpleasantness, they do no actual bodily harm as a rule in China. The forcible application of the sole of a shoe seems to be the most effective means of exterminating these pests.

Cockroaches are pounded up, and an infusion of them with boiling water is made in the same way as tea is infused. The water is then given to children suffering from fever.

CONFUCIUS AND CONFUCIANISM.—One feels a certain amount of difficulty in approaching such a vast subject, for Confucianism is so entwined and blended with all that concerns China, that it is hard to know where to begin or where to leave off. We will simply preface our account by saying that Confucianism is a system of philosophy and ceremonial observances to which its founder and followers ascribe the highest possibilities, if carried out rigidly and faithfully to every jot and tittle. Its originator was *par excellence* the sage of China.

Confucius's father 'was a military officer eminent for his commanding stature, his great bravery, and immense strength.' The birth (552 B.C.) of the sage has been surrounded by mythical legends. 'From his childhood he showed ritualistic tendencies,' and 'delighted to play at the arrangement of sacrificial vessels and at postures of ceremony.' He 'bent his mind to learning.' He married young, his experience of the married state not being a happy one, nor did he appear to bestow much affection on his son. Confucius early took public service in the State, holding different offices at different times, such as Keeper of the Stores of Grain, Guardian of the Public Fields and Lands, Magistrate, Assistant Superintendent of Works, and Minister of Crime; and applied his principles to the government with the most signal success.

These appointments were not all held in succession, but were interspersed and followed by years spent in imparting instruction to disciples (at one time as many as 3,000), in gaining knowledge himself, and in the compilation and editing of books, as well as in journeyings amongst the different petty States into which the China of that time was divided, in the hope that the rulers would give him the opportunity of putting his principles of government to the test, when, such confidence had he in them, that he was convinced that, instead of anarchy and confusion, peace and harmony would reign supreme. He died, (479 B.C.) feeling that he was unappreciated, at the age of seventy-two. His disciples had the highest admiration for him, and exhausted attributes in the expression of it.

The best title which has ever been bestowed on him is that of 'The Throneless King.'

'Probably no man has been so contemned during his lifetime, and at the same time so worshipped by posterity, as Confucius. In both extremes there has been some exaggeration. His standard of morality was high, and his doctrines were pure. Had he, therefore, had an opportunity of exercising authority, it could but have resulted in good to an age when the notions of right and wrong were strangely confused, and when both public and private morality were at the lowest ebb. On the other hand, it is difficult to understand the secret of the extraordinary influence he has gained over posterity, and the more the problem is studied the more incomprehensible does it become,' when viewed from a European standpoint. 'His system of philosophy is by no means complete, and it lacks life (if we may venture to say so), in face of the fact that it has supplied the guiding principles, which have actuated the performance of all that is great and noble in the life of China for more than twenty centuries.'

In is impossible in the short space of this article to give a digest of the doctrines of the sage. We will content ourselves with giving a summary of the essential points as adapted to the requirements of modern everyday Chinese life by the great Emperor K'ang Hi:—

'1. Esteem most highly filial piety and brotherly submission, in order to give due prominence to the social relations.

'2. Behave with generosity to the branches of your kindred, in order to illustrate harmony and benignity.

'3. Cultivate peace and concord in your neighbourhoods, in order to prevent quarrels and litigations.

'4. Recognise the importance of husbandry and the culture of the mulberry-tree, in order to ensure sufficiency of clothing and food.

'5. Show that you prize moderation and economy, in order to prevent the lavish waste of your means.

'6. Make much of the colleges and seminaries, in order to make correct the practice of the scholars.

'7. Discountenance and banish strange doctrines, in order to exalt the correct doctrine.

'8. Describe and explain the laws, in order to warn the ignorant and obstinate.

'9. Exhibit clearly propriety and yielding courtesy, in order to make manners and customs good.

'10. Labour diligently at your proper callings, in order to give settlement to the aims of the people.

'11. Instruct sons and younger brothers, in order to prevent them from doing what is wrong.

'12. Put a stop to false accusations, in order to protect the honest and the good.

'13 Warn against sheltering deserters, in order to avoid being involved in their punishment.

'14. Promptly and fully pay your taxes, in order to avoid the urgent requisition of your quota.

'15. Combine in hundreds and tithings, in order to put an end to thefts and robbery.

'16. Study to remove resentments and angry feelings, in order to show the importance due to the person and life.'

These, with commentaries, were until recently, read to the people on the 1st and 15th of the month.

Divine honours were paid to the sage by the Emperor twice a year, and by every school-boy throughout the length and breadth of the land. The ceremonial has been continued by the President of the Republic.

Confucius is generally represented in the temples to him by a wooden tablet with his name and titles on it, but in some cases there is an image of him. There is a temple in every district city and one in every departmental city, consequently there are three in Canton: in two of these there is a tablet, in the third, an image. In the district city of Kit Yöng [Chieh-yang], in the Ch'ao Chau Department, there used to be both an image and a tablet. The image represents a sage as black as a negro, for he is described as being of a swarthy complexion. Besides Confucius himself, his disciples, to the extent of some hundred and seventy, are also honoured by images or tablets in the immediate presence of 'The Perfect Sage' himself, or in the precincts of the same temple that he occupies, and they are likewise worshipped.

References.—Douglas, *Confucianism and Taoism;* Legge, *Religions of China; Imperial Confucianism;* and *The Chinese Classics;* Du Bose, *The Three Religions of China;* Faber, *Digest of the Doctrines of Confucius,* and a review of the latter in the *China Review,* i. 260; Alexander, *Confucius, The Great Teacher;* Watters, *A Guide to the Tablets in a Temple of Confucius;* Parker, *Studies in Chinese Religion; Variétés Sinologiques,* Vols. xiii and xiv.

CORMORANT FISHING.—The Chinese have long used cormorants for fishing purposes; for the journal of the friar Odoric (A.D. 1286-1331) mentions this strange method of fishing, and it is largely carried on at the present day in some parts of China. To show the admirable adaptation of this bird for the pursuit, we quote from a lengthy article in *The Encyclopædia Americana*:—

'The cormorant is most admirably adapted for swimming, . . . having the great toe united to the others by a common membrane, . . . yet they are among the very few web-footed birds capable of perching on the branches of trees, which they do with great ease and security.' Cormorants, of which there are quite a number of species distributed over different parts of the world, are closely allied to the pelicans in conformation and habits. They 'are very voracious feeders. . . . They dive with great force, and swim under water with such celerity, that few fish can escape them. . . . Should a cormorant seize a fish in any other way than by the head, he rises to the surface, and, tossing the fish into the air, adroitly catches it head foremost as it falls so that the fins, being properly laid against the fish's sides, cause no injury to the throat of the bird.

Their use is not confined to one part of the country. Amongst other places where they may be found at work may be mentioned the North River above Canton, the river above Ch'ao-Chau-fu and the river above Foochow. The following passage from Miss Gordon-Cumming's *Travels in China*, describes this method of fishing:—

'The simplest form of fishery is when a poor fisherman has constructed for himself a raft consisting only of from four to eight bamboos lashed together. On this he sits poised (crowned with a large straw hat), and before him are perched half-a-dozen of these odd uncanny-looking, black birds waiting his command. The cage in which they live and the basket in which he stores his fish complete his slender stock-in-trade. The marvel is how he contrives to avoid overturning his frail raft. Sometimes several fishers form partnership, and start co-operative business. They invest in a shallow punt, and a regiment of perhaps twenty or more of these solemn, sombre birds sit on perches at either end of the punt, each having a hempen cord fastened round the throat just below the pouch, to prevent its swallowing any fish it may catch. Then, at a given signal, all the cormorants glide into the water, apparently well aware of the disadvantage of scaring their prey.

'Their movements below the surface are very swift and graceful as they dart in pursuit of a fish or an eel, and giving it a nip with their strong hooked beak, swallow it, and continue hunting. Sometimes they do not return to the surface till they have secured several fish, and their capacious pouch is quite distended, and sometimes the tail of a fish protrudes from their gaping bill. Then they return to the surface, and at the bidding of the keepers disgorge their prey, one by one, till the pouch is empty, when they again receive the signal to dive, and resume their pursuit.

'Some birds are far more expert than others, and rarely fail to secure their prize, but sometimes they catch a fish, or more often an eel, so awkwardly that they cannot contrive to swallow it, and in the effort to arrange this difficulty, the victim manages to escape. If one bird catches a large and troublesome fish, two or three of its friends occasionally go to the aid of their comrade, and help him to despatch it. Such brotherly kindness is, however, by no means invariable, and sometimes, when a foolish young bird has captured a fish, the old hands pursue and rob him of his prize. At other times a bird fails in its trick, and after staying under water for a very long period, comes up quite crestfallen without a fish.

'When the birds are tired the strap is removed from their throat and they are rewarded with a share of the fish, which they catch as it is thrown to them. It is reckoned a good day's fishing if eighteen or twenty cormorants capture a dollar's worth of fish; and as so many birds represent about half-a-dozen owners, it is evidently not a very lucrative business.

'The birds are quite domestic, having all been reared in captivity. Curiously enough, the mothers are so careless that they cannot be trusted to rear their own young; and furthermore, the said young are so sensitive to cold weather that only the four or five eggs laid in early spring are considered worth hatching, as only these can be reared in the warm summer. They are taken from the cormorant and given to a hen, who apparently must be colour-blind, as she calmly accepts these green eggs in lieu of her own. She is not, however, subjected to the misery of seeing her nurslings take to the water, as they are at once removed from her care, when after a month's incubation, the poor little fledglings make their appearance. They are then transferred to baskets which are kept in a warm corner; the young birds being buried in cotton wool and fed with pellets of raw fish and bean-curd.

'When they are two months old their nursery days are over, and the sorrows of education must begin. They are therefore offered for sale, a female bird being valued at from 3s. to 5s., and a male bird at double the price. This difference is due to the superior strength of the latter, which enables it to capture larger fish. Thenceforth the professional trainer takes them in hand; and fastening a string to one leg, he drives them into the water and throws small live fishes, which they are expected to catch. They are taught to go and return subject to different calls on a whistle, obedience being enforced by the persuasive strokes of a bamboo—the great educational factor in China! When thoroughly trained, a male bird is valued at from 20s. to 30s., and its fishing career is expected to continue for five years, after which it will probably become old and sulky.'

Cormorant fishing was practised in both France and England in the seventeenth century; and an attempt to revive it has lately been made in England.

COSMETICS.—These were largely used by the Chinese, no girl or woman above the very menial classes being considered as dressed without a plentiful application of rouge to the lips and patches of it on the cheeks. A sign, even if others were wanting, that the present race of Chinese have descended to the warmer regions of the south of China from a climate where rosy cheeks and ruby lips were natural. No art was displayed in applying the rouge, nor was concealment ever dreamt of. At the first glance, a Chinese lady was seen to be painted by the coarse big daub on each side of her face. On festivals and gala occasions it was even more freely applied. White powder was also used to render their dark faces more fair. The lavish use of cosmetics spoils whatever complexion a Chinese lady may possess. Within the last few years, however, a change has come over the fashion; a little line across the lower lip in the middle serves for the lips in the way of rouge, if rouged at all, and the cheeks are now left to their natural colour, as a rule.

COTTON.—The introduction of cotton as a textile plant into China is an interesting subject. 'The art of spinning and weaving cotton, as far as Central China is concerned,' is traced to 'a lady of high rank, who introduced the art B.C. 400.' It has been supposed that the ancient Shü King [*Shu ching*] (The Book of History) mentions cotton, but 'the weight of proof is, however, strongly adverse to this view.' It seems to have been called *po tieh* (a Turki derivation). There is no doubt that a historical notice, about A.D. 500, 'refers to cotton robes,' and in A.D. 670 we find it bearing the name of Kih-pei [*chi pei* or *ku pei*], derived from the Sanscrit *Karpasi*. This early knowledge of cotton amongst the Chinese was confined, it is believed, to what was brought into the empire as tribute, for it was not until the Sung dynasty that the plant was grown in China.

'Early in the eleventh century the plant was brought over and cultivated in the north-western provinces by persons from Khoten. . . . The opposition to cotton cultivation on the part of silk and hemp growers was so persistent that the plant had not fairly won its way into favour until the Yuen [Yüan] dynasty. The great cotton region is the basin of the Yangtzŭ Kiang, where the white and yellow varieties grow side by side. The manure used is mud taken from the canals and spread with ashes over the ploughed fields, in which seeds are sown about the 20th of April. The seeds are planted, after sprouting, five or six in a hole, being rubbed with ashes as they are put in, and weeded out if necessary. After the winter crops have been gathered, cotton fields are easily made ready for the shoots, which, while growing, are carefully tended, thinned, hoed, and weeded until the flowers begin to appear about August. As the pods begin to ripen and burst, the cultivator collects them before they fall, to clean the cotton of seed and husks. The weather is carefully watched, for a dry summer or a wet autumn are alike unpropitious, and as the pods are ripening from August to October, it is not uncommon for the crop to be partially lost. The seeds are separated by a wheel turning two rollers, and the cotton sold by each farmer to merchants in the towns. Some he keeps for weaving at home; spinning-wheels and looms being common articles of furniture in the houses of the peasantry. Cotton is cultivated in every province, and most of it is used where it grows. Around Peking the plant is hardly a foot high; the bolls are cleaned for wadding to a great extent, while the woody stalks supply fuel to the poor. Minute directions are given in Su's "Encyclopædia of Agriculture" respecting the cultivation of this plant, whose total crop clothes millions of the empire.'

'Cotton is not cultivated in China as in the United States. The preparation of the soil and the planting and cultivation are different. The ridges are wide, like the ridges of an American wheat field, and the seed is sown as an American farmer sows wheat. Consequently the plants are very thick, and the Chinese cotton-farmer cultivates every plant to the full maturity possible. The necessity for sufficient space for the plant to grow and branch is not admitted, and, when matured, the stalk is small and the limbs comparatively few. This thickness of growth necessarily results in small bolls and a short staple. To look at an acre of Chinese cotton when full-grown, leaves an impression favourable to great yielding capacity, which the actual yield is far from fulfilling. The thickness of the plants, standing so close together, keeps off the action of the sun, and causes many of the bolls to wither in the shade, and also prevents many from maturing. The hoe used for working cotton is very narrow, in order that the labourer may thread his way, as it were, between the thick standing plants. When the Chinese are taught the advantage of properly spacing their cotton rows and thinning the cotton plant, so that the warm air and the rays of the sun can freely penetrate, the change from the present system of cultivation will be rewarded by an increased yield per acre and a much finer staple.'

'The durable cotton cloth made in the central provinces called *Nankeen* by foreigners, because Nanking is famous for its manufacture, is the chief product of Chinese looms.' 'The so-called "Nankeen" cottons are said to be "colour variations" of the herbaceous cotton plant.' 'It is now seldom sent out of the country, and the natives are even taking to the foreign fabric in its stead. Cotton seed in that part of China is sown early in June, about eighty pounds to an acre; in a good year the produce is about two thousand pounds, diminishing to one-half in poor seasons. It is manured with liquid bean-cake, often hoed, and the bolls gathered in October, usually by each family in its own plot. The seeds are separated by passing the pods between an iron and wooden roller on a frame, which presses out the seeds and does not break them. The clean cotton is then bowed ready for spinning, and the cloth is woven in simple looms by the people who are to wear it after it is dyed blue. The looms used in weaving cotton vary from twelve to sixteen inches in width; they are simple in their construction; no figures are woven in cotton fabrics, nor have the Chinese learned to print them as chintz or calico. . . . The only attempt to estimate the product has been in Kiangnan, at 28,500 tons, a figure below rather than above the truth.'

The amount for all China is given as 500,000 tons in 1916.

'Owing to the great difficulty of obtaining any reliable statistical information, it is impossible to give anything approaching accuracy as to number of pounds of cotton produced annually, or number of acres devoted to the cultivation of the cotton plant' in China. 'There has been within recent years a great increase in the weight of the cotton crop as well as in the acreage. The type of plant most generally cultivated is the herbaceous, and the cotton resulting is only poor in quality. Little or no preparation is made before sowing seed, which is generally done broadcast. As a result there is much overcrowding, and as is inevitable, there is produced a stubby plant with small bolls and much unripe cotton. On the terraces of the hillsides something approaching cultivation is pursued, with the result of a better crop. Usually twenty weeks intervene between planting and picking, this latter operation being mostly the work of children and women. The old cotton stalks are afterwards collected and dried for fuel. Very few large plantations exist in China, most of them being only a few acres in extent.'

The cotton plant is grown all over China at the present day, but chiefly in the basins of the Yangtzŭ and Yellow Rivers; the Shensi product being the best. It has been thought that it may have been introduced 'by foreigners trading with the Chinese' 'by way of the southern sea' 'as well as by the Mongol usurpers coming in from the north-west,' for, though first cultivated during the Sung dynasty, it was only under the Mongols that it was grown to any extent. One writer describes the spread of the cotton plant in China as being very rapid on account of its being able to stand the northern winters and the southern mildness of climate. So common has it become now that it is the staple article for dress in China, especially amongst the poorer classes, as it can be more cheaply made than silks. Not content with their own native-produced article, cotton and cotton goods form the largest import into China, an import which is continually increasing in value. In 1892 it was represented in value by 53,290,200 taels, grey and white shirtings from England accounting alone for 15,693,081 taels of that amount. In 1916, the import of cotton goods was valued at Tls. 136,679,386; while the export of raw cotton in the same year was valued at Tls. 17,091,973. The

Indian yarn thus imported 'is suited to make coarse fabrics which are strong and wear well.' 'China greatly values cheapness, and, if she procure these [Indian yarns], she will supply her own coarse textile fabrics for the time by the cottage loom system, and suit her own taste in strength and quality.' But a new phase recently came over the cotton industry, and a number of mills fitted with the latest appliances for the manufacture have sprung up at Shanghai, and a few other important centres of trade and industry in China; this is accompanied by an increased cultivation of cotton. It would seem that the Indian yarn is better suited for manufacture than the native.

'Mr. Tratman, referring to the manufactures of the Hupeh cotton mill at Wuchang, says:—"These goods have had a fair trial throughout these provinces during the past few years, but they are not appreciated to anything like the same extent as similar goods of foreign manufacture. The yarn is short and difficult to work with the primitive appliances in use here. The shirtings have not the same toughness as even the most common kind of English goods, and they tear very easily. This inferiority of the Hupeh goods is not, I am told, to be in any way attributed to the manufacture, but simply to the fact that the cotton used is much below the standard of Indian cotton."'

Though of short staple, Chinese cotton 'is suitable for mixing with other qualities.' The Hon. T. H. Whitehead, from whom we have quoted the last sentence, in his speech at the Royal Colonial Institute in 1895, proceeds to say:—

'In the Shanghai River in December, 1893, there were at one time no less than five ocean-going steamers taking in cargoes of China-grown cotton for transportation to Japan, there to be converted by Japanese hands into yarn and cotton.' 'The Chinese have millions of acres of land admirably adapted to the cultivation of cotton.'

The starting of these cotton mills, to which we have already referred, will obviate the necessity of carrying the cotton to Japan and then bringing the yarn back to China, since the conversion of it into yarn can be carried out on the spot. There are more than seventy modern mills in China, the principal ones being at Shanghai, Hankow, and Wuch'ang. Shanghai, being the centre of the cotton growing districts, bids fair, if the industry is not throttled by Chinese officialdom and officialism, to 'be one of the greatest manufacturing centres in the world.' It has already proved a commercial success in Shanghai where a testing-house was established in 1911, and companies for starting mills at other places are every now and then being promoted; some time ago it was announced that a 'weaving enterprise on a somewhat large scale' would 'shortly be inaugurated in Honam, Canton.' There were twenty-three mills running in Shanghai and Northern China with about 400,000 spindles in 1916, and at the present time (1924) there are at least a million and a quarter spindles, producing three hundred million pounds of yarn; and 5,000 looms producing more than fifty million yards of cloth per annum.

In Shanghai in 1903 there were more than 1,000 employed in the native primitive method of weaving cotton-cloth. It takes about twelve days to make one piece of 11 chang in length (about 43 yards), and the pay for this is 380 cash, the masters providing board and lodging for the workmen, but charging them for it. Throughout China the average wages for this class of work range from 8 to 45 cents per day with board or from 16 to 72 without board. The cotton is carded by means of a large bow several feet in length, which is held by, or fastened to the body of, the workman who vibrates the string amidst the cotton, thus producing a very light floss.

The war in the North of China seriously affected the cotton mill industry in China, and other troubles, incident to new ventures of the kind in China, have handicapped it, but 'other industries, as silk and sugar, have had the same difficulties to surmount, and have surmounted them successfully,' and cotton would probably have done the same but for the war. These initial trials over, the industry will probably become a permanent one in China.

'The cotton and yarn merchants in Kiangsu province have [1924] decided to extend to the cultivation of cotton plants there for the supply of the various cotton spinning mills. During the late European War the yarn market in China was captured by the Japanese: but owing to the bad feeling existing between Chinese and Japanese, the former have since erected many cotton spinning mills in Shanghai and Tientsin. It is estimated that the original number of 100,000 spindles has now been increased to 700,000, and it is still increasing all the time. According to the latest investigation not only the Japanese but Indian yarn has been crowded out of the Chinese market. Therefore during the last few years efforts have been made to increase the production of cotton. In 1910 the Chinese Yarn Association organized a Committee for the improvement of the cultivation of cotton, and an experimental station was established in a suburb of Nanking and a branch of it in Hsuchow. Since then the native farmers in the districts in the vicinity have been very much encouraged by the profits they have made in cotton cultivation. In 1923 the Education and Industry Association of Kiangsu decided to encourage cotton cultivation on a larger scale at Hwaichow, Hsuchow and Haichow, where the soil is especially fitted for the cultivation. More than one hundred piculs of foreign cotton seed were then distributed, but the result was not so good as expected. Recently a conference was held among the experts, who came to the conclusion that the best American seed should be purchased and that one hundred mou of land should be secured at Hsuchow to make a trial of the new seed. If successful, it will be distributed among the farmers for cultivation.'

The cotton tree is not to be confounded with the cotton plant. It is a large, splendid tree, growing to a considerable size, with immense limbs branching out from it, and in spring it has a large red flower. A white silky down covers the seeds, whence its name. This cotton is 'equally good looking' as the true cotton, its staple is too short to be woven into cloth; consequently it is only used to stuff cushions, etc. A rough cloth is capable of being produced from it, so it is said, but this statement is doubtful.

References.—Williams, *Middle Kingdom;* Smith, *Chinese Materia Medica; ibid., Natural History;* Edkins, *Modern China;* Hirth and Rockhill, *Chao Ju-kua.*

CREMATION.—Cremation is opposed to the principles of the Chinese. They believe that unless the whole body goes intact into the next world, it will not be in a perfect condition in a future state of existence. It is only Buddhist monks whose bodies are thus disposed of at the present day. Until A.D. 1370 the bodies of the Buddhist laity were cremated also. It was, however, a common practice, in some parts of China, at all events, during the twelfth and thirteenth centuries, for Marco Polo says: 'The people have paper-money, and are idolaters and burn their dead.' Ibn Bututa also says:—'The Chinese are all infidels: they worship images, and burn their dead just like the Hindoos.' A memorial was presented against it in A.D. 1261 to the Emperor, 'praying that the erection of cremation furnaces might thenceforth be prohibited.' It is a great pity that the practice was not continued, as the neighbourhood of a Chinese city is converted into a vast necropolis, to say nothing of solitary graves scattered over the hills and mountains, even at a distance from human habitations. There is no intramural burial. No places of worship are turned into charnel-houses, to the detriment of future living worshippers, as with us, but an equally, or even more, reprehensible custom is in vogue of preserving the coffin in the house or some convenient temple for weeks, months, and years, until either a favourable site with propitious influences is found, or until the family can afford the expenses of a funeral befitting their social position. This is in the South; in the central portions of China, as at Shanghai, one sees coffins standing even in the corners or centres of fields. All these insanitary customs would have been done away with had the more scientific and health-preserving practice of cremation been allowed to continue. The Man-tzŭ aborigines in Western Sz-chuen [Ssŭch'uan] cremate their dead. The bodies are placed in a sitting position and bound with cords. The funeral pyre is built, and, after the body is burned, the ashes and unburned wood are buried on the spot.

Archdeacon Gray thus describes a cremation at Honam Temple:—

'As I entered the inner gates my attention was directed to an apartment, the doors of which were crowded by a number of priests arrayed in sackcloth, and wearing white bandages round their foreheads. The corpse, attired in a cowl, and with the hands fixed in the attitude of prayer, was placed in a bamboo-chair in a sitting posture, and carried to the pyre by six secular monks. All the monks were in attendance, and walked two abreast, immediately behind the remains of the departed friar. As the long procession advanced, the walls of the monastery echoed with the chanting of prayers and the tinkling of cymbals. When the bearers reached the pyre, they placed the chair containing the corpse upon it, and the fagots were then kindled by the chief priest. Whilst the body was enveloped in flames, the mourners prostrated themselves upon the ground in obeisance to the ashes of one with whom they had been accustomed to join in prayer and praise. When the fire had burned itself out, the attendants collected the charred bones and placed them in a cinerary urn, which was then deposited in a small shrine within the precincts of the monastery. The cinerary urns remain in this shrine until the ninth day of the ninth month, when the ashes which they contain are emptied into bags of red cloth, which are then sewn and thrown into a large ossuary, or species of monastery mausoleum. These edifices, built of granite, are called by the Chinese *Poo-Toong-Tap* [*P'u-t'ung-t'a*], and are upon an extensive scale. That belonging to the monastery of Honam is a noble piece of masonry, and is divided into compartments, one being for the ashes of monks, and the other for those of nuns. The bags of red cloth, with their contents, are consigned to these receptacles through small apertures just sufficiently large for their admission.'

Reference.—De Groot, *Religious System.*

CURRENCY.—China presents the curious spectacle of an empire without a gold or silver currency in general use throughout the land. For centuries, with but slight exceptions, *the* medium of exchange has been the cash, a small copper coin of the size of an English halfpenny, but only a half or a third as thick, with a square hole in its centre for convenience in stringing. It has a raised broad rim round the circumference as well as one round the square hole in the centre. In the sunk space between these two rims are, on the obverse, four raised Chinese characters, two of which are the style of the Emperor's reign, and two are the equivalent of 'current coin.' At the present day the majority of the coins also have on the reverse two raised Manchu characters, one denoting the provincial mint at which the coin has been cast, and the other the equivalent of the word 'currency.' For some centuries before Christ, and until the present time, this has been, in its general features, the circulating medium of China. Larger coins of the same character have also been coined, but, as a rule, it may be said that China has had no gold or silver coinage. A few attempts to coin silver have been made once or twice in the past, but they have been failures. Edkins says 'Arabian trade brought to China the use of silver by weight, as European trade at a later period brought the dollar.' 'A thousand years ago the people in Central China kept their accounts in copper cash.' It is now the general practice, at all events in the South, for accounts to be kept in silver—taels, mace, candarins, and *li* (a decimal system: ten *li* making one candarin; ten candarins, one mace; and ten mace, one tael); there being actually no such coins in existence. But in Hongkong and places where the dollar is common, they are often kept in dollars and cents. Hence arises sometimes a curious mixture, the shop-keeper at times puts down some of the items in taels, etc., and in other parts of his books items will occur in dollars and cents. Paper notes have at different periods been issued by the Government, and in later times by private firms. They have been much in use in certain parts of China—Foochow for example. Marco Polo devotes a whole chapter to an account of the paper-money in use in China in his time. (See BANKS and BANK-NOTES). The Chinese readily used the Mexican, South American, and other dollars—half a century ago Spanish dollars took the place that the Mexican subsequently held, but, except in the neighbourhood of Hongkong, and often there as well, they always weighed them, and they were generally stamped, as they passed through the hands of merchants and shop-keepers, with a private mark of the firm, till they fell into pieces and became what is known as broken silver, and had to be weighed as each transaction took place to know their value. For this purpose a small money scale is a part of the equipment of every one going shopping; in time, no doubt, a regular silver coinage will drive this practice out. The Japanese, Hongkong, and Straits Settlements subsidiary coins, such as the five, ten, and twenty cent pieces, have been much in circulation, especially in Hongkong and its neighbourhood. The Japanese yen and Hongkong dollar are also used more now. In 1890 a mint was established at Canton. This mint is a very fine one, and in one respect, that of stamping machines, is the largest in the world. It was at first under the superintendence of a Scotchman, but all the other officials and workmen are natives. The following extracts from Consul Brenan's Report may prove of interest in this connection:—

'This mint has not so far [1893] taken upon itself the duty of providing the people with a standard of value at the expense of the Government. It only cares to work at a profit. . . . No assayer is employed, and the provincial treasury silver is taken to be pure, the Canton dollar [few of which have been coined] is not of even fineness. Some of the first dollars coined there were found in the London mint to be actually 884 instead of 900 fine. . . . There is a steady demand [for the subsidiary coins] because of the convenience, their passing above their intrinsic value being an exemplification of Ricardo's proposition that the value of a coin depends on demand and supply. . . . There is certain to be in time an immense demand for such small silver pieces all over the Empire.'

(Sir Thomas Wade, a former British minister to Peking, actually recommended that Hongkong should coin taels when it was proposed to issue a Hongkong dollar, and this when the Chinese were familiar with foreign dollars.

The Chinese, as will be seen below, have given in their adhesion to the use of the dollar themselves.)

The coins issued by the Canton mint have been dollars, half dollars, twenty, ten, and five cent pieces in silver, copper cents and cash. The Government of the Fokien [Fukien] Province had a large quantity of silver coins minted for them at this establishment in Canton. The same Viceroy, Chang Chih-tung, who introduced this first mint into China, also established one at Wuchang [in 1895] for the benefit of the Hupeh and Hunan Provinces. Mints were opened at Peiyang and Foochow in 1896, and two years later at Nanking, Hankow, Anking, Ch'êngtu, Mukden, and Kirin. Other mints will soon doubtless supply other portions of the empire with silver coins. The ten and twenty cent pieces issued by the Canton mint are largely in circulation in Hongkong, though not now received at the Government offices, such as the Post Office, etc. Generally, the coins have only a local circulation in the provinces where they are issued, and none rival the Mexican dollar in popularity. In Peking, the Yüan Shih-k'ai silver coins have a higher exchange value than others issued by native mints.

CUSTOMS, MARITIME.—In 1853, owing to the T'ai P'ing rebels capturing Shanghai, the collection of customs duties on foreign bottoms entering that port was placed in the hands of foreigners, as a temporary measure until order should be restored (the actual date of the notification issued by the Consuls of Great Britain, the United States of America, and

France being July 12th, 1854), but what was intended as a *modus vivendi* for the time being, proved so well adapted for the purpose, that it became a permanency, and has increased with the extension of trade and the opening of new treaty ports, until it is now a most important department, with a large and efficient staff recruited from most of the European nations, though the English are in the majority.

The following is the *personnel* of the establishment:—At the head of all are the Inspector-General and the Deputy Inspector-General; immediately below them are the Commissioners, 42 in number, who are generally in charge of each Custom-house. They are assisted by Deputy Commissioners, of whom there are 22, including 6 extra for Likin; the next ranks being 10 classes of Foreign and 11 classes of Chinese Assistants, to which must be added Clerks, Miscellaneous, and Surgeons connected with the Customs, who have private practice as well. The ranks of the foreign Outdoor Staff are Tide Surveyors, Assistant Tide Surveyors, and Boat Officers; Chief Examiners, Examiners, and Assistant Examiners; Tide Waiters, and Watchers, and Miscellaneous, etc. In 1916, the total of Indoor and Outdoor officers was 1,321 foreigners and 6,325 Chinese. There are also five armed cruisers built in England, most of them by Armstrong, commanded and officered by Europeans, and styled the Coast Staff (46 in number), and manned by Chinese; also belonging to this Coast Staff is a small fleet (10) of armed launches with 19 officers, and an Engineer's Staff, 7 in number. The lighthouses on the China coast, with the exception of those kept up by the Hongkong and Macao Governments, owe their inception and maintenance to this same department, employing 58 foreigners and 222 Chinese. There is a Marine Staff as well; the Lighthouse Staff coming under the heading of Marine makes a total of 129 foreigners. There is a small Educational Department. The Postal Department is now a separate institution. The Nationality of the staff some years since was roughly stated, as follows:—There were, before 1914, about 550 British, about 125 Germans; American, 80; French, about 40; Danish, 30; Norwegian, some 30 or so; Portuguese, nearly 30; Swedish, 20; Russian, Spanish, Italian, Belgian, Austrian, Dutch, Siamese, Turkish, Hungarian, and Venezuelan below 20 each, some nations having only one in the service. The totals and proportions, however, vary from time to time.

About £400,000 a year was allowed by the Chinese Government for the support and upkeep of this entire service of the Maritime Customs, but the sum has doubtless been increased, as the establishment is constantly growing and the expenses increasing. The patronage is in the hands of the Inspector-General, whose nomination is required for appointment.

Mr. H. N. Lay was the former Inspector-General, but he came to grief in 1863 over the Sherard Osborne fleet, and was succeeded by Sir Robert Hart, and, on his death, by Sir Francis Aglen.

The receipts of a most important department are thus handed over intact to the Chinese, and, notwithstanding the large salaries necessarily paid to the foreign employés, the Chinese government reaps a larger benefit from it than it would from one in purely native hands, so difficult is it for money once in the hands of Chinese officials to leave their possession without a large percentage being deducted for the benefit of each one who has had to do with it. This revenue is likewise honestly collected, a thing impossible of accomplishment were natives employed, as bribes and presents are in continual use in China. Could this same system be enlarged and extended to the collection of the whole of the Customs revenue of China, it would prove of incalculable benefit to the nation; but the Provincial authorities are opposed to this, the Provincial and Central authorities being mutually suspicious of each other. (See LIKIN).

A further advantage of this service is the moral lesson it gives to Chinese officials. Hong Yaú-waí, one of the leaders of the Chinese Reform Party, speaking, some years since, of the enormous loss of revenue that occurs in China, stated that in his own native district, that of Namhoi, out of a total amount of $240,000 a year, only something over $20,000 reached the Imperial Purse. It is perhaps, also exerting an improving influence on the government system of keeping accounts.

CUTTLE-FISH.—This is a most common article of diet amongst the Chinese, and is eaten both fresh and dried. 'In the latter case the ink-bag is cut away, and all impurities having been removed by water, the animal is submitted to pressure and then dried in the sun. Bundles of one catty each are tide up and placed in cases holding ten catties or more each, for export' (Dennys) from the Straits Settlements.

The fresh cuttle-fish is fried over a quick fire, while dried cuttle-fish is boiled to prepare it for the table. The bone is used as a medicine.

A curious idea was prevalent at one time in the West, that the so-called Indian ink (really Chinese ink) was prepared from the colouring matter of the cuttle-fish, instead of being made from lampblack as its principal ingredient.

CYCLE.—From a remote antiquity the Chinese have used a Cycle of 60 years. This sexagenary cycle is formed of two sets of characters: one set consisting of twelve (the Earth Branches) and the other of ten (the Heaven Branches), which are combined together in sets of two, *i.e.*, each year of the sixty is represented by two characters which distinguish it from the other fifty-nine. A sexagenary division also existed in early times in India and Babylon.

The Chinese employ both this cycle as well as the year of the reign of the sovereign. The latter is preferable, as at times the use of the former causes some uncertainty. For example, if a book has the name of one of the years of the cycle on the title-page as the date of its being written or of its publication, the question may arise as to which series of sixty years the date refers—whether it is the year in the present cycle of sixty, or the year in the last, or a former cycle of sixty years. There is not the precision about it, under any and every circumstance, which there ought to be in anything connected with dates.

Since the institution of the Republic, dates are reckoned from the first year of its establishment.

Of recent years, however, the Gregorian calendar has been largely used, sometimes alone, sometimes alongside of the older system.

DECORATIONS AND PRESENTATIONS.—Mayers, who is the great authority on all matters connected with Government titles, etc., says most justly that:—

'Although rewards for distinguished service, or marks of Imperial favour, the conception of which resembles in some degree that of the European system of Royal or National Orders and Medals of Distinction, are to be found in China, nothing in the shape of an actual Order of Merit approximating to the European type has been adopted by the Chinese Government (but see *infra*). . . . Isolated distinctions have indeed been conferred in China on foreigners of various nationalities, principally for services rendered in the command of the drilled troops during the T'ai P'ing rebellion, and subsequently in the collection of the Customs' revenue, . . . but as these are bestowed for the most part by provincial authorities, and without the sanction of any established rule or recognised statutes. such as are required to constitute what is commonly known as an "Order," the badges thus conferred can scarcely be regarded as having a real value as authentic marks of distinction.'

There was, however, during the latter years of the Monarchy the newly established Order, in its various grades, originally reserved solely for foreigners, namely, the Order of the Double Dragon; it was divided into five grades, the first, second, and third being subdivided into three classes. It was bestowed for services in connection with naval, railway, revenue, and other matters. In modern times, its place has been taken by the Order of the Excellent Crop, that and one or two others being occasionally bestowed upon foreigners.

The purely native decorations and privileges are many in number. We note a few of them below.

The Riding Cape or Yellow Riding-Jacket (má k'wá) [*hsing kua* or *huang ma kua*], though so styled was not necessarily, though generally, of that colour. It was only worn 'when in personal attendance upon the sovereign, in the field, or upon journeys.' Only two Europeans have been honoured with its bestowal—General Gordon and M. Giquel. 'It is in colour of a gorgeous golden hue, lined with sleeves of peacock blue—all of the richest silk. It is very capacious . . . reaching down far below the waist.'

Another honorary distinction, conferred upon eminent public functionaries, was the privilege of being allowed to ride on horse-back 'for some distance within the outer gateways of the palace, when summoned to an audience.'

Another class of distinctions was that of the feather. The feathers allowed were those of the peacock and the crow (the latter also known as the Blue Feather). They were placed in the back of the hat, and stuck out, sloping downwards. The peacock feathers were three-eyed, double-eyed, or single-eyed. The first was conferred on Imperial princes, 'nobles of the higher degrees, or for the most signal military achievements'; the second was reserved for lower officials or dignitaries; and the third 'is bestowed as an ordinary form of reward for public service, and during the last few decades [dating back from 1900] has been indiscriminately obtainable by purchase.' The Crow Feather or Blue Plume was for the soldiers of the Imperial Guards, and officials of the seventh, eighth, and ninth degrees of rank were rewarded by it. The peacock feather has been conferred in a few instances upon Europeans.

A peculiar feature in connection with these distinctions amongst the Chinese was the withdrawal of them as a sign of Imperial impatience or displeasure. A notable instance of this lately was in the case of the late Viceroy Li Hung-chang in connection with the troubles with Japan, his three-eyed peacock feather and yellow riding-jacket were the honours of which he was deprived temporarily; for 'the slight is often quickly repaired,' not only by the re-bestowal of the lost honours but by the fresh granting of even greater ones.

General Yeh, who distinguished himself in battle, was ordered by the Throne to be rewarded with 'Imperial gifts consisting of a white peacock-feather-holder, a small knife, a pair of large purses, and a couple of tinder-boxes.'

The Bát'uru Distinction, derived from the Manchu word for 'brave,' was something like the French *Légion d'honneur* and was 'conferred solely for active service in the field.' There is no outward sign of its possession, but each recipient got a distinguishing title either in Manchu, Mongolian, or Chinese, the first being the most honourable. The title given, for instance, might be 'Bát'uru, with the title Magnanimous Brave.' The bestowal of the title gave the right to wear the peacock's feather, though the brave soldier had generally obtained that privilege before. Enhanced allowances were also the result of the Bát'uru, when on active service. General Mesny, who was in the service of the Chinese army, is the only European who has obtained this honour; it was bestowed on him for services in the province of Kwei-chow.

Another privilege was the Manchu one, of having the sword-scabbard covered with yellow bark from the *Robinia pygmœa*—a tree belonging to the Acaciæ family. The Seventh Prince, on the accession of the Emperor, Kwong Sui [Kuang Hsü], had this bestowed on him.

Another honour granted was 'the permission to use scarlet or purple reins when riding . . . on horseback . . . and to use the same colour for the props of the sedan-chair.' These privileges 'were believed to be reserved exclusively for the Imperial family,' but the Viceroy Li had them conferred on him. Yet another honour bestowed on the same high official was a robe made of throat-skins of sables, sent as a birthday present to him by the Empress Dowager; special permission from the Throne was required for the wearing of these.

The title of 'Instructor of the Emperor' was a posthumous one, and it is said was 'never given a man in his lifetime, and only to the most distinguished officers after death.' The great Tsêng Kwo-ch'üan, deceased, and his brother had it: 'it is unprecedented in history that two brothers should be so honoured.'

Among the honours conferred upon the late energetic Admiral (and General) Fong [Fang] by the Throne was the Order of the Yellow Flag—'an honour possessed only by some half-dozen recipients in the whole Empire. It carried with it the despotic power to order the execution of any subject, if of subordinate rank, without reference to Peking.'

Presentations or testimonials to officials by the people take a different form in China from what they do in the West.

Some of the older forms were as follows:

There was the presentation of the official umbrella, which was a distant cousin of the Italian *Baldacchino*. It was a circular canopy with a deep border and fringe dependent from it.

'It is made of scarlet silk, and on the deep borders which encircle it are embroidered in yellow or black silk the names of the donors.'

'At other times, tablets bearing complimentary inscriptions are given as testimonials, and these are much prized by the recipients, and used to decorate their best receiving rooms.'

'Another and more comical method of exhibiting the public estimation of official probity and worth is for a deputation of the inhabitants to wait upon a mandarin at one of the gates of the city at the moment of his making his farewell exit, and to beg the gift of his boots, which are thenceforth reverently cherished in some temple as public property.'

Decorations of foreigners were made through the instrumentality of the then Viceroy Yüan Shih-k'ai of a number of missionaries, mostly Roman Catholic, in connection with the rendering and settling of the missionary claims arising out of the Boxer disturbances of 1900—buttons, peacocks' feathers, and stars—stars doubtless of the double dragon.

Under the Republican system, there are ten Civil Orders, the 'Grand Cordon' and nine grades of the 'Excellent Crop,' and two military or naval decorations, the Order of the 'White Eagle' and nine grades of the 'Striped Tiger.' A Badge for Meritorious Service is an additional order of merit, said to correspond with the Victoria Cross.

DEMONIACAL POSSESSION.—The Chinese believe that madness and many forms of disease are due to possession by evil spirits.

The idea of evil spirits and their wicked machinations pervades the whole of Chinese society: it crops up in all sorts of unexpected places, and permeates and pervades their whole round of existence. Does a parent's love go out toward some little child, and, as year by year goes by, increase in strength, until suddenly some disease takes the little darling away from the home it has made bright and happy? Then the miserable solace the bereaved parents have, is that it was not a proper child of their own at all, but some spiteful spirit, that, after ingratiating itself into their affections, ruined all their fond hopes, and dashed their anticipations of future bliss by suddenly showing itself in its true colours in returning whence it came.

More than twenty years ago some most curious instances of apparent demoniacal possession forced themselves upon the attention of the missionaries and their native assistants in the South of China, bearing, seemingly, a close analogy to those mentioned in the New Testament in the time of Christ. Some of the native preachers treated these cases in the same way that the Apostles did, and in several instances with marked results of improvement.

At Foochow, according to Doolittle, yellow paper charms are used, with different devices on them, in a number of various ways, to counteract the evil influences when sickness is believed to be caused by an evil spirit; and, in the same part of the country, whips made of branches of the peach or willow, or a scourge, made, in the shape of a snake, out of hemp, are employed to beat the bed, and drive away the evil spirit.

There are several different kinds of demoniacal possession, according to the Chinese. There is, first, the possession of the body, produced by demons, who are capable of inducing any of the ordinary diseases to which flesh is heir in China. Vows and offerings to the gods are the remedies for those who suffer thus involuntarily. The next form is more serious, for the demon in this class is supposed actually to dwell within the possessed, whose case is, however, diagnosed by the Chinese as being different from that of an ordinary lunatic. Dennys in his 'Folklore of China,' quoting from an article by Gardner, treats at some length of these, and his account tallies in several respects with those given in the Bible of the demoniacs in the time of Christ. A still worse case is that of those who, thus possessed, yield to the demon, the consequence being that on their worship of him riches flow in; but, notwithstanding all, ill-luck, in the way of retributive justice, follows; and the ill-gotten gains take to themselves wings and flee away. There are besides 'devil-dancers' or spiritual media, who profess to be possessed, going into 'a sort of ecstatic frenzy, and, when in this state, they answer questions as to the disease and remedies to be applied for the relief of those on whose behalf they are consulted.' They also believe in demons, who to all outward appearance are mortals, and who are missionaries from the nether world to warn mankind, amongst whom they live, of the evil consequences of indulgence in wrongdoing.

China would appear to present a better field for the manifestation of such delusions, as the people are so ignorant and superstitious and are naturally susceptible. Mania, dementia, and hysteria, will probably account for all, or nearly all, so-called instances of demoniacal possession.

'Many of these cases of possession are, doubtless, due to suggestion. Persons of susceptible temperament, seeing or hearing of others so afflicted, are tempted to worry or annoy their friends, and are carried away and frightened by their own emotions into an hysterical state bordering on actual mania.'

Story after story might be given under these different heads, as well as of superstitions about foxes, which last prevail more in the North than in the South of China, but for the latter see in the North than in the South of China. (For the latter see FAIRY TALES).

References.—Dennys, *Folklore of China; Chinese Recorder*, 1881; *Chinese and Japanese Repository*, 1863. Doolittle, *Social Life of the Chinese;* Giles, *Strange Stories from a Chinese Studio;* Coltman, *The Chinese, their Present and Future—Medical, Political, and Social;* Nevius, *Demon Possession and Allied Themes;* De Groot, *Religious System.*

DIALECTS.—When one travels on the continent of Europe one expects, every few hundred miles, to find a different language spoken, but because an extent of country larger than Europe is all part of one empire, it is generally supposed that one language (the Chinese) is spoken throughout its length and breadth. It is quite true that it is Chinese that is spoken in Peking, as well as in Canton, and it is equally true that the inhabitants of Shanghai, Foochow, and Amoy as well, all speak Chinese; but it is also true that not one of the inhabitants from any of those places could understand those from the others any more than a Londoner could a Berliner; or a Parisian, a Dutchman; or a Spaniard, an Italian. It might convey a livelier sense of the difference to suppose that the speech in Liverpool was as different from that in London as one European language is from another, so that any merchants from London, who settled in Liverpool, would have to learn the language of the people of that city, and would be strangers in a strange land, as far as the speech was concerned. Again, suppose that Gaelic was the speech in Edinburgh or Glasgow, a native of those cities settling in London would find that to be understood he had to pick up the language of the South of England. Again, let Welsh be the only language spoken in the principality, a Welshman would then not be understood in York, or anywhere else in England or Scotland.

This, then, represents the position of the Chinese in his own land, for different so-called dialects are spoken in it. It is a pity that they have received this name, for it gives such a wrong impression as to their range, the number of people that speak them, and the very great difference that exists between them.

As Carstairs Douglas says in speaking of one of them:—

'But such words as "Dialect" or "Colloquial" give an erroneous conception of its nature. It is not a mere colloquial dialect or *patois;* it is spoken by the highest ranks just as by the common people, by the most learned just as by the most ignorant; learned men indeed add a few polite or pedantic phrases, but these are mere excrescences' (and even they are pronounced according to the so-called dialect of that part of the country) 'while the main body and staple of the spoken language of the most refined and learned classes is the same as that of coolies, labourers, and boatmen. Nor does the term "dialect" convey anything like a correct idea of its distinctive character: it is no mere dialectic variety of some other language; it is a distinct language, one of the many and widely differing languages which divide among them the soil of China. . . . They are cognate languages, bearing to each other a relation similar to that which subsists between the Arabic, the Hebrew, the Syriac, the Ethiopic, and the other members of the Semitic family; or again between English, German, Dutch, Danish, Swedish, etc.'

To generalise then, there are throughout China the following main divisions of speech or language, generally called dialects. We arrange them with some attempt at relative age, or the greater or less remains of age contained in them:—

1. The Cantonese.
2. " Hakka.
3. " Amoy.
4. " Swatow.
5. The Hainanese.
6. " Shanghai.
7. " Ningpo.
8. " Mandarin.

(In the Straits Settlements No. 2 is known as the Kheh, No. 4 as Tíú chíú, and No. 5 as Hylam, in this pronunciation following that of the Swatow and Amoy people.)

Mandarin and its cognate branches being the youngest, it will thus be seen that another fallacy, viz., that Mandarin is the language of China, and the others dialects of it, is untenable; Cantonese being more akin to the ancient language of China (spoken about 3,000 years ago) than the Mandarin, while the Hakka also contains traces of a high antiquity, and is supposed to mark a period long anterior to that represented by Mandarin, but, in some respects, subsequent to that period of which the Cantonese contains remains, although in other points it has traces of as high, or nearly as high, an antiquity. This is true also to some extent of Swatow, Amoy, and Shanghai, as well probably of others; so that it may rather be said that the languages spoken in the South-East of China have traces of the ancient speech, whereas the Mandarin is modern; in fact, one appears to have 'elements in it which seem to be remnants of a dialect of greater antiquity than even the ' Cantonese ' can boast of.'

Having thus spoken of the grand divisions, we have further to draw attention to the fact that, besides these main divisions, there are lesser ones, into which they are subdivided, for which, if we give the main divisions the name of languages, we have the more fitting term of dialects; for to adapt what Dyer Ball wrote some years since in ' Cantonese Made Easy,' they have their real dialects, some of which are spoken by tens of thousands or hundreds of thousands of natives, and which, if they were spoken by the inhabitants of some insignificant group of islands in the Pacific, with only a tithe of the population, would be honoured by the name of languages. We quote again from a monograph by the same author (on the San-wúi Dialect) :— At the same time, however, there are wheels within wheels in the matter of these Chinese dialects: that is to say, the dialect of one district is not one homogeneous whole, though the district may be so small as geographically to equal in square miles a few English counties only. It will readily be understood that there is scope for a considerable variation, without this variation being so marked as to become a separate dialect or sub-dialect. Considerable changes can thus be rung, while yet the changes are not so great as to put the dialect or sub-dialect out of harmony with the general characteristics of the particular dialect, or language, of which it is a branch. Every now and then one comes across villages and towns, which seem almost a law to themselves as to their speech, for all the peculiarities of the district are so accentuated, and so many new varieties of pronunciation introduced, new idioms and words used, as well as a difference in the tones employed, as to result in a lingo more or less unintelligible, even to inhabitants of the same district, and a perfect jargon of unmeaning sounds to a stranger to that part of the country.

It will thus be seen that the ramifications are numerous, for after the division of dialects proper, are the lesser divisions of sub-dialects, variations and local *patois*. The most minute divisions of all are those which present a curious spectacle when found to exist in a city itself, as, for instance, there are two or three of these minute subdivisions found in the city of Canton, with a population estimated sometimes at a million. It is as if about a dozen different minute divisions of English were to be found in London: the inhabitants of that city south of the Thames having certain peculiarities, which would mark them out as different from those in other parts of London, while the West End, the City itself, the East End, and, not to carry the comparison any further, half-a-dozen other districts of London would each have some few local peculiarities of pronunciation distinguishing them from the rest of London.

The above will help to explode another fallacy, that if a man knows one of the so-called dialects, such for instance as Cantonese, he is then perfect master of all that may be said by people speaking that language. The real facts of the case will be better understood if one instances the bewilderment of a cockney, when landed amongst a crowd of Yorkshiremen speaking the Yorkshire dialect in its broadest.

So many are the changes in the language in China that it may be said that every hundred miles the language differs to a more or less material extent—in some places every twenty miles—and a rough estimate has been made that there are as many dialects in China as there are days in the year. The word China, when applied geographically, covers such an aggregate of country, that practically a knowledge of one of the languages of China is sufficient to carry one over hundreds and thousands of miles, though, when it comes to a minute and accurate knowledge of all that is said, much is left to be desired, and ludicrous mistakes occur.

It may be of interest to have some general idea, imperfect though it must necessarily be, of the range of the different languages and some of the more important dialects. To begin with Mandarin (known as *kuan hua*, 'official language') as being the most widespread. It is the speech, in one form or another, in fourteen or fifteen out of the eighteen provinces into which China is divided. Mandarin is divided into the Northern and Southern. The standard dialect of the former being Pekingese, owing to the accident of Peking being the seat of the Central Government, while Nankingese holds the same position with regard to the southern division. A third marked variety is that of Western China, which has its centre in Ching-tu [Ch'êng-tu] in the Sz-chuan [Ssŭch'uan] province. Besides these, there are a number of smaller divisions, such as the Hankow; but, amidst all these varieties, there appears to be a better chance of one being understood through a much wider extent of country in that part of the empire, where Mandarin is spoken as the language of the people, than is the case in other parts of China. Taking the population of China as 360,000,000, a population say of 300,000,000 are Mandarin speaking. This is, of course, a mere rough estimate, and, to be accurate, would require a considerable amount of adjustment, as there are large Hakka-speaking communities amongst them, while, on the other hand, there are Mandarin-speaking people amongst some of the other provinces. In the city of Canton alone there are 100,000 Mandarin speakers. All high officials require a knowledge of Mandarin; those who do not know it have therefore to learn it, and the consequence is that almost all who aspire to office, or to come in contact with official life, acquire it to a greater or lesser extent. Many of the plays put on the stage are in Southern Mandarin, consequently ardent play-goers have a more or less smattering of that variety of it.

The other languages of China are spoken by smaller populations, but by still large enough ones to command respect. For example, the people who speak Cantonese, in some form or another, number 20,000,000, a population falling not far short of that of Italy. This language is in use throughout the larger part of the Kwang-tung, or Canton province; one authority considers that 12,000,000 speak it there. It has been estimated that about one-third of the people of the province speak Hakka, while in the north-east of the same province there is a considerable population speaking the Swatow and its variations. The Cantonese speakers then are in the majority, but they are not confined to this province, for in the next, Kwang-si, it is also largely spoken, especially in the South, some of it being of a comparatively pure type, while in other parts it is mixed with Mandarin.

It is impossible, without writing a book specially dealing with the subject, to give an account of all the dialects coming under each separate language. The following short notice of some of them in Cantonese may give an idea of what may be expected to be found under each grand division. The Cantonese has numerous dialects and groups of dialects. One group consists of the San-wúí, San-ning, Yan-p'ing and Hoí-p'ing, a most peculiar class of dialects, containing much that is very different from the pure Cantonese, and any one of which, when spoken in all its broadness, is, to a great extent, difficult of comprehension. Another group consists of the Tung-kwún, San-on, Pok-lo, and Tsang-sheng dialects. Besides these, there are a number of other dialects, such as the Höng-shán, or Macao, the Shan-tuk, the Shíú-hing, and others too numerous to mention, each district having more or less differences which segregate it and its inhabitants to a greater or lesser extent from the neighbouring districts. It must be remembered that each of these dialects has, as has already been said, smaller divisions or subdivisions. For example, the San-wúí dialect may be divided into three, whilst besides this three-fold division there are numerous smaller divisions still. The ramifications are most minute; not only are there several slight variations in one city or even in one town;

not only does the speech of the boat people differ from that of those on land; not only is there baby-talk; but there are even certain words which are used by women and never by men—in fact, the men would be laughed at if they used them.

With regard to the Hakka, there do not appear to be such differences between the speech of those living in different parts of the country, in Kwang-tung at least, as there are amongst the Cantonese. To mention some of these Hakka dialects, there are the Ká-yín-chú, the Sin-án, the Ch'ong-lok, and others. Again, with regard to this language, we have constantly been met with the supposition that a knowledge of Hakka means a thorough knowledge of Hakka in all its dialects. Such knowledge is almost impossible for one man to acquire, be he native or foreign. The difference between the dialects of Hakka is still sufficiently marked to confuse one considerably, until familiarity with speakers from different parts of the country overcomes the difficulty. In the Canton province alone not a few millions speak this language; perhaps about four millions says one authority, but this same curious people are found in other provinces as well; at present there is no accurate knowledge of their number as a whole.

The next so-called dialect up the coast is that of the Swatow and neighbouring districts, which is spoken by some millions, perhaps three, in one or other of its variations or dialects, such for example as the Hoí-fung, Luk-fung, etc.

Next after this comes the Amoy, which has about the same affinity to the Swatow that Spanish bears to Portuguese. There are numerous dialects of it, and it is spoken by a large population of say 9,000,000, or so. Again, further up the coast, but still in the same province, is the Foochow; it is spoken throughout an extent of country of approximately 130 miles by 270, and by a population of 5,000,000. Like all the others, it has variations, some twenty, or so, main ones. Of it, as spoken a few hundred miles inland, a writer says:—'But what a Babel of tongues and dialects there is among these wild mountaineers! A native can hardly pass the limits of his own village but his speech will betray him.' This is, of course, what one would expect in such a mountainous district; the country which the Mandarin occupies is, much of it, of a more level type.

Besides these, there are the languages of Shanghai and Ningpo, and others less well-known to the foreigner, and consequently, whose divisions into dialects have been less studied.

The Hainanese is spoken in the island of Hainan, where numerous other speeches are in use, Hainanese being, however, the *lingua franca;* it has also numerous variations, the dialect of

Kiung-chau [Kiungchow or Ch'iungchou] being the standard. It is allied to the Amoy and Swatow, but is very different in some respects, having some peculiarities, incident also to the Japanese, in the change of letters in the pronunciation of a word. It is spoken by three millions of people, being used in the Luichow [Leichou] peninsula.

The number of syllables in some of the different speeches of China are as follows:—

1. Amoy, 846.
2. Cantonese, 780.
3. Foochow, 786.
4. Hakka, 700.
5. Hankow, 316.
6. Ningpo, 444.
7. Pekingese, 430.
8. Shanghai, 660.
9. Swatow, 674.
10. Wênchow, 452.
11. Yangchow, 415.

Professor E. H. Parker, a great authority on Chinese dialects, says:—

'It is plain that 1,500 years back the Chinese dialects had for centuries been almost as numerous as they are now,' and he says further, 'from the earliest historical times, widely different dialects have been spoken in China.' 'Between the dialects of Peking, Hankow, Sz-Ch'uan, Yangchow, Canton, Hakka, Foochow, Wênchow, and Ningpo . . . there is complete homogeneity; and though the variations between this and that dialect are often greater . . . than the differences between Portuguese and French (as one extreme), and no greater than between Flemish and Dutch (as another extreme), yet the rigid adherences of all to theoretical standards is more perfect than in the European languages or dialects.'

The so-called dialects are, however, in many respects as different as one European language from another. These differences are partly due to climatic and tellural influences, individual, and local peculiarities of utterance which have been perpetuated, and the effects of succeeding waves of migration from different parts; possibly the influence of preceding residents, as well as other more obscure causes have also been responsible to some extent. Some of the reasons for these divergencies in languages or dialects can be seen, but the whole subject is one that would repay study. We may here draw attention to a few of the causes: the mixture of people speaking different dialects produces a new form; old forms are retained in one dialect, while other dialects may discard these and retain others; localisms are perpetuated, and new terms are sometimes brought back by those who have been in other districts and found a permanent home away from their original habitat; migrations take place from, and to, different parts of the country, so that districts wide apart are more similar in their speech than the intermediate country is to one or the other. 'There can be little doubt that the corruption of old Chinese into the modern "Mandarin" dialects was caused chiefly by the immense admixture of Tartar and Thibetan blood during the period 300-900 A.D.'

It is a dream of some Chinese to introduce a uniform language in place of the numerous so-called dialects that exist throughout the length and breadth of the land. About 200 years ago the Emperor Káng Hí [K'anghsi] caused schools to be established in Canton, and elsewhere, for this purpose. We question if the result the scheme was meant to accomplish is much nearer fulfilment now than at that time. In the future, doubtless, it will be brought about to a greater or lesser extent, but by other means than that, for there is but little reasonable doubt that when the railway shall have drawn the distant parts of China together by the meshes of its network, the unification of the language will proceed with more rapid strides, as the nation by it, and other means dependent upon and accelerated by it, becomes welded into a homogeneous whole.

What then will be the speech that will succeed to this confusion of tongues in China? We believe that, if China is not subdivided, but continues as one nation in the future, in the course of time (it may take centuries to accomplish it) one language will gradually, either take the place of the others, or the others will, modifying the one, give place to a new language, which will perhaps contain the best features of all, and be an advance on any now spoken. The language that bids fair to take this prominent position in the future would seem to be the Mandarin, at all events it stands as good a chance as any, if not a better than many, of taking this enviable position.

Besides the above, Manchu was, from A.D. 1644 to 1912 the language of the rulers of China, who caused many books to be translated into it, and tried to foster it, and galvanise it into literary activity. It is not, however, a language that the Chinese take much interest in. Mongolian is also used in Mongolia, and to some extent, of course, in Peking. Tibetan, which is of Sanscrit origin, is not used by the Chinese outside that division of the Chinese territory. The different aborigines to be found in many parts of China also speak their own languages or dialects.

References.—Numerous articles have appeared in the *China Review* and *Missionary Recorder*, amongst which may be instanced those by E. H. Parker, Don, and Dyer Ball; also see the valuable 'Philological Essay' by E. H. Parker, in Giles's *Chinese—English Dictionary*,' first edition.

DIVORCE.—There are seven reasons for which, according to Chinese law founded on the old ceremonial recorded in the *Chia yü*, "Sayings of Confucius," a man may divorce his wife; they are barrenness, lasciviousness, jealousy, talkativeness, thievery, disobedience towards her husband's parents, and leprosy. These seem sweeping enough in all conscience; and to those unacquainted with the inner life of the Chinese, it would seem simple enough for a man to bring his wife to book under one or other of these, and rid himself of an uncongenial companion, but that is not the case in practice. The wife's relations have to be considered in the matter; and again, if she has no parents, she cannot be put away, as they are not living to receive her back again; further, for the lesser offences, he cannot put her away if he be in mourning for a parent; and yet again, it is much simpler for a Chinese (and causes much less ill-feeling to all parties concerned), in case no son is born to him, to take a concubine or secondary wife (not a second wife except by courtesy, for a Chinese has only one legal wife—See MARRIAGE) and increase the number, one after the other, until he obtains the longed-for heir or future worshipper at the family tombs; or, failing this, he may adopt a son (See ADOPTION). In short, the seven reasons for divorce are subject to three conditions, namely: (1) if the wife has no home to return to; (2) if she has mourned the customary three years for her husband's parents; (3) if the husband, once poor, has become rich. Divorce was not an official matter, but was left entirely to the husband. All these different expedients and restrictions nullify, or render unnecessary, the provisions as to divorce, which, like everything Chinese, is theoretically easy of accomplishment, but in practice is something very different. Statistics are difficult to obtain in China, and, when obtained, are very unreliable, owing to the inexactitude of the Chinese mind—one of their most common characteristics. No reliable statistics have been obtained on this particular subject; but, the opinion of many long resident among the people is that divorce is not any oftener resorted to than in England, probably less often by far.

Besides what has been said above, a married couple may mutually agree to separate; again, by law a husband is liable to be punished if his wife is convicted of adultery, and he does not put her away. But there is as high a standard of chastity among many classes of Chinese married women as there is among women of the West, and such a rule among the middle and higher classes, at least, does not often require application.

This is the law and custom as between husband and wife. It is very different, however, when the wife has to complain of her husband. She has then practically no redress or safeguards (unless he break her bones, when he is amenable to law), except the small and uncertain modicum of public opinion, which may keep her husband from transgressing too much, or better still, the punishment which his wife's family will take in hand, should he act so as to bring disgrace on them.

The case is quite different with the so-called secondary wives. They are not a man's wives in the sight of the law, that is to say, they do not stand on a footing of equality, though recognised as concubines, for there is only one first legitimate wife; and a man is free to dismiss these concubines from his bed and board, and treat them in a way he would not dare to adopt toward his first wife (though a man may be cruel enough to her in China, if he choose). This treatment may be modified more or less by the prospective counteraction of the socalled wife's relations and her social position, presuming she has any. If she has none, or if her position is of no account, as is more than likely often to be the case with a secondary wife, beggary or prostitution stares her in the face unless she is fortunate enough to enter another family in a similar position. (See also WOMEN and MARRIAGE).

References.—Faber, *The Status of Women in China;* Staunton, *Penal Code of China.* Most books on China also contain longer or shorter paragraphs on the same subject; see, for example, Williams, *Middle Kingdom;* Gray *China; etc.*

DOCTORS.—The native doctor of the old type is a curious character: he passes no examination; he requires no qualification. He may have failed in business and set up as a physician, for which he requires no stock in trade, medical instruments being almost unknown (See ACUPUNCTURE). If he can get an old book of prescriptions from another retiring practitioner, so much the better for him. He is now fit to kill or cure as chance may will it, or as his ignorance, or fortuitous circumstances may decree. The doctor most entitled to confidence in the sight of his countrymen is the man whose father has been one before him, and the confidence increases should his grandfather have followed the same calling. This it might be supposed was due to a belief in the influence of heredity; but, as it is stated by the Chinese, the value in their eyes consists in the son or grandson possessing all the books of prescriptions of his sires. Thus provided, he is ready to begin his empirical career. Fees vary according to the class of man and his patients, and according to the place of residence, whether it be a fashionable quarter or a poor suburb, or whether it be town or country. The enormous sum of perhaps thirty cents or half a dollar may be charged per visit, if he comes in his sedan to see his patient, and of this amount a large proportion would go for the chair and the rest for the doctor himself. Should he belong to the humbler ranks and come on foot, his fee is proportionately cheaper. He puts on a solemn air and has quite an owl-like look, as he peers out of the semi-darkness of a Chinese bedroom through his great goggle-shaped glasses—each lens of which is two inches across and set in huge, uncouth, copper frames. The thing of the greatest importance is feeling the different pulses of the human system, of which the Chinese count a number. The pulse at each wrist is felt, and each is divided into three, which, according to the light or heavy character of the pressure, indicates a different organ of the body, so, by thus feeling the pulses, the states of a dozen real or imaginary organs are determined. Having then learned by the pressure of these three at each pulse the seat of the disease, a few questions may be asked by the doctor, but these are scarcely considered necessary. A prescription, sometimes composed of the most horrible and nauseous compounds, is prepared in large doses, for the native idea is that the larger the dose, the more likely it is to prove efficacious. In prescribing for natives, the foreign doctors have to be most careful, as most ludicrous cases have occurred, such as the paper being swallowed by the sick ignoramus, as well as the powder, or pill, it contained.

The forms of medical treatment employed were diet, drugs, herbs, physical exercises, and acupuncture. A large number of works exist on the latter method, which has been used with marked success both by Chinese and foreign doctors (as in the case of enlarged liver, etc.).

Amongst their medicines, besides some that are to be found in our Western Materia Medica, are snake skins, fossils, rhinoceros or hartshorn shavings, silk-worm and human secretions, asbestos, moths, oyster-shells, etc. Almost anything that is disgusting is considered good as a medicine. Apothecaries' shops abound where the doctors' prescriptions are made up, or where the patients themselves procure medicines as they think they require them. Quack advertisements are placarded on almost every blank wall.

The manner in which the Chinese treat their physicians is rather peculiar. Should a speedy cure not result from the doctor's treatment, the patient calls in another, and, if no better, yet another, and so on in rapid succession, until, all human aid failing, he perchance at last goes to his gods, if he has not already tried them before.

It is not an uncommon sight to see a woman waving a child's jacket in her hand in the street, while she croons in a monotonous voice to the spirit of the sick child to return to the body from whence, the child being in an unconscious or comatose, condition, it is supposed to have fled.

In seasons of epidemic, large processions are got up by the different commercial guilds, every shopkeeper and householder being called upon for a subscription.

It is interesting to note that Chinese physicians, using Chinese methods, have large practices among Europeans in Australia and New Zealand. There are now, on the other hand, a very large number of fully qualified Chinese doctors who have been trained in Western medical and surgical methods, and practise in China either under or in connection with Western physicians, or independently.

References.—Williams, *Middle Kingdom; Journal N.C.B.R.A.S.*, 1864.

DOGS.—The dog is so much in evidence in China that he deserves an article to himself. From the erroneous impression that dogs form one of the principal items of the diet of the Chinese, the common variety has been dubbed the 'chow dog.' The origin of this name, however, is doubtful, but the most probable explanation is that it means simply "a Chinese dog," the Chinese at Canton having at one time been known as "Chows." A glance at one of this species is enough to show its great likeness to that depicted in books of Arctic travel, and known as the Esquimaux dog. This Chinese dog approaches much nearer to the original wolf type than the more highly bred species to be found in our Western lands. That they are not more highly developed is doubtless due to the apathy of the Chinese with regard to them, for though kept by many families as a watch-dog, the animal is not petted and made so much of as would be the case amongst us; for instance, he is not made a companion of his master's walks, nor when his owner often does not appreciate the luxury or necessity of a bath, is it likely that his dog would be given one. He lies at the outer door, or in the shop, or prowls about the street very much uncared for, according to our ideas of the treatment of our pets, dogging the steps of the foreigner, scarcely ever attacking him boldly; but retreating before him in a cowardly manner, and seeking safety at his master's door, to be reinforced with fresh courage as the stranger passes, when he issues out behind his back with his irritating bark, which has been described as a 'short, thick snap, very unlike the deep, sonorous baying of our mastiffs.' He begins with several of these and runs off into a quick succession of them for a few seconds, a series of these short refrains producing a most monotonous effect, especially when lasting for a long time. The vigorous greeting thus received from the whole pack of village dogs is extremely unpleasant when one is out for a country walk; though apparently very fierce, there is generally but little danger to be apprehended. The chow dogs are all about the same size, a foot in height and about two feet in length. The colours are uniform in one individual, and consist of light brown, black, and creamy yellow.

'Without being handsome, the chow . . . is strong, the colour varying from black to tan, brown, ruddy-brown, etc.' 'It is most uncertain in its temper,' says another writer, 'disobedient, and liable to fits of savageness. It has almost none of the repose of our good English breeds. It has also an inveterate survival of old habits, the propensity to attack domestic animals.'

The following gives rather a different view of the chow dog, being from an account of the fourth annual exhibition of the Chow Chow Club at the Royal Aquarium in London. It is taken from one of the London dailies of 1st December, 1898:

'The chow-chow, which is known by a briefer name east of Suez, is undoubtedly the fashionable dog. Every dog has his day, and the chow-chow is having his just now. Nevertheless, we venture to predict a long life for the club, because it is certain that when the chow-chow is bred from good stock and domesticated, it is a very jolly dog and quite unlike the specimens which you meet with in the Far East. It may even attain courage in time, just as the Egyptain soldier has done under British training. Most of the chow-chows now shown are of English breed, and have thus lost—to a certain extent—their native habit of barking and running away to bark another day. They are very handsome dogs, without doubt, and curiously like the Esquimaux breed, with which certainly they may claim kinship.'

A writer in *Home Notes* on dogs thus describes them:—

'Black chows, or the edible dogs of China, are very fine animals of the size of a small collie, and of the Pomeranian type, the desirable points being almost indentical. The tongue and roof of the mouth are black, and the eyes very small and keen. They are faithful creatures, and become greatly attached to their owners.' The good points in Pomeranians are 'thick, long hair, a well "feathered" tail (styled the plume), long hair on the back of the forelegs, small ears, fox-shaped head, and a frill of thick fur round the neck.'

The tongue of the best chow should be "as if it had been licking ink."

The ears do not hang down, but are sharp and upright, except in a variety to be found in the province of Ngan-hwui [Anhui], which 'has pendent ears of great length.' One peculiar feature in these dogs is the abrupt rise of the tail from the insertion, whence it curls up over the back, never hanging down. This is so marked that a wag has said that the tail almost assists in lifting the legs from the ground. This abrupt rise is heightened, doubtless, in appearance by the unusually straight hind legs, giving a somewhat ungainly look to the animal. The chow is not a very rapid runner, probably this style of hind legs handicapping it. The bitch has dew-claws on her hind legs, one on each, but the male has none. The Chinese say of the dog that it 'can go on three legs,' as indeed all dogs are seen to do occasionally.

'The dogs of Peking are very clannish, and each set jealously guards its own street or yard; they are fed by the butchers in the street and serve as scavengers there, and in all large towns. They are often mangy, presenting hideous spectacles, and instances of *plica polonica* are not uncommon; but, as among the celebrated street dogs of Constantinople, hydrophobia is almost unheard of.' [It occurs, however, in the extreme heat of the summer.]

A writer in *Cornhill* for July, 1896, speaks about—

'A large chow-dog from Northern China, which a freak of fashion has decreed shall be kept as a pet by English ladies. These dogs are not suited either by nature or training for domestic pets. They are only half-civilised dogs, very excitable, often savage, and so little considered as household companions in their native Manchuria that they are bred for the sake of their fur, and killed, like seals, when the fur is in season. But they are born sledge-dogs, immensely strong in the shoulder and short in the neck, with pulling powers far greater than those of any of the breeds used in Holland and Belgium for drawing carts. If the laws against the use of dogs for draught are repealed, just as the laws against road-engines and steam-carts are about to be repealed, the "chows" would form the basis of a new breed of cart-dogs for minor traffic.'

There is another breed of dog, the Pekingese pug, or sleeve dog; the latter name has been given to it from the masters carrying this pretty little pet in their capacious sleeves. Dr. Rennie says of it:—'The breed is a very peculiar one, something between the King Charles and the pug.' What are termed in England 'Japanese spaniels,' which appear, if not identical with, to be very similar to the Pekingese dog, and some specimens of which were taken from the Summer Palace at Peking to England, are thus described:—

'They are docile, playful, and affectionate, and of unusual intelligence. Their long silky coats, delicate and finely-formed paws, large, lustrous eyes, massive heads, and long, feathery tails, proudly curled over their backs, make them beautiful pets. . . . Smallness is an important point, as they are carried in the large sleeves of Japanese ladies and called "sleeve dogs."'

There is a large breed of dogs in Thibet which are mentioned by numerous authors:—

Marco Polo says of them:—'They have dogs of the size of asses, strong enough to hunt all sorts of wild beasts, particularly the wild oxen, which are . . . extremely large and fierce.' Turner describes them as:—'Huge dogs, tremendously fierce, strong, and noisy . . . so imperiously furious, that it was unsafe, unless the keepers were near, even to approach their dens.' Again he says:—'Up started a huge dog, big enough . . . to fight a lion.' Captain Raper describes one:—'A remarkably fine animal as large as a Newfoundland dog, with very long hair, and a head resembling a mastiff's. His tail was of an amazing length, like the brush of a fox, and curled half-way over his back.' Mr. Hosie speaks of them as:—'Fine, powerful dogs. . . . The animal brought to me for inspection required the whole strength of a Thibetan to keep him in check. Had I bought the dog, which was offered for ten taels, I should have had to engage his keeper also.'

References.—Collier, *Dogs of China and Japan in Nature and Art;* Williams, *Middle Kingdom;* Gray, *China;* Hart, *Western China; Asiatic Researches,* xi, 529; Turner, *Embassy to Thibet,* pp. 155-215; Hosie, *Three Years in Western China,* p. 134.

DRAGON.—The dragon (*lung*) was the Imperial emblem of China—the emblem of Imperial power—and symbolical of what pertained to the Emperor: his person was called 'the dragon's person'; his countenance, 'the dragon's face'; his eye, 'the dragon's eye'; his hands 'the dragon's claws'; his sleeve, 'the dragon's sleeve'; his children 'the dragon's seed'; his pen (that is the Emperor's autograph), 'the dragon's pen'; his throne 'the dragon's seat'; when he mounted it, the action was spoken of as 'the dragon's flight' ; his bed, 'the dragon's bedstead'; his decease was euphemistically termed 'the Emperor ascended upon the dragon to be a guest on high'; and his ancestral tablet was called 'the dragon tablet.'

The dragon, which was reserved for Imperial use in designs on furniture, porcelain, and clothing, was depicted with five claws; that in use by the common people had four. A Chinese author thus describes the dragon:—

'Its head is like a camel's, its horns like a deer's, its eyes like a hare's, its ears like a bull's, its neck like a snake's, its belly like an iguanodon's, its scales like a carp's, its claws like an eagle's, and its paws like a tiger's. Its scales number eighty-one, being nine by nine, the extreme (odd or) lucky number. Its voice resembles the beating of a gong. On each side of its mouth are whiskers, under its chin is a bright pearl, under its throat the scales are reversed, on the top of its head is the *poh shan,* which others call the ' *chek muk.* 'A dragon without ' a *chek muk* ' cannot ascend the skies. When its breath escapes it forms clouds, sometimes changing into rain, at other times into fire.'

Having thus given an accurate description of this wonderful creature (one of the four supernatural [or spiritually endowed] creatures, according to the Chinese, the others being the Tortoise, the female Unicorn and the male Phœnix), it only remains to be said that 'it wields the power of transformation and the gift of rendering itself visible or invisible at pleasure.' Another Chinese authority informs us that 'the dragon becomes at will reduced to the size of a silkworm, or swollen till it fills the space of Heaven and Earth. It desires to mount—and it rises till it affronts the clouds; to sink—and it descends until hidden below the fountains of the deep.' The Chinese most thoroughly believe in the existence of this mysterious and marvellous creature: it appears in their ancient history; the legends of Buddhism abound with it; Taoist tales contain circumstantial accounts of its doings; the whole country-side is filled with stories of its hidden abodes, its terrific appearances; it holds a prominent part in the pseudo-science of geomancy; its portrait appears in houses and temples, and serves even more than the grotesque lion as an ornament in architecture, art designs, and fabrics. It has, however, been less used for ornamental purposes since the overthrow of the Monarchy.

There are numerous dragons—too numerous to enter even into a succinct account of them in the space of a short article. Volumes might be filled with a history of this wonderful, antediluvian creature, embalmed in Chinese literature and memory.

Among other rôles that the dragon fills is that of a modern Neptune to the Chinese. In this character, he occupies a palace made of pearls at the bottom of the sea, sends rain, and waters the thirsty land.

A story is related of an old gentleman in England, interested in China, who was firmly of the belief that the Chinese worshipped the devil, because they paid divine honours to the dragon; only another instance, out of many, of the fallacy of reasoning on Chinese subjects from European premises. They worship the dragon, but it does not follow that their dragon is 'that old dragon,' the devil.

Another dragon is the bobtailed dragon, which causes whirlwinds; a frightfully destructive one in Canton city, a number of years ago, was believed to be due to his agency.

The district of country on the mainland immediately opposite the English colony of Hongkong is called Kaú-lung (generally written, Kowloong, or Kowloon, but in Wade's transliteration Chiu-lung), or the Nine-Dragons, probably so named from the numerous ranges of hills, which, like gigantic monsters, spread their sinuous course along the coast, the nine dragons being a favourite number with the Chinese, and represented in some of their ancient works on standards.

The national flag of China adopted with, and by, the navy of foreign-built ships, was a triangular yellow flag with a dragon on it, now changed to an oblong one more in keeping with the shape of other national flags, at first with the same device, but, under the Republic, to a striped flag of five colours. See FLAG.

The conventional representations of the dragon, as we have already said, are commonly divisible into two. On Imperial China we see a snake-like body mounted on four legs, with an enormous head; the feet are five-clawed. This is sprawled over the dish, or whatever it may be, and covers the greater part of it. On vases used by the people as ornaments, a scope is given for ingenuity by the introduction of a number of similar saurians (but only with four claws) in different positions on the vase—front views being given as well, in which the two horns are seen. On mural pictures and in paintings on wood, inserted above doorways, the rain dragon is the one usually represented. Here what is seen of the hideous monster conveys more the impression of an enormous python, as folds of a very thick and large snake-like body are visible amongst masses of clouds, the half-suggestive revelation of what is seen increasing, if anything, the impression of size, while a frightful head fronts one, full-faced, with all its gigantic repulsiveness. In books printed under Imperial sanction or auspices, two dragons encircle the title, striving, not like the lion and the unicorn for the crown, but for a pearl. There are again two kinds of dragons which were carried in some of the processions of which the Chinese are so fond. They are at such times represented as long serpentine creatures of great girth, and 150 or 200 feet long, made of lengths of gay, bright-coloured crape and sparkling with tiny spangle-like mirrors. Every yard or so a couple of human feet—those of the bearers—buskined in gorgeous silk, are visible, the head and shoulders of the men being unseen. The whole is fronted by an enormous head of ferocious aspect, before the gaping jaws of which a man manœuvres a large pearl after which the dragon prances and wriggles. The difference between the two kinds is that the one is resplendent with gold scales, while the other gleams with silver ones. That this different way of representation is not due to simple fancy, appears from the fact that in India they distinguish three varieties of dragon: one of which lived in the mountains, and had golden scales; and the other in caves or flat country, and had silver scales; while the third dwelt in marshes and fens, and was of a black colour. The rain dragon used in mural representations appears more like the last. We give the following account of the supposed origin of the dragon, from the learned pen of Mr. Charles Gould:—

'It [the dragon] is more likely to have once had a real existence than to be a mere offspring of fancy. . . . We may infer that it was a long terrestrial lizard, hibernating and carnivorous, with the power of constricting with its snake-like body and tail; possibly furnished with wing-like expansions of its integument, after the fashion of *Draco volans*, and capable of occasional progress on its hind legs alone, when excited in attacks. It appears to have been protected by armour and projecting spikes, like those found in *Moloch horridus* and *Megalania prisca*, and was possibly more nearly allied to this last form than to any other which has yet come to our knowledge. Probably it preferred sandy, open country to forest land; its habitat was the highlands of Central Asia, and the time of its disappearance about that of the Biblical Deluge. . . . Although terrestrial, it probably, in common with most reptiles, enjoyed frequent bathing, and when not so engaged, or basking in the sun, secluded itself under some overhanging bank or cavern. The idea of its fondness for swallows, and power of attracting them, mentioned in some traditions, may not impossiby have been derived from these birds hawking round and through its open jaws in the pursuit of the flies attracted by the viscid humours of its mouth.'

References.—Gould, *Mythical Monsters; China Review*, Vol. xiii; Doré, *Recherches sur les Superstitions Chinoises*, Vol. vii; Werner, *Myths and Legends of China.*

DRAGON-BOATS AND THE DRAGON-BOAT FESTIVAL.— This festival is the nearest approach to an annual regatta that the Chinese possess. It is held on the fifth day of the fifth moon, and is known as Tuan Yang, but the preceding days shadow forth the feast day as well.

It took its origin in the search for the body of a virtuous minister of state, Ch'ü Yüan (332-295 B.C.), whose remonstrances were unheeded by his unworthy sovereign, and whose only reward was degradation and dismissal. He committed suicide by drowning himself in the Mi-lo River, an affluent on the south-east side of the Tungt'ing Lake, in the province of Hunan, and on the first anniversary of his death, the ceremony of looking for his body was begun; it has been continued on succeeding anniversaries ever since, and has resulted in this festival, observed in all parts of the country where there are streams, rivers, lakes, sea, or any suitable water. Little packages of boiled rice, done up in bamboo leaves, are eaten at this time, as such offerings were cast into the river by the fishermen who tried to recover the body.

The dragon-boats are long narrow boats from fifty to one hundred feet in length, broad enough to seat two men abreast. The craft is propelled rapidly with paddles, accompanied by the sound of a drum and gongs which are placed in the centre of the boat. Impromptu races are got up, not unattended with accidents at times, as the boats are slight and dangerous when paddled by well-nigh a hundred excited Chinamen, wild with enthusiasm and sometimes also unsteady with spirits. Large crowds of spectators line every vantage ground on the banks of the river; and prizes of no intrinsic value are often offered by them, which are eagerly contested for, the bare honour of winning spurring the men on in their efforts; the crews are occasionally treated by wealthy hongs on the banks. For hours and days nothing is heard but the unceasing monotonous clang of the gongs, and the boom of the deep-toned drums in the numerous boats.

Since the advent of plague, the Chinese think that the dragon-boats brought out and paddled about at, or near, the time of the festival will drive it away.

This Dragon-Boat Feast is one of the four festivals at which settlements of accounts take place amongst the Chinese; the others being New Year's Eve, occurring sometime in our January or February; the Moon Festival on the 15th day of the 8th moon, in September or October; and the Winter Solstice Festival, a variable feast in the 11th moon, November or December. The Dragon-Boat Festival is the second of the series, occurring on the 5th day of the 5th moon, in June or July.

References.—Gray *China;* Doolittle, *Social Life of the Chinese;* Mayers, *Chinese Reader's Manual;* De Groot. *Les Fêtes annuelles célébrées à Emoui.*

DRAMA.—See THEATRE.

DRESS.—The foundation, or starting point, of all Chinese dress is the loose pair of trousers and the almost equally loose-fitting jocket; with these two articles on, a Chinese is completely dressed: all the rest are not necessaries, but luxuries. The fundamental idea is simply displayed in these two; the other articles which are piled on to a greater or lesser degree, owing to the weather, or the length of the owner's purse, are merely, with the exception of the head-gear and that for the feet, an elaboration of that simple idea. Take any article of male attire. The long gabardine, or robe, is only the jacket which has overgrown to the ankles, instead of stopping short a little below the middle of the body: it has not an entirely different shape, as with our various shapes of coats and jackets, or what difference there is, is but slight; and even what, for want of a better term, one calls a waistcoat, is not quite another style of article, but simply a short straight jacket without sleeves, buttoning up as the common, close-fitting, sleeveless one (worn occasionally by the labouring classes) does. There are two varieties of it; one so buttoning, and one fastened at the side. A riding-jacket has wide sleeves, but is still a jacket. The jackets of the women are of a different shape from that of the men, being longer, reaching well towards the knees, and having much wider sleeves.

If one proceeds to the lower extremities, there are, as said above, the loose-fitting trousers. These sometimes are tucked into long stockings, which are neatly bound with garters below the knee, and presto! our boy or waiter is in knickerbockers—the same pair of trousers doing duty for both styles of dress Is the weather cold? Then a pair of leggings is put on. These are simply single legs of pegtop trousers diminishing gradually in calibre, as thy proceed downwards, till their extremities are tied round the ankles. They are fastened up to the girdle at the waist; but there is a void space behind, where they do not meet, and where the inner jacket hangs in folds, presenting a most untidy appearance unless a long robe is worn over all to hide it. A woman's trousers are exactly the same shape as a man's. They do not wear knickerbockers, but the middle and upper classes often wear, especially when dressed up, what for want of a better name, are called skirts. These are the very embodiment of the divided skirt, for the simple reason that their different component parts have never been united, and, at the same time, they have a trace of the trousers still about them—trousers unfinished, as it were, for one piece hangs in front down to the ankles, like an apron, and another piece hangs behind in the same way; they are buttoned up at one side, and open at the other, while embroidery and numerous pleats in vertical lines adorn them.

There are several varieties of dress besides those named above, adapted to different uses, as well as to the changes of weather. For instance, Nature's garb appears to be often all-sufficient for the Swatow fisherman or farmer, and even many of the boatmen at the city of Tie Yöng, near Swatow, wear nothing else at times. In other parts of China, the savage state is not so nearly approached, except in the case of young children of the poorer classes, who run about naked for several years, the several years being of longer duration when they are boys. In Amoy and Swatow it is not at all uncommon to see a boy with nothing on at all but a purse. It must, however, be explained that the purse is more of an apron or pinafore than with us, and is fastened round the neck, covering as much of the front of the body as decency requires in a hot climate—though this last is not always even attended to. The common coolie or labourer considers himself sufficiently attired for his work in hot weather, with a loin cloth and a pair of straw sandals, but the latter are optional. Others make shift with a pair of short trousers, only reaching half-way down the thighs, or roll the longer trousers up that length, or as far as they will go. In the purely native dress, nothing in the form of a shirt or singlet is worn, though now of late years, from contact with foreigners, the latter is being adopted by a few, and must be much more comfortable in cold weather than the loose-fitting jacket. Coats, jackets, and trousers, varied only by robes and leggings, are piled one on the top of the other as the weather gets colder. More layers are worn than by most Western peoples, because the inner garments are made of cotton instead of wool. The upper garments are readily cast off in the middle of the day, or in a warm room, thus offering a great advantage, in this one particular, to our style of dress, where a top-coat is the only thing one can throw off on entering a house.

The women's innermost garment is of thin stuff, close fitting, and closely buttoned up the front, but above this, the usual piling on of jackets takes place if the weather requires it. The women wear no long robes in the South.

Less care is taken of the legs with both men and women, and fewer thicknesses appear to satisfy them there. There is a considerable variety displayed in sandals, boots, and shoes. Besides the straw ones, already mentioned as worn by men, simple soles of leather, with a loop for one of the toes, and strings to tie them round the ankles, are worn by those of both sexes, who labour out-of-doors in carrying burdens, etc. Men's and women's shoes, on the contrary, are quite distinct; one of the most marked differences being in the thickness of the sole. The large-footed women are perched up on a thick white sole, two or three inches in height. Of late years, Shanghai shoes with thin soles have come into vogue amongst those who are well dressed, and many wear shoes of foreign type. And again a curious style is in fashion: it consists of the whole foot being poised on a round pedestal a few inches high, fixed in the centre of the sole. This is the Manchoo shoe; but it is going out, if not quite out, of fashion again. Common shoes are made of cloth, but silk and satin and embroidery are also largely employed. The cramped-up little feet are enclosed, after being wound up in long bandages, in small shoes of from two and a half to four or five inches in length, coming to a point at the toe. The pain that this foolish fashion entails on the poor girls is well shown by the common Chinese saying: 'For every pair of small feet there is a *kong* [jar] full of tears.' No stockings can be put on with such feet, but they are worn on the natural feet by women as well as by men, or rather, to be correct, socks and stockings are both worn by men, the former principally in summer, and socks are generally used by women, though stockings are also put on. Those of foreign manufacture are coming into use at treaty ports and other places; the native ones consist of pieces of calico sewn together. It may be mentioned that both sexes wear a girdle of cord round the waist to fasten their trousers up, by hitching them over it. There are no openings in the trousers, except for the legs and waist. A collar, or rather stock, made of satin, is worn 'round the neck by men in winter, and when in 'dress.'

Before marriage a Chinese girl's hair is plaited in a queue, but on marriage it is done up into a curiously shaped coiffure.

The ladies wear no bonnets or hats, neither do the common women, as a rule, except those who are out in the sun and exposed to the weather. Their hair is combed and plastered with a gum, and, thus made up, forms a sufficient head-covering in a hot climate. But an endless variety is seen in this style of head-dress; now a modest set of protuberances in connection with the tea-pot-handlelike coiffure at the back of the head; now enormous butterfly wings project from the side of the head, or lie closer to it; again back wings project to a greater or lesser degree; and yet again various adjuncts are added to eke out the quantity of hair, or to raise it like a small horn on the head. In some places the styles differ in every bit of country-side. In Swatow, in a group of from twenty to forty women, nearly a score of different coiffures were seen. The boat-girls in Macao, and some in Hongkong, go with a bright coloured handkerchief over their heads, tied under their chins. The Hakka women also often bind a cloth round the head, looking something like an old-fashioned bonnet. In Swatow and the surrounding country a number of different kinds of head-cloths are worn by the women, according to the districts they come from. A curious one was observed at the district city of Tíe Yöng, near Swatow. It was a long narrow cloth thrown over the head, and the ends were brought round the face when its wearers wished to hide their countenances from the passers-by. In winter a broad band, either plain or embroidered, is often bound across the forehead by women, and prevents that cold, aching feeling which an extremely low temperature produces. The men wear a skull-cap of satin with a cord button of red or black on the top in winter, but go bare-headed in summer, though some wear large hats made of thin straw or bamboo. Felt hats are likewise seen; they have a turned-up brim, and some of the better kind have gold thread on the edge; their use is restricted to the lower classes. In very cold weather a peculiar headgear is worn by some. It consists of a pointed cap, which, with a flap falling down behind and buttoning under the chin, covers up not only the neck but the whole head with the exception of the face. Little boys are often seen with these on, as well as some men and a few women. Large bamboo hats, nearly a yard in diameter, effectually shed the rain off, and as effectually protect the head from the rays of the sun. Several other varieties of bamboo hats are worn, some by men alone; others by women alone; while others are patronised irrespective of the sex of the wearer. In rainy weather the lower classes in the South put on a cloak made of bamboo leaves sewn together, presenting a veritable Robinson Crusoe appearance; but in Swatow a similar one made of coir fibre is substituted, looking somewhat like the *capude palha*, or straw cloads, worn by the peasantry, in the northern provinces of Portugal. At such times labourers go bare-footed, as for that matter they do at nearly all times; shop-keepers and others splash about through the mud and rain on shoes with wooden soles a couple of inches thick (for the usual felt sole acts as a sponge in wet weather), a poorer style consists of a ruder chump of wood with a network of string for the toes. A still better class, such as official underlings, and some gentlemen, put on boots made especially for damp and wet, reaching half-way, or even further up toward the knees. Wooden clogs, with leather uppers, are used by women and girls.

We have already spoken of jackets, robes, waistcoats or sleeveless jackets, and close-fitting ones. There are besides, double jackets or lined ones, and fur jackets. A dress-suit consists of a robe opening at the bottom of the centre line, both before and behind, with sleeves shaped like a horse's hoof, a jacket is worn over this, and satin boots with thick white soles, a sash round the waist, and an official hat with a button at the top, are put on.

Earrings are quite a part of Chinese female dress; every woman and girl wears them; and so accustomed does one get to see them in a woman's ears, that it looks almost as queer to see a Chinese woman without these indispensables, as it would to see an English lady going barefoot; and a Chinese woman would feel as ashamed to appear in the one condition, as an English lady would in the other. The earrings differ in style in different parts of China, and there is as great a dissimilarity between them as there is between those of one country and another. Among the Hakkas, a common earring is a silk tassel. The Foochow women have enormous rings, several inches in diameter, in their ears. The Cantonese earring is often formed of two parts: the earring proper—a round metallic (gold, silver, or brass) ring, broadened out into a flat ornamental surface in front, into which a flat ring of jade, or other stone, or composition, is hung.

Fashions in dress do change in China, but so slight and gradual are the changes—except when some dynastic overthrow revolutionises everything—that to the foreigner no difference is visible, but to the initiated into these mysteries an extremely gradual change is perceptible, so that, in the course of forty or fifty years, ladies' sleeves are noticed to be wider than before, and, in the course of a quarter of a century, quite a new style of dressing ladies' hair is seen. Some fashions even can be seen to change every two or three years.

The style of dress, it should be noticed, is not quite the same in different parts of China. What has been written above applies principally to the South of China, in the neighbourhood of Hongkong, Macao, and Canton: even in these neighbourhoods, the dress of the Hakkas is not quite the same as that of the Cantonese (See HAKKAS). The mode of doing up the hair by the women, the kind of earrings worn by them, as well as the dress itself, are so distinct as to mark anyone, at the first glance, as coming from some other part of China. The men's dress has, however, but little or nothing to differentiate it, the greatest exception being in the case of the Swatow and Hokkien men, who often wear a turban, whereas other Chinese are seldom seen with it. The short jackets of these same men are sometimes longer than those in the extreme south.

The colour of the clothing worn also differs. White is never seen as an outer garment on women in Canton or Hongkong, except to please Europeans; this colour being reserved alone for undergarments, in which, of course, a woman would be ashamed to appear in public. In Amoy, however, this does not seem to be the rule, and in that part of the country bright red, and other colours are worn by young ladies, a thing which is never seen in Canton amongst respectable women. In Swatow, white also is worn, but the young ladies do not appear to come out in such brilliant hues as in Amoy. These may be taken as instances of the variations in style of dress in China.

Though the Chinese men go often in a state of semi-nudity, the women make up for it by a severe modesty in their dress. There is no exposure of their person, as there is in the evening dress among European ladies; neither is tight-lacing a vice among the Chinese. They sedulously hide all the contours of the figure, and in fact tie down the breasts.

The chief difference between the costumes above described and those worn in the north is the use of fur or skin garments and fur or skin hats and caps in the winter, but the old-fashioned fur-lined ear-caps are now hardly even seen, their place being taken by the flaps of caps, by mufflers, or by the turned-up collars of coats. The older type of winter hat was round, turned up with a brim of black velvet or fur.

Within the last twenty years, the Western, or foreign, style of dress (which, however, is less suitable to the climate than the native style) has been adopted by many Chinese youths and men, mostly those in schools and colleges, or in foreign employ. Many of the women have modified the native type of dress worn by them by adopting a skirt to cover the trousers and by wearing foreign shoes and caps. The vast majority of Chinese, however, still (1924) retain the native style of dress. The foreign type of costume is, as a rule, more prevalent in those parts of the country in contact with foreign trading centres, missionary stations, etc.

Reference.—Werner, *Descriptive Sociology—Chinese.*

EARTHQUAKES.—An earthquake is not a phenomenon often experienced by the foreign resident in China. Very slight shocks have been felt a few times in Hongkong, but so insignificant have they been as to be unknown to the majority till the next day's papers contained a notice of them; but in some other parts of China they are not such a trivial matter. They are recorded as of frequent occurrence in Hainan; earthquakes in conjunction with storms, famine, and pestilence have materially decreased the population at one time; but, as a general rule, earthquake shocks would appear to be infrequent in China, and not of serious import; though within the last few years serious shocks have occurred in Kansu. In 1888, a violent shock wrecked about a thousand native houses in Peking, in which district severe shocks are said to occur about once a century. We give a short, but unfortunately not a complete list, as the subject has not yet received the study and attention it merits.

A.D. 1037.—A severe earthquake 'that affected Honan and Shansi and caused the death of 22,000 people, and the wounding and maiming of between 5 and 6,000 more.'

A.D. 1295-1308.—During the latter years of this period 'severe earthquakes in T'ai-yüan and Ta-t'ung in Shansi. In the former town over 800 houses were thrown down, and a large number of people were killed. Ta-t'ung, however, suffered still more severely. There 5,000 houses were shattered into ruins, and 2,000 people were buried beneath them.'

A.D. 1334.—Earthquakes; also during the next few years.

In the early days of the Ming dynasty (this dynasty lasted from A.D. 1368 to A.D. 1644), a 'terrible earthquake visited the plain of Chien-ch'ang. . . . The old city of Ning-yüan sank bodily into the ground, and gave place to the large lake which lies to the south-east of the present city.'

A.D. 1662.—One in China, when 300,000 persons were buried in Peking alone.

A.D. 1731.—Another, when 100,000 persons were swallowed up at Peking.

A.D. 1847, November 13th.—An earthquake at Shanghai.

A.D. 1850.—The city of Ning-yüan, in western China, already mentioned, was again ruined by an earthquake.

A.D. 1852, December 16th.—There was a shock of some violence at Shanghai, at 8.13 P.M., and another slight shock at 10 P.M. There were no serious effects. These were felt at Ningpo at 8.9 P.M., and three hours later. There were other shocks at Shanghai on two subsequent days.

A.D. 1854.—A shock felt in Canton, and about the same year at Chinkiang, where people were thrown on their faces.

A.D. 1867.—A sharp shock at Ningpo, at a few minutes after 10 A.M. on the 17th December. Bells were set ringing, clocks stopped, chandeliers swayed, and water in earthen jars rippled violently. A slighter shock was felt at Shanghai.

A.D. 1871, April 11th.—A severe earthquake to the west of Sz-chuan [Ssŭch'uan], at about 11 A.M., at Bathang, when 'government offices, temples, granaries, store-houses, and fortifications, with all the common dwellings,' were overthrown, and most of the inmates killed. Flames burst out in four places, and were beaten down on the 16th, but rumbling noises underground continued like distant thunder, and the earth rocked and rolled. In about ten days the earth quieted. For several days before, the water had overflowed the dykes, the earth cracked, and black fetid water spurted out. The region affected by this earthquake was over a circuit of four hundred miles, and, it occurring 'simultaneously over the whole of this region,' 2,298 people were killed. 'In some places steep hills split and sank into deep chasms, in others mounds on level plains became precipitous cliffs, and the roads and highways were rendered impassable by obstructions.'

1874, June 23rd.—A slight shock in Hongkong.

1888, June 13th.—A severe shock in Peking.

1890.—Five distinct shocks during the year in the province of Shansi; the heaviest was in the spring, and upwards of a hundred persons were killed in it. On the 15th October two shocks were felt at Fênchau-fú. This year was exceptional. It is said that earthquake shocks are only felt once in ten years in that province.

1891, April 12th or 13th.—Three shocks of earthquake felt during the day at Taiyuen-fú [T'ai-yüan Fu] in Shansi.

1891, April 17th.—A severe earthquake shock occurred at Fênchau-fú in Shansi, at half-past six o'clock in the morning, the worst that has happened in that region within thirty years. A number of houses were thrown down in the city and suburbs, and some eight or ten persons were killed. There was a great destruction of houses in the villages. The shock extended at least 100 *li* in all directions. 'It is somewhat surprising that more damage was not done, as the whole country rocked like a ship on a wave of the sea. The earthquake lasted one minute only, but some of the houses that were shaken by it fell during the following afternoon. The people say that earthquakes are caused by a large fish, which wakes up after a sleep of some years and gives a flop.'

1891, August 3rd.—A slight shock felt by a few residents at Hongkong, at 2.10 P.M.

1892, April 22nd.—A distinct and continuous series of shocks, lasting for a few seconds in Hongkong, with lateral vibrations and a rumbling sound. but doing no damage; also felt in a number of the other coast ports in China.

1892, July 21st.—A slight shock felt at the Peak (Hongkong) and Kowloong, at 6.40 A.M.

1892, July 28th.—A heavy earthquake shock at Hoihow 'that shook the whole place, houses being seen and felt to stagger and shake in a most terrifying manner, . . . accompanied by a subterranean roar far louder than thunder. . . . It is said by the natives that Hoihow has not been visited with a similar shock for a century: even a slight one is an unusual occurrence.

1892, August 4th.—A slight shock in Hongkong.

1892, December 16th.—A shock at 3 A.M. at Amoy, by which people were awakened, and lasting for several seconds.

1893, August 14th.—A slight shock felt in T'ai-ku-hsien; no damage.

1893, August 29th.—An earthquake of great magnitude, devastating an area of 9,000 square miles in the Tibetan district of Kada, bordering the province of Sz-chuan [Ssŭch'uan]. The Dalai Lama's Grand Monastery of Hueiyuan, and 7 small Lamaserais were buried in ruins, and 804 houses, belonging to the native and Tibetan soldiers and their families, met the same fate. 74 Lama priests, and 137 Chinese and Tibetans were killed, with a large proportion of wounded.

1893, October 17th.—Severe repeated shocks at Taipeh-fú [T'ai-pei Fu] in Formosa, and on the 16th a strong shock was felt in Amoy and Kulangsu, at 2.30 A.M.

1893, December 8th.—A severe shock at Foochow, at 11.10 P.M.

1894, June 20th.—A sharp shock of earthquake felt in Amoy and Kulangsu, at 6.30 or 6.45 A.M.; a very slight shock had been noticed two days previously, at about 2 P.M. Three houses were wrecked.

1894, August 11th.—There were slight shocks at Hongkong, at 10.55 A.M. and 1.20 P.M.

1895, August 30th.—Earthquake shocks were felt in Hongkong, Swatow, Waichow [Huichow], and Haifung. The earthquake was severe at Swatow, where it occurred at ten minutes to six P.M. It was preceded by an excessively hot day, with a dull, oppressive feeling in the air, rain falling heavily just before. It lasted between fifteen and twenty seconds, by one account, and two minutes by another; a slight shock had been experienced about 3.30 P.M., a continuation of minor shocks followed it as well, up until 3.15 A.M. on Saturday. Considerable damage was done on shore to native property, and a little to foreign in the way of cracked walls and ceilings. The vessels in harbour were shaken from truck to keelson, the colour of the water in the river was changed from blue to brown by the agitation of the mud, and the sea had a very confused appearance south of the Lamocks. The direction from E. to W. It was the severest shock ever felt in Swatow. It was thus described in Hongkong:—'Horizontal vibration between E. and W. roughly; there was no vertical motion, and hardly any perceptible travelling direction. The first distinct oscillation was felt a minute or so before a quarter to six, and lasted about 30 seconds. Fainter tremors were felt for some minutes afterwards; and another distinct shock occurred about 11.30 P.M.' Persons sitting or lying down felt it plainly, and it interferred a little with writing. It was felt most in high buildings. Two gentlemen in upper floors of the Hongkong Hotel felt dizzy, and thought the place was coming down. Bottles and glasses rattled in some buildings. 'A coolie sitting on the pavement in the streets rushed into the roadway, shouting that the houses were falling.'

1895, August–October.—Earthquake shocks at Kit Yöng, 30 miles from Swatow, from the 30th August till 11th of October, 'the country round for eighteen miles seeming to be within the district of disturbance.' Two small shocks toward the end of September at Swatow, but no damage. At Tsing Hai City in the Chao Chow Prefecture there were several earthquake shocks with disastrous consequences, more than a hundred houses falling, and about forty persons being killed by their collapse, the shocks in Kit Yöng being slight in comparison.

1896, July 22nd.—A pretty severe shock at Tientsin, about 8.52 P.M. 'A tremor, accompanied by a rumbling or grating noise, as if a large quantity of bricks had been shot from carts, was, after an interval of two seconds, followed by a very distinct earth oscillation, which lasted for two or three seconds. . . . The most severe shock that has been felt at Tientsin since 1888.'

1897, January 17th.—A slight shock in Hongkong; and January 18th, a severe one at Foochow, at 6 A.M., direction about north and south.

1898, November 12th.—A shock in the city of Shíú Hing (about 70 or 80 miles from Canton) and the surrounding villages. Houses, windows, furniture, and hanging lamps shook with a creaking noise as if about to fall; and people were startled from sleep by a phenomenon which they had never experienced before. The elders made enquiries as to whether it portended good or evil.

1901, June 7th.—'Two shocks of earthquake at Foochow, at 8.5 A.M., the second of which was severer than any for many years.'

1903, January 6th.—A slight shock at Weihaiwei at 6 A.M., and at Shanghai at 6 h. 2 m. 2 s. A.M., stopping two clocks looking north.

1925, March 16th.—Tali Fu, Yünnan, destroyed, 5,000 people killed.

The above examples give a good idea of the average nature and frequency of earthquakes in China. In 1909, a catalogue of earthquakes recorded in China from 1767 B.C. (the year of the great slide of Mount T'ai) to A.D. 1896 was published by Pére Hoang as volume xxviii of the series *Variétés Sinologiques*, his work being continued by Pére Tobar in a second volume of the same series and number.

References.—Variétés Sinologiques, Vols. xxviii and xxviii *bis*; Werner, *Descriptive Sociology—Chinese;* Biot, *Catalogue Générale des Tremblements de Terre . . . observés en Chine depuis les temps anciens jusqu'à nos jours* (1841); Omori, *Tremblements de Terre en Chine* (1899); Parker, *A List of Chinese Earthquakes* (1909).

ECLIPSE.—The common idea amongst the Chinese of an eclipse is that some monster is swallowing the sun or moon; hence gongs and drums are beaten and an uproar and noise is made to drive the monster dog away. That these efforts are successful is proved by the sun or moon emerging intact after each encounter. Though some of the high officials know the absurdity of this notion, yet the farce, as far as the Government is concerned, was, until recently, kept up by an occasional notification like the following:—

'A Notification in the matter of saving and guarding the Sun and Moon:—

'On the 10th day of the 9th moon [21st October, 1901] Yune, Intendant of Circuit (invested with power of control over military forces) of Suchow, Ts'ung Kong, and T'ai Ts'ong, issued a Notification suspended in front of his yamên, to the effect (stated in general terms) that on the 15th day of the 9th moon (26th October, 1901), being the Mò Yan Day (of the Diurnal Sexagenary Circle), there will be an eclipse (*lit.* an eating) of the Moon, and that on the 1st day of the 10th moon [11th November, 1901], being the Kwai Tsz Day, there will be an eclipse of the Sun. On the arrival of these dates, all Civil and Military Officers are directed each and all to save and guard the Sun and Moon.'

The above was issued by the Shanghai Taotai.

Various eclipses are recorded in the Chinese classical books; most of them have been verified by modern mathematicians.

EDUCATION.—The Chinese owe everything to their system of education. It is this which, amidst all the changes of dynasty, has kept them a nation; it is this which has knit together the extremes of this vast land, and has caused the same aspirations to rise, and the same thoughts to course, through people differing in vernacular, and in many customs and habits; it is this that has been the conqueror of the conquering hosts that have swept over the land, and set up an alien dynasty more than once in her history.

The following paragraphs describe the system of education which prevailed until the introduction of schools, colleges, and universities on Western models.

The Chinese child was heavily handicapped when he began his educational course, for 'the language of the fireside is not the language of the books'; nor had he all the auxiliary aids which first launch a child on the sea of learning. and make the acquisition of knowledge a pleasure in happy Western homes, with the present-day beautifully illustrated books, and language simplified to encourage the youthful beginner: there was no 'Reading Made Easy,' no 'Laugh and Learn,' no 'Peep of Day,' nor any of the other numerous books, which are the delight of the little ones amongst us. Though one often saw a bright, intelligent infant among the Chinese, the absence of all aids, similar in their design to those mentioned above, must have been a terrible want to the poor little Celestial. Were the first book put into the youngster's hands (the *San-tzŭ ching*, or "Three Word Classic") named 'Reading Made Difficult' it might then convey some idea of the nature of its contents; for, barring the fact that it is in rhyme and in lines of three words each, there is nothing in it to smooth the rough path for little feet. It begins with a statement that might tax all the mental powers of a philosopher to fathom, to wit:—'Men at their birth are by nature radically good'; after this tough introduction, instances are adduced of youthful learning and precocity, all tending to show the necessity of education. Categories of the numerical series, of which the Chinese are so fond, follow, such for example as the three powers—heaven, earth, and man; the five cardinal virtues; and six kinds of grain. A list of books to be learned is next enumerated, followed by an epitome of Chinese history in the tersest form possible; and the book ends with what, if it were only in an intelligible form for the boy, would be the most interesting part of all, viz:—instances of the pursuit of knowledge under difficulties, which are used to goad the future aspirant for literary fame on his course.

At first scarcely anything he read was understood by him, but he had to learn it off by heart, so as to say it without a single error. For four or five years he learned the names of the Chinese characters, but the great majority of them were meaningless signs to him. Book after book had he to get up in this wearisome manner, and page after page of copy-book characters had he to trace in a listless round, which knew no Sunday rest, nor Wednesday, nor Saturday half-holiday: a Chinese school was for work, and not play; play was considered a waste of time, and, as such, to be discouraged as much as possible; no variety of studies; nothing to break the monotony from daylight till dark, only enough time to take meals being allowed. Verily it is no wonder that the Chinese school-boy appeared heavy and dull, grave and dignified, and that he had his company manners always at hand, appearing the pink of propriety like all the fossilised youngsters he had read about. At last a little light was allowed to glint into this mental darkness, for he was initiated into the mysteries and privileges of knowing what the thousands of seemingly arbitrary signs meant. And here is the reason why, though nearly all Chinese (at least in the more civilised parts of the empire) can read to a greater or lesser extent, so many of them understand but little of what they read; for many of them are unable from poverty to pursue their course of education beyond the initial stage. Many of them are in the position of Milton's daughters: the blind poet taught them to read Latin to him—simply to read it, without a knowledge of what it meant; and the Chinese that is spoken in everyday life is nearly as different from much of that contained in the books, as a dead language is from a living one.

There was no class system in Chinese schools; each boy formed a class by himself: there were as many classes as there were boys. A dull scholar was thus not drawn on faster than he was able to go by the quicker boys, nor did the brighter pupils have a drag on their progress in the persons of the dull ones. As each boy learned his lesson he went up to say it (turning his back to the teacher while he said it), the long school-hours also making it necessary for him to learn the greater part, if not all, of his work in school-time. A Chinese school made itself heard long before it was seen: a confused babel of sounds warned you of your approach to it; for each boy was learning his task off by heart, repeating it over and over again, till fixed in the memory, in a loud sing-song tone of voice; the effect of thirty or forty boys (for few schools were fortunately much larger than that) all doing their best to outvoice each other in this manner, being better imagined than described, and, once heard, never forgotten. In England, schools are a nuisance to their neighbours at play-time; there was no play-time in Chinese schools—they were, on the contrary, a nuisance when the boys were at their lessons.

If a boy's studies were continued, he was taught, as we have said, the translation of this wonderfully recondite literary style into more intelligible language. Besides this, the following subjects found a place in the curriculum: composition, where rules of grammar were conspicuous by their absence, and position was everything, and precedent or ancient usage established the proper collocation of words. Intimately connected with this was the construction of antithetical sentences, where meaning, word, and phrase, as well as tone, were matched together with wonderful care, precision, and musical rhythm. One or two other forms of composition were also taught, and the scholar learned the art of letter-writing, where almost every possible idea was already provided for in cut-and-dried expressions redolent with the flowers of allusion, classic lore, and fable. This was a most important branch of Chinese education, and required special study. *Belles-lettres* also took a place in the more extended course of study. A collection from ancient authors, forming a course of Chinese literature, was placed in the hands of the student; a smattering of Chinese history, valuable for the sake of allusions it placed at a writer's disposal, was acquired; artificial verse-making claimed a share of attention; and the composition of those wonderful essays, where the reasoning proceeded in a circle, and ended where it began, which were valuable as preparing the student for the Civil Service examinations; this last being the final stage for which all the preceding had been preparatory; this, the goal which had necessitated all the arduous toil, with, in the event of success, its resultant office-holding. (See EXAMINATIONS.)

The whole of the classics (the Four Books and the Five Classics) were mastered, as well as the commentaries thereon, in the school and collegiate course, extending over some years. It will thus be seen that geography, arithmetic, algebra, mathematics, and all branches of science, were utterly unknown in a Chinese educational course. What then was the result? Not the acquisition of knowledge, or the training of the mind, so much as the turning out of successful essayists; a marvellous training of the memory, and the extraordinary development of the imitative faculty—these two at the expense of everything else—no originality, no scope for individuality; the production of literary machines, the manufacture of mental type-writers, where the stereotyped forms of antiquity were reproduced with but scant variety. It speaks well for the Chinese nation, that, with all this tight-lacing of healthy aspirations, with all this binding of the feet of progress, it has been impossible entirely to curb all individuality, to check all variety. It has been well said that though this system 'has considerable educative value' it yet 'limits the mental and moral vision to the horizon which confined the mind of Confucius twenty-four centuries ago, cramps the intellect, stunts the growth of moral feeling, and bends the will into an antagonism to everything non-Chinese.' It has also been stated with truth that, 'the vast majority of the educated men in China do not know to this day what is the meaning of the most common terms in our educational vocabulary, and much less do they know the use and value of the things designated, or how they are to be studied.'

China had, until recently, no school-boards, nor even anything in the place of the National and British schools in England. Schools were opened by masters to gain their living, or established by the gentry, or one tutor was employed by several families to conduct a private school for their children, while colleges,or, strictly speaking, higher schools, established on pretty much the same principles, abounded in all cities.

We have thus far only mentioned boys, and we might close without any reference to girls; for the attitude of the nation, as a whole, with regard to the education of this sex, was, until within the last few years, almost that of complete neglect. Notwithstanding this, not a few instances are adduced in Chinese history of blue-stockings; and a very small minority of the girls either managed to pick up such a smattering of the characters as to be able to read cheap novels, or, very rarely, had the advantage of a teacher provided by their parents, who were stimulated to give them an education, in some cases by the example of the mission schools. The education of girls has, however, now become part of the national system, and girls are in many cases admitted into the schools, colleges, and universities on the co-education method of many Western countries. Until recently it was the rarest thing to find a woman who was able to sign her own name, and when that was laboriously accomplished, it was perhaps all that she could write; whereas, on the other hand, a preponderating majority of men in the extreme south of China, in the cities at all events, were able to do this. To state it broadly: it is a great exception if a woman can do ought but make her mark, while it is an exception if a man cannot.

It is very hard to form an estimate as to the number of men who can not only read, but mentally understand what they read. The proportion differs in different parts of the country, and even in the same part, it will vary greatly in the citizen and the rustic. Dr. Martin estimated it at one in twenty. But these estimates are very unsatisfactory, as in different parts of the country and in city and town there are great differences. Again a great many have a little smattering of this knowledge and can manage to get along somehow when reading is made easy to them by the use of a simple style, but are soon out of their depth if the reading extends beyond the simplest characters. One recent writer estimates that only one-tenth of the entire population is able to read.

An account of education in China would not be complete without a closing allusion to the dawn of better days. Mission schools and colleges are to be found at the different centres, and these have done a good and appreciable work; there are likewise the schools in Hongkong, under the fostering care of the British Colonial Government; and, what is more encouraging still, there are, here and there at several important centres, either schools established, more or less under the auspices of the Chinese Government, such as the T'ung Wan Kwên [T'ung Wên Kuan], at Peking (1862) and Canton, where a thoroughly good training is given in English; or again, such establishments as naval and other colleges, in connection with arsenals, where a technical education is imparted; and, lastly, a most significant fact, at one of the provincial examinations in the City of Wu-chang, the examinees were asked to give a comparison between ancient and modern mathematical methods, the former being native, and the latter foreign; other centres of examination have taken the same subject up, doubtless in consequence of the decree issued about the year 1895 by which the Literary Chancellors of the provinces were ordered 'to admit candidates to a competition in Mathematics at each annual examination for the first degree [See also *infra*].' If successful, these were to undergo a special examination at Peking, in Physics, Applied Mathematics, Practical Mechanics, Naval and Military Tactics, Gunnery and Torpedo Practice; or, instead of these, in International Law, Political History, etc. 'If successful they shall be admitted to competition for the second degree in Peking, which shall be conferred in the ratio of one to twenty, the total not to exceed three in one year. Those who obtain the second degree may compete for the third.' (See EXAMINATIONS.) As an instance of this introduction of a new subject in the stereotyped Chinese examination the following will be found interesting:—

'In Western Shantung in the Tung Ch'ang Prefecture, two problems were propounded at the examination for the hsiu-ts'ai degree in 1892, the first or B. A., one of which asked for the superficial area of a globe eighteen inches in diameter. The other was of a more complicated character, and adapted to fit the aspirants for the post of Grain Commissioner. Problem.—If eight thousand piculs of rice are carried at thirteen tael cents per picul, and if the freight is paid in rice at taels two and a half per picul, how much rice is expended for the freight? It is said that this question was propounded to not less than ten thousand students in the Tung Ch'ao Prefecture, and that only one man tried to give any answer at all, and he was snubbed by the Chancellor for an ignorant pretender. Yet if any one could have given the correct answer which a Western lad of ten years would be ashamed not to be able to do in three minutes, he would probably have been passed on that account! The result, as often happens in such cases, has been a great increase in the number of applicants to the foreigner for a formula . . . which will evolve correct answers. The absurdity of proposing problems in regard to the nature of which students have had no opportunity of learning must be as evident to the Chancellor as to the candidates. But by another three years, some mathematical books will have probably been pored over not in vain.'

Another hopeful sign is the sending students to Western lands to prosecute their studies in the modern centres of learning and thought. The young Emperors Kuanghsü (1875-1908) and Hsüan T'ung (1908-1912), and the Empress Dowager Tzŭ Hsi, all began the study of English.

'The Tsung-li Yamên have promulgated [1896] a verbal edict of the Emperor to the provincial authorities, commanding that the study of foreign mathematics and the various branches of polytechnical science shall from henceforth be compulsory in all colleges of the country. Candidates at the literary examinations will now have to qualify in at least one of the latter subjects, while mathematics must be one of the standing subjects at these competitions for literary degrees.'

This gradual progress in the betterment of this wonderful system of examinations was followed by orders from the Emperor for a radical change, only to be again upset by the reactionary measures of the Empress Dowager. This is all a matter of history of the year 1898.

The dreadful events in the North of China in 1900, fit to be printed with lurid letters of blood on pages of Cimmerian darkness, followed, to be succeeded by a further appreciation (to a greater extent than previously) that her educational system was a drawback to the desire of the progressive party in China to be in a line with Western nations.

The following extracts will serve as instance of things attempted, not always to be accomplished, for progress is comparatively slow in China:—

'Upon the joint memorial of H.E. the Victory Tao and the Provincial Governor Tak, Imperial sanction has been granted to establish colleges and schools in Kwongtung for the teaching of both foreign tongues and Chinese to the native youth; in the large districts colleges will be established, and in small ones schools, where smart and intelligent students will be admitted and educated, and after a course of study be chosen by examination for Government Service. With this aim in view there will be no literary examination in any of the villages for the year' [1901].

'The Reform Decrees of the Court order, amongst other things, a provincial College in every Capital. The first to be opened was one by Governor Yün Shi Kai [Yüan Shih-k'ai] in Chinan-fu' [1901].

It was evident that the antiquated wên-chang's, or the literary essay's, days were numbered, and during the first twenty years of the twentieth century universities, colleges, and schools for both sexes, functioning on Western principles, were established at Peking and elsewhere throughout China, some supported by government funds, others by private or corporate enterprise.

References.—Werner, *Descriptive Sociology—Chinese;* Lewis, *The Educational Conquest of the Far East; Variétés Sinologiques,* Vol. v; P'ing Wên-kuo, *The Chinese System of Public Education;* Martin, *Han Lin Papers.* Also see extract from a paper by Rev. J. C. Ferguson in the *Hongkong Daily Press,* January 7th, 1892. Most of the text-books on China also contain more or less full accounts of the old Examination system of China.

EIGHT DIAGRAMS, THE.—The mythical emperor Fu Hsi is said to have had these revealed, or suggested to him, by the markings on the carapace of a tortoise. He copied them down, and subsequently they underwent various developments. They are called in Chinese the *Pa Kua,* and consist of arrangements of divided and undivided lines in different combinations up to sixty-four, though some native writers have extended them to millions. It is on the permutations of the sixty-four combinations that the classical Book of Changes (*I ching*) is founded. This is a book of divination, each diagram standing for some active or passive element or force in nature, for example, heaven, earth, fire, water, etc.

In Chinese metaphysics the origin of the *Pa Kua* is traced from the *Wu Chi,* Formless, through the *T'ai Chi,* Supreme Ultimate (represented by a dot), and the two *I* (*Yang, Yin*), to the four *Hsiang* (*T'ai Yang, T'ai Yin, Shao Yang, Shao Yin*), from which the Eight Diagrams (*Pa Kua*) are produced.

The names given to them are: Heaven (*Ch'ien*), Earth (*K'un*), Water (*Kan*), Fire (*Li*), Moisture (*Tui*), Wind (*Sun*), Thunder (*Chên*), and Hill (*Kên*). They are arranged in several forms; and in that of a circle are used as a charm. They form the text-book of the street fortune-teller. Some have even found in them the origin of the Chinese written character, and of the science of mathematics.

EIGHT IMMORTALS, THE.—The eight genii of Taoist legend who, having successively attained to immortality, have since been associated in one group, are worshipped jointly and severally, and are frequently represented in Chinese art—on porcelain, teapots, teacups, fans, scrolls, embroidery, etc. Images of them are made in porcelain, earthenware, ivory roots, wood, metals, etc. Their names, in the order in which they became immortals, are: Li T'ieh-kuai, Chung-li Ch'üan, Lan Ts'ai-ho (by some said to have been a woman, though generally recorded as a man), Chang Kuo, Ho Hsien Ku (a maiden), Lü Tung-pin, Han Hsiang Tzŭ, and Tsao Kuo-chiu.

'The term "Eight Immortals" is figuratively used for happiness. The number eight has become lucky in association with this tradition, and persons or things eight in number are graced accordingly. Thus we read of reverence shown to the "Eight Genii Table," "Bridge," "Vermicelli," "Wine-cup," etc. 'They are favourite subjects of romance, and special objects of adoration. In them we see "the embodiment of the ideas of perfect but imaginary happiness which possess the minds of the Chinese people." Three of them (Chung-li Ch'üan, Chang Kuo, and Lü Tung-pin—also known as Lü Yen) were historical personages; the others are mentioned only in fables or romances. They represent all kinds of people—old, young, male, female, civil, military, rich, poor, afflicted, cultured, noble. They are also representative of early, middle, and later historical periods.'

The legend of the Eight Immortals as a group is probably to be assigned to the Yüan dynasty (A.D. 1280-1368); but some at least were previously celebrated as Immortals in the Taoist legends.

Reference.—Werner, *Myths and Legends of China.*

EMBLEMS.—Chinese art is enriched with many emblems full of significance to the initiated and the native; but generally conveying nothing but an idea of quaintness or ornamentation to the foreigner. As illustrative of a handmaid of native art which gives meaning to flower and bird and animal depicted or carved or embroidered with such lavish profusion by the painstaking Chinese, we shall merely note a few of the emblematical symbols used.

Bamboos, chrysanthemums, plum-blossoms, and epidendrums represent the four seasons—summer, autumn, winter, and spring.

The same sound stands in China for 'noble rank' and 'birds,' hence the latter are emblems of the former. Storks mean longevity. As the same sound represents 'lotus' and 'continuous' as well, the use of 'lotus,' is obvious. The peony is the king of flowers and the pictorial synonym of wealth. The bamboo also does duty for 'peace,' and the lotus for 'a perfect gentleman, too.' Besides the seasons they typify, the plum is expressive of purity and the chrysanthemus of longevity

Reference.—Edkins, *Ancient Symbolism.*

EMBROIDERY.—The Chinese are famous for their skill in embroidery. Men and women are both employed in the production of numerous articles for home consumption as well as for exportation. Official robes for mandarins and their wives; petticoats for ladies; purses for rich and poor; shoes for men and women with natural feet, as well as for those with golden lilies—the cramped-up deformities which do an imperfect duty in place of the natural growth; caps for men and boys; adjuncts of dress, such as spectacle-cases and numerous other articles are all adorned and ornamented with embroidery. Banners, altar-cloths, the gorgeous robes donned by the ragged boys in a procession, are all rich with it.

'There are many styles with thread, or floss, and an infinite variety in the quality, pattern, and beauty of the work.' The 'motives,' are of the usual style of Chinese art-work—heavy bats, long convoluted dragons, splendid phœnixes, geometrical patterns, insignia of the genii, fruit, flowers, and butterflies; these are blended together in a galaxy of richest colours, or studded in more diffuse splendour on glowing backgrounds of cerulean blue or emerald green, or numerous other shades in which the gorgeous East delights to clothe itself. But it should be mentioned that, owing to the introduction of aniline colours, the loveliness has, in a great measure, departed, and harmony of tint almost entirely, from the needlework of tne present day

Girls are taught to embroider as an accomplishment and a necessary duty, for their own tiny shoes are worked by themselves, and not bought ready-made in the shops, while many a woman, seated in the narrow street at the door of her humble dwelling, adds to the slender means of her family by her skill in fancy work of this description. Peddlers go through the streets whirling a small rattle, and, from the stock-in-trade of these peripatetic dealers, the domestic stocks of silk for embroidery are generally replenished. Most lovely shades of the finest floss silk, running through the whole gamut of the richest colours, are displayed in the numerous small drawers of these itinerant merchants, while gold and silver thread are also for disposal, to be added to the needlework to enhance its beauty.

Numbers of men are employed in the production of shawls, table-covers, and fire-screens for exportation. The latter are made 'of divers colours of needlework on both sides,' the screen at which the men work being set upright between the two who are producing the piece, and the needle pushed through from one man to the other alternately, and thus the same pattern is produced on both front and back. Time is of no consequence when effect and beauty are to be the results, while patience and perseverance are the two principal factors employed without stint by the Chinese in all their industrial arts, nor are they absent in the production of embroidery. It is said that, in a spectacle-case, six inches by two, there will sometimes be not less than 20,000 stitches; and theatrical costumes, mandarin robes, and ladies' dresses will take ten or twelve women four or five years' constant work to finish. Uuder such conditions it will be readily seen that fashions cannot change from year to year. 'Wall hangings made of such work are very costly. In Canton where it is carried to its highest development, they have frequently brought several thousand dollars. Nevertheless such extra fine work is rare. The buying public demand good, effective tableaux at prices not over $100 each and the supply naturally equals the demand.'

Large stores of old embroidery are to be found in the pawnshops of Chinese cities; nor are the robes, there to be seen, all of modern make, but some splendid specimens of a style no longer in fashion, or ordinarily procurable, are occasionally met with. Many foreign ladies who would not touch a Chinaman's clothes yet buy these old and soiled robes, and different articles of dress worn by generations of Chinese, and utilise the embroidered pieces in ornamenting cushions, chair-backs, etc.

These may appear cheap, and they are certainly 'nasty,' yet it is the fashion in this least suitable climate to drape the furniture and walls of drawing-rooms with the equivalent of what a greasy old-clothes-man at home carries off in his bag. How much more sensible it would be if ladies sought after specimens of the Art made years ago for Art's sake. The following description of two pieces will give some idea of the best work. Both were circular and about a foot in diameter; one representing a white eagle perched on the rugged branch of a pine tree, with a stanza in beautiful characters in a column on one side, and so exquisite was the work it was almost impossible to discover that they were not written with a brush and the richest ink. Every feather of the bird was articulated, every needle of the pine was given in natural shades. The other, probably more interesting, was a dancing female figure, her robes and ribbons fluttering in the air, whilst all manner of flowers strewed the ground, a marvel of delicate work and refined colouring. But, alas! the features of this Nymph or Goddess were, as is not unusual, painted upon the satin ground, and the artist was not in touch with the embroiderers. The face was quite one-fifth of the whole figure and very unbeautiful, with, shocking to relate, a nose of Bardolphian proportions impossible in Nature and execrable in Art, but in every other respect this work was a masterpiece.

'Embroideries, ancient and modern, are always in demand among Orientals, the former being much more expensive. Many skilful artisans take advantage of this fact, and by an accurate imitation of colours faded by age and also by secret chemical treatment turn out embroideries which seem worn with age. The counterfeits are not easily detected. Even when they are, the discovery is to the benefit of the dealer and not the collector. A bogus antique of this class was recently sold in Hongkong for $500, for which two weeks previously the dealer had paid $15 to the maker. As a matter of fact, modern embroideries in China are just as good as ancient, so that it is folly to pay ten times for one picture what you might for a second of equal merit and beauty. This is especially true when a fine embroidery is to be exposed in the drawing-room of a house which uses coal and gas. . . . So ruinous are the gases produced by the combustion of both coal and illuminating gas that the only safe rule is to frame embroideries air-tight between glass plates. Thus protected they will retain their brilliancy unimpaired, where left exposed they become dull and dingy in a few years.'

As an instance of the uses ladies put Chinese embroideries to, see the following, written by one of themselves in 1901.

'The short Chinese Mandarin coats have also served successfully as evening cloaks; but all the Eastern embroideries are worth buying, being adaptable to household decorations, cushions, mantelpiece covers, and footstools, with special charm, while they are allowed to decorate simple blouses.'

There are a number of different stitches employed. In one a fine raised effect is produced by winding the thread round the needle and then taking the stitch. No foreigner, as far as we are aware, has made a special study of this subject. Great skill is shown in producing marvellous fantasies of colour. 'The East' seems 'to have been the natural home of embroidery,' and Mr. Walter Crane proceeds to say that 'to-day China and Japan produce the most beautiful renderings of flowers and birds.'

'The consummation of art textile work came in the reign of Ch'ien Lung (A.D. 1736-95), when the most beautiful tapestries, brocades, damasks and embroideries were produced. The subsequent decline of taste and art craft was gradual, but during recent years the decadence has been accelerated since the country was flooded with factory-made goods. Perhaps the last stage is represented by the so-called "Canton embroidery" made to meet a "foreign taste," which is synonymous with vulgarity, and for the special delectation of the globe-trotter, whose pockets the Chinese know too well how to empty. The average globe-trotter likes realism and prefers pure imitation of natural forms to the formal fancies of earlier date which have made Chinese art the individual thing that it is held to be to-day. It is scarcely necessary to say that the modern "Canton embroidery' with its meretricious ornament has practically no artistic merit and is merely a product of a period of crude commercialism. Art textile work, so far as China goes, has sung its swan song and it will probably be many years before the art spirit will again descend among the people.'

ETIQUETTE.—The Chinese have an elaborate system of etiquette, which is most punctiliously observed on state occasions and at festivals, and on the whole there is more polish and outward politeness than is common with English or Americans; it approaches more to the French style. The suavity of manner and urbanity with which common street coolies address one another, and even the beggars, is most noticeable, and the graciousness with which the boat-women accost each other when shouting orders and requests to different craft in the intricate navigation of the crowded rivers, is most pleasant to hear. The like is never seen in the West, though, at the same time, should a quarrel arise, the choicest 'Billingsgate' and a rare collection of obscene epithets is employed, these latter taking the place of profane oaths in the West.

We cannot call it with mock, because it is with real, solemnity that young John Chinaman copies his elders in his ceremonious observances, especially in his bows at New Year's time, performed with all the gravity of an old man with the weight of many years on his shoulders, and the full sense of the responsibility of a due and right performance of all the rules of etiquette.

Chinese etiquette has many points quite different from English, as the following examples will show:—

Scene.—A breakfast table at which is seated a new arrival who has not yet spent a winter in Hongkong. Enter the boy, his shaven pate graced with the usual Chinese winter skullcap.

The foreigner loquitur:—'A-sam! What foh you puttee on that piecee cap come waitee table? That no b'long plopah; no b'long polite!'

Answer by A-sam—'O! that b'long numbah one plopah, numbah one polite. S'pose you see Mistah——'s boy, he hab got cap all same same.'

More than forty years ago a party of six young Englishmen went out for an excursion in the country in the neighbourhood of one of the Treaty Ports. They were entirely ignorant of Chinese etiquette and custom, and while walking along one of the narrow paths at the side of a paddy-field, they met an old man carrying a load, whom they thought very rudely insisted on the path being given up to him and his burden, until he had passed with it. They pushed him out of the way, and struck him with their sticks for his rudeness, entirely unaware that they were the offenders, and gross offenders too. The path being narrow and there being no room for the encumbered and the unencumbered to pass at the same time, the Chinese, with commendable common-sense allow the burden-bearer in such cases, the right of way, while the unencumbered, who can easily step off the way, do so; those carrying a lighter weight make way for the more heavily laden, as, for instance, one man bearing a burden will step out of the way for two men carrying a sedan-chair. In this case the foreigners were also guilty of disrespect to an old man, whom the Chinese reverence—the old man also being an elder of the neighbouring village, further increased the offence. The villagers, indignant at the insult, rose, took the young Englishmen into custody, and avenged their wrongs by putting them to death, after some days of imprisonment.

The Chinese are very fond of sending presents as acknowledgements of favours received. They often consist of a multitude of different articles of tasty food, fruit, or tea, etc., and when received from a native, who knows nothing of foreign customs, a selection is only intended to be made by the receiver. An acquaintance of ours was in the habit of keeping the whole assortment, no doubt to the disgust of the sender, who also, doubtless, formed a very low opinion of the greed and rudeness of foreigners.

We here give a few unwritten rules of Chinese etiquette, which will serve to give an insight into the subject:—

Standing.—In standing, stand at attention with or without the heels touching each other, and the hands down at the sides. Do not stand at ease with one foot placed at right angles to the other; nor with arms akimbo. In talking to a man in a position superior to yours (such as a high official, while you are a lower one), do not keep your eyes fixed on his, but let them rest on the button on the lapel of his coat at his left breast, only occasionally raising them to his face.

Entering a Room.—In entering a room with a number of persons seated in it, do not bow to each separately; but give a grave bow first to the right, then to the left. If a particular friend of yours happens to be in the company, he is at liberty to advance two steps towards you, and you, in like manner, may advance two steps further into the room, each then saluting the other with clasped hands and a bow.

Etiquette

Sitting down.—The left hand is the place of honour. It is given to the guest, and the host takes the right; but the greatest caution is necessary, in sitting down, not to do so before your guest; and if either should get up, or even rise slightly, the other must follow suit at once. It is most amusing to see how Chinese visitors bob up and down at the least movement of their foreign host. Another important rule is never to sit while any one else who is your equal is standing.

Answers to Questions.—Like the French, the Chinese do not consider it always polite to simply answer 'Yes' or 'No,' but often turn the interrogative form of a question into the affirmative, using the same words, as far as possible, in the reply that have been used in the question. Foreigners are apt to think that Chinese are boorish when they answer in this manner, but they are only acting in accordance with their code of politeness.

Enquiries as to Age, etc.—It is not considered rude for a Chinese to make most particular enquiries as to a stranger's personal affairs. In fact, the making of such enquiries often evinces great politeness. 'How old are you?' 'Are you married?' 'How much money do you make a year?' 'Where are you going?' 'What are you going to do?' 'How much did you pay for this?' These questions and others of the same character are constantly on a Chinaman's lips.

Dunning.—It is not considered polite to ask a man, whom you may meet in the street, for a debt due by him to you. One of the most polite forms in which to request repayment is to ask your debtor for a loan of money for your own use.

Noises, etc.—Guttural sounds, hawking, clearing the throat, spitting, using the fingers to blow the nose, and eructations, are not necessarily considered impolite by the Chinese. It must be remembered that they look upon such things in quite a different way from what we do nowadays. We say nowadays, for it is not more than a few centuries ago that a book was published in England containing, among other things, directions how to blow the nose neatly with the fingers. But we will not offer any more remarks on such a nauseating subject.

Want of Dress.—A Chinese official will not allow his chair-bearers to carry him in the half-naked manner which the Chinese coolie so delights in. The Mercantile classes and others are not particular in this respect.

Spectacles.—It is considered impolite to wear spectacles before a guest or superior. A short-sighted man must be ready to submit to any amount of awkwardness rather than infringe this rule of etiquette. It is very amusing to see a witness in a

Court of Justice looking at some document which he is unable to see properly, not daring to put on his glasses lest it should be construed into a sign of disrespect to the judge, perhaps mildly saying he is short-sighted, but in other cases never giving a hint that he cannot see properly without putting them on. If it is absolutely necessary that something should be looked at, an apology having been offered, or permission given to put them on, they must be taken off as soon as possible afterwards. Some even hesitate to put them on when told to do so.

Hats.—There are great differences in Chinese hats, some may, or rather must, be tolerated in a room or house, and others under no consideration whatever. The common skullcap with a red or black knotted knob (or blue if the wearer is in mourning) is *au fait.* It should be worn in winter, in-doors or out, and is only dispensed with in summer for the same reason that Indian judges do not wear wigs in that country. The official hat, with the button indicative of the rank of the wearer, is dress, and is hastily donned to receive a visitor; neither do the official hats of the mandarins' servants need to be removed on entering a house; but the case differs *in toto* when we come to the ordinary rain and sun-hats, whether they are as large in size as an umbrella, or only about the size of a gong, or the small conical ones worn by the native soldiers and coolies, like those provided for the Chinese policemen in Hongkong. The same holds good of the felt hats used in winter by coolies and tradesmen, etc. Hoods also should not be kept on inside one's house. If the hat is only of the right kind, it is politeness for a Chinese gentleman to put it on to receive his guest; to appear bareheaded before a visitor is considered impolite.

Queue.—Unless the nature of his work, such as carrying a chair or washing the floor, requires, or makes it convenient for his queue to be wound in a coil round his neck or shoulders, or to be done up in any fashion in a bunch at the top or back of his head, no Chinese servant or inferior ought ever to appear so before his master or superior, but the queue should always hang down behind. Since 1912, however, the queue has been officially forbidden, and is generally discarded, though still worn by many, chiefly old, men.

Finger-Nails.—Long finger-nails are not considered a sign of dirtiness, but of respectability, and of being above manual labour, which, if necessary, would of course prevent them from attaining such length as an inch and a half, two inches, or even three, though it is seldom one sees them all of equal length on all the fingers. It is well that such is the case, as two or three on one or both hands give such a claw-like appearance to the fingers as to make them sufficiently repulsive; fortunately hand-shaking is not in vogue in China, as it would be extremely unpleasant to feel the long talons gripping one's hand.

Shaking Hands.—A Chinese clasps his two hands together and moves them up and down a few inches in front of himself several times. In cases of excessive politeness they are raised up as high as his forehead, while he makes a profound bow. Ladies do not do this, but clutch the left-hand sleeve with the right hand, and imitate the same motion.

Handing Things.—Both hands are used to pass anything, therefore a Chinese is not to be considered clumsy who hands any small articles, such as a cup of tea, in this manner: it would be thought the height of rudeness to do otherwise, for it would evince an unwillingness to take the little trouble necessary. The same rule of etiquette is observed in receiving anything from anyone.

Meals.—At meals men and women never eat together, unless the women are bad characters, even a husband and a wife should take their meals separately. This is the strict rule, but it is occasionally more honoured in the breach than in the observance. The children, or younger members of the family, wait till the grown-up people are seated, the latter nod an assent to 'a show of asking permission to eat.' Each one has his own bowl of rice, and he picks up pieces of meat and vegetables, etc., from the common dishes in the centre of the table, but it is considered polite only to help oneself from the side of the dish nearest to one.

After each meal it is the custom to wipe the face and hands with a wet cloth wrung out of hot water. In the family circle each one will leave the table and do this washing; but at a dinner party the servants will bring a cloth, so wrung out, to each diner, a separate one being given to each if the guests and hosts are not very familiar, otherwise the same cloth may be used. In the Chit--kong province (where Soochow is) the same basin and cloth are used, as it shows that they are brotherly.

One having finished may ask the others to 'eat leisurely,' which is the equivalent of saying 'excuse me,' and he is then at liberty to leave the table. It is etiquette to remain sitting at meals till all have finished, but, in the event of urgent business, etc., demanding one's attention, a guest may, before the others have finished, lay his chopsticks across his empty bowl, this being an indication of his desire to leave; the host on observing it, lifts them down, places them on the table and says 'hò háng [*hao hsing*],' (which is equivalent to our 'good-bye,' though it really has the meaning, if freely rendered, of 'I hope you will have a safe walk') to the guest, who is then free to depart.

The above form of procedure takes place with strangers, or when everybody is on their best behaviour; for, though it is incumbent on all to sit down together at the same time to their meals, it is unnecessary, in unceremonious intercourse, that all should rise at the same time. At formal dinners or meals, however, the host cannot leave the table till he sees that all his guests, having all finished, wish to do so.

VISITING—*Arrival.*—It is an act of impoliteness to walk quickly or far ahead of the host when proceeding toward the reception hall or room, though, on account of the slow, dignified pace at which Chinese officials walk and the often very long distance to the reception hall, newly-arrived foreigners, or those uninstructed in Chinese etiquette, are apt to do so. In fact, foreigners find the Chinese ceremonial, if observed in detail, tedious, and resent the waste of time it involves; yet non-observance of it is to risk being considered ignorant or impolite.

Tea Drinking.—The etiquette about tea drinking in connection with paying visits is curious. When paying a visit to an official, if a servant should bring in a cup of tea, there is no necessity to take any particular notice of it; allow the servant to put it down where he likes near you, and continue your conversation with the mandarin. Should, however, he consider you a good friend, or, even in the case of a first call, should he desire to treat you with great respect, or evince his great pleasure at seeing you, he may hand you the cup of tea with his own hands. In such circumstances it is incumbent upon you to rise to your feet and take it from his two hands with both of yours.

A cup of tea in an official call (be you either a civilian calling on an official, or even if you are both officials) is destined to play an important part. Your business over, or your conversation done, you invite your host to drink tea (ts'ing ch'á [ch'ing ch'a]), which he thereupon proceeds to do with you, and the visit is over. Should you, however, be taxing the patience of your host by overstaying your welcome, or should a pressure of business make it necessary for him to shorten the call as much as possible, he begins to touch the cup with his fingers, expecting you to take the hint. Are you such an obtuse individual that hints are entirely lost upon you? Then he may sometimes—though it is not quite the correct thing for him to do so—give you the invitation to take tea with him, when you will have to retire, feeling mortified at having transgressed the rules of politeness, and at being treated with rudeness in return. It must be remembered, however, that this tea is never to be touched until it is time to go. These rules as to the *congé* do not hold good with people who are not officials.

Marks of Friendliness.—When seeing a mandarin in his hall for transacting business, should he invite you into his private apartments, then any subjects can be discussed, and any amount of freedom, consistent, of course, with self-respect, may be enjoyed; coats even may be thrown off till a state approaching nearly to the *in puris naturalibus*, so congenial to the Chinese in hot weather, is arrived at.

Whispering.—The Chinese mode of using the hand to cover the mouth when whispering to anyone is different from the Western style; for, instead of simply covering the mouth with the hand spread open, the fingers of the hand are bent towards each other just as if a very large orange were being held in the hand, and in a position midway between a clenched fist and an open hand. The ends of the fingers are put close up to the mouth, or touching the lips, thus muffling the sound. This muffling is intensified if it is cold weather and a number of sleeves come over the hand.

Beckoning.—In beckoning, the Chinese do not use one finger pointed upwards and curved towards one, as we do; but the hand is reversed, the fingers hanging down and the whole hand is used to beckon towards one with a sweeping motion, in a most energetic manner.

Names.—A curious rule holds good with regard to names in a family: it is against Chinese etiquette to name a child after his father or grandfather, in fact the name of any member of a former generation must not be used by a descendant. The now defunct official *Peking Gazette* many years since contained an application forwarded by the Viceroy of Canton from General Hsieh Hung-chang to be allowed to alter his name to Hsieh Tê-lung, as it had been discovered from his family register that a remote ancestor of his had a name identical with his own.

Wives.—The way in which a Chinese treats a wife is, according to our Western ideas, peculiar. One or two instances of it have already been noticed. It is not amongst many Chinese considered a proper thing to write a letter to one's wife if absent from home. The family idea comes into play here as it does in so many matters connected with Chinese social and domestic life. The man's mother is the head of the family when he is away from the 'family house.' What then, according to this Chinese way of looking at things, more natural and proper than that he should write to his mother? The next best thing is to write to his son, though an infant, or even to his daughter, for all signs of affection between husband and wife are to be deprecated, not that such indications are simply bad form, but they are looked upon as even indelicate. Failing any proper person to send his letter to, the Chinese may send to the one whom the Englishman would think first of all of writing to; even in this case, however, the letter must not be addressed on the cover to his wife though it may be inside, but the envelope is directed 'To be handed to the family.' Some of the Chinese are better than their rules of etiquette or propriety, and write direct to the wife, even if there be a mother or child. A wife again in writing to her husband does so in the name of a son, or failing a son, of a daughter.

The following extract will show how incongruous the Western and Eastern codes of etiquette are:—

'Foreign ignorance of the customs of the Chinese is another cause of a feeling of superiority on the part of the Chinese. That anyone should be ignorant of what they have always known, seems to them to be almost incredible. Many Chinese unconsciously adopt toward foreigners an air of amused interest, combined with depreciation, like that which Mr. Littimer regarded David Copperfield, as if mentally saying perpetually. "So young, sir, so young!" . . . . There are multitudes of details in regard to social matters, of which one must necessarily be ignorant, for the reason that he has never heard of them, and there must be a first time for every acquisition. . . . Inability to conform to *Chinese ideas and ideals*, in ceremony, as well as what we consider more important matters, causes the Chinese to feel a thinly disguised contempt for a race whom they think will not and cannot be made to understand "propriety." It is not that a foreigner cannot make a bow, but he generally finds it hard to make a Chinese bow in a Chinese way, and the difficulty is as much moral as physical. The foreigner feels a contempt for the code of ceremonials, often frivolous in their appearance, and he has no patience, if he has the capacity, to spend twenty minutes in a polite scuffle, the termination of which is foreseen by both sides with absolute certainty. The foreigner does not wish to spend his time in talking empty nothings for "an old half day." To him, time is money, but it is very far from being so to a Chinese, for in China everyone has an abundance of time, and very few have any money. No Chinese has ever yet learned that when he kills time, it is well to make certain that it is the time which belongs to him, and not that of some one else.'

'With this predisposition to dispense as much as possible with superfluous ceremony because it is distasteful, and because the time which it involves can be used more agreeably in other ways, it is not strange that the foreigner, even in his own eyes, makes but a poor figure in comparison with a ceremonious Chinese. Compare the dress, bearings, and action of a Chinese official, with long flowing robes and graceful motions, with the awkward genuflections of his foreign visitor. It requires all the native politeness of the Chinese to prevent them from laughing outright at the contrast. In this connection it must be noted that nothing contributes so effectively to the instinctive Chinese contempt for the foreigner, as the evident disregard which the latter feels for that official display so dear to the Oriental. What must have been the inner thought of the Chinese who were told that they were to behold the "great American Emperor," and who saw General Grant in citizen's costume with a cigar in his mouth, walking along the open street? Imagine a foreign Consul, who ranks with a Chinese Taot'ai, making a journey to a provincial capital to interview the Governor, in order to settle an international dispute. Thousands are gathered on the city wall to watch the procession of the great foreign magnate, a procession which is found to consist of two carts and riding horses, the attendants of the Consul being an Interpreter, a Chinese acting as messenger (t'ing ch'ai), and another as cook! Is it any wonder that Orientals gazing on such a scene should look with a curiosity which changes first to indifference, and then to contempt?'

The modern Chinese not only understand the "foreign barbarian's" differences of custom and ignorance of the details of Chinese etiquette, but in some cases have abandoned their own too-elaborate ceremonial for the simpler laws of intercourse in vogue in Western countries.

References.—*Chinese Recorder*, vols. xxvi, xxix, xxxvii; Walshe, *Ways That Are Dark;* Werner, *Descriptive Sociology—Chinese.*

EURASIANS.—The children of European fathers by Asiatic mothers, or *vice versâ*, are, by a union of the first syllables of both words, called Eurasians. (This mixture of races existed in Eastern Europe and Western Asia as early as pre-Christian times.) Some dress in the foreign style and some in the native; the former look more like their Chinese mothers than their fathers; the latter look very white and foreign-like. Their eyes are generally black, though the results of the second and third generations of such alliances are often very fair, have brownish hair, and occasionally lighter-coloured eyes. The union of the two bloods seems, as far as the men are concerned, to produce a more sprightly race than the Chinese, and one whose organs of speech are better adapted to pronounce English than those of pure Chinese breed; for it is a very rare thing for a Chinese to speak English accurately, though he may have resided for years in England, as rare almost as for an Englishman to speak Chinese like a native, though he may have lived for years in China. Some Chinese, however, acquire a mastery of English that is really astonishing. One of these was the late Lo Fêng-lu, afterwards Minister to the Court of St. James. It was of him in his earlier career that Gladstone remarked that he "spoke

English rather well for an interpreter"! Some of the girls who have a preponderance of English blood in them are very pretty and fair. Unfortunately the majority of the daughters are brought up to lead an immoral life, and sold like slaves into it.

There is a Eurasian school in Shanghai, a great number of the children in the Diocesan Home and Orphanage in Hongkong belong to the same class, and there are a very large number of them in the Government Central School (now called Queen's College) in the same Colony. They are drafted from these establishments into the lawyers' and other offices, where they make very useful clerks and interpreters, from their knowledge of both Chinese and English.

It is not all the half-castes that come under this class, as numbers of them are swallowed up under the name of Portuguese. This, in the Far East, is not restricted alone to those worthy of that name, but is used to designate all, who, having some drops of foreign blood in their veins, elect to call themselves such, dress in foreign clothes, and talk a smattering of the *patois* glorified with the name of Portuguese. But this, in reality, is a sort of pidgin-Portuguese, and not understood by new arrivals from Portugal, who require an interpreter to explain it to them. Macanese is perhaps a better term, as the majority of them are either born in Macao or have descended from residents in that city. They are of all shades of colour, and their complexions show traces of Indian (Goa), Chinese, Japanese, and European ancestry in all degrees of proportion. The mercantile offices are full of them. They write a good hand, and act as clerks, but seldom rise to any position of great trust and confidence. They work as a rule for a mere pittance, and the poorer classes herd together after the manner of Chinese. A very few are engaged as merchants in business.

Steps have recently been taken to abolish the disabilities and injustices to which, through no fault of thin own, Eurasians are subjected in British and other possessions.

EXAMINATIONS.—We have treated of the end and aim of education in China in a former article (See EDUCATION). Here we will write more fully of the final step to this goal, namely, the system of Civil Service examinations in China as it was until abolished in A.D. 1903, and then add some forther remarks on the changes which have since taken place. In the matter of competitive examinations, the Chinese present one of those unique spectacles which are alike the wonder, as well as the admiration, of those who understand them.

Examinations

In this strange land there was in vogue for centuries, and even millenniums, a system of examinations, which, originally started with the object of testing the ability of these already in office, gradually widened in scope till it became all-embracing in point of geographical extent, and was the test of ability which all had to undergo who desired admission into the Civil Service of the immense empire with its thousands of officials; with this end in view, boys were incited to learn their lessons and be diligent; with this aim, men pursued their weary course of study, year in and year out, till white hairs replaced the black, and the shoulders, which at first merely aped the scholarly stoop, eventually bent beneath the weight of years of toil. No other country in the world presents the curious sight of grandfather, father, and even son, competing at the same time. Failures seemed only to spur on to renewed trials, until, after many times having formed a unit amongst the annual two millions that passed through one or other of the ordeals of this gigantic examination scheme, the old man of seventy, or eighty, who had been unfortunate enough not to appear among the small percentage of one or two out of a hundred, that was allowed to pass, finally attracted Imperial notice, and, as an honour, and the meed of his untiring perseverance and indefatigable toil, received the coveted reward.

The scheme was widespread as the empire: every petty district city even had its Examination Hall, where the initial trials were conducted under the supervision of the Imperial Chancellor, a sub-chancellor being in residence, who subjected the candidates to a preliminary examination. Out of the two thousand or so, only twenty of the best received the degree which the Chinese term 'Síú-ts'aí [hsiu-ts'ai],' meaning 'budding genuis,' but which for convenience is generally termed by foreigners the B.A., though, except for the analogy of being the first degree obtained in both East and West, there is scarcely any point of similarity, and so it is throughout the whole series of degrees. An original poem and one or two essays by each candidate on the subjects assigned to them were the exercises of this examination. A night and a day were spent in their production. The results to the successful student were as follows:—no office, or appointment, but admission was granted him into the charmed circle of those who were entitled to wear the lowest grade of gold button on the tops of their hats, and who were protected 'from corporal punishment; it raises him above the common people, renders him a conspicuous man in his native place, and eligible to enter the triennial examination for the second degree,' held in the provincial capital, the successful candidates at which took the second degree, styled the 'Chü-jin [*chü-jên*],' 'promoted scholar,' or M.A. This examination lasted through 'three sessions of nearly three days each.' The examiners were the Imperial Commissioner and ten provincial officers. Some six thousand, more or less, according to the size of the province, entered for this examination. Essays in prose and verse were required, but, of course, there was much more given to be done, and a higher style was required than in the former, and much strictness was exercised with regard to the slightest errors in the essays. The small percentage that passed still got no appointment, nor office, but rose higher in the public estimation, wore a higher grade of gilt button, when in dress, and put a board over the front doors of their houses with the mystic characters 'Promoted Men,' as well as the date of attaining this distinction. One step more entitled the scholar eventually to obtain office. This next higher degree was taken at Peking. It was termed 'Tsun-sz [chin-shih],' 'Entered Scholar,' or LL.D. Lots were drawn for vacant posts, and the successful candidate might, perchance, begin his official career as a district magistrate.

Another degree might, however, be taken, success in the examination for which entitled to admission to the Hanlin College. The members of this College were 'constituted poets and historians to the Celestial Court, or deputed to act as Chancellors and Examiners in the several provinces.' The highest on the list, after two special examinations in the Emperor's palace and in the presence of the Emperor himself, was styled the 'Chuang-yuen' or 'Laureate.'

The above is a rough sketch of this wonderful system; the details of which, as regards the subsidiary examinations, might be filled in at great length. Enough has been written to convey some idea of the system as a whole, but it is difficult to describe the enthusiasm which pervaded the whole country with regard to the examinations. Congratulations were showered on the successful students; they dined with the highest officials after the event, and the Emperor himself entertained the most celebrated of all. It is naturally to be expected that the family of the successful candidate should feel honoured, but those who took the highest honours were looked upon as conferring distinction on their native places; and it was quite a sight, on going through a Chinese city, to see the red boards, with gilt characters, placed over certain doors, proclaiming to all passers-by the degree, or degrees, taken by the inmates, separate boards being used for those who had taken the higher positions, such as senior tripos, etc., in each respective examination. On the blank walls of the fronts of the houses would often also be seen large yellow or red papers with red or yellow letters on them; for it was customary when any one had been successful at an examination to send a poster with large characters on it announcing the fact to all one's friends and relatives. For examinations at which one had been successful in the provinces, red paper with yellow characters, but for those held in Peking yellow paper with red characters, was used.

Besides the legitimate interest taken in these literary contests, they formed the Goodwoods and Derbys of China; for not only was the news of success spread far and wide as fast as swift messengers, rapid boats, and fleet couriers could carry it to waiting friends and expectant relatives; but it was as eagerly received by utter strangers, who, having staked on the issue, were excited to know the result.

Like everything Chinese, these trials of literary skill of the future governors of the people were held in far different surroundings from what a Westerner would expect. The buildings covered a large extent of ground, that in Canton occupied 16 acres. After the main entrance (which was within the entrance of the outside wall) was passed, a broad avenue led up to a congeries of buildings for the use of the Examiners and others connected with them and their work. On each side of this main avenue were narrow lanes, giving access to the 8,653 cells in which the students were confined. These cells were 5 feet 9 inches by 3 feet 8 inches wide, their height being a trifle over that of a man. There were two grooves in the walls for two planks; one formed a table, the other a seat for the solitary student shut up in each cell. It was a species of imprisonment, no communication being allowed with the candidates, under penalty of severe punishment. They entered the Examination Hall with provisions, fuel, candles, bedding, and writing materials, being searched to see that no 'cribs,' or other means of assisting their labour, were smuggled in, it being the constant practice for some to do this: a specially small miniature edition of the classics was printed for the purpose and secreted about the person. The confinement must have been extremely irksome and disagreeable; deaths occasionally occurred from excitement, the privations and exposure being greater than old age could endure. In other places the Examination Hall was not of the same construction. In the district city of Kít Yöng, near Swatow, the students had long forms and tables provided for them. In the departmental city of Ch'aú-chaú-fú, the Examination Hall was fitted up in a similar manner.

The Chinese have been wise in thus giving the people a share in their own government, nor was it in the way of pandering to the democracy; but it was bestowed as a right on those who were fitted for it by an education, which, though not on a par with a modern Western course of study, was by no means to be despised when compared with that in vogue in Europe a few centuries since. Thus ambitious spirits had a career open before them, which might lead them up to the very foot of the throne itself; the extra exuberance of youth was toned down by a course of study which must have had a great effect in producing the grave and reverend seniors, which Chinese mandarins were. It produced likewise a conservative element, as it was to the interest of the whole body of *literati* to conserve the existing polity and resist all violent change which might overthrow their position and prospects. China also by this admirable plan—admirable, taken as a whole, alike in its conception, development, and working—prevented herself from being overburdened by an aristocracy, with all its concomitant evils, which, had it existed, would, as in most European countries, have monopolised all that was worth having in the government, until driven inch by inch from its unfair position—a work long in operation, and difficult of accomplishment.

Here then was a mighty system, complete in all its details, ready, as soon as Western science took a fair grasp of the nation, to be used as a means of disseminating scientific knowledge and methods throughout the length and breadth of the land, as well as literary style and polish. Some faint indications that such might eventually be its function have already been given.

Besides the literary examinations, military examinations for officers of the army were held, in which skill in gymnastic exercises, such as lifting heavy weights and shooting with bows and arrows, were the tests required. But the Chinese have shown their wisdom in considering warlike exercises as far inferior to literary ability: military officers, as compared with civil functionaries, were despised, and under the heading of military officers are included naval officers as well.

Before the system above described was abolished, there was a tendency to introduce a few mathematical and other questions at some of the centres of examination, and this attempt to employ Western knowledge culminated in an edict by the Emperor Kwong Suí [Kuang Hsü], dated the 23rd of June, 1898, directing that at the literary examinations from those of doctor down to those for licentiates, the candidates should write short practical essays, instead of using the Chinese classics entirely as heretofore. A similar attempt made by the Emperor Kanghi [K'ang Hsi], to vivify with the touch of knowledge the stagnant pool of Chinese ancient lore, resulted in a short time in a return to the old state of affairs, as public opinion was against any innovation; and an even quicker reversal of the Emperor's plans took place in this case, for the Empress Dowager, with a fatuity fraught with the greatest danger, upset this as well as the other beneficent plans inaugurated by Kwong Suí. (See, however, EDUCATION).

'The standard essay—wên-chang—has been the chief cause of the working of the minds of the *literati*, and causing them to labour ceaselessly, in the same old tread-mill. It has held absolute sway for a millennium over China's intellectual life, and its baneful effects can be seen everywhere in the literature of the last three dynasties. Scholars have learned what they could not afterwards make use of in actual life, and they have had no time left for learning what could be used. The scholars of the Sung dynasty bequeathed in this legacy of the wên-chang a burden of such weight upon the mental life of China that it has been steadily crushing out its very existence. Originated to perpetuate classical learning it has been the liveliest factor in suppressing the desire for such knowledge. It has absolutely nothing to be said in its favour, unless the remark of an eminent living statesman of China be given to its credit that 'it has repressed rebellion by keeping the minds of ambitious men cramped by the pursuit of useless knowledge. The main reason that has kept it alive has been that it was supposed to be the essence of orthodox Confucianism.'

After being alternately given up and restored to the list of subjects for examination, it was finally abolished, as already noted.

Under the *wên-chang* system, about 14,000 bachelors were added to the list every year. There were probably close on 700,000 Chinese graduates living at the end of the nineteenth century. It was the expectants of office who were one of China's greatest dangers, men embittered by feeling that they had themselves been unjustly passed over, who had never been given opportunity to show what they could do, and who were incapable of doing what alone lay before them.

EXTRATERRITORIALITY.—As the laws and judical system in force in China partake more of the character of those in operation in Europe in the Middle Ages, Europeans and Americans in China, as well as in other Asiatic countries, have insisted on being amenable to their own laws, and exempted from the legal process of the country in which they dwell.

The right was established only after wars and treaties, the first recognition of it being with Russia in 1620 and with

England from 1842 onward. 'Its full expression is found in the Chefoo Convention of 1876.'

There is a Supreme Court, with a Chief Justice and other officers under the Foreign Office of England, which sits in Shanghai, and proceeds on circuit to the different treaty ports when cases arise, demanding its attendance amongst British subjects or in which one party is British. The Consular Courts, presided over by the British Consuls, take cognisance of the local cases within their jurisdiction, or hold a preliminary enquiry in cases reserved to be dealt with by the Supreme court.

On the other hand, if a Chinese is sued by an Englishman, the trial takes place in a Chinese Court, at the instance of the English Consul. In Hongkong, of course, this rule does not hold good, for, being an English Colony, it is an integral part of the British Empire. Chinese criminals sometimes escape from the mainland to this island. Before their rendition to the Chinese authorities an enquiry is held by the Police Magistrate, who, on *primâ facie* proof of the crimes, sends up the cases to the Governor of the Colony, who decides as to whether the criminals are to be handed over to the Chinese or not. Nevertheless the Chinese authorities at Canton until recent years used to feel a considerable amount of soreness on the subject, as it was difficult for them to understand (with their system of torture of prisoners and witnesses, and the forced confessions extorted from the former and even at times from the latter) the importance of unshaken, truthful evidence, and of genuine eye-witnesses. The uncertainty of English law, and the jealous care exercised over the prisoner in case he should be innocent, were incomprehensible to them. Applications have been made to the Supreme Court of the Colony, on a writ of *habeas corpus*, for a release of the prisoners on some alleged technical flaw; but these have rarely succeeded. (See also LAWS).

Referenecs.—Piggott, *Exterritoriality. The Law relating to Consular Jurisdiction and to Residence in Oriental Countries;* Ferguson, *Jurisdiction et Exterritorialité en Chine.*

FAIRY TALES.—There are many fairy tales to be found in Chinese literature, but different in detail to those of the West. The animal world, like the wolf in Red Riding Hood, comes in, but in a more artistic form than in the old nursey tale, as the foxes assume human shape at will, not being detected till well on in the story, and they are beneficent as well as malignant. 'Our Chinese foxes, which are represented as the frequenters of the ancient sepulchers, turn into the Elves of the Forest, and by moonlight imbibe the ethereal essence of heaven and earth. They dig up the graves of the dead and place their skulls on their foreheads. They then look up to the North Pole and bow to the Starry Host. If the skulls do not fall off while they perform this rite they change into lovely and fascinating females.' Love often plays an important part in some of these stories, showing that, though not considered proper by the prudish Chinese, human nature and the ruling passion will yet reveal themselves even under the most repressive circumstances. Besides this class of fairy tales, much of the Taoist mythology might be classed under this category, when the marvellous and miraculous doings of the gods, demi-gods, and genii are told at garrulous length and with tedious detail.

In China it is not only the children that believe in sprites, fairies, dryads, nymphs, demons, and goblins, but the children of an older growth nearly all firmly believe in them; for the whole universe to the average Chinaman is peopled with unseen denizens, who occasionally appear to the good or evil, and reward or punish them in quite the orthodox story-book style.

References.—Giles, *Strange Stories from a Chinese Studio;* Anon., *The Fairy Foxes; China Review,* vols. xi; xii; xiii; Werner, *Myths and Legends of China.*

FAMINES.—Famines are common in this mighty land, where in one part there will be a superabundance, while want and death are prevalent in another, It is due often to the absence of railways (See RAILWAYS) and means of rapid intercommunication, that famines are more frequent in the more northerly provinces, where the great waterways that bless the South are rarer. But famines in China are due to various causes, as often as not to the failure of the crops. As has been well remarked 'there is always a lamentable lack of intelligence in dealing with the emergency.' Taxes are sometimes remitted, and the Government in its *quasi-paternal* relations to its people professes the greatest commiseration, but any assistance that is rendered is docked on its passage through the hands of the officials. As has been truthfully remarked by one of the Hongkong papers:—'The most efficient relief work is generally done by missionaries,' who have laboured heroically in distributing the funds generously subscribed by the foreign residents in China, going in fact to the famine-stricken districts and personally attending to the relief of the famishing natives. Cases of cannibalism are known in famine times—people even eating their own children.

FANS.—There can scarcely be any other nation on earth that uses such quantities of fans: amongst us, the use of the fan is confined to the gentler sex; with the Chinese, fans are used as much by the one sex as by the other, and particular makes or forms are confined in their use to the male sex. All sorts of materials are employed in their construction, the palm leaf, which Nature seems almost to have designed as an object-lesson and a hint, being one of the most common; silk, paper, bamboo, feathers, and other things, such as bone, bone and feather, feather, ivory and bone, feather and Sandal-wood, feather and tortoise shell, ivory and satin, lacquered wood and paper, lacquered wood and silk, mother-of-pearl, bamboo with paper or silk, peacocks' feathers, are also used. The orbicular shape, has a neat rim braided round it, the stalk forming the natural handle. This gigantic size is placed in the hands of slave-girls and other female domestics, to perform the duty which the poet inveighed against so strongly in the well-known lines:—

'I would not have a slave to till my ground,
To carry me, to fan me while I sleep,
And tremble when I wake, for all the wealth
That sinews bought and sold have ever earned.'

The smaller kind of the same shape, and of which such large quantities are exported to America—the common palm-leaf fan —is used by the lower classes, and it is curious to notice the variety of uses to which this fan is put in China: it serves to blow up the wooden or charcoal fire in the earthenware furnaces, instead of a pair of bellows; old torn-down-looking seamstresses pin it on the top of their hair to serve as a hat; it also does duty as a sunshade; it is used, in common with other fans, as a duster to fan or flap away the dust off a seat, or to cool the chair before offering it to a visitor; to drive the mosquitoes out of the mosquito net; to fan the restless baby to sleep; to cool the hungry youngster's food; and it comes in handy for many another purpose.

There is a great variety of fans, and the following classification embraces many, though not all of them, viz:—feather fans, folding fans, and screen fans; the latter are of a variety of shapes, 'round, octagonal, sexagonal, or polygonal.' The young Chinese, exquisite in his robes of silk and satin, generally carries, at the proper seasons, one of them in his hand, the gift perchance of some artistic and literary friend who has embellished it with a landscape in black and white, and (or) a few lines from his pen in either prose or poetry. We give an inscription on one of these fans which was presented to a European. It not only gives an idea of what such inscriptions may be, but also shows what a Chinese complimentary letter is like. We have changed the names from what they were in the original:—

'The noteworthy visit you paid me some time ago has filled my humble cottage with glory. I believe you are a virtuous man whose object it is to benefit the world with your kind heart, which is ready to afford free services to the distressed it comes in sight of. This being its policy, many a poor sufferer has had his chronic disease removed and got immediate relief from great difficulties. How greatly in need is this class of people! Furthermore, our unexpected meeting has quickly made us bosom friends. That a man so forsaken by the world as myself can gain so true a friend as you is rare. It has given me great consolation to hear of your promotion to the post of Chief Medical Officer. Your success is the result of your repeated good deeds which always multiply one's blessings: the Eye of Heaven clearly sees our human actions. Though I am not worthy of your friendship, I sincerely hope you will not forget me after you have left here for your new appointment. Send me advice and instruction to amend my defects. True affection forbids me to forget you or to cease thinking of you. May there still be a time for our future meeting and companionship is my earnest prayer.

'Kwong-suí, 16th year, 9th moon in autumn. Written in the Tsing Ming Taí Tak Fort, Kwong-tung province, for the use of Dr. Chöng Léí. Scribbled by Chaú Yaú *alias* Sik Ping.'

The silk of which some of these fans are made is actually spun by the silkworm on the bamboo frame which surrounds the fan. This may seem incredible, but a specimen has been seen in a foreigner's collection in Hongkong consisting of a small disc of silk, a few inches in diameter, spun in the lid of a tin canister, and given to him by a relative in whose house it had actually been produced. It therefore requires no credulity to believe that a fan somewhat larger could be thus made. The folding fan (which originated in the Far East) is universal throughout China from the cheap affair of coarse bamboo splints and black paper with a few splashes of gilt to the more expensive kinds; the very gorgeous folding-fans that are sent to Europe and America are not used by the Chinese themselves—they are simply made to please the outside barbarian. In Canton simple white ones can be bought with maps of the city on them; the Chinese map-maker has, however, adapted his map to the shape of the fan. Many of the feather fans are lyre-shaped, with a white bone or ivory handle, and eight, ten, or a dozen long feathers ranged in order—a fan fit to meet the requirements of fastidious gentlemen. A lady sports one in which perhaps nearly a score of feathers are employed, and which, unlike the the gentleman's long narrow shape, is broader than long. A curious fan which used to come from Formosa was made of a fibrous, somewhat lyre-shaped leaf having a few leaves or sprays as ornamentations burnt into it with a hot iron. The Swatow fan is another sort that is well known: a bamboo tube, about the thickness of a small finger, serves as the handle; to form the framework, the bamboo above the handle is split into very thin slips; the surface is paper, pasted over these slips, on which some elegant figure or two, a bird or some scene from Chinese history, or mythology, is depicted; the top is slightly bent over. This is one of the best of open fans to use.

It is amusing to see the vigorous way in which a Chinese fans himself: not content with a languid stirring of the air in front of his face and chest, he inserts the fan under his jacket, both front and back, and applies it vigorously till cooled, when his legs and arms will come in for an equal share of attention.

The ordinary way to carry a fan is in the hand, but another convenient place for a folding one is the back of the neck, or it is sometimes stuck by a tradesman into the top of his stocking. It takes the place of a walking-stick with a Chinese gentleman, as it gives him something to hold in his hand, and to flutter and wave and gesticulate with, when excited. With schoolmasters, it is constantly at hand to rap a boy over the head or to call attention by tapping the desk with it. It serves to give point and emphasis to the public speaker's periods; when he has warmed up to his subject and his heated oratory has had its effect, and a cooler frame and quieter manner will suit his next periods better, he opens its folded ribs and with a few leisurely motions brings down his temperature to its desired state; it adds grace to the faultless get-up of the *jeunesse dorée;* while the youthful bride is sheltered from the too inquisitive stare of the crowd by her attendant's fan; the over-heated coolie cools himself with it as he rests a moment or two from his arduous toil; and the sweltering half-naked blacksmith has his apprentice fan him when engaged before the glowing forge; the mandarin used to have a huge, imitation screen-fan of wood carried in with whom he had no time to waste in salutations by the way, his retinue, which came in useful when he met a fellow-official for their attendants interposed these wooden fans, and neither official had seen the other, thus obviating the necessity of stopping the processions and descending from the sedan-chairs.

Folding fans may be used at any time of the year; but certain other fans are only to be used at certain seasons. Thus palm-leaf fans and those made of goose feathers are for summer, while when the weather is neither very cold nor very hot—as in autumn, and likewise towards the latter part of spring—circular silk fans are seen. Winter has no distinctive fans assigned to it, for the obvious reason that fans are not generally required in cold weather.

Fans are used in decorative art: papers for fans are painted, mounted, and framed as pictures; open-work spaces are left in walls of that shape. Even the gods and genii are sometimes represented with these indispensables of a hot climate, some of them being capable of all sorts of magic.

A deserted wife is, by that happy periphrasis so constantly employed by the Chinese, known as 'an autumn fan' from the inscription written on a fan, and sent to her royal master, by a lady of the Court, who found herself in this unenviable position two thousand years ago. The pathetic lines written on this memorable fan have been rendered into English by Dr. Martin, as follows:—

LINES INSCRIBED ON A FAN.

(Written by Pan Tsieh Yu, a lady of the Court, and presented to the Emperor Ch'êng Ti of the Han Dynasty, B.C. 18.)

Of fresh new silk, all snowy white,
And round as harvest moon,
A pledge of purity and love,
A small but welcome boon—

While summer lasts, borne in the hand,
Or folded on the breast,
'Twill gently soothe thy burning brow,
And charm thee to thy rest.

But ah! when autumn frosts descend,
And autumn winds blow cold,
No longer sought, no longer loved,
'Twill lie in dust and mould.

This silken fan, then deign accept,
Sad emblem of my lot,
Caressed and cherished for an hour,
Then speedily forgot.

Hangchow produces 3,000,000 folding oiled-paper fans per annum. At Nanking the industry of fan-making employs 70,000 people. In addition to the palm leaves produced in China, 50,000,000 are imported annually from the Straits Settlements.

References.—Werner, *Descriptive Sociology—Chinese;* Giles, *Historic China and other Sketches; Little* (Mrs. A.), *Intimate China.*

FENG-SHUI.—See GEOMANCY.

FERNS.—Some parts of China abound in ferns, especially is this the case in Hongkong, where they are to be found growing in every nook and cranny, as well as along the roadside and amongst the grass. In other parts they are rarer. (See BOTANY.) In Hongkong there are 24 different genera with 75 species.

References.—Forbes and Hemsley, *Index Floræ Sinensis;* Bretschneider, *History of European Botanical Discoveries in China.*

FILIAL PIETY.—Filial piety is the greatest of all virtues in the Chinese eyes, while disobedience is the greatest of all crimes. From his early childhood the child is trained up, as far as books are concerned, in this idea, while at the same time he is spoiled by the doting love of fond parents, mixed with such a portion, however, of severity, that the compound of bitter-sweet treatment produces on the whole better results than might reasonably be expected; the bitter, generally coming after the sweets of spoiled infancy, has some effect in toning down the over-indulgence so lavishly acted on. Filial piety is very wide-reaching in its application among the Chinese. It concerns itself with a proper care of their bodies, as these being received perfect from their parents, it is their duty to preserve them. As regards one's parents, it is their duty to preserve them. As regards one's parents, it is, according to our Western ideas, most exacting, though at the same time there is no doubt that if the Chinese have erred too much in going to one extreme, we have likewise erred in going to the other. Confucius said, 'while a man's father is alive, look at the bent of his will; when his father is dead, look at his conduct. If for three years he does not alter from the way of his father, then he may be considered to be filial.' He also taught that filial piety should be accompanied by reverence, and that its duties should be performed with a cheerful countenance. It is not confined to parents and children, but was the basis of the political structure, and indeed, is traceable throughout the body politic. It is thought to militate against rebellion, and is considered to be the source of loyalty to the Sovereign. The way in which it works is thus expressed in the 'Classic of Filial Piety':—

> 'Filial duty is the root of virtue, and the stem from which instruction in the moral principle springs. . . . The first thing which filial duty requires of us is, that we carefully preserve from all injury, and in a perfect state, the bodies which we have received from our parents. And when we acquire for ourselves a station in the world, we should regulate our conduct by correct principles so as to transmit our name to future generations, and reflect glory on our parents. This is the ultimate aim of filial duty. Thus it commences in attention to parents, is continued through a course of services rendered to the prince, and is completed by the elevation of ourselves.'

As Archdeacon Gray remarks in his book, 'China': 'The Chinese Government is only to be understood through the relation which exists between a father and his son.'

Instances of extraordinary self-denial are constantly occurring amongst the Chinese on the part of children towards their parents. They undergo imprisonment at times in their stead; but, what is still more strange, they cut out pieces of their own flesh, cook it, and give it to them to eat, when seriously ill and when other remedies have failed; it seems to be a never-failing cure, to judge from the accounts that appear in the native newspapers concerning it. The youths are incited to these and other acts of devotion by the recital of instances of self-denial on behalf of parents. There are twenty-four of these stories of paragons of filial piety. One thawed through the ice on a pond, by lying naked on it, and then caught carp of which his mother was fond. Another went into the bed at night to let the mosquitoes have their fill on him before his parents should retire to rest. Another, though seventy years old, played like a child to amuse his aged father and mother. As an instance of the great lengths to which the Chinese go in this respect, a father was preparing to bury alive his only child of three years of age, as poverty was so pressing that there was a difficulty in supporting his mother, when Heaven intervened, for when digging, he came across a pot of gold. One sees in ancestral worship the fullest development of filial piety, as the parents and ancestors are deified and divine honours are paid to them with, however, it must be confessed, a very selfish feeling for the great part, for the *raison d'être* of ancestral worship is founded mainly upon a desire to propitiate the departed spirits, and thus ensure prosperity to themselves. (See ANCESTRAL WORSHIP).

A great deal of filial piety is mere ceremonial observance with but little real heart at the bottom of it, and there are as unfilial sons to be found in China as in our own land, still, at the same time, it must be good for the youth of this vast country, teeming with future men and women, to have such a high standard, on the whole, held up for their guidance.

References.—Legge, *Chinese Classics;* Milne, *The Sacred Edict; Chinese Repository,* x. 164; Doolittle, *Social Life of the Chinese,* i. 452 *et seq.*

FIRECRACKERS AND FIREWORKS.—The Chinese are essentially a noisy people—all Orientals are. Spending so much time out of doors has doubtless something to do with their noisy way of talking; for they will shout at each other when a quiet whisper would serve their purpose as well, if not better. Their music, much of it at least, is noisy—what with clash of cymbals, clang of gongs, the loud sounding drum, the harsh untuned flageolets and the shrill flutes, and the entire absence of *piano* effects. One must suppose that to them the constant *forte* and *fortissimo* is as entertaining as the softest and sweetest song without words is to our ears. And the crackers—the firecrackers—here is a perfect apotheosis of noise. A perfect carnival of uproar and deafening sound is produced, especially at New

Year's time, by their almost continuous discharge, for at that joyous season a perfect pandemonium reigns rampant. Woe betide the foreigner in a native city then, or even in the British Colony of Hongkong itself, where their discharge is limited to a certain period of shorter duration than the unrestrained jubilation of the unfettered Chinese is content with. Sleep is almost out of the question at night while house after house and shop after shop lets off its strings of firecrackers, the rattling of the small artillery being accentuated by a louder boom every little while from a bomb of larger size. The only grain of comfort to the foreigner, while this uproarious din is in full swing, is that the foul spirits of disease are exorcised by the plentiful supply of sulphur fumes floating in the air and penetrating into every nook and cranny. His matter-of-fact nature refuses to believe that the monotonous fusillade of crackers will put to flight the fell and foul spirits that love to lurk about the haunts of men: for such is the supposed rationale of their use by the Chinese; therefore, at all joyous events—such as marriages, processions, saints' days, and feasts —immunity from ill has to be purchased by their explosion. In most districts they are even discharged at the grave after the burial. The cylindrical stem of the bamboo has, perhaps, given the idea of the form of the firecrackers, and the crack made by the splitting of bamboo may also have been suggestive. The manufacture of the universally used firecracker occupies the time, and helps to fill the purses, of many women and children in some parts of the country. The cracker-frames are tied, ends up, in wheel-shaped bundles, and women and girls fill in the powder. Numbers of them may be seen thus employed, as well as busied with the other processes of the manufacture, in most large towns, but especially in those of Kuangtung, Hunan and Kiangsi.

The following account of the manufacture of firecrackers in Shanghai will doubtless prove of interest:—

'Out of 26,705,733 lbs. of fire-crackers exported from China during 1897, over 20,000,000 lbs. came to the United States.' 'A small quantity went to England. Other countries' 'took only infinitesimal amounts.' 'In making crackers only the cheapest kind of straw paper, which can be produced in the immediate locality where the crackers are made, is used for the body of the cracker. A little finer paper is used for the wrapper. A piece of straw paper 9 by 30 inches will make 21 crackers 1½ inches long and 1/4th of an inch in diameter. The powder is also of the cheapest grade, and is made in the locality where used. It costs $1.50 to $1.75 per catty or 6 to 7 cents gold per lb. For the fuse a paper (called "leather" in Shanghai) is used which is imported from Japan, and is made from the inner lining of the bamboo. In other places a fine rice-paper is used, generally, stiffened slightly with buckwheat-flour paste, which, the Chinese say, adds to its inflammability. A strip of this paper 1/3rd of an inch wide by 14 inches (a Chinese foot) long is laid on the table, and a very little powder put down the middle of it with a hollow bamboo stick. A quick twist of the paper makes the fuse ready for use.' 'The straw paper is first rolled by hand round an iron rod, which varies in size according to the size of cracker to be made. To complete the rolling a rude machine is used. This consists of two uprights supporting an axis, from which is suspended by two arms a heavy piece of wood, slightly convex on the lower side. There is just room between this swinging block and the top of the table to place the cracker. As each layer of paper is put on by hand, the cracker is placed on the table and the suspended weight is drawn over the roll, thus tightening it until no more can be passed under the weight. For the smallest "whip" cracker, the workmen uses for compression, instead of this machine, a heavy piece of wood, fitted with a handle, like that of a carpenter's plane. In filling crackers 200 to 300 are tied together tightly in a bunch. Red clay is spread upon the end of the bunch and forced into the end of each cracker with a punch. While the clay is being tamped in, a little water is sprinkled on it, which makes it pack closer. The powder is poured in at the other end of the cracker. With the aid of an awl, the edge of the paper is turned in at the upper end of the cracker, and the fuse is inserted through this. A variety has two chambers separated by a plug of clay through which runs a connecting fuse. There is also a fuse extending from the powder in the lower chamber through the side of the cracker. When the cracker is to be fired it is set on end and fire set to the fuse. The powder exploding in the chamber throws the cracker high in air where the second charge is exploded by fire from the fuse extending through the plug between the two chambers. In the manufacture of these the clay is first tamped in with a punch to form the separating plug. The lowest chamber is then loaded with powder and closed by turning over the paper at the end. The upper chamber is loaded and closed with clay. A hole is punched in the side of the lower chamber with an awl, and the fuse inserted through this opening.' The hours are 6 A.M. to 11 P.M. The work is largely done by women and children. Thirty women and ten men can make 100,000 per day, women getting 5 cents and men 7 cents a day. An apprentice to the business serves four years, only having his board. At the end of that time, if a fairly good workman, he receives 150 cash a day, an expert getting 200. The business is said to be unhealthy and dangerous. 'The fumes of the powder and other things used in the make-up of the cracker bring on dread diseases which soon end the careers of the poor creatures engaged in the work.' (*Leslie's Weekly*, 12th July, 1899.)

The following description of a pyrotechnic display will give an idea of Chinese fireworks:—

'The Chinese are proficients in the pyrotechnic art, and the fireworks which were exhibited at the end of this entertainment were *chefs d'œuvre* of all skill—the four elements having been called into requisition to furnish animals, birds, fishes, and reptiles, both real and imaginary; from whose bodies issued streams of flame. Five dragons ascended into the air, and were metamorphosed into fire-vomiting lions; a huge bird, of some unknown species, fluttered in the air in a sheet of flame, presently a huge serpent crawled from out of the beak of the bird, and was lost to view in many-tinted flames; one large lantern ascended, in a mass of fire, from which smaller lanterns issued, which in their turn sent forth various and innumerable forms. On the back of an enormous fish was seated a portly mandarin, from whose aldermanic corporation burst forth streams of fire, which appeared to cause intense delight, and excite the greatest merriment amongst the spectators. The last firework was by far the most beautiful and perfect, being completely artistic in its details; this represented a mandarin's house with the whole of the adjacent buildings belonging to the residence, the roofs being ornamented with bells and figures; this burned for some time, and then changed into a mandarin seated in his sedan-chair, with the usual train of attendants, bearing flags, beating gongs, and carrying lanterns; the effect of this mass of many-coloured flames, defining the outline of the various forms, baffles description; and as the last sparks died away, we could have been tempted to follow Oliver Twist's example and asked for more.'

FIVE ELEMENTS, THE.—According to Chinese ideas these are Metal, Air, Fire, Water, and Wood. In the Sung philosophical system they spring from the interaction of the *Yin* and the *Yang*; but Chu Hsi regarded them not as those five objects, but as essences manifested by them.

FIVE RELATIONS, THE.—Confucianism recognized the following five relations as existing among human beings, namely, sovereign and subject (or prince and officer), father and son, elder and younger brother, husband and wife, and friend and friend.

FLAG.—Flags in China were originally distinctive banners used by warring States or in the chase, etc. A distinctive national flag for China is comparatively only a recent thing. When China got a foreign-built navy it was necessary that a flag should be devised for the ships. The first flag thus used was triangular in shape, yellow, with a dragon after a pearl, a most fitting emblem for the national flag of a country in which the dragon was the sign and symbol of the ruling power. Later, a flag of an oblong shape was adopted, and, on the establishment of the Republic, an oblong flag composed of five horzontal coloured stripes,—red, yellow, blue, white and black, representing the Manchus, Chinese, Mongolians, Mohammedans, and Tibetans respectively,—became the national emblem.

FLOODS.—Floods are of frequent occurrence in China. No idea of the evils of deforestation appears to be realised by the people, to many of whom a broken twig or stick is an important factor in the preparation of a meal.

The enormous rivers are fed after the winter by the snows melting at their sources, hundreds or thousands of miles from their mouths, and the mighty streams rise sometimes 40 or more feet above the height they attain during the rest of the year, with the result that vast tracts of country are flooded. Here is part of a telegraphic summary of one of the floods on the Yellow River in 1898:—'Nine counties devastated, hundreds of villages submerged, thousands of homes ruined.'

Modern engineering skill, if applied to these catastrophies and to the proper embankment of this river, could and would succeed in curbing its course, and restraining its wanderings; but the weak attempts of the natives, further palsied by the persistent peculations of the dishonest mandarins charged with the labour of supervising the work, who divert much of the money entrusted to them to their own benefit, increases the feebleness of the efforts to master this unruly river. It has been well termed the River of Death.

'The River of Death:—The Yellow River, which has been named the "Sorrow of China," is probably the most destructive stream on the face of the earth. In less than a hundred years it has changed its channel four times, and the point where it empties into the sea has from time to time been moved up and down the coast a distance of three miles. It runs through a vast alluvial plain, and is fed by streams from a great system of mountains in the north. When the snow melting on this range comes at a time of heavy rains, the result is sure to be a terrible flood. It has been estimated that in the past three centuries over ten million human beings have perished in the floods of the Yellow River. For destructiveness, both of life and property, this stream is unparalleled, and the soubriquet bestowed upon it is amply justified by its history.

Of late years important work on confining the river by modern scientific methods has been successfully carried on by American engineers.

FLOWERS.—The inhabitants of the 'Flowery Land,' as China is called, are fond of flowers. No lady is dressed without sweet-scented beautiful flowers stuck in her glossy black hair, and the lower classes are glad to copy their superiors whenever a holiday, or any event out of the common, gives them the chance to bloom forth in Nature's own adornments. Failing the natural, they have recourse to artificial flowers, some of which are very well made, especially the pith flowers at Amoy, for which the place is famous, and the paper and cloth ones to be seen almost everywhere. In most houses, and even shops, a vase or two is found, if nowhere else, at least in front of the idol's shrine, where some lovely chrysanthemums, if they are in season, white, yellow, or red, add a touch of colour or beauty to the formal primness of the set and stiff furniture.

At the Chinese New Year, flowers are all the rage. The beautiful white and yellow narcissus with its long, lance-shaped, stiff, green leaves is *par excellence* the New Year's flower. It is considered lucky to have the first bud open on New Year's Day. Another variety has the leaves all gnarled, being trained like crab's claws, and the plant, instead of being tall and upright, is reduced by art into a curled and curious-shaped looking object. Another essentially New Year's flower is the *tíú-chung fá* [*tiao chung hua*] (*Enkyanthus reticulatus*). Each blossom, about half an inch in length, hangs down like a miniature bell from the woody branches, while the delicate green of the new springing leaves forms a fine shade of contrast to the pink and white of the innumerable tiny flowers. These are not grown in the house, as the first is, but branches of them are stuck into the quaint-looking vases. A branch of flower culture which we quite neglect in the West is that of fruit-blossoms. The Chinese cut off the branches of fruit-trees as they burst into bud, and the delicate tints of the peach, the white flowers of the plum, and the tender blossoms of the almond, are all eagerly sought for, to decorate their homes at that festive season of the year. Another common form of flower-decoration is the employment of flower-baskets. A wire framework, made into the shape of a basket, is used, and the buds and blossoms artistically arranged on it so as to hide it completely. These are hung up in the room or at the doors, and diffuse a grateful odour through the heated apartments on a warm summer's day. They are largely employed at weddings, as well as at other times, nor are the designs confined only to flower-baskets.

There are no window plants, so esteemed by the better class of artisans amongst us, as well as by others higher in the social scale, but their place is sometimes taken by a solitary plant, often some woody non-flowering shrub, which has been dwarfed with much ingenuity, and is tended with constant care—the whole object only some six inches in height, but a perfect little tree in its way. This idea is further developed at times, and a little rockery is produced, frightful in its ruggedness,—an idealised bit of mountain scenery—on projecting points of which toy arbours in earthenware are perched, little paths meander from one to the other, crossing the lilliputian gorges and ravines on equally small earthenware bridges, while below, and in front of all, lies a tiny piece of water, in which gorgeous and grotesque goldfish swim about. The heights above are covered at every vantage point with small clumps of dwarf bamboo, and numerous other equally small trees and shrubs clothe with greenness the bare masses of the dry rugged rock, all in proportion with the minuteness of this morsel of quaint imitation of Nature's beauties, looked at from a Chinese standpoint—the whole affair only being a foot or two in height. Infinite care and tender pains are taken in planting, watering, and tending this microcosm of a landscape, thus revealing that the Chinese are not wanting in a love of Nature, as seen through their goggle-like spectacles.

Amongst flowers, the tree-peony is highly esteemed, being called 'the King of Flowers.' The skill of the Chinese has been exercised in producing many varieties. Another flower much thought of is the lotus. There is a white, as well as a red variety, and they are so highly cultivated as to cause the petals to spring from the seedholes even. They are magnificent flowers, with their delicately veined petals, quaint-shaped seed repositories, and curious peltate leaves. They are much used in Chinese decorative art, and form a fine throne for a god or goddess to sit on in a state of ecstatic and nirvana-like contemplation.

It is impossible even to enumerate all the beautiful flowers in which the Chinese delight: the white tuberoses laden at the evening hour with heavy perfume, roses with but little scent, beautiful, double dahlias, lovely sweet-smelling magnolias, pure white lilies, superb camellias, chrysanthemums of different shades, and many others with no English names, a mere list of which would fill pages, and the use of such terms as *Tabernæmontana Coronaria flore plena* would frighten the majority of our readers.

Most Chinese cut flowers are short-lived compared with those in the West. Bouquets and button-holes have not reached the Far East yet, as far as native use is concerned. Many Chinese flowers have been introduced into the lands of the West, and it is to be hoped that as foreign residents have many varieties of English flowers in their own gardens, the natives will in time add them to their stock of cultivated plants, the best of the floral productions of both sides of the globe being thus given in exchange. In Hongkong many foreign flowers are cultivated by the flower gardeners for sale to the exile from home lands.

Much attention is bestowed on plants by the Chinese, and not a few monographs on flowers, such as the peony, and chrysanthemum, have been written describing the varieties and mode of culture, etc.

FOOD.—Most erroneous notions are current as to the food of the Chinese, for it appears to be a generally received opinion in Western countries that their common food consists of rats, cats, dogs and mice. It would be almost as true to say that the only meat the French live on is that of horses, or that the English are fond of snails, because some people in both countries esteem these as delicacies. Pork is the chief meat of the Chinese in the south—in fact, in some of the southern languages of China, the word meat is used to mean pork. The consumption of fish, both fresh and salt, is enormous. Fowls are a favourite article of diet, and a little beef is also eaten.

There are one or two restaurants in Canton where dogs' and cats' flesh can be bought; but both are rarely consumed in comparison with other kinds of meat and food. At the races in Hongkong, stalls for the sale of dogs' flesh are opened for the three or four days, confirming the foreigner in his opinion that Chinese live on dogs, but at no other time are any stalls of the kind to be found in the Colony. Our cats in Canton used to disappear, and one of them came home one day all wet, as if it had just escaped from the pot, but then we lived on the banks of the river, and the boat people are not so very particular as to their food as some of the higher classes would be. Many of the respectable Chinese would feel as much disgust at the idea of eating dogs, cats, rats, and mice, as we do. At one time in a foreigner's employ at Canton was a boy, a young fellow named A-ling, who got the sobriquet of 'Ratty A-ling' from his fellow-servants, probably for the twofold reason of his father being a rat-catcher, and because when at home, he used to enjoy a meal of which the chief dish consisted of these rodents; but none of the other servants would have touched one. It is not an uncommon sight to see dried rats hung up in shops with dried ducks and a number of other dried meats. A favourite dog belonging to a foreigner was once killed by a snake, and when committing his body to the river, in Canton, a miserable leper seized hold of it and took it into his wretched little sampan, notwithstanding a warning as to the cause of the dog's death. But in spite of all these facts, which only show that some Chinese eat such food, we repeat, it is not the case that dogs, cats, rats, and mice, form the staple articles of diet of the people as a whole.

At the same time, there are other articles of food which to us appear as disgusting as our fondness for butter and cheese does to the Chinese. It is not every foreign stomach that can stand the sight of hundreds of greenish-brown worms, fresh from the rice fields, hawked about the streets for sale; nor do salted and pickled eggs, getting discoloured by age, and eggs high from long keeping, prove agreeable to our palate, though why we should so take our game and turn with disgust from an egg in a similar condition is a mystery to a Chinese. Silkworm grubs do not sound very tempting to a foreign ear, yet the Chinese are very fond of them.

In some parts of China the poor people eat snakes; for instance, in the neighbourhood of Amoy; but as far as could be ascertained, it was the non-venomous ones that were eaten. In some districts of the Canton province, the same horrible reptiles form articles of diet, but it is a question whether, under the same name, other reptiles of a similar shape and form may not be included as well. One of our English friends, on a trip in the country, has tasted what his host considered a dainty dish, viz., cooked snake; and poisonous ones appeared to be relished in that district. In Swatow, was seen a man hawking long, brown snakes in a basket for food. There were three or four of them tied with strings round the neck, the strings being fastened to the top of the basket to prevent their escape. They are rather an expensive article of diet, costing about seventy cents each. They are used to make soup.

Birds' nests, sharks' fins, and fish maws, come more under the name of curious articles of diet, than disgusting: for the first are gelatinous and not like 'ordinary' birds' nests (See BIRDS' NESTS); and the second and third are so cleaned and washed that they are as pure as any articles eaten by us.

In the south of China, rice is the principal vegetable food, but instead of vegetables being an adjunct to the meat, as with us, the meat is taken as a tasty article with the rice, which is the staple article of diet. Either dried, salt, or fresh vegetables are eaten at nearly every meal.

The Chinese, like the French, have nominally two meals. One about 8 or 10 o'clock in the morning, and the other at 5 or 6 in the evening, or thereabouts. With the poorer classes these consist of a number of bowls of rice—cooked till so dry that each grain is separate—a little pork or fish, salt or fresh, and some fried vegetables. Everything of the meat kind is chopped up fine, or cut into pieces, as the Chinese would think it barbarous to carve anything at the table, and also to enable the chop-sticks to pick it up it has to be in little morsels, or at all events of such dimensions as to be easily picked to pieces by them, or lifted to the mouth and a bite taken off. A drink of tea from the rice bowl finishes the frugal meal. The dinner is the same as the breakfast. This then is the ordinary everyday food of millions in China, and costs only about a couple of dollars a month; or, of late years, say three dollars or more. The more a man has, the more he expends on his food, both as regards quality and quantity, and as a consequence he has a more varied fare. Though nominally only taking two set meals a day, nearly every one takes a snack about the middle of the day; it may be only a few cakes, as the Chinese clerks in the Government offices in Hongkong indulge in; it may be a bowl of fish congee, or some other tasty soup or dish from the numerous restaurants, or from some of the many refreshment stalls, stationary and peripatetic.

Some of the hard-toiling labourers, when there is a constant demand on physical strength or muscle, take a number of meals to prime them up for their work, such, for instance, as some of the boatmen on the rivers in the South of China, who work from daylight to sunset, and to whom five meals a day are allowed, when in work.

Chinese food, like French, does not consist of roasts, but of a multitude of made-up dishes. Peanut oil and soy are added to them, and soups and broths are much taken.

Chinese bean sauce, a dark-coloured salty liquid, has been one of the most important ingredients used in Chinese cooking for ages, as well as a tasty condiment for the table. Its use and production extend throughout China.

The Chinese, as far as their own food is concerned, are born cooks. Among the lower classes almost any man can turn his hand to preparing the simple dishes, and in workmen's messes it is the youngest hand (the apprentice) who has the drudgery of the cooking to do.

The dinners to which foreign residents or travellers are sometimes invited by the Chinese, bear about the same relation to an everyday dinner, that a Lord Mayor's or Fishmongers' Hall dinner does to an ordinary one partaken of by *paterfamilias* in the bosom of his family. As a sample of these grand dinners in Hongkong, the menu of the one to which the Duke of Connaught was invited will be found below. We must, however, state that some of the dishes were added for the benefit of the foreign visitors, who wanted something more substantial than the numerous broths and slops of a Chinese fine dinner; for one rises from such a function with a vague feeling of having tasted of an infinite variety of unknown dishes, but, notwithstanding the hours spent at the table, with an unsatisfied feeling that a good English dinner of solid food would remove.

MENU.

1. Birds' Nest Soup. 2. Stewed Shell Fish. 3. Cassia Mushrooms.
4. Crab and Sharks' Fins. 5. Roast Beef (à l'Anglaise).
6. Roast Chicken and Ham. 7. Pigeons' Eggs.
8. 'Promotion' (Boiled Quail, &c.). 9. Fried Marine Delicacies.
10. Roast Turkey and Ham (à l'Anglaise).
11. Fish Gills. 12. Larded Quails. 13. Sliced Teal.
14. Peking Mushrooms. 15. Roast Pheasant (à l'Anglaise).
16. Winter Mushrooms. 17. Roast Fowl and Ham.
18. Bêche-de-Mer. 19. Sliced Pigeon.
20. Snipe (à l'Anglaise). 21. Macaroni (à la Peking).

SIDE DISHES.

Cold Roast Sucking Pig.
Cold Roast Fowl. Cold Roast Duck.
Cold Roast Mutton.

TABLE DISHES.

Cold Sausages.
Prawns. Preserved Eggs. Livers.
&c., &c., &c.

FRUITS.

Preserved Apples.
Citrons. Tientsin Pears. Pomegranates. Carambolas.
Greengages. Pine Apples.
&c., &c., &c.

PASTRY.

Sweet Lotus Soup. Almond Custard. Rice.
&c., &c., &c.

WINES.

Champagne (Krug).
Claret. Orange Wine. Rice Wine. Rose Dhu.
'Optimus' Wine. Pear Wine.

'The delicacy known as shark's fins is neither shark nor fin. . . . . Shark's fins are bits of sword-fish, delicate portions under the giant fins carefully scraped and fashioned dextrously by hand into the pattern of fins. Southern Chinese waters yield only a small number of swordfish, far incompatible with the demand. Obviously, therefore, the materials for this wedding piece de resistance must be imported from parts of the world where there are plenty of swordfish. Gloucester fishermen procure swordfish which are exported to China be way of Boston. The rest of the continuous supply demanded by China is caught off Nova Scotia and sent by way of Vancouver.

According to tradition shark's fins are the third course of the wedding menu. If one's pocket be well lined with taels in China the wedding feast has 46 courses. If, however, one's heritage be more humble one contents oneself with giving a feast of a mere 18 courses. In either case, however, there must be shark's fins, because it is unseemly for any son and daughter of any household to marry without the auspicious presence of that traditional delicacy at the feast.'

We give a few Chinese receipts which we have translated from a Chinese Cookery Book:—

STEAMED SHARKS' FINS.

Sun-dried sharks' fins are to be washed clean [as follows]:—First take the fins [as bought] and place in a cooking pan, add wood-ashes and boil in several waters. Then take out and scrape away the roughness [on the fins]. If not clean, boil again, and scrape again, until properly clean. Then change the water and boil again. Take out, remove the flesh, keeping only the fins. Then boil once again. Put in spring water. Be careful in changing the water, and thoroughly soak them, for it is necessary that the taste of lime should be taken out of them. Then put the fins into soup, stew three times till quite tender. Dish in a bowl, placing meat of crabs below them, and add a little ham on the top. The taste is clear, neither tender nor tough, something like the taste of pomeloes at times.

CHICKEN WITH THE LIQUOR OF FERMENTED RICE.

Take the bones out of a Chicken and steam till just ready. Then take it out and let it cool. Cut into thin slices. Take gelatinous rice, which has been fermented with yeast and water added, and cook with this for two hours, afterwards add the juice expressed from fresh ginger, soy, sesamum, and oil, of each a little. Mix together with boiled peanut oil. Dish and add fragrant herbs.

GENII DUCK.

Take a fat duck. Open and clean. Rub two mace of salt all over it, both outside and in. Put into an earthen dish and take of *fan* spirits one cup, and put the cup with the spirits inside the duck. Do not let the spirits spill on to the duck; only the vapour of the spirits is wanted. Steam over water till quite tender. Lift out the wine-cup into a bowl. Done in this way, there is no need of minor vegetables.

Enormous quantities of rice and flour are imported annually from abroad. Four is rapidly replacing the use of rice, especially in Northern China.

FOUR BOOKS, THE.—See LITERATURE.

FOREIGNER IN FAR CATHAY, THE.—If the record of Chinese intercourse with the West is interesting, it must be admitted that the accounts of the adventures and travels of foreigners in the distant land of Cathay are also full of interest and adventure. Are they not to be found recorded in the innumerable volumes, published during the past few centuries; are they not chronicled in the old-fashioned language of mediæval writers, so full of wonders as to astound their contemporaries who often would have none of these travellers tales, and treated them as Baron Munchausens?

The achievements of commerce, though in the general written in a soberer strain, sometimes almost approach the interest of a romance. There are fragmentary records of the early trade of the Chinese with neighbouring and distant nations in the dim remote periods of antiquity; but the origin and earlier transactions of this primitive period are lost in the hazy oblivion of ancient times. The *Serica vestis* tempted the practical Roman merchants to undergo hardships and difficult journeys of which the majority of our present-day merchants know but little; nor less adventurous were the long journeys of the Arab traders. The Portuguese, who took such a leading position in the van of nations in the sixteenth century, had the honour of being the pioneers of modern European commerce in China, in the year A.D. 1516. They were followed in later years by the Spanish, Dutch, and Russians. 'The intercourse of the English with China, though it commenced later than' that of 'other maritime nations of Europe, has been far more important in its consequences, and their trade greater in amount than all other foreign nations combined.' It began in A.D. 1635. American trade with China began in A.D. 1784. (See TRADE.)

At the present day there are different settlements of foreigners at different ports on the coast and on the large rivers, while, scattered here and there throughout the empire, may be found some solitary individuals and families.

The larger proportion of foreigners in China at the present day are British subjects. In 1890 the different nationalities in China were represented as follows:—

Austrians	65	French	589	Spanish	304
Brazilians	2	Germans	648	Swedes and Norwegians	155
Belgians	28	Italians	74	United States, Citizens of the	1,153
British	3,317	Japanese	883		
Danish	81	Portuguese	610		
Dutch	41	Russians	131		

making a total of 8,081. In 1880, 4,000; in 1899, about 17,000.

It must be remembered that Hongkong and Macao are not included in this return, as they are not a portion of the Chinese empire politically, though as far as geography is concerned they are. The total of Europeans and Americans in the British Colony of Hongkong, by the census of 1891, was 8,545, or total British and Foreign community 10,446. In 1911 the total civil population of Hongkong and Kowloon was 456,739; in 1915,

509,160 (of which 495,840 were Chinese and 13,320 non-Chinese); and in 1921, 625,166. According to returns made in 1879, there were 4,476 Portuguese in Macao, and 78 of other nationalities not Chinese. The census of 1910 gives the total population of the colony as 74,866, of which 71,021 were Chinese, 3,298 Portuguese, and 244 foreigners.

The following table shows the foreign population of China in 1921:—

American	8,230
Austrian	40
Belgian	505
Brazilian	42
British	9,298
Danish	547
Dutch	486
French	2,453
German	1,255
Hungarian	8
Italian	587
Japanese	144,434
Mexican	1
Norwegian	227
Portuguese	3,493
Russian	68,250
Spanish	286
Swedish	434
Non-treaty Powers	193
	240,769

The number of foreigners resident in the different Chinese Treaty Ports in 1898 and 1899, were as follow:—

	1898	1899
English	5,148	5,562
Japanese	1,698	2,440
Americans	2,056	2,335
Russians	165	1,621
Portuguese	1,082	1,423
French	920	1,183
German	1,043	1,134
Spanish	395	448
Scandinavian	200	244
Belgians	169	234
Danes	162	178
Italians	141	124
Dutch	87	106
Other	155	161
Total	13,421	17,193

Port Arthur, Hongkong, Tsingtau, etc., are not included in the above statistics.

Foreigner in Far Cathay, The

The following table is one of the foreign firms at the Treaty Ports.

	1898	1899
English	398	401
Japanese	114	195
German	107	115
French	37	76
American	43	70
Russian	16	19
Portuguese	20	10
Belgian	9	9
Italian	9	9
Dutch	8	9
Spanish	4	9
Austrian	5	5
Danish	3	4
Scandinavian	—	2
Total	773	933

The number of foreign forms in China in 1921 was as follows:—

Nationality	Firms
American	412
Austrian	—
Belgian	27
Brazilian	6
British	703
Danish	28
Dutch	31
French	222
German	92
Hungarian	—
Italian	42
Japanese	6,141
Mexican	—
Norwegian	12
Portuguese	152
Russian	1,613
Spanish	7
Swedish	9
Non-Treaty Powers	14
	9,511

There were 3,839 foreigners in the large Treaty Port of Shanghai in 1895; in 1915, 20,924 (7,387 Japanese, 5,521 British, and 1,448 American); the whole foreign community of Amoy was stated to be 400 or 500 in 1899; in later years this seems to have slightly decreased; other smaller ports have many less.

In 1924 there were 3,364 foreign residents in Peking, comprising 2,568 men and 796 women. Of the total number, 1,500 were Japanese.

The foreign population in the British and American concessions at Shanghai were as follows:—

'The recent censuses of foreign residents in Shanghai (exclusive of those living in the French Settlement who numbered 2,405 in 1915) give the following figures, with which may be compared those for 1895:—

	1895	*1900*	*1915*
British	1,936	2,692	4,822
Portuguese	371	978	1,323
Japanese	250	736	7,169
American	328	562	1,307
German	314	525	1,155
Indian	119	296	1,009
French	138	176	244
Manila and Malay	32	157	—
Spanish	154	111	181
Austrian and Hungarian	39	83	123
Danish	86	76	145
Swedish	46	63	73
Italian	83	60	114
Russian	28	47	361
Norwegian	35	45	82
Turkish	32	41	108
Dutch	15	40	55
Swiss	16	37	79
Belgian	21	22	18
Various	21	28	151
Total	4,424	6,774	18,519

'The preponderance of British subjects in Shanghai remains, therefore, as great as ever it was. In 1870 there were 894 British subjects, 255 Americans, 138 Germans, 46 Spaniards, and 16 French, no other nationality running into double figures.' The French concession also contains a considerable foreign population.

References.—*China Review;* Williams, *Middle Kingdom; Chinese Repository;* various statistical tables; De Jesus, *Historic Shanghai.*

FORFEITS.—The Chinese have a noisy game of forfeits often played at the dinner-table at feast times. It consists in the player flinging out one or more fingers of the hand, and shouting out a number, when the other, who is playing with him, must instantly fling out as many of his fingers as will, if added to the number mentioned by his opponent, make up the total to ten, and while doing this he also shouts out the number of his fingers that he throws out. If a mistake is made, the one who makes it has to drink a cup of spirits as a forfeit. As they proceed, the party of six, eight, or ten, get more and more excited and boisterous, and the shouting at the top of their voices proves very annoying and exasperating to Europeans who may unfortunately have their residences near to those of the Chinese. Such a nuisance is this noisy game, that the playing of it after 11 o'clock at night is prohibited in Hongkong by Ordinance.

Looking at it from another point of view, this game of *chái-múi* (chiee mooee) [*ts'ai mei* or *mu chan*] is a most interesting one, as the Italians have a similar game, which they call *morra;* in France it is known as *mourre,* while the ancient Egyptians had some corresponding game, as represented on their sculptures, and the Romans had their *micare digitis* over which butchers and their customers gambled for bits of meat, from which game descended the Italian one already mentioned.

FROGS.—The batrachians of China have not been fully treated of. There are a number of varieties. The edible frog—*Rana esculenta*—is an article of European diet in Hongkong as well as of Chinese. Tree-frogs are found in Hongkong, Macao, and Swatow, and doubtless in other places as well. Bull-frogs are common, at all events in the South. The rice-fields in the southern provinces of China afford ideal breeding places for frogs, as their constant croaking fully testifies.

'In Mid and North China the Common Frog of Europe (*Rana temporaria*) and the Common Toad of Europe (*Bufo vulgaris*) are met with. The genus of Fire-bellied toads (*Bombinator*) consists only of three species, of which two are European and the third Chinese. The little green Tree Frog (*Hyla arborea*) also extends from Europe right across the temperate part of the continent to China, where also a closely allied form (*Hyla arborea sinensis*) is found even as far south as Formosa. The Edible Frog (*Rana esculenta*) is another European form found in China, extending certainly as far south as Fukien. The green Toad (*Bufo viridis*) from southern Europe extends through the middle of Asia along the Himalayas to South China.

Of the tropical forms the common toad of India (*Bufo melanostictus*) is found all over South China, certainly as far north as the Yangtze valley, and is the common toad found around Shanghai. The largest Indian frog, the Tiger Frog (*Rana tigrina*) is also found as far north as the Yangtze. The commonest Shanghai frog (*Rana limnocharis*) is also the commonest species in Formosa and extends throughout the Malay Peninsula and India. The tree frogs of the genus *Rhacophorus* also extend from India through China up to the Yangtze; while a few species of the family *Engystomatidæ* extend from the Tropical Orient into South China.'

FRUIT.—One of the advantages of living in a hot climate is the quantity of fruit that one gets. After a long residence in the East, one notices on a return to Europe, unless it be in a plentiful strawberry season, how much more readily one can get fruit morning, noon, and night in the East than in the West.

There is quantity in the East, but quality (with regard to many fruits) in the West; for, after all, few fruits are superior to those grown in hot-houses in England. This is, however, not so much the fault of the fruit, as the fault or misfortune of the cultivator; for it is often due to circumstances over which he has no control. As a rule, unless the fruit is plucked when yet unripe it will spoil with the heat before the slow means of locomotion available will allow of its being conveyed to its destination. One can try to imagine what would become of our vaunted hot-house productions were they all plucked while green—pears picked while hard, strawberries gathered before they were ripe, and a week taken in carrying them to the market.

In the South of China, at Hongkong, Canton, and Macao (for in some other places, such as Amoy, fruits are scarcer, though in Swatow they seem plentiful and of fine quality) there is a succession of fruit nearly the whole year through; for not only is there such a variety of it indigenous to the soil, but so many different kinds have been introduced during the last few centuries from foreign countries, that before one has had time to get tired of one sort, another has succeeded it—sometimes all too soon. Oranges are very common in the South, having been introduced from that part of China into Europe in A.D. 1548 by the Portuguese, and are also to be had, at some seasons of the year, in most other parts. The German name *Apfelsina*, shows their origin, while the Italian name, *Portugallo*, points out their introducers in the West. The common coolie orange, however, differs rather from those brought to England from Spain at the present day, perhaps the change of soil, climate, and cultivation, have caused a difference in the fruit. The small *kat-tsaí* [*chieh tzŭ*], as they are called in China, but erroneously named 'mandarin oranges' in London ['coolie' and 'mandarin' being colloquial expressions formerly used by Europeans at Canton for 'inferior' and superior'], have a fine acid taste, and were only brought into Europe in the present century: they are like Tangiereens. The real mandarin orange, or *chü-shá kat* [*chu sha chieh*], is a much larger fruit—larger even in diameter than the common coolie orange, which last is about the shape and size of the ordinary kind in England. It is the finest of all, having a skin of a cinnabar red colour very loosely adherent to the fruit itself, the segments of which are much larger in every way than the small *kat* (though the shape of the two varieties is much the same), and without the acid taste, but very juicy and sweet. It is much dearer and rarer than the smaller one, or than the coolie, or 'tight skin.' The Swatow orange seems to be a variety between the mandarin and the loose-skinned orange as known in Canton and neighbourhood.

Of plantains there are numerous varieties, amongst which may be named the coarse large ones—almost unfit to eat raw—the 'dragons' tusks,' 'fragrant plantains,' 'over-the-hill plantains,' and others. One sort or another, with but few breaks, carries one through the year, while the oranges are a winter fruit.

Amongst other indigenous fruits in the Canton province, may be named:—first, the whampee [*kuang-p'i*], a yellow-skinned fruit, as its name implies, and pendent in clusters from the glossy-leaved trees which produce it, about the size of a small grape, tart, and nearly filled with two, three, or four, comparatively speaking, large and greenish stones. Second, the li-chi [*li chih*], better known in England by the dried ones, which are exported there in some quantites, but the pulp of which, being shrivelled into a dryish, sweetish, black substance round the dark stone, gives no idea of the taste of the fresh fruit. The skin, when fresh, is more like a shell, being rough and of a bright, red colour, like a very large round strawberry, when seen at a distance. Inside this is a thin white membrane, enclosing the watery, translucent pulp of a sweetish taste, surrounding the brownish-black ovoid stone. The colour of the fruit is like that of a glass of water with a few drops of milk mixed in it. There are two or three kinds of li-chis; the best variety has a very small stone. Third, the lung-ngan [*lung-yen*], or 'dragon's eye,' is a fruit about the size of a li-chi, with a yellowish-green skin, a large stone, and a watery pulp of a disagreeable, rawish taste, though the Chinese and a few Europeans are fond of it. Fourth, the lo-quat [*lu chü*], which Williams describes as a kind of medlar. There is a thin yellow skin adherent to the fruit, and within, in a cavity in the centre of the fruit, is a large seed or two. The fruit is not unpleasant in taste.

The peaches, when ripe, are good, though smaller than the English hot-house ones. There are two or three varieties of the common kind, one being the eagle-bill, with the point prolonged, and a curious kind, somewhat like a very small apple in shape, but more flattened, the stone inside partaking of the spheroid form.

There are two varieties of pear; one hard, like a turnip, rather sweet in taste, but better when cooked, and growing in the South: the other comes from Tientsin, and is much nicer, being sweeter and more juicy in its turnipy substance. Grapes are also brought from the North, a few are grown in the South, but very different are both pears and grapes from English ones. Apples come from the North of China, but many are very spongy in taste.

The mango is a flattish, oblong fruit of a bright yellow, gold colour, and very nice, having however, a slight turpentine taste. It is a fruit overflowing in its juiciness. The best come from Saigon and Manila, whence they are brought over in steamers.

China has not only given the orange to Europe, but has on the other hand benefited by the introduction of not a few fruits from other parts of the world, amongst which may be mentioned the pineapple, which was cultivated as early as A.D. 1594 in China, 'to which it was brought from the Western shore of America through the Philippines.' The delicious custard-apple also, as its name in Chinese—*fán-laí-chí* [*fan li-chih*], foreign li-chi—implies, is a foreign introduction, and is identical with the sweet-sop of the West Indies. Besides this, there is that most curious of fruits, the carambola, called by the Chinese the *yöng-t'ò* [*yang t'ao*], or foreign peach, though why this name should have been selected is a mystery, for when cut through, it looks like a star with five rays. By Europeans it is also known as the Cape gooseberry. There is another variety called the *sám-ním* [*san nien*], which is sourer than the other. These belong 'to the belladonna, or deadly nightshade family, without having, of course, its poisonous qualities.'

There is also the guava, having a smell something like onions. The Amoy pumelo is a fine fruit, the shaddock of the West Indies. There are two or three varieties of persimmons; a yellow, hard kind, a bright red, soft sort, about the size and shape of a middling-sized apple, and a small, red variety somewhat like a small egg. There are also several varieties of plums, some very nice, and the sour arbutus, too sour at Canton and neighbourhood to be eaten as a fruit, but making a good fruit-syrup; it, however, is sweeter and better at Swatow than at Canton. The jack-fruit is also found in China, and the roseapple, a highly scented fruit, giving one the idea of eating solidified scent, about the size of a small apple and of the form of a hollow sphere, the seeds being inside the hollow part. Besides the above mentioned fruits there are citrons, cocoanuts in Hainan, limes, melons of various kinds, papaya, pomegranates which are a mass of dried seeds in the South of China, and consequently not eaten, pumpkins, etc. In the north of China the fruits are more of the European type—apricots and strawberries, besides some we have already mentioned.

FUN.—Although the Chinese look so serious and grave, they enjoy a bit of fun immensely. The lower classes enter heartily into jokes, and practical ones are constantly to be seen practised in the streets by the chaircoolies waiting for hire. Even what seems to most Europeans a cumbersome language lends itself to puns. Hilarity reigns at wine and dinner-parties. Comedies are in great vogue at theatres. Jest-books are to be bought at the street book-stalls; but, unfortunately, many of the broad jokes in them verge on the indecent and some of them are quite obscene.

FUNG-SHUI.—See GEOMANCY.

GAMBLING.—See AMUSEMENTS and PO-TSZ AND OTHER GAMES OF CHANCE.

GARDENS.—Here is again a word, like many other words, which represents a different idea in China from what it does in the West. One who comes to China prepared to see the beautiful beds, the grouping of colours, and blending of shades, the massing of foliage, the parterres, the trim gravel-walks, the grass-lawns, and the *tout ensemble* that goes to make up the idea represented by the word garden amongst us, must be prepared to be disappointed. In their place are fantastic masses of artificial rockwork, or pools filled with the large, rich, green, disc-like leaves of the lotus, while the formal but lovely red flowers give some warmth or colour to the scene. A Chinese garden must have a suggestion, at least, of water: if nothing else, a tiny pond with artificial rockwork and a bridge—a veritable arch—up which one climbs to its top and descends on the other side. At times, as on the earth's surface, water abounds more than the dry land, for numerous sheets of water take up the space which would be occupied in Western lands by flower-beds; but still the flower-beds are not foregone; in other words, the Chinese have no flower-beds on land, but their flower-beds are in the water; for the still surface of the ponds is embellished with the large, round peltate leaves of the lotus, having a still beauty of their own, relieved in the summer months by the many petaled, purple, chalice-like flowers borne on their long, green stalks above the leaves, and rising from the underlying mud—a Buddhist emblem; for 'as it lifts up its buds out of the slimy ground to a greater or less height above the water, unfolding its leaves and flowers, on whose spotless petals no traces are to be found of the mire from which it has sprung, so the souls of men . . . rise from the slime of sin, by their own power and effort, to different heights, and reach the blessedness of Nirvana.' Later on, when the petals are scattered and have floated away like tiny boats, the green and curiously shaped seed-vessels are seen. Bridges, as we have said, cross these ponds, while kiosks, or summer-houses, are placed here and there, in the midst of the water or on land, as fancy suggests. Here picnics or summer parties are held, and the literary tastes of the guests are met by the quotations, or excerpts, from the classics hung up by the hundreds under the roofs of the sheltered walls, while the votaries of the histrionic art have their tastes provided for by a stage erected especially for that purpose. Larger buildings are scattered about the grounds, fitted with the straight-backed and antique-looking blackwood chairs, matched with teapoys and sofas, while rustic-looking stools stand about, formed each of an irregular stone, supported on a wooden stand of three legs.

The plants are ranged in rows in hundreds of course earthenware pots, or at the best, green glazed ones supported on similar stands or on wooden ones. Very few, if any, flowers are planted in the ground. Plants of privet are trained into figures of animals and men, to which eyes, hands, feet, and hats of earthenware are added. Long rows of these, interspersed with flowers and shrubs, all in flower-pots, line the walks. Trees are allowed to grow in certain places, but there are no ferneries, no glass-houses, and, though the minutest care is taken in the cultivation, the results do not produce what we would look upon as a garden. Gardens, in this Chinese sense of the term, are attached to temples, to ancestral halls, or form the pleasure-grounds of wealthy gentlemen, and are sometimes, in the latter case especially, of considerable extent. Most Chinese who can afford it, or who have the space for it, have a few flowers, or shrubs, in pots, some rockery work, and a little water with goldfish, in the inner part of their house, or congeries of buildings which do duty for a mansion.

The following account of a native garden, the Lotus Gardens, the former residence of the Literary Chancellor in Pao-ting fu, will give some idea of what they are like, even to the touch of decay so often present:—

There are 'extensive rockeries, fine old trees of several varieties, grottoes, an irregualar lake covering an acre of ground perhaps, while in the buildings are collections of tablets engraven from texts written by different Emperors for this place. It has been a fine place in its day, but is now much out of repair. Until recently the "lake" was a stagnant pond, but this spring it was deepened, the ways opened, so that the water flows at a very slow pace, which could hardly be otherwise on this plain. This necessitated the removal of the Lotus roots, and doubtless with them the removal of the cause of much sickness. The whole place needs renovating, and might be made a lovely spot. There are wistarias said to be 600 years old, and trees perhaps equally aged.'

Reference.—Wên Chên Ming, Kate Kerby, and Mo Zung Chung, *An Old Chinese Garden.*

GEOGRAPHY.—The China of to-day is not the China of ancient times; its boundaries have extended greatly while the history of the Middle Kingdom was being made. Unlike England, which had to go beyond the sea to add to her empire, the nucleus of the Chinese people had all around them their grand future, and having acted well up to their possibilities, these have developed into the actualities of their present extended dominions—dominions which, with all their tribute-bearing neighbours, form the most extensive 'ever swayed by a single power in any age or any part of the world.' The germs of this mighty realm are supposed to be found some thousands of years before Christ, in a nomadic people in the present province of Shensi. Settling in villages, they became tradesmen and agriculturists, and from the dim mists of myths and tradition, amidst which scarce anything can be seen clearly or with certainty, we find the empire growing, getting the sea-board as a boundary, and extending its limits. We do not intend in the course of this short article to give a historical account of the geographical growth of the empire. It would lead us, were we to do so, far beyond our limits, and its scope would necessitate an account of all the petty states into which, at times, China was divided. Suffice it to say, that for many centuries China did not extend beyond the great River, the Yang-tsz-kiang. Eventually an offshoot was sent south into the eastern portion of the present Kiang-nan, and, like the rootlets from the banian tree, grew and formed finally another trunk to support the tree of empire, which was destined gradually to cover the whole land. For a long period the extreme South of China was not embraced in the realm except as a tributary state or with spasmodic attempts at Government, but at last the bonds which united it with the northern portion were strengthened until it formed an integral portion of China.

The last (Manchu) dynasty recovered much of the territory that was lost under the Ming; till now it is nearly equal to what it was under Kublai Khan, when Marco Polo wrote of him 'in respect to number of subjects, extent of territory, and amount of revenue, he surpasses every sovereign that has heretofore been or that now is in the world.' In 1840, it was estimated than the Chinese Emperor ruled over 5,300,000 square miles, from lat. 48° 10′ N. to long. 144° 50′ E. in the N.E. part of the empire, to the island of Hainan in the south, in lat. 18° 10′ N., and on the extreme West to long. 74° E. It has since lost about half a million square miles, which have gone to add to the dominions of the other colossal empire of the world, Russia, which is China's neighbour in the North, while more is apparently going the same way in the shape of Manchuria. England and France in their colonial empires also touch her territories in the south. 'Of the 12,000 miles which form the land girdle of China, 6,000 touch Russian territory, 4,800 British territory, and only 400 French, while 800 miles may be described as doubtful.' Japan has also, by the acquisition of Formosa and Corea, been brought into near neighbourhood to China. Since the greater part of the above was written, Germany has likewise established herself on the coast of Shantung at Kiao-chao, afterwards taken by English and Japanese forces and now (1924) returned to China. Russia has obtained Port Arthur, afterwards taken by Japan, and the French, Kwong Chau Wan in the South. England has also, besides Wei-hai-wei now (1924) about to be restored to China, obtained a lease of land at the back of the Kaulung (Kowloon) Peninsula, Hong-kong, and some islands. What the near future has in store for China remains to be seen. Will this great country so loosely knit together remain intact, or will it fall to pieces from the combined pressure from without and the corruption and disintegrating forces from within? Efforts are being made to preserve it as a nation, as *vide* the late Anglo-Japanese alliance.

In shape, China approaches a rectangle, whose circuit is 14,000 miles, or more than half the circumference of the world; her coast-line is roughly stated to be 4,400 miles. This vast dominion naturally divides itself into the three divisions of China proper, Manchuria (363,700 sq. miles), and the Colonial Possessions.

China proper embraces the whole of what used to be the eighteen provinces, now increased to twenty-two, as well as the large island of Hainan; Manchuria lies to the North of Corea and part of China proper; and the Colonial possessions include Mongolia, Ili, Kokonor, and Tibet.

The twenty-two provinces known as China Proper cover about 1,532,800 square miles. It would take seven Frances, or fifteen Great Britains and Irelands, to cover the same extent of ground. China is surrounded by different mountain chains, forming a wall almost all round it, with their different ranges, such as the Altai, the Stanovai, the Tien-shan, and others; also four large chains occur inside the boundaries, assisting in delimiting territory, the highest peaks of some of which are snow-clad the whole year through.

The three great basins form a great part of China. These are drained respectively by the Yellow River, say 2,500 miles long, the Yang-tzŭ-kiang, 3,200 miles long, while the Canton River and its numerous tributaries drain 130,000 square miles. We cannot mention the other rivers, though they are by no means insignificant nor few, for 'the rivers of China are her glory, and no country can compare with her for natural facilities of inland navigation.'

Among the lakes may be mentioned the Tung-ting, about 220 miles in circumference (75 miles in length and 65 in breadth, with an area of 2,000 sq. miles), and the picturesque Po-yang, with its numerous islands, 90 miles long by 20 in breadth, and an area of 1,800 sq. miles.

Besides the three basins drained by the three great rivers, there is the Great Plain of 700 miles in length, varying in width from 150 to 400 miles, having the same area as the plain of Bengal, drained by the Ganges. It supports an enormous population; in 1812, the number was 177,000,000, that is two-thirds of Europe, being the most densely settled portion 'of any part of the world of the same size.'

China may likewise be 'divided into the mountainous and hilly country and the Great Plain.' (See GEOLOGY.) The mountainous is nearly half of the whole of China, the hilly is in the south-east, another Great Plain is in the north-east.

From the Yang-tsz to Hainan, the whole coast is studded with numerous islands and rocky islets.

The most important Channels are that of Formosa, between the Island of Formosa and the mainland, and the Straits of Lúí-chaú [Lei-chou], between the Island of Hainan and the Promontory of Lúí-chaú.

The most noteworthy gulfs or bays are the Gulf of Liao tung in Manchuria, the Gulf of Pei-chih-li [or Chihli] in the province of the same name, and the Gulf of Tonquin [Tongking] in the extreme south.

Among the principal promontories may be named that of Liao-tung, forming the Gulf of the same name, the Shantung promontory, and the Lúí-chaú promontory, already named.

The principal seas are the Yellow, between Corea and China; the Eastern, between Japan and the Lew-chew Islands and China; and the China Sea to the south.

In political geography, China proper is divided into the twenty-two provinces, these again were sub-divided into prefectures, the latter being formed of different kinds of districts, which may be compared to the counties in England. The prefectures, however, have recently been abolished, and included in the divisional unit, the *hsien*, or district. It is not an uncommon thing to group two of the provinces together for administrative purposes, such as the two Kwang—Kwangtung and Kwangsi; the two Hu—comprising Hupeh and Hunan.

Of the principal cities, it is impossible to give an enumeration, so numerous are they. The capital of each of the eighteen provinces would come under this category, some of them boasting of a million or more of inhabitants, such as Peking, Canton, and others. Every province has numbers of important centres of commerce and government, such as the district cities and marts; the former taking the place of county towns, and often having tens or hundreds of thousands of inhabitants; the latter forming centres of commercial activity, and distributing centres for agricultural produce, etc., to the surrounding country districts.

References.—Richard, *Comprehensive Geography of the Chinese Empire;* Parker, *China;* Oxenham, *Historical Atlas of the Chinese Empire;* Armstrong, *Shan Tung: a Chinese Province*; Rocher, *La Province Chinois du Yünnan;* Davies, *Yünnan.*

GEOLOGY.—The geology of China has not been fully investigated. When it is remembered that vast tracts of country have not yet been trodden by the man of science, it will be seen how much remains to be done toward the acquisition of a full knowledge of the geological conditions of the large portion of the globe ruled over by the Chinese.

In the centre of China is the great alluvial plain produced by the large rivers, the Yang-tzŭ-kiang and the Yellow River, as Egypt has been created by the Nile. The great quantities of silt brought down by the Yellow River, combined with other causes, such as deforestation, etc., produce the periodical floods (See FLOODS) and cause 'China's Sorrow,' as it has been aptly termed, to seek new means of reaching the sea. The Yang-tzŭ-kiang, which has been styled 'The Girdle of China,' carries its silt more out to sea than the Yellow River does. The land it has made during its existence must have been enormous, for it has been estimated that it discharges 770,397 cubic feet of water per second into the sea, and the 'amount of suspended material carried down every year to the sea at 6,428,858,255 cubic feet.' An island 32 miles long by 10 broad has been formed since the fourteenth century, in its estuary. This mighty river takes the third place in the list of the largest rivers in the world, the Amazon and the Congo heading it, and the Mississippi coming fifth. It has been calculated that the

Yang-tzŭ, the Yellow River, and the Pei Ho, would in sixty-six days form an island a mile square in the sea, and in 36,000 years the Gulfs of Pei-chih-li and Liao-tung, the Yellow Sea, and the Eastern Sea as far south as about half-way between Ningpo and Wênchow, and as far east as about midway between the coast of China and Japan, would become solid ground. Passing from the future to the past, it has been reckoned that it has taken 20,000 years for the delta of this gigantic river to be formed. The oscillations of land level do not appear to have had much share in its formation, as they, in this portion of China, seem to have been of the slightest, during this period at all events.

Even during the historical period, the changes appear to have been great, for the Shü King [Shu ching], which contains the most ancient account of Chinese geography, mentions three mouths of the Yang-tzŭ, though only one now remains. At the time of Christ a 'great part of the Shanghai plain was not yet reclaimed from the sea; and the Woo-sung River or Soo-chow Creek was also anciently a large river twenty *li* (6 or 7 miles) broad at what is now the city of Shanghai.' The land has extended further out into what was then the sea, by 50 miles. With regard to the underlying stratum, or strata, Dr. Macgowan said: 'Whether it rests immediately upon granite, which forms the basis of the nearest mountain; or immediately upon new red sandstone, of which some of the adjacent hills are composed; or upon limestone, which is found protruding at the Great Lake (Tái-hú) [T'ai Hu], it is impossible for us without more information to determine.' In A.D. 1865 an artesian well revealed, at a depth of 248 feet, grey sand beneath 10 feet of loam, and a few feet lower, pebbles; at 240 feet, a fragment of limestone.

At one time the Shantung promontory with the contiguous mountainous portion of the province was an island, and the province of Kiangsu had no existence. The steppe-like plains of Pei-chih-li show their recent elevation above the sea. On the other hand, there are evidences of the encroachments of the sea on the land to a no less remarkable extent. The eastern border of the continent has experienced a slight depression, and the real eastern border included Sumatra, Java, Borneo, the Philippines, Formosa, the Liu Chiu Islands, Japan, and the Kuriles, to Kamtschatka.

Among the most interesting features of the geology of North China is the loess. It covers a vast extent of country, 'extending over thousands of square miles and often hundreds of feet in thickness,' and is a brownish-coloured, yellowish-brownish, or greyish earth; it is split up into numerous clefts; is of a terrace formation, and steppe-like contour; but admirably adapted for agricultural purposes; and lends itself to the picturesque most effectively. One opinion about it is that 'it is a subaerial deposit, dating from a geological era of great dryness before the existence of the Yellow and other rivers of the northern provinces.' Another, and the latest, is that it is a sedimentary deposit, and probably of marine origin.

'Its striking peculiarity is that, while so soft and friable that it may be powdered between the fingers, it is of such firm consistency that, when excavations are made in it, walls hundreds of feet high will remain standing like granite, though quite perpendicular. Its particles are so fine that they are said to disappear on being rubbed into the pores of the skin. In China roads become worn out to depths of 70 or 80 feet, the walls being quite perpendicular. . . . Its greatest thickness in Europe and America is 100 to 200 feet. But in China it reaches a depth ten times as great, and it is held responsible for the frequent shiftings of the Yellow River.'

In Southern China, between Canton and Hankow, the succession of rocks is first, granite; second, grits and slates; these are covered by old limestones, on which rests another series of limestone strata, and over some coal-beds lies red sandstone. Of this part of the country it has been written:—

'The whole country is . . . divided into several isolated basins, any one of which can be studied by itself, whilst in most instances, the lines of demarcation follow roughly the political divisions of the empire. Amongst these natural divisons of the country, we may adduce the provinces of the two Kwang, Kiang-si, Fuh-kien and Che-kiang, Ngan-whui. Kwei-chau, Kiang-su, etc.,—all forming separate districts, divided by ranges of mountains and distinguished each by geological characteristics.

'The central and eastern portions of Kwang-tung, contain, within a limited area, a connected sequence of formations, ranging upwards from the early paleozoic rocks of Hongkong and the adjacent coast and islands, to the new red sandstone of Canton and the delta of the Pearl River, intermixed with some traces of still later formations, and being accompanied by masses of rocks of igneous origin extending probably over a still more prolonged epoch.' 'From the neighbourhood of Canton to the sea, the rocks are composed of red sandstone resting on granite, until, on reaching the clusters of islands that line the coast, these are found to consist of a coarse granite only, crossed by perpendicular veins of quartz., over the irregular surfaces of the islands, and at the summits of the highest, are strewn immense rounded blocks of the same rock. They are generally imbedded in the coarse earth, which is a disintegration of the general substance of the islands, and, as this is washed from under them, roll down the steep declivities until they reach a level space, and commonly stud the sandy margin of the islands with a belt of piled rocks, some of them many tons in weight. The scenery of these islands has often been compared to that of the Hebrides, and is quite as barren.'

'The island of Kulangsu (Amoy) is typical of the coast formation of Southern China; granite is its principal feature, and it seems to be a general, but by no means unexceptional, rule that along the coast, from South to North, the granite becomes coarser grained, less micaceous and more felspathic.'

The following is an account of the country north of Amoy:—

'Considerable diversity of the geological structure of the district from Amoy to Tam-si,—the most northern portion of the province visited—obtains; this is not, however, the case with the Physical Geography, as in the latter respect the whole country is a series of high mountains, the general character being physically very persistent, although geologically ranging from the ingenite or granitic, plutonic, and volcanic rock at Amoy (as observed along the greater portion of the East Coast of China and typically represented in the island of Hongkong) the Transition or Metamorphic sedimentary rocks being developed in proceeding northwards, culminating in the Derivate rocks, the Subaqueous containing the whole series of the Paleozoic period, the Devonian, Carboniferous, and Permian systems being highly developed, particularly the Carboniferous; and the Sub-aerial being represented in the Mesozoic period, principally by the upper new red sandstone in the Triassic system. The whole country must have been subject, long after the Mesozoic period, to extraordinary convulsions of Nature. One "fault" in the Carboniferous Group, which the writer had a good opportunity of studying, extended a distance of 8 miles; the mountain in which the "fault" appeared being over 1,500 feet above the adjacent valley, standing at a scarped angle of about 8 degrees, exposing, amongst other groups of the system, the coal measures in numerous seams fully 300 feet thick.'

Shantung is a most interesting province from a geological point of view.

The following extract from 'Across Shantung,' by S.B.J. Skertchly, F.G.S., M.A.I., puts in a succinct form an account of the geological formation of the Eastern portion of China:—

'Travelling northwards from Hongkong by Amoy, Foochow, Ningpo, Shanghai to Chefoo, we pass, speaking generally, from older to newer rocks. The granites of Hongkong with their associated beds of diorite and felspar porphyries are the oldest rocks of China, the backbone, geologically speaking, upon which has been laid down the newer beds which take the surface over by far the greater part of this vast empire. These rocks are again seen at Amoy and Foochow, are hidden beneath newer volcanic rocks at Ningpo, where the beautiful mottled volcanic agglomerate yields the fine building stone which adds such beauty to the architecture of Shanghai; then the land sinks down to the broad plain of the mighty Yangtsz, to be succeeded by old crystalline rocks, probably of Laurentian age, which run all the way to Chefoo on the Gulf of Pechihli, whose northern shores in Manchuria and Chihli are largely made up of beds belonging to the Carboniferous system.

'Travelling inland a similar series of rocks is found, the granites being overlaid by crystalline schist, and gneiss and quartzites, over which again lie the carboniferous beds, with patches of volitic rock here and there, yielding as in Eastern Shantung beautiful fossil fishes.

'The granite rocks rise in bold hills and mountains, weathered into rounded masses, which ofttimes become quite isolated, and stand like boulders upon the hill-sides, or lie embedded in the well-known "decomposed granite" . . . ; these boulders are simply harder masses of granite which have withstood the dissolving action of the elements; they tell neither of frost-bound coasts, nor changes of level, nor volcanic outbursts, but are stolid witnesses of the silent forces of rain and river, of tropic showers and burning suns and chilly nights.

'In marked contrast to the swelling contours of the granite series, are the jagged and gnarled hills and mountains of the crystaline schists, which beautify the landscape with every variety of crag and peak and sierra, the rocks themselves bent, twisted, and crumpled, as though, instead of being tough enough for nether millstones, they were plastic as dough.

'Very different again are the limestone hills of the carboniferous system with their gentle flexures, fretted into picturesque castellated ramparts, and running in long lines along the dip.'

The province of Shansi is rugged. The southern part 'presents a geological formation of great simplicity. . . . There are coal formations and limestone,' and a plateau of later rocks —sandstones, shales and conglomerates of green, red, yellow, lilac, and brown colours. Some granite peaks rise to a height of 8,000 feet. 'On the eastern side . . . rocks are made up of ancient formations or deposits of the Silurian age.'

There are most extensive coalfields in China; for she is credited with possessing the largest coal mines in the world 'covering 200,000 square miles,' 'Most of the rocks belong to the paleozoic or early secondary ages; the later deposits in the central and seaboard provinces at least being confined to a few sandstones and clays.' The great coalfields of China stretch from 'near Peking along the frontiers of Pei-chih-li and Shansi, and thence through Honan and Hupeh, into the great coal and iron district of Hunan.' 'The less important fields are those of Kiangsi, Hupeh, Nganhwui [Anhui], Kiangsu, Chêkiang, Fukien, and Kwangtung.' They all belong 'to the true "coal measures" of the carboniferous system.'

Geologically the General Structure is divided into (i) North-eastern China; (2) Central China; (3) The Yangtzŭ Valley; (4) The South-eastern Coast; (5) South-west China.

The Stratigraphical divisions are (i) Azonic and Proterozoic; (2) Palæozoic; (3) Mesozoic; (4) Caenozoic. The igneous rocks are granite, syenite and diorite, alkaline rocks, diabase and basalt, and prophyry.

All kinds of minerals and precious stones are found in China.

References.—Pumpelly, *Geological Researches in China, etc.;* Richthofen, *China;* Obrutchov, *Central Asia, Nanshan, and Northern China;* Willis and Blackwelder, *Researches in China;* Yokoyama, *Plant Fossils from China;* Yabe, *Fossil Corals from China;* Brown, *Contributions to the Geology of the Province of Yünnan; Chinese Recorder; Journal N.C.B.R.A.S.; Notes and Queries on China and Japan;* Williams, *Middle Kingdom; Hongkong Daily Press,* Sept. and Oct., 1892.

GEOMANCY, OR FUNG-SHUI (FÊNG SHUI).—This superstition in connection with the worship of ancestors has the greatest hold on the Chinese mind. To them the whole of Nature is alive with influences for good or evil, revealed to those who have made their indications a study: the course of a stream, the trend of a mountain, the position of a clump of bamboos, the curve of a road, the site of a grave, and a number of other things too numerous to mention, all form the visible manifestations to the initiated eye, of Nature's future actions, or the good and evil intentions of the departed dead. The term geomancy, though used in most books on China, is, however, not a correct description of the ideas embodied in *Fêng-shui.*

The rudiments of this magic art are to be found in ancient China, being manifestations of the *yin* and the *yang,* but it was not till the twelfth century that it was elaborated into the system of science, falsely so-called, that has now such a hold on the Chinese. Adopting what was popular and attractive in the modern school of Confucianism, and being already in consonance with the Taoistic and Buddhistic philosophies, this system, based to some degree on the rudiments of natural science, has subtly laid hold of the whole being and existence of the Chinese people. They believe not only that the comfortable sepulture of their ancestors will redound to their own comfort, but that if the union of the elements, the nature of the soil, the configuration of the ground, and all the other things which enter into this farrago of nonsense are such as to produce a felicitous combination, that riches, honour, and posterity will be vouchsafed to them. It is these beliefs that cause the coffin to be so often kept for months or years unburied, for a site is being searched for which shall combine all that is productive of good to the children and grandchildren. Even when the eldest son has discovered such a site, and is confident that happiness and prosperity will be his lot, it may be that another son has found out that what will benefit his brother will not be productive of good to him, but of evil; consequently the whole search will have to be gone over again till one favourable to all parties can be discovered. So many different elements come in, in determining the lucky sites, that the professors of geomancy are easily able to make a living out of the gullibility of their employers. When it is added that in building a house, in fixing on a site for an ancestral hall, in commencing a temple, and in numerous other projects and businesses demanding the attention of the Chinese, these doctors of geomancy have to be consulted, it may readily be seen that, in the hands of clever and designing men, much room is open for earning an honest (?) penny.

The forms of hills, directions of watercourses, forms and heights of buildings, directions of roads and bridges,—these and other features are supposed to modify the *ch'i*, or universal spiritual breath, the plenum of the universe. *Fêng-shui* is the art of adapting the residences of the living and the dead so as to harmonize with the local currents of the cosmic breath.

The compasses exposed for sale in such numbers in the streets in Chinese cities are not mariner's compasses, which are seldom to be met with, but geomancer's compasses, which contain the elements of their mystic art, by the aid of which they largely determine their judgments on sites and localities.

Just one instance of how *Fêng-shui* is troublesome to Europeans in China: in the phraseology of this occult science 'when two buildings are beside one another, the one on the left is said to be built on the green dragon and the one on the right on the white tiger. Now the tiger must not be higher than the dragon, or death or bad luck will result.' Supposing now a European or American gets a site for a residence next to, and on the right-hand side of, a native dwelling. Here then are all the elements ready for trouble; for, to begin with, the foreigner will naturally desire to erect a house more suited for habitation than the low abode which would satisfy the average Chinaman.

Another curious instance of the reasonings, or shall we rather call them insane vapourings, that its professors indulge in, will give a practical illustration of the workings of *Fêng-shui*: when it was proposed to construct a telegraph between Canton and Hongkong, the ground of the opposition against it was as follows:—Canton is the 'City of Rams,' or 'Sheep,' the mouth of the river is known as the 'Tiger's Mouth; the district opposite Hongkong is the 'Nine Dragons' (Kaú Lung). What more unfortunate combination could be found—a telegraph line to lead the Sheep right into the Tiger's Mouth and amongst the Nine Dragons!

It is this pseudo science which has so strenuously opposed the introduction of railways, telegraph lines, and foreign innovations, in the past, or was made to do duty as an objection to them. But it has not been an insuperable obstruction; for whenever the Chinese Government has made up its mind to the introduction of any of the inventions of Western science, *Fêng-shui* has not been allowed to be an obstacle: while pandering to its absurd ideas as far as is practicable without hindering the feasibility of their scheme, the populace, if obstructive, has usually been made to feel that the will of the rulers has to be obeyed.

References.—Doré, *Recerches sur les Superstitions en Chine;* De Groot, *Religious System;* Eitel, *Fung Shui;* Du Bose, *Dragon, Image, and Demon;* Williams, *Middle Kingdom;* Gray, *China;* Doolittle, *Social Life of the Chinese.*

GINGER.—Most of the ginger produced in the world is furnished by the root of the *Zingiber officinale* (Roscoe); but that from China, as well as Siam, is the product of another plant, the *Alpinia galangas,* 'yet, considering the wide distribution of *Zingiber officinale,* it is quite possible that the true ginger may also be cultivated in some parts of China.'

It is grown largely in the Kwangtung province, where it is found in nearly every part, the Miau-tzŭ aborigines even cultivating large quantities of it. The best and most, in the neighbourhood of the city of Canton, coming from the Nám-hoí [Nan-hai] District itself, in a portion of which the provincial city is partially situated.

In another district, some days' journey from Canton, three-tenths of the flat land, and seven-tenths of the cultivated soil in the hills are planted with ginger.

'A distinction is made between the flat-land ginger . . . which is generally soft and tender, and mountain ginger . . . which is brittle and very pungent. This is generally used for home consumption; the Chinese pickle it in vinegar. The expensive . . . —syrup ginger—is almost exclusively consumed by foreigners, or exported.'

'Ginger is collected from many small up-country growers and brought to the Canton ginger factories by a few Chinese dealers. Stem ginger, or the young, tender roots of the plant, is cut up into small sizes suitable for sale. Cargo ginger is treated as it comes from the growers and is brought into Canton in pieces weighing from one fourth of a pound to a pound.

After arrival at the factory the ginger is given a preliminary washing in the river and then put into a vat with a capacity of about 360 catties (equivalent to 480 pounds) and boiled for about an hour. After draining off the water, ginger and sugar are mixed in equal proportions, with enough water for boiling. This mixture is boiled in the vat for an hour, and the resulting preserved ginger is packed in casks of 168 catties

(224 pounds) for shipment abroad. It is also shipped in cases containing jars packed in straw. The cases are made of local timber.

The same process, up to the boiling with sugar, is followed in the manufacture of dry ginger. In the case of dry ginger, very little water is added after the ginger is mixed with sugar. The ginger is boiled until dry, after which it is removed from the vat and packed in one pound tin boxes which are also made locally. The small tin boxes are packed in wooden cases for shipment abroad. For the China trade a wooden case contains twenty-four, twelve, or six one pound tins. For export abroad the ginger is packed in a bamboo-leaf wrapper and is placed in tin boxes. Wooden cases containing 50 or 100 pounds of the tinned ginger are prepared for the foreign trade.

The largest consuming centres for Canton ginger are England, the United States, the Netherlands, Germany, and Australia. Ginger is packed in various ways to meet the demands of the various markets.'

Ginger is also grown to a large extent in Hu-peh and Kiangsi, where it is largely eaten in the green state. This ginger of mid-China is said to be very fragrant, but 'too sticky' to make 'a very excellent preserve.' It is also found in all parts of Ssŭch'uan.

Ginger is used as a medicine in China. It has been seen to cure a violent headache when applied in the Chinese fashion, which is to heat fresh ginger in the fire, and slice it in thin pieces which are stuck on the forehead and temples.

The *Alpinia galangas* grows wild in Hongkong, and forms when in flower a conspicuous object in the glens and on the hill-sides, with its narrow, long leaves and bright panicles of flower, each flower being nearly an inch in length.

GINSENG.—Kaempfer says that next to tea ginseng is the most celebrated plant in the whole Orient, on account of its root. It has indeed well been termed the cure-all, as the Chinese have a most wonderful faith in curative and strengthening properties, for which reason it has been also styled 'the chinchona of China.' The older the plant, the greater the value set on it. The wild is incomparably more valued than the cultivated root. It is considered to be 'a cure for fevers and weaknesses of all sorts—the chief and most costly medicine.' The name, *jên ts'ên,* is taken from its supposed resemblance to the human form.

The plant belongs to the family of the *Araliaceæ,* and the scientific name for it is *Panax Ginseng* or *Panax repens.* It is found 'wild in the mountain forests of Eastern Asia, from Nepal to Manchuria.' It formerly grew in Fukien, Kiangnan and Shansi; 'their stock would seem to be extinguished, or the plan of cultivation by seed, described in the *Pên ts'ao*, might have been given up in the face of the growing favour of the Manchurian wild plant.' Ginseng is one of the treasures of Manchuria. Dr. Lansdell, in his book 'Through Siberia,' thus writes of it:—

'Ginseng is found chiefly in the valleys of the Upper Ussuri, where it is cultivated in beds, planted in rows. The earth must be a rich, black mould, and loose; and when the plant has attained the height of four or five inches, it is supported by a stick. The beds are carefully weeded and watered and protected from the sun by tents or sheds of wood. Wild ginseng is said to be the best. From May to September hundreds go out to seek the plant. . . . The prices named . . . for this root were almost fabulous, a single root being valued in Manchuria at from £250 to £300. I was told on the river that ginseng sells for £30 per Russian lb., but that in a bad year the Chinese count it as valuable as gold, and give up to £40 per lb. . . . The root is straight, spindle-shaped, knotty, and up to half an inch in diameter, and eight inches in length. The leaves are cut off, and the root is boiled in water, apparently to remove some injurious quality; and when it has undergone fitting preparation its colour is a transparent white, with sometimes a slight red or orange tint; its appearance then is that of a stalactite. It is carefully dried, wrapped in unsized paper, and sent to the market.'

'Ordinary ginseng is prepared by simply drying the root in the sun, or over a charcoal fire. To prepare the red or clarified ginseng, the root is placed in wicker baskets which are put in a large earthen vessel with a close-fitting cover and pierced at the bottom with holes. This is set over boiling water, and the roots are steamed according to their age, about four hours being an average time.'

Dr. Porter Smith, in the course of a long article on ginseng, says:—

'The root is carefully hunted for by Manchus, who boast that the weeds of their country are the choice drugs of the Chinese. The pieces, after carefully trimming with a bamboo knife and drying in still air, are made to assume something of the form of the human body. They generally do resemble a miniature human hand, the larger pieces being of the size of a man's little finger, with some two to four finger-like branching rootlets. They are yellowish, semi-transparent, firm, brittle to some extent, and of a sweet mucilaginous taste, accompanied with a slight bitterness. . . . Fabulous stories are told of the finding of special depôts of this root, which is associated with guiding voices, stars, and other good and peaceful omens. . . . The trade in the drug is a speciality. Great care is required to preserve choice specimens from the effects of damp and the attacks of worms, to which the drug is very liable. This drug is prepared as an extract, or as a decoction, in silver vessels as a rule. . . . . Several cases in which life would seem to have been at least prolonged by the taking of doses of this drug, so

18

as to allow of intelligent disposition of property, indicate that some positive efficacy of a sustaining character does really exist in this species of Ivywort.'

Manchuria does not supply sufficient quantity to meet the constant demand for it, and Corea and Japan furnish it as well, but they (the Japanese and Corean) are not considered equal in quality to the first-named variety. That found wild in Chinese Manchuria is a government monopoly, and is gathered 'by detachments of soldiers detailed for this purpose.' The Emperor sometimes made presents of it to high officials, as a mark of great favour. There is even a variety of it which is indigenous in the Appalachian range, and which is exported from Philadelphia and Baltimore (U.S.A.) (and also from the Western States as well) to China. In 1877 nearly $700,000 worth were sent to the Celestial Empire. The trade is not increasing, of late years, remaining 'stationary owing to the gradual extinction of the plant [*Panax Quinquefolius*], which cannot be grown artificially with success.'

GODOWN.—Godown is a word in use, amongst the foreign residents in China, for a storehouse or warehouse where cargo or goods are stored. It is a corruption of the Malay gĕdong, or gadang.

GOLDFISH.—The original habitat of the goldfish appears to have been China: according to the Chinese the native place is Lake Tsau [Ch'ao], in the province of Ngan-hwui [Anhui], but it is doubtful if it is ever found in a state of nature. They were taken to Europe in the seventeenth century.

Williams says of them:—

'The effects of domestication in changing the natural form of this fish are great; specimens are often seen without any dorsal fin, and the tail and other fins tufted and lobed to such a degree as to resemble artificial appendages or wings rather than natural organs. The eyes are developed till the globe projects beyond the socket like goggles, presenting an extraordinary appearance. Some of them are so fantastic, indeed, that they would be regarded as *lusus naturæ,* were they not so common. The usual colour is a ruddy golden hue, but both sexes exhibit a silvery or blackish tint at certain stages of their growth, and one variety, called the silver-fish, retains this shade all its life. The Chinese keep it [the goldfish] in their garden ponds, or in earthen jars, in which are placed rocks covered with moss, and overgrown with tufts of ferns, to allow them a retreat from the light. When the females spawn, the eggs must be removed to a shallow vessel, lest the males devour them, where the heat of the sun hatches them; the young are nearly black, but gradually become whitish or reddish, and at last assume a golden or silvery hue. Specimens upwards of two feet long have been noticed, and those who rear them emulate each other in producing new varieties.'

Japanese in Japan produce these double-tailed goldfish, known as *Carassius auratus* or *Cyprimus auratus*, by taking the eggs of the single-tailed variety and shaking or disturbing them. The result of which is that unnatural developments take place and double monsters result, some having double tails and some single tails and *mirabile dictu* double heads. Those with a pair of tails are likely to live and perpetuate in their offspring this peculiar feature. For this to become a fixed trait, it would appear that all that was required was care taken in selection of the fish to breed.

GOVERNMENT.—The following is a description of the governmental system as it was until its replacement by the republican form in 1912. The Government of China is that of an absolute, despotic monarchy. The Emperor rules by virtue of a divine right derived direct from Heaven, and he is styled 'The Son of Heaven.' This divine right he retains as long as he rules in conformity with the decrees of Heaven. When the dynasty falls into decay by the vices of its rulers, Heaven raises up another who, by force of arms, the virtue of bravery, and fitness for the post, wrests the sceptre from the enfeebled grasp of him who is unfit to retain it any longer. This idea has exerted a beneficial effect on the sovereigns of China, who feel that on the one hand they are dependent upon high Heaven for the retention of their throne, and who humbly and publicly confess their shortcomings in times of floods and drought. On the other hand, though there is no House of Commons to exercise a check on the unrestrained power of the Sovereign, there is the general public opinion of the people, who, being educated in the principles that underlie all true government, are ready to apply them to their rulers when they forget, or act grossly in opposition to, them. To see the system of patriarchal government carried out in its entirety, one must come to China. The Emperor stands in *loco parentis* to the common people, and his officers occupy a similar position. The principles which have formed the framework of government for millenniums among these ancient, stable, and peace-loving people, may be found in a study of the rule of the ancient kings, Yao and Shun, and their successors, and in the precepts inculcated by Confucius and Mencius. With all its defects, their system appears to be better adapted for the punishment of the criminal classes amongst them and the prevention of their fraudulent bankruptcies than our systems, which are the outgrowth of centuries of civilisation, not yet passed through by the Chinese, who consequently are not yet educated up to our standpoint. The unit in China is not the individual, but the family, therefore it is impossible for a fraudulent bankrupt to settle his goods on his wife or family, as the family must make good his losses; in the same way a family is responsible for the good behaviour of its members; a neighbourhood for its inhabitants; and an official for those governed by him. Thus results a system of 'mutual responsibility among all classes.' This acts as a great deterrent of serious crime and defalcations; and it is much to be regretted that in our rule of the Chinese, such a system could not have been carried out, with such modifications as to free it from its defects, instead of introducing a new system foreign entirely to their feelings and understanding.

The right of succession to the throne in China 'is hereditary in the male line, but it is always in the power of the Sovereign to nominate his successor from among his own children.' This nomination, most wisely, is not made public during the lifetime of the reigning Sovereign, thus preventing intrigue and obviating all necessity for those bloody scenes which disgrace the accession of so many Eastern potentates to their thrones.

The Emperor has two councils to advise him and to consult with. One is the Cabinet, or Imperial Chancery (the Nuí Koh) [Nei Ko]. A more influential body is the Council of State, or General Council, approaching more to the Ministries of Western nations, though necessarily quite unlike them. It meets in the Emperor's palace daily. Under these two councils are the Six Boards—Luk Pò [Liu Pu]—their names give a pretty good idea of their functions: The Boards of Civil Office, Revenue, Rites, War, Punishment, Works—and a Naval Board has been added in recent years, and still more recently a Board to deal with the foreign relations of China, forced reluctantly into the comity of civilised and enlightened nations.

There are other departments of government, one of which, the Censorate, deserves more than passing notice. On account of its peculiar duties it has attracted much attention from Western writers. In conjunction with some of the other Boards, it forms a Court of Appeal; and, with other departments of government, it deliberates on important affairs of State; it exercises an oversight over all criminal cases and superintends the affairs of the metropolis. These duties call for but little remark, but it is the extraordinary powers that are vested in its members of censuring, not only the manner in which other officials have performed or neglected their duties, but even the conduct of the Emperor himself—powers that are often availed of in the interests of justice, with a boldness and courage most unusual under a despotic rule, that at times meet with their reward, and at other times call forth overwhelming censure and punishment from the Sovereign himself. When rightly used by a high-minded and conscientious official (for such are to be found in China) in the consciousness of right, and with the best interests of the country at heart, and with broad and enlightened views, these extraordinary powers must be productive of good, though many must be loath to use these privileges of outspoken speech for fear of the consequences which may recoil on their own heads, often indeed so serious, as to make the best intentioned hesitate before committing themselves.

For the government of the provinces there is a perfect ramification of officials from superior to inferior, from the ten or twelve Viceroys of one or two provinces each, down to the petty officials.

One very curious feature in Chinese official life is the manner in which judicial, military, naval, and fiscal duties are performed by one and the same official at different stages of his official life. He is transferred from one post to the other, irrespective of former experience in the particular duties of his appointment. With the introduction of Western naval vessels and military armaments this eclectic system of filling offices is bound in the long run to give way. Were bribery and corruption absent from official ranks, this complete system of officialdom, with all its business-like methods of accomplishing work, would produce much more beneficent results; but a premium is put on 'squeezing,' as no official is paid a sufficient salary to meet his necessary expenses. Notwithstanding this, there are noble exceptions to the general rule of corruption, and these honest mandarins meet with honour from the people, who justly appreciate such conduct. They have no other rewards but this, and that of their own self-approving consciences, for such probity brings no pecuniary benefits in its train; indeed, it often lands the noble man in the lowest depths of poverty.

'A Viceroy in the provinces gets as his yearly official salary about £100, and allowances amounting to £900 or £1,200 more; but he has to defray out of these sums all his yamên expenses, including stationery, etc., salaries and food to his secretaries, writers, and A.D.C., his body-guards and general retinue, to entertain his innumerable guests, and send his annual tributes to the various high officials in the capital, to say nothing of supporting his high station and his numerous family [doubtless consisting of a number of wives and sons and daughters] and relations. As a matter of fact, to meet his expenditure he would require no less than £10,000 or £15,000 per annum. . . . From these high magnates downwards, the Chinese officials are underpaid in the same proportion, until we get to the lowest grade, the petty mandarin, whose, official pay is scarcely better than that of a well-paid Hongkong coolie, and the soldiers and sailors who receive four to ten shillings a month, subject oftentimes to various unjust deductions and squeezes by their superiors.'

As an indication of a peculiarity in Chinese life, the following extract, taken from a paper written by a Chinese in the *Asiatic Quarterly Review*, is given. It touches lightly on the people being allowed to a certain extent to govern themselves so long as no flagrant breach of the laws comes to light:—

'The Central Government does not do its plain duty, and the people have in consequence been compelled to evolve some sort of local administration for themselves. The authorities do not interfere with this, because it is not their interest to do so. It is a cheap and easy way of getting some sort of administration carried on, while the money which should go in administering the country is squandered in other ways.'

The names of the various departments of the above now obsolete system may be found in Mayers' *Chinese Government*. With the establishment of the Republic in 1912 the administrative offices were arranged as follows:—

The Presidency (Ta Tsung T'ung).
The Vice Presidency (Fu Tsung T'ung).
The Senate (Ts'an I Yüan).
The House of Representatives (Chung I Yüan).
The Cabinet (Kuo Wu Yüan).
The Office of Military Governors of Provinces (Chiang Chün Fu).
The Audit Office (Shên Chi Yüan).
The Nine Ministries (Chiu Pu).
The Peking Gendarmerie (Pu Chün T'ung Ling Ya Mên).
The Central Salt Administration (Yen Wu Shu).
The National Tobacco and Wine Administration (Ch'üan Kuo Yen Chiu Shih Wu Shu).
The Revenue Council (Shui Wu Ch'u).
The General Staff (Ts'an Mou Pên Pu).
The Supreme Court (Ta Li Yüan).
The National Conservancy Bureau (Ch'üan Kuo Shui Li Chü).
The Department of Mongolian and Tibetan Affairs (Mêng Tsang Yüan).
The State Historiographer's Office (Kuo Shih Kuan).
The Government of the Metropolitan District (Ching Chao).
The Governments of the Provinces (Shêng) and the Special Administrative Areas (T'ê Pieh Ch'ü Yü).

GRAPES.—Grapes are very poor in the South of China, and but little cultivated or eaten. Those from Tientsin or the North are much better, but still far behind the English hothouse production in every respect. The grape is not indigenous to China, but was imported from Central Asia about 126 B.C.

There are now several varieties: the elongated white grape produced near Hsüan-hua; the seedless white grape of North China; purple grapes, chiefly from Shansi; etc.

Reference.—Bretschneider, *Botanicon Sinicum.*

GUAVA.—This fruit (*Psidium cattleyanum*) is very common in the South of China, but unknown in the North, though occasionally seen in Central China as a pot plant. Its strong odour when fresh is much disliked by many foreigners. Whatever may be the opinion concerning the fruit itself, the jelly made from it is highly esteemed by all. The Chinese have not yet taken up the manufacture of this delicious article.

GUILDS.—Guilds (lit., "meeting houses") are unions of merchants in any particular branch of business with the object of promoting the business operations of each individual member. They are of two chief kinds: (i) *Kung-so*, "public hall," the trade union proper; (2) *Hui-kuan*, the club of fellow provincials in an alien province.

The former are supposed to have originated in the Han dynasty. The latter are said to be of still earlier origin.

They consist each of members of one trade, have an organized administration and revenue, and settle their disputes by arbitration at the guild meetings. They have their own meeting or guild halls, in which is a shrine of the patron deity of the guild.

There is also met with (but very rarely) a third kind, the Hanse or Guild Merchant, an association of all the merchants of a locality to regulate trade. Those of Newchwang, Swatow, and Canton are the chief known examples.

References.—Morse, *The Gilds of China; Journal N.C.B.R.A.S.*, N.S. Vols. xii; xxi.

HAKKAS.—Who the Hakkas are is a question of some interest. They are often situated in the midst of a population, quite distinct from them in language, differing in customs, to a slight extent in dress, and even in some of the idols worshipped. Those found in the South of China were not originally of that region, but their family genealogies show that they have come from the North, being the last wave of immigration from the North to the South, settling in some cases in different places till they have finally established themselves in their present surroundings. In certain districts they have monopolised the whole country-side, as in the prefecture of Ká-yin-chü [Chia-ying], in the Canton province, 'which is entirely peopled by Hakka,' while in other places they form a half, a third, or more, of the population, being interspersed among the Pún-téí [Pên-ti], as the older Chinese inhabitants are termed. In some places, partly peopled by them, they have settled on the higher land, leaving the Pún-téí to the low-lying lands, and from this circumstance they have been called Chinese Highlanders by some, but the name is a misnomer, as it is only capable of local application, for in other places they are spread over the plains as well as the hilly ground. They are not confined to the Canton province, where they are considered to form a third of the inhabitants, but are found in different parts of China—in Kwangsi, in Fukien, and in Chêkiang; it has also been said that 'the chief part of the Kiangsi province' is Hakka, and that the language spoken in the capital of that province, Nán-ch'ang, is Hakka. They number altogether probably about fifteen millions.

Their language is more akin to Mandarin, being a halfway house between Cantonese and Mandarin: 'the Hakka dialect is the remnant of a phase of transition through which the common Chinese language passed in developing itself from Cantonese to Mandarin.' It is perhaps spoken by about four millions of people in the Canton province alone (*See* DIALECTS). The German Missionaries and English Presbyterians have some most successful missions among this interesting people.

The sexes are not so strictly separated in domestic life as is the case with some of the other Chinese; nor do the women bind their feet. Perhaps this last might be taken as an indication that they left their original home before foot-binding came into vogue, and, not having practised it at first, never took to it.

Taken as a whole, they are a poor people, having to work hard for their living, though there are rich men among them, as well as literary graduates. In dress the women differ somewhat from the Cantonese, their jackets being longer and reaching down nearly to their knees; their shoes have squarer toes; they wear a peculiar hat consisting of a broad brim with a valance of cloth round it; the bunch of hair, done up on the top of the head, goes through the open crown. The women's ornaments are somewhat dissimilar, such as their bangles, which are made of thick silver, and of different patterns from those in use among the Pún-téí population. The earrings are also of curious construction; one kind, of silver, hooking through the ear and thickening up to the other end, while every short distance they are embossed with rings of silver; another kind of earring is formed of tassels of silk. The Hakka children often have a ring of silver round their neck; Cantonese children do not wear the same, but one or two of the attendants of the Chinese idols have such a ring.

In the Straits Settlements there were, in 1891, as many as 16,736 Hakkas, out of a Chinese population of 227,989.

The Hakkas are a simple people, but very contentious, and show a litigious disposition in the few cases which occur in the English Courts in Hongkong; for there are a great number of them in the colony: the barbers, stonecutters, and foreign ladies' tailors being mostly Hakkas.

The word Hakka means 'strangers (in Chinese k'o chia),' and refers to their origin. In the Straits they are known as Khek, or Kehs, so called from the Swatow and Amoy pronunciation of the word Hak.

We give a short summary of the history of this curious people as far as is at present known about them:—

The North of China is 'the original home of the Hakkas' where, about the third century before Christ, they were located in Shantung principally, as well as to a slight extent in Shansi, and Nganhwui [Auhui].

They were subjected to a bloody persecution in the time of the Ts'in dynasty (B.C. 249-209), and this started them off on their travels. Settling in Honan, Nganhwui, and Kiangsi, some changed their names, but a more prosperous time followed. Another persecution under another Ts'in dynasty (A.D. 419) finally scattered them entirely from that part of China. This resulted in a general stampede 'which carried some of them even into the mountainous regions in the south-east of Kiangsi and to the very borders of the Fukien province.' At the beginning of the T'ang dynasty (A.D. 618) they were compelled to move again, the majority took 'refuge in the mountains of Fukien, whilst a few hovered on the high mountain chains which separate the Kiangsi and Kwangtung (Canton) provinces.'

Under the Sung dynasties (A.D. 960-1280) many became soldiers, and thousands of them perished with the last Chinese prince of the Southern Sung, in A.D. 1280, west of Macao, when the Mongols were coming into power. Under these last they 'made their first appearance within the borders of the Canton province,' but not settling down permanently here, or in large numbers, until the beginning of the Ming dynasty (A.D. 1368), when the Fukien Hakkas, after centuries of residence there, were compelled by disturbances to seek a new home. They came in such overwhelming numbers 'that they drove everything before them' in the Ká-yin-chü prefecture, which has remained their headquarters ever since. About the same time others came from Kiangsi and settled to the north-west of the Fukienese Hakkas. From these places they have spread more or less over different parts of the province.

The change of dynasty, which resulted in the Manchu house being established on the throne, caused them to spread to the west and south-west of Canton. The nucleus of the great T'ai-P'ing rebellion was formed of Hakkas from the Canton province, and it was among them that it started. During the Manchu dynasty many became soldiers and were employed by government, gaining admission to the competitive examinations for both literary and military degrees. A dreadful internecine strife, in which 150,000 at least, perished, took place between the Hakkas and Pún-téís in the south-western districts of the Canton province, from A.D. 1864 to 1866, and arms and even armed steamers, were procured from Hongkong by both parties. Finally, the Chinese Government took vigorous measures, the half-hearted schemes hitherto pursued having proved ineffectual, and, with the aid of money to assist immigration of the Hakkas to waste lands, succeeded in getting some of them to move to the province of Kuangsi, the Island of Hainan, and other parts of the country.

References.—Notes and Queries on China and Japan, Vol. i; *China Review*, ii. 160; *Chinese Recorder*, Vol. xxiii.

HISTORY.—Chinese history deserves more attention than it has received from Western scholars; it has been both unduly lauded and unduly depreciated. Like all histories, it may be divided into the mythological, ancient, and modern.

The line of demarcation between the first and second is blurred and indistinct. The mythological period covers from 45,000 to 500,000 years, and commences with 'the opening of heaven and earth,' as the Chinese say. Different accounts have been given of the creation, one of the most popular is that of Pwan-ku [P'an Ku], who is represented with hammer and chisel bringing the rude masses of chaotic matter into shape and form. His labours lasted for 18,000 years, and day by day he increased in stature six feet, while the heavens rose, and the earth expanded and thickened. His task completed, and the earth roughly fitted for its future inhabitants, Pwan-ku by his death benefited the world as much as by his life, for, as the story goes:—

'His head became mountains, his breath wind and clouds, and his voice thunder; his limbs were changed into the four poles, his veins into rivers, his sinews into the undulations of the earth's surface, and his flesh into fields; his beard, like Berenice's hair, was turned into stars, his skin and hair into herbs and trees, and his teeth, bones, and marrow, into metals, rocks, and precious stones; his dropping sweat increased to rain, and lastly (*nascitur ridiculus mus*) the insects which stuck to his body were transformed into people!'

The Chinese believe that there were giants in the earth in those days, for Pwan-ku was followed by three sovereigns, named the Celestial, the Terrestrial, and the Human, who were of gigantic form. Another 18,000 years was occupied by their reigns, during which numerous inventions and improvements were effected for the good of mankind, such as good government, the union of the sexes, and, what must have been of paramount importance, men learned to eat and drink, and sleep was invented. Two more sovereigns succeeded these, Yu-chau [Yu Ch'ao] and Sui-jin [Sui Jên]; the latter brought fire down from heaven, and mankind had the blessing of cooked dishes.

The ancient or legendary history commences with Fu-hsi: he and his four successors are called 'The Five Sovereigns.' Now begins the 'highest antiquity' of the Chinese, 2852, 2953, or 3322 B.C., according to different authorities, which is about the same time as the commencement of the Assyrian Monarchy. Amongst other blessings conferred at this period was marriage; the bounds of the kingdom were extended to the eastern sea; and Fu-hsi's capital was in the present province of Honan. His successor was Shên-nung, who shortly changed his capital to Shantung. Fuhsi and his six successors reigned 596 years, or an average of 85 years each. This period has, of course, much of the mythical about it, but standing out very prominently is the reign of Huang Ti. He triumphed over his several rivals, and divided his territory according to the decimal system, as follows:—

10 towns=1 district.	10 departments=1 province.
10 districts=1 department.	10 provinces=the empire.

Weights and measures were also fixed on the same principle. He is credited with having regulated the calendar, and having introduced in the sixty-first year of his reign the cycle of sixty years, which in its sexagenary periods bridges over the thousands of years from that time (2698-2598 B.C.) to the present, namely, seventy-five revolutions of sixty years. He made roads and built vessels for inland waters, as well as for the open sea. He is looked up to as the founder of the great empire, and his dominions are said to have extended from Sha-chow, in the west, to the sea; and from the modern Pei-chih-li, in the north, to the Yang-tzŭ Kiang in the south. He was succeeded by his son, and the latter by his nephew, who is said to have widened the borders of his empire to Tongking in the south, and to Manchuria in the north.

Two hundred and forty-one years (four reigns) intervened between the periods of Huang Ti and a galaxy of China's greatest worthies, the Emperors Yao, Shun, and Yü. Confucius and Mencius have held up to all future time the perfect character and virtues of Yao and Shun—they are two of China's greatest sages. During this period occurred the great deluge in China, which the best authorities concur in considering to be an overflow of the Yellow River, possibly when changing its channel. Years were spent in coping with this great disaster, which must have wrought terrible havoc and destruction, and unremitting toil and energy were expended in remedying it. It was about this time that the first Chinese settlers arrived in their future home, namely 2200 B.C., driving out the earlier settlers into more remote parts of the country, where some of them are now still to be found as aboriginal tribes. (See ABORIGINES.)

The history preceding the time of Yao, it has been suggested, must then be considered either as that of the previous inhabitants of the land incorporated into Chinese history, or their own previous history brought over with them to their new home; for though much, if not a great portion, of what is narrated of the present period under review is mythical, unsubstantial, and unreal, we cannot help considering it the height of folly to agree with the sceptical school of Chinese sinologists, who reject everything because the greatest proportion is incredible. It seems wiser, in our eyes, to believe that amidst all the chaff, some grains of wheat are to be found. The great Yü was the founder of the Hsia dynasty (2205-1766 B.C.); and with this period the throne became hereditary—having hitherto been more or less elective—seventeen rulers belonged to the same family; one was dethroned by the people, and another by a minister, but the heir-apparent was preserved alive in a massacre that ensued in an attempt to recover the throne, and, after many vicissitudes, ascended the throne of his ancestors. (The whole population of China at this time was only between one or two millions, forming, so it is supposed, stations of colonists dotted about amidst the aborigines. The greater part of 'China was then, except in Honan and along the Yellow River, overrun by luxuriant vegetation.' Wild beasts abounded, and their trails formed the roads. In certain senses life must have been a harder struggle for existence than at the present day.) Yü's son was worthy of such a sire, but the succeeding nine monarchs were of so little account that but little record is left of their doings. In 1818-1766 B.C., Chieh-kuei and his consort spent all they extorted in unbridled voluptuousness. A pond of wine was formed, able to float a boat, at which 3,000 men could drink at once; when drunk, they were allowed to attack the pyramids of delicate viands surrounding the lake; and the vilest orgies were held in the palace. Public opinion was outraged, and one of the ministers, a descendant of Huang Ti, assumed the throne, and founded the new dynasty of Shang in 1766 B.C., which lasted for 644 years. The Shu King [*Shu ching*] contains fragments of the annals of this time which show the high standard aimed at by China's rulers. Twenty-eight sovereigns, good and bad, ascended the throne, the fortunes of the State fluctuating in response to the hand that held the helm, the wickedness culminating in the person of Chou Hsin, the last of the line. Two instances of his wanton cruelty may be noted:—Several women who were gathering shell-fish, bare-legged, on a river's bank, one winter's morning, had their legs cut off, that the inhuman monarch might see the marrow of those who were so insusceptible to cold: and he, likewise, had the heart of a bold minister, who reproved him, brought, that he might see the difference between it and that of a cowardly statesman. Such conduct in China naturally produced its inevitable result, the passing away of the dynasty; and the founders of the Chou dynasty (1122 to 255 B.C.) were the agents in establishing a better order of things. Some sinologists would blot out all that precedes this dynasty and make this the starting-point of Chinese history. We have already expressed our opinion on the subject.

The founders of the Chou dynasty, Wên Wang, Wu Wang, and Chou Kung, 'are among the most distinguished men of antiquity for their erudition, integrity, patriotism, and inventions.' Wên Wang united the principal men against the reign of misrule, but, dying, left to his son the completion of the work he had begun, while the uncle of Wu Wang, Duke Chou, advised the actual sovereign. These men were praised and held in the highest esteem by Confucius. Notwithstanding all his ability and reverence for the Supreme Ruler, Wu Wang committed a grand political blunder by dividing the empire into petty states; and, harassed by attacks of the Tartars, a later sovereign, P'ing Wang, committed an equally grave error of judgment in abandoning his eastern capital to one of his nobles, to form a buttress against the incursions of these nomads, while he retired to the western capital, thus dividing it into the Eastern and Western Chou. These fatal mistakes paved the way for the weakening of the central authority; and the result, of the first especially, was a multiplicity of feudal states —little kingdoms in themselves, engaged in internecine strife, the weaker succumbing to the stronger, and all belittling the authority of the ruling sovereign. The number of these states varied at different times, 125, 41, and 52 are numbers that are given. Begun so auspiciously, this dynasty, like its predecessors, reached a period of decadence, though it has the honour of having lasted for 867 years, with 35 rulers, the longest time known in history.

'A series of wars, intrigues, diplomacy, conspiracies, and plots, much resembling what has been occurring in the empires of Europe during the last 200 years, ensued.' 'The Chinese Empire consisted of Shansi, Honan, and Shantung, and it gradually threw out tentacles to embrace the rest of modern China, just as Rome threw out its tentacles, from Italy, Greece, and Spain, to embrace parts of Asia, Africa, Teutonia, and Sclavonia.'

Eunuchs probably followed the introduction of the imperial harem at the beginning of this dynasty, the tributary princes copying the bad example of the emperors.

This period is, however, glorious for having given birth to two of the most remarkable men the world has ever seen, Lao Tzŭ and Confucius. Dissimilar as two men could possibly be—the one, to his contemporaries, a wild visionary, the other a man who occupied himself with ceremonies and moral precepts—they were both destined to exercise an important influence on the country. Nor must we forget that Mencius lived during this time:—

'There can be little doubt that the competition in arms, in diplomacy, in military discipline, in material civilisation, and in education, caused the Chinese of that period to reach a very high level of ability, of skill, and of material progress. It was so, under similar circumstances, in Greece, in Arabia, in Italy, and it is so in modern Europe; and we can no more wonder at the fond pride with which the Chinese regard that famous time than we can at the European for his admiration of ancient Greece and Rome. Against Plato and Aristotle place Confucius and Mencius; whilst China had then statesmen and orators not greatly inferior to those of antiquity.'

Millions were slain during the constant wars which lasted during the whole of the Chou dynasty; but out of all this continued strife between the feudal princes themselves and between them and their own subjects grew the material on which a greater China should be established, for before the Chou, China was, without doubt, but of limited extent. The end of that dynasty saw the southern border-line of the Chinese Empire extended to the south of the Yang-tzŭ.

Some foreign writers are again inclined to reject as incredible the greater part of this period, but when archæological researches are carried on in a systematic manner in China, confirmatory evidence of the Chinese records may be found similar to the ten stone drums of the period 827-782 B.C.

One of the most powerful of the feudatory states, that of Ts'in [Ch'in], subdued the sovereign; and the son of the conqueror assuming the imperial power, destroyed the last vestiges of the famous Chou dynasty, but died in three years, thus forming a dynasty with only one Emperor. His son, ambitious and powerful, took the name of the first Emperor, Shih Huang-ti (221-209 B.C.), and was the first of the Ts'in [Ch'in] dynasty. A man of consummate skill and ability, he consolidated the empire, dividing it into thirty-six provinces. His name is known throughout the habitable world by the gigantic work with which it is associated, viz., the Great Wall of China; but this stupendous labour was not accomplished entirely during his reign, as the beginning of it seems to have been made in 240 B.C., and even as late as the Ming dynasty, in the year A.D. 1547, between 250 and 300 miles of wall were added to that then in existence.

Were this the only work that had received the impress of his genius, his name would doubtless have lived to all time as that of one of the great benefactors of the empire, but the restless activity of this Napoleon of China also expended its energy in the construction of palaces, public edifices, canals, and roads. The latter, like the Roman roads in England, remain during 2,000 years to this day. Again, had he contented himself with these engineering triumphs and architectural undertakings, supplemented by his vigorous sway, his name and exploits would have been had in everlasting remembrance; but one act of his has blasted his reputation to all eternity in the eyes of the Chinese; and they have nothing but ill to say of him. Desirous of blotting out all records of a former China, and wishing to pose before posterity as the First Emperor, he ordered the destruction of all classical works by fire, as well as of five hundred scholars.

The texts were recovered by transcribing them from the retentive memories of the *literati*, and a few copies were discovered which had been secreted. To a literary nation like the Chinese, such a crime was never to be forgotten, nor forgiven.

On a complete survey of all the facts of the case, the Emperor, though the act was cruel, was not so much to blame as the Chinese make out, for the integrity of the empire was jeopardised by the *literati*. His son reigned but seven years, and was unable to cope with the feudal chieftains. With this period closes the ancient history of China.

A soldier of fortune, a commander of the forces of one of the chiefs, captured the capital, and started the Han dynasty (206 B.C. to A.D. 25) and the modern history of China.

In the North of China, Men of Han (Han-jin) [Han-jên] and Sons of Han (Han-tzŭ), are still the names by which a Chinese is known, thus perpetuating this glorious epoch, whether looked at from a literary, historical, military, commercial, or artistic point of view. Many public works were undertaken, prominent among which were bridges. The capital, being difficult of approach, had roads cut through mountains, valleys filled up, and suspension bridges built to it. It was, the 'formative period of Chinese polity and institutions, official and formal.'

The present competitive examinations for which China has been so famous were started. (See EXAMINATIONS.) A penal code was drawn up, which has formed the model for subsequent codes in China. (See LAW.) This dynasty is famous for the introduction of Buddhism; it was 'one of the most popular which ever ruled the Chinese'; years of peace, during which the nation prospered, alternated with incursions by the restless Tartars. The modern Fukien, Yünnan, and Canton, etc., and the greater part of Sz-chuen [Szŭch'uan] became Chinese provinces, other territory was incorporated with that of the empire, and tribute-bearers came from remote countries. Chinese armies marched across Asia, and China occupied a foremost position among the nations of the world.

The short reign of a usurper, who tried to found a dynasty of his own, under the name of Sin [Hsin], divides the Han dynasty into the Western, or Former, and Eastern, or Later, Han (the Eastern Han lasted from A.D. 25 to 221). Commercial relations are supposed to have been established with the Roman Empire at this period. The two Hans lasted 427 years, with a total of twenty-eight monarchs.

Contemporaneous with the latter part of the Han, and extending to a later period, viz., from A.D. 200 to 280, is one of the most interesting periods of Chinese history, and it has been immortalised and a halo of romance thrown over it by the famous historical novel called 'The History of the Three States.' Were any instance needed of the utility of works of fiction, it might be found in this entertaining book which has spread a knowledge of what took place in those troublous times in a way in which no cut-and-dried history, though it might have proved more veracious, could possibly have done.

The Ts'in and Eastern Ts'in dynasties ruled for 155 years (from A.D. 265 to 420) under fifteen monarchs—a time big with disasters and wars. A General then succeeded to the throne, and started the dynasty of the Northern Sung, but, as at former times, the country was divided among separate states, and it did not always happen that the house which the historians have considered as the legitimate one was the most powerful. This observation also holds good with regard to some of the succeeding periods. The dynasty ended in a series of crimes, and the Ch'i followed it. Both of them were uninteresting and inglorious, and the line was again extinguished in murders. This brings us to the year A.D. 502. Several small dynasties succeeded, the Empire being re-united under the Sui dynasty (A.D. 589-618).

We come, in the T'ang dynasty (A.D. 618-907) to another of those most illustrious periods in Chinese history, which lasted for nearly three hundred years. 'Under that beneficent imperial sway, the peasant tilled his land and the trader sold his goods in peace. The fiercer and more martial spirits found an outlet for their energies in extending the western boundaries of the empire, and the triumphs of war and the tranquil pleasures of peace were sung and hymned by some of the greatest poets which China has produced.' It augured well for this dynasty that its founder did not cement the foundations of his empire with the blood of his predecessors, as was so frequently the case with those who started a new house in China. Of the second Emperor, it has been well said that:—'no ruler of any country has had sounder claims to the title of great.' His military exploits, with but one exception, were always attended with success, while his genius, military knowledge, and courage, were tempered with the gentleness which maketh great. He gave peace and settled government to the troubled land, while his conquests ensured the same to some of the neighbouring peoples. He patronised literature; and it was during his reign that the Nestorian table was erected. (See MISSIONS—NESTORIANS.) It was during this dynasty that, after a century of struggle and hard-bought victory, Corea became a possession of China; and so powerful was China that even Persia solicited aid from the Middle Kingdom.

We find the empire placed at this time in what would be considered an anomalous position for China to be in, namely, under the rule of a woman; this however, was not so very uncommon, especially in ancient times; but the most notable instance of it was the Empress Wu, who ruled with a masculine hand, and whose reign, notwithstanding her cruelties, was one of benefit to the people for more than forty years.

The siege of Tai-yuen ([T'ai-yüan] claims notice from the use of cannon for its defence, which threw twelve-pound stone shot to the distance of three hundred paces. Civil wars and troubles with Tibet and other neighbouring nations—wars which lasted for two centuries—dimmed the lustre of the earlier reigns, and the vigorous hands which held the sceptre were succeeded by weaker ones unable to grasp the kingly power with regal grip and pass it on intact to their successors. The eunuchs arrogated to themselves the character of king-makers, and took far too much on themselves, as has often been the case in the course of Chinese history. The closing chapters of this period are melancholy—a desolate country, ruined towns, and the capital in ashes. It had lasted for 289 years, and twenty emperors and one usurping empress sat on the throne.

The people of the South of China have immortalised this dynasty, and marked the time of their civilisation and incorporation into the Chinese rule, by calling themselves T'ong-yan [T'ang jên], or Men of T'ong.

In contrast to the dark ages of Europe, China presented the brightest spectacle to the nations of the world. Mohammedanism was introduced; the Greek Emperor, Theodosius, sent an envoy, in A.D. 643, with presents of precious stones; as also did the Persians.

We next come to a series of petty dynasties—'The Five Dynasties' or 'Ten States' (A.D. 907-60), as the Chinese call them; the centre of the empire on the Yellow River formed their arena, while the rest of the country was held by different generals—'a period of wasting and incessant civil war, discord, invasions, and commotions.' The whole time occupied by them is less than sixty years; the most noteworthy thing was the invention of printing. (But see PRINTING.)

The Sung (A.D. 960-1127) is another of the great dynasties of Chinese history. It is divided into two, the Sung and the Southern Sung (A.D. 1127-1280). There was a greater centralisation of power in the Supreme Government, the almost autocratic power of the governors of the provinces being curtailed, and more peaceful times succeeded, though fierce wars were still waged with the Tartars. The empire was reunited, and literature and the arts of peace were cultivated. Chinese history contains the record of many great names as shedding lustre on this period; the Sung dynasty, however, lacked the military prowess to hold its own against the warlike ancestors of the modern Manchu-Tartars, the Kins; these first acted as treacherous allies, then showed their true colours, and eventually founded a kingdom (A.D. 1115-1234) which was more powerful than that of the Sung; and the two held concurrent sway in China.

The rise of the Mongol power prevented what might perhaps have happened five centuries sooner, namely, the establishment of a Manchu dynasty over the South as well as the North of China. Constant wars took place between the Chinese and the Kins, the latter compelling the conquered people to shave their heads, as during the recent Manchu dynasty, until their waning power sank before the rising glory of the Mongols, who overthrew them, though they offered a stubborn resistance. The Sung ruler allied himself with the Mongols, out of hatred to the Kins, but no sooner were the latter conquered, then it became evident that the Chinese and Mongols could not rule together in China. After a war carried on for seventy years, during which parts of China were subdued, the Mongols, under different leaders, but finally under Kublai Khan, gradually conquered China. Among many memorable battles, the siege of Sian-yang [Hsien-yang], which was defended for four years, is worthy of note. After the conquest of Hankow and its neighbouring cities, the conquerors proceeded in their victorious course, subdued the country, and gained possession of the Yang-tzŭ Kiang, while the Court retreated to the south of China. Mementoes of the last Emperor's flight are to be found in British territory on the mainland opposite Hongkong, while the last scenes of his life were enacted in one of the estuaries of the Canton River, to the west of Macao, where, after a disastrous naval encounter, one of his courtiers sprang into the sea with him in his arms. Thus ended, after a possession of the legitimate throne for a space of 320 years, the Sung dynasty in its two divisions of Northern and Southern. This House was not equal to that of T'ang. One very interesting feature was the trial of socialistic principles, after long discussion and opposition. They, however, were not of such a nature as to be adapted for a successful issue, and proved a failure.

'An elaborate experiment in Socialism was tried in the Province of Shansi,' 'in the time of William the Conqueror; the poor were exempted from taxes, and to every man a plot of land and seed for it was given, with the result that, according to the Chinese historiographers, Shansi became a desert, no man caring to work.'

The Mongol sway (A.D. 1280-1368) was a foreign one to the Chinese, and the latter being the superiors of the former in civilisation, though not in military prowess, the Mongols very naturally allowed the Chinese laws to remain in force, and retained all the advantages of the superior state of the Chinese. To those who are anxious to learn fuller particulars of the 'vigorous and magnificent' sovereign, Kublai Khan, the gossipy pages of the mediæval Venetian traveller, Marco Polo, will afford many details of interest, both of the vast domains and the splendour of the Court of the great Khan at Peking; this city was first made the capital, and it and the Court were at that time the most splendid in the world. Not content with all his victories on the mainland, this born conqueror resolved to win Japan, but his efforts only met with disaster and defeat; his armies, though encountering a similar fate in Annam, were successful in Burma. He evinced a toleration of all creeds. The rule of the invader (the Mongol dynasty was named the Yüan) was not popular with the Chinese, but the grandson, Timur, who succeeded him, endeavoured, with some success, to make it more so. A number of princes of the same house succeeded to the throne, whose reigns were of short duration; Mongols were put into office in disregard of the Chinese rule of that event following upon literary distinction. This innovation caused disgust to the natives; abortive insurrections followed one another, gaining strength and force with each renewed effort, until at length the Heaven-sent man arose, and the Mongols were finally expelled, in A.D. 1368, after a sway of 88 years over China. The dynasty had become effete and powerless through luxury, misrule, and weakness, and had to give way to one more vigorous and powerful—a native dynasty that changed its capital to Nanking.

The founder of the Ming dynasty (A.D. 1368-1644) having been left an orphan at seventeen, and without any means of support, became a Buddhist priest, according to some accounts. He afterwards joined one of the rebel forces as a soldier, and was soon in a forward position in the strife between the Chinese and Mongols. In A.D. 1356, he made himself master of Nanking, and, continuing to extend his authority for some ten years, he finally, in A.D. 1366, commenced 'the war for the expulsion of the foreign rulers.' Very little opposition was experienced, so that in a short time Peking was captured, and the last of the Mongol emperors fled, though wars, necessary for the consolidation of the power of the empire, lasted for some years longer, the Mongols still giving trouble by their continued raids. Hung Wu, as the first Ming ruler was called, was a man of ability and prudence, wisdom and moderation; a man of peace, he promoted literature, which the Mongol rulers, with the exception of Kublai Khan, had foolishly slighted. Among many other deeds conducive to this end, he caused libraries to be placed in all the large cities; not this act alone, but many others, not least of which was the distribution of salt, showed he had the welfare of his people at heart.

Hung Wu was succeeded by his grandson, who, after a short reign, was displaced by one of his uncles, who reached the throne after a protracted and frightful civil war. His son was

Emperor for a few months only. The Ming dynasty was more firmly established. Envoys bearing presents came from Bengal and Malacca. The son of the last Emperor succeeded to the throne, and during his reign Tongking, which had been a Chinese province for ten years, was given up, owing to the difficulty of its administration. The next reign but one gave another forcible illustration of the ill effects of allowing a eunuch to hold the reins of power, for, owing to the incapacity of one of this class, the Emperor was well-nigh brought to the verge of ruin, he even being taken captive by the Tartars.

Periods of incessant warfare succeeded—wars with the Tartars, insurrections, seditions, movements, and disturbances. One of the Emperors was foolish enough to start a Council of Eunuchs—a species of Chinese star-chamber, but the public outcry against it was so loud that it was suspended after five years. Another bad measure by the same Emperor was the granting of lands to several members of his family, thus tending to build up Feudal States. This was one of the 'chief causes that operated towards effecting the overthrow and destruction of the Mings.' The Court was extravagant, and orders were given to work the gold mines in Central China, but the result was next to nothing. Of undertakings that were of use must be noted the repair of the Great Wall.

The difficulties that surrounded the Ming dynasty were increasing: troubles in Cochin-China, further wars with the Tartars, and raids by the Japanese, all kept them occupied; and the misfortunes culminated in the long reign of Wan Li, when the troubles began with the Manchus, though several Emperors succeeded to the throne before the final overthrow of the native dynasty. The Portuguese arrived in China in the reign of Chia-Ch'ing (A.D. 1522-67), and Jesuit Missionaries in that of Wan Li (A.D. 1573-1620).

A small Tartar tribe, presided over by a chief of ability, gathered strength and amalgamated its power with other branches, until, after a long and desultory warfare, the opportunity arose in the success of a rebel chieftain who ascended the Chinese throne, and the last of the Ming Emperors committed suicide. Wu San-kuei, a renowned general, called in the aid of the Manchus to expel the usurper, and they, in their turn, after a long contest of forty years, succeeded in conquering the whole empire, notwithstanding that several Ming princes were proclaimed Emperors and fought against the conquerors. Numerous uprisings also took place, but the Manchus were victorious over all. A great part of the reign of the first emperor (A.D. 1644) of the Manchu, or Ts'ing [Ch'ing] dynasty, was occupied by these wars; and it is interesting as being the time when several embassies from the West arrived in China. Shun Chih, for that was the name which the first sovereign of the Ts'ing dynasty was known by on the throne, was succeeded by the renowned K'ang Hsi. These two reigns were also famous for the exploits of the semi-piratical and naval hero Koshinga, who expelled the Dutch from Formosa. The Jesuit missionaries held high positions, on account of their mathematical and astronomical knowledge. A bold rebellion, headed by the redoubtable Wu San-kuei, complicated amongst other things by a threat of the Mongols to attack China, was quelled by the Manchus, and as a result Manchu garrisons were placed in the cities, where they are still maintained at the present day. Formosa was conquered, and a protracted struggle took place with the Eleuths under Galdan, but the Chinese army met with success. This was followed by much trouble over the Central Asian question; and Chinese authority was rendered paramount in Tibet. K'ang Hsi reigned for sixty-one years, during which period the Manchu rule over China and the neighbouring States was firmly established. 'The public acts and magnificent exploits of his reign . . . show him wise, courageous, magnanimous and sagacious.' 'In the smallest affairs he seems to have been truly great.'

His son Yung Chêng followed him, but his reign was short compared with that of his father. He was a man who cared not for military glory and aggrandisement; his reign is noted for the restrictions placed on the growing power and influence of the Jesuit missionaries, and after Ch'ien Lung succeeded to the throne they suffered persecution. The first few years of this latter monarch's reign were tranquil; but they were succeeded by a long war in Central Asia, where his authority was set up amongst the turbulent tribes; and for nearly a century and a half the wisdom of Ch'ien Lung's able and far-seeing policy has been visible in peaceful frontiers. Wars were also carried on against the Burmese and the Miao-tzŭ with success, and also against the bravest of the Indian tribes—the Goorkhas in Nepal—who had attacked Tibet. An insurrection in Formosa was put down, as well as some others. This long reign of sixty years is also noted for the close relations that were entered into between China and the nations of Europe. We cannot leave our short summary of some of the principal events of this period without adding our tribute to the universal voice of praise of the energy and thoroughness of this Emperor, and the assiduity with which he devoted himself to the subjects requiring his attention. The Manchu power was brought to the zenith of its glory, and had as able rulers always sat on the throne as K'ang Hsi and Ch'ien Lung, much of the misery of later days might have been prevented.

The succeeding reign, that of Chia Ch'ing was not one of peace and quiet: there were secret combinations against the Government, and insurrections and piracies abounded; a formidable force of pirates infested the coast of Kuangtung for some years; the Portuguese assisted the Chinese in attacking them, but the two piratical leaders quarrelled, and finally submitted themselves to the Imperial Government.

Chia Ch'ing's son Tao Kuang was a more energetic and just ruler than his father. Many local insurrections and disasters took place, among which was the first war with England, which, however, resulted in one good thing, the opening of China to foreign trade. The frightful T'ai P'ing rebellion broke out at the close of this sovereign's reign, and demanded the prowess of a K'ang Hsi or Ch'ien Lung to subdue it, but Hsien Fêng, who succeeded Tao Kuang, was not cast in the same mould as his grandfather, or great-great-grandfather. A second war with England took place, and resulted in the country being still further opened to Western nations.

In the next reign, that of T'ung Chih, the great T'ai-P'ing rebellion was subdued, Chinese Gordon having a very great share in the matter; this rebellion had lasted from A.D. 1850 to 1864 and had desolated several provinces. A Mohammedan rising was also quelled; and diplomatic intercourse was started with the Treaty Powers.

His cousin succeeded T'ung Chih, under the style of Kuang Hsü. A slow progress toward Western civilisation was initiated: the construction of railways begun; cotton mills established; mints opened for the coining of copper and silver after the Western fashion; a navy of foreign-built vessels acquired; bodies of troops trained in European style; arsenals started; and various other minor improvements effected. But the almost universal corruption and inefficiency of the mandarins resulted in a series of disastrous defeats of the army and navy, the results of which amongst other things were seen in the loss of the magnificent Island of Formosa, the dismantling of Port Arthur, and in the destruction or taking of the vessels of the Northern Fleet by the Japanese. These were followed by the Boxer rising, fomented by the Chinese Government or officials, finally culminating in the siege of the foreign legations in the heart of the capital by the Boxers and Chinese soldiery, and massacres of missionaries and foreign residents and native converts in the North. The Audience Question was at last settled (see AUDIENCE.) The Anglo-Japanese Alliance was for the purpose of preserving the integrity of the Chinese Empire: a politically polite way of saying 'hands off' to all who would desire the dismemberment of China.

The despotic government of the Manchus, continuing under the mask of constitutional reforms, at length provoked the revolution of 1911 which overthrew the dynasty. Hsüan T'ung, a child, had, on the death of Kuang Hsü in 1908, been placed on the throne under the supervision of the Empress Dowager, and on February 12th, 1912, an edict proclaiming his abdication was promulgated. Meanwhile the prime mover of the revolution, Sun Wên, also known as Sun Yat-sen, had been elected President of the Chinese Republic set up in the provinces south of the Yang Tzŭ River. On the abdication of the Manchus he resigned in favour of Yüan Shih-k'ai, a general who, having been recalled from exile to help the Manchu cause, had become Premier and Commander-in-Chief. The North and South being united, the Republic now embraced all the provinces of China. The first Chinese Parliament met on April 8th, 1913. An abortive attempt on the part of Yüan Shih-k'ai to revert to the monarchical form of government led to his illness and death on June 6th, 1916. He was succeeded by Li Yüan-hung, and, after another abortive attempt to restore the monarchy by Chang Hsün in July, 1917, by Fêng Kuo-chang, who was superseded at the election of September, 1918, by Hsü Shih-chang (his inauguration dating from October 10th of that year). On the latter's resignation in June, 1922, Li Yüan-hung was reinstated, but in June of the following year fled to Tientsin under military pressure of his rivals, and on October 5th Ts'ao Kun was elected President, and retained the post until deposed in favour of Tuan Chih-jui, as the result of a short civil war between the chief military Governors in the autumn of 1924.

We have thus traced in the shortest manner possible the history of the Chinese nation from a mythological period to a mythical and semi-mythical one, until, under the House of Chou, the facts of Chinese history are more reliable. We have seen the ebb and flow of dynastic changes; how, with the new vigour of a fresh dynasty, the power of China was extended for a few centuries, to be succeeded, when effete rulers followed, by an ebb of dominion and influence, until, with each successive change, a higher tide of power reclaimed what weak hands had lost, and the boundaries of the empire were again expanded with each rise of fortune to a greater extent: how the Feudal States of China, with a nominal paramount lord, were succeeded by 'the foundations of a coherent empire' under the first Emperor of Ts'in; next, have seen 'the stately House of Han,' 'making vast strides towards a more settled state of prosperity and civilisation'; the troublous times of the Three States and other dynasties from which China rose in the brilliant epoch of the T'ang; another ebb and transition period of the Five Dynasties, when the recurring tide of prosperity came in with the Sung, to be followed by an efflux, and another stormy wave of conquest under the Mongols, which quickly retired, to return, with renewed force, with the great Ming dynasty on its crest again, to again retire, and with fresh energy, to once more return with the conquering Manchu. The Republican government established in 1912 has still to stabilize itself, but at the present time (1925) is in an unsettled condition, owing to its subjection to its military, and the corruption of its civil officials.

References.—Chavannes, *Mémoires Historiques;* Cordier, *Histoire Générale de la China;* Parker, *China; Ancient China Simplified;* Werner, *China of the Chinese; Descriptive Sociology-Chinese;* De Mailla, *Histoire générale de la Chine;* Macgowan, *The Imperial History of China;* Li Ung-bing, *Outlines of Chinese History; Chinese Recorder; China Review; Chinese Repository.*

HORNBILLS.—

'These answer to the "Toucans" of America. Their apparently cumbrous beaks and helmets are in reality very light, only one species having the portion above the head solid. It is from this—a yellow, wax-like-looking substance—that the Chinese carve brooches, earrings, etc.'

HOK-LO.—This name is applied to the inhabitants of certain parts of the north-eastern portion of the Canton province, who differ in speech, manners, and customs, from the rest of the population. Their language (see DIALECTS, under SWATOW) is near akin to the Fukienese, but has several dialects. The Swatow is spoken at that port, and the Hoí-fung and the Luk-fung in the districts of country so named, and some other dialects would probably be discovered were the subject fully examined into.

The Hok-lo occupy the whole of some districts, and are scattered through other parts, having migrated from the Fukien province a few centuries since. It is estimated that within the Canton province there are about three million Hok-lo speakers. There are some traces of a very ancient origin in this speech; it is not so soft and musical as the Cantonese, having many nasal twangs.

In dress they differ slightly from the Cantonese; the jackets of the men are rather longer at times, and they often, in common with the Fukienese, wear turbans. They are a rougher, wilder set of men than the Cantonese. There are other points of difference between them, into which we cannot enter.

The American Baptist and English presbyterian Missions have many stations in the Hok-lo country.

There are a number of Hok-lo in Hongkong, many of the chair coolies belonging to that part of the country. They make good bearers, being physically stronger than the natives further south. Many Hok-lo have gone abroad, and are to be found in different parts of the world. By the census of 1891 there were 43,791 Teo Chews in the Straits Settlements: Teo Chews is the term applied generally to them in Singapore, Penang, and the Malay States, while Hok-lo is the name by which they are generally known by the Cantonese speakers in China; the former name being derived from the Departmental city of Ch'ao Chao [Chou] fú (in the local dialect Tíú Chíú fú, or Teo Chew fu), to which the different districts, from which many of the Hok-los come, belong; while Hok-lo means 'Men from the Fuk' (or, as it is locally, Hok) 'province,' *i.e.* Fukien province. The inhabitants of this portion of the Canton province, as we have already said, having been settlers from that, the Fukien, province.

INFANTICIDE.—The longer one lives in China the more one feels the necessity for caution in saying what does and what does not exist here. Some authors have been egregious sinners in thus writing about a small portion of China in which they have resided: they have judged of the whole of this vast empire, with its diverse inhabitants, manners and customs, from a small part of it, reversing the mathematical axiom that the whole contains its parts, into 'one small part contains the whole."

About no subject is this perhaps more strikingly true than that of infanticide, for what holds perfectly good of one small district, is entirely false when applied to other large tracts. Also what happens at one time, an exceptional period possibly, may not happen again, even in the same district, for years.

To form an approximately correct estimate of this evil and crime in China, a systematically carried out investigation, extending over a number of years, all over the land, would be necessary.

To premise, as a general statement, it may be said that in certain parts of the empire, and (or) at certain times, this crime is only too alarmingly practised. One writer says, 'thousands of female babies are destroyed every year.'

That it is prevalent in some regions it is useless to deny. There is a *quasi* sanction given to it under certain circumstances by the tale of one who had not sufficient to support his aged parent and his own family, and who thereupon came to the resolve, with his wife, that the infant should be sacrificed in order to have enough for its grandparent. Taking the child for the purpose of burying it alive, the misguided and wicked parent—but, according to Chinese ideas, most dutiful son—was rewarded by Heaven, and restrained from this murderous act of filial piety by discovering a pot of gold in the hole he had dug for his own offspring. And this is held up as an example, it being one of the twenty-four moral (?) tales to encourage others to a performance of filial duties. What wonder if some follow the example thus held up to them. Were it not also a known fact that infanticides take place, proof of it might be found in the proclamations which are sometimes issued against it by the officials. And even another corroboration of its practice may be found in the Chinese mothers, who have acknowledged putting their own children out of the way. Again there used to be published a small tract issued under the *imprimatur* of the Goddess of Mercy, containing illustrations of the methods of committing the crime, and inveighing against it.

On the other hand, it must not be supposed that all the dead bodies of children that float down the rivers are the victims of infanticide, nor that those which are found exposed at the road-side or on the hills are necessarily thrown there by heartless hands, for the Chinese do not go to the trouble of burying little children with the same care that they do older people, and the dead children are often thrown into the river, or cast out in the country. The mortality amongst infants in China is awful. With death statistics in Hongkong, if reliable, it is possible to form some idea of what it must be in China where no statistics are available. Out of 1,000 Chinese infants born in this colony, only 72 survived for a period of twelve months in 1900.

One of the great causes of infanticide is poverty; another is the low estimation in which girls are held, and all the evils which necessarily ensue from such an inferior position in the social status, for it is seldom, indeed rarely, that boys are killed; and that brings us to another reason, for if a boy is made away with, it is probably due to some physical defect, this reason also causing the death of some girls.

'In his pamphlet on "The Diseases of China," Dr. Dudgeon says (on p. 56):—"One thing is certain, infanticide does not prevail to the extent so generally believed among us; and in the North, whence Europe derived her ideas chiefly from the Jesuits of the last century, it does not exist at all." These remarks do not apply to Shansi, where the practice is quite common. The teachers deny that female infants are thus killed, but the common people readily admit that they destroy many of their girl babies. There are comparatively few old women of the poorer classes who have not been guilty of this crime. The writer himself is aware of some instances of the kind.'

'It has been calculated that of every thousand girls born in China, sixteen are smothered at birth, to avoid the "calamity and disgrace" of another girl in the house.'

Infants were drowned, suffocated, buried alive, allowed to die from neglect, or the newly-born fœtus was thrown to the scavenger dogs.

In the neighbourhood of Hankow there are many cases of it among the poor and rural population. It is also said to be prevalent among the Hakkas. It is prectised in Canton, but is much rarer there than in some places. It seems to prevail in certain parts of the Fukien province. From enquiries made in some villages in that part of the country, it was ascertained that an average of 40 per cent. of the girls were thus murdered, as we call it, but neither Chinese law nor opinion seem to consider it as such.

At the prefectural city of Ch'ao Chou, near Swatow, some years ago could be seen, outside the walls of the city, a basket hanging against a wall, looking from a distance something like a cradle. A piece of matting was fastened above it, forming a sort of pent-roof to shelter it from the rain and sun. In this basket, was put any baby whom its parents did not care to preserve, and should any charitable person have been so disposed, he, or she, might lift out the forsaken infant and take it home. Failing such rescue, the child ultimately met the fate of so many of the inhabitants of babydom in China. The provision made for infanticide in a large and important departmental city near Amoy was not so merciful, as it was simply a large hole in the city wall into which the infant was cast. In the north of China, baby towers are provided, perhaps amongst other reasons, for the same purpose, though they are principally used for receiving the dead bodies of infants. Occasionally a separate hole is provided on different sides of the tower to keep the sexes distinct, and thus prevent any incentives to immorality amongst the ghosts of the little babies! No wonder the Chinese consider themselves so far superior to us in this all-important virtue of morality!

References.—Journal N.C.B.R.A.S., N.S. vol. xx; Werner, *China of the Chinese.*

INSECTS.—Insect life is rampant in China. To one who is accustomed to its abundance in the East, it appears as if man had to look for it in the West, the opposite being the case in China; here the insects find out the man; for hide as he may from their advances, they follow him everywhere, and all his subterfuges to avoid them are unavailing. There is no need for the enthusiastic entomologist to look under stones for beetles, for beetles abound everywhere; nor need he sally forth at night to catch moths, the moths come, attracted by his lamp, into the room to him. And when the white ants are in full flight, they fly in at the open window in such quantities that the table is soon littered with the wings which the pupa-like insects drop, without the least reluctance, at the slightest hint: they come off in the hands, they are shed on the lamp-globes, anywhere and everywhere, while the wretched little creatures crawl over your book or paper, and, if the lamp is not too attractive, they proceed to explore the genus *homo* with a persistency worthy of a better cause. A grand thing is to set the lamps into large basins of water, when hundreds of them lose their lives in the moats which thus surround the lights.

And these same white ants, when in another stage of their existence, are a worse nuisance than ever, for they are not simply an annoyance then, but a pest. Nothing is secure from their depredations. Have you a trunk full of valuable documents? You may, after keeping them for years intact, suddenly discover, on opening the trunk, that the papers and pamphlets have been transformed into trash, glued together into one mass and riddled with the tunnelled roads of these indefatigable workers in the dark. Are you fond of books and is your collection a valuable and priceless one of old editions? With all your care, you may discover some day that these respecters of nothing have eaten up through one of the legs of your bookcase, and run riot here and there throughout all the accumulated treasure of years. Is there anything left untouched by white ants? One's house is attacked in the flooring and the beams of the roof, and suddenly and unexpectedly collapses; clothing, carefully packed away for future use, is found, when wanted, to be eaten into holes.

The only fault to be found with the white ant is, that he has a superabundance of energy that is misapplied, but unfortunately misapplied energy is not appreciated by man, and thwarts his plans in a most aggravating manner. Were the white ant amenable to instruction, he might be yoked in the service of man instead of being his antagonist; but he has views of his own on the subject, and probably prefers to work on his own lines, instead of drilling holes in wood for the carpenter, or making button-holes for the seamstress.

From white ants to ants is not a far cry, though they are not relations, not even thirty-second cousins. We want a Sir John Lubbock to study Chinese ants. We do not know how many species there are, but the most casual observer cannot help noticing that, at the very least, there are several: black ants and red ants, tiny ants, small black ants and large black ants. In a country where everyone and everything is busy, the ants do not prove an exception to their world-wide reputation for diligence. It is most interesting to notice how these busy little scavengers perform their work; a dead cockroach will not lie long on the floor before it begins to move, and an investigation will show that tens of ants are supporting it and carrying it off; also how carefully and systematically they bring up the earth from the neat little holes, which are occasionally seen in one's path; one by one they bring up a small piece, and, climbing up on the encircling mound, select a little hollow, or what seems to be a suitable spot to them, to deposit it—not dumping it down just anywhere. All sorts of devices have to be resorted to, to keep these industrious little creatures out of the stores: the sugar is black with them, and all sorts of edibles are attacked. To keep them away, the feet of cupboards are set in bowls of water, but this water must be often changed, else a scum will coat the top, and the ants cross over as human beings would on ice.

Cockroaches are even worse plagues than ants in many places. They swarm everywhere, hiding in the daytime in any dark corner, whence they emerge and run riot after dark, running and flying all over the room, much to one's discomfort. They attack clothing, especially that with starch in it, as well as edibles, and books. Woe betide the newly-bought book, nicely bound in cloth, lying on your table; its fine binding will be blotched all over with stains (if you have not already given it a dose or two of anti-cockroach varnish), and a week of such treatment will reduce the volume to so disreputable a condition, that it will look as if a heavy shower of rain had besprinkled it. The female cockroach displays a considerable amount of ingenuity in her endeavours to hide her eggs. These consist of an oblong case, with one edge serrated, of about half or three-quarters of an inch in length and about three or four times as long as broad. This is naturally of a dark, brownish colour; but if it is laid on a white pith hat, the mother collects some of the whiting off the hat and partially covers the egg-case with it to conceal it; and to a lesser degree this is also done where the colour of the substance on which the egg is deposited differs much from that of the egg-case itself.

Insect life knows no rest in the East. Speak not of the silent voices of the night here! The voices of the night are as many as the day, if not more. This is particularly noticeable to the newcomer on his voyage out, when perhaps he spends a night on shore at Singapore, and first realises that insect life in the East is more intense, more persistent, and universally prevalent.

We have seen a book called 'Songs in the Night,' but the insect world in Eastern countries provides incessant 'songs without words,' both day and night. In North China, however, this is noticeable only in the summer.

A walk along a country road after nightfall is through a perfect chorus of chirps and chips, scissors grinding—but sufficient words have not yet been invented in the English language to describe accurately all the shrill little voices, pitched in different keys; soprano, alto, and tenor are present, and, to make up for the want of a bass, the bullfrogs in the neighbouring pond join in a deep, full, well-sustained note, brought out at regular intervals.

All else being quiet, doubtless the insects have a better chance of being heard. But the day is not silent either. It is sufficient to mention the cicada, an insect about an inch and a half to two inches long. The outline of its shape is somewhat like that of the shot of a breech-loading cannon, for its head is nearly straight across, and its abdomen tapers to a point. In colour it is black, touched with brownish-orange, especially on its under surface; it has four transparent gauze wings, two long, and two short, and absurdly small antennæ for an insect of its size; as to its voice—well, to put it mildly, it is not pleasant, though we read in a recent book of travels in Africa a charming account of its angelic notes! Solitude must have had a soothing effect on the family of cicadas which settled in that dark land, and perhaps the cruel treatment they receive from the Chinese boys has produced an irritating one on those in the Celestial Land; for young John Chinaman delights, with a long bamboo pole, some sicky substance having been placed on the end, to poke among the upper branches of the trees and capture the insect, which then does duty as a rattle, protesting with his strident 'sz-sz-sz-sz' when he is fingered; but it is when he is at liberty 'on the tree-top' that he is in full voice—no other insect approaches him in that respect—and, as if apparently rejoicing in a knowledge of what his voice is capable of, he starts off with a preliminary flourish, and then settles down to business. This ear-deafening din is kept up for several minutes (its distressing nature is intensified if half a dozen cicadas are within earshot), then, after a short rest, he starts off again with a wearying iteration through the hot hours of the day. It is only the male which possesses the musical apparatus, consisting of two membranes over air-tubes in its throat, with hollow-sounding cavities behind each, which increase the volume of its notes.' (See CICADA.)

But time, as well as space, would fail us to bring all the insect creation found in China before our readers: the useful silkworms; atlas moths, nearly as large as two palms of the hands joined together; smaller moths, quaint in contrasts of colours unusual in the West in such insects; tiny mites of ones like little pieces of marbled paper flying about; lovely butterflies like bits of rainbow floating in the breeze, and fluttering over the flowers; gorgeous beetles of all shapes and sizes; and the ubiquitous mosquito (of which there must be a good many species out of the 150 species which are known to exist in the world), the plague of one's nights—what aggravated torture and torment it is capable of inflicting!—then the hosts of grasshoppers of all sizes and modification of shape and habits, some tiny morsels about a quarter of an inch in length which walk sideways. What myriads there are of them all! Where do all these insects come from, and where do they all go? Is it any wonder with their ingenious habits, their wonderful adaptation to their surroundings, their marvellous instinct, their wondrous beauty—is it any wonder, with all these, that the Oriental has endowed them with immortality, and has given them a place in future stages of existence?

As to the insects which it is not considered polite to mention in respectable society, they also abound, and the Chinese appear to have no scruples in speaking of them, or in allowing them board and lodging free of expense, though they try to keep down over-population by a judicious thinning-out. The means employed to this end are not always pleasant to a squeamish taste, as the operation is carried on, especially by coolies and beggars, in the open street, the lowest classes using their teeth as the executioners, for the Chinese do not feel any shame at their persons being inhabited.

As to the Westerner in China, personal contact with these parasites is perhaps, if anything, less common even than in England, where a ride in a London 'bus may introduce one to a stray member of their community, *nolens volens*.

With the advance of medical science it has become more and more apparent that man has more to dread from insects, such as the mosquito, than the mere discomfort of its bite or its buzz; for it is well known that the mosquito spreads malaria. (See MOSQUITO.)

'Man . . . may become infected by drinking water contaminated by the mosquito, or, and much more frequently, by inhaling the dust of the mud of dried-up mosquito-haunted pools; or in some similar way.' 'The later researches of Surgeon Ross of the British army have not only proven that malaria can be acquired from a mosquito bite, but that the malaria parasite is mostly one of insects and only an occasional visitor to man. Particular species of malaria parasites even demand particular species of mosquitoes—a fact at least partly explaining apparent vagaries in the distribution of malaria. When all is known, Europeans may be able to live in climates now made deadly by this pest.'

Flies and other insects may likewise help to spread that awful disease the plague.

'One can understand . . . how lice, fleas, bugs, and perhaps flies may act as carriers of the virus from person to person, inserting it with their bites. Yersin found that the flies in his Hongkong plague laboratory died in great numbers, their bodies being crowded with the specific bacillus. Sablonowski . . . remarked that during the Mesopotamian epidemic (in 1884) a certain species of fly appeared and disappeared concurrently with the plague; he considered that this insect was an active agent in spreading the disease.'

'Mosquitoes infect water with the germs of the disease, to prevent it we have to keep the mosquitoes down, to prevent their preying on already infected individuals, or, and this is the simple plan, to keep them from getting access to our drinking water, or by boiling or filtration to kill the germs which our drinking water may contain.'

Nor is the deadly list complete of the dreaded diseases which this apparently harmless, though troublesome, insect, the mosquito, may disseminate, for elephantiasis is to be considered as another.

And now, still later, it has been discovered that the mosquito carries the germs of yellow fever.

References.—Donovan, *Natural History of the Insects of China;* Manson, *Tropical Diseases.*

ISINGLASS.—A large quantity of isinglass is consumed in China, under the name of fish-maws. It is used to make soups, and is an article of considerable export from Malaya. Chinese traders also send large quantities from the Straits to China.

'The isinglass or fish glue of the tariff is said to be made from the noses and sounds of a species of carp caught in the Ganges. This fish glue is prepared in thin, diaphanous sheets, which are used in water colours for porcelain painting, in giving a lustre and surface to silks, and in the manufacture of Indian ink; it has countless uses, but is not employed as an article of food. In addition to this import, a large quantity of clarified seaweed from Japan is also introduced into China and known by the name of isinglass. This is used entirely as an edible.'

Isinglass proper, however, which is manufactured from the dried air bladders of fish, is not imported into China.

Dennys gives the names of the following fish as furnishing this isinglass, *Arius arius, A. militarius, A. truncatus, Johnius dracanthus, Lates heptadactylus, Lobotes erate, Otholithus argenteus, Otolitus brauritus, Otholitus maculatus, O. ruber, Polynemus indicus.*

Reference.—Williams, *Commercial Guide.*

JADE.—The mineral held in the highest estimation in China is jade. Under the name yuk (pronounced yook in the South; in the North, *yü;* also called *pi yü,* or *fei ts'ui*) the Chinese not not only include 'the three varieties of the silicate of alumina called jade, nephrite, and jadeite by mineralogists,' but they also apply the same term to a number of different stones. Sonorousness and colour are the two qualities which enhance its value, the best coming from Khoten and Yünnan. It is also supplied to China by the Burmese mines, 'through Bhamo, which is the entrepôt for the trade.'

There are two kinds: nephrite and jadeite. The former is a silicate of calcium and magnesium, varying in colour according to the amount of iron it contains. Of this the Chinese distinguish nine kinds.

Jadeite is a silicate of aluminium and sodium. It is more translucent than nephrite. Jade is not now mined in China.

'A greenish-white colour is the most highly prized.' Williams gives the following description of jade:—

'Its colour is usually a greenish-white, or grayish-green and dark grass-green; internally it is scarcely glimmering. Its fracture is splintery; splinters white; mass semi-transparent and cloudy; it scratches glass strongly, and can itself generally be scratched by flint or quartz, but while not excessively hard, it is remakable for toughness. The stone when freshly broken is less hard than after a short exposure. Specific gravity from 2.9 to 3.1.'

The Chinese look upon jade as 'emblematical of most of the virtues'; and from the excessive admiration they have for it, it is natural that they should have largely used it in their ceremonious language; for instance, in addressing a man, his daughter is styled 'a jade girl,' his hand is 'a jade hand'; 'a jade foot' means his coming, or 'I hope you will transfer your jade' means 'I hope you will come.' etc.

It is the ambition of every girl and woman, amongst the Cantonese, to have a pair of jade-stone drops for her earrings, and a pair of jade-stone bangles for her arms. Failing the genuine article, imitation ones are worn. Long pins, six or eight inches in length, having from one to four inches of jade forming the upper part, are stuck into the hair of women; hair-presses, a curious kind of ornament holding up part of the coiffure; rings for women; large thumb-rings, an inch broad, for gentlemen; vases, sceptres—these and many other articles of jewellery, of ornament, and of *virtu*, are all made of this stone.

The jade-stone shops are amongst the neatest and finest-looking Chinese shops. The jade in its different shades, from rich green to white, as well as other specimens of precious stones, already made up into the ornaments so highly esteemed, are tastefully arranged on white paper in glass-covered boxes. Much labour and pains are taken in the production of these different articles, time being of little consequence to the Chinese lapidary, and expense being lavishly incurred by the moneyed man for their purchase, for the adornment of his wife, concubines, and numerous daughters, as well as for his own wear, and for seals and *bric-à-brac* of various kinds to be placed in the halls of his rambling mansion.

The Chinese, it is said, will not purchase jade brought from foreign countries. Williams says that a cargo load, brought from Australia, was rejected by the Cantonese, owing to its origin and colour. Giles says that 'whole shiploads of it have been brought from other countries to China, but have found no market, the Chinese declaring it was not the same article as their own.' It was thought at one time that jade was only to be found in three places: New Zealand, the northern slopes of the Karakorum mountains, and Northern Burma, but it has since been found *in situ* in Silesia, Monte Video, British Columbia, and Alaska. It also probably exists or existed somewhere in the Alps, as 'jade has often been found in the remains of Swiss lake dwellings,' which are supposed to be at least 3,000 years old, and it has also been found in Asia Minor, in Mexico, the West Indies, and South America—particularly in Venezuela and Brazil.

'The jade of Turkestan is largely derived from water-rolled boulders fished up by divers in the rivers of Khotan, but it is also got from mines, in the valley of the Karákásh River . . . The jade of Khotan appears to be first mentioned by Chinese authors in the time of the Han dynasty under Wuti (B.C. 140-86).'

References.—Bushell, *Chinese Art;* Laufer, *Jade.*

JEWS.—Considerable excitement was caused, a number of years since, by the discovery of a colony of these ancient people in the interior of China, in the city especially of K'aifung, a departmental city in the province of Honan. They are said to have established themselves in China in the Han dynasty (probably soon after the persecution in Babylon, A.D. 34), though there is great uncertainty as to the time of their arrival.

Several visits have been made to them in K'aifung-fú, and copies of Hebrew manuscript have been obtained from them, but 'no variations of any consequence have been found between the text of these rolls and that found in the printed Hebrew Bibles of Europe.' These manuscripts have been deposited in different institutions, such as the City Hall Library in Hongkong, the British Museum, and the Bodleian.

The descendants of this Jewish colony at K'aifung-fú have sunk into a state of ignorance and poverty; not one of them can read Hebrew; their synagogue is no longer in existence; no services are held; their creed has faded out; and in a few years the last traces of this Jewish community, of from two to four hundred souls, will probably be lost in the mass of their heathen and Mohammedan surroundings. This appears, since the above was written, to have become almost if not quite true.

Besides this colony of Jews in this distant land, others existed in different places. Amongst other cities in which communities of them lived were Ningpo and Peking. Tradition is credited with the statement that they settled in China 249 B.C., but it is thought that the more probable period was between A.D. 58 and A.D. 75. Their language consisted of a jargon of Hebrew and Chinese with a trace of Persian. What seems a more reliable supposition is that 'the first Jewish refugees are supposed to have reached China in company with the last Sassanian King of Persia, whose flight before the Caliph Othman is placed by Gibbon in A.D. 651.'

References.—Foster, *Christian Progress in China;* Williams, *Middle Kingdom;* Finn, *The Jews in China; The Orphan Colony of Jews in China; Facsimiles of the Hebrew Manuscripts obtained at the Jewish Synagogue in K'ae-Fung Foo;* Adler, *Chinese Jews;* Perlmann, *History of the Jews in China;* Smith, *The Jews at K'ai-fêng Fu; Chinese Repository,* Vol. xx; *Variétés Sinologiques,* Vol. xxvii.

JINRICKSHAS.—Though not used in the purely native parts of China, as a rule, yet these convenient vehicles are largely employed in several of the Treaty Ports, as well as in Hongkong, not only by Europeans, but also by Chinese. They have been described as a cross between a bath-chair and a hansom cab.

The Jinricksha (from *jén-li ch'ê,* 'man-power vehicle') is not a native invention. One account says an inventive American missionary in Japan produced the first one, while one of H.M. Consular Chaplains in Yokohama, Rev. M. B. Bailey, is credited with having originated what has now become the national vehicle of Japan.

They appear to have been introduced into the Shanghai foreign settlements from Japan, and some years later into Hongkong, where there are 500 or so. An attempt to introduce them into Peking in the early nineties was frustrated by the cart guilds, nominally because it was considered deregatory for a man to take the place of an animal, really because their interests were threatened. The streets of native cities are generally not of such a character as to suit vehicular traffic of any kind, and special roads would usually have to be prepared if it were inteded for them to run outside the foreign settlements. This has been done in Nanking where a good carriage road has been constructed by the viceroy, Chang Chih-tung, a great many houses having to be pulled down for it. A score of carriages and a thousand jinrickshas are running on it.

There are now (1924) seventy thousand in Peking, and they are to be seen in many other inland cities also. Generally, the ricksha coolies, except where under foreign administration, are a low, dirty, abusive class, who extort from the foreigner far more than is accepted from the native, any protest being met with vulgar abuse.

'The police in taking the annual registration of Peking rickshas [in 1924] announced that thirty-six thousand vehicles have been counted already, and it is estimated that on this basis, the total in the capital will reach seventy thousand. All but seven thousand of these rickshas belong to companies that lease them out to the coolies, who pay between twenty and thirty coppers per day hire.

It is estimated that ever two hundred thousand people are dependent upon the livelihood gained by these ricksha coolies, who average about a hundred coppers per day, out of which they have to pay the hiring fee to the owner. Thus, out of sixty or seventy coppers per day the coolies support themselves and dependents.

In commenting on the present condition of these ricksha coolies and the effect the tram car lines will have on them, the Chinese press states that less than five per cent. of the coolies ever get enough money saved up to set themselves up in trade. The others either die, every often of starvation, or turn criminals to keep themselves alive. Nevertheless, many farm labourers are attracted by the seemingly higher profits from pulling rickshas than working on the farms, and that has caused a labour shortage on the land, thereby raising the price of food, so that it in turn reacts on the poor people generally.

While the police have more or less strict regulations as to the pulling of rickshas by too young or too old men, they are generally allowed to lapse either for the purpose of increasing the tax collections or to help the person who needs the employment from which he would be barred by law. As a result many of these unfit coolies die from exertion.'

It must, however, be remembered that an aggregate very large amount of the fares paid to ricksha coolies is spent in gambling and prostitution.

Outside the foreign settlements and concessions there is no fixed tariff, and the charge thus becomes a matter of arrangement between the fare and the ricksha coolie, the latter invariably asking not what he knows would be a just amount, but, judging by the appearance of the former, what he thinks the latter is able to afford. Foreigners cannot make a contract of this sort, because the first demand is always from twice to five or ten times or more the proper fare; consequently there are often disputes when then destination is reached.

The Chinese are not such good ricksha coolies as the Japanese, who think nothing of drawing tandem a heavy man fifty miles in one day up and down hill; but still the Chinese, though not such swift runners or possessing such powers of endurance, make very fair ones.

To those who have not seen it, the ricksha may be described as a small two-wheeled vehicle, capable of seating one, or sometimes two, persons, with a pair of shafts, between which the coolie runs and drags the vehicle. Private ones have sometimes two or three coolies, the other one or two pushing from behind. They are fitted with hoods which can be raised or lowered at pleasure, and waterproofs to cover the legs are part of the outfit. The rates of hire in Hongkong are—quarter-hour, 5 cents.; half-hour, 10 cents.; and one hour, 15 cents. In Macao the fares are even less.

One enthusiast has proposed that they should be introduced into London. They are already half-way there, as their use has not only extended to Singapore, Ceylon, and India, but even to South Africa, where at 'Cape Town, Durban, and Pietermaritzburg they are well patronized, and are crowding out the cabs and public buggies. Kaffirs furnish the motive power.' They are even extending nearer Europe now.

JUNK.—A name applied by foreigners to the largest Chinese trading vessels. Its derivation is from the Portuguese *junco,* which was a corruption of the Malay *ajong,* abbreviated *jong,* a ship or large vessel. There is a tendency which has now become so established as to lead to the application of this name to all Chinese vessels above the size of boats, though this was not the original use of the word.

KINGFISHER.—There are three varieties of this bird in the colony of Hongkong: one the black cap, one white-breasted, and another beautifully coloured one. They are frequently to be seen in various parts of China. The kingfisher feather jewellery is made from the back feather of the common kingfisher (*alcedo bengalensis*). The black-capped variety (*halcyon* *pileata*) is found in summer all over China, and a rare kind, *alcedo grandis*, in Hainan.

KITES.—China is *par excellence* the land of kites. They are not relegated here to youthful hands alone and considered as simply childish toys; they are looked upon as fit for children of an older growth—not scientific apparatus a Benjamin Franklin might employ to bring the lightning down from the skies, or such as aeronauts used for experiments in attempting to solve the problem of a flying machine, or for meteorological purposes; but as simple objects to amuse themselves with.

With this higher view taken of kite-flying, it is natural that more pains should be employed in the construction of kites and more ingenuity in their design than is usually the case with us.

The convenient bamboo in its natural growth of different sizes, tubular and light, easily split, should the whole stick be too large, and almost as easily bent into circles, strong, yet flexible—seems specially adapted for the framework, be the kite a crude and conventional imitation of a bird to amuse a child (for the pastime of kite-flying is not entirely monopolised by those of maturer years in China), or be it a wonderful structure, the joy and admiration of not only its owner, but of a gaping crowd and of the whole neighbourhood. The framework is covered with paper and silk, but no Chinese would think of using old newspapers for such a purpose: any unwanted written or printed paper is reverently burned. Such importance do the Chinese attach to this that men perambulate the streets for the express purpose of rescuing any scraps of such paper from being trodden under foot, little wooden boxes are also stuck up on the walls to receive anything of that nature thrust into them.

But to return to kites—so lifelike are some of them made, and so well does the trained hand manipulate them (or rather their strings) in their tethered flight that the simulated hovering of a bird of prey in the air is good enough to deceive, at first sight, even a naturalist. It has well been said that 'the skill shown in flying them is more remarkable than the ingenuity displayed in their construction.' Butterflies, lizards, gigantic centipedes, a pair of spectacles, a huge cash, fish, men, and many other objects may be seen disporting themselves in mid-air, while at the other end of the strings will be found young men, or even middle-aged ones perchance, gravely enjoying themselves, and a group of boys watching them and doubtless wishing they had grown old enough to fly such beauties of kites. A mimic game of warfare is also played, the flyer of one kite endeavouring to capture that of another by entangling the strings.

The festival on which kite-flying is indulged in largely is the ninth day of the ninth moon, and this throughout China.

'Doolittle describes them [the kites] as sometimes resembling a great bird, or a serpent thirty feet long; at other times the spectator sees a group of hawks hovering round a centre, all being suspended by one strong cord, and each hawk-kite controlled and moved by a separate line. On this day he estimates that as many as thirty thousand people assemble on the hills around Foochow to join in this amusement if the weather be propitious.'

A delightful concomitant to the kite in Chinese eyes, or rather ears, is a small contrivance which is so placed that the wind rushing through it produces a humming sound.

We wonder if there is anything in China which is not connected with their religion in some way or other, even the thieves and prostitutes have their deities whom they devoutly pray to for success and protection. What wonder then that the innocent kite is often used as a species of scapegoat, as with string deliberately cut for that purpose, it floats on its downward erratic flight, freighted with an imaginary load of disasters, thus carried away from those who otherwise would bear the weight of ills unknown and dreaded. With such a simple expedient to get rid of the dark to-morrow, who need be unhappy even in wretched China?

LACQUER-WARE.—M. Paléologue, in his admirable work on 'L'Art Chinois,' while giving full credit to the perfection to which the Japanese, originally the scholars of the Chinese, have carried this art 'une perfection que les Chinois n'ont jamais égalée,' says further:—'Mais, pour relever d'un art moins élevé et d'une technique moins parfaite, les laques Chinois comptent quelques spécimens qui sont remarquables par la qualité de la matière, par la douceur des tons, par la puissance de la composition, par la largeur et la sévérité du style.'

The lacquer is originally a resinous gum obtained from the lac or varnish tree (*Rhus vernicifera*), cultivated both in China and Japan for the purpose. Its foliage and bark resemble the ash; it grows to a height of fifteen or twenty feet; and at the age of seven years furnishes the sap, which is collected in July and August from incisions made in the trunk of the tree near the foot. These incisions are made at night, the sap being collected in the morning. Twenty pounds from one thousand trees in the course of a night is a good yield. The lacquer sap is of a very irritating nature, especially to some constitutions; and the Chinese, when preparing it in cakes to enclose in tubs to send to the market, take the precaution to cover up their faces and hands to prevent contact with it. Lacquer 'in any stage, except when perfectly dry, is capable of producing' the following symptoms:—'Blood to the head, swelling, violent itching and burning, and occasionally small festering boils.'

The best kind of sap is of a tawny or dark-brown colour when in its inspissated state, and tarred paper is used to protect it from the air, but all lacquer turns jetblack on exposure to the light. Other ingredients are added, as wood-oils obtained from plants such as *Augia sinensis* and others. These, combined with the *Rhus vernicifera,* form the different qualities of lacquer-ware. Sz-chuen [Ssŭch'uan], Hunan, and Kuangsi, produced the finest.

The preparation, of the best qualities especially, takes a long time, and one reason assigned for the deterioration in quality supplied to the foreign market in China is the ignorance, or ignoring, of this fact by Europeans, who, when giving orders, will not wait the necessary time for producing a first-class article; and the Chinese manufacturer, from being forced to supply the articles required at short notice, has got into the way of producing inferior workmanship, which meet with as ready a sale amongst the uneducated in the mysteries of lacquer as the better specimens did.

The varnish is prepared for use by the addition of oil of the *Vernicia montana* or *Camellia oleifera,* sulphate of iron, and rice vinegar; these ingredients vary according to the condition and transparency required. Different tints are given to the lacquer, likewise, by the introduction of different substances, such as pig's gall and vegetable oil, ivory black, animal charcoal, and tea oil.

The wood to be varnished is first planed and polished, the the joints are stuffed with a kind of fine oakum, narrow slips of paper are pasted over them, and fine paper, or thin silken material is put over the whole surface. A mixture of emery powder, red sandstone, vermillion, or of gamboge, and of cow's gall, is then applied with a hard brush, and when dried in the air it is polished with sandstone, pumice-stone, and powdered charcoal.

This double operation is repeated several times. The preliminary work, which takes several weeks to accomplish, forms the foundation for the lacquer, which is applied in a room closed on all sides from wind and dust. A very fine, flat brush is used to apply a light and very equal film of it. The drying room next receives the article, or articles; here the atmosphere must be fresh and damp, for it is under such conditions that the lacquer dries most quickly. It next receives a polishing with a kind of soft schist. Each layer of lacquer is subjected to the same slow and minute operations: the least number of layers applied is three, the most eighteen.

The ornamentation of figures, flowers, and gilding, etc., is done in more than one way:—

'The gilding is performed by another set of workmen in a large warkshop. The figures of the design are drawn on thick paper, which is then pricked all over to allow the powdered chalk to fall on the table and form the outline. Another workman completes the picture by cutting the lines with a burin or needle, and filling them with vermilion mixed in lacquer, as thick as needed. This afterwards is covered, by means of a hair-pencil, with gold in leaf or in powder laid on with a dossil; the gold is often mixed with fine lamp-black.'

'Quand, sur le fond uni de laque, l'ouvrier veut peindre un d'écor, personnages, fleurs, arabesques, etc., il esquisse directement au blanc de céruse le sujet qu'il va traiter, ou bien encore il le décalque en suivant avec une pointe de bois les lignes de son dessin, sur lesquelles il a préalablement passé, au verso de la feuille de papier, un trait d'orpiment liquide. Il commence alors á peindre sur ce croquis avec les coleurs dont dispose sa riche palette.'

Much skill, dexterity, lightness of finger, and long practice are necessary to ensure that fineness and requisite delicacy, which at the first touch will produce the effect desired without repetition, for this last is not allowed, the gummy consistency of the lacquer likewise forbidding it; notwithstanding all these difficulties, some of the lacquer produced by the Chinese is characterised by distinctness of line and a freedom of composition.

Besides gold and silver spangles, incrustations of ivory, mother-of-pearl, jade, coral, malachite, and lapis lazuli, are employed in the ornamentation of lacquer-ware, rough mosaics of flowers, animals, etc., being formed of them, and then varnished.

Foochow lacquer equals the Japanese; the latter people, it is said, having taught their original teachers, the Chinese, the production of this superior quality. Some fine specimens also come from Ningpo, and command a very high price. In Foochow a special kind of vases, etc., is made consisting of a background of canvas on which the lacquer is spread, giving the article a surprising lightness when lifted up.

Carved lacquer is either not now (during the present century) made, or but little is produced, as it requires great labour, rendering its production too expensive. Its mode of preparation is as follows:—A dark paste is made of *Urtica nivea*, of 'papier de *broussonetia*,' and egg-shells; these are beaten together, pounded, and camellia oil added to thicken them. After being applied to the wood and becoming perfectly dry, it is carved by the artist, who requires a firm hand, as no repetition is possible. Several coats of red varnish, the composition of which is unknown, are afterwards applied. The defect, to a European eye, in this style of lacquer is the overburdening of the decoration with entangled dragons, phœnixes, the lotus, etc.

There are no names of Chinese artists to mention as in the case of the same art in Japan. In China it is not the individual that is to be noted, but the schools, differentiated by style, tradition, and tendency. At present, at all events, but little has been discovered of the history of the art. Carved lacquer was known during the early part of the Christian era, though no very ancient specimens are extant, the oldest being of the comparatively modern date of the end of the sixteenth century (Ming dynasty). 'Les laques sculptés de cette époque sont fort rares, et les Chinois les estiment à très haut prix: le vernis en est très épais, le travail en est ferme, d'un style sobre et sévère.'

Great improvement was effected in the reign of the Emperor K'ang Hsi (A.D. 1662-1723) of the present dynasty, both in quality of material and decoration; and in Ch'ien Lung's time (A.D. 1736-1796) some fine carved lacquer was produced, as also some exquisite specimens of other lacquer, the best of these being made in the imperial manufactories. We cannot resist the temptation to quote once more from M. Paléologue's interesting work, 'L'Art Chinois,' as to the last:—

'M. de Semallé possède une dizaine de pièces ayant, sans aucun doute, cette origine; ce sont des coupes formulées en calices lobés, légères à la main et delicatement modelées: l'une est d'un bleu paon à reflets verts, chatoyant et intense comme un émail; une autre est d'un rose très pâle que rehausse un rose de corail, et l'ensemble est d'une douceur de tons incomparable; une autre encore est d'un noir uni et profond, de ce beau noir si apprécié des Japonais; signalons enfin, dans la même collection, un laque aventuriné, à incrusatations d'or et d'argent figurant des lotus, qui est une merveille de goût et de finesse. Ces pièces comptent à nos yeux pami les rares objets de laque chinoise peinte qui mériteraient de figurer dans la collection d'un amateur au Japon.'

Generally, there are two chief kinds of lacquer, the painted (from Canton and Foochow), and the carved (from Peking and Soochow). Both kinds are sometimes inlaid with precious stones or mother-of-pearl. The art has declined since its culmination in the middle of the eighteenth century.

References.—Paléologue, *L'Art Chinois;* Williams, *Middle Kingdom;* Bushell, *Chinese Art.*

LANGUAGE.—As the Chinese have been outside the comity of nations, so their language has been relegated to a position of its own with no certain relationship to the other speeches of mankind; and as the exclusiveness of the nation is being slowly broken down, so it is to be hoped that, before long, in response to the toil of not a few scholars, the affinity of Chinese with that of other languages in the world will be more clearly established and the wall of partition separating it from the others be a thing of the past. Most divergent views have been held on the subject and clearly proved to the satisfaction of those who held and advanced them, but not to the equal satisfaction of their readers.

There would appear to be some connection between Chinese and the so-called Aryan languages; to prove this Edkins, Schlegel, and others, have laboured. The idea of the late Professor Terrien de Lacouperie, and his co-labourers in the same field, was that of an affinity between the languages of China and Babylon. These views still await general acceptance, the feeling of many being one of suspense: a waiting till convincing proofs are produced before acquiescing in any of the theories put forth; there are still immense fields for the patient worker to explore.

The connection between Chinese and the languages of some of the surrounding nations is deserving of further attention, in order to fix with a greater amount of certainty the relationships which exist between certain of them.

Some people go so far as to say that Chinese has no grammar. If grammar only consisted of declension and inflection, such a statement might be true; but the Chinese most cleverly use the relative position of words to express what we, to a great extent, and some continental nations to a greater, and the dead languages of Europe to the greatest extent, show by case, mood, tense, number, and person: position is everything in the construction of Chinese sentences, and does away with those troubles of school-boys, carried to such an excess in the classical languages.

In addition to position, the use of auxiliary characters is employed, and, in the written language especially, a general symmetry of construction, and use of words in sentences and clauses, which are either in antithesis or juxtaposition to each other, assists materially in the correct development of ideas.

Chinese is one of the simplest, while at the same time one of the most difficult, languages in the world: most simple from the almost entire absence of these inflectional forms; most difficult from the combination of different languages under the one heading of Chinese; such for instance as the book language in its two or three different forms, the Colloquial or spoken language in its different vernaculars, and in its tones, the bugbear of most European readers and speakers of it.

The Chinese have spent much time and labour in the cultivation of their wonderful and interesting language. The Shu King [*Shu ching*] mentions writing as being practised in the time of Shun (2255-2205 B.C.). Some doubt, however, has been cast on the genuineness of these passages in the Shu.

There is no doubt that writing was in use a little later, in connection with Government matters, and in the Chou dynasty it was in common use among the official class. Colleges and schools existed, books were made and libraries formed. Writing was a laborious task, the language at this early period not having attained the rich collection of written characters it now possesses. The nucleus or prototype of the first Chinese dictionary, the Urh-ya [*Erh-ya*], is referable to this period.

The violent attempt of the execrated monarch Ts'in Shih Huang Ti to introduce one language throughout China, by destroying all trace of the past, was unsuccessful. It was about this time that the transition from the mainly pictorial or symbolic representation of the language took place, and more attention was paid to sound.

The period of the Han dynasty, or from 206 B.C. to A.D. 221, witnessed the commencement of the study of the language, its exciting cause being the elucidation and determination of the characters of the books which had escaped the wholesale destruction. Many of the works of the renowned scholars of these ancient times have disappeared during the lapse of ages. Amongst two to be noted as still extant are the Fang-yen, a comparative vocabulary of dialectic varieties, and the Shuo-wên, an etymological dictionary (A.D. 121), which dealt with the writing of the character. The language at this period 'acquired a considerable degree of exactness and polish,' and many additions were made to the characters in use. The Buddhist missionaries about this time also assisted in bringing into general future use the spelling now in vogue to explain the pronunciation of words.

During the troublous times even of the Three States some sensible men busied themselves with the cultivation of the native tongue. An epoch is marked in this cultivation, in the period known as the Northern and Southern Dynasties, or from A.D. 420-589; and the study of etymology began to flourish. The four tones were first noticed in published works, though doubtless previously known to scholars. The Sui dynasty (A.D. 589-

618) still saw much attention paid to tones and the sounds of characters. The tones are accentuated modulations of the voice by which words of different meaning but of the same phonetic value are distinguished from one another. Their number has varied at different times and in different parts of the country, their tendency being to diminish. In some of the southern dialects there are now nine, and in the Peking dialect four. The T'ang dynasty (A.D. 618-907) gave an impetus to this study so congenial to the Chinese nature. The Emperors encouraged learning, and even cultivated it themselves. Renewed enthusiasm was shown in the study of the classics: much learning and ability were displayed; the tones and sounds of characters received much attention; and acquaintance with such subjects was required from the competitors for government employment. Books were also written on Sanscrit grammar and its alphabet by Indian Buddhist missionaries, or Chinese monks who had studied the language in India, and the knowledge thus acquired was of use to native authors in the study of their own language. 'In several respects the period of the T'ang dynasty forms an era of great importance in the history of the cultivation of the language. It was the time in which China began to have a popular literature. . . . Plays also now began to be written and performed, and romances to be *composed in a style often but little removed from that of every-day conversation.*' This fixed the style and made fashionable the dialect—the Mandarin—in which they were written. Printing was first invented at this time in China, though it was not till succeeding dynasties that it exerted its full power.

It is under the Sung dynasty that the language 'is supposed to have reached its acme; to have become complete in all its formal and material equipment, having everything needful to make it an effective instrument for expressing the national mind'; and works on philology of great and permanent value were produced.

About the time that the Mongols prevailed, a book was published which has been rendered into English under the title of 'The Six Scripts.'

'The founder of the Ming dynasty (A.D. 1368-1399) was a patron of all kinds of learning, and promoted efforts to recover and preserve the valuable treatises which had been lost, or become very rare.' One of the most widely used works, and the standard dictionary, of the present time, is the K'ang Hsi dictionary, prepared by direction of the Emperor of that name. A revived interest was taken during the eighteenth and nineteenth centuries in the philological works of antiquity.

Language

The Chinese, as far as at present has been ascertained, have confined their studies nearly entirely to 'sounds, meanings, composition, and history of the written characters'; and the study is not generally pursued for its own sake, but for the purpose of elucidating the 'orthodox canonical literature.'

'The Chinese language is very rich in . . . nature sounds and "vocal-gestures"'; while the interjectional element appears to have had its full share in the formation of some portion of the language. Many of the words and terms in use are imitative of sounds in nature, of noises of falling objects, of calls and cries of animals, birds, and insects; and of actions by man himself; these have all had their share, and still have, in forming the language.

On the whole, the Chinese, however, take comparatively little interest in such researches. The Buddhist missionaries, who introduced Buddhism, did a good work, first, in interesting the Chinese in Sanscrit with its alphabet and grammatical forms, and, secondly, in inducing a study among the Chinese of their own language, leading them to examine and appreciate it.

The Chinese consider the faculty of speech to be man's natural endowment: expressive sounds are uttered by the promptings of nature; but as to the development of speech, they believe that the most highly endowed men have been its nursing fathers.

It would be highly instructive and interesting were a history of the rise, development, and progress of the Chinese language down to the present time possible. The materials seem at present to be fragmentary. Doubtless with the combined study of numerous scholars, much more may be known of it than at present. The Chinese language retains, to a great extent, the primitive simplicity of early speech; and this is what makes it of advantage to the student to attempt to peer into its past depths, and to study its present state.

The Manchu, Mongolian, and Turkish tongues are descended from one source, and this parent language may likewise have been the progenitor of the Chinese, in common with that of these other languages.

The speech of the Chinese was preceded in China by numerous dialects and languages of what are termed the Aborigines. It seems impossible not to suppose that these former speeches must have had some effect on the language of the new-comers, though, if a policy of extermination was adopted towards the former inhabitants, that effect would not be much. Traces are now found in some of the so-called Chinese dialects of relics of some of these former languages. In the Amoy language, a few words are instanced as being remnants of a previous race, the same is supposed to be the case in the Swatow language, and in Cantonese also a word or two is spoken of as being thus taken over into the present language.

The Chinese language would appear, at first sight, to be, like the Chinese themselves, separated from the rest of the world and self-contained; though this is true to a great extent of the people as regards their communication with Western nations, yet it must not be forgotten that there has been considerable intercourse between China and the countries whose borders are conterminous with her own; and so, instead of the language having no admixture of foreign words in it, some such words are to be found. These words of foreign origin are generally of a technical character: names of countries, official designations, names of fruits, spices, woods, reminiscences of foreign intercourse, conquest, and commerce. The use of these words has not been confined to modern times, but imbedded in the language are found a few fossil remains—relics of ancient foreign relations or wars, now well-known matters of history. These words are met with here and there in books and in conversation; for example, to take a modern one, Ho-lán-shöü [*Holan shui*], or Holland water=soda water, because it was first introduced by the Dutch.

Buddhism has introduced in its train many words into Chinese. They consist of Sanscrit words brought into the language, translations into Chinese of such Sanscrit words, and new phrases in Chinese due to Buddhism, but not translations of Sanscrit words or terms. This religion has also given new meanings to words and phrases which were in use before.

The Han, T'ang, and Manchu dynasties, especially increased China's knowledge of the outside world, while other periods even bore their share, though a smaller one, in exchange for the arts of peace, and at times for the horrors of war, with the neighbouring states of Japan and India; even distant Persia, as well as many other kingdoms, too numerous to mention, all being known to a greater or lesser extent; and, latterly especially, the countries of Europe have come within the horizon of Chinese ken. It is not surprising therefore to find a small amount of terms derived from the languages of some of these countries. 'Certain terms even in a comparatively early period of the Chinese language . . . seem to have at least a common origin with their equivalents in Greek and Latin'; Spanish, English, Malay, Persian, Arabic, Turkish, Manchu, Mongolian, Tibetan, as well as Sanscrit and other Indian languages, have each assisted in giving new words in the past, while with the advance of science and learning this must be more especially the case in time to come. Of recent years, many Japanese idioms and expressions have also been introduced. But after all that can be said, these foreign words form but a very small proportion of the whole.

The language of China may be divided as follows:—

1. The ancient style in which the classics are written; sententious, concise, vague, and often unintelligible without explanation.

2. The literary style: more diffuse, and consequently more intelligible; it might be described as poetry written in prose on account of a '*rhythmus*,' as it has been termed, in which it is written, the ancient language having less of this—both forms having a number of particles either difficult or impossible of translation into English. The essays written by candidates at the literary examinations were composed in this style.

3. The business style which is plain enough to be intelligible: it is prose without, or with but little of, the poetry element, and few, if any, of the troublesome particles. It is in general use for commercial purposes, legal documents, official and business correspondence, and governmental, statistical, and legal works are written in it.

4.—The Colloquial, or the spoken languages. They are divided into numerous dialects (see DIALECTS), but unfortunately they are despised—there is scarcely even one book written in them in the South of China, and yet it is impossible to speak in any other language; and to the great majority of the lower classes, no other is intelligible in its entirety. When we learn to speak a Western language, we nearly always learn consequently to read it; but a knowledge of Chinese, as spoken, only places one on the threshold of the Chinese of books. This has not inaptly been compared to a man who knows French fluently, but who, if he wishes to read Latin, has, after his knowledge of French, to apply himself to Latin; the French in this instance being the colloquial and the Latin the language of the book. Again, let us suppose the ancient language, as compared with the business style, to be that of the English of Chaucer as compared with that of the modern writer.

The difference between the book style and the colloquial might be likened perhaps to the difference between a common English book and some highly scientific or technical work so bristling with scientific terms, or technical expressions, or mathematical formulæ, that it would be entirely, or nearly entirely, incomprehensible, except to one who had been specially educated for years, making such a subject a speciality. This way of putting the matter may throw some light on what seems such a mysterious matter to English-speaking people, and show how difficult of comprehension the book language is to all except those who have received a special and sufficient training.

One well known Chinese scholar, at least, now advocates the use of the colloquial in books, and abandonment of the old book language. To those who know, and appreciate the beauty and value of, the book language this would seem to be an unnecessary act of iconoclasm. Books and newspapers could be written in the colloquial for those who do not understand the book language,—as many, in fact, are,—but to make the scholar write his books in the "vulgar tongue" would surely be a retrogressive step.

Writers on the Chinese have differed as to the richness, or otherwise, of the language. Putting aside all prejudiced statements, it may fairly be affirmed that in some respects its vocabulary is very full, where some of our languages are poor, and *vice versâ*. The Chinese have no difficulty in expressing themselves so as to be understood by their own countrymen and others, though Europeans and Americans have not sometimes the patience to make the good listeners which the want of mood, tense, and all inflections occasionally requires in order to get at the meaning.

On the other hand, the statements are often more concisely expressed than is the case in the general run of European languages. What strikes a foreigner as strange in the language, is the ease with which a word does duty as a noun, or verb, an adjective, adverb, or preposition. Marshman says: 'A Chinese character may in general be considered as conveying an idea without reference to any part of speech: and its being used as a substantive, an adjective, or a verb depends on circumstances.'

References.—Watters, *Essays on the Chinese Language;* Chalmers, *The Structure of Chinese Characters;* Chalfant, *Ancient Chinese Writing.* There are chapters on language in standard works, such as Williams' *Middle Kingdom,* Parker's *China,* etc.

LARKS AND OTHER SONGSTERS.—The lark is one of the most prized of song-birds among the Chinese. Their fondness for birds and flowers, as Williams has well noted, being 'one of the pleasant features of Chinese character.' No Chinese gentleman, at least in the South of China, takes a dog out to walk with him; but on a fine day numbers may be seen with a lark in a cage in the outskirts of a town, or sauntering leisurely along the streets, or standing in some square, or squatting on their haunches on some green spot, while their favourite bird enjoys himself, occasionally even with a little ramble on the grass. His master *cum dignitate* gravely taking his pleasure in watching his pet, or even unbending so far as to occupy himself with the pursuit of grasshoppers amongst the turf, though more frequently such a hunt is left to the boys or to the wretched grasshopper hunters, who, armed with a bunch of twigs and tiny baskets to hold their victims, from dewy morn till darkest twilight, wander up and down the hills, beating every tuft of grass for the active, springing, startled insects, which, when caught, they sell for a cash or two apiece, to the bird shops or bird-fanciers; their ultimate fate, of course, to be gobbled up by pet birds. Chinese houses are so often, in cities especially, shut out from the breezes, that it must be a positive pleasure to these active songsters to get such airings; but caged up as they are in close and narrow streets they may often be heard pouring out their melodious sonnets from the purlieus of some confined shop, trying in shrillest notes a musical contest with some imprisoned neighbour—such emulation is there that they get almost frantic at times.

The lark's cage is round, made of neatly rounded splints of bamboo, and varnished brown, with a removable bottom sprinkled with sand and furnished with a perch, in shape like a large mushroom, the Chinese evidently knowing that the lark does not alight on twigs or branches.

Williams informs us that 'the species of wagtail and lark known amount to about a score altogether.' Amongst them may be noted the field lark (*Alauda cœlivox and arvensis*). Large numbers of Chihli larks are brought down every year to the South of China, where they are preferred. The Mongolian lark commands a high price—$25 being a common figure for a good one; it is called the *pák ling* [*pai ling*], or 'hundred spirits.' Various species and sub-species are found in North, Mid, and South China and Formosa at different seasons, some migrating from Mongolia at the beginning of winter and returning in the spring.

Next in importance, if not in equal favour, as a songster is the thrush. Amongst the most common in the neighbourhood of Canton is the *wá méi* [*hua mei*], a greyish-yellow thrush (*Garrulax perspicitatus*), a 'well-trained bird is worth several dollars.' The spectacle thrush derives his name from a black circle round each eye; it is very graceful and lively, though not a very sweet singer. Another thrush (*Suthoria webbiana*) is kept for fighting—death or victory being its song. Of many members of the sub-family of thrushes *Merula naumanni* is probably the one most commonly met with in China, especially in the north and west. In Peking in the winter it is seen everywhere; in summer it retreats to Manchuria and Siberia. This and the abundant *Merula fuscata,* the Dusky Ouzel, are often found in company.

The canary is a great favourite, large numbers being reared and even exported as far as England. Its colour is not only yellow but some seem to display a tendency to revert to the dusky hue of the original bird in the Canary Islands. It is commonly known as the white swallow, its usual light yellow, or canary colour, being a near enough approach to white to satisfy the Chinese philologist. The canary is generally kept in a round cage made of bamboo and varnished, with a removable bottom and perches of twigs. The cage is rather larger than the English wire canary cage, but smaller than the Chinese bird-cage used for larks. Besides this cage very neat canary cages of the same materials are made in imitation of houses and boats, as well as large squarish cages of unvarnished bamboo, these last being especially useful for breeding purposes.

The prices of canaries vary with the season of the year. In Hongkong about 70 cents is an ordinary price charged for one to a European. It is said that large numbers of canaries are sent to China every year from Germany.

Many other birds, some of which might fairly be entitled to the name of songsters, as well as others which can only boast of one or two notes, are kept as pets by the Chinese.

References.—Journal N.C.B.R.A.S., O.S. No. III; David et Oustalet, *Les Oiseaux ,de la China.* See also a comprehensive bibliography in Couling, *Encyclopaedia Sinica,* under "Ornithology."

LAWS.—It has been observed that:—

'The laws of a nation form the most interesting portion of its history.' 'The laws of the Chinese, if taken in the most comprehensive sense of the term, framed, as they have been, by the wisdom and experience of a long series of ages, and suitably provided as they are for the government of an empire, unparalleled in the history of the world in extent and population, must, it will readily be imagined, be proportionally numerous and complicated. They are also, which is still more embarrassing, generally intermingled in such a degree with details, concerning the ancient history and actual condition of the civil, political, and ceremonial institutions of the empire, that individual works on these subjects are sometimes extended to the enormous length of a hundred volumes, and the aggregate is, of course, enormous in proportion.'

The Chinese code of penal laws has been described as, 'if not the most just and equitable, at least the most comprehensive, uniform, and suited to the genius of the people for whom it is designed, perhaps of any that ever existed.'

'The civil and military establishments, the public revenue and expenditure, the national rites and ceremonies, the public works, and the administration of justice, are, each of them.

regulated by a particular code of laws and institutions; but the laws of the empire in the strictest and most appropriate sense of the term, and which may be denominated Penal Laws by way of contradistinction, are the peculiar and exclusive province of the last of these departments.'

The Chinese, as in nearly everything of importance that concerns their commonwealth, carry back the first promulgation of their system of laws to a remote antiquity, namely, the time of Yao (2357-2255 B.C.) and his successor Shun, though according to their account of that sovereign (Yao), there would appear to have been but little need of any repressive legislation; for his rule was the *beau ideal* of perfect government in China—a state of almost perfect blessedness due to the virtues of the ruler or official, for such an one by his conduct and precepts changes the thief into an honest man, and produces such a state of security, that a bag of money, dropped by the wayside, will be left untouched or carefully put in a place of safety till the return of the loser. Yet, notwithstanding the resplendent virtues of these early monarchs, the second, Shun, is credited with having established the following five punishments:—Branding on the forehead, cutting off part of the nose and feet, castration, and death. So innocent and virtuous, however, were the people at that period, that many centuries are said to have passed before it was necessary to enforce them. This traditional high state of civilization is, however, irreconcilable with the prevalence of crime, dishonesty, etc., elsewhere recorded.

Each change of dynasty in China may be compared to a new geological period, for, notwithstanding the entire dissolution of the government and abrogation of the constitution established by the preceding dynasty, yet, as in the deposit of new strata, the same general conditions and principles are adhered to in the formation, or laying down of the new laws, a new code being generally made with each successive change of family on the throne. That in use during the late Manchu dynasty came into force when the Manchu Tartars assumed the rule over China; but, to use again the same illustration as above, imbedded in this new code, as in the newer geological strata, are to be found remains of antiquity; and, if a minute investigation be substituted for a cursory survey, it will be found, as in the material forming the later deposits on the earth's surface, that the mass of the laws are of the same stuff and substance as the more ancient ones, codified and altered in conformity with the changed conditions of time and life, some of the older forms dying out, and more recent enactments, necessitated by the progress of events, giving fresh life and vigour to the whole. The advent of written laws was supposed to denote decay of government, but by 650 B.C. codes began to appear. The earliest were engraved on iron tripods.

The first regular code of penal laws to have any permanent influence is attributed to Li-kwai [Li K'uei], fourth century B.C. It is described as ' simple in its arrangement and construction, having been confined to six books only, two of which appear to have been introductory and treating of practice, the third relative to prisons, the fourth to the administration of the police, the fifth to the lesser or miscellaneous offences, and the sixth to all the great and capital offences against public justice.' This code is supposed to have come into operation under the Ts'in [Ch'in] dynasty in 255 B.C. Though codified at this period, the principal characteristics belong to a remoter antiquity. Alterations and enlargements took place with the advent of each successive dynasty, both in the plan and divisions of the code, viz.:—under the Han, Ts'in [Ch'in], T'ang, Sung, Yüan, Ming, and some of the lesser dynasties, and the latest, under the Ts'ing, or Ch'ing. The laws of latter times are referred to at the end of this article.

As in European codes, the building up of new material on an old structure, and in conformity with an antiquated plan, instead of pulling down and rebuilding on a new scheme better adapted for the requirements of an altered and progressive state of society, gives rise to ambiguity, confusion, complications, intricacies, and inconveniences. The artificial and complex construction of the Manchu code (*Ta Ch'ing lü li*) was another cause of obscurity. It is not to be supposed that all those principles, some of which are excellent, contained in our English system of laws, the result of many years of a progressive struggle towards the attainment of justice, and the outcome of a different system of life and its surroundings, will be found in a body of laws produced under such different conditions. Yet, on the whole, the Chinese Penal Code was admirably adapted to the requirements of its teeming population of law-abiding subjects, taking into consideration the great difference in the fundamental principles on which the superstructure was founded.

The parental authority is clearly seen as one of the great conditioning causes in operation from remote times to the present. From the small circle of the family of a few individuals it spreads in ever-widening circles to the clan, composed of the aggregate of many families, and reaches its final limits in the Government which is based upon the same principle, that of parental authority; and to this principle is doubtless due, in union with some others, the conservative and preserving force, which has, amidst, and in spite of, many heterogeneous elements, knit the Chinese people together as one through so many past ages; and which still preserves its unifying power, and may for countless generations to come.

The following extract from a Chinese newspaper, published in the colony of Hongkong, viz., *The Chung Ngoi San Po*, will give some idea of what process of law entails in China:—

'Governor Luk Chuen-lam has given instructions to the Magistrates of Nam-hoi and Pun-yü districts that they are not to detain people connected with the cases brought before them, whether the prosecutor or prosecuted, except in cases of emergency. The order is warmly appreciated by all the Chinese, for the detention of people in the yamêns, pending the investigation of the cases concerned, afforded chances to the yamên people to make their squeezes, and it is a fact that the Chinese are willing to stand any amount of suffering rather than present themselves before the mandarins to be maltreated and squeezed by the yamên people, who do not receive any wages from the mandarins and simply watch for chances of squeezing. People ordered to be detained by the Magistrate in the yamên are kept under the custody of the yamên people, who lock them up in exceedingly dirty rooms, . . . giving them no food and no bedding until their friends and relatives come forward amply to bribe the custodians. Sometimes a person is detained in the yamên for many years, although the case may be only a minor one, if there is no influential Shan-sz to stand bail, which bail is represented by influence and not by money. It is not uncommon for the Chinese successfully to bribe the yamên runners not to take them before the Magistrate if a warrant is issued for their arrest.'

The prisoner, whether he may turn out to be innocent or guilty, is not treated with that tenderness incident to our twentieth-century civilisation: every effort is not made to prove his innocence, if possible, and points are not strained in his favour, which would be dropped if against him. The Chinese law would appear to be better adapted to ensure the punishment of a greater number of guilty persons than the English law; but it is probable that occasionally an innocent person is caught in its meshes, and, unable to escape, is punished; but English law is not free from this defect, even when such a sacred thing as human life is at stake. There is no doubt that, notwithstanding misfortune overtaking a few innocent ones in China, the well-being of the mass, on the whole, is better conserved than in a system where sentiment is apt to get the upper hand. This for the moment leaving out of sight the universal bribery and corruption prevalent and the infliction of torture (only recently abolished by law).

The English principles of a man being considered innocent till proved guilty, and of no man criminating himself, are unknown; but on the other hand, a prisoner was always required to confess before he could be punished; for no criminal case was complete without this confession. Unfortunately, however, the utility of this safeguard was somewhat, if not entirely, nullified by the introduction of torture, if necessary, to induce confession. The application of this necessarily depended a good deal upon the character of the official within whose power the criminal chanced to be. A cursory examination of the penal code might lead one to infer that corporal punishment, and, as a consequence, torture was universal; but, before arriving at such a hasty conclusion, several things which have a tendency to modify such a decision have to be considered:—In the first place, the Chinese should be compared with other Asiatic nations, whose punishments will often be found to be of a most ferocious character. Viewed under such circumstances, the use of torture to extract the truth does not seem so awful for an Eastern people; it must also be remembered that it is only a few centuries since torture was in use in our enlightend lands in the West; and, finally, there are so many exceptions and grounds of mitigation, that universality of corporal punishments, and consequently of torture, will be found to be much affected thereby.

The law in China likewise interferes with many acts which in Europe are without its pale; on this point it has been remarked that:—

'In a country in which the laws have not in any considerable degree the active concurrence either of sense of honour, or of a sense of religion, it may perhaps be absolutely requisite that they should take so wide a range. Experience may have dictated the necessity of their interfering in this direct manner in the enforcement of all those national habits and usages, whose preservation, as far as they are of a moral or prudential tendency, must undoubtedly be of essential importance both to the security of the government and to the happiness of the people.'

We quote again from Staunton's 'Penal Code of China' (Introduction):—

'Another object which seems to have been very generally consulted is that of as much as possible combining, in the construction and adaptation of the scale of crimes and punishments throughout the Code, the opposite advantages of severity in denunciation and lenity in execution.'

The laws of this Penal Code are divided into the *lut* [*lü*], or fundamental laws, and *lai* [*li*], supplementary laws: the former are permanent; the latter, which are liable to revision every five years, are the 'modifications, extensions, and restrictions of the fundamental laws.' Each article of the fundamental laws has been likewise further explained or paraphrased by the Emperor Yung Chêng, 'and the whole of the text is further illustrated by extracts from the works of various commentators. These appear to have been expressly written for the use and instruction of magistrates, and accordingly form a body of legal reference directly sanctioned for that purpose by government.'

The laws are classified as follows:—'General, Civil, Fiscal, Ritual, Military, and Criminal Laws, and those relating to Public Works,' comprised in 436 sections of the original laws, and a more numerous quantity of the supplemental laws, or 'Novellæ, which bear the same relation to the code as the judiciary law and subsequent enactments in France, and the new laws and authoritative interpretations in Prussia, respectively do to the Code Napoléon and Code Fredéric.'

Staunton characterises the Penal Code as remarkable for the conciseness and simplicity of its style of language, at the same time he calls attention to the difficulty, without 'various references and considerable research,' of ascertaining the punishment which a criminal 'is actually liable to suffer.' He proceeds to say:—

'That the sections of the Chinese Code may thus, perhaps, not unaptly be compared to a collection of consecutive mathematical problems with this additional circumstance of perplexity that a just and entire comprehension of each section individually requires a general knowledge of those that follow, no less than of those which precede it.'

'By far the most remarkable thing in this code is its great reasonableness, clearness, and consistency, the business-like brevity and directness of the various provisions, and the plainness and moderation in which they are expressed. There is nothing here of the monstrous *verbiage* of most other Asiatic productions—none of the superstitious deliberation, the miserable incoherence, the tremendous *non-sequiturs* and eternal repetitions of those oracular performances—nothing even of the turgid adulation, accumulated epithets, and fatiguing self-praise of other Eastern despotisms—but a calm, concise, and distinct series of enactments, savouring throughout of practical judgment and European good sense, and, if not always conformable to our improved notions of expediency, in general approaching to them more nearly than the codes of most other nations. When we pass, indeed, from the ravings of the Zendavesta or the Puranas to the tone of sense and business in this Chinese collection, we seem to be passing from darkness to light, from the drivellings of dotage to the exercise of an improved understanding.' The legal maxim *de minimis non curat lex* is not known in China; much minute attention is paid to trifles. 'We scarcely know any European code that is at once so copious and so consistent, or that is so nearly free from intricacy, bigotry, and fiction. In everything relating to political freedom or individual independence it is indeed woefully defective; but for the repression of disorder and the gentle coercion of a vast population, it appears to be equally mild and efficacious. The state of society for which it was formed appears incidentally to be a low and wretched one; but how could its framers have devised a wiser means of maintaining it in peace and tranquillity.'

'The people have a high regard for the code,' 'and all they seem to desire is its just and impartial execution, independent of caprice and uninfluenced by corruption. . . . It may be observed, as something in favour of the Chinese system, that there are substantial grounds for believing that neither flagrant nor repeated acts of injustice do, in point of fact, often, in any rank or station, ultimately escape with impunity.'

'Besides these laws and their numerous clauses, every high provincial officer has the right to issue edicts upon such public matters as require regulation, some of them even affecting life and death, either reviving some old law or giving it an application to the case before him, with such modifications as seem to be necessary. He must report these acts to the proper board at Peking. No such order, which for the time has the force of law, is formally repealed, but gradually falls into oblivion, until circumstances again require its reiteration. This mode of publishing statutes gives rise to a sort of common and unwritten law in villages, to which a council of elders sometimes compels individuals to submit; long usage is also another ground for enforcing them.'

'The Chinese customary law . . . undoubtedly rests, as did the Roman Law before the publication of the Twelve Tables, upon the *mores majorum*, "that is,' as Lord Mackenzie says of the latter, upon "customs long observed and sanctioned by the consent of the people." We are inclined to think it improbable that the Chinese have added to, or more than superficially changed any of their fundamental social principles since the compilation of the "Ritual of Chau" by *Chau Kung*, and that of the "Record of Rites" by Confucius, both of which collections . . . most probably reduced to a definite code the social principles of the Chinese, whilst blending them with those of the then ruling dynasty, and to this day continue to exercise a profound influence upon the Chinese mind. We mean by fundamental principles, those such as the Patriarchal Principle . . . and the Fraternal Principle . . . which, especially the former, apparently the progenitor of the others, pervade the Law and Customs of the Chinese as completely as the *Patria Potestas* ever did the Jurisprudence of Rome. The Chinese customary Law furnishes a standing "caution" (in the language of Sir Henry Maine) "to those who with Bentham and Austin resolve every law into a *command* of the law-giver, and *obligation* imposed thereby on the citizen, and a *sanction* threatened in the event of disobedience."' 'The principle of *hiao*, which, in its broadest sense, we think we may take to include friendship (*sin*), and loyalty (*chung*), as well as filial (*hiao*), fraternal (*yu* and *kung*), or (*t'i*), and conjugal piety or duty (*shun*), is undoubtedly the substratum of the Chinese social and legal fabric.'

'The Chinese Law, both Customary and Statute, furnishes an immense amount of collateral evidence in support of Maine's theory, that the movement of the progressive societies has hitherto been a movement from Status to Contract, or from families as units to individuals as units. It is particularly fruitful in illustration, perhaps more so even than the Hindoo Customary Laws. . . . The numerous illustrations are the more valuable, inasmuch as China has not yet emerged from Status; and, as regards the *Patria Potestas*, the Testamentary Power, the position of women and slaves, the fiction of adoption, and the almost entire absence of any written law of contract, remains in the position of the Roman Law,—not of the latter Empire, not even of the Antonine era; not even, again, of the early Empire, or the Republic at its prime; but of the Roman Law anterior to the publication of the Twelve Tables—2,200 years ago. In fact, with the Chinese law, as with the Chinese language, we are carried back to a position whence we can survey, so to speak, a living past, and converse with fossil men.'

'The law secretaries . . . whether Provincial or Metropolitan,' are 'the true and almost sole depositories in China both of the life of the law and the life of official language. They are the jurisconsults of the officials, as the Roman lawyers were those of the people. True, most Chinese officials are thoroughly cognizant of the main principles, and fairly acquainted with the details of their not very voluminous codified law, but the law secretaries are they who search out and apply the law in each case, and who draw up the records for submission to the Courts of Appeal at Peking,—The Grand Court of Revision and the Board of Punishment, . . . and to the Supreme Tribunal, consisting of the Emperor, either alone, or aided by such commissioners as he shall see fit to appoint—which commissioners, again, are assisted by their secretaries. A highly paid class, possessing immense indirect power, and usually plying their vocation with the least possible outward show, they furnish not unfrequently some of the ablest statesmen in the Empire. *Tso Tsung-t'ang*, the strategist who . . . recovered Kashgaria to the Empire, may be cited as an illustrious example; and a . . . memorial presented by him to the Throne, praying for posthumous honours to be conferred on four of his secretaries, evidences the value which is attached to the services of these men and the important part they take in the concerns of the Empire.'

The punishments inflicted for an infringement of these laws were:—Flogging with the bamboo; banishment within a limited distance for a limited time or permanently; death—of which there are two modes—by strangling and decapitation.

Manacles of wood, and iron fetters were used, and the cangue, a species of stock consisting of a heavy framework of wood in which the neck and hands were confined. Two instruments of torture were legally allowed: one for compressing the ankle-bones and one for the fingers, but others were used as well, though perhaps not to the extent that is sometimes supposed.

It was not every crime that was brought up before the Courts, but some, such as trifling thefts, were summarily punished by the people of the neighbourhood, the thief being whipped through the streets of the locality where his larceny was committed.

In cases coming before the officials, the prosecutor had to file his charge at 'the lowest tribunal of justice within the district,' from which, if not summarily dealt with, it might proceed on to higher Courts. There were no lawyers in our sense of the term, though there was a class of men who assisted the parties, unknown to the judge, by preparing witnesses and drawing up petitions, etc:—

For these 'lawyers are a disreputable class in China, not recognised by law, and not allowed to appear in Court. They can simply prompt their clients from behind the scenes, and write out their petitions and counter petitions for them.'

'Everything connected with law and law matters is so different in China that a European is in constant danger of misunderstanding and misjudging the people in connection with such matters. In the first place, hearsay evidence is perfectly permissible, and a man would suffer the extreme penalty of the law even if such were the only evidence against him. No oath is taken in a Chinese Court. The oaths, if a matter is in dispute, take place in the temple before the gods, or out in the open air in the presence of Heaven, and consist of worshipping and either the chopping off of a live cock's head, or the burning of imprecations written on yellow paper. In the country something earthen'—a 'vessel—is sometimes broken by way of an oath. The appeal to Heaven is undoubtedly the best.'

Consequently in our Courts of Justice in Hongkong when a suitor fears his case is going against him, or sees that his opponent as strongly sticks to his version as he does to his, he often suggests a reference to what are more binding to him than the simple declarations of our Courts, viz., an oath on a cock's head, which is chopped off.

Again a Chinese suitor in a native Court does not bring his witnesses with him or subpœna them to attend. That is the magistrate's or judge's duty, or function: he sends his lictors for them if it appears, either in the course of giving evidence or earlier, that their presence is necessary, consequently in our Courts of Justice, litigants are constantly coming up without their witnesses and they often, *more Sinico,* ask the judge to send for them.

The lengths to which the Chinese idea of the sanctity of the life of the parent carries them may be seen from a cutting from the *North China Daily News* in 1897:—

'A child, barely eleven years old, was escorted by a number of *yamên* runners into Soochow city on the 20th August, having come from the district city of Chinkuei, not far from Soochow, for his final trial before the Provincial Judge on the fearful charge of murdering his mother. As a matter of fact the affair was a simple accident. The child was swinging a small bamboo stool about him when he accidentally struck his mother on the left side with it. She died almost immediately, with the result that her son will have to suffer for his so-called "crime" at the hands of the executioner, not merely by simple decapitation, but also by the "slicing process"—the penalty for parricides and matricides, no matter how accomplished, whether accidentally or premeditated, for the Chinese laws do not recognise any difference where life has been taken.'

A Chinese judge acts as prosecutor as well as judge, more in the French style (there being no lawyers in our sense of the term [but *v. infra*], there is consequently no prosecuting counsel, or Solicitor-General, or Attorney-General), and he sometimes allows the parties to set to and bandy words and recriminate each other while he quietly sits by and listens to see if he can pick up any more facts about the case.

Amidst all the anomalies of the Chinese administration of justice there is one good point, and that is, that the magistrate or judge endeavours, if not influenced by bribery, etc., to give a reasonable common-sense verdict. Though there are both law and custom to guide him, he is not bound by the iron bands of precedents, and law and custom, within certain limits, may go to the wall should he be sufficiently clear-sighted to see a better and more reasonable course to pursue.

The following extracts will illustrate one or two more traits of Chinese character with regard to legal matters:—

'Though there is an elaborate Penal Code and there are distinctions between different kinds of murder and homicide, yet it is all one to the common people, and a life for a life is their cry. However, a money compensation often pacifies wounded feelings in a case of accident. Though if the relations insist on revenge, the matter must come before the mandarins.'

'When a Chinese witness comes into the box he 'expects the magistrate to ask him the name of his native district, his own name, his age, the age of his father and mother (if alive), the maiden name of his wife, her age, the number and ages of his children, and many more questions of similar relevancy and importance, before a single effort is made towards eliciting any one fact bearing upon the subject under investigation. With a stereotyped people like the Chinese, it does not do to ignore these trifles of form and custom: on the contrary the witness should rather be allowed to wander at will through such useless details until he has collected his scattered thoughts, and may be safely coaxed to divulge something which partakes more of the nature of evidence.'

'No provision is made for fresh legislation as such. The Penal Code, which is the only body of statutory law in existence, is supposed to contain enactments to meet every possible case, but if by chance some difficulty occurs for which there is no precedent, it is referred to the Board concerned, which in turn reports to the Throne. A decree or rescript is thereupon issued, which settles the case. Periodically the Code is revised, and these various decrees are consolidated or incorporated, and become part of the Statute Law.'

Toward the end of the Ch'ing (Manchu) dynasty, as a result of the "Reform Movement" arising out of the fear that China would be unable longer to resist foreign aggression and defeat (as in the war with Japan), a code of laws, based on Western systems was drawn up. It was named *Chan Hsing Hsing Fa Lü*, "Provisional Criminal Code." It substituted hanging or strangling for decapitation and imprisonment for bambooing. It remained in force until the end of the dynasty, was adopted in large measure by the Republican régime, and has continued to be the recognized legal instrument to this day, though ignored at will by Yüan Shih-k'ai (who had planned to supplant it by a code of his own) during the suspension of Parliament (1913-6). The following extracts give further particulars of the changes which have taken place in recent years.

'After the collapse of China that followed upon the Japanese and "Boxer" wars, the question of legal reform was seriously taken up, one of the chief motives being to imitate Japanese success and get rid of extraterritorial jurisdictions. The numerous memorials presented to the Emperor by the most distinguished Manchu and Chinese statesmen and viceroys, central or in the provinces, are all recorded in full, and amply prove the literary, logical, and even legal capacity of the writers, if only their colleagues intrusted with the carrying out of excellent laws could honestly and fairly administer the laws so well understood and approved.

The first point was to expose clearly the difference between executive and legislative functions, and to lay stress upon the unwisdom of continuing these two separate functions in the hands of one and the same man or group of men. The second reform of supreme importance was to secure the independence of judges and to establish proper courts of first and second instance, appeal, and so on, both in the capital and in the provinces. The precise legislative and executive rights of Parliament on the one hand and the Boards and Supreme Law Courts on the other, were shrewdly discussed. This useful work began in 1905, and was proceeding apace when the Empress-Dowager and the Emperor died in 1908. Meanwhile Wu T'ing-fang, the present (end of 1916) Secretary of State for Foreign Affairs, was commissioned to draw up a code. . . . After some elaboration the Code was drawn up largely after the Japanese model, and from a European point of view a very fair code it was, apart from the fact that it got rid of many anachronisms. But it met with serious viceregal opposition on account of the novelty, not to say coarseness of its style, its use of ill-understood semi-foreign definitions, and its failure to recognise the ethical principle of Chinese Law, based on *hiao*, or the natural family rights, duties, and responsibilities as defined in the Confucian classics.'

'China's unsuccessful war with Japan in 1895 may perhaps be considered as the chief historic event which definitely started the general reform movement on its way. . . . In China attention is at present almost entirely concentrated on providing a sure and legal foundation for other changes which must come later. This in itself constitutes as epoch in Chinese history. It is the result of an acute struggle, a sharp contest between the demand of a conservative, traditional autocracy for absolute obedience and the growing restlessness of an expanding intelligence claiming a share in the management of the nation's affairs. Public opinion, when it understands its own aims, is always irresistable, and the Manchu Court felt impelled to recognize the new national spirit. On October 27, 1907, an Imperial edict announced that the old order would end, that a constitution would be adopted, and that a Parliament would be convened nine years later. A "Scheme of Proposed Reforms" from 1908-1917 was published. A number of laws were actually enacted some of which are still provisionally in force. The programme was ambitious, but gradually it became apparent that while promising lavishly the Government was steadily concentrating power in the hands of the royal family. Autocracy grew while constitutionalism was held up as the prize. There was no confidence in the Government's promise, and in 1911 the Revolution began. The republic was established in the following year, the fate of the monarchical idea sealed, and the fundamental principles of the constitution based on republican ideals settled.

Legal reform is now the immediate work of the future. It started in the closing years of the Manchu régime, and may be traced to two causes, a general awakening and complications arising from extraterritorial jurisdiction.

The first definite step towards the desired goal was China's formally expressed wish "to reform the judicial system and to bring it into accord with that of western nations." She met with a ready response. On September 5, 1902 Great Britain engaged to surrender her extraterritorial rights "when the state of the Chinese laws and the arrangements for their administration warrant us in so doing;" on October 8, 1903 the United States of America concluded a similar treaty, followed by Japan on January 29, 1904.

In pursuance of the reform policy Prince Tsai Chên, Yüan Shih-k'ai and Wu T'ing-fang were appointed Imperial Commissioners to compile a code of commercial laws, and in 1904 they submitted a draft containing nine articles on general law regarding merchants, and 131 articles on company law. This was shortly afterwards sanctioned by Imperial mandate. The code for the first time introduced the principle of limited liability and in the main followed the general principles of English company law. Drafts were also drawn up regarding trade-marks and mining, but owing to certain objections by foreigners they did not come into force.

In 1906 a " Code of Civil and Criminal Procedure for the Chinese Empire " was prepared. It distinguished between civil and criminal proceedings, instituted trial by jury, and provided for pleadings by lawyers in court. Another important feature was the introduction of the Anglo-American practice of cross-examining witnesses by counsel, in contradistinction to the well-known continental inquisitorial procedure. The Code, however, was at the time, felt to be too radical a change, and consequently it did not pass beyond the stage of an official draft.

The late Mr. Shên Chia-pên, Vice-President of the Board of Justice, having been appointed Imperial High Commissioner for the Revision of Laws, and later, head of the Bureau for the Investigation of Constitutional Principles, prepared a number of important laws, such as the Bankruptcy Law, the Mining Law, the Police Offences Law, the Press Law, the Law of Associations, the Nationality Law and the Transportation Law. The Bureau translated a large body of western law which was afterwards published in thirty odd volumes. These formed the basis of a comparative study of the whole subject, and the following codes were drafted, namely the Criminal Code, the Civil Code, the Codes of Civil and Criminal Procedure, and the first part of the Commercial Code. Their provisions were taken from Japanese law, which, in turn, is largely influenced by German law.

Of these drafts the Criminal Code deserves more than a passing notice, as it is the only modern Chinese code that has been enacted. It was drawn up during the closing years of the Manchu Dynasty, and with the exception of certain matters pertaining to the Imperial family and a few amendments added in 1914, it has been in force since March 30, 1912. Including those which have been deleted, it contains 411 sections.

A new principle introduced into Chinese criminal jurisprudence is section 10, by which no person can be convicted of an offence not expressly provided for. This, though a legal maxim in the west, is a change of wide import. In China it was formerly possible so to stretch the law as to cover many acts not expressly made criminal.

The Code divides punishments into main and additional. Main punishments are:—

(1) Death.
(2) Imprisonment for life.
(3) Imprisonment from two months to fifteen years.
(4) Detention from one day to two months
(5) Fines.

Additional punishments are:—

(1) Deprivation of civil rights.
(2) Forfeiture of articles which have been put to a criminal use.

Without discussing details, it may be noted that the principle of maximum and minimum punishments is followed. By this means the judge has discretionary power to pass sentence according to circumstances.

Commercial enactments.—The old commercial laws of 1904 were repealed in 1914 by two statutes: the General Law regarding Merchants, and the Law of Business Associations. According to the latter, business associations are divided into four kinds: the first is partnership, the second is limited partnership, introduced into England as late as 1907, the third resembles the English limited liability company, the fourth has no prototype in English law, being in fact a combination of the partnership and limited liability company. Other commercial statutes are: Business Registration Law, Law on the Registration of Business Associations, Law on Chambers of Commerce, Commercial Arbitration Law, and Mining Law.

The Judiciary.—One very tangible result of China's legal reform is the present judiciary, which owes its existence to a law passed in 1910, and which, subject to certain verbal alterations, is still provisionally in force. Its fundamental principles are the independence of the judiciary and the punishment of judges guilty of misconduct in office. The Act creates four grades of courts: (i) Courts of First Instance for the trial of minor civil and criminal cases; (2) Local Prefectural Courts to decide ordinary civil and criminal cases and appeals from Courts of First Instance; (3) Provincial High Courts; (4) the Supreme Court (*Ta Li Yüan*) at Peking. There are also four grades of procurator's offices. These represent the State in criminal matters and in civil cases of public interest, *e.g.* reduction of a person of full age to the status of an infant, marriage, etc.

Trial by jury.—Trial by jury is practically unknown. Provisions for this form of trial were inserted in the Draft Code of Civil and Criminal Procedure (1906) which, however, never went into effect. One or two trials by jury were held in Shanghai in the first year of the Republic, but this form of procedure has not since been seriously considered. The fact that jury trials have been abolished in Japan is indicative of the inadvisability of transplanting this western institution into China. [Probably the risk of bribery and the liability to favour rich complainants or defendants would be too great.]

Lawyers.—A further great change in the legal history of China is the admission into the courts of lawyers to represent litigants. Every practising lawyer must hold a certificate from the Ministry of Justice and be a member of the Bar Association in his own judicial district. There are now over 2,500 registered Chinese lawyers scattered throughout the country.

Prison reform.—The movement for the erection of modern prisons was initiated in 1909. It received a fresh impetus from the report of the Chinese delegates to the International Prison Congress held in Washington in 1910. Since that date model prisons have been erected in most of the provincial capitals, including juvenile and women's prisons. As funds permit, it is proposed to erect similar institutions in other cities. The entire prison system is under the central control of the Ministry of Justice, to which appeals from decisions of prison inspectors may be made. A few of the regulations for the government and administration of prisons may be mentioned as illustrative of the general treatment of the inmates: educational facilities are provided for juvenile offenders, and for other prisoners suitable labour is allotted according to their social standing, crimes, age, physical condition, and possible future. The work assigned may be printing, carpentering, weaving, toy-making, basket and bamboo work, and other handicrafts. Wages are paid at thirty to fifty per cent. of the usual rate. By good behaviour prisoners may under certain circumstances obtain a conditional release.'

'The Ministry of Justice has issued an explanation of the work done toward reforming the prison system in China since the establishment of the Republic. Three new prisons have been built in Peking and fifteen throughout the provinces. It is planned to construct another forty in various places. In addition considerable change has been wrought in the old barbaric jails by reforming those which have not been entirely rebuilt. The houses have been renovated, sanitary systems introduced and factories and workshops added, so that the life of the prisoner is not the painful existence it was under the Empire.

According to the statement of the Ministry, strides have been made in the way of reformatory and educational measures whereby the prisoners are taught to do manual and skilled labour and thus take their position as responsible citizens when leaving the jails. The reports of prison superintendents on those leaving bears out the fact that good is being accomplished.

The report of the Ministry also comments on the reform schools where children under eighteen are taught reading, writing, singing and arithmetic. Another departure is the segregation of women and juvenile prisoners from the men. The former are under the control of women superintendents.

One of the hardest tasks has been the employment of prison officials and guards who were not subject to bribery or corruption. That has been got around by getting reliable men and giving them responsible and high ranking positions which enjoy equal rank with other civil officials.'

Continental Law.—'Chinese legislation shows a distinct tendency towards the Continental legal system. One or two attempts were made to follow Anglo-American principles, such as the Commercial laws of 1904 and the Draft Code of 1906. As already stated the first gave way a few years later to new statutes based on the Continental commercial codes, and the second was still-born. Since then German law has filtrated into China through Japan. To attribute this to the large number of Chinese students trained in Japan is only an approximation of [to] the truth. The real reason must be looked for in the fact that Anglo-American law emphasizes the individual as against the family, while the Continental system inherits something of the old Roman *familia*. The unit of Chinese society being the family, reform naturally seeks to preserve this institution and to modernize it as far as possible after the Continental idea. Another reason why China turns from English jurisprudence is the prevalence of case law. To imitate a law, developed by judicial interpretation, is difficult, if not impracticable. It is easier to adopt a ready-made system of comprehensive rules clearly and concisely set forth section by section.'

Revisions and additions. — 'A review of what has been accomplished shows that a great deal has been done in a comparatively short period. Codification is by no means a simple task, and much praise is due to the Imperial Commission for the pioneer work performed. Many of the provisions in drafts it prepared were borrowed *en bloc*. It in no way derogates from the value of the work of the Commission that revision is to-day necessary. The work of the Law Codification Commission is to reconsider and revise these drafts and to frame certain other important statutes. There are two points of view which the Commission will always have to keep before it. On the one hand, there is the difference between the East and the West, and the ideals of both ought to be preserved. On the other hand there is the great variety of Chinese customs, some of which must be followed in the new code, while others must be sacrificed in favour of uniform legislation. Only thus can sacrificeo in favour of uniform legislation. Only thus can codification be successful, and the laws become a controlling factor and not a dead letter. It will therefore be neccessary to consider the applicability of foreign institutions to Chinese conditions, methodically and thoroughly to investigate local customs in the important provinces, and to embody their principles in the form of a code. The assistance of foreign experts will be sought. All this will take time, but the Commission will, it is hoped, like the prow of the vessel which cuts the resisting wave and makes a path for the wealthy cargo in the vasty holds [*sic*], open the way for China to share her rich inheritances with the rest of the world and, in return, to receive valuable contributions from her neighbours' garnered stores of experience gathered in other fields of endeavour, thus fulfilling the ancient adage, "All under heaven are one family."'

'Things are in such a state of flux under the Republic that it is hardly safe to say what law is actually followed by Chinese judges; what is the juridical capacity of those judges; and what is the *ratio decidendi*. So far as I can judge, whatever the law and the judge may theoretically be, justice to the average claimant is as far off as in past times, and the Chinese courts are as unfitted to replace the extraterritorial consular courts as ever they were.' (See EXTRATERRITORIALITY.)

That serious efforts toward definite progress and just administration are being made cannot be denied. The two chief instruments of this progress are the Law Codification Commission and the Supreme Court.

'Apart from the fact that the Constitution of the Republic separates the governmental powers, so as to make the judiciary independent, the Supreme Court has very definite accomplishments to its credit. In the first place it has prepared five codes, Civil, Criminal, and Commercial, and two codes of Procedure, one for civil and one for criminal cases. These various codes have not all yet been fully promulgated, but they have been carefully adapted from those of the most advanced nations in such a way as to be workable in and applicable to conditions in this country. In the second place, three new grades of courts have been established, namely District Courts, High Courts or Courts of Appeal, and the Supreme Court in Peking, and side by side with these there has been established also a system of procurates with three corresponding grades. In the third place, there have been numerous cases of improvement of legal proceedings, such as the separation of civil and criminal cases, the publicity of all trials and judgments rendered, and in criminal cases the consideration given to circumstantial evidence and personal testimony and the abolition of corporal punishment as a means of extracting evidence; and in addition to these may be mentioned the definite status given to the legal profession. In the fourth place, the judicial officers of all courts, high and low, are required to have received regular legal training. In the fifth place, the prison and police systems have been reformed and the success of these reforms is generally acknowledged.

It is not pretended that the judicial administration throughout China is perfect. There are still miscarriages of justice, there are still prisons that lack something of the sweetness and light that are considered indispensable in the best type of modern prison, penitentiary or reformatory. But Roman law was not built in a day, any more than was Rome itself; and new machinery requires delicate handling, if it is to work without a breakdown. It says much for China that in spite of many difficulties, to only a few of which we have referred above, so much progress has been made already.

The progress that has been made has not been made without overcoming much opposition and ignorance. Even the legislators of the land have at times tried to divert the reforming activities from the path of true progress; but they have not succeeded. For example, take the question of the absolute independence of the judiciary. In the fifth year of the Republic, when Parliament was reconvened after the death of Yüan, the majority of its members contended that the Supreme Court, as Court of Appeal, should not have power to try and to decide election cases. In the Election Law of the two Houses of Parliament it is not expressly stated that an appeal can be made to the Supreme Court, nor is it expressly stated that an appeal cannot be made to the Supreme Court, but in interpreting the provision in the Election Law itself it seems proper that such an appeal should be permitted. The Supreme Court therefore took up certain Election cases in spite of the contention of Parliament, which thereupon passed a resolution denouncing the decision of the Supreme Court and reported it to the Government of the day. The majority of the Cabinet supported the view of Parliament, and the Cabinet's view was communicated to the Supreme Court. In its reply the Supreme Court contended that as it had the power to interpret the law, its decision was final and could not be disturbed even by Parliament itself, Parliament, according to Article IX of the Provisional Constitution, only having the power to pass resolutions and make laws, and having no authority over the judiciary. Finally, Parliament withdrew its contention and its resolution. The result is that the Supreme Court stands absolutely independent: though the Ministry of Justice is responsible for the administration of Justice throughout the whole country, the Supreme Court is equal in rank with it, and so, although such matters as the appointment and fixing of the grade of the officers of the Court and the presentation of its budget have to go through the formal channel of the Ministry of Justice, they are actually settled by the Court itself; and as to other matters concerning the Court, the Court itself has absolute power.'

References.—Staunton, *Ta Tsing Leu Lee; Being the Fundamental Laws and a Selection from the Supplementary Statutes of the Penal Code of China;* Williams, *Middle Kingdom;* Alabaster, *Notes and Commentaries on Chinese Criminal Law and Cognate Topics;* Couling, *Encyclopædia Sinica;* Parker, *China; Journal N.C.B.R.A.S.*, N.S. Vols. xxxvii; xlv.

LEPROSY.—One of the most loathsome diseases to be met with in China is leprosy; and one that the civilised world has had prominently brought before its notice of recent years. The symptoms and suggestions for cure are described in ancient Chinese medical works. 'As to the cause of its prevalence, the poverty of the great bulk of the people, poor food, overcrowding, generally dirtiness, absence of segregation [in some districts], and the hot, moist climate, provide a chain of conditions very suitable for the propagation of leprosy.' China is not a land where statistics are available; the Chinese mind needs a considerable tonic of Western science and ideas before it will be braced up to that definite and precise form of statement which will prepare the way for this useful branch of knowledge. At present the Chinese delights in a vague statement of even facts well known to himself. He calls certain of his relations brothers, which term includes real brothers, cousins of more than one degree, and clansmen. He tells you a thing took place between 2 and 3 o'clock, when he might as well say 2.15 P.M.; he says there were between ten and twenty present, when he might as well say fifteen or sixteen. Statistics from such an individual, it can be readily understood, are well-nigh impossible, else China would present a splendid field for an array of facts on leprosy; for not only is it existent all over China, but it prevails extensively in the South, especially in the Canton province, where cases are very numerous in the silk districts. The Government has Leper Asylums at different centres of population in the South for the purpose of segregation, and doles from the Emperor's bounty used to be granted to the lepers. These asylums are badly managed, as unfortunately most native charitable institutions are. The village for lepers at Canton is situated about two or three miles north of the city; there is accommodation there for 400 or 500, but it is not sufficient; they are allowed in boats on the river as well, and outside the east gate of the city.

The lepers in the leper village occupy themselves in making rope of cocoa-nut fibre, and brooms, etc., which, though the inhabitants of the city are in mortal dread of the afflicted inmates, yet find a ready sale; females, who have lost the outward symptoms of the disease, sell them in the market. Lepers also waylay funerals and demand alms, which are given, for fear that leper ghosts may torment the departed. The sums demanded are on a varying scale, and fixed by the lepers according to their idea of the rank and wealth of the deceased. Such exorbitant sums are asked that they are sometimes refused, and then the lepers leap into the grave and prevent the interment. They accept promises of payment, but, if these are not kept, they exhume the corpse and retain possession of it until their demands are met. These payments to the lepers form an item in the funeral expenses.

In the leper boats, a single leper often resides who paddles about seeking charity; in such cases the boats are tiny little canoes with mat-covering over the centre. They sometimes strip the dead bodies that float down the river, and, if they find one respectably dressed, occasionally advertise it for the reward that they hope to obtain. In the silk districts there would appear to be no asylums on land, but the lepers are restricted to the boats, from which they solicit cash by means of a long bamboo pole with a bag at the end. In some of the districts they occupy certain shrines on the river bank, and beg alms with rod and bag.

The Chinese at Canton will have nothing to do with lepers; and if the family of a rich man who has taken the disease tries to hide it, the neighbours, as a general rule, soon compel his segregation. They are unable to cure it; and ascribe it to different causes; one reason given is the rain-water dropping from a certain kind of tree on anyone; another is, that the droppings from spiders cause it. They suppose it to work itself out in three or four generations, and it would appear to be a well-established fact that in some of the large leper villages the proportion of lepers is but small, the disease having died out in the course of a century or so. Lepers in Canton marry amongst themselves, but not with others. When the disease is well developed, the sight is sickening; the parts affected, such as the face, ears, hands, and feet are enlarged, and red, smooth, and glossy. At certain stages of the disease, spontaneous amputation of the fingers and toes takes place, for they rot and drop off. An improvement in diet, and tonics, better the condition of the patient, but there is still much to be learned as to the cause and treatment of this dreadful scourge. In two and a half years 125 lepers presented themselves at the Alice Memorial Hospital in Hongkong.

'Throughout the greater part of the province of Shangtung leprosy is seldom seen, and where it does exist it is mainly anæsthetic leprosy. But in the prefectures of Yi-chou Fu and Yen-chou Fu leprosy is quite common. The majority of cases met with in missionary hospitals through the province come from these two prefectures, the one including the home of Confucius and the other, Yi-chow, lying to the south of it. The cases exhibit all the characteristics of true leprosy, and often in an extreme stage. It is not uncommon for villages in Yi-chou prefecture to have several lepers. Dr. Hunter, of Chining-chou, who has kindly furnished facts, regards the causes of the prevalence of leprosy in one section of a province, most parts of which are free from it, to be mainly climacteric.'

In Soochow the lepers live in their own homes and mingle with other people without any restriction. In the North of China there are no leper villages, and, it would appear, no attempts at segregation whatever. It is stated to be 'comparatively rare in the northern provinces of China, excessively common in the southern.'

On the basis of the number seen at the Soochow Hospital, a calculation has been made that there are probably 150,000 lepers in China; but this must be very much a guess. China is supposed to be the country in which there is the largest number. 'In India there are said to be 500,000.' Again it is stated that 'according to the census of 1891, after making allowance for error, it is estimated that in British India there were 105,000.' 'Judging from what is seen in the coast towns and treaty ports [in China], the number of lepers there is even greater than in India.' It is questionable whether a place such as Soochow, where 'less than one in two thousand of the sick are afflicted with this disease,' affords a reliable basis to form an estimate of the prevalence of the disease throughout China. (Another estimate puts the number in China, India, and Siberia as 1,000,000. In Russian Turkestan there are said to be 2,000.) Another of these attempts at guessing puts the lepers in China as 300,000. As an example of districts where leprosy is more common, it may be mentioned that during a week at Chao Chow-fu from two to three or four a day, so diseased, appeared amongst about forty or more patients, and this was not an exceptional week. In the tract of country round Swatow with a population not much less than that of Scotland, it is estimated that there are 25,000 lepers; and, to one accustomed to the horror the Cantonese have of the disease, it was extraordinary to see the utter carelessness the natives evinced in their contact with the subjects of this loathsome malady. Just outside the city of Chao Chow-fu a leper lad was seen sitting at the roadside and eating out of a bowl which had evidently been obtained from a hawker's stall, such a thing being utterly out of the question at Canton. In a shop in one of the principal streets of the same important city, a leper was pointed out busy at work in a tailor's shop. The utter *nonchalance* with which the people in this part of the country regard the lepers, and the utter absence of all precautions in their intercourse with them is most extraordinary. There are leper villages in some of which the disease is said to have died or to be dying out; some poor miserable huts and temples are also tenanted by lepers on the roadside.

Leprosy does not appear to be on the increase in China, though in some parts every opportunity is given for its spread. Doubtless were every precaution taken against the possibility of contagion from it, and a rigid system of segregation enforced throughout the empire it might be stamped out, as it is said it was in England some centuries since.

From historical references to it, it seeme to have been known in China some two or three hundred years before the time of Confucius; the sage himself had a disciple who died of this dreadful disease. It is very curious to find some districts of country quite free from this horrible infliction while other parts in the neighbourhood are affected with it. It is a great comfort to the European residents in China to find that its power of contagion is, comparatively speaking, so slight. It is, however, contagious and perhaps communicable in some way or other as well, so that it behoves those that are brought into contact with cases of it to take every precaution instead of being so foolhardy as to ignore its communicability. In one notable case the disease was taken by an American missionary, who died after some years in all the horrors incident to it; the cause evidently, in this case, being a Chinese who had the disease having his quarters in the same dwelling as the missionary. After his removal from the house a Chinese woman, who occupied the same room that the leper had previously had, also took it. It is said that some European women in Australia have taken it from their leprous Chinese husbands. There were a few years ago 19 Chinese lepers in Little Bay, N.S.W. lazar-house amongst a total of 36. The bacillus of leprosy is 1-100,000th of an inch in diameter. 'In length it is from half to two-thirds, and in breadth about one-sixteenth, the diameter of a blood-corpuscle.' There are 2,000 lepers in Crete; the disease is said to be spreading in Russia, over 600 new cases a year, in the Eastern Province of Prussia, in North Prussia.

as well as in the Austrian Province of Bosnia, and even some cases have occurred in England.

It is with delight we hail the change of front that has taken place with regard to the communicability of leprosy during the last few years, amongst the medical profession, as the result of the conference on leprosy held in Berlin in 1897, for we have always felt it was a most dangerous disease.

'The conference declared [and rightly so] that leprosy is a contagious disease, and that every leper is a danger to his surroundings. The conclusion come to is, in short, that, as leprosy is dangerous and incurable, lepers should be isolated.' 'The communicability of leprosy, by direct or indirect means from lepers to the healthy must now be accepted as an established fact, the evidence in support of this belief being conclusive; . . . there is no evidence of the disease arising or spreading in any other way.'

'Hospitals were originally intended for the reception of lepers.' The number of lazar-houses in Great Britain testifies to the prevalence of the disease there at one time.

There are 30,000 lepers in the Philippine Archipelago, where it was introduced in 1663 by a shipload of 150 lepers sent to the Romish priests there to be cured by the Emperor of Japan. The Spaniards, it is said, took no measures to cure or cope with the disease. Another estimate says there are 10,000 in these islands.

The want of cleanliness and contact appear to be the causes of the disease. 'In Norway there were 1,600 lepers in 1880, out of a population of 1,850,000.' In the Sandwich Islands 1,800, in Greece 100 lepers, and 60 leper deaths a year in Mauritius. There are supposed to be 714 cases in Ceylon.

It is generally believed that leprosy is incurable, but we note that in 1900 inoculation for leprosy in Hanoi was being carried out with satisfactory results; and Sister Gertrude states positively that she has known several cases of leprosy cured. A curious cure for it in China is noted by one writer. A buffalo was killed and the leper was placed inside its body and remained in it for some time. To all appearance he was cured; but most people will doubtless require stronger evidence before accepting this or other statements of the cure of this loathsome and apparently incurable disease. Isolation has been tried with marked success in Norway.

We close this article with a short extract from Dr. Manson's work, 'Tropical Diseases':—

'Seeing that leprosy is caused by a specific germ, there must have been a time in the history of every leper when the infecting germ entered the body. In the case of many specific diseases

. . . the time of infection can usually be ascertained. So far as present knowledge goes, this much cannot be affirmed of leprosy. . . . We are equally ignorant as to the condition of the infecting germ, whether it enters the organ or organs through which it gains access as spore or as bacillus; and, also, as to the medium in or by which it is conveyed. We cannot say whether it enters in food, in water, in air; whether it passes in through the broken epithelium, or whether it is inoculated on some broken breach of surface, or, perhaps, introduced by some insect bite. But, though we are in absolute ignorance as to the process of infection, we may be quite sure that in leprosy there is an act of infection, and that the infective material comes from another leper. Leprosy has never been shown to arise *de novo*.'

There are homes for lepers at Hangchow, Foochow, Pakhoi, Hokchiang, Tungkun, Wuchow, Siaokan, (40 miles from Hankow), and T'êng Hsien (Shantung), all maintained by missionary organizations. The British Mission to Lepers assists various Protestant Missions in work for their relief.

References.—Thin, *Leprosy;* Cantile, *Leprosy in Hongkong;* Gray, *China;* Coltman, *The Chinese, their Present and Future; Medical, Political, and Social;* Manson, *Tropical Diseases; Chinese Recorder,* Vol. xlvi; *China Medical Missionary Journal;* Reports of different Medical Missionary Hospitals in South-eastern China.

LIGHTHOUSES.—The lighthouse system in Chinese waters is under a department of the Maritime Customs. 'The lighthouses on the China Coast have a luminous intensity equal to that of the best non-electric lighthouses in the world. The lighting and maintenance are attended to with the greatest punctuality, and there has never been a complaint as to the regularity of working and amount of safety afforded.' Some of the most important positions have been selected for their display; and these indispensable aids to the navigator extend from Newchwang in the North to the island of Haiman in the South, and along the Yang-tzŭ and Canton Rivers. They are mostly on land, though a few are lightships; and they are either fixed, fixed and flashing, or group-flashing, revolving, or occulting; the illuminating apparatus is either catoptric or dioptric. Besides these, there are a number of buoys and beacons, light-vessels and light-boats. The lights, etc., are being added to, and the department increased as time goes on. Since the first lights were started in the years 1855, 1859, and 1863, up to 1895 or 1896, there have been but nine years in which a new light has not been exhibited, while in a few years the total of new ones for the year rose as high as nine or ten. At the end of 1897 there were 105 lights, 4 light-vessels, 82 buoys, and 65 beacons, making a total of 256 under the control of this department. In 1901 there were a total of 288.

Lighthouses

The sub-joined table shows the number of Lights, Light-vessels, Light-boats, Buoys, and Beacons in Chinese waters in 1921:—

Customs district.	Lights.	Light-vessels and Light-boats.	Buoys.	Beacons.	Total.
Pakhoi . . .			3		3
Kiungchow . .	4		3	1	8
Kongmoon . .	3			2	5
Samshui . . .	2	1		1	4
Wuchow . . .			16		16
Canton . . .	25		16	17	58
Swatow . . .	6		3	1	10
Amoy	4		10	16	30
Foochow . . .	5		17	14	36
Santuao . . .	2		1	1	4
Wenchow . . .	2		2	3	7
Ningpo . . .	6		1	5	12
Shanghai . . .	16	3	38	36	93
Chinkiang . .	10	6	9	11	36
Wuhu	10	4		6	20
Kiukiang . . .	19	16		12	47
Hankow . . .	16	21		8	45
Yochow . . .	6	2	26	5	39
Ch'angsha . .	4		2	10	16
Ichang . . .			2		2
Chefoo . . .	9		4	6	19
Tientsin . . .	6	3	1	8	18
Newchwang . .		1	8	13	22
Harbin . . .	37		114	794	945
Total . .	192	57	276	970	1,495

Leaving out those on the Canton River as well as those at Chinkiang, Kiukiang, and Hankow, there are approximately about one light to every hundred and two miles of coast line. A few years ago there was a lighthouse to every fourteen miles of English coast, one to every thirty-four of Irish coast, and one to every thirty-nine of Scotch shore line. It must, however, be remembered that about two-thirds of the Chinese lights are at those ports mentioned above. The staff required for the maintenance of the lights is composed of both foreigners and natives; the former numbering fifty-eight and the latter two hundred and twenty-two.

Besides these there are three lighthouses in the British Colony of Hongkong, and one in the Portuguese Colony of Macao.

LIKIN AND SOME OTHER TAXES.—The incident of taxation in China seems stange and mysterious to the stranger, who finds it difficult to understand the various taxes.

Likin [lit., contribution of a thousandth, *i.e.*, one-tenth of one per cent.], which may be termed 'Inland Transportation Tax,' 'is a tax originally of one cash per tael on all sales, voluntarily imposed on themselves by the people, among whom it was very popular, with a view of making up the deficiency of the land tax in China, caused by the T'ái P'ing and Nien Féi troubles. It was to be set apart for military purposes only—hence its common name, "war tax"; and was said by the Tsung Li Yamên to be adopted merely as a temporary measure.' It has been 'collected at rates differing in different provinces and at different times. The Chefoo Agreement makes the area of the foreign concessions at the various Treaty Ports exempt from the levy of Lekin. This tax has been a bone of contention between Chinese officials and European merchants, and no small amount of irritation, on both sides, has been excited thereby. The Transit Pass System, stipulated by Treaty, arranged that all foreign goods, which entered the interior of China, under this regulation, should be freed from further taxation.'

'It has been continued in defiance of promises that when the finances of the country had recovered their normal condition the likin should be abolished.'

'As a guarantee for a portion of China's indebtedness, it was agreed that the likin collection at the Yangtsz ports and at Ningpo should be placed under the control of the foreign customs.'

The present [1924] position as regards likin is stated at the end of this article.

The Lotishui, destination or laying-down tax, is levied on goods when they arrive at their destinations inland, having run the gauntlet of the different *likin* stations *en route* and been mulct the duties charged at these stations, but it is commonly levied 'to save time,' at port of departure.

This Lotishui 'was not especially provided for in the earlier treaties, and has nothing to do with transit *lekin* as such. And it is these unforeseen taxes which have figured so largely in public discussions, though they have all been lumped under the general heading "likin."'

There is also the Cheng-fei, or Ching-fei, or military defence tax.

All the numerous stations for paying taxes offer much friction and hindrance to goods in transitu. Some of the barriers only collect likin, or lekin, as it is often written, sufficient to pay for the staff employed to collect. This, however, cannot be a very common practice.

Likin and some other Taxes

It is feared by some that the abolition of lekin and the substitution of 7½ per cent. on all sea-borne commerce will prejudicially affect foreign mercantile interests in China.

Likin was in its incipience a temporary measure, but it has developed into a permanent burden, very onerous on account of its lack of definition.

'It has been estimated that of every $100 collected under the old likin organisation $10 reached the State coffers, and $90 stuck on the way, whereas, when judiciously managed, the result ought to be precisely the converse. The levy of likin was most unfortunately and mistakenly recognised by the British Government long ago, and, having been so long tolerated, it will be difficult, if not impossible, to get rid of it, except on a basis of compromise. . . . The Kowloon Customs collect the Chingfei, or military defence tax, for the Viceroy of Canton, on the trade with which they have to deal; the amount of that tax may be varied from time to time, and all the Customs have to do is to collect it and account for the proceeds.'

The following paragraphs explain exactly the incidence of taxation under the imperial régime as it affected the Collectors —the Provincial Authorities, and the ultimate receivers—the Imperial Authorities, or the Court at Peking.

'The great principle underlying the financial administration of the Chinese Empire up to the present is that the Imperial Government makes demands on the provinces in lump sums, leaving the Provincial Governments to apportion the details. Experience in a rough way has pointed out the proportionate sum each province is capable of transmitting, and beyond this there is at present no machinery whereby the provincial levies can be controlled either in amount or in incident. To add to this difficulty, there exists on the part of the Provincial Governments and Peking a profound want of confidence. Each deeply mistrusts the other, and tries to deceive as to its income and expenditure.'

The Imperial Government has drawn the revenues to be derived from the sea-borne commerce—it has always 'been looked upon as an appanage of Imperial power, and the provinces have never openly ventured to interfere in the Imperial arrangements; but when the cargo was once landed for local consumption, the position was at once altered, and the Imperial Government had no more right to interfere than had the provincial in the first instance. Such has been the theory.' Imterference has, however, taken place from time to time on both sides, when either found itself more powerful than the other, but with normal conditions the interference ceased.

'When one considers the delays, the squeezes, and above all the uncertainties to which goods are subjected in China, one is inclined to marvel, not that the trade of China is so small in proportion to its population as compared with other countries, but that any trade exists at all. One of the greatest curses of China is the detestable system of likin barriers which everywhere obstruct the trade.'

It was proposed 'that in return for the raising of the import tariff, from 5 per cent. *ad volorem* to 15 per cent.,' the Chinese Government should 'abolish entirely all internal taxation, whether Imperial, provincial, local, or municipal, on all merchandise, foreign or native, whether for import, export, or internal consumption (salt and native opium alone excepted), and' 'remove all likin and other barriers, . . . the British Government to reserve to itself the right to cancel this arrangement and revert to the now existing conditions, should the Chinese Government fail to carry out the stipulation of the agreement.'

Hazell's Annual for 1903 thus puts the position of affairs at that time, with regard to the Scheme proposed by Sir J. L. Mackay, and approved by several high Chinese Officials, as well as Imperially sanctioned:—

'The Scheme was embodied in a Commercial Treaty with Great Britain . . . by which it was provided that all likin dues, stations, and barriers, and every form of internal taxation on British goods should be abolished in return for a surtax equivalent to a duty of one and a half times the duty leviable' under the 1901 Protocol. This to 'become effective in January, 1904,' should the other Powers likewise agree.

'The first mention of it [likin] in its present form was in 1852, when the Governor of Shantung instituted it in response to demand made on the province for funds to suppress the T'ai P'ing rebellion. The idea of the tax is, however, said to have originated with the Tao-t'ai Yao some years earlier. It was extended throughout China about 1863. . . . The tax was originally one tenth of one per cent. on the value of the goods; it is now estimated that goods passing through one province pay five per cent., and passing through several provinces as much as twenty per cent. of their value.

By treaty stipulation foreigners importing and exporting goods pay to the Maritime Customs seven and a half instead of the regulation five per cent. duty and are then exempt from the likin tax; but this has never been adhered to. The foreign Powers have long tried to get the tax abolished, in the interests of all trade, both local and foreign, paying extra duty to the Maritime Customs.'

The Mackay Treaty of 1902, between Great Britain and China, and the Commercial Treaty between the United States and China of 1903 both proved abortive, but by a treaty between the United States, Belgium, Great Britain, China, France, Italy, Japan, the Netherlands, and Portugal, dated at Washington on February 6th, 1922, it was agreed that "immediate steps shall be taken, through a Special Conference to prepare the way for the speedy abolition of likin."

The following table shows the estimated amounts under the respective headings:—

	$
Likin proper	39,250,000
Goods tax (on trains)	2,200,000
Main and subsidiary taxes (such as tea, sugar, bamboo, lumber, fishery, live stock, mining, and other similar taxes)	11,720,000
Excise tax	1,600,000
Total	54,770,000

The Peking Octroi Revenue (a tax which has given rise to much opposition and is illegal as regards foreign imported goods) averaged $200,000 per month in 1923 and 1924.

References.—Wagel, *Finance in China;* Edkins, *Revenue and Taxation of the Chinese Empire.*

LITERATURE.—'Untold treasures lie hidden in the rich lodes of Chinese literature.' This may be considered a sufficient answer to those who question if there is anything worth seeking for in what has been termed by another equally learned sinologist the barren wilderness of Chinese literature.

Numbers of books of great antiquity have left no remembrance behind them but that of their names, or, at the best, but little else. Some fragments are reputed to have survived from before the time of Confucius (552-479 B.C.). The sage said of himself that he was a transmitter, not an originator, and, as such, he utilised material, that was in existence to a great extent previously, in the production of the works which are attributed to his hand. From the time of Confucius onward, for some centuries, the numerous writings produced by the different philosophers give evidence of mental vigour and activity. The power of the literary class, backed up by their arsenals of learning, and their muniments of classical lore, were forces that threatened to thwart, by their conservative and other tendencies, the iron will of the monarch, who rendered himself infamous in Chinese history by his despotic and cruel attempt to sweep the obstructive *literati* and their books out of his path of progress. Works on medicines, divination, and husbandry, were the only ones that were exempt from the storm of destruction that swept over the land, with the exception of those, not a few in number, that surreptitiously weathered the tempest buried in mountain holes and hidden behind walls, or stored up in the memory of some who prized them better than life itself. After the night of desolation rose the brighter dawn of the Han dynasty, when every effort was made to recover the lost treasures, and with such success that considerably over ten thousand volumes, or sections of books, the work of some hundreds of authors, were gathered together. But unfortunately this library, collected with such care, was destroyed by fire at the close of the dynasty, and other destructions of valuable imperial collections have taken place more than once since. It has, however, been the pride of succeeding dynasties to follow the example of the Han, and every encouragement has been given to literature.

The T'ang dynasty especially deserves notice for its patronage of letters. The classification now extant was then adopted, viz.:—The four divisions of Classics, History, Philosophy, and Belles Lettres; but these are so numerously subdivided, that a mere list of them would occupy a page and a half. It will thus be seen that, except in a work especially devoted to that purpose, it would be impossible to give even a *résumé* of the vast field thus covered. We must content ourselves with the indication of a few of the more salient points.

The Classical writings occupy the foremost position not only as regards antiquity, but they are also regarded as the foundation of all learning by the Chinese; and they have been the cause of the production of not a small proportion of Chinese books.

The 'Four Books' and the 'Five Classics' are the chief amongst the classical works of the Chinese. The 'Four Books' consist of 'The Confucian Analects,' 'The Great Learning, 'The Doctrine of the Mean,' and 'The Works of Mencius.' The 'Five Classics' consist of 'The Book of Changes,' 'The Book of History,' 'The Book of Odes,' 'The Book of Rites,' and 'The Spring and Autumn Annals.' The last is the only one of which Confucius is actually the author, though he compiled 'The Book of History' and 'The Odes.' 'The Book of Changes' is regarded with almost universal reverence, both on account of its antiquity, and also for the unfathomable wisdom which is supposed to be concealed under its mysterious symbols.

'The Four Books,' which rank next after 'The Five Classics,' are composed, for the most part, of the words, conversations, and opinions of Confucius and Mencius, as recorded by their disciples. Around these, and a few other works, has gathered an immense collection of commentaries and works elucidative of the Classics; among these the Chinese class dictionaries, over the production of which much labour has been spent by eminent Chinese scholars, in order to conserve the purity of the language.

'The Bamboo Books' are a collection of bamboo tablets covered with more than 100,000 seal characters, said to have been exhumed in A.D. 279 from the tomb of Hsiang, King of Wei, who died in 295 B.C. They contained fifteen different works, some of which have probably been lost, but included the *I ching* and a book of annals in 12 or 13 chapters from the reign of Huang Ti to 298 B.C. Their authenticity is doubtful.

Historical works, or dynastic histories, are sub-divided into a number of divisions. These have been compiled dynasty after dynasty on a general plan, dealing first with the Imperial Records, then the Arts and Sciences, followed by a Biographical Section. The latest compilation of them is called 'The Twenty-four Histories,' comprised in 3,264 books by over twenty different authors, commencing with Sz-má Tsin [Ssŭ-ma Ch'ien], the Herodotus of China.

HISTORICAL ANNALS.—This class of histories contains a concise narrative of events on the plan of 'The Spring and Autumn Annals.' Among the most celebrated of these is the Tsz Chi Tung Kiu [*Tzŭ chih t'ung chien*], of the famous historian Sz-má Kwang [Ssŭ-ma Kuang,] in 294 books, which occupied the author nineteen years in writing.

Another division of historical works is that of 'The Complete Records' in which a general view of a particular subject is taken, 'The Historical Classic' being taken as the example.

Besides these, there are several other divisions of Historical Works, such as 'Separate Histories,' 'Miscellaneous Histories, 'Official Documents,' and 'Biographies,' which last are very numerous and some ancient, one being more than two thousand years old. Added to these, are 'Historical Excerpta,' 'Contemporary Records,' which deal with other co-existent states, and 'Chronography,' this last heading comprising a small category. 'The Complete Antiquarian Researches of Má Twan-lin,' A.D. 1275, is a most extensive and profound work.'

Another division is of Geographical and Topographical Works. Among these is the famous 'Hill and River [or Topographical] Classic,' containing wonderful accounts of countries inhabited by pigmies and giants; of men with a hole through the middle of their bodies, who when going out for an airing have a pole thrust through it and are thus hoisted on the shoulders of two men and carried along; of one-sided people, who have only one arm and one leg, and who have to walk in couples, as they cannot stand alone; of tiny pigmies who, like Alpine travellers, rope themselves together to prevent large birds carrying them off; of numerous wonderful and strange objects in the animal creation, as well as fish and snakes with many heads, and fish with many bodies to one head. It is very amusing to look through an illustrated edition of this book, and originally a *bona fide* attempt at an account of what were though it contains many strange vagaries, it was probably actually considered to exist; it is a work of great antiquity. In this connection it is interesting to note that Pliny speaks of the Blemmyans, an African tribe that were headless, the eyes and mouth being in the breast—'Blemmys traduntur capita abesse, ore et oculis pectori affixis.' 'Historia Naturalis,' Bk. V. ch. 3. See also the 'Tempest,' Act. III. Sc. 3.

> 'When we were boys,
> Who would believe that there were
> . . . . . . such men
> Whose heads stood in their breasts?'

[The origin of the idea of headless people is to be found in the mistake, handed down by tradition uncorrected through paucity of language, of headless tribes for headless ancestors.]

Every small division of the empire has its topographical work dealing with its own history, antiquities, towns, curiosities, and anything of interest connected with it; one on Kuangtung, being a historical and statistical account of that province, is in 182 volumes. The late Dr. Wylie well said of this department of Chinese literature: 'The series of topographical writings in China are probably unrivalled in any nation, for extent and systematic comprehensiveness.' Works on the water-courses also find a place in this section.

There are categories under which come bibliographical and other works. 'One of the finest specimens of Bibliography possessed by this or perhaps any other nation . . . is a descriptive catalogue (in 400 books) of the Imperial Library of the present [Manchu] dynasty.' The Index Expurgatorius is also contained in this division, and several tens of thousands of volumes are prohibited in whole or in part. The Historical division ends with the section of 'Historical Critiques.'

The third great division, that of philosophers, includes, not only that class, but writers on Religion, the Arts and the Sciences, etc. Original thinkers are found amongst the Chinese authors, who have not subscribed to the Confucian teaching, and some of our modern Western ideas have already seen the light of day in the Far East, long before they were ever dreamt of by our Western moral philosophers.

The immense mass of matter to be found under this grand heading may be judged from its subdivisions, viz.:—

1. Literati.
2. Writers on Military Affairs.
3. Writers on Legislation.
4. Writers on Agriculture.
5. Medical Writers.
6. Astronomy and Mathematics.
7. Divination.
8. Arts.
9. Repertories.
10. Miscellaneous Writers.
11. Cyclopædias.
12. Essayists.
13. Taoism.
14. Buddhism.

Under this heading come 'The Sacred Edicts': moral maxims written by the second Emperor of the present dynasty for the instruction of the people. Taking these maxims for texts, a series of homiletic sermons were composed on them by his successor, and they were read aloud to the public on the 1st and 5th of every month throughout the empire.

Medical works claim attention from the numerous writers on this branch. The oldest work was written several centuries before the Christian era. It has been supposed from their minute account of the human body, that the Chinese, at one time, practised dissection. If so, however, the remembrance of it has long been forgotten, and their medical works are characterised by groundless theories, which, considering the low state of science until recent years even in the West, is not much to be wondered at. (See DOCTORS.)

ASTRONOMY AND MATHEMATICS.—The Chinese in ancient times represented the starry firmament by three different methods. First, as a concave sphere; secondly, a globe is taken to represent the universe, and stars are placed on the outer surface; the third method is supposed to bear a close analogy to that of the West. The Jesuit missionaries assisted the Chinese materially in righting their calendar, and in other matters connected with astronomy, contributing their quota also to the books on astronomy and other mathematical matters. One of the native books on Mathematics has quite an interesting history. It is supposed to have been in use in the Chou dynasty, was destroyed in the general burning of books by Ts'in Shih Hwang-ti, after which imperfect fragments of it were gathered together during the Han dynasty, when additions were made to them; a commentary was written on it, and an exposition; it was well known in the T'ang dynasty, preserved as a rarity in the Sung, and entirely lost in the Ming; but fortunately it was possible to gather up the fragments that were found in one of those gigantic cyclopædias, which the Chinese have been so fond of forming, containing copious quotations from thousands of books, and taking years of toil to compile. The copy now in existence has thus been gathered together piecemeal in this way, and has been found to agree with quotations and with the description given of the book. 'It is divided into nine sections, viz.:—Plain Mensuration, Proportion, Fellowship, Evolution, Mensuration of Solids, Alligation, Surplus and Deficit, Equations, and Trigonometry.' It contains 246 problems. The illustrations have unfortunately been lost.

Under the heading of Divination are not a few works; books on dreams coming under the same section, the counterparts of 'The Napoleon Dream-book' and 'The Egyptian Dream-Book' in English.

As to books on Arts, Wylie remarks:—

'However the Chinese may differ from Western nations in matters of mere convention, the fact that they have methodical treatises, of more than a thousand years' standing, on Painting, Writing, Music, Engraving, Archery, Drawing, and kindred subjects, ought surely to secure a candid examination of the state of such matters among them, before subjecting them to an indiscriminate condemnation.'

Under Repertories of Science are Cyclopædias. The most remarkable under this heading is the *Yung lo ta tien*, prepared by direction of the second Emperor of the Ming dynasty; two thousand two hundred scholars were employed on the work, which was to include the 'substance of all the classical, historical, philosophical, and literary works hitherto published, embracing astronomy, geography, the occult sciences, medicine, Buddhism, Taoism, and the arts.' It was published in 22,877 books, and the table of contents filled 60 books. Wholesale selections were made of some books; in this way '385 ancient and rare works have been preserved, which would otherwise have been irrecoverably lost.'

A fine specimen of the voluminous encyclopædias the Chinese so delight in is to be found in the British Museum. Its title is *T'u shu chi ch'êng*. It consists of 6,109 volumes. The Museum authorities have had it rebound in 1,000 volumes, which require ten tablecases to accommodate it.

ESSAYISTS.—Works of fiction are despised, as a rule, by the Chinese *literati*, but they form a most interesting and valuable portion of the vast body of literature which has, for more than twenty centuries past, been in ever-increasing volume seeing the light of day. The most popular is the historical romance. 'The San Kwok Chi' [*San kuo chih*], dealing with the period from A.D. 168 to 265. The plot 'is wrought out with a most elaborate complication of details,' it abounds with the marvellous and supernatural, and is laid amidst the stirring scenes after the fall of the Han dynasty. 'The Dream of the Red Chamber' [*Hung lou mêng*] is another popular novel dealing with domestic life, but not moral in its tone. Another holding the highest estimation, in the opinion of all classes, from the purity of its style, is 'The Pastimes of the Study' [*Liao chai chih i*], full of tales of wonder and mystery. This has been translated into English by Prof. Giles, under the title 'Strange Tales from a Chinese Studio,' in two volumes. Chinese novels contain much that would be considered tedious by an English reader. Minute details are entered into about the characters and the localities; trifling particulars and lengthy conversations are given; long digressions, prolix descriptions, and sermonising are all indulged in; but the 'authors render their characters interesting and natural.' The characters are well sustained at times; there is, of course, a plot, and much of what goes to make up the main portion of a tale in Western lands is also introduced, such as the troubles of the hero and heroine, complicated by the evil machinations of the villain, and all the accessories of plot and counterplot, and at last the grand finale in a happy marriage. All showing that human nature is alike the wide world over, the surroundings, of course, having an Eastern cast in the one case. There is, however, a large class of this literature which cannot be commended.

BUDDHIST LITERATURE.—Buddhist books include many translations of Buddhistic works from the Sanscrit, as well as original compositions.

TAOIST LITERATURE.—The Tao Teh King [*Tao-tê ching*] is the only work known to be produced by Lo tsz [*Lao Tzŭ*]. The aspect of Taoism has changed since its early days; its votaries, who believed in achemy, and the subduing of animal propensities, have been succeeded by a set of most base charlatans (see TAOISM). Books dealing with the gods and genii are found under this heading. One of the most popular of all Taoist works is 'The Book of Recompenses and Rewards' [*Kang ying p'ien*] (of a future state), which has gone through innumerable editions, and is sometimes issued embellished with anecdotes and illustrated with woodcuts. It is thought a great act of merit to distribute it.

BELLES LETTRES, in which are included Polite Literature, Poetry, and Analytical Works. There are numbers of divisions. The class of 'Individual Collections' deserves attention, as it is 'one of the most prolific branches of Chinese literature,' but short-lived. In this class may be noted the collections of the two celebrated poets of the T'ang and Sung dynasties, Li T'ai-po and Su Tung-p'o, comprised in 30 and 115 books, and that of the celebrated historian and statesman Sz-má-Kwang [Ssŭ-ma Kuang] in 80 books. Most of the emperors of the Manchu dynasty contributed their share to this branch of Chinese literature.

Under the heading of 'General Collections' are classed selections of choice specimens of acknowledged merit from the pens of various authors. One of 'the greatest enterprises in the history of book-making' may be noted in this connection; it saw the light of day in the time of the Sung dynasty, and consisted of 1,000 volumes, being an 'extensive collection of all specimens of polite literature subsequent to the Liang dynasty. . . . Nine-tenths of the whole were made up of the writings of the T'ang scholars.'

RHYMES AND SONGS.—(See POETRY.)

DRAMA.—The Drama is not included in native book catalogues, though considerable works are found of that nature. It was developed at a comparatively late date—the latter end of the T'ang dynasty saw its origin. It continued to improve until the time of the Yüan dynasty, when the best collection of plays was published as 'The Hundred Plays of the Yüan Dynasty [*Yüan jên po chung ch'ü*].' (See THEATRE.)

Professor Douglas thus writes of Chinese literature as a whole:—

'In the countless volumes which have appeared and are appearing from the many publishing centres, we see mirrored the temperament of the people, their excellences, their deficiencies and their peculiarities. Abundant evidence is to be found of their activity in research and diligence in compilation, nor are signs wanting which point to the absence of the faculty of imagination, and to an inability to rise beyond a certain degree of excellence or knowledge, while at the same time we have seen displayed the characteristics both of matter and manner, which most highly commend themselves to the national taste.

'As a consequence of the very unplastic nature of the language, there is wanting in the literature that grace of diction and varying force of expression which are found in languages capable of inflection and of syntactical motion. The stiff angularity of the written language, composed as it is of isolated, unassimilating characters, robs eloquence of its charm, poetry of its musical rhythm, and works of fancy of half their power; but in no way interferes with the relation of facts, nor the statement of a philosophical argument.

'And hence to all but the Chinese mind, which knows no other model of excellence, the poetical and fanciful works of Chinese authors offer fewer attractions than their writings on history, science, and philosophy. Unlike the literatures of other countries, one criticism applies to the whole career of Chinese letters. It is difficult to imagine a nation of busy writers pursuing a course of literature for more than 3,000 years, and yet failing to display greater progress in thought and style than Chinese authors have done. That their works vary in quality, no one who has read two Chinese books can doubt; but the variations are within limits, and . . . the width of thought and power of expression have in no wise increased, at least, since the revival of letters under the Han dynasty, B.C. 206-A.D. 25.'

It is unfortunate that many of the finest passages of Chinese literature lose, when translated, their epigrammatic force, the play of words loses its sparkle, the glittering poetry is transformed into prosy periods, and what is full of life and spirit falls flat and tame on the foreign ear. The freshness of the flowers of speech is gone when the ideas of the original are plucked and transferred into the Englishman's receptacle of thought. In other words, just as the Chinese himself looks best in his native costume, the thoughts of his mind appear in their best when clothed in his native language—the foreign dress often fits them badly; and, in short, many of the productions of a Chinese pen have to be read in the original, if the reader would appreciate to the full the brilliancy of some of these jewels of the first water; for not a few stray passages, ripe with the love of the beautiful, are to be found scattered through the pages of Chinese literature, instinct with true poetic genius—glowing with the deep feeling caught from a communion with the hills and mountains, rivers, streams and babbling brooks, woods and forests, sunshine and storm, in solitudes away from the busy haunts of men. These ecstatic raptures of the true child of nature strike a responsive chord in the breast of the Western barbarian. So charming are they in their simplicity, so in unison with every touch of nature, that one feels that the ardent lovers of the beauties of God's beautiful world speak but one language, equally understood by all who have revelled in such simple delights, and that there is no place round this wide, wide world 'where their voice is not heard,' whether it be in the confines of the Middle Kingdom, or in what was the *Ultima Thule* of barbarism when many of these fine passages were penned.

It is, however, in comparison either with the literature of other Eastern countries, or with our own some centuries since, remembering at the same time their isolation and the want, to a comparatively great extent, of the vivifying influences of the competition of other countries pursuing the same researches and branches of knowledge, that the most just view can be taken of what Chinese literature is as a whole. With the patient toil, love of research, and passionate ardour for literary pursuits, it is an interesting speculation to give rein to one's fancies—to wonder, in short, what would have been the result had the Chinese possessed all the advantages we have been blessed with in the West, instead of presenting the unique spectacle of a nation self-contained and self-sufficient in all its requirements. The few chances they have had of assistance from the West, when once appreciated (for the Chinese, unlike the Japanese, are slow in accepting what is offered to them until fully proved and approved of), have been accepted and made good use of, as in the case of a knowledge of Sanscrit introduced by the Buddhist priests, and more lately in the introduction of Western knowledge and science, which no doubt is destined eventually to exercise a wonderful effect. One of the greatest boons that can be conferred on this ancient and conservative empire, will be the knowledge that true wisdom consists in the publication of books in the language of the people, and not in the book style—a style as remote from that of the former almost as Latin is from that of English. Then knowledge and learning will be the property of everyone instead of being confined to the lettered classes.

References.—Wylie, *Notes on Chinese Literature;* Giles, *Gems of Chinese Literature.* We cannot give a list here of the native works which have been translated into English and the other European languages: they are legion.

MALT SWEETS AND OTHERS.—Malt sweets are made by soaking grains of wheat in water for three or four days (a day longer is required in winter and a day shorter in summer) until they send out sprouts a couple of inches long or so. They are then washed in water, when the husks float to the surface and are thrown away, not being wanted. They are next boiled with glutinous rice and form a sweetmeat which is sold in little black pots. The Chinese are very fond of sweets, and candied melon rind, cocoa-nut strips, ginger, and many other kinds of sweetmeats too numerous to mention.

MANCHUS.—The family that occupied the throne in China from A.D. 1644-1912 was not a native one, but one of Manchu Tartars, being a small branch of the Tungusic nomads. Their original habitat was in the neighbourhood of the Long White Mountain. Transplanted thence by the ambition of a capable leader, they flourished in the wider area of China, which gave greater scope to their abilities than the narrow confines of Manchuria.

The history of the whole of the region is a long one, and is blended with that of China through many generations and dynasties.

Repeated waves of incursions have swept into the North of China, or beaten against its borders to be driven back, and, losing their power for a period, have finally gathered strength and united their forces for another effort; this, perhaps, proving more successful than the last, has resulted in a partial or complete sway over the Middle Kingdom, which with its riches, has ever proved a tempting prey for its nomadic neighbours.

The Manchus (who, in the earliest historical times, occupied the region around and to the north of Shêngking) have been known by various names; in their quiescent periods by that of Sishūn, Sooshūn, or Nüjin [Nüchên], as well as by their numerous dynastic titles assumed when, under the vigorous guidance of a skilful chieftain, their power was consolidated and a simple tribal rule was developed into that of an incipient state, having within its comparatively small bounds the potentialities of mighty empires and kingdoms. History has only repeated itself in their case, as in that of many others; for the incursions of the Huns are only the movements in Europe of the same species of tribes who originated from the same neighbourhood, and who, on account of their selection of modern Europe as their stage in the one case, brought themselves more prominently before the eyes of the Western historian than the Manchu Tartars did when they overthrew the native Chinese dynasty in the other case. That overrun of Europe is more akin to the partial conquest of China—that part of it lying to the North of the Yellow River—by the Nüjin or Sooshūn, the ancestors of the present Manchus, where they ruled as the Kin (or Chin) dynasty for more than a century, A.D. 1115 to 1234, contemporaneously with a native dynasty in the South of China, until both were deposed by another foreign dynasty, named Yüan, that of the Mongols under Genghis Khan.

In common with the other nomadic neighbours of China on her Northern frontier, the ancestors of the Manchu Tartars play a conspicuous part in the history of ancient China. Wars, intrigues, subterfuges, plots and counterplots, treachery, cruelty, and lies, fill up the pages of this history as much as they do those of the West, and, except to those specially interested in such incidents, prove but dry reading. The Manchu power enlarged its realms, swallowing up neighbouring states, until it extended between the Gulf of Liao-tung and the Amur; and Manchuria was more populous than at any subsequent period, though the emigration into it now bids fair to raise it to an equally populous condition. Nor at this time could it have been in a low state of civilisation, as we are told that 'learning flourished and literature abounded.' This strong and extensive kingdom was battered to pieces by the Khitans; and broke up into a number of small independent clans under separate chieftains, which, it would appear, relapsed again into a nomadic, rude, and primitive style of life. Consolidating again under the name of Nüjin, they commenced activity once more and became a force and factor in the ceaseless wars with, and against, the divided states of China, as well as the neighbouring kingdoms. In passing, we may notice that such seems to be the history of all the Mongolic tribes, viz.: first, a nomadic, primitive state, followed by increase of numbers and power, and a settled and highly civilised condition, to be followed, on final defeat and overthrow, by an abandonment of literature, cities, and agriculture, and a return to the primitive nomadic condition.

But to return to the Nüjin, who were rapidly developing into the second condition when their chief took the word Gold, *Kin,* for the title of his dynasty in contradistinction to that of the *Liao,* or Iron dynasty, that of the Khitans or Mongols, then ruling in Northern China, and whom he had defeated in battle, 'for iron, if strong, rusted; while gold always remained bright.'

By the combination of the Sung and the Kin, the Liao dynasty was driven from the throne out of Northern China, and the Kin substituted for it. The Yellow River had been the boundary between the Liao and Sung, whereas the Yang-tzŭ was the boundary between the Kin and the Southern Sung, which succeeded the broken-down Sung. The Amur was the northern boundary of the Kin. They 'established themselves at Peking in A.D. 1115, whence they were driven, in A.D. 1234, by Genghis Khan, and fled back to the ancestral haunts. on the Songari and Liao Rivers.' Their modern descendants, after some centuries, again established themselves at Peking, and reigned longer than their ancestors—from A.D. 1644 to 1912—and over a larger extent of country, for it embraced the whole of the China of the present day. (See the article on History, where, under the Ts'ing, or Ch'ing dynasty, the name they have elected to rule under, some short account will be found of their doings).

Amongst the modern Manchus, Buddhism is in vogue, and spiritualism is believed in—in the shape of the fox, the stoat, or the tiger. They seem more religiously disposed than the Chinese, and Christian missions have also met with success amongst them. They are not so opposed to Western innovations as the Chinese were until recently.

Their peaceful life and dependence upon charity has eaten much of the hardihood and bravery out of the men as a nation, but the rulers are still able men. They do not bind the feet of the women.

References.—Ross, *The Manchus;* Howarth, *History of the Mongols;* Klaproth, *Mémoires sur l'Asie;* Ross, *Corea, its History, Manners, and Customs; The Phœnix,* 1871; *Records of the Missionary Conference held at Shanghai,* 1890; *China Review,* xv, 263; xiv, 281-5; xv, 23; Parker, *A Thousand Years of the Tartars;* Grosier, *Description de la Chine; Revue d'Orient,* 1844; *Chinese Recorder,* xxiv, 501-13; *Geographical Journal,* London, 1893-4; 1904-5; Du Halde, *Description of the Empire of China and Chinese Tartary;* Hosie, *Manchuria: its People, Resources, and Recent History;* Mayers, *The Chinese Government.*

MANCHU LANGUAGE.—The Manchu language belongs to the Turanian stock of languages, is entirely unlike Chinese, and is polysyllabic. It has been inferred that all the languages of Mongolia, Manchuria, and Corea, were originally one language—at all events they were polysyllabic 2,000 years ago. It will thus be seen that this language boasts of a considerable antiquity; but knots in strings, notches in sticks, and such like devices of unlettered people were the only means of record. When a pressing need of a more intelligible mode of perpetuating their speech by visible signs was felt, the Manchus, in the time of the T'ang dynasty, turned to the Chinese and studied Chinese letters and literature; a desire to have a writing of their own arose amongst them, the Khitanes being the first to adopt some of the Chinese characters to stand for the syllables of their own language. This was in A.D. 920. Two kinds of characters were employed, but, though it is not a thousand years ago, not a trace of them, as far as is known, has been left behind.

'It [the Manchu language] is of Tungusic origin, sonorous and easily learned. It is composed of dissyllabic roots, the meaning of which is modified (especially in verbs) by agglutinative suffixes. The alphabet is syllabic, and of Syro-Uigur origin. The latest form has been borrowed, in the XVIth century, from the Mongols. There are 6 to 8 vowels, 18 consonants, and 10 diacritical marks. Like the Chinese, it is written in vertical columns, but from left to right. The Manchu language has no indigenous literature.'

It would appear, however, that the Khitans only perfected former attempts made by others. The ancestors of the present Manchus used both this Khitan and Chinese writing, but, after conquering half of the Khitan empire, the Emperor ordered a new style of writing to be devised, and, pretty much in the same way as before, parts of Chinese characters were used to express the sounds. In A.D. 1119 and 1135, two different styles were invented, and, as with the Khitans' former essay, were extensively used. This second written language was again forgotten and disused; and the modern Manchus only learned from Chinese history that their ancestors possessed a written language of their own. Unfortunately it also appears to be irretrievably lost. These two written languages were written horizontally. The Mongols, successors of these ancient Manchus (Nüchên), used Uigur writing for governmental matters, which is very like the ancient Syriac, or Sabæan (whether it was introduced to this part of the world by the Nestorian missionaries [see MISSIONS], or earlier, is not known); and the Nüchên or Manchus, who were subject to the Mongols, used this Uigur writing. They also used the Mongol language until the foundations of the Manchu empire were laid, when they discarded it, still using the Mongol alphabet to write the Manchu language; but when many Chinese works had been translated into Manchu, it was found that it, the Mongol alphabet, was not a suitable medium to employ in writing Manchu. Improvements were then introduced, by which the 'Manchu writing acquired an alphabet distinct from Mongol; and, although for two hundred years no further radical changes have been introduced, it has during that time, in the course of long and extensive use, developed a roundness, elegance, and grace which still further distinguish it from its rude parent.' Modern Manchu is, like Chinese, written in vertical columns.

Every effort was made by the Manchu Government to foster the acquisition of their own language by Manchus: books were translated from the Chinese, for they had no literature of their own, and every means taken to make the Manchus a literary race, but all to no purpose, for the conquered race, the Chinese, have vanquished their conquerors. Though numbering five millions in 1848, they live scattered in garrisons amongst the Chinese, and having to learn Chinese, and possessing no indigenous native literature, they have turned to Chinese books. 'There exist in all about 250 works in Manchu, nearly all of which are translations from the Classics, some historical and metaphysical works, literary essays, collections of famous writers, novels, poetry, laws and regulations, Imperial edicts, dictionaries, phrase-books, etc. Most of these translations are excellent, but they are all literal.' Not only with the common people, but with the Manchu Government itself, Chinese was of more importance, for what are five millions of people compared with three or four hundred millions; so the consequence has been that Manchu is being rapidly forgotten, and is becoming an extinct language in China, though probably spoken in the wilds of Manchuria.

References.—Chinese Recorder, March & April, 1891; *China Review,* Vol. xxv; *Journal N.C.B.R.A.S.,* N.S. xxiv, 1-45; Wylie, *Translation of the T'sing Wen K'eung: a Chinese Grammar of the Manchu Tartar Language, with Introductory Notes on Manchu Literature;* Möllendorff, *A Manchu Grammar with Analysed Texts.* In an Appendix at the end of the last work, is a list of the principal European works for the study of Manchu.

MANDARIN.—The nomenclature applied to certain things Chinese has cast a glamour round them which a simpler naming would have avoided. A case in point is the term mandarin: with the rhythmic flow of the word and with its foreign flavour, a certain *soupçon* of the poetic and the mysterious is imported into it, so that the distant Westerner is apt, when reading about mandarins, to picture in his mind's eye some highly exalted and privileged class, the members of which are born to the purple, and dwell amidst halls of pleasure surrounded by affluence and luxury and ministered to by the poor down-trodden populace. A better appreciation of what mandarin means would doubtless have resulted had the terms used been officers of governments, or civil and military officials.

The method by which the ranks of the civil and military services were and are recruited, and some details about them, will be found in the articles on ARMY EXAMINATIONS, GOVERNMENT, and NAVY.

The word mandarin is derived from the Portuguese *mandar*, to command. The term mandarin is only applied to such officials as are called kwún (kuan) by the Chinese, and not to the subordinate class of officials. In other words, it is restricted in its application to those officials who were entitled to wear a button. There were nine ranks of such officials; the buttons which distinguished them were as follows:—for the first and second ranks, a transparent and opaque (ruby and coral) red button respectively; for the third and fourth, a transparent and opaque blue (sapphire and lapis lazuli) button respectively; for the fifth and sixth, a transparent and opaque white (crystal and stone) button respectively; for the seventh, a plain gold one; and for the eighth and ninth, a worked gold one. Since the abolition of the Monarchy they have lost their meaning and gone out of use, though occasionally still worn by some old-fashioned ex-officials.

These buttons, as they have been called in English, were commonly of a round shape, about an inch in diameter, and formed a knob on the apex of the conical-shaped official, or dress, hat.

The different grades of civil and military officials also wore, as insignia of their rank, certain birds (in the case of those in the Civil Service) and certain animals (in the case of those in the Army and Navy), embroidered in a large square, of about a foot in size in its two dimensions, on the breast and back of their robes, as well as girdle clasps of different materials—both branches of the service using the same. The following is a list of these insignia:—

	Civil.	Army & Navy.	Girdle Clasps.
1st rank	Manchurian crane.	Unicorn.	Jade set in rubies.
2nd ,,	Golden pheasant.	Lion of India.	Gold set in rubies.
3rd ,,	Peacock.	Leopard.	Worked gold.
4th ,,	Wild Goose.	Tiger.	Worked gold with silver button.
5th ,,	Silver pheasant.	Bear.	Worked gold with plain silver button.
6th ,,	Egret.	Tiger-cat.	Mother-of-pearl.
7th ,,	Mandarin duck.	Mottled bear.	Silver.
8th ,,	Quail.	Seal.	Clear horn.
9th ,,	Long-tailed jay.	Rhinoceros.	Buffalo's horn.

Mandarin, when applied to language, refers to the *lingua franca* in use throughout China in official intercourse and in Courts of Justice; it is very poorly spoken by many, being mixed up with localisms; it is also the speech, in its various dialects, in considerable parts of China. (See DIALECTS.)

The word mandarin has also been used, by foreigners in China, to distinguish a lovely species of duck of beautiful plumage—the mandarin duck (*Anas-* or *aix-galericulata*), which is an emblem of conjugal fidelity with the natives. For the same reason probably, that of superiority over others, it has also been used to designate a species of orange, the mandarin orange. (See FRUIT.)

MANGROVE.—The mangrove is found growing largely near Swatow, and it grows on the south side of the Island of Hongkong, near Aberdeen. The following account of mangroves in Sierra Leone will show the work Nature has designed this shrub for:—

'Mr. Scott Elliot states that the effect of the mangroves in creating alluvial soil could be very clearly seen at Mahela and in the Samu country generally. Mangrove trees seem, in fact, he says, to have been designed by Nature to change any bay or indentation of the coast-line into fertile soil. As the level of the ground gradually rises above high tide, the mangroves, which require a constant supply of brackish water, die off, and the whole grove advances seaward, leaving behind it a mass of rich, vegetable, alluvial mud, better suited for rice than probably any other soil in existence.'

The above rapid growth of soil by their means is what follows apparently under the most favourable conditions.

Mangrove bark (*rhizophera Mangle*) is used for dyeing the fishermen's nets in the South of China a ruddy brown to preserve them.

MAPS.—The old purely native maps of China are most curious productions. The eighteen provinces are compressed into an oblong shape to meet the requirements of the map. Double lines mark the boundaries of the provinces where not otherwise divided by the rivers. These latter are represented by broad, wavy meandering masses, joining and separating in a most wonderfully mysterious manner, one of the junctions being due, no doubt, to a desire to represent the Grand Canal. The Great Wall runs across the top of the map, being represented by an immense battlemented structure an inch in height. The other three sides of the map are nearly surrounded by water represented by tumultuous waves. On the east is the source of the Yellow River, from which the Yangtsz seems to rise in the Sea of Stars and Constellations. Cartouche-like frames of different patterns contain the names of principal places. For foreign countries these names are found placed in the seas surrounding China. In a series extending down the east coast and close to the land are thus arranged the names of Corea, the strange Fu-song, Japan, the Great Loo-Choo, the Little Loo-Choo, and other names. To the south are Portugal, Annam, and other countries. There is a want of exactitude even in the position of places in China itself; for instance, the celebrated Lò Faú [Lo Fou] Mountains are put up at the north of the Canton Province. With the exception of these noted mountains in this province, the whole country might be a level plain instead of diversified with numerous ranges of towering hills and rugged mountainous ramparts. The same is true of other provinces for one height a piece, occasionally varied, is the *quantum sufficit* of the cartographer, and he is quite content with two or three in some of the provinces. To make up for this, a mountain range is depicted at the very top of the map, and another shares with the seas a place at the bottom. This geographer has been content with filling up the provinces with the names of Prefectures and Districts.

The Jesuits, some three centuries ago, were employed by the Chinese Emperor in trigonometrical surveys and the construction of maps of the different provinces of the empire.

Of recent years numbers of maps have been made by foreigners of the whole Empire of China, and numerous ones of districts where they have settled, or travelled, or of rivers which they have ascended, or descended.

MARRIAGE.—Marriage is the one end and aim set forth for a girl: this is the goal to which she is taught to look forward, or to which her parents look forward for her, for it matters little about the girl herself. She is almost a nonentity in the matter: her wishes are not consulted; she has often never seen her future husband; she is even sometimes hypothetically betrothed to a contingent husband, that is to say, two married couples agree that if one should have a son and the other a daughter, they shall be married when they grow up. From the last, it will be seen that the man is not much better off than the woman in these matters. Sometimes in the Swatow district, two families change girls in order that when grown-up they may be daughters-in-law in the respective families which have adopted them in this way. A great advantage in this method is its economy. It is not the parties themselves that are considered so much—for the individual is nothing in China—it is the respective families that are taken into account. A man in China does not marry so much for his own benefit as for that of the family: to continue the family name; to provide descendants to keep up the ancestral worship; and to give a daughter-in-law to his mother to wait on her and be, in general, a daughter to her. So far are these ideas carried that if her future husband die before marriage, his intended wife, if a model girl, will leave her own family and go and live with that of her deceased betrothed, and perform all the services which her position then requires of her.

Nearly all the fun of life, and very little she has at the best, is gone as soon as a girl is engaged. She retires into a stricter seclusion than ever, and has to be very circumspect in her intercourse even with her own brothers. It would not be human nature if she did not manage sometimes to get a glance at her future husband, that is to say, it is not always impossible for her to see him; but as to love-making, the prudery of Confucianism, and social customs and usages utterly forbid such a thing: it is highly immoral.

The marriage customs vary in different parts of the country, but the essential ceremonials preliminary to, and connected with, marriage are six; and even the details of these vary greatly. (See BETROTHAL.) The conditions indispensable to the actual marriage are (i) the contract signed by the parents or guardians; (2) acceptance of the weddings gifts by the bride's family; (3) the bringing of the bride to the bridegroom's house. (See also *infra.*)

All having been satisfactorily arranged, and the money agreed upon in the contract having been paid to the girl's father, the final ceremonial which hands her over to her husband is performed. She is dressed in her best, and, when the procession comes for her, is placed in the grand, red, marriage sedan-chair, in which she never rides again. This chair is a heavy cumbrous article of wood, highly ornamented with carving and kingfishers' feathers; the bride inside is completely secluded from profane gaze, and on a hot summer's day the position cannot be an enviable one, though a Chinese girl probably stands it better than an English girl (so accustomed to fresh air and freedom of motion) would; but even for Chinese girls the ordeal is sometimes greater than they can bear, and when the bridegroom opens the door, it is sometimes found that the poor little bride has escaped from all the future troubles of married life. At times the wedding chair has to cross a river on its route, and woe betide the girl if the heavy chair causes the cranky boat to capsize. Should the bride-elect die before her marriage, the future husband marries his dead bride; but as the Chinese customs with regard to men are different from those with regard to women, he is free to marry again. The young lady does not name the day, as with us; that is done by the bridegroom's father.

Her trousseau is sent to her future home before her marriage, and is made the occasion for a procession, the bearers of the various objects being clad in red jackets, and parading through the streets. For some days preceding the wedding, the girl, with her sisters and friends, 'bewails and laments her intended removal from the home of her father.' The bridal chair, which we have already mentioned, is carried last in the wedding procession; many carved wooden pavilions (carved open wooden stands with or without covers over them as the case may be) with sweetmeats, and the inevitable music, lanterns, and other objects which go to make up a Chinese procession are not absent. It wends its way to the bride's home, where the friend of the bridegroom presents a letter to her, written on red paper tinged with gold, urging the bride to come. This letter is carefully kept by the bride, and is somewhat the equivalent of 'marriage lines' in England. After certain ceremonials are gone through, the bride makes her appearance, but her features are concealed effectually, not by a white veil, but by a piece of red silk. After saluting the friend of the bridegroom, she enters the chair and is borne with the clashing of gongs and the playing of the Chinese Wedding March to the bridegroom's house. Preceding her are the only equivalents of bridesmaids, female attendants; and her younger brother follows in an ordinary chair. Arrived at her future home, the chair is set down. The bridegroom is at the door with his fan, with which he knocks at the door of the chair, which the bridesmaids open, and the red-veiled bride, still with face unseen, steps out. Sometimes the chair, still closed, is carried right into the reception hall and the door of the latter shut. If, as is occasionally the case nowadays, the bride goes in a motor car, the windows, etc., are closely screened with silk, thus effectually preventing her from being seen from outside.

'She is placed on the back of a female servant, and carried over a slow charcoal fire. . . . Above her head, as she is conveyed over the charcoal fire, another female servant raises a tray containing several pairs of chop-sticks, some rice, and betel-nuts. By this time the bridegroom has taken his place on a high stool, on which he stands to receive his bride, who prostrates herself at the foot, and does obeisance to her lord. The high stool is intended to indicate the great superiority of the husband over the wife. . . . Descending from his elevated position, the bridegroom removes the veil of red silk. Now for the first time he catches a glimpse of his wife's face. It is still, however, more or less hidden by the strings of pearls which hang from her bridal coronet. The bridal pair are conducted to the ancestral hall, where they prostrate themselves before the altar on which the ancestral tablets are arranged. Heaven and Earth, and the gods of the principal doors of the house, and the parents of the bride are the next objects of their worship. A further act of homage, which consists in pouring out drink-offerings to the ancestors of the family, having been duly performed by the bridegroom only, the happy couple are escorted to the bridal chamber, where they find the orange-tree with its strings of cash, emblems of fruitfulness and wealth, and the burning tapers, which formed a part of the procession, placed on the nuptial couch. From the top of the bed are suspended three long strips of red paper,' containing good wishes: one being, 'May you have a hundred sons and a thousand grandsons.' 'The bridegroom having now saluted the bride, they sit down and partake of tea and cake.' The bride tries hard at this time to get a piece of her husband's dress under her when she sits down, for, if she does, it will ensure her having the upper hand of him, while he tries to prevent her and to do the same himself with her dress. The strings of pearls on her coronet are now drawn aside by the maids in attendance, in order that the bridegroom may have an opportunity of seeing the features of his bride, who, that he may receive a correct impression of them, has carefully omitted the use of rouge in her toilet operations. . . . While the bridal pair are thus engaged, many of the relatives and friends assembled to celebrate the wedding, enter the chamber, and freely remark on the personal appearance of the bride.' This must be a trying ordeal to a modest retiring girl, as the observations are loud enough for all to hear. Her new relatives and friends wish her many children; and the bridegroom soon leaves her to mix with his guests. 'At seven o'clock in the evening a banquet in honour of her parents-in-law is prepared by the bride. When all things are ready, the parents enter the banqueting-hall, where the bride, after bringing the principal dish, or *capat cœnum*, from the kitchen and placing it on the table with her own hands, assumes the position of a waiting-maid. Filling the cup of her father-in-law with wine, she presents it to him with both hands, and whilst he is drinking the contents, she kneels at his feet and twice knocks her head upon the ground. To her mother-in-law, whose cup she now fills, she is equally reverential. The banquet over, and the parents-in-law having washed their hands, the bride is called upon to partake of a repast. On a table which her father-in-law orders the servant to place at the top of the steps by which the dining-ball is approached, various viands are set, and she is invited to occupy a chair on the east side of the table. Her mother-in-law fills a cup of wine and presents it to her. Before receiving it, however, she rises from her chair, and kneeling at the feet of her mother-in-law, does obeisance by twice knocking her head upon the ground. . . . In some of the districts 'round Canton it is not unusual for the bride to be kept up during the greater part of the night,' answering riddles put to her generally by the bridegroom's relatives and friends. The gentlemen sometimes get drunk, and disturbances arise.

It only remains to be said that on the third day the ancestors are worshipped again, and a visit is paid by the young lady to her own father and mother, the bridegroom also paying a visit on the same day. On the evening of the fourth day, there is a dinner party for the friends of the newly-married couple, women and men eating separately—the bride and bridegroom waiting on their guests. This is a brief account of some of the ceremonials attendant on weddings in Canton. The boat people have different customs, and each district of country differs more or less in these matters.

In Swatow the bride does not ride in a red wedding chair like the Cantonese bride. The chair is not made of wood, as it is in Canton, nor is the bride fastened up in it; red cloth hangings are put over the chair and it is a larger one than the one in common use, being like an official chair. A catty or two of raw pork is hung by a string outside the door of the sedan chair. When she arrives at the bridegroom's house she steps over a flare-up fire on the ground, made by burning a few whisps of dry grass. The idea is said to be to purify the bride from the contamination of any devils or other dangers that she may have come across on the road. The bride does not return to visit her parents on the third day after marriage, but four months after. On the third day after marriage, the Swatow bride receives a visit from her younger brother or from some boy in the neighbourhood of her parents' house in case she has no younger brother. This younger brother or boy brings a little pea-nut oil for lights (lamps). The Swatow bride goes to worship at the Ancestral Hall, on the 15th of the 1st moon, for the first three years after her marriage (a woman is a bride for three years); men as well as women, strangers as well as acquaintances, are all free to go and have a look at her. Most of those who go, go in the first year. At such a time she gives loose-skinned oranges to the children to eat, and to the grown-up people she offers tea; while the married people give presents of cash or silver in red paper parcels to her.

A curious marriage custom prevails in the province of Yünnan. Chinese call it the woman marrying the man. It has been described by a traveller as follows:—

'The ceremonies attending this kind of marriage are on a smaller scale than those observed in the case of ordinary marriages, and consist principally in the man coming to the woman's house, where she has her family and friends gathered for the occasion. The door is shut and the man must knock. His intended then asks who is there, in reply to which he gives his name and particulars. She then asks him if he wishes to come to her house and stop with her, to which he replies that he will come and live with her in good partnership. The door is then opened, the man is admitted, and the festivities commence. The wife, by marrying a man in this way, agrees to keep her husband in everything, but contracts no other obligation towards him. It is her house, and she may do in it as she likes.

On the other hand, as long as the husband stops at home and behaves like a good boy, he performs his part of the agreement, for no work is expected of him. Such marriages take place where parents, having only daughters, are sufficiently rich to keep their husband and wish for grandchildren, for the children take the wife's family name and belong to her and her family.'

When a man is absent from home and unavoidable circumstances prevent his return to be married, a strange marriage by proxy takes place sometimes in some districts of the Canton Province; we are not aware whether it prevails in other parts of the empire or not. But the curious thing about it is that, instead of a man acting as the proxy, a cock does duty for the bridegroom. This fowl is sent by the latter to the marriage ceremonies, though it is not even necessary that he should be sent by the bridegroom, the presence of the fowl at the wedding being sufficient.

A girl is but once legally married in China; she rides in the bridal chair but once, and only if she is a legal, principal wife. Not so the man, he can be married over and over again. Only one woman in a man's household holds the position of a proper wife; all the others—and he may take as many as he likes— are not principal wives, or legal ones; but secondary wives, or concubines, though their children are on an equality with those of the first wife. The women who are taken as concubines are sometimes told by their husbands, in order to humour them, that they are to be considered as equal wives with the first.

As to whether Chinese married life is happy or not, there is this to be said, that neither Chinese men nor women know any other kind of married life. One fruitful source of trouble is the polygamy allowed by custom for quarrels and fights, jealousies and envy, bickerings and disputes, are more or less the inheritance of the many-wived household; and lawsuits for property left by the much-married Chinaman are rendered more complicated by the different interests of the four, five, or six women who all own the deceased as their late husband.

It is sometimes a question with Europeans what really constitutes the binding part in a Chinese marriage. With us the kernel of the whole matter is contained in the proper preliminaries having been carried out as laid down by the law of the land and the few sentences in which the married couple promise to take each other as husband and wife respectively. If all the requirements of the civil law have been complied with, as exemplified in a civil marriage before a Registrar, the marriage is a valid one, and all the rest of the ceremony which in a religious marriage is added, often *ad nauseam*, is superfluous.

But with the Chinese there are no notices to be given to a Registrar of Marriage; there is no marriage before a priest, clergyman, minister, or Registrar; there are no such officials appointed to celebrate marriages. What then constitutes a valid marriage from the Chinese standpoint?

Before the actual marriage ceremony takes place, the most important thing is 'the Three Documents and Six Ceremonials.' Of these again, the most important is 'The Three Generations'; this must be present; all the rest may be wanting. It must again be pointed out and remembered that the standpoint of viewing the marriage is totally different from that taken in the West. With us, as we have said, the sentences, which the bridegroom and bride repeat (thus entering into a contractual obligation), are the essential portion of the ceremony; but with the Chinese it is the preliminaries, as above, which are the essentials. Without these even the different incidents, such as red sedan-chair, the worshipping of the ancestors, etc., which go to make up the complex mass of ceremonies are invalid to make it a kít fát (*keet faht*) [*chieh fa*, lit., to put the hair up] marriage. However, the time at which the woman becomes the man's wife is when they worship the man's ancestors. After this they drink a mixture of wine and honey out of goblets tied together with red thread. Strictly speaking, the marriage is only supposed to be complete after their joint visit to the bride's family, when they both worship her ancestral tablets, but in law they are husband and wife after the first joint worship abovementioned.

As has already been said, the ceremony itself is made up of a mass of minor details, out of which rise into importance several ceremonials, one of which is the bride riding in the red sedan-chair, and the worshipping of ancestors. To emphasize again the comparative importance of the preliminaries, it may be noted that should rebellion, or robbers running riot in a district of country, make the quiet (or shall we say, noisy?) carrying out of the marriage ceremonials impossible, it would be quite a *keet faht* (or proper marriage of a first wife) marriage, under the circumstances of the case, if the preliminaries having been already properly carried out, the man should take the woman without any other ceremony as his wife and live with her, nor would it be necessary at a future time to go through the ceremony. But it is needless to say that, with the love of the Chinese for a procession, this mode of taking a wife would be very exceptional.

A go-between (*chung jên* or *mei jên*) is one of the most important matters: a marriage is not a proper marriage without one. How very important this is may be seen from the following passage from the *Li Ki* [*Li chi*], one of the 'Five Classics':

'The master said, "The cermonial usages serve as dykes to the people against bad excesses (to which they are prone). They display the separation which should be maintained (between the sexes), that there may be no occasion for suspicion, and the relations of the people be well defined. It is said in the Book of Poetry (I. viii. Ode VI. 3, 4).

"How do we proceed in hewing an axe-handle?
Without another axe it cannot be done.
How do we proceed in taking a wife?
Without a go-between it cannot be done.
How do we proceed in planting hemp?
The acres must be dressed length-wise and cross-wise.
How do we proceed in taking a wife?
Announcement must first be made to our parents."

'In this way it was intended to guard the people (against doing wrong), and still there are some (women) among them, who offer themselves (to the male),' p. 297.

The first important ceremony is the bride going in the red sedan-chair to the bridegroom's house. When a bride has to be taken at once on account of her parents' death, or sometimes, in the case of poor people, the real red chair is dispensed with, and a common chair is taken and some strips of red cloth thrown over it, or with poorer people strips of red paper pasted on it.

Another important thing is for the bridegroom to receive his bride, he coming to the chair to do so.

Another thing which is always done when the proper preliminaries have been carried out, is the worship of ancestors. If the tablets are not present, then it suffices to write on a piece of red paper the words, 'The ancestors of —— for generations back,' which represent the ancestors in all their generations of that surname. The bride and bridegroom, and, if father and mother of bridegroom are present, they as well, worship together this paper or the spirit tablets.

It is important to pay obeisance to the father and mother of the bridegroom only.

It is Chinese etiquette for the guests invited to a marriage to call to congratulate the father of the bridegroom on the morning of the marriage.

With all the Chinese feelings on marriage, it is strange to find that in one district at least, the girls stand out against the fulfilment of the marriage contract:—

'The high-spirited disposition of the' women of Lung Kong is shown 'in the organisation of an anti-matrimonial league, in which the fair damsels of this fortunate district bind themselves under solemn pledges never to marry. Such a course is so contrary to the whole history and spirit of Chinese institutions and so daring a challenge to the practices of ages, that one cannot but admire the spirit of independence and courage from which it springs. The existence of this Amazonian league has long been known, but as to its rules and the number of its members no definite information has come to hand. It is composed of young widows and marriageable girls. Dark hints are given as to the methods used to escape matrimony. The sudden demise of betrothed husbands, or the abrupt ending of the newly-married husband's career suggest unlawful means for dissolving the bounds. When they submit to marriage they still maintain their powers of will.' 'One of their demands being that the husband must go to the wife's home to live, or else live without her company.'

'There is a peculiar custom in the village of Tai Leong and [other villages in] Shun Tak [Kuangtung], which may be well characterised as misanthropical, and is highly deprecated even among the natives. Nearly all the girls there have a habit of swearing sisterhood to each other and taking vows of celibacy, looking upon their future husbands as enemies. On the third morning of the wedding, which is generally contracted by their parents, they go home, and refuse to return to their husbands again. Some of them will rather pay money to their husbands to buy concubines, and others, who are poor and cannot afford to do so, prepare to die together by poison, by throwing themselves into the river, by cutting their throats, or by hanging themselves so as to be free from the thraldom of their lords."

One of the chief of these secret societies of women who bind themselves not to marry is known as the *Chin Lan Hui*, "Gold-and-Orchid Society."

This is an old-established custom. There is a small brochure, written long ago, containing a ballad about six maidens of this district throwing themselves into a pond to escape matrimony. The girls who belong to this league, if it may be so called, swear sisterhood with several others of like mind, going before the gods to do it; but it is not known what the oath is. The first object in refusing to marry is stated to be a dread of the troubles of motherhood; secondly, to escape the thraldom of serving a father-in-law and mother-in-law; and lastly, in all probability, the nuns have superadded their notions about celibacy being a purer state of existence than the married one.

Those belonging to such an association are taught by the nuns, so it is said, to kill their husbands by saying certain charms or incantations, by taking hairs out of their husbands' queues for some certain hidden purpose, by procuring the bones of dead infants or children, getting them from what are styled the Lün tsong téí [*luan tsang tui*], and these latter are buried under the bed, fireplace, and family rice-jar. The societies to which such women belong are called Maí Fú Kaú [*mai fu chiao*]. They will not enter their husbands' houses for the purposes of permanent residence (called lok ká [*lo chia*]); but on their occasional visits to their husbands' residences their food is even sent them from their own homes, and not as much as a cup of tea will they take from their husbands' houses. These girls went about formerly with four ounces of arsenic, supplied by the nuns, who, it is said, not only used to charge them ten taels for it, but often cheated them; one instance is known when some red ashes from the furnace was supplied under the pretence that it was arsenic. At the present day opium is carried on their persons, and they threaten to take their lives if forced to marry. More than half of them, after residing the most of the time with their parents, are persuaded to become good wives, and the number appears to be increasing of late years. When the rest of the whole band of sworn sisters, in number from six to twenty, as the case may be, are married, the one who is left 'sometimes ceases holding out any longer and takes up her proper position as wife.'

It is not an uncommon thing to read of girls in various parts of China committing suicide rather than be forced into marriage. Doubtless many a girl must feel it a dreadful ordeal to face an unknown husband and come under the power of a Chinese mother-in-law.

If an unmarried son dies before reaching adult age, the parents seek by means of go-betweens a family that has lost a daughter of about the same age and at about the same time. The betrothal and wedding ceremonies are gone through, the tablets taking the place of the pair. The bride's coffin is then buried in the grave by the side of the bridegroom's.

Since the establishment of the Republic the essentials of marriage have generally remained the same, but changes are to be noted here and there, such as the greater freedom of the modern girl, who at times claims the right to choose her own husband. The former seclusion of women has, of course, been abandoned. The ceremonial changes consist chiefly in the adoption in some cases of Western costumes, non-seclusion of the bride, and, absence of much of the ceremonial detail and superstition of the old régime. Concubinage, however, continues to be practised, and there are no signs of any decrease of it, even in the best educated classes.

References.—Gray, *China;* Doolittle, *Social Life of the Chinese; China Mail*, July 10, 1890; *Hongkong Daily Press*, 1861 (Hakka Marriage Customs); *Variétés Sinologiques*, Vol. xiv; Werner, *Descriptive Sociology-Chinese; China of the Chinese;* Möllendorff, *Family Law of China;* Parker, *Comparative Chinese Family Law.*

MEDICINES.—The various substances, etc., used as medicines by the Chinese may be classed under the following headings: (1) Roots; (2) Barks and Husks; (3) Twigs and Leaves; (4) Flowers; (5) Seeds and Fruits; (6) Grasses; (7) Insects; and (8) Sundries. The total number in all the classes would be about 1,400. Examples of the substances, etc., included in these categories, with the places of production, are given below.

Roots.—Turmeric (Kiangsu, Ssŭch'uan), bellwort (Anhui), yam (Hunan, Hupei), ginger root (Ssŭch'uan, Hupei), liquorice (Ssŭch'uan, Hupei), galangal (South China), sassen (Shansi), capoor cutchery (South China), foxglove (Hupei, Ssŭch'uan), rhubarb (China generally), aconite (Ssŭch'uan, Hupei), orange peel (Kuangtung, Ssŭch'uan), acorn husks (Kuangtung), cinnamon (Kueichow, Kuangsi, Ssŭch'uan), cardomom husks (South China), cassia lignea (Kuangsi), betel-nut husks (Kuangtung), mulberry bark (Ssŭch'uan), pumelo peel (Kuang tung), bryony (Anhui, Kiangsu), peony root (Anhui), etc.

Barks and Husks.—Orange peel (Kuangtung, Ssŭch'uan), acorn husks (Kuangtung), cinnamon (Kueichou, Kuangsi, Ssŭch'uan), cardomon husks (South China), cassia lignea (Kuangsi), betel-nut husks (Kuangtung), mulberry bark (Ssŭch'uan), pumelo peel (Kuangtung), melon net (Kuangtung), bamboo (Kuangtung), etc.

Twigs and Leaves.—Spikenard, Valeriana (Shensi, Ssŭch'uan), cassia twigs (Kuangsi), *clematis vitalba* (Shansi, Ssŭch'uan, Chêkiang), peppermint leaf (Ssŭch'uan, Hunan, Kiangsi), etc.

Flowers.—Chrysanthemum (Chêkiang, Ssŭch'uan), Tibetan sunflower (Tibet), magnolia yülan (Ssŭch'uan), magnolia purpurea (Hunan), lotus stamens (Hupei), lemon (Ssŭch'uan), honeysuckle (Hunan), coltsfoot (Ssŭch'uan), lotus (Shansi), hibiscus (Fukien), senna (Chihli, Hupei), camomile (Chêkiang), Chinese gooseberry (Kuangtung), etc.

Seeds and Fruits.—Camphor tree seed (Kuangsi), plantain seed (Kuangsi, Hupei, Chihli), balsam seed (Kuangtung), buckwheat (Kuangtung), mustard seed (Hupei, Ssŭch'uan, Chihli), small red beans (Kuangtung), kumquat or 'golden orange' (Kuangtung), wheat (Kuangtung), wild raspberries (Chêkiang, Kiangsu, Hupei), apricot kernels (Shantung, Chihli), linseed (Ssŭch'uan), pepper (Kuangtung, Ssŭch'uan), red rice (Kuangtung), hemp seed (Ssŭch'uan, Shantung, Chihli), stones of lichees (Kuangtung) dried pears (Chihli), stones of mangoes (Kuangtung), cotton kernels (Kiangsu), fresh quinces (Ssŭch'uan), kernels of wild plum (Chêkiang), Ssŭch'uan, Shantung, Chihli), seed of wax tree (Kuangsi), star aniseed (Kuangtung, Kuangsi), castor-oil plant seed (Kuangtung, Kuangsi), long pepper (Ssŭch'uan), areca or betel-nut (Hainan), mulberries (Kuangtung), peach kernels (Ssŭch'uan), beans of soap tree Kuangtung), jujube kernels (Hupei, Shantung, Chihli), black plums (Kuangtung), pumelo pips (Kuangtung), coriander seed (Hupei, Chihli), galls (Kuangtung), quince (Ssŭch'uan), nutgalls (Ssŭch'uan), linseed (Ssŭch'uan, Hunan), buckthorn (Chêkiang), etc.

Grasses.—Mugwort (Hupei, Ssŭch'uan), plantain (Kuangtung), clove pink (Ssŭch'uan), golden flowered or 'opium-weaning' grass (Kuangtung), spurge (Kuangtung), lemon grass (Kuangtung), crane's grass (Kuangtung), glue seaweed (Kuangtung), common horsetail (Ssŭch'uan, Chihli), vervain (Kuangtung), saxifrage (Kuangtung), dandelion (Kuangtung), rice-paper plant (Hupei, Ssŭch'uan), southern-wood (Kuangtung, Ssŭch'uan, Chihli), etc.

Insects.—Scorpions (Hupei, Shantung, Chihli), centipedes (Chêkiang, Kiangsu, Ssŭch'uan), common earthworm (Kuangtung), blistering fly (Kuangtung), willow-bug (Kuangtung), dried silkworms (Kuangtung, Chêkiang, Kiangsu, Ssŭch'uan), red cicada (Ssŭch'uan), etc.

Sundries.—Moxa punk (Kuangtung), dried toads (Kuangtung), mugwort powder (Kuangsi), tea-seed cakes (Kuangsi), skins of cicadas (Kuangtung, Chêkiang, Ssŭchuan, Shantung), camphor (Formosa), pangolin scales (South China), golden mica (Hunan, Kueichou), tabasheer (South China), sea slugs (Hainan), pipe-fish (Hainan), algae (Chêkiang), arsenic (Hunan), tigers' bones (Ssŭch'uan, Hupeh), fowls' gizzards (Kuangtung), preserved liquid manure (Kuangtung), urea (Kiangsu, Hupei), pigs tubers (Ssŭch'uan, Chihli), wasps' nests (Kuangtung), seals' kidneys (Shantung, Manchuria), realgar (Ssŭch'uan Shansi), dried lizards (Kuangsi), rice sprouts (Kuangtung), imitation dragons' blood (Kuangtung), land snails (Kuangtung), tortoise shell (Kuangtung, Hupei), cassia oil (Kuangtung), oyster shells (Kuangtung), antelopes' horns (Kansu, Mongolia), hartshorn jelly (Chihli, Manchuria), asses' penis (Shantung, Manchuria), deers' penis (Shantung, Chihli, Manchuria), deers' wombs (Manchuria), snakes' skins (Chêkiang, Ssŭch'uan), fossil ivory (Kuangsi, Chihli), fossil teeth (Ssŭch'uan), puff-balls (Kuangtung), honey (Kuangtung, Hupei), arrowroot (Kuangtung), soot (Kuangtung), peppermint cakes (Kuangtung), haw jelly (Hupei), musk (Ssŭch'uan, Tibet), loadstone (Kuangtung), fossil crabs (Kuangsi, Ssŭch'uan), orpiment (Yünnan), oil of cloves (Kuangtung), castor oil (Manchuria), verdigris (Kuangtung), silkworms' dung (Kuangtung), hedge hogs' skins (Ssŭch'uan), magpies' dung

(Kuangsi), nutgalls (Kuangsi), sheeps' penis (Chihli), medicine teas (Kuangtung), plasters (Kuangtung, Kiangsu, Chihli), medicinal powder (Kuangtung), medicinal pills (Kuangtung, Chihli), bats' dung (Kuangtung), selenite (Chihli), rabbits' dung (Kuangtung, Kuangsi), etc.

References.—Bretschneider, *Early European Researches into the Flora of China;* Tatarinov, *Catalogus medicamentorum sinensium;* Hoffmann and Schultes, *Noms indigénes d'un Choix de Plantes du Japon et de la Chine;* Bebeaux, *Essai sur la Pharmacie et la Matière médicale des Chinois;* Geerts, *Les Produits de la Nature japonaise et chinoise;* Smith, *Contributions towards the Materia Medica and Natural History of China;* Hanbury, *Notes on Chinese Materia Medica;* Bridgman, *Chinese Chrestomathy; China Mail* (Hongkong), June-Sept., 1878; *Journal N.C.B.R.A.S.*, N.S. Vol. 19.

MENDICANTS.—If numbers form any criterion, China should be the happy hunting ground for beggars. Mendicancy is reduced to a fine art—a science; backed up by the charitable tenets of Buddhism, the Chinese beggar, armed with an amount of assurance and audacity, proceeds to lay siege to a Chinese city, not in a haphazard way, but with a systematised organisation which gives him a hold on the shopkeeper, and a vantage ground to attack him with effect and perseverance. In some, if not in many, cities the beggars are united together under a head, 'The King of the Beggars,' who has complete authority over his subjects. The payment of a fixed sum to the King by any shop will secure immunity from all visits of his subjects; otherwise the collection of their tax of one or two cash will be undertaken with that pertinacity and disregard of time and convenience so characteristic of the Chinese beggar. In Nanking there is a royal order of beggars established by Hung Wu, the first Emperor of the Ming dynasty. In this city the beggars are allowed to live in certain arches in the city wall, and 'their chief is appointed by the police authorities of the district.'

Beggars in China may be divided into several classes, viz.:—Those who go in strings of three or four; solitary beggars, divided into stationary and peripatetic ones; those who inflict wounds upon themselves; those who are suffering from sores; and, last but not least, blind beggars. The demarcations between these different classes are not always strongly accentuated, as the one class may merge into the other.

A business like this requires preparation; it is commenced by some in early life, the youngsters generally being found leading the strings of three or four blind beggars, otherwise it is a case of the blind leading the blind, and, all things considered, they appear to get on very well. It is not an unknown thing, by any means, for mothers to deprive their children of eyesight in order that they may earn their living as blind singing girls; and some of the beggars may owe their blindness to the same cause. No doubt many others have lost their eyesight from disease; for different affections of the eyes are very common in China, where there is no proper knowledge of preventives, nor of curatives; the hot sun, bad air, poor living, and the reprehensible practice of the barbers of scraping and cleaning the socket of the eye must induce blindness in others. Next to blindness, open and festering sores and wounds, and deformities of limbs, of any and every kind, either form a good capital to start on, or, shutting out all other means of gaining a livelihood, reduce the sufferer to beggary of position and beggary as a calling. Failing genuine wounds, and armed with a knife, a sturdy, impudent vagabond, with strength of limb and body and good eyesight, may cut himself in a shop, with noisy and wild yells, and thus gather a wide-mouthed crowd, which, flocking in and obstructing trade, draws a cash or two from the accountant, the Chinese horror of blood being also a sufficient ready-drawer of alms. The next shop, or one a few doors further on, forms another stage for the repetition of the performance. These nuisances, for whom one feels no sympathy, but disgust, are fortunately not so common as some of the other varieties of the genius beggar.

One of the most common is the string-beggar. Almost always blind, this class goes about in small bands of three or four, sometimes five, mostly females, but one or two males are not uncommonly found in the string, each with a slender long bamboo, the equivalent of the foreign beggar's stick. They make their way, tapping with short quick taps, now uncertainly feeling with their bamboos, which serve as antennæ, lifting their sightless orbs in vain appeals for light, raising their faces with that pathetic helplessness, though possibly in the exercise of that facial perception with which those born blind are accredited—a new sense vouchsafed to those deprived of sight which enables them 'by some singular insight' to tell when they are opposite some object, as to its dimensions and characteristics, such as height, breadth, etc.

Happy are these Bartimæuses with their sisters, wives, and cousins, if some bright-eyed youngster, not smitten with the darkness of night in broad midday, is found to lead their devious course through the crowded streets. Such a one is also better able to see the white *fan kwai*, whose pockets are filled with gold, or, who, at least, has not hoarded up a store of bad cash to pass off on the beggar tribe as their countrymen have. As soon as he appears in sight, their monotonous whine is exchanged for more vigorous appeals, and higher titles of respect follow each other in rapid succession in the hope of loosing the purse-strings of the young clerk, who has instant brevet rank of Taipan, Cap-i-tan (Captain), Worship, Honour, Lordship, and everything else worth having.

Let us watch their *modus operandi.* It is a combination of street and shop begging—a general business not confined to any one branch—each shop is most carefully and religiously visited, unless exemption has been purchased by a commuted sum paid to the 'Lord of All the Beggars.'

Should the shopkeeper be a good-natured man, a cash or two may be flung to the string, who may get it without even the trouble of going further than the doorstep, but as often as not if not more often than not, more patient toil is necessary to earn even a broken cash. Then the whole string file in, each holding on to the back of the other, and the monotonous, whining, singsong appeal begins; the shopmen turn a deaf ear to everything, titles are thrown away, the pearls are cast before the swine, who in this one case, dare not turn to rend them, perhaps for fear of vengeance; though also is not one string of beggars for half an hour better than half a dozen strings of them in the same time? And, as long as one string is in possession of the place, the others pass by. Wearied, some of the band, if not all of them, crouch down on the tiled floor, waiting for their opportunity, for it is bound to come sooner or later; and here it is at last, for several customers of another sort step in—purchasers, at sound of whom the din and clatter of the beggars begins with renewed energy, and the surly shopmen, whom no amount of pity could move, hasten, for fear of losing a good customer, to get rid of the wearisome noise, by tossing a few coins into the shallow basket of the mendicants, who renew the same tactics at each shop in the street.

Better when the round happens at meal-time, for then the beggar will get some broken victuals to fill his empty stomach, receiving them in the first place in his shallow basket, or in his bowl, which latter Shakyamuni Buddha has sanctified, and his numerous priest-followers have hallowed by the use of centuries.

The solitary beggar wends his way through the mazy street, picking up an old cash, here and there, from those more charitably disposed than the rest, or from those who seek immunity from the pest that the beggar is to the whole of the respectable world.

Some select a space in a busy spot, sit down and wait for alms, with a written-out appeal spread before them, setting forth that, natives of other provinces, they are stranded in what is, to all intents, almost a strange land to them; others select some quieter spot, but where the stream of passers-by is still sufficient to give a hope of an occasional dole from unwilling hands, the donors hoping that merit for the deed, though performed unwillingly, may mitigate the horrors of a future hell. One feels a pity for some of these beggars—stranded wayfarers; broken-down tradesmen; ruined gamblers, *roués*, with the punishment of all their profligacy on them; and, saddest of all, some poor old woman whose undutiful son has turned her out on the street, penniless, and with no shelter for her grey hairs, to depend on the uncertain charity of her neighbours, who, though virtuous in their indignation, give no, or but little, practical proof of their sorrow, and who are in constant dread lest the old dame should give up the ghost on their doorsteps; harsh words and angry rebuffs, therefore, forbid her sheltering herself under what were erewhile friendly roofs: for would not the economy of Chinese social life, as well as its judicial system, render the tender-hearted, who should overstep the limits of prudence and on whose premises she might die, liable, at least, to the expense of a coffin and funeral? The presence of a ghost haunting the house would follow; and, even worse still, some trumped-up charge of having caused her death might bring the charitably disposed within the clutches of the law—a law hard to escape, with (until recently, at least) all its concomitants of torture and pre-Howard-day prisons.

It is curious how very polite the chair-coolies are to the blind beggars in the street, addressing them as 'Sir,' when requesting them to get out of the way—a nice trait in Chinese character, due to their innate politeness, and perhaps also to self-interest, as a want of it might lead to bad language. These beggars are not always most polite; the writer was once knocked, with not a light hand, by a woman in the streets of Canton, but there was some excuse for her, as she seemed to be crazy. Many of the beggars in Canton sleep in an asylum in the east of the city, and go out by day to ply their trade.

MINTS.—Nearly every provincial city had a mint for the issue of the native cash; but of late years different mints have been established at a number of the principal cities for the coinage of silver dollars and subsidiary coins and copper cents. Amongst other places where mints have been started, are Nanking, Hangchow, Anking, Tientsin, Foochow (1896), Chêkiang, Hunan, Peiyang (1896), Wuch'ang (1895), Canton (1890), Ch'êngtu, Mukden, Kirin, and Chahar. A mint opened in Ch'angsha in 1897 was in working existence for two years. Some, if not all, of these have, or had, a European Superintendent. The Ch'êngtu Mint after issuing a supply of coin, sufficient as it was thought, was closed and its Superintendent dismissed, and this may be the case with some of the others as well. The Shanghai Mint, for which loans were raised and preparations made in 1921, has so far failed to materialize.

'The Kiangnan [Nanking] Mint was closed in June, in consequence of financial difficulties, but the events in North China created a sudden demand for dollars, and it was re-opened, and turned out 20,000 to 40,000 dollars a day until the market was choked. It then closed again and the English Superintendent left.'

The dollars coined at these mints have only a provincial circulation, and have not supplanted the Mexican dollar as a national coin.

For full information regarding the Mints in Chihli, Hupei, Kuangtung, Hunan, Kiangsu, Chêkiang, Anhui, Fukien, Kiangsi, Yünnan, Ssŭch'uan, Shantung, and at Kalgan, see the *Chinese Economic Monthly*, April, 1925.

MISSIONS.—ANCIENT MISSIONS.—Tradition points to an early proclamation of Christianity in China. The apostle Thomas has been mentioned as the first missionary to this country; at all events it seems that some of the first teachers of the new faith must have selected China as their mission field. It would be most interesting to have had some particulars of this enterprise, but we must be content with rumours and detached notices in ancient ecclesiastical writings, which give but a vague and misty idea of the extent of the work and its results.

In 1262, Kublai-Khan had decreed that Erkun and others should give Military Service and pay land- and trade-taxes. (Erkun=Arkons=*ye-li-k'o-wên*, the name given by Mongols to Christians.)

In 1282, both Musuman and Erkun (Mussulman and Christian) chiefs at Quilon in India sent missions to Kublai. These Quilon missions were sent by U-tsa-r P'ieh-li-ma (?the Ustâd, or rabbi, Ephraim.)

NESTORIAN MISSIONS.—The first really solid ground that we have to rest upon is the historical fact of the Nestorians having carried on missions in China. A thousand questions present themselves to one's mind as to the work done by these men, the extent of country they travelled over, the numbers that came to China, their *modus operandi*, the success that attended their labours. But to these and many others we get answers which only whet our appetite for more information.

'The time of the arrival of the Nestorians in China cannot be specified certainly, but,' Williams states, 'there are grounds for placing it as early as A.D. 505.' One of the most interesting of the ancient monuments in China, while at the same time 'the most ancient Christian inscription yet found in Asia,' is the Nestorian monument. It is 'the only record yet found in China itself of the labours of the Nestorians.' It was discovered in A.D. 1625 by some workmen in the suburb of Ch'ang-an, a district city in Shen-si. It was erected in A.D. 781.

'The contents are threefold:—Doctrinal, Historical, Eulogistic. The first part gives a brief outline of the teachings of the religion, and of the ways and practices of its ministers; the second part tells of its first entrance into China, and of the patronage extended to it for the most part for nearly 150 years by various emperors; in the third part, to which, though it be the shortest, the two others are introductory, the Christians express, in verse, their praise of God and their religion, and also of the emperors whose protection and favour they had enjoyed.'

From this inscription we learn that a priest, Olopun by name, made his way through difficulties and perils from the West, guided by the 'azure clouds' to China, bringing with him the 'True Scriptures.' He was favourably received by the Emperor in the palace, in A.D. 635, where a portion of the Scriptures was translated in the library of the palace, and approving of the new doctrine, with that eclecticism the Chinese are so noted for, the Emperor gave special orders for its propagation, and a proclamation issued a few years after with regard to it ended with the words:—'Let it have free course throughout the Empire.' A monastery was built 'sufficient to accommodate twenty-one priests'; succeeding sovereigns vied with each other in the benefits they conferred on the new religion which had the ægis of imperial patronage thrown over it; it spread throughout the then ten provinces of China; 'monasteries filled a hundred cities.' Then came a period of persecution, for twenty or twenty-five years, from a bigoted Buddhist Empress, when another time of prosperity ensued, the buildings being restored and more helpers coming from the West. Not only did the imperial favour shine on them again, but an eminent Buddhist from India appears to have embraced Christianity, and 'threw all his wealth and influence into the promotion of the Christian cause, manifesting especially an extraordinary charity.' Thus we have a summary of the history of Nestorian Christians in China for nearly 150 years, till A.D. 781. Of its history subsequent to that date there is not much to be said; for sixty years or more it continued; during this time Buddhism made vigorous progress, which called forth spirited protests from the *literati.* The Taoists, in A.D. 841, finding their opportunity come, succeeded in getting the Emperor to launch a proscription against Buddhism, and Buddhist monasteries were destroyed; this persecution also affected the Nestorians, as they were referred to in the edict, and the Nestorianism of Si-ngan-fu [Sian Fu or Hsian Fu] never recovered from the blow. Another authority gives the date of the Emperor Wu Tsung's edict of suppression as A.D. 845. Scattered groups, however, continued to live in various parts of the country.

Marco Polo, in the thirteenth century, mentions Nestorian churches in China; but it is not thought that these were descendants of the former Nestorian Church. He found several congregations at Kashgar, Samarcand, Peking, Yangchou, Chinkiang, and Hangchou at the close of the 13th century. It is probable that the monument we have already mentioned was buried at the time of this great persecution, and so, after a period of two hundred years or more, ended an interesting chapter of missions—that of the Nestorians in China. Its failure was doubtless due to two causes: the one being the reliance on the Emperor and men in power; the other being the absence of the Gospel in their presentation of the truth. It is to be hoped that future researches may discover further evidence of this church at the different periods of its existence in China. Some have thought it possible that such may be the case, and that remains of this ancient Nestorian Church may yet be found—that converts, buried in some isolated region, with possibly the ancient translation of the Scriptures made by their first missionaries, still in their possession, will be come across, as the descendants of the Hebrew community were some half a century ago in the interior of China. (See BUDDHISM and JEWS.)

ROMAN CATHOLIC MISSIONS.—We now come to the prosecution of missions on a large scale.

The first Jesuit to set foot in China was Père Melchior Nuñes Barreto, who twice visited Canton in 1555 on his way to Japan.

Giovanni Di Monte Corvino (or Jean de Montecorvino; also known as John de Montecorvino) arrived at Khanbalig (Cambalu) in 1293, bringing letters of introduction from the Pope Nicholas IV. He built his church there about that time, but the date of his arrival is uncertain. He was sent by Nicholas in 1289, and may not have reached Cambalu for some years. He was the first Archbishop of Cambalu.

An Archevêché de Cambalic ou Péking was created by Clement V. in 1307. Jean de Montecorvino was nominated archbishop Cambaliens in that year (he had arrived some time before, and in 1305 had two large churches in Peking—then called Khanbalig—and 6,000 converts), but of the six Franciscan bishops appointed only three, Gérard, André, and Pérégrin, arrived at Cambalu, where they consecrated the Metropolitan and became bishops of the suffragan seat at Zaiton (probably Ch'üan-chou Fu or Changchou Fu). Montecorvino was consecrated in 1308, and died at Peking in 1330. In 1313, Odaric of Pardenone, another Franciscan, left Europe for China, eventually landed at Canton, and after visiting Foochow, Hangchow, Nanking, and Yangchow, reached Peking, where he stayed three years and baptised 20,000 natives.

But the founders proper of Jesuit missions in China were Michael Ruggiero and Matteo Ricci, who arrived in this Empire in A.D. 1579 (some accounts say 1581) and A.D. 1581 (some accounts say 1582, others 1583) respectively. The latter has been described as 'a man of great scientific acquirements, of invincible perseverance, of various resource, and of winning manners, maintaining, with all these gifts, a single eye to the conversion of the Chinese, the bringing the people of all ranks to the faith of Christianity.' They found it difficult to obtain a footing, but Ricci established himself at Shíúhing, Chao Ch'ing (locally Shiu-hêng), the ancient capital of the Canton Province, and worked his way up, till he finally reached the capital, where he died in A.D. 1610. He was favourably received by the Emperor Wan Li, of the Ming dynasty. He was the author of a number of learned works as well as books on Christianity, and left many converts behind him, the most noted of whom was Hsü Kwangsi, a member of the Han-lin college and an official of high rank. One of Hsü's daughters, known as Candida, built thirty-nine churches, printed one hundred and thirty books, and sent many blind story-tellers, instructed in gospel history, out in the streets to tell what they had learned.

The Church of Rome was wise in her generation in sending out at first men of the stamp of Ricci, among whom may be named Adam Schaal [properly Schall—Jean Adam Schall von Bell (1591-1666)] and Verbiest (1623-88); it was not only Jesuits, but the different Roman Catholic sects, such as Franciscans, Dominicans, and others, which sent their members to China.

'The Dynasty of Ming . . . was drawing near to its close, and the Manchus were preparing for the conquest of the Empire. Many difficulties and perils encompassed the missionaries, but Schaal was able to maintain his position at Peking by his astronomical knowledge in correcting the calendar, and by establishing a foundry, where he cast cannon to be used against the Manchus. And this position he continued to hold when the Empire fell to those invaders. He was made head of the Board of Astronomy and Mathematics, and was a favourite with the first Manchu sovereign, though he did not shrink from remonstrating with him against certain severe measures, and urging him rather to justice, forbearance, and mercy. He was able to lay, in A.D. 1650, the foundation of a grand church in the neighbourhood of the Imperial palace.

'When the second Emperor, known to us as K'ang Hsi—by the name of his reign—succeeded to his father at the early age of eight, there was trouble during the minority; but as soon as he took the Government into his own hands, he gave his full confidence to the missionaries. He was, probably, the most able and enlightened sovereign who ever sat on the Chinese throne, and his reign lasted sixty-one years. Schaal and Verbiest regulated the calendar and cast cannon for him. Regis and several others conducted for him the survey of the Empire which Rémusat correctly describes as "the most complete geographical work ever executed out of Europe."'

Owing to imperial favour shown to Schall, 100,000 Christians were received into the Church in the short space of fourteen years, but before his death in 1666 he endured the bitterest persecution.

Disputes, however, arose amongst the Roman Catholic missionaries as the correct terms to use for God (as to what words were to be applied by their Christians to the Deity); as to the worship of ancestors and Confucius— whether it were a mere homage or real worship, and whether their converts consequently might engage in it. Unable to agree amongst themselves, the dispute had grown to such a head that they referred it not only to the Pope but also to the Emperor of China; each of whom gave a different verdict. The missionaries, of course, were bound to obey the Pope, and this setting up of an outside authority over that of their own Emperor, incensed the Chinese, and the storm which was gathering burst in the next reign, when in A.D. 1724, an edict was issued against them (at the request of Man Pao, Viceroy of Fukien and Chêkiang, and of the Board of Rites), prohibiting the propagation of Roman Catholicism, and only retaining the few missionaries required for scientific purposes in Peking; all the others were required to leave the country or go to Macao. Some obeyed the edict, while others remained in secret. More than three hundred churches were destroyed. The trouble originated with the literati at Fu-an, who lodged a complaint against the Christians with the local magistrate. Many of the Chinese converts remained firm, notwithstanding the persecutions which arose now and then. Matters remained in this state for about a century, when in A.D. 1842 Christianity was tolerated by treaty. There are now numbers of priests and numerous bodies of Roman Catholics in the country. When the priests care to use a Bible, the translation they employ is said to be that of the first Protestant missionary, Dr. Morrison; for though translations of portions have been made by them, yet, like the Church of Rome, they seem never to have printed the whole Bible and given it to the people; they have, however, quite a literature of their own in Chinese. They do not seem to practise any public preaching; but retain hold of the communities of converts already made. In one point they are very aggressive, that is in the baptising of infants, for every one so sprinkled becomes a unit in their grand total of Christians.

The *Roman Catholic Register*, a paper formerly published in Hongkong, gave the following as the statistics of Romish missions in China:—Bishops, 41; European priests, 664; native priests, 559; colleges, 34; convents, 34; native converts, 1,092,818. These numbers of course vary from year to year; generally they tend toward a steady increase. One well-known writer speaks thus of their work:—

'Had they adhered to religious teaching, their converts would doubtless have been legion; but the usual rash meddling with politics soon aroused fear of foreign aggression, leading to violent opposition and terrible persecution, which have been repeated with every fresh scare of undue political influence. . . . It is this arrogation of temporal authority which has so incensed the Chinese, and accounts for much of the hostility to missionaries and converts of all Christian churches and denominations, as the ignorant masses naturally could not discriminate between Protestants and Roman Catholics. Hence, in the Edict of Toleration, proclaimed in 1886, the Imperial Government deem it necessary to state that men who may embrace Christianity do not cease to be Chinese, but, as such, are entitled to all protection from their own Government, to which alone they owe obedience. The promulgation of this Edict followed immediately on the decision of the Pope to send a Papal Legate to the Court of Peking, to represent him as the sole foreign power interested in the Chinese Roman Catholics, thereby totally disclaiming all political protection from France.'

In 1914 there were 8,034 Roman Catholic schools, with 132,850 pupils. In 1924 the number of converts is given as 2,017,056 (another record says 2,142,516), or including Manchuria, Mongolia, Tibet, and the outlying dependencies, as 2,208,800.

PROTESTANTS.—The first Protestant missionary to China was the Rev. Robert Morrison, who arrived in A.D. 1807. There was such a strong feeling against all Europeans at that time that he was unable to preach in public or carry on direct evangelistic work; but he engaged in some literary undertakings, which not only redounded to his credit, but prepared the way for future labourers. A gigantic dictionary of the language and the translation of the whole Bible have made his name famous, and it is a marvel how, confined within the foreign factories (as the European settlement in Canton was called) in a godown, and assisted by a teacher who was in terror of being discovered, this wonderful man, nearly single-handed, accomplished such tasks. It is true he had a former translation of a part of the New Testament which he used as a basis, and he had the help of Dr. Milne in translating part of the Old Testament, but with all these aids the labour must have been herculean. 'It was printed from wood blocks and published (at Malacca) in 21 volumes in 1823.' Thus Protestant Missions in China took their start on the Bible, and it is to this reliance on the word of God at their inception, that their wonderful success is due. Of his other herculean task it has well been said:—'There is no finer monument of human perseverance than the dictionary of Dr. Morrison.' Unable to penetrate into China, a number of missionaries settled in the Straits, and learning the language, were ready when their opportunity came, to land, fitted for work in China. One of the prepared founts of movable type, and these were the precursors of the numerous printing presses, which, now that the Chinese have seen their utility, are not confined to mission premises, but are used by the natives themselves, at the treaty ports, to a limited extent, for the production of their own books. In addition to the English missionaries, some came to Macao from America. After the Nanking Treaty of 1842, by which Hongkong was ceded to Great Britain and five treaty ports opened, the missionaries came up from the Straits and more arrived from home. Better translations of the Bible were made, schools established, dispensaries opened, and books printed. There were at that time only a few Chinese converts all told. Since then more treaty ports have been opened, and residence in the interior has been possible in many places, till a few years before 1903 there were forty different societies at work, and a few independent workers unconnected with any society. There were 589 men, 391 married women, and 316 single ladies, making a total of 1,296; these were British, American, German, and Canadian. Of native helpers, there were 1,657. There were 522 organised native churches (but this number may be stated as more than a thousand if each company of believers is termed a Church), of which 94 were self-supporting and nearly 50 partially so. These native churches are a sufficient answer as to whether missions have been a success in China or not, for a Chinese will not pay away money for Christianity unless he is convinced of its truth or beneficial results. There were also 38 churches which were under a general endowment scheme, the money being contributed by natives alone; beside this there was a group of sixty congregations which were to support themselves; there were other cases also which might be included, so that the number of self-supporting churches given above fall short of the reality. The amount contributed in money was $36,884.54, but 'no account is taken of the value of houses and land given by natives to the churches to which they belong.' As the work has increased, the figures are now very much larger. Since 1903 the numbers have increased, and 111 missions are named as established in 1907.

Extra to these were the concomitants of mission work, such as schools, with 16,836 pupils, and medical work—of hospitals there were 61, of dispensaries 44, with hundreds of thousands of patients passing through them annually. In 1900 there were 100 missionary hospitals and dispensaries; in 1907, 366; since then the number has largely increased. In 1914 the Protestant Missions had 3,736 schools, with 104, 986 scholars; including private schools, the number of English, American, and German Protestant schools was 4,143, with 112,834 scholars. There were 12 religious journals published by missionaries, and hosts of books are being annually issued from the mission presses—not only religious ones, but scientific manuals as well, of every kind and character. Had Protestant missionaries done nothing else in China than prepare and publish the books issued by them in Chinese; start the schools; write the books in English, containing narratives of their own travels, and accounts of the natives, and of their religious customs and manners; translate native works; instruct the youth of both sexes; and found hospitals and dispensaries—had these been the only things accomplished by Protestant missionaries, they would have done a noble work; but added to all these more secular labours is the directly religious work of preaching the Gospel, tract and Bible distribution, visiting, gathering together the converts, etc., all of which, though less appreciated by the general mercantile community of China, have been as signally successful as the other class of undertakings.

The statistics here given are, of course, subject to revision every few years. Wonderful advances are being made each year in almost all the various branches of missionary labour.

It is now more than a hundred years since Protestant missions were started in China, and at first the missionaries were but a handful in number, restricted in their operations, and confined to a few localities. They have had hard up-hill work, prejudice and ignorance opposing them, a difficult language to learn—a language requiring years of unremitting, diligent study, before a sufficient knowledge of it can be acquired for general use,—but little sympathy from their fellow-countrymen on the spot, and yet the following statistics will show what has been the result of one phase alone, of their labours:—in 1842 there were 6 communicants; in 1853, 350; in 1865, 2,000; in 1876, 13,035; in 1886, 28,000; in 1889, 37,287. At the present day there must be in round numbers some 200,000 or more communicants, and besides these perhaps an equal or greater number of a Christian community.

'If Christian missions advance in the next thirty-five years in the same ratio as in the past thirty-five years, there will be at the end of that time twenty-six millions of communicants and a Christian community of one hundred million people'—one-fourth of the Chinese nation.

As to the character of the converts—are the native Christians genuine? Unfortunately some false professors, who have joined merely for the dollars which they hope to obtain, have given a bad name to native Christians amongst certain classes of people. It ought to be remembered that it is these very hypocrites among them who obtrude themselves on public notice, as what these desire is the opportunity of making money, and they thus push themselves into prominence for that object, while the genuine ones are content to occupy the humble position they already fill. The centuries of heathenism, in which the Chinese have been steeped, must also be taken into account in judging of those just come out of it: a wild flower transplanted into a garden does not produce the beautiful flowers of the cultivated species that grows at its side, but care and labour have to be expended, and the skill of the gardener exercised, to develop its best characteristics; so we can scarcely expect one transplanted out of all the debasing concomitants of idolatry to be on a par in all respects with (in fact, sometimes they are expected to be superior to) those who have been surrounded by centuries of Christian influence in our more highly favoured Western lands. But, notwithstanding all this, there are amongst the Chinese converts those who compare favourably with any in the West. (See also SCHOOLS.)

References.—Legge, *Christianity in China; Nestorianism, Roman Catholicism, Protestantism;* Foster, *Christian Progress in China;* Broomhall, *The*

Chinese Empire; Huc, *Christianity in China;* Semedo, *Histoire Universelle de la Chine;* Du Halde, *Description of the Empire of China;* Parker, *China;* Rohrbacher, *Histoire Universelle de l'Eglise Catholique;* Wessels, *Early Jesuit Travellers in Central Asia*, 1603-1721; Louvet, *Les Missions Catholiques au* xixe *siécle;* Smith, *A Short History of Christian Missions;* Smith, *Rex Christus;* Moule, *New China and Old; Handbook of Christian Missions;* Pisani, *Les Missions Protestantes à la fin du* xixe *siècle;* Medhurst, *China, its State and Prospects;* Nevius, *China and the Chinese;* Parker, *China and Religion;* Guinness, *Story of the China Inland Mission;* Wylie, *Directory of Protestant Missionaries in China;* Smith, *China in Convulsion; China Mission Handbook; Chinese Repository*, Vol. xv, etc.; *China Review*, xviii, 152, etc.; *Chinese Recorder, passim*. There are numerous other works dealing with different sections of the mission field, which are good as far as they go. Some idea also of what has been and is being done may be gathered from a study of *Records of the Missionary Conference, held at Shanghai*, 1890.

MOHAMMEDANS.—The introduction of Mohammedanism into China is interesting, resulting as it did in the settlement of followers of that religion in China, and the consequent proselytising, till now there are large communities of the followers of the prophet scattered here and there throughout the empire. The word proselytising, used above, must, however, be taken in a mild sense, for it has not been carried on with that vigour which uses compulsion to accomplish its objects and makes its converts at the point of the sword. There is no rapid growth of Mohammedanism in China. Content with a foothold in the land, and with the achievements of the past, it is now satisfied with the increase due to the natural enlargement of its borders from within, owing to the growth of the families of its professors.

Arabia has the honour of introducing Mohammedanism into this land, and commerce was the motive force which brought the most of the early followers of the false prophet to these distant shores. An embassy is recorded as having arrived in A.D. 651. In 757 a body of troops was sent by the Caliph to assist the T'ang emperor to suppress rebels. These soldiers remained in China, and are supposed to be the nucleus of the present Mohammedan population. Wos Kassin, supposed to be a maternal uncle of Mohammed, is credited with having introduced the Moslem faith into China: he come to this country in the seventh century, with a band of followers. Its missionaries arrived at different sea-ports, especially at Canton and Hangchow; they also travelled in the caravans from Central Asia. With such a measure of success was the propagation of the Islam faith carried on, that large numbers of Mohammedans are to be found in China, especially in the Northern and Western provinces where the inhabitants of whole villages are followers of the Arabian prophet; there are 200,000 in Peking. In one of the large cities of Szchuen [Ssŭch'uan] there are 80,000. In Yünnan there are said to be between three and four millions. (This province, on conquest by the emperor, was administered by a Mohammedan). In Kansuh they are estimated as 8,350,000 in number, and in Shensi as 3,500,000. These three provinces contain nine-tenths of the whole Mohammedan population of China. (In some places Mohammedans from one-third of the population); it is estimated that there are more than 10,000,000 North of the Yang-tzŭ Kiang; there are not so many in the South. 'According to an official estimate there are from twenty to twenty-five millions of Moslems in China.' The estimates, however, vary greatly—from three to eighty millions; one of the most reliable gives between five and ten millions. There are mosques in many of the cities; Canton boasts of four, two of which were built by Wos Kassin. This apostle was buried, after a residence of fifteen years in China, outside the Great North Gate of Canton. One of the two pagodas in Canton, different rather in style from the ordinary pagoda, was erected in connection with one of these mosques, in orden that the *muezzins* might call the faithful to prayers from it. The followers of this religion would appear, in this distant land of their adoption, to have held strictly to the tenets of their faith, such as circumcision, alms deeds, observance of the feast of Ramadan, and prayers in the mosque. In all their mosques is to be found a tablet on which is inscribed in letters of gold: 'May the Emperor reign ten thousand years,' the penalty of the recognition of their faith by their sovereign (their religion forbidding worship of the tablet of the emperor); Confucian, Buddhist, and Taoist temples, if of any size, all having the same reminder of the homage due to, and worship demanded by, the Son of Heaven. His subjects may worship whom they choose, but, whether they choose or not, adoration must be paid to him, except in the case of Christians, who will not bend the knee nor offer the incense of worship to any but the one living and true God.

'Unlike' what it has done 'in other countries, Islam in China has bent itself to the national ideals, and has become Chinese, not only in habits and manners, but in patriotism and character. The treatment of their Mahommedan subjects by the Emperors of China has been characterised by the broadest toleration, provincial rulers having been often degraded or dismissed for failing to enforce equal treatment of them by their fellow-subjects.'

The approximate number of Moslems in and near Peking in 1914 is given as 30,000, there being some 5,949 families connected with the 32 mosques in or near the city. Twenty-two of the mosques with 5,069 families were inside the walls, and 10 with 880 families were within 2 miles of the city.

According to the estimate of one of the mullahs there were 25,000 Moslems in Peking in 1919, while the police census of 1917 gives the number inside the walls as 23,524. The Peking Guide Book, published in 1919, gives the number of mosques as 30, ten outside the city, and a new one has just been built on Wang Fu Ching Ta Chieh. The interiors of all the mosques are in good repair and outwardly most of them are in fair condition.

Worship is still carried on in all the mosques, the principal service being held at 2 o'clock on Friday afternoon. At that time all the worshippers must take the "Ta Ching" (large bath) and change their clothes. Women take no part whatsoever in the religious services. The average attendance at the Friday service in all the mosques is about 843. Preaching is ordinarily done in Arabic, though occasional sermons are given in Chinese. The addresses usually consist of exhortations to lead a good life, explanations of the Koran and general advice.

All but one of the mosques has an " ahong " or mullah who, at least, can read the Koran in Arabic. The two best known of the Peking ahongs are Wang Hao Jên, at Niu Chieh and Chang Ch'ing Yu at Chiao Tzŭ Hut'ung. Both of these men have made the pilgrimage to Mecca, the latter having been twice. He has also visited Constantinople, Jerusalem, Moscow, Petrograd, and other import centres.

There are also schools, an academy with more than twenty-five students, and a college with more than ten. Some of the mosques engage in charitable work.

From outward appearance it is practically impossible to tell who are Moslems in Peking. They differ from their neighbours principally in that they are apt to be cleaner and are somewhat restricted in their social intercourse. The fact that they do not eat pork cuts them off from a good many social contacts, particularily since eating is connected with so much of the Chinese life. There are some Mohammedans in government employ, some have money shops and large stores, some run dairies, but by far the majority are dealers in mutton, or camel, donkey and cart drivers, the caravan trade to the city being almost entirely in their hands.

A large literature has been brought into existence by the Mohammedans. Several works were published under Imperial auspices; on the title-page some have two dragons encircling the name of the book—this being the sign of the imprimatur of the sanction, or approval, of the Emperor. (See also MISSIONS-NESTORIAN.)

There have been several rebellions of considerable magnitude by the Mohammedans against the Government (*i.e.* against the late Manchu Government only), of which may be mentioned the Tungan of A.D. 1862-70 in Kansu and Shensi, and that in Yünnan, lasting for eighteen years (1855-73).

References.—Williams, *Middle Kingdom*, ii. 268-71; Gray, *China*, i. 137-42, *The Moslem World*, 1914, No. 4, p. 165; *Chinese Recorder*, xx, 10-18; 68-72;

(literature published by Mohammedans) xxii, 263, 354, 377, 401; Rocher, *La Province Chinoise du Yünnan* (Rebellion of 1855-73); Devéria, *Origine de l'Islamisme en Chine;* Broomball, *Islam in China;* De Thiersant, *Le Mahometisme en Chine.*

MONGOLS.—The Mongols are another of those nomadic races bordering China, who have forced themselves into relationships with that country. The Huns, or Hwing-noo [Hsiung-nu (Western Tartars of Mongolia)], were the ancestors of the present Mongols, whose home was on the upper course of the Amur River. As Attila, with his hordes of savage Hun, was styled the 'Scourge of God,' and proved to be veritably the 'Terror of the West' in the fifth century; so, early in the Han dynasty (202 B.C. to A.D. 190), the Hwing-noo [Hsiung-nu] proved entitled to a similar appellation as regards the China of that period, for they ofttimes became 'virtual masters of the Empire.'

The Heanbi [Sien-pi], another Mongolic tribe, made themselves famous in Chinese history during the Han dynasty for about a hundred years. They also proved an annoyance to succeeding dynasties, becoming a formidable State, ranging over northern China and engulfing parts of it.

A number of these Mongols, as well probably as some of the Huns and other Mongolic tribes, were settled in North China; and so not only were there foes without, but within also; and in preparation for a war with the external foes, the Emperor ordered a Chinese 'St. Bartholomew's Day' of all the nomadic tribes within his borders, so that 200,000 families were slain. To prevent them turning traitors, many Chinese also suffered in the indiscriminate slaughter; but, even after such treatment, Tibetan and Hunnish families collected in China, and harsh laws were enacted against them, which drove large numbers of them out. Before that, Hienbi Mongols had returned to China, and they continued to do so afterwards. There was a Hunnish Kingdom, one of the most powerful of the many rival ones into which China was divided, in A.D. 435.

Mongols, under the name of Too-küe [T'u-chüeh], assisted the first Emperor of the T'ang dynasty to gain the throne of China. These same Turks, as they were called, plundered the north-western and northern borders of China during the whole of the T'ang dynasty.

The Khitans, another Mongolic tribe originally, have also made for themselves a chapter in Chinese history. Harrying the frontiers and plundering the country; defeated by the Chinese, who employed 1,800,000 men to build a great wall to protect the Empire from their ravages in the time of the Ch'i dynasty; eclipsed by the so-called Turks, they rose, to be again defeated.

After acknowledging the supremacy of the Chinese, they again fought with them, and threatened the North of China after the T'ang dynasty had crippled its strength in its exhausting and foolish war against ancient Corea; two expeditions were sent against them, which proved ineffectual, and it was found impossible to oust them from the new territories they had acquired. It is impossible, however, to follow the fortunes of the Khitans through all the intricacies of the history of Chinese dealings with their nomadic neighbours. Suffice it to say, that eventually, in A.D. 926, the Khitans, after Eastern Mongolia had been formed into a kingdom, began to lay the foundations of that Empire under Abdoji, [Apaoki or A-poo-chi], 'one of the great conquerors of mankind.' Under his successors they assumed the Imperial power as the Liao, or Iron dynasty, overthrowing the Ts'in Emperor. They carried on incessant wars with the Sung, and reigned over the country north of the Yellow River, their dominion extending as far north as the Sungari and Hoorha [Hurka, or Peony] rivers. The Khitans are said to have had a curious custom, that of drinking human blood, which the husbands drank from the living bodies of their wives by cutting a small slit in the wife's back. Their higher civilisation in other matters would almost appear to throw some doubt on this strange propensity, as they were painters, and had, at the time when they entered China, a literature comprising thousands of volumes, including medical works; they were hospitable, and fond of drink. It may be here proper to remark, that 'Huns,' 'Turks,' and 'Mongols' 'differ only as the Han, T'ang, and Sung of China differ. They are but dynastic titles of the same people.' They were finally driven out of Northern China by the help of the ancestors of the present Manchus, who succeeded them as the Kin dynasty, after a reign by the Liao dynasty of 240 years. It is interesting to note that Peking was first made a capital during their time.

We next find the Kins, as well as the native Chinese dynasty in the south, swept off their thrones by the Mongols. The name, Kin, is said by Ross to mean 'silver.' Genghis Khan had gathered together the numerous bands 'of restless cavalry on the north of Shamo and the west of the Hinganlin [Hsingan (or Khingan) Lin].' Defeated tribes swelled his numbers, and he entered on a career of conquest; his sons completed his work as far as China was concerned, the Yüan dynasty, as it was called, reigning over the whole of China for a period of eighty-eight years, until the Ming, a native dynasty, was founded on the ruins of the destroyed and hated power of the Mongols. (See CHINESE HISTORY.)

MONGOLS, CHARACTERISTICS AND CUSTOMS OF—The distinguishing features of the Mongols are described, by the late celebrated Russian traveller, Col. Prejevalsky, as 'a broad flat face, with high cheek-bones, wide nostrils, small narrow eyes, large prominent ears, coarse black hair, scanty whiskers and beard, a dark sunburnt complexion, and lastly, a stout thick-set figure, rather above the average height.' The Chinese face is 'cast in a more regular mould.' The men shave their heads like the Chinese used to, but the women plait their hair 'in two braids decorated with ribbons, strings of coral, or glass beads, which hang down on either side of the bosom.' The Mongols live in felt huts or tents, and are very dirty, never washing their bodies and faces, and their hands but seldom. They drink great quantities of tea and 'milk prepared in various ways, either as butter-curds, whey, or kumiss,' and are much addicted to drunkenness. Mutton is eaten in great quantities. 'Their only occupation and source of wealth is cattle-breeding, and their riches are counted by the number of their live stock.' The Mongols are very fond of their animals, and lay themselves out completely for them, being very considerate of them; their cattle, etc., are bartered for manufactured goods. They are very lazy, never walking, always riding on horseback, and are great cowards, but are fond of hunting, and kind and simple-minded. 'A Mongol can only have one lawful wife, but he can keep concubines,' the children of the latter 'are illegitimate, and have no share in the inheritance.' 'Bribery and corruption are as prevalent as in China.' 'Religious services are performed in Tibetan.'

References.—Prejevalsky, *Mongolia;* Gilmour, *Among the Mongols; More About the Mongols;* Howorth, *History of the Mongols; Geographical Journal* (London), viii, 264-78; 356-72; xx, 576-610; etc. The titles of several hundreds of books, articles, etc., are given in Cordier's *Bibliotheca Sinica,* Part V.

MONGOL LANGUAGE.—The Mongolian and Chinese languages are quite distinct and not related: Chinese is monosyllabic to a great extent, Mongolian abounds in words of several syllables; Chinese is non-alphabetic, Mongolian alphabetic. Mongolian is said to be an easier language to acquire than Chinese, especially is this the case with the written language. Gutturals and aspirates are largely used, 'so much so that their speech seems mostly gasping and sputtering.' One very curious feature in the language is the facility with which terminations are added to the verb, and by this agglutinative process a great variety of meaning is introduced without the need of using additional words; and it is not surprising to find from the 'disproportionately large part occupied by the verb' in the language that 'sentences are run out to an indefinite length, consisting of an indefinite number of participial clauses strung together like the links of a chain.' The Mongol language 'is rich in words and several forms and dialects, which, however, are not very distinct, except as between Northern and Southern Mongolian, where the difference is strongly marked,' where 'even the construction of the sentence changes'; but, notwithstanding all, it seems a very rare thing for Mongols from different parts of the country not to understand each other, thus forming a sharp contrast to the Chinese-speaking natives. There is a great difference between the colloquial and written language, and the natives appear to find it well-nigh impossible to write the language as it is spoken. A line of Mongolian writing has been compared to a knotted cord (this form dates from the 13th century); the people themselves say of it that it is like 'a stream of water poured out from a jug.' They read from left to right in vertical columns:—

'There are a good many printed books, the Chinese Government having appointed a special commission, at the end of last century, to translate into Mongol, historical, educational, and religious works.' 'But it may be remarked, in passing, that outside of the sacred books and Buddhist liturgies, there is very little in the shape of literature to be found in the Mongolian language. The book collector may find numerous manuscript copies of parts of Buddhist scriptures, some histories of famous monks, and a few tales written with the purpose of enforcing Buddhist doctrines, but secular writings are very hard to find, religion having taken such entire possession of the Mongolian mind that it is thought a waste of time to write and copy anything that has not a religious value.' 'There are schools at Peking and Kalgan for teaching the language, and an almanac and some books are from time to time printed in it. The learned classes are the princes, nobles, and lamas, the latter also learning Tibetan, the princes and nobles, Mongol and Manchu. The common people are in general illiterate.'

There are three styles of the written language: first, that of the sacred books, 'being that in which the translations of the Buddhist scriptures are made,' stiff in its style and rendering foreign idioms literally (the liturgies are written in Tibetan); second, the documentary style characterised by 'formality and the use of uncommon words'; and, lastly, the correspondence style in which letters and business documents are written. The last is pure Mongol, and nearer to the colloquial than either of the other styles.

The Mongols appear first to have borrowed the characters used by the Uighur Turks of Kashgaria, and this style of writing was commonly used by Chinghiz Khan and his immediate successors. The Uighur character was borrowed from the old Syriac, which was probably brought into Eastern Turkestan by the Nestorian clergy. This Syro-Uighur alphabet was modified in the latter part of the thirteenth century, in Kublai Khan's time, to adapt it better for the Mongol language. Continuous lines connecting the letters vertically were introduced, but the system was not completed. After this, a square character was invented instead of the Uighur. This square character was 'founded on a Tibetan modification of the Devanagari.' This was not acceptable, though Kublai Khan tried to 'force it into use.' Finally, after a reversion to the 'Uighuresque characters' with some additions, this form was, in A.D. 1307-11, brought to perfection. 'This is substantially the character still in use among the Mongols, though some additions have been since made to it.' The Manchu alphabet, again, was modelled upon this Mongol one. 'Roughly speaking, there is about as much difference between the Mongolian and Manchu character as there is between French and English writing.' But, though very similar in their written forms, the Manchu and Mongolian languages in their spoken forms are quite different.

References.—The best books for learning Mongol appear to be in Russian. For a general account of the Mongolian language, see Lovett, *James Gilmour of Mongolia: His Diaries, Letters, and Reports*, Appendix 3.

MOSQUITO.—This apparently insignificant insect—in fact, a gnat—has always been considered a nuisance in tropical countries; of late, with the new knowledge acquired, it is now known to be not only an object of annoyance but of danger, from being one of the principal factors in the transmission of malaria (and also elephantiasis, and yellow fever), the parasites of malaria running their cycle through man and the mosquito. The result is that the science of medicine is being, or will be, revolutionised as regards its application to these diseases, for the adage that prevention is better than cure has received fresh point with the new discoveries. Millions and millions of human beings will rejoice in a fresh lease of life and health as the result of the war of extermination that has commenced against this ubiquitous insect. The history of this discovery, or series of discoveries, is one of great interest; but this is not the place to enter upon a lengthened description of how, step by step, what were originally suspicions were confirmed, and eventually the whole process as regards malaria was revealed.

The mosquitoes of the world were said, some years ago, to number over 200 species. Doubtless, with the discovery of new species made of late, due to the careful attention paid to this insect, the number of known species has increased considerably. As far as Dr. Thomson's investigations at present have shown, there are sixteen species in Hongkong and the New Territory, several, at least, of which were unknown to science before. Three out of the sixteen belong to the Anopheles, and the rest are species of Culex. All the Anopheles have spotted wings, at least this is the case in Hongkong, and the Culex unspotted. It is the Anopheles which carries the malaria germs, while certain species of the Culex give elephantiasis. Several species, one of which at least is present in Hongkong, transmit, it is believed, the yellow fever germ. The fecundity of the mosquito is a great difficulty in dealing with its extermination.

'Ficalbi said one mother mosquito might in the fifth generation be the progenitor of fifty milliards. Howard showed that one rain barrel might contain 19,110 larvæ, and that they may produce at least twelve generations in one summer. This, at seventy eggs a mosquito, would produce a number of mosquitoes expressed by twenty-five figures.'

'The proboscis of the mosquito, as revealed to us beneath the magnifying eye of the microscope, is indeed a marvellously constructed organ. It is a perfectly equipped case of the most delicate surgical instruments. Here are its contents named in order of use: the keenest of lancets; a pair of fine-toothed saws, set back to back; a powerful suction-tube, through which the blood of its victim is drawn; and lastly, an injection pipe, through which is spirted the subtle poison that causes the irritation and subsequent swelling, and which by the light of corroborated investigation, we know, holds the parasite that generates malaria, elephantiasis, or some other of the many disagreeable ills to which frail flesh is heir in the tropics. Accurately described, the wound inflicted by the mosquito is not a bite at all; for the flesh is not pinched, nipped, held, or seized in any manner either by teeth or by anything equivalent to teeth. It is rather a comparatively deep incision. The intolerable smarting sensation may be partly the result of contact of the exposed edges of the wound with the air, directly the glutted insect withdraws its proboscis; but it is more probably very largely due to the after-effects of the injection.'

'There is, it appears, a microscopic parasitic little beast—an *amoeba*—which lives and multiplies in the blood of man, and which also lives and multiplies, after another fashion, in the mosquito. The creature is, strange to say, "metoxenous"; that is to say, it emigrates. Having lived one life in man, later on it lives another life in the mosquito. Malarial fever is due to the presence and development of these parasites in the blood. Ultimately they produce "zygotes," and the mosquito, having bitten a person in whom the zygotes are present, takes them into its own system. There they develop themselves again and, passing to all parts of the insect, make their way to the salivary gland, ready for the blood of a fresh human victim. It is the injection of the secretion of the mosquito's salivary gland which causes the lump which follows the mosquito's bite. A large series of experiments has shown conclusively that malarial infection is caused by the bite of the mosquito.'

'Mosquitoes cannot fly long distances, though they may be carried by a strong wind 15 miles. . . . Another plan, where it is not desired to contaminate the water, is to introduce into the breeding waters carp and other small fish which devour the eggs of the mosquito. Another remedy is to drain the swamps, and still another is to plant eucalyptus trees. There is considerable testimony to the effect that this tree will drive them away, and that a branch of it on the pillow at night will afford protection to the sleeper. In a rather unpractical way the dragon-fly is a remedy against mosquitoes, as he feeds upon them at every stage of his varied career. When darting about in the air, as he seems to in summer, he is snapping up mosquitoes.'

There are three methods of combating malaria: one is to saturate the human system with doses of quinine; another is to have fine wire netting at all windows and doors in malarial districts and prevent the mosquitoes from entering the house; and the third is to destroy the breeding places of the Anopheles.

With regard to precautions, the following abstract, made by the Honourable Dr. Clark, M.O.H., of Hongkong, of Reports furnished to the Malarial Committee of the Royal Society by Dr. Christophers and Dr. Stephenson, is interesting:—

'I. The Anopheles larvæ breed in small sheltered pools, especially those containing organic matter in suspension. These pools may be either natural or artificial, the latter being most commonly rain-water tanks. The larvæ may even be found in deep wells when the surface of the water is some 20 or 30 feet down.

'II. Anopheles can fly a distance of a quarter of a mile or more.

'III. At the end of a dry season, living *ova* do not exist in the earth of the dried-up pools.

'IV. Anopheles usually exist in the neighbourhood of native dwellings throughout the whole of the dry season, even when it may extend to several months, and from 5 to 10 per cent. of such Anopheles will be found to be infected with the malarial organism.

'V. In tropical countries Europeans are mostly infected with malaria from the natives, not from other Europeans, so that the first means of protection for Europeans consists in avoiding the native quarters with their infected population and infested Anopheles.

'VI. European dwellings should, therefore, be distant not less than 400 or 500 yards from the nearest native dwellings other than those servants' quarters which are a necessary adjunct to the dwelling and which come under the personal supervision of the European occupants of the dwelling.'

Pools in which mosquitoes may breed should be filled up, nullahs trained so as to offer no facilities of lodgment for the Anopheles, and brushwood, undergrowth, and grass kept closely cropped, for the insect frequents such places of shelter; and in houses, dark corners cleared out and fumigation with sulphur occasionally carried out in winter months to dislodge the mosquito while hibernating in servants' quarters, basements, box-rooms, stables, etc. The following directions by Dr. Thomson, of Hongkong, who has made the study of the mosquito a speciality, are herewith appended. The directions are for the destruction of the larvæ of mosquitoes, and they are published as an appendix to Dr. Thomson's able and interesting annual report on his systematic examination and classification of the mosquitoes that prevail in Hongkong and its dependencies. This appendix is dated the 18th October, 1901, and appeared in the Hongkong Government *Gazette* for that year:—

'The one great principle to act on is to prevent or abolish all stagnant water.

'Careful search should be systematically made in the neighbourhood of all dwellings for any vessels that might contain stagnant water from rain or any other source; and arrangements should be made to keep them empty, or to have them emptied, or the water changed, once a week.

'If running streams or ravines should be near . . . efforts should be made to confine the water to a central channel. Side pools should be filled up; rock hollows should be smoothed out by cement or concrete, or a channel should be made from them by means of hammer and chisel; and a ready exit, or drainage under ground, should take the place of all oozings of water from the ground surface.

'Where this guiding principle cannot be applied, or until it can be applied, still or stagnant water surfaces should be systematically inspected for the presence of larvæ of mosquitoes, and measures adopted to destroy them. This is most conveniently done in this locality by sprinkling the water surface with kerosene oil. The oil spreads in a very thin layer over the surface and prevents the larvæ form rising to breathe the air, which results in their speedy death. About one tea-spoonful of oil to each square yard of water surface is sufficient, and, if there is little movement of the water, once a week is often enough.

'As the colour of the larvæ assimilates itself to the colour of the water it inhabits, the larvæ cannot usually be easily seen in the water-pool itself. It is necessary to dip up the water with a rapid dip of a large spoon or a saucer.'

References.—Manson, *Tropical Diseases;* Christy, *Mosquitoes and Malaria;* Giles, *Gnats or Mosquitoes;* Theobald, *A Monograph of the Culidæ or Mosquitoes.*

MOURNING.—The Chinese are very punctilious in their observance of mourning. At the funeral the mourners are clothed in coarse sackcloth, while the sons and nearest of kin wear caps of the same. Mourning, especially deep mourning, is not graceful in the East. No Chinese widow looks well in her weeds; and to enhance the unsightliness of the mourning costume, the finger-nails are not cut, and the mourner goes unshaven and unshorn for seven weeks. No marriages of course, take place in the family, nor can its members go to theatres. The two large, red, globular lanterns hung up outside the front door are changed for white ones; the pieces of red paper pasted over the door are replaced by white strips. The widow and children sit on the ground for seven days, and sleep on mats on the floor near the coffin; food is not cooked, the friends and neighbours supplying what is required; chop-sticks are not allowed to be used, but the deep sorrow, supposed to be felt, is symbolised by the employment of the hands in eating, and needles and knives must be eschewed as well. After the deepest mourning of sackcloth is discarded, white is worn as deep mourning—white shoes, white robes, a white button on the cap, and white cord braided into the queue. Blue is used as lighter mourning; it must not, however, be supposed that a simple blue jacket implies that anyone has been bereaved of friends, as a great majority of the Chinese would then be in mourning every day of their lives; but a blue knob on the top of the cap instead of a black or red one, also a blue cord braided into the end of the queue, are other signs of it, as well as certain styles of blue shoes; blue earrings are worn by women. In the North of China, white is the only mourning used (but *v. infra*). The visiting cards also show that one is in mourning, a different shade of colour being used. The whole nation goes into mourning, to a certain extent, on the death of the sovereign; no one is allowed to shave for 100 days after it is proclaimed; the poor barbers must have a sad time of it. The discomfort and distress are minimised by the natives getting a clean shave before the decree enforcing it is promulgated. In Shanghai on the death of the Emperor T'ung Chih (1862-75), it was curious to see all the wheel-barrows come out with blue clothes on their seats (for wheel-barrows are the cabs of the native population in Shanghai) instead of the red ones.

A Chinese wears mourning for his superiors and equals in relationship; he does not require to put it on for his wife, but an affectionate husband, will sometimes put on white at his wife's funeral, though it is not incumbent on him to do so, or even to attend the corpse to the grave; in the same way, some abstain from red cord in the queue, and bright colours, though it is not obligatory to do so. As some who profess horrible creeds are often better than their beliefs, so there are Chinese who are better than their heartless ceremonials, which take no, or but little, account of women or children.

A period of seven times seven days is observed in mourning, funeral rites being performed on each seventh day up till the forty-ninth.

There are five degrees of mourning, as follows:—for parents; for grandparents and great-grandparents; for brothers, sisters, etc.; for uncles, aunts, etc.; and for distant relatives in line of descent or ascent.

In the first, sackcloth without hem or border; in the second, sackcloth with hem or border; in the third, fourth, and fifth, pieces of sackcloth are placed on certain parts of the dress. When sackcloth is worn, after the third interval of seven days is over, the mourners can cast it off, and then wear plain colours, such as white, grey, black, and blue. For a parent, the period of mourning is nominally three years, but really twenty-seven months, and for all this time no silk can be worn; during these months, officials have to resign their appointments, as a general rule, and retire from public life. There is an immense amount of ceremonial connected with Chinese mourning, and different duties to be performed, certain of them devolving on the chief mourner, such as carrying a certain mourning staff in the procession. The whole subject is one that much might be written upon, as there are many curious customs connected with deaths, such, for example, as the chief mourner, supported on each side and accompanied by friends, going out with a musician playing a discordant flageolet, till they come to a well or pool, when a cash or two is flung into the water, of which some is dipped up in a basin they have brought with them, taken home, and the corpse washed in it; while lanterns with blue characters on them are hung up at the front door instead of the usual red ones with black characters; and the ornament over the front door (a curiously shaped sort of tablet suspended over the doors of officials, and at weddings and funerals) is of white paper pasted on a framework of bamboo.

It should be noted, however, that though white is usually said to be the colour of mourning in China, the fact is that not colour, but plainness, such as undyed material, is at the root of the idea of Chinese mourning,—this idea resting on the manifestation of poverty, which, again, rests on the abandonment in the earliest historical and later times, of all of the nearest relatives' possessions to the deceased.

Mourning

A shed constructed of bamboo and mats, or a roof made of the same materials, is put up over the street in front of the house in which the death has taken place; a paper stork is erected on the top of bamboo poles, rising to the height of twenty or thirty feet above the street—for it is believed that the spirits take their flight into the other world on such birds, and paper, many feet in length and a yard or two in breadth, is posted up on the outside wall of the house, giving notice of the spirit's departure and the route to be taken, and warning others from coming across the road, in case any disaster should happen. Funeral cards are sent out by the family, giving intimation of the death to friends. These are large documents, and amongst other matters, they contain the date of birth and death of the deceased and a list of the children; a slip is enclosed with them, giving the date when the reception of friends to worship the spirit of the departed one will take place. A small present of money (perhaps a sum of fifty cents., that being a very common amount) is sent to the bereaved family to purchase candles, joss-paper, and incense for the ceremonies. As an instance of what may take place, we quote from a Chinese novel the directions given by the Astrologer for the funeral rites of an official's wife:—

'(This Astrologer) decided that the coffin should remain in the house for seven times seven days, that is forty-nine days; that after the third day, the mourning rites should be begun and the formal cards should be distributed; that all that was to be done during these forty-nine days was to invite one hundred and eight Buddhist bonzes to perform, in the Main Hall, the High Confession Mass, in order to ford the souls of the departed relatives across the abyss of suffering, and afterwards to transmute the spirit (of Mrs. Ch'in); that, in addition, an altar should be erected in the Tower of Heavenly Fragrance, where nine times nine virtuous Taoist priests should, for nineteen days, offer up prayers for absolution from punishment, and purification from retribution. That after these services, the tablet should be moved into the Garden of Concentrated Fragrance, and that in the presence of the tablet, fifteen additional eminent bonzes and fifteen renowned Taoist priests should confront the altar and perform meritorious deeds every seven days.'

Further on we have, in the same novel, the following:—

'This day was the thirty-fifth day, the very day of the fifth seven, and the whole company of bonzes had just (commenced the service) for unclosing the earth, and breaking Hell open; for sending a light to show the way to the departed spirit for its being admitted to an audience by the King of Hell; for arresting all the malicious devils, as well as for soliciting the soul-saving Buddha to open the golden bridge and to head the way with streamers. The Taoist priests were engaged in reverently reading the prayers; in worshipping the Three Pure Ones and in prostrating themselves before the Gemmy Lord. The disciples of abstraction were burning incense, in order to release the hungered spirits, and reading the Water Regrets Manual. There was also a company of twelve nuns, of tender years, got up in embroidered dresses, and wearing red shoes, who stood before the coffin, silently reading all the incantations for the reception of the spirit (from the lower regions), with the result that the utmost bustle and stir prevailed.'

In this connection it may be interesting to give an account of a Chinese funeral procession, and we select for that purpose a tolerably full description of that of the late Mr. T'ong King-sing of Shanghai:—

'At the head of the procession were two gigantic paper figures, one in black and the other in red. The first represented a fierce-looking soldier, and the other a mild-looking minister of state; the functions of these being to scare away any malignant spirits that might be inclined to trouble the spirit of the deceased. Next came five men on ponies, in single file, followed by sixty dirty young ragamuffins bearing boards containing the names of the offices and titles of the deceased. Then came two flags; four more men dressed in blue on ponies, followed by an umbrella, thirteen soldiers carrying many coloured banners, twenty-four men on foot bearing weapons with pewter heads and wooden handles, two men blowing clarions, a mandarin on a pony, four soldiers with banners, twenty-three soldiers with bayonets fixed, behind them being a three-flounced umbrella and mandarin runners. Next came ten musicians very well dressed, and another umbrella and attendants. A green chair, borne by eight carriers, with a mourner on each side, and two handsome scrolls immediately preceded the Taotai's band, who were followed by thirty well-dressed soldiers, a number of tables on which were a roasted pig, a skinned goat, fruit, and pewter wine-bottles, while some paper tables had on them gold and silver mock sycee, scrolls, and representations of Chin Shan and Yin Shan,—the Gold and Silver Mountains—all these latter intended to be burnt. The handsomest part of the procession was the "myriad name umbrellas," of which there were twenty-four, presented by the people whose names appeared in velvet characters on the lower flounces, while round the upper ones were quotations from the classics. These umbrellas were very handsome, and were mostly of silk and in many colours. Then there were two more chairs, some Taoist and Buddhist priests, satin scrolls, and a chair containing the picture of the deceased, on either side of the chair being a mourner. Next came some Buddhist priests playing on flutes, and then behind them boys carrying flowers on stands. A hundred of the friends of the deceased in their official robes followed, each bearing a lighted joss-stick. Many handsome scrolls succeeded, and then came the Town Band, four mourners, the sons of the deceased, gongs, and images. The catafalque was carried by thirty-two bearers, the pole which ran through it having the head and tail of a dragon, a taken of Imperial favour, and the end of the procession was brought up by hundreds of Chinese in carriages and chairs and on foot.'

What value the Chinese attach to such matters may be judged by the saying that, 'the most important thing in life is to get buried well.'

No one who has not been married is entitled to a funeral procession. The coffin in such a case would simply be carried to the grave without all the concomitants of music, and all the chairs and open stands, lanterns, insignia, *et hoc genus omne*, which brought together into a trailing picturesque confusion form that delight of the Chinese, a procession. When children die they are not always coffined, but the bodies are often put into a box. Amongst the Cantonese this may, perhaps, be done in eight cases out of ten, and the corpses of infants which are seen floating in rivers and pools and lying by the wayside or on the hill slopes are many of them those which are thus indecently cast aside without burial, though some of them are the bodies which have been exposed or killed outright by their inhuman parents.

There are many superstitions prevalent with regard to funerals: some firmly believed in by some people, and by others thought of little account. Again, different superstitions are found in different parts of the country; some places being extremely superstitious and others less so.

The following will serve as instances:—

It is not lucky for certain people to go to a certain funeral or even to see the corpse when the encoffining takes place. The man who selects the auspicious time and date for burial, etc., states what persons of a certain age (dependent on the time the deceased died) should not be present.

There is an idea that if two coffins come together, *i.e.*, meet while going in opposite directions, should the death or deaths be recent, this will cause another death in the family; and if two coffins meet another it will cause two deaths. Such circumstances are supposed to be unlucky for the living and even for the spirit of the dead, and will prevent in the last case the family of the deceased from having good luck. (In this connection see also GEOMANCY.)

The bringing of several corpses together while only recently dead is much objected to by some Chinese.

The distinction between the sexes as to meeting one another, etc., is overlooked to a certain degree at times of death.

People of a certain age should not attend a certain funeral or even see the corpse at all; this depends on the hour the deceased died and the age of the living persons. In order to find this out, the dates and hours of birth and death of the deceased are taken to a man whose business it is to select the lucky dates for events, *i.e.*, for starting business, for encoffining, and for burial; the same man decides whether two persons should marry, and the day for boys to start going to school, and sometimes, as well, the day to start on a journey, but this is seldom done; and the people also look in the almanacs for the time for digging foundations for a house and for putting up ridge-poles. This man may be a fortune-teller as well or not. He gives directions as to what aged people are not to look at the corpse at the encoffining and not to look on at the burying. There is a propitious time for the funeral to start, and a lucky time for the corpse to be lowered into the grave. Again, in Amoy they are intensely superstitious over all these things, and funerals in consequence are fixed for all hours of the day and night—midnight, or any other hour which may turn out to be lucky.

Though the same in essentials, mourning rites have of recent years become somewhat less strict than formerly.

References.—Gray, *China* (Cantonese customs); Doolittle, *Social Life of the Chinese* (Foochow); *Hongkong Daily Press*, 1861 (Hakkas); *China Review*, xvii, 47-8 (days of official mourning); *ibid.* p. 38 (periodical funeral rites); *Li chi (Li Ki)* (trans. by Legge, *Sacred Books of the East*, Vols. xxvii-viii) (ancient mourning customs on which the modern ones are based, modified by local usages and practice). The whole subject is most fully treated in De Groot, *Religious System of China*, Vol. ii.

MUSIC:—

'Music in China has undoubtedly been known since the remotest antiquity. It is said to have been invented by the Emperor Fu-hsi (B.C. 2852). . . . It is, say the Chinese, the essence of the harmony existing between heaven, earth, and man. . . . The first invaders of China certainly brought with them certain notions of music. The Aborigines themselves had also some kind of musical system which their conquerors admired, and probably mixed with their own.'

Different systems seem to have been evolved by different emperors and were differently styled, but it assumed its 'characteristic form' with the (mythical) Emperor Huang Ti (B.C. 2697), when, amidst other innovations, names were given to the sounds, and one fixed upon as a base note. Theoretically, music holds a position of paramount importance in the good government of a State. Either this ancient music was of an extraordinary character—for Confucius was so ravished on hearing a piece, composed by the great Shun 1,600 years before his time, that he did not taste meat for three years—or the Chinese were sensitively responsive to certain combinations of sounds, in a manner unknown to Europeans. Unfortunately we have no means of testing which is true, for the knowledge of this ancient music is lost. If the descriptions of it are true to the reality, no one who has heard Chinese music of the present day will have any hesitation in accepting the statement of its being unknown now, for it has been remarked, in a comic strain, that the music of the Chinese is '"deliciously horrible," like cats trying to sing bass with sore throats.' Some most abstruse theories are all that remain for us. At the great destruction of books, those on music, as well as musical instruments, shared 'the same fate as every object which could give rise to any remembrance of past times.'

Great efforts were made to resuscitate the lost art; some of the books and instruments were recovered from their hiding places; but the times were not favourable for the cultivation of peaceful arts; the memory of the great music-master, in whose family the office had been hereditary, was not sufficient to bridge over the chasm which the great catastrophe had occasioned; different authors disagreed in their theories, and a confusion of the different systems has resulted. Two Emperors of the recent Ch'ing dynasty, K'ang Hsi and Ch'ien Lung, used their best efforts 'to bring music back to its old splendour,' but without much success.

'It must not be supposed that semitones were unknown to the ancient Asiatic nations; on the contrary, we find in their music even smaller divisions than our chromatic scale, at least in theory if not in practice.

Of the early history of Chinese music we possess an account by the French missionary Amiot, who, during his abode in Peking, made it part of his mission to collect as much information on this subject as he could possibly obtain. He consulted a large number of old Chinese treatises on the science and history of music, of which a list is given in the book containing the result of his investigations (Mémoires concernant l'Histoire . . . des Chinois, tome sixième). We learn from them that the ancient Chinese divided the octave into twelve equal parts, like the semitones of our chromatic scale, which were called *lu*. (There is, however, this difference, that the twelve Chinese divisions were strictly alike, while our chromatic scale consists of large and small semitones.) Their scale, as commonly used, consisted, however, of only five notes, which were called *koung*, *chang*, *kio*, *tché*, and *yu*, and which corresponded to our *f*, *g*, *a*, *c*, *d*. *Koung*, or *f*, was considered to be the normal key, as we consider our *c*; and it was from *koung* that the above order of intervals was transposed to any of the other keys, in a similar way as we change the scale of C major into that of G major, F major, etc. The intervals of the *fourth* and *seventh* were called *pien-koung* and *pien-tché*. The former was identical with our *e*, and the latter with our *b*. These two intervals they employed only in exceptional cases, or rather, nearly in the same way as we introduce chromatic intervals into our diatonic scale. Several of the ancient Chinese musical instruments contain only the pentatonic scale, and are purposely thus constructed. The *hiuen*, an ancient wind instrument of an oval shape, had five holes through which the notes *koung, chang, kio, tché* and *yu*, were emitted. A similar instrument is still used. The highly esteemed *kin*, the favourite instrument of the venerated Confucius, was also similarly tuned. Another very ancient one the *ou*, in the shape of a crouching tiger, possessed six notes, corresponding to our *f, g, a, c, d, f*.

Several of these instruments are no longer in use, or have become gradually changed. The Chinese, even at the present time, construct instruments in which they purposely introduce the pentatonic scale only. Of this kind is the one . . . deposited in the Museum of the United Service Institution in London. The Chinese harmonicon which Dr. Burney saw in Paris, in the possession of the Abbé Arnaud of the French Academy, was of a similar construction.'

'Modern music really dates from the T'ang dynasty (A.D. 600).' Mr. Van Aalst divides Chinese music into two kinds; 'ritual or sacred music, which is passably sweet, and generally of a minor character; and the theatrical or popular music. . . . The present Chinese theoretically admit seven sounds in the scale, but practically they only use five, and that as well in ritual music as in popular tunes.' Chinese music cannot be exactly represented on our Western musical instruments, as the intervals between the notes are not the same as ours.

Ritual music was used in the acts of worship in which the Emperor either took part himself or was represented by a deputy, such as the worship of Heaven and Earth, of Ancestors, of the Sun and Moon, etc., and of Confucius. The popular music includes all other kinds, and there are not a few. Not a procession of any importance winds its meandering course through the busy narrow lanes, that do duty for streets in a great part of China, but has bands of musicians, sometimes scores of bands, having small drums and clashing cymbals, etc. That music should take a prominent part in a marriage is naturally to be expected, but it takes an equally prominent part in funerals, the poorest of which has at least one musician, and the better ones more, playing a dirge on shrill clarionets—in the latter case also bands of performers on instruments are seen as well. Before the establishment of the Republic in 1912 no officer of a high grade proceeded on an official visit without the deep-toned boom of the sonorous gong proclaiming, by the number of beats, the rank of the 'great man,' while its other uses are not a few. In evening worship on board ship, it and the drum provide the music.

Much of the attraction of the theatre to the natives consists in the music and singing—attractive to the native, but ear-splitting and headache-producing to the foreigner. The singing on the stage 'is not unfrequently in the "recitative" style, and the way the orchestra accompanies, in broken, sudden chords, or in long notes, bears a striking resemblance to our European recitative.'

Ballad singing is much appreciated; blind men play one species of guitar, while blind singing girls accompany themselves on another. The courtesans are given a musical education according to Chinese ideas; and scarcely a boy or coolie but delights in singing to his heart's content from a book of songs of one kind or another, or screeches a song in imitation of some theatrical character. Grass-cutters and field-labourers beguile the time by singing responsive songs, the men and boys singing one verse and the girls the other. The Buddhist priests chant in their services; while the Taoists also chime their instruments and sing their liturgies.

There is quite a variety of musical instruments in use, some being confined to the Chinese sacred music in their ritual ceremonies, and other to popular music. One of the most ancient is called the 'stone chimes,' consisting of a series of sonorous stones of varying thickness, hung in a frame. There is also the 'single sonorous stone' and a marble flute. This employment of stone for musical instruments is peculiar to China. A 'conch,' a large shell, is used by soldiers, watchmen, and bands of pirates.

Bells of different shapes—square and round, and of all weights, from over fifty tons downwards—are much used, every temple of any size having one large one at least, as well as a large drum. Amongst curious ancient Chinese musical instruments may be noted the chimes of small bells suspended in a framework; and the chimes of gongs, ten in a frame; while another *outré* object is a wooden mortar struck with a wooden hammer. The cymbals in use are said to have come originally from India.

Some of the stringed instruments are also most ancient; there are a number of lutes, guitars, and violins, some of the latter with the bow passing between the strings.

Of wind instruments, there are flutes and clarionets, or flageolets.

Wooden instruments are also made; one of the most common is the wooden fish, it is shaped somewhat like a skull, and hollowed out; it is struck with a piece of wood, and is much used by priests. Of drums there are not a few varieties.

'The shêng is one of the most important of Chinese musical instruments. . . . No other instrument is nearly so perfect, either for sweetness of tone or delicacy of construction. The principles embodied in it are substantially the same as those of our grand organs. Indeed, according to various writers, the introduction of the shêng into Europe led to the invention of the accordion and the harmonium. Kratzenstein, an organ-builder of St. Petersburg, having become the possessor of a shêng, conceived the idea of applying the principle to organ stops.'

The following notes written by a scientific Professor of Music will be of interest:—

'It is strange that the Chinese found out perfect Intonation centuries before we ever dreamt of such a thing, and that the scale of music is based not upon the 1st sound of tonic, but upon the 4th. The sets of tubes kept to tune instruments by (that is the standard cones kept at the Capital, gauged by their holding so many grains of millet) are scientifically exact, with one curious exception, at the 6th, which is 81, while the true scale is only 80, the difference being a comma of 81/80, which is the cause of all our trouble in tempered tuning. The scale of Nature is in the proportion of

	1st	2nd	3rd	4th	5th	6th	7th	8th
Chinese	48	54	60	64	72	80	90	96
True	48	54	60	64	72	81	90	96

This has been caused by the fact which has stumbled all our learned musicians, viz., that the 2nd tone of the scale 54 does not bear a perfect fifth of 2 to 3, but is imperfect by a comma.

'Another misleader to all writers on Chinese Music is that the scale is used in the same way as the Moderns do, viz., from the 1st or Tonic to its Octave. Chinese Music is quite different, and, like our old Scotch, Irish, and English Music—indeed, all the old music of the world. If may begin on any note of the scale, reading the tones from the 1st to the 1st, 2nd to the 2nd, 3rd to the 3rd, and so on; for instance, if you look at "Madame Wang," page 38 of the treatise [Chinese Music], you will see it runs from the 3rd to the 3rd of the scale, that is from Mi to Mi. Page 42, "Haunts of Pleasure," is in the mode of the 1st of the scale; 44, "Oh Mamma," mode of the 2nd; so is the "Wedding March," page 46. The "Funeral March," same page, is in the mode of the 3rd; please compare this melody with Macrimmon's "Lament," or with Mackintosh's in the "Thistle," and you will see how much they are of the same character. . . . Read the Introduction to the "Thistle" . . . specially as to the modes; what is explained there of Scottish Music is equally true of Chinese.'

Chinese music, as looked upon from a foreign standpoint, has been thus described:—

'The intervals of the Chinese scale not being *tempered,* some of the notes sound to foreign ears utterly false and discordant. The instruments not being constructed with the rigorous precision which characterises our European instruments, there is no exact justness of intonation, and the Chinese must content themselves with an *à peu près.* The melodies being always in unison, always in the same key, always equally loud and unchangeable in movement, they cannot fail to appear wearisome and monotonous in comparison with our complicated melodies. Chinese melodies are never definitely major nor minor; they are constantly floating between the two, and the natural result is that they lack the vigour, the majesty, the tender lamentations of our minor mode; and the charming effects resulting from the alternation of the two modes.' 'The Chinese have, theoretically, a perfect scale and a fairly good notation; there is, however, one great lack in their system, they have no satisfactory method of expressing time. . . . This is all the more strange, seeing that in practice they are strict timists.'

Professor C. J. Knott, D.Sc., F.R.S., writes:—

'The Chinese musical school, as it is developed in Japan, is peculiar in the high pitch in which the leading female voice chants the libretto. There is melody in the airs and truthfulness in the instrumental *ensemble* of fiddles, guitars, and flutes. But there is no harmony in our sense of the term. Each piece is very long and wearisome in its apparently endless repetitions.'

The Chinese do not appreciate our music any more than we do theirs. A Chinese, who was listening to the military band playing in Hongkong, was asked his opinion of it, and he said the music lacked harmony. That they fully appreciate their own music needs but a glance at the crowd round a Chinese band performing; their writings equally show this appreciation, for example, take the following from 'Gems of Chinese Literature':—

'Softly, as the murmur of whispered words; now loud and soft together, like the patter of pearls and pearlets dropping upon a marble dish. Or liquid, like the warbling of the mango-bird in the bush; trickling like the streamlet on its downward course. And then, like the torrent, stilled by the grip of frost, so for a moment was the music lulled, in a passion too deep for words.'

Who will say after that, that the Chinese have no soul for music?

References.—Van Aalst, *Chinese Music; Journal N.C.B.R.A.S.*, N.S. ii. 176-9; v. 30 *seq.; vii.* 93 *seq.;* viii. 93 *seq.; Mémoires Concernant les Chinois,* vi. i *seq.;* 225 *seq.;* Engel, *The Music of the Most Ancient Nations;* Burney, *History of Music; Asiatic Magazine,* i. 64 *seq.; Chinese Repository,* viii. 38-54; De la Fage, *Histoire générale de la Musique et de la Danse,* i. i-400; *Notes and Queries on China and Japan,* Vol. iv; Perny, *Dict., Append.* No. xiv, pp. 143-54; *China Review,* i. 324-8; 384-6; ii. 47-9; 257; v. 142, 269; xv. 54; xi. 33; *Chinese Recorder,* xxi. 221.

NAMES.—The different names that a Chinese has are a perfect puzzle to a European; for nearly every Chinese has several names. He keeps his surname through life, of course, as we do, but at every memorable event in his life, such as first going to school, and getting married, he takes another name. It must not, therefore, be supposed that because a native gives you different names for himself he is attempting to palm himself off as someone else, though this system of a plurality names offers facilities to one who is inclined to be tricky.

The names recorded in the *Po chia hsing*, or "All the Clan Names," number four hundred and eight single and thirty double ones. The commonest names are Chang, Li, and Wang.

A Chinese surname then is unchangeable, and generally consists of one syllable, though there are a few of two or three. The surname comes first, and the other names afterwards—in fact the Chinese follow the convenient order used in our directories. A remembrance of this would prevent the foreign resident from prefixing our 'Mr.' to the personal name of a Chinese. It sounds incongruous enough to prefix 'Mr.' to a Chinese surname—an attempt to mix two civilisations which will not blend together in harmony, but it sounds ten times worse to call a perfect stranger by his personal name and then prefix a 'Mr.' to it. To illustrate:—Say a Chinese bears the euphonious designation of Ch'un Wá-fuk [Hua-fu]. Now the first, Ch'un, is his surname, and Wá-fuk is what he elects to be called by, his Christian name in fact. If the 'Mr.' must be used, then he is Mr. Ch'un or Mr. Ch'un Wá-fuk, but not Mr. Wá-fuk or Mr. Fuk any more than Mr. John Harry Jones is Mr. John Harry, or Mr. Harry, to a stranger.

Though it generally happens that the first syllable or word in the string of three words, which usually form the surname and name of a Chinese, is the surname, it does not always follow that it is, as Chinese as well as English have a few double surnames, they have even a very few trisyllabic surnames. One of the most common of these bisyllabic surnames in the South of China is Aú-yöng [A-yung], so therefore in the combination Aú-yöng Tát the two syllables form the surname and the last syllable the name.

About a month after a boy's birth a feast is given, and he gets his 'milk name (*nai ming*, *ju ming*, or *hsiao ming*),' as it is called. This name clings to him through life, as in fact all his names do after they are once bestowed. This milk name is, if anything, more especially distinctive, as it is used by his relatives and neighbours, and in official matters if he has no 'book name.' This name of infancy often consists of but one character, and in that case has, in the extreme South, the prefix Ah put before it, so that a boy named Ch'un Luk will commonly be called Ch'un Ah luk, though the Ah is not really a part of his name. In the so-called dialects, this Ah is not used.

On first going to school the boy has another name given to him, the 'book name (*shu ming or hsüeh ming*).' It 'generally consists of two characters, selected with reference to the boy's condition, prospects, studies, or some other event connected with him.' This name is used by his master and school-fellows, in official matters, and in any matters connected with literature.

On marriage the young man takes still another name, his style or 'great name,' or 'style' (*tzŭ*) and this his father and mother and relations use as well as the 'milk name.'

Another name called 'another style (*hao*)' may be assumed, which is employed by acquaintances and friends, not by relatives and parents. The latter have a right to use the 'milk name,' but with well-to-do people, who have more than one name, it is not considered the proper thing for outsiders to call a man by his 'milk name'; of course it is different with farmers, labourers, and others who only own one name.

Every *literatus* takes one or more 'studio names' (*pieh hao*). On taking a degree, on entering official life, or on having official distinction or rank conferred on him, a man takes yet another name, known as the 'official name' (*kuan ming* or *k'ao ming*).

After death he is known by his posthumous name in the Hall of Ancestors (*shih ming* or *hui ming*).

Besides all these, we may notice one or two other designations. It is a very common thing for the Southern Chinese to give a suggestive sobriquet to anyone who may have some personal defect or characteristic, and the euphonic syllable, Ah, is often used before these, leading foreigners to think that such a nick-name is a real name; it is at the same time tantamount to a real name, as everyone speaks of the person so-called as such, and calls him or her by it. The individual bears it complacently, knowing that he must accept the inevitable. Such names are called 'flowery names.' When they consist of more than one syllable the Ah is dropped: they are used in combination with the personal name or not; as instances of this class are such names as Giant Ah Yŏng (here Ah Yŏng, of course, is the man's right name), other terms of a similar kind are Dwarfy, Fatty, etc. A very common one, used alone, without any name with it, is Ah Pín=flat, meaning flat nose, another often heard is Taú-p'éí [*tou p'i*], Small-pox Marked, and there are a few others.

To cheat the evil spirits which may wish to rob a man of his son, the boy may be called by some name that will convey the idea of vilifying the young child, such as 'Puppy,' or his head may be shaved and he be called 'Buddhist priest.' It is not at all uncommon to call the children in a family Primus, Secundus, Tertius, etc., but this practice sounds rather ridiculous when it is not limited to the first few numbers, and one hears a child or boat-woman called Duodecima.

There is also yet another name, which is a very important one, it is the *t'ong* [*t'ang*] name. It is difficult to convey its import by an English translation, but it may be rendered by 'ancestral name,' or 'family name,' or 'house name,' remembering that all these terms must bear a restricted meaning if applied to the Chinese. A man of means, having a house of his own, is sure to possess such a name, and he has, in all probability, inherited it from his father or ancestors, unless he has risen from the lowest ranks of society, and has to select such a name for himself. Or it may refer to some special event in the family's history. This name will generally be found up at his door on a small board. It represents himself and it also represents his family in a way. If he dies, his sons (if they continue to live together, as the Chinese so often do, in the same family house) retain the name, and together, or separately, make use of it. This *t'ong* name is often used in business, some partners appearing under such names, while others appear under some of their other names. In such a case the *t'ong* name in the partnership may only represent one man or the whole branch of the family, with what result of confusion and shiftiness when bankruptcy occurs may readily be understood, for only one member of the family may be down in a firm's books under his *t'ong* name, and in other cases this *t'ong* name in a firm's books may not represent one man but the family, and there may be, which often happens, no proof of what it really stands for. If, however, the brothers separate and live in different houses, they add certain words to the *t'ong* name signifying 'second family,' or 'third family,' etc., as they may chance to be second or third sons, etc. The *t'ong* name has the word *t'ong* attached to the end of it, and is otherwise composed of some happy sounding combination of words, such, for example, as Wing Shín T'ong [Yung Shan T'ang], which might be rendered into English as 'The Hall of Eternal Goodness.'

One of the most ridiculous mistakes which foreign residents make in China is calling natives by the name of the business they are engaged in. True enough a Chinese when asked who he is, or 'Who you b'long?' in pidgin-English, will perhaps answer 'Sun Shing': so a man from a foreign business might say at times, 'I am Smith, Brown & Co.' It is, however, in fact more absurd to call such a man Mr. Sun Shing, or look upon that as his name, than it would be to call the other Mr. Smith Brown; in the latter case it is possible the man's name may be Smith or Brown, in the other it is almost impossible that the man's name could be Sun Shing. A clearer idea of the incongruity of thus styling Chinese might be got by supposing that a foreigner in England, seeing the name 'Royal Oak' over a public house should style the proprietor Mr. Royal Oak. At the same time, some of the very small master masons, etc., occasionally add the character Kéí [Chi] to the end of their surname and name, and take this combination as their business style; for instance, a man named Ch'an Ah Luk, might take as his business style Ch'an Luk Kéí. This is the only approach to a man's name appearing in his business on his signboard; for the majority of 'business styles' are such combinations as 'Mutual Advantage,' 'Extensive Harmony,' and 'Heavenly Happiness.'

A man engaging in different branches of business will also often take different business names for each branch, or use some other method of distinguishing the different businesses.

Girls are left out in the cold as far as names are concerned. They have to be content with a milk name, a marriage name, and nicknames. They retain their own surnames when married; that is to say, a married woman considers her maiden surname as her own, and gives it as such; by courtesy she is addressed by her husband's surname, being the equivalent of our Mrs. So and So. In official documents her two surnames are given one after the other, and the combination serves as her name; for example, a woman's maiden surname may be Léí (pronounced Lay), her married surname Ch'un. She would then be known as Ch'un Léí Shí [*Shih*], the Shí denoting that she belongs to the Léí family by birth. The 'territorial name' (*chün ming*) is hardly used except for girls on their marriage documents.

A lady will not give her name. A Chinese lady, when asked her name in Court will answer that she had no name. The stranger must be content with simply knowing the combination of two surnames, such as given above; for there is a feeling, partly of modesty, partly of fear, that an impudent stranger might, in sheer impertinence, call her by it if it were known. The wives of labourers and of the lower classes do not have the same feeling, and will tell their names freely, at least the Cantonese will; and with this experience of them it was curious to find the same class of people in Ch'ao Chow-fú not prepared to respond freely to such inquiries, the questioner having to be content with the husband's name (not surname) followed by the word sister, aunt, or mother, according to the age of the woman.

Emperors in China also rejoiced in a multiplicity of names which are very confusing to the foreign student of Chinese history. After his death the Emperor is known by his posthumous title (*miao hao;* temple name), such for example as 'The Great Ancestor,' 'The Martial Ancestor,' etc. While he is on the throne, the years of his reign have a designation which serve as the equivalent of his name. This 'year style' (*nien hao*) is composed of two characters, which, in combination, will sound well, such for example, as 'Compliant Rule.' In the last reigning dynasty, the one designation served for the whole reign, but it has not always been so, and confusion seems worse confounded when every few years in one sovereign's reign the 'year style' is changed, owing possibly to some untoward event having happened. Such changes have taken place half a dozen or more times. It will thus be seen that the name by which an Emperor is known is not one of his own personal names, as in the case of King Edward or any of our Western sovereigns. In fact, a Chinese Emperor's personal name is too sacred to be used by the general public, no one is permitted to utter it or even write it, as long as the same family remains on the throne, even though the Emperor who bore it is dead; and to prevent this difficulty, the characters composing it are changed by the alteration or addition of parts of the character. Nor is it proper for a child to use his father's own name; it is considered disrespectful. His father's name is tabooed, so is a husband's name to a wife; so far is this carried that some wives amongst the Chinese do not even know their husbands' names. After this it will excite no surprise to learn that no one is allowed to use the names of Confucius and Mencius. The surnames of these sages, however, are not considered sacred. The great sage of China has many descendants to this day bearing his honoured cognomen. But those who have got into straitened circumstances change their name, so as not to dishonour him.

Literary men are fond of the disguise of a *nom de plume* in China as well as in the West; and, when it is remembered that China is the 'Flowery Land,' it may readily be understood what a fanciful form such a name sometimes assumes.

NAVY.—In the first and second editions of this book the author wrote:—

'We have a very fine coat, but there is no man inside it,' such was the estimate of the Chinese Navy by a Chinese naval officer of the Northern Fleet, and probably a very just estimate, not only of that portion of the navy, but of the whole of the modern Chinese fleet made on Western lines; for very fine vessels they are, but the Chinese cannot yet, with all their inexperience of them and their bribery and corruption, be proper masters of their own vessels.

When we turn to the native junks, which were all the navy she had till of late, we find that for conflict with Western powers, China is as ill-prepared as a soldier of the time of the Norman Conquest would be at the present day.

We may now add she was almost as ill-prepared with her modern ironclads. A fleet of twenty-five vessels of all sizes and armaments forming the Northern Squadron, or the greater part of it belonging to that portion of the Chinese navy, some of the number being powerful ironclads built in Europe, were lost to the Chinese during the disastrous war with the Japanese in 1894. These vessels were sunk, or destroyed, or set on fire, or surrendered to the Japanese, while one or two of them were wrecked, the Japanese gaining a considerable addition to their navy. As the Chinese fleet of ships built on foreign models consisted in 1892 of 47 men-of-war of one class or another, it will be seen that half of their vessels, and of those many of them of an advanced type, were lost at almost one blow. 'The officers and men had both received much careful training'—a most complete one and of 'a very efficient standard'; but official corruption, added to the vanity and ignorance so frequently displayed by the Chinese naval authorities in recent years worked out their natural result in the first serious conflict with the foe. This is not the first serious disaster that the Chinese have suffered in trying their prentice hands at the modern game of war, for a fleet of vessels, 11 in number, built on the foreign model, was sunk or destroyed by the French in August, 1884, in the Min River below Foochow, by a fleet immensely their superiors; but this last one in 1894 was a far more severe blow and a far greater loss than the previous one. To repair this annihilation and carrying off of the major portion of their modern naval force, the Chinese began to reconstruct their navy; the first instalment of this new fleet, built in Europe, was to consist amongst other ships, of 2 battleships of 8,000 tons, 2 armoured cruisers of 5,000 tons, and 4 protected cruisers of 3,000 tons.

One writer well said, 'It may be predicted, however, that unless the Chinese improve their present system of recruiting and training, the fleet, which they are now seeking to re-form, will be exposed to . . . a disaster similar to that of Weiheiwei.'

In addition to these vessels we should mention four powerful torpedo-boat destroyers of 6,000 horse-power, to steam at the rate of 32 knots per hour.

The Chinese do not depend for their war vessels entirely on those constructed in foreign lands, but they are able to turn out new ships for their navy at the various arsenals established of late years on the models of those amongst Western nations. A steel cruiser of about 1,800 tons was completed at the Foochow (Pagoda Anchorage) arsenal. She was to be armed entirely with quick-firing guns, and was probably to be employed as a training vessel for the new graduates of the Tientsin Naval Academy. It will thus be seen that the Chinese were gradually re-building their ruined navy or at least the northern portion of it, before the last war, for with but one or two exceptions it was only the Northern Squadron that was engaged in the Japenese war; and an amusing story is told of the Captain of a vessel belonging to another portion of the Chinese navy, whon taken by the Japanese, requesting to be let off, as his ship did not belong to the Northern Squadron which only was fighting the Japanese.

A writer in 1899 thus describes the Chinese navy:—

'Little progress is being made with the reconstruction of the Chinese Navy, and unless it is taken in hand by another Lang it is feared by those who have an intimate knowledge of it, that it will be one of the biggest of the many failures in China. The mismanagement by the Chinese authorities is simply appalling. More Europeans are required—at the very least a captain and an engineer for each ship. Suitable men would be difficult to get, however, for few would have patience to endure the Chinese methods, and fewer still have the tact to work along with the incompetent Chinese officers who are appointed to the ships. It it very difficult, apparently, to get them to understand the difference between an officer and a member of his crew, and, in consequence, there is always lacking that spirit of discipline so necessary for the proper management of a warship. We hear that the higher Chinese officials are anxious to get rid of all the foreigners in the service. If this is true, then the speedy dissolution of the Chinese Navy is in sight; but we expect it will manage to weather the threatened storm. China does not know how to reward faithful service by foreign *employés*, and so it will be difficult to get another Lang; but the miraculous may happen some day, and China herself produce a clean-handed official who will reconstruct the Naval Department, and place it on a sound footing.'

'The Statesman's Year Book' for 1902 says:—

'At the conclusion of the war with Japan the *Chen Hai* and the *Kang Chi* alone remained to China, of her effective Pei Yang squadron. Some swift vessels have since been added to the fleet. Among these are the crusers *Hai Chi* and *Hai Tien* (4,300 tons), launched in the Tyne in 1897 and 1898. They have 6-inch armoured shields and a 5-inch deck, and they carry two 8-inch, ten 4.7 inch, and twelve 3 pr. Armstrong quick-firers. The speed is 24 knots. The small cruisers *Hai Yung*, *Hai Shen*, and *Hai Shew* (2,900 tons), have been launched at Stetton (1897), four destroyers, built at Elbing, have been captured, and distributed to England, France, Germany, and Russia. A French engineer, M. Doyère, has reorganised the Arsenal of Foochow, and a torpedo gun-vessel (817 tons) and a 20.5-knot torpedo-boat are in hand there [1901]. The Chinese blue-jacket is as good as any in the world.'

Besides these are three or four other protected cruisers, four torpedo gunboats, six floating batteries, twenty-two river gunboats, and twenty-one torpedo boats.

The Chinese fleet is divided into the North Coast Squadron, the Foochow Squadron, the Shanghai Flotilla, and the Canton Flotilla.

The Foochow Squadron was stated in 1892 to consist of 'nine cruisers of from 1,300 to 2,480 tons, three gunboats, nine despatch boats, and three revenue cruisers'; but this Nanyang (*i.e.*, South Coast) fleet was described in 1894 as consisting of the cruisers *Kaichi*, lost by explosion in 1902, *Huantai*, *Chingtsung*, *Namsheng*, *Namshui* (German built), *Paoning*, and the sloops *Weiching*, and *Chunho*, and the mosquito gunboats (one 36-ton gun each), *Lungsiang*, *Huwei*, *Feising*, and *Ts'etien*. The Southern Squadron has its headquarters at Foochow; its officers have a slight acquaintance with foreign methods.

The Viceroy Chang Chih-tung also possessed in 1894 'four sloops built either at Shanghai or Foochow, whose names' began 'with the characters *T'su*, denoting the provinces (Hunan and Hupeh) they are intended to protect.'

In 1892 the Shanghai flotilla consisted 'of an armoured frigate, 2,630 tons, a gunboat, six floating batteries (wood), and three transports.'

In the same year the Canton flotilla consisted of '13 gunboats . . . of 100 to 350 tons displacement.' Since then there have been added to the last flotilla three large steel cruisers, named the *Kuangchia*, *Kuangping*, and *Kuanyi*. These three ships 'are commanded and officered for the most part by young men who received their first foreign education in the United States. Their commodore is named Yü, and is reported to have seen some active service.' Most of the principal officers of the late Northern Squadron, it may be remarked, had also been taught the European methods of war, though the late Admiral Ting, who was in command, had not had such a training, being a purely native untrained Mandarin, his substantive appointment being that of a General of Cavalry; the Chinese have not yet learned with regard to Government officials, in the words of Herbert Spencer, that 'the transformation of the homogeneous into the heterogeneous, is that in which progress essentially consists'; for a Mandarin is considered to be in a general way competent to undertake any duties, civil, military, naval, judicial, fiscal, or even those connected with civil engineering. The more progressive officials see that this plan will not do with regard to a navy on foreign lines, and consequently the inferior officers have been educated in Europe as well as at different places in China, where naval colleges and arsenals have been established of late years. There has been an arsenal at Foochow (Pagoda Anchorage) for a number of years past, where Chinese youths are trained; besides this there are naval and military colleges at Tientsin, Nanking, Shanghai, and Foochow.

'Several viceroys and governors of provinces have taken in hand the reorganisation of their forces. Yüan Shih-kai has led the way, by his vigorous steps for the enrolment of 100,000 men in the capital province and the reorganisation of the Northern fleet. The Governor of Shan-hsi has now announced his purpose to enlist fifteen regiments of trained men. They are to be newly recruited and trained by competent instructors. The Governor of Shan-hsi has applied to Yüan Shi-kai for assistance in the supply of instructors, some of whom, it is presumed, will be foreign.'

A number of small gunboats are found at different ports in connection with the revenue service, the Imperial Maritime Customs, as well as others under the control of the high provincial authorities or others.

The purely native craft are uncouth-looking objects, and utterly unfit to cope for a moment with foreign vessels.

Financial difficulties have not permitted the Chinese navy to be replaced.

'The biggest man-of-war is an unarmed cruiser, twenty years old, with a tonnage of 5,000. Many gun-boats are used for coastal and river defence and for the suppression of pirates. The Ministry of the Navy can perhaps hardly justify its own existence, but it is useful as a department in charge of the training of naval officers and architects for the future extension of China's force at sea. It controls a few naval schools, and it is in charge of a few docks and shipyards, where old ships are repaired and new gun-boats of inconsiderable size can be constructed by the Chinese without foreign expert assistance. . . . It controls several wireless stations.'

References.—Brassey, *Naval Annual; Statesman's Year Book;* Roche and Cowen, *The French in Foochow* (destruction of Chinese fleet).

NEWSPAPERS AND PERIODICALS.—There are foreign newspapers at several of the Treaty Ports. In Shanghai eight or more dailies are published in English and French, the principal being *The China Press, Shanghai Times, North China Daily News, New Press,* and *L'Echo de Chine,* in the morning; and *Shanghai Mercury, China Gazette,* and *Evening Star* in the evening. There are seven or more weeklies; *The North China Herald, Celestial Empire, Union, Shanghai Sunday Times, Finance and Commerce, Weekly Review of the Far East* and *Der Ostasiatische Lloyd.* There is the *Chefoo Express at Chefoo.* In Amoy a small shipping sheet is printed, called *The Amoy Gazette,* and a weekly appears, named *The Amoy Times and Shipping Gazette.*

Newspapers and Periodicals

In Hongkong there are four dailies:—*The Hongkong Daily Press* and *South China Morning Post* morning papers, and *China Mail* and *Hongkong Telegraph*, both evening papers. The weeklies are *The Overland China Mail, Hongkong Weekly Press*, and the *Telegraph* also issues a weekly paper. The *clientèle* of these are principally foreigners, but a few natives who know English subscribe to them. At Kiaochao there is a German newspaper published daily and weekly, called *Der Deutsche Asiatische Warte*, and also the *Tsingtao Leader*. At Hankow there is the *Central China Post*. And every now and then newspapers are started at different ports.

There is a German newspaper published in Shanghai, and an Italian paper in Tientsin since 1902; the latter starting in English and Chinese, Italian to be substituted for English later on. It was stated a short time since that a paper was to be started in Peking in seven languages, surely a unique venture. These were to be Chinese, Japanese, English, French, German, Russian, and Italian, at a subscription of $10 a year.

In 1924 the Tientsin papers were the *Peking and Tientsin Times*, with a weekly edition entitled the *China Illustrated Review; North China Star* (daily), *North China Daily Mail* (evening), and *North China Sunday Times* (weekly).

A number of Chinese-owned journals are printed in the English language at the Treaty ports and in Peking. The most important are the *Peking Leader* (daily), *Peking Daily News* (daily), *Far Eastern Times* (daily, bilingual), Peking, *Shanghai Gazette* (daily, evening), Shanghai, *Canton Times* (daily), Canton.

Numerous Japanese-owned Chinese newspapers are published in China. There are also four English journals: the *Manchuria Daily News* (daily), *Light of Manchuria* (monthly), Dairen; *North China Standard* (daily), Peking; *China Advertiser* (daily), Tientsin.

There are several Portuguese papers in Macao and Hongkong, one of which publishes a portion of its contents in English.

Of periodicals, in English there is published in Shanghai *The Chinese Recorder and Missionary Journal*, issued monthly, and *Women's Work in the Far East*, issued half-yearly. (See BOOKS ON CHINA.) Besides these, there are several journals of different societies in North, Central, and South China and *The China Medical Missionary Journal*, issued quarterly. In Peking there is the *Chinese Social and Political Science Review* (quarterly).

The first European journal published in China was *The Canton Register*, issued in 1827. The first foreign newspaper started soon after the opening of Shanghai as a Treaty port. The first Chinese newspaper was the Shanghai *Hsin Pao,* a mere sheet, in 1870. It was succeeded by the *Shen Pao* under British ownership, and followed ten years later by the *Sin Wên Pao.* Both of these are still in existence. These two have a circulation of 50,000 to 60,000 a day, though they sometimes claim that it reaches 100,000.

As regards papers published in Chinese, many of which are commercial ventures, there are in Shanghai the *Shun* [*Shên*] *Pao,* already mentioned, and some two dozen or more newspapers sold at the price of ten and eight cash each; these have a very large circulation, sometimes of 10,000 copies a day. There is the monthly illustrated journal, the *Wan Kwo Kung Pao;* the *Chung Si Chao Hui Pao,* a monthly journal; the *Shin Chang Hwa Pao,* issued thrice a month; the *Hwa T'u Sin Pao,* a monthly journal. Of the numerous Chinese daily papers in Hongkong may be named the *Chung Ngoi San Pò,* issued from the *Daily Press* office; the *Wá Tsz Yat Pò,* or *Chinese Mail,* published at the *China Mail* office; the *Ts'un Wán Yat Pò,* and the *Waí San Yat Pò,* the *Chung Kwok Po* and the *Höng Hoi Yat Po.* In Canton there are the *Yüt Kíú Kéí Man,* the *On Ngá Shü Kuk Shai Shüt P'ín,* and the *Shöng Mò Pò.* After the Revolution of 1911 there was hardly a town of any importance without its newspaper. In 1921, there were about 1,200 Chinese newspapers and periodicals registered for transmission through the Chinese Post Office in all China.

A first attempt to issue a regular newspaper in Hainan was made in 1903 by the Taotai, in the form of a small daily gazette.

All these native papers mentioned are the direct result of foreign influence, as before the arrival of foreigners in China the Chinese had no newspapers according to our idea of the term. In 1895 there were only nineteen native newspapers; in 1898 this number was quadrupled, and now, as stated above, nearly every large town has its newspaper.

The Chinese living abroad have also native newspapers, both daily and weekly: in Singapore, Penang, Sydney, Manila, San Francisco, Honolulu, Japan, etc.

The Peking Gazette was the only newspaper the Chinese had till recent years, and it was the oldest newspaper in the world. It was published daily, being more of the nature of a Government Gazette than an ordinary newspaper.

'It is simply the record of official acts, promotions, decrees, and sentences, without any editorial comments or explanations; and, as such, of great value in understanding the policy of Government. It is very generally read and discussed by educated people in the cities, and tends to keep them more acquainted with the character and proceedings of their rulers than ever the

Romans were of their sovereigns and Senate. In the provinces, thousands of persons find employment by copying and abridging the *Gazette* for readers who cannot afford to purchase the complete edition.'

'The printing is effected by means of wooden movable types, which, to judge from some specimens examined, are cut in willow or poplar wood, a cheap if not highly durable material. . . . An average *Gazette* consists of 10 or 12 leaves of thin, brownish paper, measuring 7½ by 3¾ inches, and enclosed between leaves, front and back, of bright yellow paper, to form a species of binding. The whole is roughly attached or "stitched" by means of two short pieces of paper rolled into a substitute for twine, the ends of which, passing through holes, punched in the rear margin of the sheets, are loosely twisted together. [This being the usual manner of "stitching" small pamphlets in China.] . . . The inside leaves, being folded double in the usual Chinese fashion, give some twenty or more small pages of matter, each page divided by red lines into seven columns. Each column contains fourteen characters from top to bottom, with a blank space equal to four characters in height at the top.' 'As everything which the Emperor says takes precedence of everything else, his replies to memorials appear in advance of the documents to which they relate, and this produces an effect much like that a Puzzle Department, where all the answers should be printed one week, and the original conundrums the next.'

It has been well remarked that:—

'Although as a matter of antiquarian interest, it may be said that China in her *Peking Gazette* had the first newspaper in the world, yet, as a matter of fact, newspapers are but of yesterday. The . . . [native] newspapers of Hongkong and Shanghai have been the true pioneers of the native press. That work has borne fruit in a remarkably short time. Take, for example, Canton, which had until the other day four dailies and one newspaper of a more literary nature, published once in ten days. . . . The number of readers is immense, for it must be remembered that newspapers are written in the "book style" of language, which is understood throughout the Empire. Anyone who has even only occasionally glanced at these papers, must have noticed a tendency to pander too much to native tastes and ideas, that are recognised by the Chinese of any education as false and degrading. But it would not be fair to lay hold on these blemishes, not acknowledging that for the most part they have exercised a beneficial and enlightening influence over their readers. A few years ago, the one newspaper then in existence in Canton had suddenly to move from the city to the Shamien, to avoid the persecution of the officials. When the pressure passed away, that paper was again removed to the city, and in the interval three more papers have been started. A visit to the offices of these papers is an inspiration and a splendid testimony to the spread of ideas in China. Most of the printers have received their training in Hongkong. The old printing-blocks and hand-presses have given place to modern steam-printing machinery. One of the Canton papers has on its staff a Chinaman who was educated in Germany, and who is therefore well abreast of the times.' [1900 or 1901.]

Things Chinese

Several newspapers and periodicals in English and Chinese are published by the missionaries in different parts of China, some partaking more or less of a scientfic and religious character as well as detailing news. A few of these have been mentioned already. A small monthly in Romanised Colloquial has been started in Canton.

The following extract marks a new departure. There is a talk of similar enterprise in Canton, and one of the Hongkong native papers prints [1902] occasionally a piece in Colloquial. This has since extended throughout many other parts of China.

'Some time ago it was announced that Hangchow scholars were issuing a newspaper in Colloquial language. Some scholars of advanced view in Peking are emulating the example thus set them, and purpose publishing a paper in Pekingese on the same lines as the Hangchow paper, and with the same object, viz., to enlighten the people. They also think it will help people in the study of Pekingese, and thus accomplish a double purpose. They also intend to send men into the country to distribute the paper free to all who wish to read it, and for Chihli alone 50,000 will be required. The capital is at present furnished by one or two patriotic men, but as such a large enterprise requires much capital, it is hoped that others will come forward and give financial help.'

In June, 1924, the *Women's Daily News*, a Chinese newspaper for women and the first of its kind in North China, was started by several young women in Tientsin. Another, of the same name, owned, edited, and published by Chinese women, was started in Shanghai in September, 1925.

There can be no doubt that the modern newspaper is destined to be an important factor for good in China, if it falls into judicious hands. Unfortunately, a tendency very occasionally reveals itself to pander to depraved tastes in articles not conducive to public morality, and a rabid hatred of the foreigner is sometimes visible in some distorted account of them and their doings, but on the whole, the 'tendency seems towards morality, etc.'

'The Chinese Press of to-day [1924] leaves much to be desired. With a few notable exceptions it is absolutely unreliable in its presentation of domestic and foreign news. Many of the papers are notoriously corrupt, and often inflammatory and malicious. The good that they might do by exposing official incompetence and corruption is often offset by their mischievous activities in other directions. Very few of the papers are really independent or well-informed. The Chinese Press is, however, exercising an increasing influence upon public opinion, especially on international issues. Notwithstanding the constitutional guarantee of freedom of speech and publication, the militarists who have been in power under the Republic give short shrift to any editors who offend them by too outspoken criticism.'

The foreign papers published in China cannot be compared with those published in the West, either in the matter of size, cheapness, quality of paper and print, absence of literals, good writing, variety, original matter, or in any other respect. Some of them, moreover, still lend themselves to the retrogressive method of propaganda prevalent during the world war, while but few uphold the ideals of freedom of speech and justice which must be regarded as essential in civilized communities.

References.—'List of Periodicals in the Chinese Language' being Appendix F. to *Records of the Missionary Conference held in Shanghai*, 1890. 'The Peking Gazette': being an article in *The China Review*, iii, 12. See also article on 'The Peking Gazette and Chinese Posting,' by E. H. Parker, in *Longman's Magazine* for November, 1896.

NOBILITY.—There is no real nobility in China. Mayers, in his invaluable work on Government Titles, says:—

'The existing Chinese system of conferring patents of nobility, and honorary titles is linked by an unbroken chain of descent with the history of the feudal states of the sixth century before Christ, perpetuating in its nomenclature, on the one hand, the titles of the semi-independent Princes of that era, and, on the other, the names of official degrees which have ceased for many centuries to exist in practical operation. . . . The titles now conferred are not to be regarded as other than official distinctions of a peculiar class, and cannot rightly be considered as bestowing aristocratic position or privilege in the European sense. The nine degrees of nobility, indeed, which are conferred at the present day, and which are either heritable within certain limits, . . . or hereditary for ever, . . . are granted exclusively as rewards for military services.'

The five highest ranks of hereditary nobility then are Kung (Koong), Haú (Hou), Pák (Po), Tsz, and Nám (Nan), generally rendered into English as Duke, Marquis, Earl, Viscount, and Baron. Each of these is subdivided into classes or degrees. 'To the titles of the first, second, and third ranks laudatory' titles or terms 'are appended, significant of the special services by which the rank has been earned.' We are not aware whether an attempt has ever been made to render the four lower ranks into an English equivalent. Any such attempt would probably be even less successful than that already made as regards the five higher ranks. These lower titles 'have occasionally the degree next above them "annexed" . . . the bearer being thus enabled to rank "with, but after," possessors of the title immediately preceding.' All the different ranks, except the lowest, are 'hereditary during a specified number of lives, ranging from twenty-six' for a Duke of the first class, to one for the eighth rank, the next but lowest of all. Any of them also becomes hereditary by being 'conferred posthumously . . . on officers killed in battle.' Meritorious public servants are also rewarded by having hereditary official rank bestowed upon their sons, grandsons, younger brothers, or nephews. The whole principle it will thus be seen is against perpetuating hereditary rank, the son with but few exceptions—so few as to be scarcely worthy of notice—taking a lower title until at length the status of a commoner is reached. The most noticeable exceptions are the following:—the lineal descendant of Confucius, who is a Duke; and the descendants of Mencius, and of Koxinga (the Conqueror of Formosa), each of whom is a Marquis. The son of a man of exceptional renown, such as of the first Marquis Tsêng, whose son, the well-known minister to England, has the title continued; but it goes no further unless the son's deeds have been such as to merit its bestowal on the grandson.

Titles of honour are also conferred as rewards 'for merit or service, or of Imperial bounty, on occasions of rejoicing.' These are bestowed upon the official himself, his wife, parents, or grandparents while they are living, or 'as a posthumous distinction . . . to his deceased progenitors.' These titles differ for each of the nine degrees of official rank (see MANDARIN) and their subdivisions, making in all eighteen, while the wives have nine. Military officials also receive honorary titles of a martial character.

Posthumous titles of honour may be granted to officials losing 'their lives at sea or on any of the inner waters, whilst engaged in the public service,' and their eldest sons are given official rank. Most sensibly the Chinese have put before them merit as the cause of their nobility, and not the mere circumstance of blue blood. The class which in European lands would form the aristocracy, is in a very, comparatively, inferior position in China. There were certain classes who owned titles on account of kinship with the Emperor; but here again heredity was the exception, and extinction of the title (which decreased in degree from father to son) happened in the case of descendants of a prince in about twelve generations. The only exceptions to this rule amongst these classes were the eight 'Iron-Capped Princes,' who were descendants of the Chieftains who immediately preceded the Sovereigns. Another was the Prince of I, a descendant of the thirteenth son of K'ang Hsi, the second Emperor of this dynasty. These all retained the title in perpetuity.

Under the Republic, the old titles of nobility have been replaced by Titles of Merit granted by the President. They are arranged in six classes as follows: Grand Title of Merit, and First Class to Fifth Class Title of Merit, the first corresponding to the former Prince of blood-royal, and the other five to the five orders of nobility above-mentioned.

References.—Mayers, *Chinese Government;* Beltchenko, *Present-day Political Organization of China;* Werner, *Descriptive Sociology—Chinese.*

NORTH CHINA BRANCH OF THE ROYAL ASIATIC SOCIETY.—In 1857 the Shanghai Literary and Scientific Society was founded in Shanghai. In 1858 it became affiliated to the Royal Asiatic Society, and received the name of the North China Branch of the Royal Asiatic Society. It ceased to exist from 1861 to 1864, but was revived in the latter year. In 1871 buildings were erected on a site granted at a nominal rent by the British Government in 1868. Its meetings, at which papers (some of which are published in the *Journal of North China Branch of the Royal Asiatic Society*) are read and discussed, are held periodically in Shanghai. The membership subscription (which includes the subscription to the *Journal*) is five dollars a year, or fifty dollars for life membership. The annual subscription to the *Journal* for non-members is five dollars. A classified index to the articles published in the *Journal* from the formation of the Society to December 31, 1892, is to be found in Vol. xxiv of the *Journal*, New Series. Of recent years extra volumes (so far three) dealing each with a special subject, have been published. These are issued at a reduced price to subscribers. There is a museum in connection with the Society, and a large library, now comprising about 8,000 volumes, the nucleus of which was the collection of the late Alexander Wylie.

NOVELS.—There are thousands of books of this class in China, at least 18,000 well-known ones, classified contemptuously by the pedantic literary class as 'small talk.'

'"Novel," as the name of a thing came to us with the thing itself from Italy in the reign of Elizabeth.' The 'thing itself,' as this writer thus describes the novel of the West, was known in China long before the time of our good Queen Bess. '"Tell me a story" is among the earliest expressions of our wants in life,' and amongst John Chinaman's numerous children this want was early expressed. 'Stories told for their own sake,' and stories furnished with morals, all doubtless held their sway over the progenitors of the seemingly phlegmatical Chinese, who will listen spellbound to the *raconteurs* in public squares and streets. To the East is ascribed the first taste for the romance, and it is stated that there is even a Chinese variant of Petronius's 'Widow of Ephesus.' And to come to more modern times and a more recent development of the tale of the West, we have it stated by one sinologist in comparing the construction of Chinese novels with those of Richardson, that the 'authors render their characters interesting and natural by reiterated strokes of the pencil which finally produce a high degree of illusion.'

A Chinese novel is generally a finished sketch in black and white—very black and very white, no softening down, nor shading: the characters stand out in bold relief. The villains are as black as black can be, and form the deepest background to throw into relief the virtuous hero and heroine and their friends, helpers, and well-wishers. The hero is a paragon of excellence, physically, mentally, and morally. He often possesses the prowess of a warrior, the intellect of a senior wrangler, while as regards the virtues he stands at high-water mark. The heroine—but what need to describe her: it is needless to say she is charming, as seen through Chinese spectacles; her lover will generally find her—in this so different from the real Chinese women—so well acquainted with letters as to lift her from the mere position of a doll, and withal 'a clever, resourceful, and a modest young lady.' Apparently insuperable difficulties are, of course, piled up by the novelist for him to clear away by his consummate skill in the unravelling of the plots and intrigues against hero and heroine, and all comes well at the end. There are historical novels as well as social ones in China. (See LITERATURE and HISTORY.)

Novels are largely read, not only by men, but some women even manage to pick up a sufficient knowledge of the printed character to be able to enjoy them, and circulating libraries are carried through the streets with novels for the delectation of their *clientèle.*

NUMERICAL CATEGORIES.—'Number has long exercised a peculiar fascination over the Far-Eastern mind. Europeans, no doubt, sometimes use such expressions as "The Four Cardinal Virtues" and "The Seven Deadly Sins," but it is not part of our mental disposition to divide up and parcel out almost all things visible and invisible into numerical categories fixed by unchanging custom, as is the case among the nations from India eastward,' so writes Mr. Chamberlain in *Things Japanese.* The Chinese have thus grouped together any and everything into such classes, beginning with two and ending with ten thousand. The fact that Mayers' *Chinese Reader's Manual* has a second part, consisting of sixty-seven pages, devoted to this portion of Chinese literature, will show its importance, and even it is not an exhaustive list; to it we refer the curious reader, while we only give a dozen of the most common:—

THE TWO EMPERORS of Antiquity, Yao and Shun, who reigned 2357-2255 and 2255-2205 B.C., respectively.

THE THREE LIGHTS: The Sun, Moon, and Stars.

THE THREE POWERS OF NATURE: Heaven, Earth, and Man, which, taken together are used in the sense of the universe, or creation in general.

Numerical Categories

THE FOUR CARDINAL POINTS: North, South, East, and West. When the centre is included, they are called The Five Points.

THE FOUR BOOKS, which with THE FIVE CLASSICS may be called the Bible of the Confucianist. (See LITERATURE.)

THE FIVE BLESSINGS: Longevity, Riches, Peacefulness and Serenity, the Love of Virtue, and An End Crowning the Life.

THE FIVE ELEMENTS OR PRIMORDIAL ESSENCES: Water, Fire, Wood, Metal, and Earth. 'Upon these five elements or perpetually active principles of Nature the whole scheme of Chinese philosophy . . . is based.'

THE FIVE METALS: Gold, Silver, Copper, Lead and Tin, and Iron.

THE FIVE ESCULENTS OR GRAINS: Hemp, Millet, Rice, Corn, and Pulse.

THE FIVE COLOURS: Black, Red, Azure (Green, Blue, or Black), White, and Yellow.

THE EIGHT GENII, or, 'EIGHT IMMORTALS, venerated by the Taoist sect'; each celebrated for possessing some mystic power or owning some wonderful, magic-working instrument. One, if not two of them, were females. One went about with one shoe off and one shoe on. Another, having gone up to heaven, and left injunctions that his body was to be preserved for seven days for his return, found on his soul desiring to re-enter it after six days, that his disciple, who had been left to watch it, had been called away to his mother's death-bed, and consequently his master had no vitalised body of his own, but was forced to enter that of a beggar just expired. Another had a white mule, by which he was carried thousands of miles in a single day, and which was folded away and put into his wallet at night, and resuscitated in the morning by his master spurting water from his mouth on him.

THE EIGHTEEN ARHAN: Eighteen of Buddha's immediate disciples, which are found in Buddhist temples. Besides these there are THE FIVE HUNDRED DISCIPLES of BUDDHA, also found in some temples, the number is even carried up to ten thousand sometimes.

The following are in common use likewise amongst the people of Canton, and similar geographical and other combinations are doubtless used in other parts of China as well.

THE THREE DISTRICT CITIES: Nám, P'ún, and Shun; that is Nám Hoí, P'ún Yü, and Shun Tak.

THE FOUR GREAT TRADING MARTS, viz., Fatshan, Hankow, Kintak [Ching-tê Chên] (the great porcelain manufactory), Chü Sin.

THE FOUR DISTRICT CITIES: Yan, Hoí and San, in concise terms; but in full, Yan P'ing, Hoí P'ing, San Ning, and San Wúí, all in the Canton, or Kuangtung Province.

THE LOWER FOUR PREFECTURES: Kò, Löü, Lím, and K'ing, in concise terms; in full Kò Chaú fú, Löü Chaú fú, Lím Chaú fú, and K'ing Chaú fú.

Reference.—Mayers, *Chinese Reader's Manual.*

OPIUM.—The poppy seems to have been cultivated in China as an ornamental flower in the Sung dynasty, or before, and the healing virtues of its seeds were commended, while 'the medical use of the capsules was of course early known.' Opium was used for medicinal purposes as early as A.D. 973, and it was a highly esteemed drug, being imported overland from Burma and through Central Asia. There would appear not to be sufficient warranty for the opinion that the poppy was grown in China at an early date for other than ornamental purposes; everything points to a contrary conclusion. It was 'an article of trade at Canton in the middle of the last century,' but, up to nearly the close of that century, it was a limited trade.

We quote from Dr. Dudgeon, late of Peking, a short summary of the origin of that destructive vice, opium-smoking:—

'Opium-smoking was introduced from Java by the Chinese from Chien-chieu and Chang-chow in the early years of the eighteenth century and towards the end of the reign of K'ang Hsi, 1662-1723. The first edict issued against it was in 1729, (by the Emperor Yung Chêng) and was directed against the practice in Formosa, and was the result of a report of an official sent by K'ang Hsi to inquire into the unseemly proceedings in the island. (At that time the importation of foreign opium amounted to only 200 chests a year. In 1796, it was 4,000 chests. In 1800 it was made contraband). K'ang Hsi died, and his successor was some six or seven years on the throne before steps were considered necessary . . . to stop the evil there. It had been introduced by people from the above two prefectures on the mainland. From Formosa and these southern ports, the practice spread gradually, and very slowly. As late as the end of the century, the import and consumption of opium, both for medicine and smoking, was comparatively trifling. The use of opium, first as capsules and then as an extract, is of older origin, and was used solely as a medicine. Part came by land through Central Asia by the Mohammedan merchants and travellers, part by sea to Canton, and part also overland from Burmah and India. The opium which came overland was for the most part as tribute, and we read in the Ming history of as much as 200 catties for the Emperor and 100 catties for the Empress being presented as tribute. Other drugs were likewise presented. . . . At the time when smoking began, a short bamboo tube filled with coir, opium, and tobacco was the regular mode of insufflation.

'The present pipe is more modern, and is said to have been invented in the province of Canton. . . . The native growth is of still more recent origin. The cultivation of the poppy, for the sake of its extract, began about 70 years ago. Since that time it has been gradually making its way over the Empire, until now there is not a province where it is not grown. . . . The native growth and consumption of the native drug having thus largely increased in the North, it has, year by year, been driving the Indian article out of the market. This process bids fair to continue to increase, and at no distant day in all likelihood the foreign import will cease, unless it can compete with the native in price. Its superior quality and freedom from adulteration would in these circumstances always command a sale. . . . The great dimensions to which the native growth is reported latterly to have grown is only, it is evident, within the past few years. The native growth has been stimulated by the growing demand for opium and its profitable nature, the poppy not being taxed as a cereal. . . . The increase of the native growth is accounted for by the fact that it is profitable to admix with the Indian, and the proportion given is native 3/10 with foreign 7/10. . . . The consumption of opium, where it was formerly strictly forbidden, has greatly increased since the relaxation caused by the late agreement, by which the Imperial Government collects both Import and Likin duties at the ports, and opium is allowed to pass freely throughout the Empire.'

With regard to this increase of the native opium we are informed from another source that:—

'The Chinese are every quarter increasing the native-grown opium . . . the import of the foreign drug is steadily declining in consequence.' Again, 'The Customs' returns for 1895 show that the market falling in the import for 1894 was not arrested in 1895, but on the contrary, the decline in the trade was even more conspicuous in the latter year. . . . It is a question of cost. . . . The poppy is rarely met with in Kwongtung, and as the soil and climate are not favourable it is not likely to be extensively cultivated there.'

'In 1887, the value of the opium imported was Hk. Tls. 27,926,865, and the figure for 1897 stands at Hk. Tls. 27,901,056; but whereas in the former year the sum expended procured a supply of 74,350 piculs, the almost identical amount in 1897 purchased only 49,217 piculs. The cost of the foreign drug has increased since the closing of the Indian mints, and the quality of the native drug is said to be undergoing an improvement which brings it more into demand.'

It is but natural after this to find the following as a newspaper summary, made in 1905, of one item of our Indian revenue:—

'Opium.—Decrease R. 1,550,000. This represents a distinct worsening of the financial position with no corresponding gain to the people of India. This part of the revenue has nothing to do with the consumption of opium in India (which is taxed under Excise), and is in reality the profit of the Government of India as a monopolist manufacturer and exporter to foreign markets (chiefly China). At all times subject to great fluctuations, this source of income shows a steady tendency to decline.'

The following on the taxation of native opium in China, was published in 1897, and will be interesting in this connection:—

'According to a memorial of the Board of Revenue recommending a new system of taxing native-grown opium, the chief opium producing provinces in China are stated to be Szech'uan, which will produce this year a crop of 120,000 piculs; Yünnan, 80,000 piculs; Kueichou, 40,000 piculs; Chêkiang, 14,000 piculs; Kiangsu, 10,000 piculs; Kirin, 6,000 piculs; Anhui, 2,000 piculs; Fukien, 2,000 piculs; and the provinces of Kansu, Shensi, Shantung, Shansi, Honan, and Chihli, an aggregate amounting to 60,000 piculs, or a total of 334,000 piculs from 14 out of the 21 provinces which constitute the present empire of China—not including Outer Mongolia and Tibet. The memorial further states that according to the above estimate, which the Board has reason to believe to be quite accurate, having been compiled by Sir Robert Hart at the Board's request, the duty on the native opium this year should amount to at least 20 million taels, at the ordinary tax of Tls. 60 per picul; but, so far, not a third of this amount has found its way to the Imperial exchequer, the rest having gone to enrich the provincial authorities and their tax collectors. It is now proposed to begin with the provinces of Kirin, Szech'uan, Yünnan, and Kiangsu, for the collection of native opium duty which is to be handed over to the I.M. Customs at Shanhaikuan, Chungking, Mêngtze, and Chinkiang, respectively.'

When the liking for it began, the English, to their shame, be it said, continued to bring the fatal drug to administer to the depraved tastes of the Chinese, whose rulers made most piteous attempts to prevent its introduction. And the feeling of dislike to the English, and, through them, to the hated and despised foreigner in general, partially due to this cause, is not confined solely to the upper classes, as anyone may find who knows the language and mixes with the people; for it is not an unfrequent question:—Why do you foreigners bring opium to China? And the only reply that can be given is:—There are bad people (there is no use combating the idea of the badness of the people who do such a thing—it is a foregone conclusion in a Chinaman's mind) in every nation as well as good; and if you Chinese would not smoke it, they would not bring it.

It is impossible to say what proportion of Chinese smoke opium, but immense numbers of all classes of the community do so; in some parts of the country the proportion is larger than in others. From the Imperial Palace down to the lowest hovel every class has its smokers, even women and children are, in some places, preys to this insidious vice. Many smoke it, as we have already said, at the present day, and the number is increasing. It has been estimated that there are 25,000,000 of opium smokers in China; another estimate, considered to be moderate, puts them at 40,000,000, that is a ninth, or tenth, of the whole population. In the city of Foochow alone there are said to be 1,000 registered opium dens, they 'being more numerous than tea or rice shops.'

The habit is easily begun; the offering of it, as a glass of wine amongst many classes of Englishmen, easily leads the fashionable votary into the practice; the fast man takes it sometimes as an aphrodisiac; the prostitutes take it because their visitors do; others take it first to ease pain, or disease; while others are led into it by their friends and acquaintances. In this connection it is interesting to note that, 'figures taken from the Perak Hospital returns during 1893 and part of 1892 show that no protective influence against malaria can be claimed by the opium smoker.'

Once formed, the habit is very difficult to break—some try, over and over again, to wean themselves from the pipe. One man actually came to a hospital no less than five times for that purpose. Five hundred smokers in the course of one year were desirous of entering a refuge, which was opened in Foochow, in order to cure themselves.

'Terribly rapid is the ascendency of this fatal vice. A few weeks' indulgence will rivet its chains for life. Thenceforth the unhappy captive must have his stimulant at accustomed hours, or even his feeble labour is impossible, and griping pain and intolerable depression lay hold of him. Many a labourer whose wages amount to $3 or $5 a month expends twice such sums on opium. How is this contrived? The smoker borrows on all sides; the pawnbroker fattens on his wretchedness. The poor mother toils all day at embroidery to earn food to hush her little ones' hunger-cries. Clothing of wife and children, and lastly their very home is sold over their heads, even if they themselves are not bargained away for opium. Every resident in the interior of China has seen once well-to-do people changed to out-cast vagabonds by this noxious vice; " whole bands of beggars, as one has described them, "pleading on their knees for the ashes from a neighbour's opium pipe."

'"No flesh, no strength, no money," is a native proverbial summing-up of the dismal case; it is well known that three or four generations will exhaust an opium smoking family.

'The increasing frequency of opium suicide in China is awakening the anxiety of even Chinese statesmen.'

Opium was until recently the most common means of committing suicide in China, and China is said to have the unenviable notoriety of being the country in which suicides are most frequent. 'Since the introduction of opium in China, suicides have become alarmingly frequent.'

'Some twenty years ago few Chinese women smoked opium, but now it is estimated that at least one-tenth of the female population are its slaves; nor can we wonder that those whose lot in Eastern lands is so joyless should seize on such antidote for suffering and relief from ennui.'

The evils which arise from opium-smoking are many. It injures the health and physical powers, especially of the working and poorer classes, whose wages are only sufficient to meet their necessities, and who curtail the amount spent on food and clothing to gratify their craving for the vice, and, consequently, are less able to resist its inroads on their system; whereas the wealthy buy certain foods with the purpose of nourishing and strengthening their systems against it. All these factors, and others, have to be taken into account; and it must also be remembered that there are some men who have such a resolute will (though like many other vices, the opium habit weakens the will power) that having fixed upon a certain amount as the limit of their indulgence, they do not overstep it, thus staving off some of the worst effects of opium-smoking. Those who have yielded to it for years, and who are slaves to the pipe, are miserable if circumstances should arise to debar them from their accustomed whiffs: it is extraordinary to see how perfectly wretched they are; every attitude, every feature of the face, every sentence, is a living witness that they are in agony till the craving is satisfied. The opium sots or 'opium devils,' as the natives term them, are pitiable objects, emaciated almost to a skeleton, until they finally succumb to their vice.

As to wealth, it often melts away when the pipe is indulged in. In one case a man smoked away a valuable property consisting of a number of houses advantageously situated in the city of Canton, and eventually smoked himself into his grave. It is a great waste of time, as the process of smoking is a slow one and requires long preparation, and, as the habit increases, more has to be smoked to produce an effect, and consequently longer time spent over it: from a quarter, or half an hour at first, it increases till hours are required, and a great part of the night is wasted in it instead of being spent in sleep. The smokers lie down in couples across a wide couch, with a small stool-like table between them containing the opium-tray, on which are the pipe and pipe-bowls, opium-lamp, and the different instruments used in connection with the pipe. Taking up the pipe, one of the smokers lifts up a small quantity of opium on the end of a long needle-like instrument. The bowl of the pipe is held over the lamp, and the drug, which has been already prepared so as to be of the consistency of treacle, is worked by him in the heat of the flame over the small orifice of the pipe-bowl. This takes some time, and, when all is ready, a few whiffs exhaust it, so that the whole process has to be gone over again, each smoker often taking the preparation of the pipe in turn. The following account by a doctor who has paid much attention to the subject, gives with minute exactness the whole process summarised above:—

'The smoker, lying on his couch or divan, with the pipe, lamp, and other implements on a tray, takes a portion on the point of a wire and warms it carefully over the flame of the lamp. He dips it again into the little jar of opium until the requisite quantity adheres, alternately warming it over the flame and pressing it on the flat bowl of the pipe, turning it over and over and working it carefully on the end of the wire, until it is reduced to the state of a soft solid by the evaporation of a portion of the water. During this process it swells up into a light porous mass from the formation of steam within, and must therefore be heated up to the boiling point of water. When the little bolus has been brought to the exact state fitted for smoking, it is worked into a conical-shaped ring around the wire, the point of the wire inserted into the round hole of the pipe, and, by twirling the wire around while withdrawing it, the opium is deposited on the pipe, the hole in it corresponding to the hole in the bowl of the pipe. The stem of the pipe being applied to the lips and the bowl held over the lamp, the heat of the flame is drawn in over the opium, converting into vapour all the volatilizable material in the bolus. To understand what takes place, it is important to note that, preparatory to smoking, the bolus of opium has been slowly and carefully heated until steam has been generated in its substance. While in this heated state, and with water enough to prevent charring and to form more steam, the flame of the lamp passes over it, converting part of it into the so-called smoke, and leaving a solid residuum known as "yín-she," opium dross, and also as "yí-yín," seconds.'

'The vapour is inhaled into the lungs, and comes in contact with the immense surface of the respiratory mucous membrane, by which the alkaloids are absorbed into the blood, and thus act upon the whole system.'

'Notwithstanding the theory of some scientific gentlemen . . . that none of the alkaloids are carried by the smoke into the system, it is demonstrated a thousand times a day by every whiff a Chinaman takes of his pipe that *certain constituents of the watery extract of opium are converted into vapour:* and the sallow complexion, stupid visage, and wasted frame of old smokers, and especially the remorseless grip of the craving on every fibre of their nervous system, afford strong reason to believe, if they do not absolutely prove, that every inhalation of the *vapour* conveys a portion of the alkaloids into the victim's blood."

Opium-smoking induces laziness, idle habits, and unwillingness to exertion, shortens life, and diminishes vitality.

'Among the well-to-do, with healthy constitutions, good food, comfortable surroundings, and especially if there be pressing business to attend to, the drug may be used for a lengthened period without any apparent deleterious results, but at the same time it will be observed that any indulgence in the vice, even under the most favourable circumstances, diminishes functional activity in the nervous system, impairs and arrests the process of secretion, and ultimately produces structural changes in important organs, and a general undermining of the constitution all round. Although the effects are more gradual, they are none the less sure. Vital resistance to its evil effects is soon diminished as the smokers become poor, thus depriving the victims, not of opium, for the supply must increase with the craving, but of the necessary sustenance, thus enfeebling the system, and rendering it more susceptible to its evil influence. . . . Sooner or later retribution overtakes them, and they are suddenly cut off. . . . That there is no more harm in its continuous use than smoking the mildest cigarettes is an utterly absurd statement. It is pernicious in itself apart from its too frequent conjunction with other well-known social evils. In such cases opium tells with redoubled violence. . . . The reasons for believing the habit to be harmless and that it can be abandoned without suffering, have been made by some to depend upon the bodyweight of the smokers when admitted to gaol and once a week afterwards. The weight is not much affected, provided the habit is not great nor of great duration, and the material surroundings are good.'

'After the imperious craving has been established, then the smoker smokes not for positive enjoyment but to relieve the pains and aches which the non-satisfaction of the craving sets up. It is . . . foolish to read of the stalwart races which are addicted to opium. It is quite fallacious to reason thus: the Chinese are given to opium: but the Chinese are industrious, therefore, opium is beneficial. The poor, lazy, good-for-nothing people in China are the opium smokers,' and if they are not that when they begin to smoke it, the vice soon does its best to hurry them to these conditions. 'No doubt, immediately after the craving has been satisfied, there is unwonted brilliancy and activity, both physical and mental, and this requires constantly to be renewed. . . . There does not seem much hope for the rejuvenescence of China so long as this terrible evil remains in their midst, the vice is enthralling, the craving is imperious, and the abandonment of the habit extremely difficult.'

The following is from a native newspaper, the *Shenpao*, of Shanghai:—

'Opium came from abroad, but the poison is left with China. The drug wastes time, destroys energy and health, and dissipates one's property. There is no poison more deleterious. It is hated by non-smokers who merely behold its ravages in others. But even smokers also hate it, for they know its awful power to destroy them. At first all opium was contraband, for China hoped to interdict the curse. But soon it became apparent that the attempt to exclude it was hopeless. Hence China devised a new plan to check the evil, if the evil could not be eradicated, viz., a high tariff on opium. But alas! make the duty as high as we please the stream keeps flowing in, in ever-increasing volume, and every province besides grows native opium. Smokers increase apace, and sellers of the drug are more numerous every day. Our Government knows the evil of opium, but poverty makes it loth to give up this source of revenue, especially in view of the load of indemnities upon its back.'

Opium

The late Viceroy Chang Chih-tung wrote about opium:—

'In all provinces the nuisance has appeared, and causes incalculable damage. It ruins the people, enervates the soldiers, pauperises the rich, and makes the officials useless.' 'Opium has pauperised and poisoned the Chinese, and is the greatest evil of the ages.'

A new vice, that of the subcutaneous injection of morphia, appears now to be following that of opium-smoking, and the habit is spreading rapidly, in some parts of the country at all events. It was making enormous advances in Hongkong until put down by law a few years since. As an instance of what a hold the habit takes on the people already prepared for it by opium-smoking, the following facts as to the practice, taken from a British Consular Report, and the Maritime Customs' Annual Report, may prove of interest:—800 ozs. were imported in one month in 1894, in Amoy, and there was a decrease in the import of opium. Some of it was doubtless used for pills, powders, etc., and not all for hypodermic injections.

The habit of injecting morphia was greatly on the increase in Amoy in 1894, there being many establishments in the city where the practice was carried on.

'Habitual opium smokers taking to morphine injections are enabled to abstain from the opium pipe, but are by no means cured of opium smoking, as a cessation of the injection habit inevitably leads to an increased indulgence in smoking.' In 1895 the total amount of morphia imported into Amoy was 4,835, ozs. and of hypodermic syringes 128, in Shanghai for the same period 64,043 ozs. were imported, being double that of 1894 and more than four times that of 1892. The Commissioner of Customs thus speaks of it in that part of the country:—'Though partly consumed as a liquid decoction, it is chiefly used to make pills and tabloids, which are taken as a substitute for opium by those who find it inconvenient to smoke during business or when travelling. This easily becomes a habit.' The Commissioner at Canton says, 'morphia . . . is largely being availed of amongst [opium] smokers.' In the general report on the foreign trade of China for the same year (1895) we find it noted that, 'there is a large increase in the importation of morphia, which indicates a greater use of so-called anti-opium pills and that indulgence in morphinism is spreading.

It appears that the amount and consequently the habit, must be increasing, for in the Annual Returns for 1897, it is stated that in Amoy, 9,103 ozs. of morphia, valued at Hk. Tls. 15,473, passed the Customs,—the highest total yet reached. In Shanghai, for the year 1897, it had risen to 68,170 ozs.; and in Canton the amount for the same year was 1,580, value Hk. Tls. 2,429, as against a value in 1895 of Hk. Tls. 954. A large quantity of opium pills are also made, and sold under the name of anti-opium pills. Some, in the endeavour to give up opium-smoking, try these; but they seldom cure anyone of the habit; they simply, by the opium they contain, satisfy the longing of the smoker and enable him to stave off the desire to smoke for a while. Those who take them can also conceal the opium habit from their friends; they require less waste of time, as they are swallowed at once, whereas the smoking, if much is taken, runs away with hours which a poor man can ill afford. They are mostly prepared from opium dross mixed with soft-boiled rice, or paste, and various medicines, according to the different prescriptions. They would appear to be somewhat cheaper than the opium.

There are Chinese opium dens in the United States and in London. It was stated on good authority about twenty-five years ago, that 2,500 Chinese visit the port of London in the course of the year—chiefly sailors, firemen, carpenters, cooks and stewards employed on steamers running between China and England, as well as a few more permanent residents; so that there are quite sufficient out of that number to patronise these places and keep them going. Opium probably costs the Chinese at least 168,000,000 taels annually.

Of recent years stringent laws have been passed against opium smoking, and many habitual smokers have been executed. In 1917 the importation of Indian opium ceased under the terms of an agreement between the Chinese and Indian Governments made in 1907. There have also been frequent public burnings of opium and opium utensils under official supervision. But though the whole mass of Chinese enlightened opinion is against the use of opium except for medicinal purposes, and in spite of the good work done by the National Anti-opium Society and the International Reform Bureau, the poppy is still extensively grown (with the connivance of the Chinese local—chiefly military—authorities) in many parts of China.

References.—Dudgeon, *The Evils of the use of Opium;* Turner, *British Opium Policy* (account of Opium question up to about 1883); *British Parliamentary Papers, passim;* Brereton, *The Truth about Opium;* Hill and Spencer, *The Indo-Chinese Opium Trade;* Hosie, *On the Trail of the Opium Poppy;* Morse, *The Trade and Administration of the Chinese Empire;* Moule, *The Opium Question;* Shearer, *Opium Smoking and Opium Eating;* Stirling, *Opium Smoking among the Chinese;* Sultzberger, *All about Opium;* Edkins, *Opium.*

PADDY.—The Malay name for rice in the ear or unhusked, hence so styled by foreigners in China from the Malay *padi.* A paddy-field is a rice-field, and paddy-birds are a certain species of birds, the white egret, *Egretta modesta,* that frequent these fields. (See RICE.) Rice-birds are a different bird altogether.

PAGODA.—The word pagoda is descended from the Sanscrit *Chagavati* through the Persian *bootkuda* or the Hindustanee *poutkhoda* or *bootkhoda*, and means 'the house of idols,' 'the abode of God,' or 'Holy House.' 'According to the original use of the word in India, it is a name given to the various buildings where they worship idols,' and it has been employed in the same indiscriminate way by some writers on China, but the majority of modern writers restrict the use of the term to the tower-like structure common in China, described as 'a peculiar class of buildings that rise several storeys high in the form of a narrow and polygonal obelisk, whether tenanted by idols or not.'

These picturesque objects that crown a jutting eminence or stand on a swelling hill; that rise from the general dead level of the shanty-like buildings forming a Chinese city; or again are seen breaking the monotony of low-lying lands; so common that they seem almost a natural feature in a Chinese landscape: these are not native but of foreign origin, and introduced, so it is said, after the Christian era.

The great majority of pagodas in China are ancient, and in Chinese scenery take the place of the old and ruined castles to be met with in the West. The stiffness of the lines has been toned down by the kindly hand of time, in the course of the centuries which have generally passed since their erection. Decay has dislodged a brick here and there in the galleries (placed often at each storey) round the tall shaft-like structure, while sometimes the lightning in its play, or the wild winds in their sport, have robbed the ambitious tower of its topmost storeys, or, at least, of its crowning glory, an imitation of 'a big bottle-gourd.' Nature, in another of her aspects, has dropped a seed in the mother earth; unnoticed it has lain till, mixed with the other materials, it has been used in the building, and the fierce tropical sun has warmed it into maturity; or, failing that, the feathered songsters of the air have plucked the ripe berries and left the seeds on the pagoda; in either case the result is a growth of shrubs and bushes and young trees, which add to the beauty of the tower and also accelerate its decay.

Pagodas are usually of seven or nine storeys in height, though any odd numbers such as three, five, eleven, or thirteen storeys are known—odd numbers being most propitious: those above nine storeys are very rare, though there have been one or two, if not more, constructed of that height. It has been the intention to erect some of thirteen storeys, but want of funds or fear of destruction by the elements (the Chinese have no lightning rods) have caused the Chinese to desist from the attempt. With regard to their dimensions it has been stated that 'the average height of the loftiest pagodas is about 170 feet.' The famous Nanking pagoda was 261 English feet high. The highest (that at Tingchou, Chihli) is 360 feet. The walls of pagodas are of great thickness, especially at the base, reminding one of the old walls of castles in England. They decrease proportionately in circumference and in thickness as they ascend. One in Soochow (in which city there are five) is nearly 300 feet in circumference, or about 100 feet in diameter at the bottom, 'and its ninth or uppermost storey is about one-third in circumference' of the base. Some are solid; others very narrow; some have staircases inside all the way up; in others, to reach the next storey, it is necessary to go out on the balcony and walk some distance round to the door leading to the next flight of steps. The usual material is brick, sometimes glazed brick ('porcelain towers') and sometimes cast iron. They are generally hexagonal or octagonal in shape externally. The octagonal ones are the more numerous; some octagonal ones have the faces alternatively large and small; square ones are not uncommon; hexagonal and round ones are rare. Sometimes several shapes appear in the same tower. The number in China must be enormous, Williams estimates there must be nearly 2,000 in the country.

On each storey are openings—doorways, or windows—neither furnished with doors, nor glazed, adding much to the picturesque details of these interesting buildings. There are cornices at each storey on the outside, forming at times only ornamental details, while at others they are developed into outside galleries, or balconies, going round the whole pagoda. These galleries are either unprotected or railed, and the openings in the brickwork of the tower, already mentioned, give on to these cornices or galleries. From them, magnificent bird's-eye views of the city at one's feet, or of the surrounding country, are obtained, increasing in range as the visitor ascends succeeding storeys; but it is not every pagoda that is open to ascent. Some are in too dilapidated a condition to be safe, and the officials prohibit visitors going up, and close the entries; others, though safe enough, have proved too common and easy a point of departure for giddy or weak-brained mortals to essay a flight into the great unknown. As to the modes of ascent they may be divided into two categories; none, or some. In the former case, none being provided by the builders, the inhabitants in the neighbourhood appear with a long plank ready to assist, for a remuneration of course, the aspirant to giddy heights. This long plank is thrown from the windows of a lower storey to those of the next, and, once crossed, it is pulled across and the further end raised again to the next higher storey. Thus slowly, stage by stage, the traveller ascends, crossing his improvised bridge, while a slip, or a fall of brickwork, would precipitate him to the foot of the hollow tower. A trick with the Chinese in the olden days was, when half-way up, or when the top had been reached, to take possession of the plank and refuse to place it in position for the descent until their rapacity had been satisfied by the bestowal of some coin, thus cruelly extorted by them. A steady brain is required in such a mode of ascent, as well as when a staircase winds round the interior of the structure without any railing or protection whatever. In some pagodas, however, each stage has a floor (*v. supra*). In one at the District City of Tie-yea, near Swatow, this was the style, and there were separate stairways round the interior of the building for each storey. The lowest of all was unprotected for the greater part of its ascent, after which it entered the wall of the building and landed one on the first floor; the succeeding staircases being all within the thick walls. The galleries were protected by balustrades, and were of sufficient width to allow of those going in one direction to push past those going in the opposite.

Buddhist temples are often erected at the foot of a pagoda, the primary object of a pagoda having been to preserve the relics of a Buddha, or saint. The Chinese have improved on this, and firmly believe that, in order to conserve or improve the propitious geomantic influences of a place, it is necessary to have pagodas; and they consequently take a prominent position in the curious medley of superstition and glimmerings of natural science known as Fung Shui (see GEOMANCY.) Their presence is supposed to ward off evil influences and attract those conditions which go to make up the Chinese idea of a state of prosperity, so much prized by them, and for the attainment of which they will sacrifice almost everything. As a concrete example of the good they are said to produce, it may be noted that the presence of a pagoda in a city was supposed to cause numbers of its studious youths to gain literary distinctions in the Civil Service examinations.

The geomancers of Canton say that the two pagodas inside that city are like the two masts of a junk, the stern sheets being the huge, five-storeyed, barn-like structure on the walls at the north of the city. To an imaginative people, like the Chinese, such a comparison is highly felicitous. A large commercial centre is thus symbolised, and a concatenation (of pagodas and buildings) producing such a symbol is looked upon as not only being an emblem of what the city actually is at present, but as a means of ensuring (for such probably would be the train of thought evolved) a future continuance of such commercial prosperity as long as such emblems continue to exist. The prosaic Englishman spends thousands on a grand system of underground drainage to improve the sanitary conditions of the city he lives in: the Chinese knows nought of, and cares less about, sanitary science, but he firmly believes in spending money to secure long life, health, and prosperity, and to preserve him from all the evils and dangers that surround him. He, like the Englishman, firmly believes in his system, and also that centuries of experience have proved that the means of obtaining such blessings is to erect new pagodas or to repair those already in existence in his district. The four winds may blow, but under the benign influences of the pagoda they are averted; the dire waters may flow, but the pagoda wards off their evil results.

An illuminated pagoda: such a sight is worthy of fairyland, whether a mass of Chinese lanterns turns the slender, pointed tower into a tongue of fire against the dark background of a moonless sky, or whether each coign and vantage ground forms a resting-place for a glimmer of light; but we question whether the reality comes up to the ideal, as 140 lamps for the Nanking Porcelain Tower, when it was in existence, seems but a small allowance for such a large building. They are hung at the windows and from each corner of the different storeys.

The aggregate sum of money spent on the erection of pagodas in China must be something enormous. 'The entire building at Nanking cost the Imperial Treasury no less than 2,485,484 taels of silver—$3,300,000'; and the repairs of another cost $26,000. Sixty years were spent in the construction of one.

Besides the pagodas already written about, known as *fá t'áp* [*hua t'a*] flowery, or ornamented, pagodas, there is another variety, know as *mun t'áp* [*wên t'a*] *or put t'áp* [*pi t'a*], literary, or pencil, pagodas, which are very numerous in the south of China. They are often seen on the banks of rivers, and are supposed, like the others, to exert a good influence on the neighbourhood.

Some people have been misled into thinking pagodas were intended as beacon towers; but beacon towers are quite different from them.

Pagodas are occasionally erected at the present day, but not often; the first was probably built in the third century (A.D. 249-50).

References.—Milne, *Life in China;* Williams, *Middle Kingdom;* i, 102, 743; 745; Gray, *China,* Chap. 31; *Transactions of the C.B.R.A.S.*, 1855, Part V; *Journal, N.C.B.R.A.S.*, N.S., Vol. 46.

PARSEES.—A number of Parsees are found engaged in trade on their own account and as *employés* in Hongkong, as well as at many of the Treaty Ports. They are a bright, intelligent race, good business men, and well-conducted. Their original country is Persia, from which they were driven by religious persecution. They are worshippers of fire. They have cemeteries in Hongkong and Macao, where they *bury* their dead.

PAWNSHOPS.—Towering above low-lying dwellings, and pierced by numerous small windows, the massive, square erections of the pawnbrokers' strongholds, are seen dotted here and there throughout the Chinese city or town. They are the objects which first attract the attention of the stranger, who naturally is surprised when informed that they are not fortifications but pawnshops.

Conspicuous they are in material substance, and they hold an equally prominent position in the social economy of the curious and complex product of Eastern life and prudential economy, which constitute the average Chinaman's life. The Westerner must dismiss from his mind all preconceived ideas of pawnshops and pawnshop-keepers. The position these latter hold is a highly respectable one, and the business is one in which a moneyed man is glad to invest his savings, or an official his surplus cash, as a share in the joint-stock concern which many of them are. Native banks would appear to restrict their operations more amongst trade, or business people, while the pawnshop comes in for a share of the business which, in England, would otherwise be monopolised by the banks.

If its shareholders are merchants and officials—people of respectability and position—so its *clientèle* not only embraces, as in England, the spendthrift, those who live from hand to mouth, the hopelessly impecunious, who are sunk in the lowest depths of poverty, the gambler, the thief, the robber, and the burglar, the opium-smoker (who takes the place so ignominously filled by the drunkard in our countries of the West, though even the drunkard is found in China amongst those who frequent the pawnshop, for has not the poet Tu Fu sung:—

'From the court every eve to the pawnshop I pass,
To come back from the river the drunkest of men.');

but they also still further boast, in almost equal numbers, the most respectable classes of society as amongst their numerous clients. Rumour now and again whispers that even in London some of those in good positions in the world, as far as family and connections are concerned, contribute customers to the sign of the three gilded balls, but these transactions are done *sub rosâ* and most indignant would these same customers be if they were taxed with them. John Chinaman, unlike John Bull, has nothing to be ashamed of—in fact any idea of such a thing as shame entering into his mind with regard to such a common and honest business transaction would not find a lodgment in his brain.

The pawnshop is a safe repository for the gentleman's, or lady's, furs in summer, where they will be well taken care of and preserved from the destructive moth; and, again, in winter, the summer robes of thin and diaphanous material may be carefully housed in the same storehouse.

There are several classes of pawnshops (such as *chih tang*, private, licenced, and *ssŭ ya or hsiao ya*, not officially recognized), but, for all practical purposes, they may be considered as separated into these two divisions. They have different regulations as to rates of interest and the length of time unredeemed pledges are kept before being sold, etc. A very common rate of interest is thirty-six per cent. a year. A not unusual sight is a lot of pawn-tickets for sale on a street stall. Those who buy them have, of course, the right of redeeming the articles on pledge for which they are issued.

Pawnshops form a fine object of attack for burglars or robbers; and, notwithstanding all the strength of their construction, their massive doors, their narrow windows, and the piles of stones on the roof to throw down on the heads of their assailants, as well as all the precautions taken in early closing, the attacks made on them are sometimes successful. It is dangerous work to engage in, as, if caught, the penalty is death.

'Perhaps the most important financial institution of the lower class Chinese is the pawnshop, the owner of which occupies a position much higher in the social scale than does the pawnbroker in a Western country. Chinese records seem to have lost trace of the earliest dates associated with the pawnbrokers, but mention is made of them by a scholar in the T'ang dynasty (618-905), who in a poem speaks of pawning a fur coat to secure wine. Since then, or an earlier time, the business has developed until now almost every workman in China who has something of pawnable value is within reach of a shop which will take it.

"Tang" and "yao" are the general terms used to denote pawnshops in the south of China, as in Hongkong and Canton. About Shanghai there are the first and second class "tang," a third class known as "chee," and fourth grade known as the "yao," which is to be found only in the foreign settlements and in the Nantao district. These "yao" are operated on limited capital. About Shanghai it has been their practice to use the character "tang" on their signs, adding "yao" inconspicuously.

Their indulgence in certain sharp practices has caused the pawnbrokers' guild, a strong organisation having as members shops outside the foreign settlements and the Nantao district, long to refuse to allow the "yao" to operate in territory where there are members of its association. Neither the "chee" nor the "yao" are members of the pawnbrokers' guild, but they have small organisations of their own. The "tang" shops generally try to uphold their dignity more than do the shops of the lower class. A "tang" has the confidence of the public, since it is considered that trickery, sharp practices and varied interest rates to different customers will not be found in dealings with them. The same is not always true of a smaller shop, which is often on the look-out for a sharp bargain.

Recently the "yao" was permitted in Nantao, permission coming after much controversy when the representatives of the "yao" promised not to use the character "tang" on their signs again. Members of the pawnbrokers' guild, since they felt this change meant sufficient distinction between them and the smaller shops, which gave less safety, promised to refrain from interfering with them in the Nantao district.

Pawnshops are taxed in various ways in various parts of the country. Those in Kiangsu province, in which Shanghai is located, for instance, pay a fee for opening, the license not needing to be renewed. In Kiangsu a first class "tang" pays $500, silver, for an operating license; a second class "tang" pays $300, and a "chee," $200. Shops in Canton pay a city license fee.

It is said that the earlier shops were operated as philanthropic institutions for the poor who might have nowhere else to borrow money when it was needed. Pawners of goods nowadays, however, pay a sharp interest. About Shanghai a pawnshop is expected to have at least $50,000, silver, as stock in capital. This is called in Chinese "fa yuen," or origin of resources. During some seasons of the year this sum is in many cases insufficient to take care of the business which comes, and it is often necessary for the owner to borrow from the outside, or advance from his own resources, in order to inflate his working capital. The average pawnshop owner in a year makes from 15 to 25 per cent, after expenses are paid, on the capital he has in the business. The employes get a share of the profits, the percentage being on a scale which gives the higher ranking employes the most. The salary of employes has not, however, kept, pace with living costs and there is agitation among them for wage increases.

The interior of a first or second class pawnshop is barren of goods, a contrast in appearance to those in Western countries, where it is the practice to display unredeemed goods for sale. While practices in different parts of China differ, about Shanghai only the smallest and meanest shops display goods. The large shops have a large screen before or inside the door so that passers-by may not see what is going on inside. Important customers are usually invited into the inner room, so that business may be transacted over a cup of tea. A cigar, a cigarette, or the water pipe is often offered, and women customers are paid special courtesies.

When one enters the shop by the main front door, he is confronted by a counter five or six feet high. There is little in the room except some ready cash in drawers behind the counter. Names and addresses of pawners are required in some parts of China, as at Canton, when articles are left. Thus when stolen goods are located in a shop, the thief is often found by some clue contained in the name given. Shanghai shops, however, do not require the names and addresses of those pawning articles.

A need in ages past for protecting pawnshops from attacks by organised bandits has caused a type of building to be erected in Kwangtung province and in some other parts of the country resembling a feudal stronghold. These quarters are of heavy stone or brick, and stand high above surrounding buildings, their tiny iron-barred windows looking over the roofs of adjoining buildings. Some of the more influential shops have secured permission from the authorities to arm themselves, and they keep rifles and other firearms ready for possible attack by thieves.

On the staff of the present day shop is an honorary adviser, a general manager, a goods manager, a treasurer, and a " dress ornament " keeper. One of the duties of the adviser is to negotiate with the officials on various questions that may arise concerning business, and otherwise to keep his shop from falling into the ill graces of those in power. The general manager supervises the business and he is, if the shop is not run by the man who owns it, the medium between the owner and those who operate it. He takes care of the annual accounts and makes a report on the profits or losses.

The goods manager has personal charge of the goods that have been pawned and which are stored as security. The treasurer has charge of the shop's finance, and he is the accountant in charge of daily transactions. The " dress ornament " keeper is in charge of jewelry as well as other articles which are made of gold or silver or which contain jewels.

Other employes are a bond writer, a wrapper, and a sign attacher, and there are several apprentices. The business of the bond writer is to make out receipts for the goods received and to note the various details in the agreement between the shop and customers. Since the bond must be in considerable detail, a sort of Chinese stenography has been devised, and none except one skilled in this special writing is able to understand what is stipulated on the certificate.

The special business of the wrapper is to tie up in cloth goods other than jewelry. When he has finished, the sign attacher places on it a tag of wood, after which it is ready for storing. The apprentices, who are ranked as first second, third, etc., according to seniority, are general assistants to all the others holding specific jobs.

When anyone in the lower grades of the shop staff dies, or for any reason leaves, an apprentice usually steps into his place, although it is always possible that a vacancy may not be filled by an apprentice, but that someone may be brought in from the outside. In this case the candidates must await another opening before promotion. There is no time limit to apprenticeship, and one may remain as such for five or six years. But even with such a slow start, if the man is able, he may be promoted in time to the position of manager.

Actual business is done by men called " chu tan " who are experts in appraising. The goods may be furs, pearls, jade, diamonds, silver of gold ornaments, or any of many other classes of goods, including clothing. When the article is wrapped and tagged, it is put away by apprentices in one of the storing departments, such as the "dress ornament department," the "clothing department," or the "hardware department," where copper and lead utensils are kept. Some pawnshops in the interior of the country have warehouses where cotton may be pawned and stored, and some even take furniture, but this requires large storage quarters.

The pawner who takes his goods to a "tang" in Shanghai pays 18 per cent interest for ten months and 21.6 per cent for a year. The limit of the redemption period is eighteen months, after which the pawner cannot secure his goods unless he again pays interest before the expiration of the time. In various parts of China the loan period can be extended to two or three years, or even four, according to local custom. The lower class shops sometimes charge much higher rates, and the limit of a loan period is sometimes but a few weeks.

When the eighteen-month period expires, the goods are offered for sale to brokers, or to a broker. He who secures the goods is usually one who has been doing business with the shop for a long while, and often it is not the highest bidder who receives the business. Friendship between the broker and the shop manager or owner carries weight, and often an old customer receives the goods while a new one fails to have his offer accepted even though it is better. A reason for preferring an old customer is that some goods taken by the broker and sold do not return a profit, in which case the broker insists on other business in order to recoup. The matter of credit and payment also enters into consideration on the part of the shop owners.

A broker's bid is on the basis of what the shop first advanced on the goods. Thus in buying, the broker offers 10, 20 or 30 cash above the loan, exclusive of interest. For instance, if a loan advanced on something was 100 cash, the broker takes it by giving the shop 110, 120 or 130 cash.

Since the broker does not know just what goods are stored by the shop, the brokers themselves prefer to deal with shops with which they have been doing business, as only by repeated trading do they learn what good they are likely to get for their offer made without first having seen the goods.

The shops usually do not insure their goods against fire, and in case of one the shop has to pay pawners as fully as possible for the goods destroyed. A fire is the most disastrous misfortune a pawnshop may expect. It is seldom able to reimburse pawners in full, 50 or 60 per cent. being perhaps the average. Shop employes are drilled in what they are to do in case of a fire, and small brigades are formed. Of late years pawnshops have had chemical extinguishers installed. In case the shop is robbed, it is expected that the shop owner shall pay for in full or replace the articles lost.

In every important city or town there is a pawnshop guild to which qualified shops belong. It is the custom for the guild members to elect men of their trade as committee-men, of whom there are generally three, who look out for matters in the city which affect the interest of the shops and the guild members.

In Kiangsu province, in which is Shanghai, there is a provincial pawnshop guild, a higher association which discusses and deals with questions of interest to the trade in the province. The guild holds regular meetings once a year and, when necessary, special meetings to which each district guild sends its representatives.

The provincial association has established in Nanking a guild pawnshop, the capital of which is advanced by members throughout the province. The shops have a bank in Soochow, with branches in Shanghai and other important business centers. Members of the provincial guild have considered establishing an insurance company, but this has not yet been realised.

In the various localities pawnshops are expected to take an active part in charitable work. The shops hold to customs of doing business practised hundreds of years ago, and they have in recent years been criticised for their conservatism. It is said that the business requirements made on them have outgrown what they, with ancient methods, are able to take care of. The pawnshop has so far proved itself one of the most conservative and little-changing business institutions in China.'

References.—Gray, *China*, vol. ii, chap. 20; *Chinese Economical Monthly*, 1924.

PEA-NUT.—The following account of this common and well-known ground-nut, *Arachis hypogœa* (called in Chinese *hua shêng, ch'ang shêng kuo,* or *lou shêng*), is from Rein's *Industries of Japan*:—

'A very considerable botanico-geographical interest attaches to this remarkable leguminous herb. Numerous leaves appear on its low-lying branching stalk. These are elliptical or oval, inverted, and at their axils grow short-stemmed, yellow blossoms. When these have disappeared their stems lengthen out, the joints sink into the loose sandy soil, where, at a depth of 5-8 cm. below the surface, they develop into little pods, 15-30 mm. long and 10-15 mm. thick. As a rule they have a constriction in the middle, deep and gradual. . . . Their grey-white earthy' coloured 'shells contain a seed on each side of the constriction. Shorter ones, without constriction, hold only one. . . . Externally' these seeds 'are a brownish red; inside white. They yield 40-60 per cent. of a fatty oil, which serves almost all the purposes of olive-oil. . . . Brazil was formerly considered to be the original home of the ground-nut; but now that it has become known how widely distributed it is in Africa, this opinion has been relinquished, and it is held more probable that it was introduced into the New World by Portuguese slave-ships from Africa. In the Old World it is found cultivated in many tropical and sub-tropical countries, though never to the same extent as on the West Coast of Africa, from Senegambia and the regions adjacent down to the Gold Coast, where it is a prominent article of export. Marseilles is the chief market for ground-nuts and the oil they yield. . . . In Japan and China, as well as in North America, ground-nuts are usually eaten roasted, and their cultivation is very limited.'

This last sentence may be true of North China, but in the South they are a common crop. Pea-nut oil was the common illuminant before the introduction of kerosene into China; but it is now disappearing fast before it, or has been completely given up, in many places in favour of the brighter oil.

The pea-nut has only recently been cultivated in the northern half of China (see below). To produce the best crops, a sandy soil, with abundance of sunshine, and not too much moisture are necessary. They are sown in the early spring and gathered in October. There are two kinds, the large and the small. The former, called the foreign pea-nut, was introduced from the United States. The oil production is one-third by weight of the nuts. The cake is considered one of the best for live stock. The shells are used to fatten pigs. The production has increased since the suppression of opium. The foreign trade has expanded enormously since 1909. More than one-third of the exported quantity goes to France. As an export, the oil is gaining on the seed.

'The foreign pea-nut, by which name the large pea-nut now grown in China is commonly called, was introduced into China from the United States about 35 years ago by Archdeacon Thompson of the American Church Mission, says the agriculture and forestry notes of the University of Nanking. Archdeacon Thompson brought four quarts of pea-nuts to Shanghai and there divided them equally with Dr. Charles R. Mills of the American Presbyterian Mission (North), who was on his way to Têngchowfu in P'ênglaihsien, Shantung. This district was already noted as a large pea-nut growing section.

Dr. Mills divided his two quarts of pea-nuts equally with two of his church members on the condition that they should gradually increase them over a period of three years and at the end of that time use them for general distribution. One of the farmers at the end of the first year ate all his crop. The second farmer, however, fulfilled his contract faithfully and distributed them at the end of the third year. Because of their size they were acceptably received and grown as widely as the three years' increase permitted.

Hopes of the rapid spread of the large foreign pea-nut were somewhat shaken when, after trying to express the oil according to custom by grinding both the hull and the kernel previous to applying the pressure to extract the oil, it was found that the thick shell of the pea-nut absorbed practically all the oil. Then someone got the happy idea of shelling the pea-nuts before expressing the oil. This was done and the value of the foreign pea-nut was clearly demonstrated. This saved the day for the foreign pea-nut, and ever since its production has been increasing yearly until at the present time it enters into China's foreign commerce to the extent of millions of dollars annually. The introduction of the pea-nut into P'ênglaihsien was considered such an important event that a large stone tablet memorializing the virtues of the foreign pea-nut was placed in the grounds of the yamên of the magistrate of the district.

It is difficult to estimate the benefit which the farmers have derived from this missionary introduction. It has become indigenous, to say the least, and its area and production are still on the increase. Land too poor for other crops will usually produce a fair crop of the large pea-nuts.'

PEKING GAZETTE.—See NEWSPAPERS.

PHEASANTS.—Marco Polo says:—'Pheasants are found there twice as big as ours, indeed, nearly as big as a peacock, and having tails of seven to ten palms in length.' To this Col. Yule has a note on p. 271 of vol. i. of his 2nd edition as follows:—'The China pheasant answering best to the indications in the text appears to be *Reeves's Pheasant.* Mr. Gould has identified this bird with Marco's in his magnificent *Birds of Asia*, and has been kind enough to show me a specimen which, with the body, measured 6 feet 8 inches. The tail feathers alone, however, are said to reach to 6 and 7 feet, so that Marco's ten palms was scarcely an exaggeration. These tail-feathers are often seen on the Chinese stage in the cap of the hero of the drama, and also decorate the hats of certain civil functionaries.'

The order Gallinæ, including pheasants, partridges, grouse, peacocks, turkeys, fowls, etc., is represented in China by more than thirty-six chief species.

The Chinese ring-necked species of pheasant has been successfully introduced into England.

References.—David et Oustalet, *Les Oiseaux de la Chine; Proceedings of the Zoological Society of London, passim.*

PHILOSOPHY.—We do not propose to enter on a long dissertation on Chinese Philosophy, whether it be ethical as applied to everyday morals, with its five virtues; or cosmogonal, as applied to the evolution of the finite from the infinite, the conditioned from the unconditioned, and the production of light and darkness. Here one appears to be on solid ground, but when one follows out the reasonings and statements of the ancient philosophy, and comes on stalks of milfoil, and the carapax of a tortoise, the eight diagrams, the eight trigrams—notwithstanding the assurance that 'it is very probable that there is underlying' them, the trigrams, 'a definite system of natural philosophy'—it all appears to the foreign reader, who has not imbibed the true Chinese spirit, that the most of us are outside the pale of the Middle Kingdom; the feeling is but little modified though one is assured that the Grand Plan is typified in them, that the dual principles of Nature are working in their midst, and that they 'typify the transformation which the dual principle of Heaven and Earth undergoes in the phenomenal changes of nature.' This is all *caviare* to the Westerner, who has no taste for Chinese delicacies; and to the general reader it all seems incomprehensible and unfathomable, for the ancient philosophical worthy who devised these mystic combinations appears to the common mind to have lost himself in the maze of his dreams and speculations. How difficult to understand the 'Yik King' [*I ching*] ('the Classic of Changes'), which deals *ad nauseam* with these diagrams and their commutations, is, may be gathered from the fact that the late Professor Terrien de Lacouperie asserted it to be a word-book of Accadian or Babylonian words; but the Chinese, by the aid of commentaries, have read sense and meaning into what would otherwise baffle the common intellect.

One turns with more pleasure to the speculations of the heretical Micius (Mi Tzŭ), who, shunned by the unappreciative, orthodox Chinese scholars, laid it down as a principle 'to love all equally'; and the brilliant Chuang Tzŭ's paradoxes, his fables, his mysticism, are all more congenial to the Western mind—more practical in their bearings, notwithstanding all the defects and errors, than the dry sticks of the milfoil and the harder shell of the tortoise, who withdraws under his *testudo* and resists all the prying efforts of the seekers after knowledge.

We might wander amidst the speculations of different writers subsequent to the Confucian age, when many were 'distinguished for the boldness of their theories and the freedom of their utterance,' where, besides the names already mentioned, may be cited those of Licius (Lieh Tzŭ), Mencius, Süncius (Hsün Tzŭ), and others, but space will not permit; nor can we follow the mazes of the speculative philosophy, which 'sprang suddenly into existence' under the Sung dynasty. In fact, the whole subject is a vast one, diverging into many branches, and worthy of an exhaustive treatise dealing with it alone. We refer the reader to the article on Taoism in this book, for some notice of Chancius (Chuang Tzŭ), with his vivacity and remarkable fertility of imagination, whose writings have been described as 'a storm of dazzling effects.'

For so large and complex a subject it will here be sufficient to mention the chief Chinese philosophers with their leading ideas: Lao Tzŭ (doctrine of the *Tao*, the Absolute; used in two senses—the Great Principle which formed the universe, and the primordial matter from which the universe was formed); Confucius (socio-political duties; modified despotism, dependence, subordination; state economy; maintenance of the 'five cardinal relations' and proper discharge of duties appertaining to them); Mo Tzŭ (doctrine that good government and general peace and happiness are achieved by ruling class practising universality and reciprocity in 'universal love' based on utilitarianism); Yang Chu (opposed the altruistic philosophy of Mo Tzŭ with one of extreme egoism: 'each one for himself'; despondent hedonism and crude epicureanism); Lieh Tzŭ (transcendentalism; contentment in life and rejoicing in death); Mencius (Confucianism; man's nature inherently good; practice of benevolence and integrity; government by the cultured class; social order: people, spirits of land and grain, sovereign; division of labour; prosperity and education result of regulation of agriculture and commerce); Chuang Tzŭ (Taoism; anti-Confucianism; vanity of human effort; laissez-faire; life to be cared for; but indifference to death); Hui Tzŭ (subjectivism; discussions of relations of matter to mind); Hsün Tzŭ (human nature evil; morality artificial; orthodoxy; government by physical force; anti-Mo Ti-ism); Han Fei Tzŭ (Taoism); Yang Hsiung (human nature both good and evil; importance of environment); Huai Nan Tzŭ (researches into secrets of nature in light of contemporary Taoism); Wang Ch'ung (criticism of Confucianism and Mencianism); Chou Tzŭ (doctrine of the Supreme Ultimate; primordial Ether; Two Modes—*Yin* and *Yang*; Five Agents, or Elements; Man); Ch'êng Hao, Ch'êng I, Chang Tsai, Yang Kuei Shan, Lo Ts'ung Yen, Li Yen P'ing, and Chu Sung (development and transmission of Chou Tzŭ-ism); Chu Hsi (account of constitution of man's nature founded upon theory of universe; dualism supplanted by monism); Wang Yang Ming (lofty idealism).

References.—China Review, xv, 338; xvii, 26; xviii, 299; xix, 225; Legge, *Sacred Books of the East*, vol. xvi; Faber, *The Doctrines of Confucius; The Mind of Mencius;* Balfour, *The Divine Classic of Nan Hua;* Giles, *Chuang Tzŭ;* Martin, *Hanlin Papers; Journal N.C.B.R.A.S.*, O.S. Nos. 3 and 4; Meadows, *The Chinese and Their Rebellions;* Suzuki, *A Brief History of Early Chinese Philosophy;* Bruce, *Chu Hsi and His Masters; The Philosophy of Human Nature;* Werner, *Descriptive Sociology—Chinese; China of the Chinese.*

PIDGIN-ENGLISH.—When foreigners settled in China, finding the language difficult to learn, and the Chinese finding English nearly equally difficult for them to acquire, a middle course was struck, and the outcome was the mongrel talk, called pidgin-English (said to be the Chinese attempt to pronounce 'business'). We say a middle course was struck, for the words employed are generally English modified to suit the defective pronunciation of the Chinese. For example, the letter *r* is dropped and *l* substituted, while the idiom is Chinese, and, in the absence of inflection and declension, the Chinese is again copied. The result has been a most wonderful gibberish, especially when talked in its purity. It is, of course, not at all like Chinese, and so unlike English, that new-comers require to learn it. The difference between it and proper English was once unconsciously and wittily expressed by a Cantonese shopkeeper, who, finding himself at a loss to understand the correct English spoken by a new arrival, turned to his friend, an American, and said: 'Moh bettah you flen talkee Englishee talk, my no sabbee Melican talk.' A very few of the words employed in pidgin-English are Chinese so distorted as to be almost past recognition, while Portuguese, Malay, and Indian have also added a few words to the vocabulary. Some residents have occasionally amused a leisure hour by putting a few of the gems of English literature into this jargon, with the result that diamonds of the first water have been changed into ashes. The soliloquy in Hamlet commencing, in pidgin-English, 'Can do, no can do, how fashion,' as well as 'Excelsior,' and other poems, have shared this fate. We give a specimen at the end of this article, but very few of any of the pieces put into this lingo represent it as it is really spoken, as *bs*, *gs*, *ds*, and *rs*, are all left in, letters which, when the Chinese speak it, are not pronounced, but *ps*, *ks*, *ts*, and *ls*, are used instead. The pidgin-English, as usually written, represents it as it is pronounced by the foreigner, but not as it is spoken by the majority of Chinese, and the latter we would maintain is the proper pidgin-English.

Fortunately for all concerned, this dialect of English, which has had an existence of more than half a century, now seems doomed. The extended acquisition of some knowledge of English on the part of the Chinese, is superseding its use. One very curious feature regarding the use of pidgin-English, is to find Chinese from different parts of the empire, who, on account of the difference in the dialects spoken by them, are unable to converse together, occasionally forced to use it.

EXCELSIOR.

That nightey tim begin chop-chop,
One young man walkee—no can stop.
Maskee snow! maskee ice!
He cally flag with chop so nice—
Topside Galow!

He too muchey solly, one piecee eye
Look-see sharp—so—all same my,
He talkey largey, talkey stlong,
Too muchee culio all-same gong—
Topside Galow!

Inside that house he look-see light,
And evely loom got fire all light,
He look-see plenty ice more high,
Inside he mouth he plenty cly—
Topside Galow!

Olo man talkee ' No can walk,
By'mby lain come . . . welly dark,
Hab got water, welly wide.'
' Maskee! My wantchey go topside,'
Topside Galow!

' Man-man,' one girley talkey he;
' What for you go topside look-see! '
And one tim more he plenty cly,
But allo-tim walkee plenty high.
Topside Galow!

' Take care t'hat spoil'um tlee, young man,
Take care t'hat ice. He want man-man.'
T'hat coolie chin-chin he ' Good-night,'
He talkee ' My can go all light.'
Topside Galow!

Joss-pidgin-man he soon begin,
Morning-tim t'hat Joss chin-chin,
He no man see—he plenty fear,
Cos some man talkee he can hear.
Topside Galow!

T'hat young man die, one large dog see
Too muchee bobbely findee he,
He hand blong colo—all-same ice.
Hab got he flag, with chop so nice—
Topside Galow!

MORAL.

You too muchee laugh! what for sing!
I tink so you no savvy what ting!
Supposey you no blong clever inside!
More betta *you* go walk topside!
Topside Galow!

References.—Leland's *Pidgin-English Sing Song* contains a vocabulary, and many pieces put into pidgin-English.

PIRACY.—It must be difficult for those living in our Western lands to understand how piracy on water and highway robbery on land render to a certain extent life and property insecure in China as compared with countries like England, where nowadays such hindrances to travel and trade are rare.

In a land where living is to many a bare point above absolute want, if harvests fail or floods come, numbers of erstwhile honest villagers may be driven to beggary, or, emboldened by despair, turn into sea robbers or land thieves; in a land likewise where rebellions are common occurrences, bringing destitution and starvation in their train, it needs but little to drive some of the desperate characters, robbed of all resources, to such a pitch that the life of a gentleman at large preying on the resources of others seems a beneficial change to themselves at least if not to others; in a land where the soldiery are kept at starvation wages or not paid at all for months at a time, it is but little wonder that when disbanded such troops, accustomed already to loot, should turn to brigandage as only a shade worse morally than the life they have been driven to by their corrupt officers and the effete government. The following extracts will give some idea of the state of things:—

'Time was . . . when the Two Kwang were the chosen haunt of pirates who were a terror in all the southern seas from Amoy to Java, including the Philippines, Borneo, Malay Peninsula, etc. The establishment of the British sea power in these waters, however, soon proved the destruction of piracy, British gunboats making it so warm for these freebooters that in the end they practically disappeared, or became merged in the population pursuing lawful avocations afloat. That the old free-booting spirit still survives among many who are now apparently peaceful traders and fishermen, we occasionally get startling proofs in some unexpected daring act of piracy on the high seas or along the coast.'

With regard to piracy, the British Consul for Canton thus writes in his report for 1894:—

'While piracy on the coast has nearly disappeared, the inland waters of the province are still infested with robbers. Even in the immediate vicinity of Canton, acts of piracy are committed every day. The passage-boats are armed as if they were going into action. On the roofs of the cabins where the passengers are confined (or what may be called the upper deck) may be seen half-a-dozen old-fashioned muzzle-loading cannon well depressed, so as to hit a boat close alongside, and also racks full of modern rifles ready at hand for the use of the crew. Old fishing-nets are hung in folds on each side ready to be spread out as a screen against bullets, and passenger-boats are now being fitted with a grating to separate the men who tread the stern-wheel from the rest of the boat, for the first act of the robbers, whether they push out from the river bank, or rush out from the cabin where they have been posing as honest passengers, is to disable the wheelmen and bring the boat to a stop. On shore there is not much more security. But, with all the lawlessness, foreigners live in perfect safety. In their excursions by land or water they are never [or rather, we should say, scarcely ever] molested. Robbers know that foreigners will make a stouter resistance than the timid Chinese, and that the native authorities would not be allowed to wink at the outrage as they do when the victims are Chinese.'

The steam-launches which ply between Canton and different cities and villages in the country are armed, and some have a grating of wire-netting round them to prevent pirates getting on board.

Within the last few years further outrageous acts of piracy have been committed on board foreign and native steamers and launches, the foreign captain, officers, and several of the passengers having, in some instances, been murdered in cold blood.

Connected with the subject of piracy is that of banditry, which has increased in many parts of China in proportion to the disbandment and non-payment of the soldiers. The worst example on record is the attack on the 'Blue Express' from Shanghai to Peking at Lin Ch'êng, Shantung, in May, 1923, when one foreigner was murdered and many foreigners and natives marched off to the bandits' stronghold at Pao Tzŭ Kou and held to ransom for many weeks, during which they suffered terrible privations. One or two escaped, and the rest were ultimately released owing to diplomatic pressure and the exertions of voluntary intermediaries, indemnities to the victims being paid by the Chinese Government. The last of the leaders of this band died (by suicide after betrayal by his friends) in May, 1924.

PLAGUE.—This disease, long known under different names, is variously said to have originated in Scythia, India, Tartary, and China. In China it is known as *shu i* (rat disease), *wên i, i chêng*, and *pai ssŭ tu.*

At the end of the nineteenth and beginning of the present century a mysterious disease, which, from the reports received, appeared to be a species of malignant fever, was prevalent in the province of Yünnan, and excited the curiosity of a few of the foreign residents in China, who eagerly scanned any accounts by travellers in the hope of acquiring a fuller knowledge of this fatal malady, which seemed to have made its home in the mephitic valleys of that distant province. No fears were ever entertained that this unwelcome guest of the Yünnanese would start on its erratic rambles and visit with its malign presence and virulent persistence the south-eastern coasts of the empire and commit its ravages beneath the very eyes and, in the British colony of Hongkong, in the actual midst of those who had wondered what it was, thus throwing its defiance indeed in the teeth of Western medical science; but this was the case, and the unknown visitant proved to be either the black plague of mediæval days, or closely akin to it. That black plague which we read of in our history books, in magazine articles, and in Defoe, and whose dread presence caused a stagnation of civic life and commerce, spreading a dark pall of misery and distress over merry England, making our centres of life veritable cities of the dead, and finally reducing the population of the country to one-half of what it had been before it expired, according to general opinion, amid the lurid glare of London in flames.

'Though not necessarily confined to such, in modern times plague, like leprosy, had become practically a disease of warm climates. The hygienic conditions which advancing civilisation has brought in its train have forced back these two diseases from Europe, where, at one time, they were even more prevalent than they are in their tropical and subtropical haunts at the present day. They are typical examples of that large group of acute and chronic germ diseases whose spread depends on social and hygienic, rather than on climatic, conditions, and more especially on filth and overcrowding; conditions which nowadays are found, to an extent and an intensity sufficient to ensure the endemic prevalence or epidemic extension of these diseases, only in warm countries.'

'The most potent circumstances which predispose to the epidemic outbreak of plague are extreme filth and overcrowding. In such circumstances, the virus, once introduced, tends to spread. These conditions, however, are not all sufficient; for even in the filthiest and most crowded Oriental towns and without any apparent alteration in the habits or circumstances of the population, the disease, after having become epidemic, dies out spontaneously. It may be difficult to indicate the exact way or ways in which filth and overcrowding operate, but certain it is, as experience has shown, that in sanitary hygienic conditions plague does not spread, even if introduced, and that in opposite conditions it may for a time spread like wildfire.'

'Filth and overcrowding imply close proximity of the sick and the healthy; an atmosphere saturated with the emanations of the sick; a lowered tone of the general health; abundant saturation of soil and surrounding media with animal refuse, fitting them as a nidus for what might be termed natural culture of the germ; abundance of bodily vermin of all kinds [see INSECTS]; abundance of other vermin, such as rats and mice, which serve as multipliers of the virus; carelessness about personal cleanliness, about wounds of the hands and feet, about clothing, and about food, dishes, and water. One can understand how in such circumstances the germ has opportunities to multiply and spread.'

'Plague, though "catching," is not nearly so infectious as are scarlet fever, measles, small-pox, or even typhus. Medical men, and even nurses, in clean airy hospitals rarely acquire the disease, provided they have no open wounds and do not remain too long in close proximity to their patients. In cities, the cleanly districts are generally spared. This was well exemplified in the late epidemics at Canton and Hongkong, where the airy, cleanly European quarters and the relatively clean, well-ventilated boat population were practically exempt; whilst the disease ran riot in the adjoining filthy, overcrowded native houses only a few yards away.'

It is thought that the disease may be conveyed to man in food and drink.

Things Chinese

'As far as present knowledge extends, it seems certain that plague is also communicated by the breath, inasmuch as the special bacilli were found in the saliva of the Vienna victims.' 'The most hopeful branch of the inquiry, as far as we can see at present, is that which relates to the preparation and administration of preventive or curative serums.'

'The study of the bubonic plague in India has thrown light upon a bit of Biblical history hitherto not understood. When the Philistines restored the sacred ark to Israel, they sent with it, as an atonement to JAHVE, "five golden tumours and five golden mice" (1 Samuel vi. 4, R.V.). What the mice had to do with it has been the mystery. The Montreal *Medical Journal* elucidates it in an article by Dr. J. G. Adami. A peculiar thing about the plague in India is, that it attacks rats and mice. This was noticed at Hongkong in 1894. These vermin, when infected, desert their holes without fear of man, a phenomenon noticed by an old chronicler in England in the seventeenth century. What is said in 1 Samuel v. 12, "the men that died not were smitten with the tumours," exactly corresponds to the fact that the swellings characteristic of the disease (called "bubonic," from Latin *bubo*, a tumour) are more noticeable in cases that are not fatal. The breaking out of the disease in one Philistine city after another, as the ark was carried from place to place, marks the infectiousness of the plague, and so does the fact that those who carried the ark back to Israel carried the plague with them. This is described in 1 Samuel vi. 19 as a Divine judgment: "Because they had looked into the ark of the Lord, He smote of the people seventy men and fifty thousand men." The Authorised Version in this passage translates the Hebrew for swelling by "emerods" (hæmorrhoids, or piles), which renders the account of a great mortality incredible; the Revised Version "tumours" is correct enough, but unintelligible. The mouse, which in the fable gnawed the cord that fastened the lion, has once more done service in freeing this story of mystery, and given an unmistakable realism to what many have regarded as merely a legend from three thousand years ago.'

'The first bubonic plague of which we have authentic record is placed by two physicians of N.S.W. in the year 1141 B.C., or more than eight centuries earlier than the date usually assigned. It is concluded that the epidemic described in the 1st Book of Samuel was true bubonic plague.'

Before proceeding to an account of its manifestations in China in recent times, it may be interesting to give a short summary of the known history of the plague.

'Plague is perhaps the one disease of which we have an authentic description at periods of time coming down from 430 B.C. to mediæval times (1348) and so through the Great Plague of London (1665-66) to this last epidemic in 1894 [in Hongkong and adjacent country]. The character of the disease seems not to have altered in any way since the time of Thucydides. The sudden invasion and the other symptoms, the buboes and hæmorrhages, are all as plainly marked in the Hongkong epidemic as they were in Athens 2,500 years ago. There is one similarity between the epidemic at Athens and the plague of 1665 which we do not find mentioned in Dr. Lowson's report of the Hongkong epidemic, so perhaps the same conditions did not obtain—*i.e.*, the absence of other diseases.' The Emperor Julian's physician mentions the plague. We learn from him that it was 'endemic in Egypt and Syria from the beginning of the second century before Christ.' It appeared in Europe in the sixth century. This, it is said, was the first time in history when 'this formidable disease assumed the character of a great epidemic. Breaking out in Justinian's reign (A.D. 542) the disease quickly occupied the whole of the known earth, and began a tragic course which has continued even to our own time.' The black death which swept over the continent of Europe in the fourteenth century had several of the symptoms of bubonic plague, but it differed essentially from it (but see Dr. Manson's opinion below), so one writer informs us, and he proceeds to tell us that Egypt seems to have been the seat of origin of bubonic plague, and Cathay some centuries later of the black death. The ravages of the latter in London in 1665, when 70,000 died of it, are well known, as well as the outbreak in 1720 in Marseilles, after which it appeared in neither England nor France, retiring to the easternmost part of the Turkish Empire in the beginning of the nineteenth century, and disappearing altogether from the continent of Europe in 1841. 'Prior to 1661, there are almost continuous records from year to year of the presence of the disease in Northern Africa, Asia, and Europe generally, and it is worthy of note that as first one country and then another in Europe adopted some systematic form of drainage and improved habits of life, so soon did the plague disappear from these countries.' To epitomise:—'For 1,200 years it was pre-eminent among pestilential maladies. In the sixteenth century, when quarantine was established, 69 outbreaks were recorded in Europe; in the seventeenth century, 56; in the eighteenth, 28; in the first half of the nineteenth, 15. In 1844 it apparently became extinct. But about ten years afterwards it again showed itself in the Levant, and has since occurred in various parts of Asia and North Africa and even in Europe.'

A most interesting account is also contained in 'Tropical Diseases,' pp. 144-6, of the history of the plague, which does not quite agree with the extract given above, and is fuller, in fact too long to be inserted here.

After the foregoing, especially after the last sentences, a few notes by Dr. Manson in 1878, prefatory to a translation of M. Rocher's account of the plague in Yünnan are very interesting. Speaking of M. Rocher's statement, he says:—

'They prove unmistakably the existence of bubonic plague in China, and that this dread disease has spread over a larger area of late years than is generally known. They are of great value as showing that the disease did not entirely disappear between the years 1844 and 1873 as some epidemiologists believe, and thus do away with the supposition that in the latter year there was a re-creation of the plague virus.

'In 1844, the plague disappeared completely from Egypt and Turkey in Asia, and we were told to congratulate ourselves on being finally rid of the most terrible of all epidemic diseases. For years there was no sign of it in its favourite haunts, and there seemed good reason for the belief that it had become a thing of the past. But in 1873, after an absence of nearly thirty years, it once more broke out in Mesopotamia, and ever since has been steadily extending its area, till last year it reached the shores of the Caspian. To account for this re-appearance after so long a period of complete absence, some epidemiologists have propounded their belief in the spontaneous generation of the plague virus, as it is absurd to suppose that parasites could retain their infective powers for nearly thirty years. But in the light of M. Rocher's notes such a thing is unnecessary, as his dates bridge over twenty years at least of the thirty during which the disease was supposed to be dead, and show that an extensive epidemic may rage in Mid-Asia, and Europe be in complete ignorance of the fact. In such a country as Central Asia, where the distances are great and travelling very slow, we can understand that such a disease as plague would take a long time to pass from west to east and back again from east to west, and that an interval of thirty years might elapse before the disease returned again to the place whence it started. Our knowledge of the countries to the north of the Himalayas is so meagre, and communication with them so difficult, that the plague might pass through them without our hearing about it at all, and one can readily suppose that it did actually pass thus from Yünnan to Mesopotamia or Persia to originate the epidemic at present raging in these countries. M. Rocher's description of the disease is sufficiently clear to justify us in calling it plague.'

The first time we are aware of it in China was in 1844, but it did not work so much havoc as in 1894. One of the first authentic accounts, as far at all events as is known at present, of it in this land is contained in the following paragraph from the *Overland Friend of China*, of 23rd May, 1850:—

'The city of Canton and the neighbour-towns and villages are afflicted by a malignant fever. It is commonly called typhus; some European physicians are of opinion that it is akin to the yellow fever of the West Indies; *others think that it resembles the plague which desolated London two centuries ago.* The disease is said to be fatal invariably, its victims linger three or four days, though in some instances they have died in twelve hours. More than one European doctor cheerfully tender their services,—but the Chinese are obstinate in their adherence to old custom—old ignorant quackery. The distemper has not made its appearance at the Factories, and as it may arise from a want of cleanliness among the people, we are in hopes that it will not extend to Europeans.'

We are unable to say what the death rate was during this visitation, though hundreds are said to have died, nor can we tell whether there had been previous epidemics of it in Canton. Chinese accounts, with their utter ignorance of all medical knowledge, are so meagre and untrustworthy when dealing with historic invasions of sickness that they are extremely unsatisfactory, and the diseases they mention are difficult of identification, especially would this be the case were the plague the subject-matter of a terse, short paragraph by a Chinese historian. We should almost suppose that had it approached at all to the horrors of the epidemic at Canton in 1894, more extended notice of it would have been taken by the foreign papers published in the South of China. For even before the end of its duration in Hongkong in the epidemic of 1894, the deaths in the city of Canton alone were estimated, from the beginning of the outbreak until the 18th of June, at 35,000, while the number of deaths in the villages around could not be ascertained.

We learn from a missionary lady, resident for some time in the Pok-lo District, Canton Province, that in that district or in the Hakka country near there, the Chinese say they have had the plague several times; but it had never been so fatal as in 1894, ninety per cent. dying in that year, whereas only sixty or eighty per cent. of those who took it died previously. We have endeavoured to learn from inquiry amongst natives of different districts of country whether there were local traditions of visitations of the plague in their respective districts; but all the evidence we were able to gather, and it was but small in quantity, was of a negative character. There would appear to be 'very little literature on the subject.' One would fancy there would be not a few notices of such a dreadful disease; some may yet be discovered; but we have examined book after book to try and find some little mention of it. They almost all display a most wonderful unanimity in keeping a discreet and profound silence on the subject. We carefully looked through a standard Chinese work, on the Canton Province, only to be disappointed. Authorities appear in their voluminous tomes to flee all references to epidemics almost even as their authors would fly from the plague itself.

Before proceeding to an account of this 1894 epidemic, which brought the plague under the immediate purview of European medical science and knowledge, it would be more historically correct to call attention to its ravages in the province of Yünnan. We are indebted for accounts of it in that province to the narratives of travellers, and notices by one or two of the few residents in that distant portion of China. From the notes on the route followed by Mr. Grosvenor's Mission through Western Yünnan, from Tali-fu to T'êng-yueh, reprinted from the Parliamentary Report, China, No. 3 (1878), we extract the following:—

'Another strange disease which haunts this and some other of the valleys of Yünnan bears, in some respects, a resemblance to the plague of London described by Defoe.

'Its approach is indicated by the eruption of one or more minute red pustules, generally in the arm-pits, but occasionally in other glandular regions. If several pustules appear, the disease is not considered so hopeless as when there are few. The sufferer is soon seized with extreme weakness, followed in a few hours by agonising aches in every part of the body; delirium shortly ensues, and in nine cases out of ten the result is fatal.

'It often happens that the patient suddenly, to all appearance, recovers, leaves his bed, and affirms that, beyond a slight sensation of weakness, he feels thoroughly convalescent. This is invariably a fatal sign; in about two hours the aches return, and the sufferer dies.

'True recovery is always very gradual. This is the account given us by a French missionary, who has spent half a lifetime in Yünnan. The native version includes all the above facts, but involves them in a cloud of superstitious accessories; for instance, all parts of the sick-room are occupied by devils; even the tables and mattresses writhe about and utter voices, and offer intelligible replies to any one who questions them.

'Few, however, venture into the chamber. The missionary assured me that the patient is, in most cases, deserted like a leper, for fear of contagion. If an elder member of the family is attacked, the best attention he receives is to be placed in a solitary room, with a vessel of water by his side. The door is secured, and a pole laid near it, with which twice a day the anxious relatives, cautiously peering in, poke and prod the sick person to discover if he retains any symptoms of life.

'Père Fenouil . . . had himself witnessed many cases of the disease, and lived in infected towns. He attributes his own safety to the precautions he took of fumigating his premises and keeping charcoal braziers constantly burning, to such an extent, indeed, that his house on one occasion actually took fire. He states that not only human beings, but domestic animals and even rats are attacked by the pestilence.

'Its approach may often be known from the extraordinary movements of the rats, who leave their holes and crevices and issue on to the floors without a trace of their accustomed timidity, springing continually upwards from their hind legs, as if they were trying to jump out of something. The rats fall dead, and then comes the turn of the poultry; after the poultry have succumbed, pigs, goats, ponies, and oxen successively die off.

'The good father has a theory of his own that the plague is really a pestilential emanation slowly rising in an equable stratum from the ground, and as it increases in depth all animals are, as it were, drowned in its poisonous flood—the smaller creatures being first engulfed, and man, the tallest of Yünnan animals, suffering last.

'The Christian converts suffer less than their pagan countrymen from the superior cleanliness which, as we were informed, their faith inculcates.

'We ourselves never saw any cases of the plague; but we met one native of South-western China, no less a personage than the Governor of the Yünnan province, Ts'ên, a quiet, sober-spoken veteran of a hundred battles, deeply marked between the eyes with a scar inflicted by a rebel bullet. He had undergone two attacks; the second was less violent than the first. He remembered nothing of the acute period of the illness, but in both cases his recovery was gradual and protracted.

'He attributed it to the influence of demons; and we afterwards heard a characteristic instance of his faith in his own diagnosis. The headquarters of his division during the Mohammedan rebellion were situated in a plague-stricken town, and when the infection began to attack his troops, Ts'ên had all the gates closed except that in the southern wall, and then sent in his soldiers with orders to slash and pierce the air in every corner that could possibly harbour a demon. After this preliminary slaughter the men were formed in line against the inside of the north walls, and gradually advanced upon the south gate, hemming in the invisible fiends, and ultimately driving them with a final rush through the gate, which was immediately closed and a strong guard placed outside. But somehow or other the goblins contrived to regain the interior of the city; by what means has not been ascertained; but it is surmised that they climbed over the wall.'

The following summary of M. Rocher's account of the Plague was prepared by the late Mr. Dyer Ball, and appeared in one of the Hongkong local papers in 1894:—

Some interesting notes on the plague are appended to M. Rocher's 'La Province Chinoise Yünnan,' as well as some observations on it in the body of the work itself.

M. Rocher informs us that the plague is known in that part of the country by the name of *yang-tzŭ*. In Hongkong, however, we find the Chinese speak of it as *wan-yik* [*wên-i*], the epidemic. Not only does it claim numerous victims each year in Yünnan, but it also commits its ravages amongst the Laos, as well as on the frontier of the neighbouring province of Kueichou.

From the information given to M. Rocher, he was led to believe that this disease came from Burmah by means of the caravans passing between that country and China. The time of its first advent seems uncertain, some being of the opinion that it first showed itself in the centre and east of the province at the time of the great Mohammedan rebellion; while a few hold that it was known in the west of the province at Ta-li-fu some years before that event.

A very curious feature noticed in Yünnan is the susceptibility of the lower animals to what is believed to be the malignant miasma which causes the disease (but *v. infra*). The inhabitants of the sewers or the dwellers underground are the first that are attacked by this fell plague. The rats, driven from their holes, rush into the houses, maddened by the mephitic vapours which they have inhaled, and shortly give up the ghost; but more often the foul odours from their dead bodies under the flooring is a proof of the deadly work which is going on. All animals, large and small, are subject to the same infection: buffaloes, cows, sheep and goats, and the poultry to a lesser extent. Some, at all events, of the animals seem to suffer less than man from it.

On his arrival in these parts, M. Rocher refused credence to the stories of the natives, believing them to be due to the effect of imagination or to superstitious fears; but on the pest bursting forth in the very district in which he was, and having then ocular demonstration of the truth of the reports he had heard, his unbelief was changed to faith.

The precautions taken nearly everywhere were to light fires in all the rooms in order to purify the houses; and the people in certain cities and districts abstained from the meat *par excellence* of the Chinese—pork.

M. Rocher describes this bubonic plague as beginning with a high fever 'accompanied by an intense thirst; some hours after a deep red tumour appears in the armpits, the groin, or the neck; the fever increases and the patient soon loses consciousness; the tumour usually increases in size until the second day, after which it remains stationary. The patient then appears to recover his senses, but he is still in great danger; for, if the tumour which up to that time has been very hard becomes soft and if the fever does not diminish he is considered as lost; on the contrary, if the tumour is pierced on the outside, which rarely happens, there is hope of saving him; but at this stage the patient is so weakened that although the tumour may have broken he dies of exhaustion.'

Strange to say, notwithstanding the extreme repugnance the Chinese have to the surgeon's knife, M. Rocher tells us that some of the Chinese doctors have tried the effect of cutting or excising these tumours; but whether it be that the operation is put off too long or unskilfully performed, very few of the patients have survived the amateur efforts of their physicians. The strongest remedy that they employ under these circumstances is musk, which is prescribed in strong doses as a last resource. Dr. Porter Smith informs us that musk is 'believed by Chinese authors to be a rousing, stimulating, anti-spasmodic, deobstruent, expectorant, diaphoretic, ecbolic, anthelmintic, and vulnerary remedy, . . . and enters into the composition of ointments for dressing ulcers and sores.'

M. Rocher saw a great many cases of the plague in Yünnan, and most of them had a fatal result. The proportion of the inhabitants affected by it differs in different places; in some spots, where it may be described as simply passing, from 4 to 6 per cent. were attacked by it; while in other localities the population was completely decimated by this awful scourge, whole families even being swept away by it. The inhabitants in such districts, driven from hearth and home, even leave their crops, and flee from the fell foe to the heights. Nor does flight ensure their safety at all times, for we are told that even to these upper regions the plague very often follows them, invading the mountains after having ravaged the plains, and on these higher levels likewise claiming numerous victims, the neighbouring heights near the cities also suffering from it.

The insanitary habits of the Chinese with regard to the disposal of those who succumb to the disease—so much in accord with similar methods prevalent in many parts of the Celestial Empire, where the dead are often of more importance than the living — contributes greatly to aggravate the situation, so M. Rocher informs us is his opinion; and we can readily believe it when we are told by him that instead of burying the bodies of those who have died from the pest, the natives are content to place the coffins in the open air, either on the slopes of the hills or on the plains, exposed to the fierce rays of the tropical sun, with what results it does not need even the help of a lively imagination to picture. (It is known, however, that the direct rays of the sun are fatal to the plague germ).

In the years 1871-2-3, the plague began in May and June, the time of the planting of the rice; the summer season, which is the rainy season, seemed to check its activity; but it redoubled its energies and claimed the most of its victims during the period extending from harvest till the end of the year.

A strange circumstance noted by M. Rocher is that the epidemic at several places in the middle and north of the province overleapt certain spots in its course, or passed them by, and left them untouched until several months after or even until the following year, when it returned to the places thus apparently forgotten. Having attacked nearly all the villages in the plains, the plague sought new fields for its devastations by ascending to the mountains and committing numerous ravages amongst the aborigines. M. Rocher gathered, from what he had seen and from the irregular manner in which the disease appeared, that it must have been imported into these higher localities by the men and women who go at certain times of the year to work in the plains. More colour appears to be given to this view from the fact that it is after the rice has been planted or when the harvest is ended that this scourge leaves the low-lying country for the heights.

An interesting sketch-map is given in the book to illustrate the course of the plague in 1871-2 and in 1872-3, showing the places where the most victims succumbed and the spots where the visitation simply passed with slight mortality. This map was prepared from official sources of information and from other knowledge of the matter obtained by M. Rocher. It appears to have followed a most curious zigzag route on both occasions in its erratic course. M. Rocher also informs us in a note on the map that certain cities and principal towns of the west of the province have been successively visited by the pest, and in some districts it has remained during several years permanent amongst the troops which were carrying on operations against the rebels.

The late Mr. Happer, Commissioner of Customs at Mêngtzŭ for some years, thus writes about it in 1889:—

'In spite of such a favourable climate, Mêngtzŭ, in common with other parts of Yünnan, has suffered annually, for a period of years, from the plague . . . which has carried off a number of its inhabitants. Indeed the presence of fallow land in the near neighbourhood of the city is attributed to the decimation of the farming population by the pest. . . . A curious fact about the disease [in Yünnan] is, that it never descends to places under 12,000 of altitude above the sea, and it rarely scales heights over 7,200 feet high. Strangely enough also, it seldom attacks people sojourning in Yünnan from other provinces, its victims being confined to the aborigines, and to native-born Chinese.'

With regard to it in 1895, it is stated:—

The season in Mêngtzŭ in 1895 'up to July had been very dry, but the first few days of that month were wet, and shortly afterwards the plague began with its wonted virulence. The disease was prevalent and fatal during July and August, and remained till towards the end of September. Various estimates of the number of victims, are given from 800 to 1,500. The neighbouring towns suffered severely, the malady even raging in Lo-lo villages considerably over 6,000 feet above the sea level. At the commencement of the epidemic the Chinese thought it would disappear with the arrival of the autumn (8th August), but the disease prevailed till it had run its course, which requires about three months' time, as shown by the records kept since the establishment of the Mêngtzŭ Customs in 1889.'

'The plague appeared in Mêngtzŭ as usual [in 1897], but it was not, apparently, as virulent as in former years, and ran a shorter course. The first death was reported on 31st May, and no deaths were reported after 6th August. The estimated mortality from plague in the city was from 250 to 300.'

It still continues at Mêngtzŭ. It is said to have been worse in 1896 than it had ever been before. The deaths were then estimated to number thirty per day out of a population of

30,000. 'Every evening the Taotai has his troops drawn up in the courtyard of the Yamên to fire their rifles in all directions to frighten the plague demons.'

A more recent report (1899) says that it appears to be dying out in that neighbourhood, though this has been denied.

The plague has been endemic for many years at Pakhoi, a small treaty port situated in the Kuangtung Province and on the Gulf of Tongking; but takes an epidemic form there at intervals of five or ten years or even more frequently. It first occurred there in 1867, recurring at certain intervals; severe outbreaks took place in 1877, 1882, and 1894. In the last year it began in 'March, continuing with lessening severity till the end of June, but at Lien Chow city, twelve miles distant, it lasted till August.' The mortality was estimated at Pakhoi in 1882 to be 400 or 500 out of a population of 25,000, the average a day, when at its height, being ten. The people were almost panic-stricken at its commencement and fled the town. Rats were attacked, but no other animals. There were three groups of symptoms of the disease as it manifested itself respectively in Pakhoi, Yünnan, and India. In 1894 it was worse in point of mortality than ever before—300 or 400 having died at Pakhoi by the middle of May when it was abating. From Chinese sources it is learned that before 1875 only about 100 people had died in any year of plague at Pakhoi; in 1884, 50 or 60; in 1891, about 40 or 50. We have already mentioned the mortality in 1882 and 1894. 'Native doctors in Pakhoi prescribed what they call "cooling remedies" such as rhubarb. It appears they do not treat the bubo locally.' The natives at Pakhoi 'burn joss-stick and a plant, the sweet flag, which are supposed to have prophylactic power as disinfectants.' In 1894 they bought a great deal of foreign disinfecting fluid. Dr. Deane of Pakhoi says of it:—

> 'The disease appears in one locality and seems as restricted as though it were in a bottle. One house may be so bad that anyone entering it will be seized, but the next house quite free from all danger.' 'Many perfectly healthy men take the disease and die next day.' 'It is endemic to a particular locality.' 'In Pakhoi it does not appear as an epidemic generally, but only in the most evil-smelling quarters.'

Pakhoi escaped the epidemic in 1895, being practically free from it, though Kotak, a village near the port, had a slight visitation.

It is curable in Pakhoi when brought to the missionary hospital as soon as the symptoms appear, but 'nothing can be done in the advanced stages.'

The plague is essentially a disease that delights in 'filth and insanitary surroundings.' The simple drainage systems in vogue in Chinese cities are periodically flushed by nature at the season of the year when they would prove most dangerous to the inhabitants, viz., during the hot and sultry summer which is the rainy season in the South of China. So effectively do the torrential rains sweep away the accumulation of weeks and months that it would be extremely difficult for man to compete with them. But their work is stultified to a large extent by the crass ignorance of all sanitary matters by the Chinese and by their utter indifference to the offensive odours which give warning of the dangers to life and health around them. No, or but very little, supplementary aid is given to the cleansing rains, so when a period of draught ensues, the inhabitants naturally suffer from their neglect of the filth which surrounds them and the effluvia therefrom, whose subtle essence permeates the whole atmosphere which they breathe. Given such conditions, the plague, if once introduced, runs a wild riot in its congenial surroundings, resisting and defying all the puny efforts put forth by the natives for its extermination. It revels in its filthy haunts; it ensconces itself in the malodorous districts and fetid precincts of a Chinese city, town, or village, where filth is never wanting, where the soil is saturated with the escaped drainage of centuries, where every street corner is a dustbin, where every vacant lot is a dirt-heap, where the frontage of the houses on the rivers is a rubbish-shoot, and the banks are a dumpage-ground for all refuse, where every house is an *omnium gatherum* of dust, dirt, and cobwebs; where in some cases the kitchen is a urinal and the market gardens are fertilised with night soil, and where in the midst of houses the public latrines scent the whole neighbourhood with their filthy odour, where in the early hours of the forenoon the scavengers almost render the family streets impassable to a foreigner by their necessary offices for the houses in which the modern conveniences of Western civilisation are unknown; where the most elementary sanitary laws are never dreamt of and utterly ignored by the inhabitants, where even the well-to-do are often unclean and filthy in their habits, in their clothing, in their surroundings; where the poorest wear their scanty clothes in rags and alive with vermin till it almost drops in pieces from them; and where overcrowding prevails to the utter disregard of ventilation and fresh air. What wonder then that with such a welcome reception ready for it, the plague, like the evil spirit in the parable, returns again, not often, however, like the evil spirit, to find the place swept and garnished, but with the same filthy conditions even present, inviting its return. What wonder also that year after year the visit is repeated.

'Plague is developed under three sets of conditions, (*a*) local conditions affecting communities, (*b*) certain relations between persons sick of the disease and healthy persons, (*c*) particular seasonal influences. (*a*) . . . The conditions "which determined and favoured" the disease among communities were dwelling upon alluvial and marshy soils, notably those found near the shores of the Mediterranean, and on the banks of certain great rivers, such as the Nile, Euphrates, Danube, and Yangtsz, a warm and humid atmosphere; low, badly ventilated and crowded houses; great accumulation of putrefying animal and vegetable matter in the vicinity of dwellings, unwholesome and insufficient food, excessive physical and moral misery and neglect of the laws of health as well public as private. Although outbreaks of plague occur in marshy soils, it is not confined to them, as evidenced by its persistence in Kumaun on the Himalayan mountains and the . . . outbreak in Hongkong. Colvill and Cabiadio ascribe poverty as the influential condition in promoting plague. (*b*) Persons living in the same house are peculiarly liable to suffer, while those who are only brought into occasional contact (as the physician) are rarely affected. . . . (*c*) Seasonal changes. In Mesopotamia, it was notified that the disease became dormant with the setting in of the hot weather, re-awakening in the winter and gathering force with the advancing spring. In Constantinople, on the contrary, the disease was dormant in the colder months and active during the hotter. The same was true of the great plague of London, the records showing that September was the month of greatest prevalence, the disease rising through July and August.'

The plague would appear to be one of Nature's scourges for the punishment of those who disobey her laws and for instruction in the elementary rules of sanitary science. Unfortunately, Orientals find the lesson a difficult one to learn, and the innocent dwellers amongst them also suffer with the guilty.

We now come to the terrible visitation of the plague in Hongkong in 1894. It was probably introduced into this British Colony from the city of Canton, only distant 90 miles, between which places there is constant daily communication by native boats and foreign steamers, there being 11,090 passengers every week from Canton; many patients were fleeing from the plague in that city where it had began in the February of that year. The deaths in Canton from it during the first four months of 1894 were to be numbered amongst the tens of thousands.

The first official knowledge of the plague in Hongkong was in May, 1894, though it is suspected that it had been present in the Colony for some weeks at least before that, though unknown to the authorities, any cases of death from it having probably been registered as due to fever or other causes, no medical certificate of death being required from the Chinese. The native quarters of the city presented an exceptionally favourable field of operations for it, and it spread with great rapidity through the narrow streets, in the blind alleys, amid the crowded tenements, claiming its victims from young and old alike whether at home or abroad, for several cases occurred of men dropping down dead in the streets.

No rain had fallen for a considerable time and there was a scarcity of water in the Colony, an intermittent supply being furnished to the inhabitants; the drainage system, which had been begun without any system in the early days of Hongkong and had not kept pace with the requirements of the population, was in a transition state towards a complete renovation. T'áip'ingshán, which formed the headquarters of the epidemic, was built at the foot of a steep mountain side and facing the north, the breezes being kept off, as in a great part of the city, to a considerable extent by the Peak. The filth which had accumulated in the dwellings is almost indescribable, and would scarcely be credited by those who do not know how the Chinese live; the soil was saturated and reeking with half a century's sullage water and leakages from sewers; while the ground floors, really no misnomer in many cases, as whatever flooring tiles there might originally have been, were often covered by inches of dirt and hardened mud, a compost teeming with germs of disease; underground basements were occupied not only by workmen during the day as workshops, but were used as sleeping dens at nights; the rooms, small and ill-ventilated enough already, were in the majority of cases further diminished in size and the atmosphere rendered more foul by being subdivided by low board partitious into cubicles, and, not content with this, a horizontal division of the apartments was effected by cocklofts, or mezzanine floors, and these latter were in some cases even partitioned off into little tiny rooms, and in some rooms, a second cockloft would even be found; the streets and lanes were narrow and intricate; the houses which had originally been built low and of only one or two storeys, of late years had in many cases been replaced by higher dwellings, and every available piece of ground in the city was being rapidly built over, so that what was once a sparsely populated district was soon converted into a congested mass of buildings with but little means of ventilation; where even in some houses an open verandah would offer some chance of fresh air, the Chinese would, unless under constant supervision, quickly economise the space by either enclosing the verandah or putting up bedrooms in it.

The enhanced price of land, the raising of rents, the attempts to solve the problem of how to live upon next to nothing—all tended in the one direction, that of rendering the native quarters a hotbed of disease, by favouring the overcrowding of houses on the land, and the overcrowding of the inhabitants in those houses. Every facility was thus offered for the spread of the disease, and once fairly started it continued to hold its ground all through the summer, the number of cases rapidly increasing, the deaths keeping almost equal pace with it, until the latter reached the number of 70 or 80 per diem; but by this time half the Chinese population had fled the Colony in terror, ill and well, all attempting to get away from the plague-infected city; the streets presented a very different aspect from the period when a full tide of life flowed through them, business was seriously affected, the foreign trade of the Colony greatly hampered, the outlook was dismal in the extreme, many steamers were afraid of calling at the port, the law courts were nearly deserted, the schools were almost forsaken; in the foreign offices, pots of chloride of lime stood at every desk, or disinfectants were freely used about the premises. The plague proclamation was in force in Hongkong for nearly four months, from the 10th May until the 3rd September, 1894, and during that time there were 2,547 deaths in the Colony from it. How many really died of it will, however, never really be known, as many fled the Colony, going up to Canton and the neighbouring country while ill.

As soon as the Government and the foreign residents realised what this dreadful disease that had come amongst them was, energetic measures were taken to cope with it. A committee was formed to advise and direct operations, bodies of the troops, residents, police, and officials formed 'whitewash brigades,' which went to the infected houses, tore down the cocklofts and partitions, cleared out the rubbish, and burnt the *débris;* a burial party was formed, in which sailors under the leadership of an official did gallant service. The greatest praise is due to all we have mentioned and to many others unknown to us, for with the greatest bravery they ran terrible risks for the benefit of their fellowmen. Several of the soldiers and one officer succumbed to the infection—if there be any glory in death itself, theirs was a more glorious death than on a field of battle. Doctors came from different places to assist, and much was added to our knowledge of the plague during this visitation in Hongkong. A Japanese doctor, Dr. Kitasato, a student of Koch's in Berlin, first discovered the plague bacillus in Hongkong in 1894, and Yersin, a French doctor afterwards, while another of the Japanese who came to the Colony to investigate the disease died from it.

The efforts of the Europeans were often misunderstood by the ignorant Chinese, and the strong hand of the law was required to enforce obedience; in fact, many of the natives had fled from the Colony in consequence of the measures taken to cope with and overcome the plague.

Concerning infection from this much dreaded disease, Dr. Lowson says that it is stated that 'skin to skin infection is impossible unless the one to be infected has some wound and the infecter's skin has been soiled by fæces, blood, or the contents of buboes,' but there are sufficient other methods of infection known, or suspected, to render the horrible dread the Chinese had of it well founded. The period of incubation may extend to nine days, or even less, though in the case of rats it is two or three.

In the beginning of the plague infection, the symptoms may be varied, an anxious terrified expression is common, and fever and buboes are also signs, but not of course infallible, the temperature as a rule rises gradually, 'and in most severe cases the tendency is for the temperature to keep about the same level for some time'; but we cannot go into a full report of the symptoms. Those who are interested in them will find them fully described in Dr. Lowson's valuable paper. The death rate amongst those attacked in Hongkong in 1894 was as follows:—

Chinese	93.4 per cent.
Indians	77 „ „
Japanese	60 „ „
Eurasians	100 „ „
Europeans	18.2 „ „

The Chinese lacked efficient medical attendance—in many cases they would have nothing to do with foreign doctors, while Europeans called in properly trained physicians, and that, in most cases, right early. At the same time there is no doubt that the European constitution was better able to withstand this fearful disease. Judged by the percentage of deaths in those attacked, the Eurasians would appear to have the worse constitutions of all.

'About ten acres of the most densely populated part of the city was closed by the Government at the height of the epidemic, and the inhabitants turned out of their dwellings and housed elsewhere. The streets were walled up, and constables were stationed to prevent egress to the "forbidden city." In this quarter of the city, T'áip'ingshán, nearly every house had plague in it, and most of the houses were unfit for habitation. The

Government resumed all the land and houses in this portion of the city, giving compensation to the owners; the wretched dwellings were eventually pulled down, and the streets are now laid out on an improved plan.

During the next two years the plague played havoc in the neighbourhood of Canton, Hongkong and Macao, now visiting, during the hot months of the year, one part of the country and now another. Hongkong escaped in 1895, except for a few sporadic cases, amounting to some 44 in number, but Macao was visited by a severe epidemic of it in April and May, 1895. The city of Canton was reported to be practically free in 1895.

In Canton, when the plague was raging in 1894, a reward was offered for the bodies of rats that had died from it, and in consequence 21,000 were collected. The plague during these last few years also visited Amoy, Swatow, and other places in the south eastern part of China, reaching as far north even as Shanghai, where a few cases occurred.

A recurrence of the bubonic plague took place in Hongkong in 1896. It began early in the year:—

'The disease was at its worst stage in April and May, and was not finally stamped out till the end of September. The total number of cases brought to notice was 1,204, of which 1,097 ended fatally. Europeans attacked numbered fifteen, of whom seven, including two soldiers and one Inspector of Nuisances, succumbed to the disease. . . . One of the two sisters who were engaged in nursing at the Plague Hospital was also attacked by the disease, but fortunately recovered. The largest number of fresh cases in one week was 100, from the 23rd to 30th May, and the greatest number of deaths was 87, for the week ending 9th May.'

But it has spread so over different places in China that to give an accurate and full account of its visitations would require more space than we have at our disposal. Several hundreds are said to have died of it in Kaúlung [Kowloon] City in 1898. Visitations occurred in Hongkong in subsequent years (see below), several Europeans dying of it in 1901.

The plague also visited Formosa in 1896; and considerable alarm was caused in 1896 and 1897 by a serious outbreak of it in Bombay and elsewhere in India. A new phase of it in Bombay was that pigeons were attacked by a disease which presented points of resemblance to the plague, and died in large numbers. In this connection the following extract from the *Bombay Gazette* as published in the London *Daily Chronicle* of the 14th January, 1897, proves of more than passing interest:—

'Mr. Hankin has set himself to investigate an important branch of the subject—the means by which the pest becomes diffused, and is brought in contact with the population which becomes subject to its ravages. The time has not come to enter into details, but it is permissible to state that there is evidence proving beyond all doubt that rats, living and dead, and ants play a large part in diffusing the disease and establishing it in buildings which become in their turn centres of infection. Rats which have the plague, deposit the germ of the disease on the floors over which they pass. When they die their bodies are eaten by ants, which absorb the germs and deposit them in cracks and crevices, especially when there is any lurking moisture. Ants require water, and consequently they frequent the neighbourhood of taps and sinks. The bacilli have been found in ants a fortnight after they received them from preying on dead rats. A house near Dhobie Talao, in which two deaths took place, was searched for dead rats. Their bodies were dug out and the holes closed up. The man employed on that work took the plague. Some days afterwards Mr. Hankin succeeded in picking out from crevices ants which were found to have the bacilli. Some of the surface of the ground near the sink had bacilli, though it had been flushed with phenyle the day before. The bacilli were doubtless deposited by the ants after the phenyle had become dry. It is not to be supposed that ants have any monopoly in the diffusion of bacilli. Insects which have never been held in such general esteem for industry and self-help have unquestionably their share in that deadly work. But keeping in view the proved fact that rats get the plague and die of it in large numbers, that their dead bodies under the floors and among the rafters of old buildings are sources of infection, intensified by the action of myriads of ants, Mr. Hankin has come to the conclusion that the segregation of human beings who get the disease can have but a very small effect in preventing the spread of the disease. The danger lurks in the house, and he recommends that the other inmates should be removed whether the patient elects to stay there or not. In the Himalayas and in all countries the segregation of the healthy has been the one effective means of stopping the spread of the plague.'

'The bacillus pestis, discovered by Dr. Kitasato,' is 'now universally recognised as the essential cause of the plague. It belongs to the group of parasite or disease-producing bacteria which find a home in the bodies of certain animals. It is so minute that Dr. Woodhead has estimated that it would take about 500,000,000 of such organisms, laid side by side, to cover a postage stamp. They multiply by fission, and each divided portion is a new plant; reproduction thus proceeds in a rapid geometrical progression. The greatest enemy of the bacillus' is 'sunlight.'

Monkeys and squirrels and snakes, especially the rat-catching snakes, are also affected by plague.

With regard to the plague amongst the lower animals, Dr. Manson says:—

'It seems to me that they have to be reckoned with in the future, more than they have been in the past, in devising schemes of quarantine, and in attempts at stamping out the disease in already infected localities. It seems to me that the wholesale destruction of domestic vermin should go hand in hand with the isolation of plague-stricken patients.'

'In an article on the plague in the *Annales de l'Institute Pasteur*, Dr. Simond says that both amongst rats and men the infection is carried by fleas, which are the chief instrument in the propagation of the disease.'

Dr. Yersin, a French physician who went to Hongkong in 1894 to study the plague, has since made a series of experiments with the plague bacillus which has resulted in his discovering what he believes to be a cure for the plague. By the injection of the serum he prepared, he cured one case in Canton; of twenty-three cases in Amoy, fifteen were cured, two died, and of the remaining six cases he unfortunately left before a cure was effected, though he had every hope that it was in progress. It takes twenty-four hours to effect a cure, and it must be taken at once as soon as the symptoms develop. 'Haffkine practised during the Bombay epidemic a system of prophylactic inoculation,' the figures were encouraging in 1897; in 1899 the accounts were very encouraging:—

'Inoculation against plague bids fair to become universal in India; one town of a population of about 40,000 having only about 5,000 uninoculated, while many have been inoculated twice. The results justify the practice, a report for one week in September [1898] showing only 69 attacks among 32,000 inoculated persons, and 417 attacks among 8,500 uninoculated.'

The bubonic plague is 'known in India by various names. In the Bombay Presidency it is called "Pali plague' because it was very rife in Pali in 1836.' As a general rule the following may be said to be fairly demonstrated by experience, namely, 'that the attacks of the plague fail upon subjects living wholesome lives under good sanitary conditions, and succeed . . . upon those living in unhealthy surroundings or whose system has been weakened by other disease.' As a rule, doctors seem to escape, though not always. It is those who are constantly with patients that are more liable, though the immunity that nurses and others usually enjoy seems wonderful, a few cases have occurred of even these taking it.

'The German Commission sent out to India in 1897 to study bubonic plague, attribute the comparative exemption from plague of Europeans and of the wealthier population generally, not only to better general conditions of life, but more especially to the greater protection afforded by their clothing. The evidence seems to show that it is usually abrasions or perforations of the skin, even of the most insignificant character, that afford the plague bacillus an entry into the body, whereas the poison is much less rarely absorbed through the lungs or the digestive apparatus. The Commission also came to the conclusion that plague had long been endemic in certain districts of Northern India.'

In some epidemics of plague it is said that patches are seen on the surface of the body after death, hence one name it formerly got was that of the Black Death.

In the epidemic of 1898, in Hongkong there were 1,315 cases, 75 of which were non-Chinese; 26 of these latter being Europeans two of the nurses at the hospital being victims of this frightful disease. Though a less severe epidemic than that of 1894, the cases in some instances were more severe. 65.3 per-cent. of non-Chinese who took it died; whereas amongst the Chinese the mortality reached the high figure of 89.6 per cent. Dr. Clarke, the Medical Officer of Health in Hongkong, in his report makes the following interesting statement:—

'I am strongly inclined to apply tentatively Sanarelli's theory concerning the bacillus of Yellow Fever, to the infective material of this disease also, namely, that the vitality of the bacillus, outside the living bodies of men and animals, depends largely upon the co-existence of vegetable moulds by which it is nourished. It is already well known that a moist atmosphere, defective ventilation, a moderate amount of heat, and the absence of sunlight are the most favourable conditions for the development of the Bubonic Fever bacillus, while they are the conditions which encourage the free growth of the vegetable moulds, and it is not unreasonable, therefore, to surmise that this property of symbiosis, which has been observed by Matchinkoff in connection with the bacillus of cholera, may have not a little to do with the persistence of the bacillus of Bubonic Fever in damp and ill-ventilated dwellings.'

Dr. Atkinson, the Principal Civil Medical Officer of Hongkong, writes:—

'The conclusions to be drawn from our experience of plague in 1896 and 1898 are that the occurrence of plague is favoured by (1) long prevalence of drought or of abnormally low rainfall; (2) atmospheric temperature below 82 F., as the months of maximum mean temperature were in each year followed by a material reduction in the number of cases; (3) the absence of sunshine; (4) the dampness of the atmosphere, during the months in which there were most cases the mean humidity of the atmosphere was high.'

Professor Simpson writes:—

'Plague is in fact primarily a disease among rats, the infection of which can be conveyed to human beings, but once established in human beings, the infection is communicable to others by means of the expectorations, by the discharges from the bowels and by the urine, and by discharges from the buboes or glandular swellings which form in this disease. The clothes, the food, and surroundings of a plague patient are likely to be infective and also spread the disease. Accordingly no measures are complete which do not include the prevention of the disease in rats as well men.'

'M. E. Duclaux, Director of the Pasteur Institute, speaking (in the *Revue de Paris*) of the means of protection against plague afforded by bacteriology insists strongly on the necessity of destroying rats, fleas, and bugs as an essential preliminary. The extermination of rats and their parasites is, he says, a more effectual barrier than is generally believed against the invasion of the disease.'

The plague recurred in Hongkong in 1899, the mortality gradually rising to some forty or fifty deaths in the course of a week in the beginning of May, one European being attacked by it, while the following account of it at about the same period of the year shows the ravages it was committing in the neighbourhood of Canton:—

'The plague is more than recrudescent in many of the towns and villages of the delta. In Canton and Fatshan, it is reported as "bad" but not so bad as in some of the inland cities.

'The city of San Ning might correctly be named, at present, "The City of Death." The plague is ravaging with special virulence, and carrying off its victims in large numbers. Shops and dwelling houses are closed, and their inhabitants have fled into the country, carrying the infection with them. Business is, for the present, paralysed. The streets, meanwhile, are reeking in filth and all drains choked with rubbish. Behold the remedy employed! In one street, I observed no less than three matsheds erected, in which were seated, in calm complaisancy, many idols which are implored to exert their power to stem and turn back the tide of death. Moreover, over almost every door are hung branches of cactus, or other thorny shrubs, also a piece of fine netting, and a bag of small cockle shells. It is believed that the malignant devils cannot well avoid all these obstacles and enter the house! They *may* be frightened by the rattling of the shells, as boys used to frighten birds from the cornfields by the rattle of a tin pan. If the devils yet attempt to enter, they must pass through the mass of thorns, but can scarcely avoid the small netting.

'It is almost past belief that men's minds are so dark, minds, too, that have spent years in America or Australia. Yet, there it is. It is altogether tragic to see such things, and to look behind and contemplate the sorrow, bereavement, and blank despair that hover over the houses and paralyse the hearts of those who crouch in terror within. One may well ask oneself the question, can such things exist? Furthermore, can it be possible that those enshrouded in such mental darkness can dare to assert, and venture to dream, that they stand on an equality with the people of the West? In the interests of humanity, there is every reason why all agencies, religious, educational, and commercial, should continue their propaganda, and endeavour to penetrate and dissipate this terrible gloom.'

The plague was also at Kuangchouwan, the new French port in the Kuangtung province, in April or May, 1899: it was prevalent among the natives; one European soldier died of it, and another who was attacked with it, was cured by the Yersin serum.

'Speaking of the persistence of the contagion of the plague microbe, which is causing so much anxiety in Austria and Germany, the journal *La Suisse*, Geneva, cites a characteristic case. "In 1660 the Dutch city of Haarlem was devastated by the plague. Whole families perished, among them a family by the name of Cloux, whose various members were buried in the Haarlem Church. Thirty or forty years ago it was found that the masonry of the tomb was out of repair, and the vault was entirely rebuilt. The masons in charge of the work descended into the vault and remained there during more than a day. Now although more than two centuries had passed since the epidemic, all these workmen were attacked with the infectious bubo [characteristic glandular swelling] of the plague, and had to undergo long treatment at the hospital. Nevertheless, there were no symptoms of the plague proper, and all recovered." '

The plague seems to have spread fairly over the world of late years, being conveyed even to the cities of Europe by commerce, though, thanks to the comparative cleanliness of European cities, its attacks have always been repelled. (It has reached even such an apparently out-of-the way place as Uganda.)

The following extract will show what dense crowding in the East means:—

'The most densely populated metropolitan districts of the city of London are St. James', Westminster, Whitechapel, and St. George's, in the East, but none of these have a population of more than 200 persons to the acre. Yet here in Hongkong, in No. 5 District, which is situated in the centre of the city, we have almost 1,000 persons to the acre, and the adjoining Districts, Nos. 6, 7, and 4 are in nearly as bad a state.'

This was in 1899.

'In a public lecture in the Sassoon Institute, Bombay, Dr. G. Waters disposed of the theory that the bubonic plague had been imported into Bombay from Hongkong by rats in ships. He inclined to the belief that it was not introduced from other ports, but had its origin in the large granaries of the Mandvie quarter of the town. The first outbreak was among the granary *employés*, and rat murrain was first discovered there. Surgeon-Colonel Cleghorn, who has made a special investigation for the India authorities, holds the same opinion. It is stated as a curious fact by both doctors that wheat and rice eaters have enjoyed almost complete immunity from the disease, which has been most prevalent amongst the millet eaters (the Hindoos)—millet being a generic term for various kinds of inferior grain. Limewashing is advocated as the absolutely best preventive of the plague.

References.—The local papers published in Hongkong contained, during the prevalence of the plague, many interesting particulars about it. Trever, *Diseases of India; Encyclopædia Britannica*, art. Plague; Davidson, *Tropical Medicine;* an article in *London and China Express*, quoted in *Hongkong Telegraph* 9th July 1895; Dr. Manson, *Report on the Health of Amoy* for the half-year ending 31st March, 1878; and *Notes of an Epidemic Disease observed in Pakhoi*, by Dr. Lowry, in *Medical Reports of the Imperial Maritime Customs*, for the half-year ending 30th September, 1882; *The Imperial Maritime Customs Decennial Reports*, pp. 654 and 671; Rocher, *Yünnan;* Dr. Lowson's Report on *The Epidemic of Bubonic Plague in Hongkong, 1894*, published in the *Hongkong Government Gazette; Report on the Outbreak of Bubonic Plague in Hongkong to the International Congress of Hygiene and Demography held at Buda-Pest, 1894*, by Dr. Ayres and Dr. Lowson; Sir Wm. Robinson's speech reported in the *Hongkong Weekly Press*, 9th Dec., 1896; *Tropical Diseases: A Manual of the Diseases of Warm Climates*, by Manson, from which we have made large extracts; also see *Annual Reports by the Medical Officer of Health for Hongkong* for years 1897, 1898, and subsequent years; *A Treatise on Plague: the Conditions for its Causation, Prevalence, Incidence, Immunity, Prevention, and Treatment*, by Major G. S. Thomson and Dr. J. Thomson; *Plague: How to Recognise, Prevent, and Treat Plague*, by Dr. Cantlie; *Encyclopedia Sinica*, art. Plague.

PLANTAIN.—'Botanists declare the banana and plantain to be the same plant.' In the Straits the distinction is said to be as follows:—'The plantain . . . never becomes sufficiently ripe to eat without cooking.' This fruit is too well known to require description. There are many varieties in China. (See FRUIT.)

POETRY.—The whole subject of Chinese poetry is one that is worthy of a more thorough treatment than it has yet received. One peculiar characteristic is the tones, constituting in the Chinese language an element unknown in foreign languages, which has to be paid attention to by the Chinese poet apart from the identity of sound required for rhyme.

The Chinese are passionately fond of poetry. The East is the land of poetry. Here Nature is found in her happiest moods: she lavishes all the tints of her wonderful palette on here gorgeous sunrises and sunsets; she instals her electric lights—the bright stars in the blue depths of the unfathomable sky—and so pure is the atmosphere, that one can see beyond their clear shining into the illimitable space; her full-orbed moon floods the whole landscape with a silvery light but seldom seen in the West; the sun glows with such an intense heat, that aided by the tropical showers, the earth is clad with a hothouse growth of plants and shrubs; nor are her grander moods unrevealed to man, for towering crag and rugged mountain hem in the meandering river, and the soft lights of sunset play amidst their gloomy rocks and sheltered ravines, while the noonday clouds cast passing shadows on the lovely scene; anon, amidst the thunder of the storm and the vivid flashes of the lightning, the God of Nature reveals Himself, while all the latent forces of destruction seem let loose in the howling, whistling wind, the dashing wave, and the fierce battling of the elements of the dreaded typhoon.

The Chinese have been worshippers of Nature for centuries and millenniums, both in the literal and figurative sense of the term: long before we in the West awoke to her wild charms and sylvan beauties; ages before the ponderous Dr. Johnson saw nothing to admire in the wild Hebrides and the rugged mountains of Scotia, the Chinese had sung the praises of similar scenes in their native land; 'Chinese poets manifest a passionate love of nature thousands of years before Scott or Wordsworth.' A suggestion, a reference, a line, or a word points to some aspect of nature, such as—

'The white clouds fly across the scene,'

to find its response in the next line of—

'The distant hills are clothed in green,'

while others will revel in some descriptive piece of solitary scenes.

But, unfortunately, much Chinese poetry is incapable of translation: it loses its essence in the transfer into another and barbarian speech, and becomes tame prose and prosy at the best. As the wild flowers which adorn the hill-sides in this land, with their bright pinks and rich crimsons, soberer mauves and clear pure whites, when gathered by the enthusiastic botanist and treated by his careful hands with the greatest tenderness, fade and wither, lose their fresh bloom and bright tints, turn to a uniform brown and black, and smell musty and dry; so the flowers of Chinese poetry lose their freshness and beauty—the sparkle of wit and the point of allusion are lost to unappreciative Western ears, the rhyme and rhythm are gone, and they are interesting alone to the sinologist's ear. Occasionally, however, by a happy chance, the brightness and sparkle of a ballad or song are retained, or even improved upon, as in Stent's or Giles's translations.

The Chinese language lends itself readily to the poetic art—harsh consonantal sounds are wanting, and the combination of consonants and vowels is often musical. Though largely monosyllabic, the diphthongs give a somewhat dissyllabic character to many of the words. The cadence and modulation required are to be found in the tones of the Chinese language, and every word takes the place occupied by a metrical foot in our Western poetry.

Poetry

'In the hands of an accomplished writer, the Chinese language is capable of a condensed picturesqueness and vigour such as can be rendered into no foreign language less ideographic in its mode of writing, unless by means of wordy paraphrases. Each character in its (often numerous) component parts carries a wealth of imagery to the sense, and whole series of metaphors are embodied in a single epithet. A language of this kind lends itself especially to the description of the scenery, and the most superficial analysis of Chinese poetry reveals the fact that the productions which are most applauded in this branch of literature consist simply of elaborate word-painting whose beauty resides rather in the medium of expression than in the author's thought. Hence is happens that when odes, renowned for centuries among Chinese readers, are transposed into the naked languages of Europe, it is found that their charm has vanished, as the petals of a flower are dropped from the insignificant and sober coloured fruit.'

As Giles puts it they are:—

> 'Strains that to alien harps can ne'er belong,
> Thy gems shine purer in their native bed.'

One of the classical works of the Chinese, the Shi King [*Shih ching*], (500 B.C.) is a collection of ancient songs, etc. 'The bulk of these curious vestiges of antiquity . . . do not rise beyond the most primitive simplicity, and their style and language, without the minute commentary, would often be unintelligible.'

Here is one translated by Dr. Martin:—

A speck upon your ivory fan
  You soon may wipe away;
But stains upon the heart or tongue
  Remain, alas! for aye.

Another put into English verse by Mr. Jennings:—

BRIDAL SONG.

Ho, graceful little peach tree
  Brightly thy blossoms bloom!
Go, maiden, to thy husband;
  Adorn his hall, his room.

Ho, graceful little peach tree
  Thy fruit abundant fall!
Go, maiden, to thy husband;
  Adorn his room, his hall.

Ho, graceful little peach tree
  With foliage far and wide!
Go, maiden, to thy husband
  His household well to guide.

The reader is referred for further specimens of these 300 Odes to the Shi King, or Book of Odes, itself. It has been well said by Professor von der Gabelentz, 'that in this whole collection of Odes . . . there is not a line to be found which may not be read aloud without any hesitation in the most prudish society.'

Epics and pastorals are not found in Chinese poetry; but almost every other description is to be seen, as well as poetic effusions of a character unknown in the West, such as proclamations by the magistrates in rhyme.

It is very extraordinary to find an Edgar Allan Poe in Chinese literature, 200 B.C. The Chinese prototype was an eminent statesman, Kia Yi [Chia I] by name, who was also 'no mean poet.'

A CHINESE 'RAVEN.'

THE FU-NIAO, OR BIRD OF FATE.

'Twas in the month of chill November,
As I can very well remember,
In dismal, gloomy, crumbling halls,
Betwixt moss-covered, reeking walls,
An exiled poet lay—

On his bed of straw reclining,
Half despairing, half repining;
When athwart the window sill,
Flew in a bird of omen ill,
And seemed inclined to stay.

To my book of occult learning,
Suddenly I thought of turning,
All the mystery to know,
Of that shameless owl or crow,
That would not go away.

'Wherever such a bird shall enter,
'Tis sure some power above has sent her,
(So said the mystic book), to show,
The human dweller forth must go,'——
But *where* it did not say.

Then anxiously the bird addressing,
And my ignorance confessing,
'Gentle bird, in mercy deign
The will of fate to me explain,
Where *is* my future way?'

It raised its head as if 'twere seeking
To answer me by simply speaking,
Then folded up its sable wing,
Nor did it utter anything,
But breathed a 'Well-a-day!'

More eloquent than any diction,
That simple sigh produced conviction,
Furnishing to me the key
Of the awful mystery
That on my spirit lay.

'Fortune's wheel is ever turning,
To human eye there's no discerning
Weal or woe in any state;
Wisdom is to bide your fate;'
This is what it seemed to say,
By that simple 'Well-a-day.'

A poem of great repute among native scholars is 'The Dissipation of Sorrows [or "Falling into Trouble"]' written by Ch'ü Yüan (332-295 B.C.), whose untimely end is commemorated by the annual Dragon Boat Festival (See Article under that heading).

Here is a husbandman's song as rendered by Prof. Giles:—

Work, work—from the rising sun
Till sunset comes and the day is done:
  I plough the sod
  And harrow the clod,
And meat and drink both come to me,
So what care I for the powers that be.

Here is a little ode addressed by 'Su Wu to his wife on setting out on an embassy to the Court of the Grand Khan of Tartary,' 100 B.C. The English is from the rendering by Dr. Martin:—

Twin trees whose boughs together twine,
  Two birds that guard one nest,
We'll soon be far asunder torn,
  As sunrise from the West.

Hearts knit in childhood's innocence,
  Long bound in Hymen's ties;
One goes to distant battle-fields,
  One sits at home and sighs.

Like carrier bird, though seas divide
  I'll seek my lonely mate;
But if afar I find a grave,
  You'll mourn my hapless fate.

To us the future's all unknown,
  In memory seek relief;
Come, touch the cords you know so well,
  And let them soothe our grief.

Poetry flourished most in the T'ang dynasty (A.D. 618-907) in the ninth and tenth centuries, which have been described as the Augustan age in China of peotry and letters. 'The collected poems of the . . . T'ang dynasty have been published by Imperial authority in nine hundred volumes.' Among the most celebrated poets of this time is Li T'ai-po (A.D. 705-62), an anacreontic poet whose adventures are famous, as well as his sonnets. His works were published in thirty volumes. He attained high government distinction, but was drowned, falling overboard from a boat when under the influence of his favourite wines. He is thus described by one writer: 'the best known of China's countless host of lyric poets, famous for his exquisite imagery, his wealth of words, his telling allusions to the past, and for the musical cadence of his verse.'

Dr. Edkins describes Li T'ai-po's characteristics as a poet, as follows:—

'This poet is fond of deep passion, fear and pathos. All his power is devoted to the production of these sentiments in the reader's mind. He loves quick transitions, and one touch is enough for one thought. Another thought crowds after it, and then a third . . . Burns collected old songs, and infused them with the fire of his genius. That class of Western poets, of whom Burns is a shining example, would be the fit companions of Li T'ai-po, whose poems are often filled up with lines gathered from the wide range of early-song literature. . . . Li T'ai-po had a consciousness of power, and this made him careless in regard to rules. He uses short lines whenever he pleases, and it is often hard to punctuate his lines. His nation admires him so much, that when he is irregular in the choice of his words and the length of his lines, they still praise him. His genius was intuitive. No one took less time than he to write. No one made such leaps from one subject to another as he did. This recklessness was a great aid to him, because he did not need to take time to polish his style and smooth down his roughnesses. He vaulted over difficulties and expected his reader to follow him, without asking: Why this leap? or, Where is my master intending to go? He left the reader to fill the gap, and he himself always wrote brilliant sentences, and dealt in the pathetic and the sublime. All faults are readily forgiven if a writer can do this, for there is nothing that readers so much delight in as in having the tender sentiments of the heart stirred from their depths. Our poet wrote verses as he travelled, and his poems are a running comment on his visits to various localities in his native country.' The manner in which he was able 'to find in the rounds of nature the interpreter of his thoughts, and to throw himself into nature. . . . is proof of his high character as a poet. Here he seems to resemble Wordsworth, who, with Coleridge, passionately loved every wild and sublime scene in nature, but was not less moved by quiet landscapes. His heart was open to every suggestion that could be made to spring from wheat-field, grove or sunset glory. . . . But he greatly exceeds Wordsworth in popularity, having a whole nation at his feet, and there is to the present time no diminution of his fame.'

Of him, it has been said that he was 'without doubt the greatest of Chinese lyric poets.' One of the emperors said of him that 'a god had become incarnate in his person.'

We give a few specimens of Li T'ai-po put into English, first an impromptu which shows his early genius, being produced at the age of ten:—

TO A FIREFLY.

Rain cannot quench thy lantern's light,
Wind makes it shine more brightly bright;
Oh why not fly to heaven afar,
And twinkle near the moon—a star!

A VISIT TO THE CLEAR COLD FOUNTAIN.

Alas, that day should lose itself in night!
I love this fount so clear, so passing cool;
The western glow pursues its waters' flow:
The wavelets symbolise my silent thoughts,
And murmur forth a wordless hymn of praise.
I watch the moon among the clouds so grand,
The waving pines, athwart the sky so tall
Anon do blend their rustling with my song.

A VISIT TO THE RAPIDS OF THE WHITE RIVER.

I cross the stream just as it starts to life,
From man and all his deeds afar I roam.
The isles are clad in nature's living hues,
And set in scenes of sweetest beauty rare.
The deep-blue sky is mirrored in the stream,
Whose broad expanse reflects the passing clouds.
I watch them as they sail away to sea,
My leisured mind next wanders where the stream
Is full of fish that dart adown its course,
The setting sun doth end my day-long songs,
By silv'ry moon-lit rays I hie me home
To where my humble cot a-field doth lie.

THE POET.

You ask what my soul does away in the sky,
I inwardly smile, but I cannot reply;
Like the peach-blossom carried away by the stream,
I soar to a world of which you cannot dream.

Here is a short lyric translated by Dr. Martin which he describes as 'characterised by simplicity of expression and naturalness of sentiment, rather than by strength and elevation':—

A SOLDIER'S WIFE TO HER HUSBAND.

'Twas many a year ago,
  How I recall the day!
When you, my own true love,
  Came first with me to play.

A little child was I;
  My head a mass of curls;
I gathered daisies sweet,
  Along with other girls.

You rode a bamboo horse,
  And deemed yourself a knight,
With paper helm and shield
  And wooden sword bedight.

Thus we together grew,
  And we together played—
Yourself a giddy boy,
  And I a thoughtless maid.

At fourteen I was wed;
  And, if one called my name,
As quick as lightning flash
  The crimson blushes came.

'Twas not till we had passed
  A year of married life
My heart was knit to yours,
  In joy to be your wife.

Another year, alas!
  And you had joined your chief;
While I was left at home,
  In solitary grief.

When victory crowns your arms,
  And I your triumph learn,
What bliss for me to fly
  To welcome your return.

Tu Fu (A.D. 712-70) was another poet of the T'ang, and one of some distinction, who has been described as 'one of China's greatest men in poetic genius.' The Chinese rank him 'as second only to Li T'ai-po.' 'He lived in the eighth century, dying of hunger in A.D. 768 [or 770] . . . in a temple in which he had been compelled to take refuge.' We give some specimens of Tu Fu's poetry:—

IN ABSENCE.

White gleam the gulls across the darkling tide,
  On the green hills the red flowers seem to burn;
Alas! I see another spring has died......
  When will it come—the day of my return?

The Chinaman's ardent desire to return to his native land, dead or alive, though due to a very great extent to the cult of ancestral worship and all the customs that group themselves round this central idea, setting and crystallising into a rigid system through the course of long ages—though his wish to return is apparently almost entirely based on this; may it not be that underneath the frost of ice-bound custom, frozen stiff in the bonds of conventional expression, there yet flows the natural love of home which the ordinary Celestial is unable or unwilling to give utterance to (perhaps because the deepest feelings are silent), but which wells up from the heart of the poet? Other selections might be made which express this longing in stronger language than the above.

THE DESERTED WIFE.

Once fair beyond the fairest dame on earth,
Within the mountain dell I live perdue;
And scion of a virtuous house I am,
Though shrubs and trees are now my sole support.
Our troubles came within the walls amain:
Not long ago my brothers met their end.
Their rank was high. Alas! it mattered not;
For e'en their stiff, cold clay was lost to us.
I care not for the present age, no charms
It hath for me. Life flickers like a wick:
A passing breath blows all our joys away.
A new fair wife, as fair as clearest jade,
Is now my husband's love in place of me.
The libertine hath turned away from me.
Th'acacia knows the hour to close its leaves,
The turtle-dove without its mate doth pine;
He only sees the new wife's witching smile,
He heeds not how his former love doth weep.
Upon the mountain top the rill is clear;
But at its foot the stream is muddy, thick.
My maids go out to sell my lustrous pearls;
And with a wisp they mend the patchèd roof.
I pluck the wayside flowers, but wear them not;
And then I gather cones from off the firs.
My broidered sleeve is thin for gusty winds,
As morn and eve I lean my pensive form
Against the tall bamboos with drooping sprays.

Another name to be mentioned is that of Han Yü (A.D. 768-824) 'foremost among the statesmen, philosophers, and poets of the T'ang dynasty, and one of the most venerated names in Chinese literature.' From his pen are the following:—

THE WOUNDED FALCON.

Within a ditch beyond my wall
I saw a falcon headlong fall.
Bedaubed with mud and racked with pain,
It beat its wings to rise, in vain;
While little boys, threw tiles and stones,
Eager to break the wretch's bones.

O bird, methinks thy life of late
Hath amply justified this fate!
Thy sole delight to kill and steal,
And then exultingly to wheel,
Now sailing in the clear blue sky,
Now on the wild gale sweeping by,
Scorning thy kind of less degree
As all unfit to mate with thee.
But mark how fortune's wheel goes 'round;
A pellet lays thee on the ground,
Sore stricken at some vital part,—
And where is then thy pride of heart?
What's this to me?—I could not bear
To see the fallen one lying there.
I begged its life, and from the brook
Water to wash its wounds I took.
Fed it with bits of fish by day,
At night from foxes kept away.
My care I knew would naught avail
For gratitude, that empty tale.
And so this bird would crouch and hide
Till want its stimulus applied;
And I, with no reward to hope,
Allowed its callousness full scope.
Last eve the bird showed signs of rage,
With health renewed, and beat its cage.
To-day it forced a passage through,
And took its leave, without adieu.
Good luck hath saved thee, not desert;
Beware, O bird, of further hurt;
Beware the archer's deadly tools!—
'Tis hard to escape the shafts of fools—
Nor e'er forget the chastening ditch
That found thee poor, and left thee rich.

HUMANITY.

Oh spare the busy morning fly!
Spare the mosquitoes of the night!
And if their wicked trade they ply
Let a partition stop their flight.
Their span is brief from birth to death;
Like you they bite their little day;
And then with autumn's earliest breath,
Like you too they are swept away.

The poetic taste is present in what seems to many a Westerner the unpoetic Chinese, and the English poet's love for May, or for Springtime, as especially in the case of Chaucer, Langland, and other poets of the Middle Ages, was not wanting in their Chinese brethren.

TASTE.

The landscape which the poet loves is that of early May.
When budding greenness half concealed enwraps each willow spray.

That beautiful embroidery the days of summer yield,
Appeals to every bumpkin who may take his walk afield.

YANG CHÜ YÜAN (8th & 9th Cent. A.D.).

Another famous poet was Su Tung-p'o (A.D. 1036-1101), of the Sung dynasty, which has been described as the Elizabethan age of Chinese letters. His poems are contained in one hundred and fifteen volumes. He was 'an official of remarkable talents, a statesman, poet, essayist, and man of letters,' who spent many of his latter years under a cloud, being banished to the south of the empire, a punishment he partly brought on himself, owing to his satire. Of him it has been written that, 'under his hands, the language of which China is so proud, may be said to have reached perfection of finish, of art concealed. In subtlety of reasoning, in the lucid expressions of abstractions, such as in English too often elude the faculty of the tongue, Su Tung-p'o is an unrivalled master.' We give also a few specimens of Su Tung-p'o's poetry. The first we extract from 'Gems of Chinese Literature.'

THE SONG OF THE CRANES.

Away! away! My birds, fly westwards now,
To wheel on high and gaze on all below;
To swoop together, pinions closed, to earth;
To soar aloft once more among the clouds;
To wander all day long in sedgy vale;
To gather duckweed in the stony marsh.
Come back! Come back! Beneath the lengthening shades,
Your serge-clad master stands, guitar in hand.
'Tis he that feeds you from his slender store:
Come back! Come back! Nor linger in the west.

Su Tung-p'o's eulogies of departed worthies are fine specimens of writing. He 'never failed to clothe his thoughts in beautiful language,' 'with great facility he collects all the meritorious deeds of his heroes, and places them in a very strong light; he then makes some allusion to the ages long gone by, and traces their resemblances to celebrated personages, concluding with his own panegyrics. These eloquent pieces were not only printed but also engraved on solid stone.' We give one of these eulogistic inscriptions.

IN MEMORIAM: HAN WÊNG KUNG.[1]

High mounted on the dragon's back he rode
A loft to where the dazzling cloudlands lie;

[1] The same as Han Yü.

The glory of the sky he grasped amain;
The splendour of the stars, his sparkling robe.
The zephyrs' breath him gently wafted on
From earth's domain up to the throne of God.
On earth his practised hand swept off the chaff,
The husks which hid the grains of truth from sight.
He roamed the wide world o'er from pole to pole,
From east to west his rays so bright were shed,
And nature's darkness clothed upon with light.
The third amidst the three of genius great,[1]
His rivals strove in vain to reach his height,
And panted, dazzled by his glory's glare.
Buddha was cursed by him; his priests denounced.
His sovereign's wrath was poured upon his head.
He journeyed to the distant South afar:
And passed upon his way the grave of Shun;
And wept o'er the daughters of ancient Yao.
The spirit of the deep before him went,
And stilled the noisy waves' tumultuous roar,
As 'twere a lamb the monster fierce he drove.[2]
In heaven above the golden harps were still,
And God was sad, and called him to his place
Beside His throne. I now salute him there,
And now present to him my off'rings poor;
The red lichee, the yellow plantain fruit.
Alas! Why lingered he not then on earth;
But passed so soon away with flowing locks
Into the future world the great unknown?

Here are two other pieces from Su Tung-p'o, translated by Dyer Ball:—

THE STORK.

In my garden dwells a stork,
  Docile, coming at a word.
'Hark! I call thee; come my stork,'
  But the proud and lofty bird
Stood stock still with look askance
  Though he heard me, heeding not,
Head aslant with sidelong glance.
  'Is it true thou knowest a lot?'
Said I then, 'Like Ka Yi's owl,
  Dost thou wish to talk with me?
Art thou then no earth-born fowl?
  Heaven thou'st left this world to see?
Canst thy soul with mine commune?
  Tell me, tell me, now I pray.'
Soon his thoughts with mine attune,
  And I heard him slowly say:
'Lone I stand above the throng
  (Not for long below I stay).
Perched on legs so tall and long,—

---

[1] The other two were Tu Fu and Li T'ai-p'o.

[2] Referring to the crocodile which he is said to have driven away.

Listen as you will or nay,—
Spare my frame and spare my need;
'Am I then a toy for thee?
Yield I not though thus you plead.'
Solemn, silent, still stood he.
'Wilt thou baulk me thus?' I cried,
'Drive him up to where I sit.'
Stately stood he then, nor sighed
Gesture none, nor spake, as fit
Sovereign man be served by brute.
Flung I then some grains of corn,
Guerdon fit for birds, and fruit;
But he moved not, as one born
Thrones to fill, not meekly stand
At my whim, and at my call
Pick up food from my right hand.
'Oaf,' he cried, and off he went.
'Bird, Oh! Bird, Oh!' then I thought
'Why? Oh! why, thus am I sent—
Sent to office, it not sought?
Yet I stay, nor try to go,
As thou goest when thou would'st.
Always to myself a foe.
Would I could as, oh! thou could'st
Leave my master's side and fly;
Hie me from my office cares.
By the brooklet then I'd lie,
Catch the finny tribes with snares.
In my cottage in the wood,
Read my books and dream and think,
Love o'er all the past to brood
And the present with it link.'

KUO LUN: A FORGOTTEN KNIGHT OF OLD.

A warrior bold,
In Ho Sai old;
Alas! but no one knows him now.
Athwart the stream
Where waters gleam,
He sees the boats through billows plough.

His piebald steed
Has run to weed;
Nor bears his master to the fray.
His lance so long,
In arm so strong,
A beam, nor man, nor elf could stay.

And now the toll,
This noble soul,
Must count the livelong summer's day.
And fret himself,
With hoarded pelf;
And wear his wasted life away.

From Western lands
Our beaten bands
Return; but he our land could save;
He'd mount his steed,
And take the lead
Before ten thousand troopers brave.

And foemen die,
As arrows fly,
And sheath themselves in quiv'ring flesh.
Then from my car
I'll watch afar
My hero's valour rise afresh.

Sentiment is not wanting in the Chinese, though suppressed to a great extent by their customs and manners:—

MY NEIGHBOUR.

When the Bear athwart was lying,
And the night was just on dying,
And the moon was all but gone,
How my thoughts did ramble on!

Then a sound of music breaks
From a lute that some one wakes,
And I know that it is she,
The sweet maid next door to me.

And as the strains steal o'er me
Her moth-eyebrows rise before me
And I feel a gentle thrill
That her fingers must be chill.

But doors and locks between us
So effectually screen us
That I hasten from the street
And in dreamland pray to meet.

Poetry is held in high estimation by the Chinese. Capping verses is a pastime of scholars; and at the competitive examinations the candidates had to try their hands at the composition of verse. This mechanical art they had first to learn at school, as, with us, boys waste their time at public schools and colleges in composing Latin verse. The consequence is that all the educated men were verse-makers—we cannot call them poets. To this cause is partly due the mechanical structure of much of Chinese poetry, but it is also due to the peculiarities of its construction. Nor is the art of poetry confined to men. China has had her burning Sapphos who loved and sang, and her lyric Corinnas. The lower classes are passionately fond of the recitations of ballads by men who go from house to house for the purpose.

We append a piece translated by the late G. C. Stent:—

CHANG LIANG'S FLUTE.

'Twas night—the tired soldiers were peacefully sleeping,
The low hum of voices was hushed in repose;
The sentries in silence a strict watch were keeping,
'Gainst surprise, or a sudden attack of their foes.

When a mellow note on the night air came stealing,
So soothingly over the senses it fell—
So touchingly sweet—so soft and appealing,
Like the musical tones of an aërial bell.

Now rising, now falling—now fuller and clearer—
Now liquidly soft—now a low wailing cry—
Now the cadences seem floating nearer and nearer—
Now dying away in a whispering sigh.

Then a burst of sweet music so plaintively thrilling,
Was caught up by the echoes who sang the refrains
In their many-toned voices—the atmosphere filling
With a chorus of dulcet mysterious strains.

The sleepers arouse and with beating hearts listen,
In their dreams they had heard that weird music before;
It touches each heart—with tears their eyes glisten,
For it tells them of those they may never see more.

In fancy those notes to their childhood's days brought them,
To those far-away scenes they had not seen for years;
To those who had loved them, had reared them and taught them,
And the eyes of those stern men became wet with tears.

Bright visions of home through their mem'ries come thronging,
Panorama-like passing in front of their view;
They were *home-sick*, no power could withstand that strange longing,
The longer they listened, the more home-sick they grew.

Whence came those sweet sounds? Who the unseen musician
That breathes out his soul which floats on the night-breeze
In melodious sighs—in strains so elysian—
As to soften the hearts of rude soldiers like these?

Each looked at the other, but no word was spoken,
The music insensibly tempting them on:
They *must* return home:—ere the daylight had broken,
The enemy looked, and behold, they were gone!

There's a magic in music—a witchery in it,
Indescribable either with tongue or with pen;
The flute of *Chang-Liang*, in that one little minute,
Had stolen the courage of eight thousand men.

References.—Davis, *The Poetry of the Chinese* (gives an account of the structure of Chinese poetry, with examples of poems); *China Review*, i, 32 (Su Tung-p'o); iv, 46; vi; ix; xii, 31; xvii, 35 (Li T'ai-po); etc.; Stent, *The Jade Chaplet; Entombed Alive, and other Verses; Chinese Repository*, xi, 132; Martin, *Chinese Legends and other Poems;* Giles, *Chinese Poetry in English Verse;* Legge, *Chinese Classics*, Vol. iv; *d'Hervey Saint Denys, Poésies Modernes;* Budd, *Chinese Poems;* Allen, *The Book of Chinese Poetry;* Wayley, *A Hundred and Seventy Chinese Poems; The Temple and other Poems; More Translations from the Chinese;* Waddell, *Lyrics from the Chinese*; Schott, *Chinese Poetry;* Fletcher, *Gems of Chinese Poetry;* Gauthier (trans.), *Chinese Lyrics from the Book of Jade;* Toussaint, *La Flûte de Jade.*

POPULATION.—Much has been written on the population of China, and various surmises and estimates have been made of the number of the inhabitants.

If it is well-nigh impossible to find the exact number of any one people in our Western lands, much more difficult is it in the East. There are several things that militate against an exact return being made of the population in a country like China. To begin with, the object of taking a census in this land has often been simply for the purposes of revenue, and infants and young children as well as very aged men were not included, though, at the present day, a fuller method of taking the census is in vogue. Then again, people who do not have the fullest confidence in their rulers are not willing to give the fullest returns to these rulers. And, again, anyone who knows anything about Orientals can readily understand how difficult it is for them, brought up with such a want of precision in their habits of thought and expression, to realise the importance of contributing their quota of statistics with the care and exactitude they demand. Notwithstanding all these things, the different censuses taken by the Chinese in the past are worthy, on the whole, in many instances, of a considerable amount of credence; and, in fact, form the only returns available for the entire empire. Compared with estimates made by foreigners, they are tolerably trustworthy.

There have been considerable fluctuations in the number of people in China at different periods: wars, rebellions, famines, and floods have exerted a most depopulating effect on large tracts of country, and have acted as a drag on the continual tendency to increase.

Notwithstanding all these minimising effects, during the centuries and millenniums the empire has been in existence, the inhabitants have increased from some 21,000,000 to the 380,000,000 which some eighteen or nineteen years ago formed what was considered on the best native data to be the present population of this immense country.

Had it not been for the gigantic T'ái-p'ing rebellion its population might now have been reckoned at 450,000,000. To this figure of 380,000,000 must be added the population of

Manchuria, and of the vast regions of Ili and Tibet, which may be anything from 15,000,000 to 27,000,000 more: so that, perhaps, all things considered, the round sum of 400,000,000 may be taken as that of the whole of the dominions comprising China; it is, probably, not much less, and by latest figures seems to be considerably more than that — some 420,000,000 (but *v. infra*).

As to the population to the square mile, it is said the Eighteen [now Twenty-two] Provinces have an aggregate of 1,348,870 square miles, though this statement is not supposed to be accurate (*v. infra*). With a population of say 380,000,000, and the total of square miles given above, there would be nearly 282 Chinese to a square mile of their territory (but *v. infra*). But the density of the population differs greatly in different parts of the country: 'that of the nine eastern provinces in and near the Great Plain, comprising 502,192 square miles, or two-fifths of the whole' is nearly three times that of 'the nine southern and western provinces constituting the other three-fifths' of the erstwhile Eighteen Provinces of China. 'The surface and fertility of the country in these two portions differ so greatly as to lead one to look for results like these.' Taking the countries of France, Germany, Great Britain, Italy, Holland, Spain, Japan, and Bengal for comparison with China, we find that only two of them—Great Britain and Bengal—exceed the density of the average population of China 'taken as a whole, while none of them come up to the average of the eastern provinces,' but fall far short of it. From an estimate of one district in Shantung, it was calculated that in that spot the population to the square mile was 531, 'or considerably above the average of the Kingdom of Belgium (the most densely populated country in Europe), which had in A.D. 1873 an average of only 462 to the square mile.' In another spot the actual number of families in each village was taken, so far as the number was known to the natives, the number of individuals to the family being reckoned as five, though it is often far larger than that. This other spot gave a result of 2,129 to the square mile.

'So far as appearances go, there are thousands of square miles in Southern and Central Chili, Western and South-Western Shantung and Northern Honan, where the villages are as thick as in this one tract, the contents of which we are thus able approximately to compute. But for the plain of North China as a whole, it is probable that it would be found more reasonable to estimate 300 persons to the square mile for the more sparsely settled districts, and from 1,000 to 1,500 for the more thickly settled regions. In any case, a vivid impression is thus gained of the enormous number of human beings crowded into these fertile and historic plains, and also of the almost insuperable difficulties in the way of an exact knowledge of the facts of the true "census."'

The province boasting the largest population is Chihli; the inhabitants are 32,571,000 in number; from this they dwindle down to between five or six and a half millions in each of the two provinces of Kansu and Kuangsi; and in Chinese Turkestan to one million and a third.

'Living as the Chinese, Hindus, Japanese, and other Asiatics do, chiefly upon vegetables, the country can hardly be said to maintain more than one-half or one-third as many people on a square mile as it might do, if their energies were developed to the same extent with those of the English or Belgians.' 'The social and political causes which tend to multiply the inhabitants are numerous and powerful. The failure of male posterity to continue the succession of the family, and worship at the tombs of parents, is considered by all classes as one of the most afflictive misfortunes of life; the laws allow unlimited facilities of adoption, and secure the rights of those taken into the family in this way. The custom of betrothing children, and the obligation society imposes, when arrived at maturity, to fulfil the contracts entered into by their parents, acts favourably to the establishment of families and the nurture of children, and restricts polygamy. Parents desire children for a support in old age, as there is no legal or benevolent provision for aged poverty, and public opinion stigmatises the man who allows his aged or infirm parents to suffer when he can help them. The law requires the owners of domestic slaves to provide husbands for their females, and prohibits the involuntary or forcible separation of husband and wife, or parents and children, when the latter are of tender age. All these causes and influences tend to increase population, and equalise the consumption and use of property more, perhaps, than in any other land. The custom of families remaining together tends to the same result.' 'The reasons just given why the Chinese desire posterity are not all those which have favoured national increase. The uninterrupted peace which the country enjoyed between the years 1700 and 1850 operated greatly to develop its resources. Every encouragement has been given to all classes to multiply and to fill the land. Polygamy, slavery, and prostitution, three social evils which check increase, have been circumscribed in their effects. Early betrothment and poverty do much to prevent the first; the female slaves can be and are usually married; while public prostitution is reduced by a separation of the sexes and early marriages. No fear of overpassing the supply of food restrains the people from rearing families, though the Emperor Ch'ien Lung issued a proclamation, in 1793, calling upon all ranks of his subjects to economise the gifts of heaven, lest, erelong, the people exceed the means of subsistence.'

'The density of the population of China differs greatly in different parts of the country. The great plain of N. China, the Yangtzŭ basin, the Ssŭch'uan tableland, the coast region, and the Si-kiang delta, are the most densely populated parts of the country.

Population

The provinces which have the largest population are Ssŭ-ch'uan, Shantung, Hupei, Kuangtung, Kiangsi, Kiangsu, Anhui, and Fukien [?]. In each of these eight Provinces, the number of inhabitants ranges from 60 [? 30] to 20 millions. The Provinces which are least populated are Yünnan, Chêkiang[?], Kansu, Shensi, and Kueichou. Here the number of inhabitants in each Province dwindles from 12 down to 7 millions' (but *v. infra*).

According to the census of 1902, the population of China amounted to 428,710,000 inhabitants, distributed over 4,278,352 square miles, as follows:

	Population.	*Square miles.*
China Proper (18 provinces)	410,000,000	1,532,800
Manchuria	8,500,000	363,700
Mongolia	2,580,000	1,367,953
Chinese Turkestan	1,200,000	550,579
Tibet	6,430,000	463,320
	428,710,000	4,278,352

The following table shows the estimates according to the official census of 1910, and includes the provinces of Shêngking, Kirin, Heilungkiang, and Chinese Turkestan (or the New Dominion), which now raises the number of Provinces to twenty-two:

Province.	*Area in square miles.*	*Population.*	*Inhabitants per sq. mile.*
Anhui	54,826	17,300,000	315.
Chêkiang	36,680	17,000,000	463.
Chihli	115,830	32,571,000	281.
Fukien	46,332	13,100,000	282.
Honan	67,954	25,600,000	376.
Hunan	83,398	23,500,000	282.
Hupei	71,428	24,900,000	348.
Kansu	125,483	5,000,000	40.
Kiangsi	69,498	14,500,000	208.
Kiangsu	38,610	17,300,000	448.
Kuangsi	77,220	6,500,000	84.
Kuangtung	100,000	27,700,000	277.
Kueichou	67,182	11,300,000	168.
Shansi	81,853	10,000,000	122.
Shantung	55,984	28,600,000	528.
Shensi	75,290	8,800,000	116.
Ssŭch'uan	218,533	23,000,000	105.
Yünnan	146,714	8,500,000	58.
Shêngking Kirin	363,700	14,917,000	41.
Heilunkiang Chinese Turkestan	550,579	1,350,000	2.
	2,447,094	331,438,000	136.

It has been stated that 'from 1651 down to the present time the figures of the returns vary with such extraordinary rapidity, so unlike anything noted in the earlier enumerations, that they must be regarded as fanciful.' The maximum and minimum figures for recent years, including Manchuria, Mongolia, Sinkiang, and Tibet, are 544,760,000 and 289,510,000.

It may be interesting here to remark that 'recent statistics (1901) give the population of the British Empire as 400,000,000.'

To give some idea that the brain can easily grasp of what a population like that of China means, it may be stated that 'it would take over twelve years for the population of China to walk by a given spot, one person passing each second.'

References.—Williams, *Middle Kingdom*, i. 258-88; *Chinese Recorder*, January, 1893, etc.; Parker, *China*, pp. 191-294; *China: Past and Present*, Chap. ii; Werner, *Descriptive Sociology—Chinese;* Richard, *Comprehensive Geography;* Morse, *Trade and Administration of the Chinese Empire; British Consular Report on the Trade of Kiangsi*, 1903; *Report of the Smithsonian Institute*, 1904, pp. 659-76; *Journal of the Royal Statistical Society*, vol. lxii, Part I.

PORCELAIN AND POTTERY.—The word porcelain, it is said, was introduced by the Portuguese (in the sixteenth century), who first brought such ware in any quantity to Europe from China. The name 'refers to the exterior appearance resembling the shining white of the *Cypræa* or porcelain shell (Portuguese *porcellana*)' 'so called from its carved upper surface being supposed to resemble the rounded back of a *porcella*, or little hog.'

Marco Polo saw the manufacture of it in China in A.D. 1280, and informs us that it was sent all over the world, and evidences of this early trade in it are found in India, Persia, Egypt, Malayia, and Zanzibar.

'The Chinese from the most ancient times have cultivated the art of welding clay, and they claim the invention of the potter's wheel, like most of the great nations of antiquity.' Like the origin of many Chinese things, the invention of porcelain is shrouded in mists of antiquity, and no certain date can be assigned to it. 'It is generally ascribed by them to the ancient Emperor Shun, who is supposed to have reigned during the third millennium B.C.; but some attribute it to his more famous predecessor, Huang Ti, who is given a Director of Pottery,' among the officers of his court.

In a book published in the Chou dynasty, 'there is a short section on pottery, in which the processes of fashioning on the wheel and moulding are distinguished. Among the productions we read of coffins, sacrificial wine-jars, and altar dishes, cooking utensils and measures, all made no doubt of simple pottery, and it is doubted whether this was ever covered by a vitreous glaze—the employment of which is so ancient in Egypt. Different potteries are mentioned in the Wei and following dynasties.' 'The manufacture of articles of pottery for domestic use then was known to the Chinese as early as B.C. 1700.'

This is one view, but, unfortunately, the term used for porcelain in Chinese is one of those words which every language possesses, namely, words which have changed from their original significance—this word, having first been applied to all pottery, affords no sure clue for fixing dates as to the original production of porcelain. St. Julien places the invention as early as between B.C. 185 and A.D. 83. 'It has been objected to this, with justice, that the Chinese statements on which he bases his theory, are, like those of Marco Polo, very superficial and indefinite, and most probably relate to quite other clay-wares.' Therefore, the statement that porcelain was produced in the Han dynasty (206 B.C. to A.D. 220) is unfortunately incapable of proof. Were it possible to discover any indubitable production of that epoch, all doubt might be set at rest, but at present it is not known that any exist. Were archæology more of a science among the Chinese than it is, some hope might be entertained that this would be the case. Some have been sceptical enough to suppose that it was not known 'long, if at all, before the Ming dynasty (A.D. 1368),' while again, on the other hand, it is asserted that porcelain was invented when, in the middle of the ninth century, certain pieces were produced of a white colour, like ivory, and giving a clear sound when struck.

It is supposed that the Chinese endeavoured to imitate ivory in their whole porcelain, which is known in France as *blanc de Chine*.

The cups, produced at Ta-i, of this ware, have had their praises sung by Tu Fu, a poet of the T'ang dynasty (see POETRY). The decorations were effected before the baking, and were not elaborate, being confined to such subjects as fish, flowers, etc.

'This was the time when the cobalt decorations under glaze were first employed, which from then till now have played such an important part in the ornamentation of Chinese porcelain, especially for domestic use among the Chinese themselves.'

'At whatever period or by whatever happy chain of circumstances porcelain was invented, we have tangible evidence that the Chinese potters produced wonderful works at a very early period of our era, and have gone on producing them up to our own day. Speaking on this subject, M. Phillippe Burty remarks:—"The Chinese ceramists succeeded to a marvellous degree in their manipulation of porcelain; in their hands it became a truly magical substitute, receiving every form and gradation of colour that caprice could dictate. In their porcelain productions we have proof that the decorative taste and imitative skill of the Chinese artists are almost faultless. You see, for instance, a carp and carplings with descended gills slipping amongst a clump of reeds; a garden rat devouring a peach; a toad crawling up the involuted root of a bamboo; or a beautiful water-lily in full bloom, forming a cup, of which the tea-pot is so constructed that not only have its concentric, movable rings been carved out of a solid mass, but they revolve upon each other, causing us to wonder how adherence could have been prevented in the firing. The origin of the great superiority of the Oriental potters is, that they start, in nearly all instances, with a more or less free or capricious imitation of some natural production; and the article, peculiar in outline and treatment, will, however, readily suggest to the mind some affinity with the real object. All the productions of the natural world, and, indeed, the beings and monsters with which they crowd the supernatural world, are alike resorted to for fresh inspiration; and their habits of careful observation of nature supply them with countless delicate subtleties."'

'It is unquestionably to this great appreciation for, and unremitting study of the works of nature that we are indebted for the marvellous variety of works produced by the artists of China and Japan. No one can review a collection of Oriental porcelain without being struck with the masterly handling of form and colour it displays. In flower vases, perfume burners, and water vessels, every shape that the mineral, animal, and vegetable kingdoms could suggest has been adopted, and the colouring studiously imitated.' 'The early porcelain of the Chinese appears to have been remarkable for its form, and the beauty of its material. At one time, it is probable, white porcelain only was made; but it is evident that at a very early date the art of covering the pieces with a rich coloured enamel had been invented, and also the mode of producing the crackled appearance in the enamel discovered. Many varieties of white porcelain have been produced by the Chinese potters, and some are of great beauty, not only on account of the perfection of their paste, but likewise from the tasteful manner in which they are decorated. Some have flowers or conventional designs, carefully modelled in relief, while others have designs so engraved that they are visible only when held up to the light.'

'The old Chinese potters do not appear to have worked in grooves, or styles, beyond what a limited demand on the part of their patrons rendered necessary. No sooner had some experiment or accident introduced a new colour, combination of colours, or some peculiar surface decorations, than articles were produced suitable for the display of the same; and we are of opinion that in many cases such essays were never repeated, until attempted in the recent periods of imitation to meet the demand of European collectors. There are, no doubt, such things as unique Chinese porcelain in the cabinets of collectors in China and Europe, and it is highly probable that they have been unique from the day of their fabrication. Many specimens, now so much prized, may have been spoiled pieces in the eyes of their makers, and, not turning out to be what was desired or expected at the time, were never repeated. This argument applies to the highly curious, and at times extravagant specimens of the splashed or enamelled ware which are met with, and which carry with them evidences, in their distorted shapes and slag-vitrification, of their accidental decoration.'

The paste of porcelain-ware is prepared usually from two ingredients; these are finely mixed and pulverised; the one is known as *kaolin,* so called, it is said, from a hill to the east of the Chinese Imperial Porcelain manufactory, King-teh-chin [Ching-tê Chên], *kao* meaning high in Chinese, and *lin* (properly *ling*), a ridge, or high peak, 'which hill, however, does not yield the product of decomposition which we in Europe call *kaolin* ("porcelain or pipe-clay"), but a phyllite, whose chemical composition resembles that of the Swedish Hälleflinta (?)'; the other ingredient consists of some mineral 'rich in silicic acid, the so-called flux—usually felspar or pegmatite, porcelain stone (. . . these porcelain stones, which are wanting in our porcelain industry, contribute greatly to that of China and Japan), or some other white-burning form of quartz is used in the finer ceramics.' The proportion of the two and the degree of heat in firing depend upon whether porcelain or faïence is to be produced. Some of the colours which were used by the Chinese six hundred years ago to decorate their porcelain 'we are not yet able to imitate.'

The white Ting porcelain would appear to have been in existence during the seventh century. The Ting-Yao was made at Ting Chau in Chihli, whence its name. It was also known as white Ting porcelain from its colour being mostly of a brilliant white. It is probably one of the oldest kinds. There were three varieties of it—plain, smooth, and that having ornaments in relief. The sign of its being genuine is that of having marks like tears on it. It is to be distinguished from the creamy white of another species of porcelain, the kien-yiu made in Fukien. Commencing with the beginning of the seventh century, it seems probable that the manufacture of porcelain 'began to flourish in various parts of the Empire.' Of the different kinds produced during the T'ang dynasty, no specimens, as far as is known, are extant, but those of the Sung period are to be found in the market; these, from their age, command a good price. Unfortunately, however, many of this period were of such a delicate make as to be unfitted for survival during the centuries that have intervened. Some, especially those of an indestructible nature, have been handed down; the others are only known from the descriptions given of them in books. Amongst the best of them were the Ch'ên and Ju kinds. The Ju was of a pale 'bluish-green.'

At the same time as the Ta-i cups, mentioned above, were produced at Yüeh-chou for the Emperor's use, the class of porcelain styled Pi-sê was made, the colour described as 'a hidden colour' has given rise to some discussion as to the precise meaning. So fine was certain porcelain made here that it was described 'as transparent as jade and so resonant as to be used in sets of twelve to play tunes upon.' But few, if any, specimens of these ancient examples of ceramic art are in existence. No kind of painted decoration appears to have been used before the Sung dynasty, as writers are silent about anything of the kind.

The tenth century is marked by progress, both in the perfected operations and in the art of the decorator, which felt the influence of Buddhism bringing Indian art in its train, and improving the taste of the natives. The Chinese describe the porcelain produced at this epoch (A.D. 960-1280) in the following terms:—'Blue as the sky, bright as a mirror, fragile as paper, and sonorous as a plaque of jade-stone; they were lustrous and of a charming delicacy; the fineness of the crackle and the purity of the colour are distinguishing features of them: they eclipse by their beauty all preceding porcelains.' They were called by the highly poetical name of *yu kwo tien tsing* [*yü kuo t'ien ch'ing*], 'cerulean blue in the cloud rifts as it appears after the showers'; they were highly valued, and even broken fragments were treasured up as jewels would be, and formed into ornaments. We shall find that later on these were imitated with good effect.

Amongst numerous manufactories opened then throughout the empire, that of King-teh-chin [Chin-tê Chên] in Kiangsi, established in A.D. 1004, takes pre-eminence. This manufactory still 'supplies all the fine porcelain used in the country.' It was almost wholly destroyed by the T'ái-p'ing rebellion. A million workmen were employed there previous to that event, when they were dispersed, either joining the insurgent ranks or dying of want; but according to latest accounts these manufactories are resuming their prosperity; five hundred kilns, it is said, are constantly burning

'And bird-like poise on balanced wing
Above the town of King-te-tching,
A burning town or seeming so,—
Three thousand furnaces that glow
Incessantly, and fill the air
With smoke uprising, gyre on gyre,
And painted by the lurid glare,
Of jets and flashes of red fire.'

—LONGFELLOW, *Kéramos*.

Rapid progress was made in the art, and at the end of the tenth century coloured enamel was first applied on the pieces baked in biscuit, and various colours, such as several shades of violet and blue, as well as yellow were used. Buddhist and Taoist figures, flowers, and the Chinese written characters, which have for so many centuries lent themselves readily to decorative art, all were employed, as well as fillets in relief.

The Chün is another of the oldest kinds of porcelain. The factories for its production were in existence in the tenth century, at the beginning of the Sung dynasty. One native work says:—

'The highest quality consists of pieces having a colour as red as cinnabar, and as green as onion leaves and kingfisher's plumage, . . . and the purple brown colour of the skin of an egg-plant fruit, or of pieces red like rouge, green like onion leaves and kingfisher's plumage, and purple like ink-black,—these three colours being pure and not in the slightest degree changed during the firing.'

Kuan-yao, mandarin porcelain, as its name implies, was produced in certain Government factories.

Dr. Hirth describes the specimen seen by him as 'of a peculiar brownish green, a sort of bronze colour,' called by the Chinese ch'á-ch'ing, tea green, but the varieties described as of the Sung dynasty are 'white and thin like paper'; 'another was very much the same as *Ko-Yau* [the ancient céladon crackle] with three gradations in colour constituting their value, viz.: (1) a pale *ch'ing*-green; (2) a fallow white; and (3) grey. The *Ko-ku-yao-lun* speaks of *ch'ing*-green playing into pale scarlet, the shades being very different though; the best ones having the "crab's claw pattern," and "a red brim with an iron coloured bottom."'

Another division of porcelains was the *Lung-ch'üan-yau* and *Ko-yau*, 'the real old céladons' described as of 'a sea-green mixed with bluish or greyish tints, neither a decided green nor anything like blue.' The qualities it possesses are 'thickness, heaviness, rich olive or sea-green enamel, white paste, and a . . . ferruginous ring on the bottom'—the paste, which was originally white, turned red in the fire. These were produced in the Sung and Yüan dynasties (A.D. 960 to 1368) and seem to have been carried by the current of mediæval Chinese trade into 'Arab possessions and other foreign countries.'

We quote from Gulland's work the following interesting account of crackle, that curious characteristic of many specimens of porcelains:—

'This [*crackle*], like the following class [céladon], consists of a glaze, white or coloured, generally covering a coarse paste resembling stoneware, which is sometimes of quite a red colour. Although now artificially produced, it is said originally, at an early period, to have been discovered by accident. Crackle, it is said by the Chinese, was known during the southern Sung dynasty (A.D. 1127-1280). There seems to be various ways of producing this effect, which appears in the main to have been caused by exposing the piece to a sudden drop in temperature, thus causing the glaze on the surface to contract faster than the paste or biscuit, and so break into sections, which, when baked become crackle. In these small cracks in the glaze, Indian ink or a red colour were sometimes rubbed, thus heightening the effect. The Chinese were so completely the masters of the process, that they could turn out at will crackle of any size, now known as large, medium, and small crackle, the latter being called by the French truité, from its resemblance to the scales of a trout.'

The crackled porcelain known as *tsui-k'i* in the thirteenth century, was also a product of this first or primitive period of the ceramic art in China. 'The beautiful coloured ground tints, chalcedony, dull violet, yellow and Turkish blue, so much valued by collectors, began to be used in the thirteenth century.'

The second period, the Hsüan Tê, comprises the reigns of Hsüan Tê, Chêng T'ung, and Ching T'ai, lasting from A.D. 1426 to 1465. Ceramic art was still in a formative stage at the commencement of this period, notwithstanding the advances made in the last period. Its characteristic type was the decoration of blue flowers under the glaze. This blue was the su-ni-po, and took after the firing a pale blue. This porcelain is highly esteemed by the Chinese. M. Paléologue describes the pieces thus produced in the following terms:—'Elles ont, en effet, un charme doux de coloris et de composition, une pureté de ton, une delicatesse d'aspect qui n'ont jamais été surpassés.'

Red was also put into the enamel for the first time before the glaze was applied, being 'painted on the paste so that the red designs shone through the glaze, dazzling the eyes. It is described as obtained by powdering rubies from the West, but this is impossible.' It was a copper silicate; and the red for painting over the glaze was prepared from sulphate of iron and carbonate of lead. 'This mixture produced a fine coral red,' and, to procure a deep enough red, cornelian was employed.

Amongst other work produced at this time may be mentioned some pottery known by the Portuguese as *boccaro*: the fine kind of this ware was formed into teapots and other objects, while the coarser sort was employed as ornamentation on walls, it being used in the famous Porcelain Tower of Nanking, which was built A.D. 1415-30.

The reign of Hsüan Tê 'is celebrated for its porcelain, which is held [by some] to be the finest produced during the Ming dynasty: every production was of the highest artistic value. Cups were made of a bright red or of sky blue. The surface on some cups was granulated like the skin of a fowl or the peel of the sweet orange. There were vases crackled like glass, or with veins as red as the blood of the eel, rivalling in beauty the porcelain of Jou-chou and the Kuan-yao. The bowls decorated with crickets were of extraordinary beauty.'

'The most flourishing period of Chinese porcelain making, however, like that of most other branches of its art industry, was during the Ming dynasty, especially in the second half of the fifteenth century. During this period its manufacture occupied a new position, owing to the employment of many coloured decorations upon glaze after the article had been baked. This was a new development, and was called "the five-coloured porcelain," because more than one colour was employed, but the number was not necessarily confined to five. We shall refer again to these under the K'ang-Hsi period. With this advance the artist proceeded to more difficult subjects for decorative purposes, such as the human figure, historical, legendary, and religious scenes and landscapes. Porcelains in which green predominated were particularly prized.' 'Gold and gold purple were not used till the year 1690.'

The third epoch, that of Ch'êng Hua, includes the reigns of Hung Chih, Chêng Tê, Chia-Ching, and Lung Ch'ing, and lasted from A.D. 1465 to 1573. Blue porcelain was still manufactured, less pure materials being employed in place of the su-ni-po.

At the same time advances are noticeable in other points, such as arrangements of colours and skill in designs, etc. An improved quality of cobalt seems to have been used (A.D. 1521) and a new dark blue was produced; the objects made in it commanded a high price.

'In the Ch'êng Hua period [that of the reign of that sovereign A.D. 1465-87] lived several celebrated artists. One made jars which he decorated on the upper part with the *moutan* [tree peony] in flower, and below a hen and chickens full of life and movement. There were also cups with handles, painted with grapes; wine cups, ornamented with figures and the lotus; others as thin as paper, painted with blue flowers; others with locusts. The enamelled were especially esteemed. The blue on the ware of this period is inferior to the Hsüan Tê, but its paintings and colours surpass any that preceded them.'

Gilding, which was first employed during the Yüan dynasty, was brought to perfection during the reign of Ch'êng Hua (A.D. 1465-89).

'In the Chia Ching period (A.D. 1522-66), the dark blue vases were alone in favour.'

Immense quantities of porcelain were ordered to be manufactured for Imperial purposes, in A.D. 1571: no less a number than 105,770 pairs of different kinds of articles, and in 1583 as many as 96,000 pieces, but remonstrances were made by the censors, and in some instances, at all events, the amounts were reduced. This wholesale ordering and consequent enormous production flooded the streets of Peking with porcelain of that date, 'where a street-hawker may [might] be seen with sweetmeats piled on dishes over a yard in diameter, or ladling iced syrup out of Ming bowls, and there is [was] hardly a butcher's shop without a large Ming jar.'

The fourth period is styled the Wan Li period, though it covers the reigns of T'ai Ch'ang, T'ien Ch'i, and Ch'ung Chêng of the Ming dynasty, as well as that of Shun Chih of the Ts'ing, or Ch'ing dynasty, and lasted from A.D. 1573 to 1662.

Green and the 'five coloured porcelains' were the chief products. Two drawbacks were experienced at this time: one was the giving out of the clay employed for the fine porcelain; and the other was the cessation of the importation of the blue—the Mohammedan blue as the Chinese termed it—just, as a century before, the su-ni-po blue had failed. To meet the new condition of affairs and to hide the greyish character of the only products procurable with the materials at their disposal, a rich brilliancy of enamel was employed, and the importance attached to the outer surface hid the inferior products below.

During the reign of Lung Ch'ing, the last Emperor of the last period, as well as during that of Wan Li, the first of the period now under review, 'the Imperial manufactory produced pieces which showed the greatest artistic skill.'

The latter Emperor 'had cups for the altar as white as jade, and of extraordinary beauty. The glaze of the vases was creamy, "like a layer of congealed fat." The surface was granulated, as if covered with grains of millet, or like the flesh of a fowl; some are said to appear as if covered with buds of the azalea, and others shagreened like the peel of an orange.' During this same reign there 'lived a celebrated artist of the name of Au, who excelled in poetry, writing, and painting. . . . He withdrew from the world and retired to a manufactory where he produced, in secret, porcelain, remarkable alike for its quality and the beauty of its colours. Among these the most sought after were large cups, ornamented with red clouds, brilliant as vermilion, and egg-shell cups, of dazzling whiteness, and so fine that some of them did not weigh more than twelve grains.' 'The white pieces of the Wan Li' reign 'were very celebrated.' 'The manufacture of porcelain continued at the King-teh-chin Imperial Potteries under the present dynasty (the Ts'ing, or Manchu Tartar, A.D. 1664) with equal success.' During Shun Chíh's reign, however, as well as the latter part of the Ming dynasty, 'there seems to have been a great decline in the manufacture of fine porcelain; therefore little artistic work is found during this period.'

'The Monochrome porcelain of the Ming and Ch'iên Lung period, the ruby, *sang-de-bœuf*, Imperial yellow, crushed strawberry, peach-bloom, moonlight blue, camellia-green, apple-green, and other rare enamel porcelains of old China always have been, and still remain, inimitable.

'The secret of the Chinese coloured enamel porcelain vases' consisted in 'the art of using vitrifiable enamels, which required the second firing over the glaze at a low temperature.'

The fifth epoch is that of the reign of the Emperor K'ang Hsi (A.D. 1662-1723), in which the art of the manufacture of porcelain attained its greatest eminence, as M. Paléologue says about it:—

'C'est la belle époque de la porcelaine. Les procédés se sont perfectionnés, les ressources des céramistes et des peintres sont plus riches; d'autre part, les formes sont plus heureuses et mieux pondérées, la composition plus savante et plus variée; les colorations ont une harmonie douce ou une puissance d'éclat que les pières anciennes, avaient rarement réalisés.'

Mr. Gulland calls attention to the fact that:—

K'ang Hsi 'seems to have been a very able man, fond of art and science, willing moreover to avail himself of the assistance of the Jesuit missionaries, and it was probably their aid that led, as Sir A. W. Franks says, "to many improvements in the porcelain manufacture and to the introduction of several new colours." It is said that two Jesuit lay-brothers were at this time employed at the royal factories of King-te-chin.'

Ysbranti Ides, ambassador to China from Peter the Great in A.D. 1692, speaking of the porcelain of the country, says:—

'The finest, richest, and most valuable china is not exported, or at least very rarely, particularly a yellow ware, which is destined for the Imperial use, and is prohibited to all other persons. They have a kind of crimson ware [probably the *sang-de-bœuf*], which is very fine and dear, because great quantities of it are spoiled in the baking. They have another sort, of a shining white, purfled with red, which is produced by blowing the colour through a gauze, so that both the inside and outside are equally beautified with crimson no bigger than pins' points; and this must be very expensive, since for one piece that succeeds a hundred are spoiled. They have a kind of china purfled in the same manner with gold. Also a kind which looks like mosaic work, or as if it had been cracked in a thausand places and set together again without cement. There is another kind of violet-coloured china, with patterns composed of green specks, which are made by blowing the colours through a frame pierced with holes; and this operation succeeds so rarely, that a very small basin is worth two or three hundred pounds. They have a kind of white china, excessively thin, with blue fishes painted on the material between the coats of varnish, so that they are invisible except when the cup is full of liquor.'

The most of the porcelain of this period may be grouped under the four heads of white porcelain, green, rose, and coloured glaze.

This white porcelain was made in Te-hoa [Tê-hua] in the Fukien province; the Chinese call it *peh-tsz* [*pai tz'ŭ*] that is 'white porcelain.' It 'is very lustrous and polished,' but it is very thick. It was used with good effect in the construction of statuettes of Buddhist idols. M. Paléologue thus describes one that he saw:—

'Certaines statuettes faites de cette pâte ont un charme singulier; une déesse Kouan-yin, que nous vîmes à Pékin, avait, dans son immobilité hiératique, une délicatesse de formes, une grâce pensive, une douceur de physionomie et une suavité d'expression que n'ont jamais dépassées les plus beaux bronzes sacrés.'

The white is not confined to one shade, but runs through all the varieties.

With regard to the green porcelain, two schools sprang up: one, while following the models of antiquity, introduced a grace and beauty and an improvement in style wanting in the old works. Flowers, sprays of trees, grasses, flights of birds, beetles, and dragon-flies, all lent their aid to the decorations of these objects, and the love of nature, so inherent in the Chinese, had full scope, while in combination with the dominant green, appeared red and touches of yellow, blue, and violet; the other school, while paying less attention to colouring, had able brushes and skilful hands, which were employed in depicting 'historical or religious scenes, full of life and movement,' but unfortunately an Imperial edict in A.D. 1677 put an end to the production of such scenes.

Several new colours were discovered about A.D. 1680. The rose-colour had different shades of 'exquisite sweetness.' The commonest subjects employed were flowers and birds, amongst the former, the lotus and chrysanthemum were favourites. This kind of porcelain, however, was further perfected in the following period. Of the remaining porcelains, of this epoch, the céladons and the flambés are to be particularly noticed. With regard to the former they were not first produced during this epoch, but some manufactured now were perfect gems in brilliancy. 'Turquoise-blue, sea-green, and a suspicion of violet' is one description of what céladons are, and all these tints are often met blended in one.

'Gulland describes céladon as '"single coloured glazes," known as "whole" or "self" coloured pieces. To lovers of colour this is probably the most interesting class. It was much appreciated by the collectors of last century, and still brings long prices. Of all the various descriptions, it is, perhaps, the one that lent itself best to French skill in ormolu mounting. The distinctive feature of this class is that the coloured glaze was applied to the "paste," and thus exposed to the extreme heat of the first firing. This often caused the glaze to change colour, hence the variegated hues to be met with, known to the French as *flambé*, and to us as "splashed." In course of time the

Chinese, no doubt, could produce this effect pretty well at will, and perhaps sometimes used glazes of more than one colour to obtain their end. The word céladon is unfortunately used in two senses—as a general term, where the substance of which the vessel is made is hid from view by the coloured glaze with which it is covered; in the other, as indicating that particular range of greens known by this name. . . . In no class do we find greater variety or brilliancy of colouring than in this; nearly every colour and shade thereof is to be met with.'

The list of shades, thirty-four in number, given on page 139 of Mr. Gulland's book (first edition), will show what a variety of colours are to be met with in this interesting division of porcelain.

We must again quote M. Paléologue, who is so in love with his subject that he would make an enthusiast of almost any one. He says of these céladons:—

'Les céladons dits "bleu de ciel après la pluie," en souvenir des porcelaines, de Che-tsong dont ils étaient l'imitation, nous offrent les plus délicats spécimens de ce genre. Mais les céladons ornés de dessins gravés ou imprimés en relief dans la pâte du fond sont encore plus séduisants peut-être par les effets de modelé et de coloration que réalise la couverte accumulée sur le décor: la fluidité des teintes, la sorte d'ombre dont elles s'enveloppent par places n'ont jamais pu être reproduites dans les porcelains de fabrication européenne. Notons enfin, dans le même groupe céramique les céladons bleu empois dont la couverte, préparée au cobalt, a un aspect lumineux, semi-translucide.'

Che-tsong named above is Shih Tsung, or Chia Ching.

'Céladon porcelain is manufactured by applying the green glaze to the ware before it has been fired at all; by this means, the peculiar depth of surface is given to it, the burning process thoroughly incorporating the glaze into the body.'

The spotted céladons which were the rage in France in the eighteenth century were also the products of this period.

There were some beautiful specimens of flambés at this time: one is described as resembling precious stones blended together; but it is in the next period that these works were the most finished.

During K'ang Hsi's reign crackled china was brought to perfection (see also *supra*):—

'Perhaps the most characteristic ware produced by the Chinese potters is the crackled. Many varieties of this ware exist. but they are all produced by the same means, namely, the unequal contraction of the glaze and the body. There is little doubt that the first crackled piece was the result of an accident, or what might as properly be called a blunder; the glaze had not been of the usual quality, and in cooling, contracted so much more than the body, that it split into a thousand pieces.'

The crackle glaze is highly esteemed by the Chinese, and in their hands has been made in many varieties quite decorative. There is a style of large crackle with the intervening space filled with a fine crackle, the fine cracks never passing beyond the enclosing lines of the coarse. There are other specimens with zones of fine crackle, with intervening spaces without crackle, ornamented with markings to suit the fancy of the artist. But one of the most decorative crackles is produced by making the fissures of the first glaze as wide as possible, and then rubbing colouring matter into the interstices; the piece being again fired to fix these colours, after which a smooth transparent enamel is applied over all, often giving the piece the appearance of mosaic work.'

Amongst other noteworthy productions of this epoch are to be named the *tsang*, the enamel of which was serpent green, gold yellow, pale yellow, violet or light green; and this variety took all the colours of bronze.

A very curious coloration is produced on vases by the workman blowing the colouring, 'after the base colour' was applied, which was matter 'usually of a reddish brown' colour, 'through a piece of gauze fastened at the end of a tube of bamboo.' 'This metallic colouring strikes in a spray, and, after firing, the specimen has a fine metallic lustre not very unlike what is known as gold stone.' Some vases have been subjected to this mode of treatment more than once, receiving a miniature shower of different coloured rain. This kind of decoration is known by the name of soufflé, and the finest of it was produced during the K'ang Hsi period.

Quite a variety of these decorations were produced, one of which at least is very beautiful. By some means the colouring material was 'blown from the tube' and lighted 'upon the piece in small bubbles, some remaining as such, while most of them' broke and formed 'rings, many of the rings, in turn,' broke 'at their lower side, the colours running a little, often giving a beautiful agate appearance, in fact, such pieces are called agate specimens. Soufflé porcelain was also made in the Ch'ien Lung period, but not of so fine a quality' as that just described.

'The best blacks were made in the reign of K'ang Hsi, and with their fine enamel some specimens are quite beautiful; the black is produced by uranium oxide. Plain reds were not much used, it seems, during the time of K'ang Hsi, but a lovely tint was employed in connection with other colours in the decorations. . . . What is known as the five-coloured decoration, was introduced during the Ming dynasty, but brought to its greatest degree of perfection during the time of K'ang Hsi. The five colours are red, yellow, green, blue, and black. These are all produced from metallic oxides or minerals; no other colouring matter will stand the high degree of heat required to produce underglaze decoration. In using these colours in combination it required a great amount of experience and manipulative skill, and so the range of colours must necessarily be limited, for all material used must be of a character to fuse, on the one hand, before the fusing point of the paste, and, on the other, not evaporate and spoil the shade required, while enduring the heat necessary for the underglaze firing; and then again, some colours are much more refractory than others; no two fuse at the same temperature. Therefore the most refractory colours must in all cases be applied first, then the piece fired to the fusing point of this colour; then, for the shading of this colour, more must be added to points requiring the heavy shades, and fused again until this colour and its tints are satisfactory; then the next refractory colour is applied in the same manner, fired to the fusing point, and so on until the last and most easily fusible colour has been applied, whereupon over all an enamel is fused which is less refractory than any colour. The fine specimens of the five colours have probably been fired from fifteen to twenty times. Then if the piece comes out at the last finished, without break, crack, warp, or the colours having run, and possessing all the brilliancy and shading desired, the piece is valuable; many are spoiled during this fiery ordeal. With very limited exceptions, the finest artists that ever existed in China lived during the K'ang Hsi period.' During this 'time Chinese porcelain was brought to its highest degree of perfection and artistic beauty, with perhaps the exception of the beautiful Ming greens. The exquisite *sang-de-bœuf* when perfect is of great beauty. To describe its brilliancy would be most difficult, yet, if attempted, one might say, take a plain, undecorated porcelain vase and immerse it in the freshest arterial blood, and, while dripping, fix the colour with a deep transparent enamel. While one piece is nearly perfect, a thousand are more or less spoiled in the firing. They come out of the kiln from the beautiful colour above described to a much darker red, often badly blotched; from the latter they run through all the shades until lost in an ash colour tinged with only the slighest blush of red. There is a beautiful blue which seems engraved into a creamy paste over which a liquid enamel is fixed, the enamel often being crackled, and also an exquisite white described as having the appearance of congealed fat. Perhaps with these exceptions, no Ming porcelain or decorations equal, in quality of paste, beauty of form, purity of enamel, brilliancy and happy combination of colours, and high artistic decorative skill, the porcelain made during the reign of K'ang Hsi.'

'With the exception of the beautiful blue and the creamy tinted white (often crackled), which belong to the Ming dynasty —these specimens are often rare—all other fine old blue and white china belongs to the K'ang Hsi period, often inaccurately marked Ming in Chinese characters on the bottom. Many of the specimens are very beautiful; they have a clear white ground and brilliant blue ornamentation, and have this virtue, that in whatever light, and from whatever distance the colour of the piece is seen, it is always blue. These blues are formed from cobalt oxide. All the fine yellow with a deep transparent enamel which lights up with a delightful brilliancy, was also made in the K'ang Hsi period; these are often decorated with a lively green, usually with a dragon,' a lion, 'or some mythical creature.'

'Yellow is the present Imperial colour. The turquoise variety was probably first made during this reign, and is among the most highly prized. The colour is derived from a copper oxide, and like the *sang-de-bœuf* of the Mings, it seems to have been somewhat incorporated with the glaze, which is translucent, and, if it can be properly expressed in words, would appear as though you were looking into a depth of brilliant colour; when pure it is very beautiful, and has the property of retaining its character in artificial light. Green was the Imperial colour of the Mings, and was brought to a fair degree of perfection, having a jade-like brilliancy; in fact real jade was reduced to a fine powder and incorporated with ordinary colouring material, chromic oxide, so that in firing, a good jade green was the result. These fine greens were well preserved, but very much improved upon in true jade brilliancy during the K'ang Hsi period. The plain green of the Mings called *truité* is highly prized.'

'Towards the end of the reign of K'ang Hsi a new style of decoration appears in the "famille rose" distinguished by a totally different tone of colouring, with its prevailing half tints and broken colours, including pink and ruby enamel derived from gold.'

This kind of porcelain attained its highest excellence during the following reign, that of Yung Chêng.

The sixth epoch is that of Yung Chêng and Ch'ien Lung, A.D. 1723 to 1796. The beginning of the period marked a new era in ceramic art, and the modern school may be said to have then begun. The artists of the modern school as regards the processes and technical skill are the equals of their predecessors, 'in some points they are even superior to them,' as for example in the egg-shell china produced by them; but at the same time there are distinguishable the causes which resulted in the decadence of the Chinese porcelain later on, for the ornament is overdone, the tendency being to cover the whole surface with arabesques, branches, and foliage.

During Yung Chêng's reign, a period of thirteen years, 'the ceramic art declined, and very little fine work was done.' Yet what was done is of interest. There is a fine egg-shell specimen, very thin, often decorated. Some pieces were of the colour of an egg, and as shining as silver. Others were imitations of the ancient wares, especially the five-coloured Ming, true to the colour of the porcelain, which is of a greyish white, but rather coarse in appearance, instead of a clear white, like the K'ang Hsi work. The colours used and the style of decoration are so exact that it would be difficult to detect the difference, were it not, perhaps, for the introduction of certain fruits, the peach and pomegranate, for instance, and the peculiar modified shapes of at least the beakers.

'The "hawthorn pattern"—really the "prunus," which produces its blossoms before its leaves—is to be met with bearing very early date-marks; but it is now generally held that none are genuine previous to Yung Chêng (1723-36), "and the finest and most prized examples were probably made about this date."

In Ch'ien Lung's reign many varieties of china were produced, but 'the principal types may be ranged into four classes':—the rose porcelain, egg-shell, flambé, and that for exportation. We have already mentioned the first under the reigns of K'ang Hsi and Yung Chêng; the egg-shell porcelain which reached its perfection about A.D. 1732 was a most delicate production; the flambé porcelain presents the appearance of a play of colours and, as we have already said, of precious stones fused together; currents of air were rapidly directed on the vase while it was in the fire; the Chinese have taken their inspiration as colourists of porcelain from nature, whenever rich tones or a play of colours presented themselves; the porcelain for exportation consists of several varieties, such as Mandarin porcelain, where these functionaries figure as the decorations. This porcelain is sent to Europe, and is very inferior in character. There is also porcelain with Persian designs, for the Persian market; and Chinese porcelain, exported and decorated in Europe.

During the reign of Ch'ien Lung (A.D. 1736-96) 'the ceramic art was brought nearly to the perfection it was left in by K'ang Hsi; yet altogether it fell a little short. However, one artist, named T'ang, decorating in the five colours, surpassed all others, before or since, in his wonderful skill in drawing flowers and fruit. He represented fruit in all stages; sometimes the skin of the ripe grape or peach was broken, the juice running on to the stand or table on which it was lying; even a broken bit of this porcelain is of value, while a perfect specimen brings a large price.' The Ch'ien Lung as a whole is a little below the K'ang Hsi 'in quality and decoration. There is, however, a great variety of plain reds called dragon's blood; many are fine specimens, but not equal to the *sang-de-bœuf* of the Mings, though perhaps better than any K'ang Hsi red. Also a good turquoise was made, but inferior to the brilliant K'ang Hsi specimens, and a very large variety of flambés. Probably this flambé was at first an accident caused by one colour running into another; evidently the cue was taken from the accident, and a high degree of ornamentation followed. One of the most charming effects, perhaps, is produced by streaks of whitish blue running down over a dragon's blood red, giving one something of the sensation of delightful minor music. The other coloured enamels are almost countless, an endless variety being obtained by admixture of different tints, by dusting, sprinkling, and splashing. These enamels appear to be laid upon the porcelain while it is in a biscuit state, and fused at a great heat; the firing does really the artist's duty in works of this class, changing the tints, combining and running them over into one another in the most fantastic manner. It seems every attempt was made in mixing colours to produce new tints; even new colours were discovered among them, violet and pink. It is probable that the endeavour to get a greater variety of tints by mixing colours was one reason of the Ch'ien Lung decoration falling short in brilliancy of the simple colour decoration of K'ang Hsi.'

The seventh epoch is the present period commencing with A.D. 1796. It has seen no progress, but is rather a period of decadence, partly due to the excessive demand for Chinese porcelain of any style or character in the West, and also to the diminution of artistic judgment in China.

The marks on Chinese porcelain chiefly consist of a date, or rather the name of the reign of an Emperor, or that of a dynasty, or both combined. The workman's name does not appear, as 'in China every piece passes through the hands of a number of workmen, each contributing his fraction to the decoration. All these decorators being other than the potter who turned the vase, and the workman who glazed it, no single specimen could be marked as the work of one man.'

With the Chinese collector, age is the first requisite, and beauty is a secondary consideration. It is amusing to hear the laughter from a Chinese crowd round a stall when the Chinese stall-keeper offers an ugly ginger jar of a hideous glaring yellow, with the recommendation of its age, and the European despises it for its ugliness.

The following epitomised account of some of the principal points of interest with regard to porcelain is from the pen of the late Dr. Edkins:—

The history of Chinese porcelain goes back to the year B.C. 189, as to the farthest limit; but it is best to say it dates from B.C. 185 to A.D. 87, and the locality was Hwai Ning Hien in Honan, an arrondissement enclosed within the walls of the prefectural city Ch'en Chow. This place is nearly one hundred English miles south-south-east of Kai-fong-fu. Here the first porcelain was made, while in Europe it was in A.D. 1706 that hard porcelain was first made in Germany. The Portuguese had in A.D. 1518 brought Chinese porcelain to Europe, for they had then begun trading to China. In 1695 soft porcelain was first made in France, and in 1768 or 1770 the manufacture of hard porcelain was begun at Sèvres, near Paris. Stanislas Julien in his 'Translation of a Chinese History of Porcelain' gives these facts from Brongmart's 'Traites des Arts Céramiques.' He also observes that the discovery of a mode of manufacturing porcelain by the Chinese preceded that of Europe by about 1600 years. During the Han dynasty the progress of the ceramic art in China was slow, but it reappeared in the Wei period, A.D. 220 to 264, in the neighbourhood of Si-an-fu in Shensi and at Lo-yang in Honan. The residence of the court in those cities promoted the advance of the art at that time. A little later the blue porcelain of Wen-chow, south of Ningpo, was held in high estimation. This was in the Tsin dynasty, which reigned A.D. 265 to 419. The manufacture at King-te-chen in Kiangsi began about A.D. 583, in the Ch'ên dynasty, when Nanking was the capital for South China, while Loyang was the Northern metropolis, and was held by Tartar chiefs, who called their dynasty the Wei. The old glass-ware of China called *lieu-li,* a Sanscrit word introduced by the Buddhists, must indicate that Indian workmen came with the Buddhist priests.

There are from two to thirteen towns producing ceramic ware in fourteen out of the twenty-two provinces, but Ching-tê Chên (in Kiangsi), Tê-hua (in Fukien), and Shih-wan (in Kuangtung) are the most important centres, the two first being noted for their porcelain, the latter for its pottery. The following extracts, chiefly from the valuable report of Mr. W. J. Clennell, formerly H.B.M. Consul at Kiukiang, give the fullest information concerning the city and its industry.

'The industry was started at these places at an early period and the output steadily increased. There has been little change in the organisation of the works. Even now the work remains a hand industry, being carried on by small factories and household workers. Nearly all the numerous kilns in the Ching-tê Chên district, for instance, are owned and operated by separate individuals. Most of the clay workers do not have kilns themselves. The few manufacturing companies recently organised on a modern basis have not been very successful in their efforts at quantity production with the use of machinery.

The Ching-tê Chên kilns were started as the imperial porcelain works of the Sung Dynasty, and the city has developed into the most important porcelain center in China. The city has thus been famous since the eleventh century for this ware. It is said that its name was derived from that of Emperor Ching-tê, who is reputed to have founded the city in A.D. 1004. It is in the northeastern part of Kiangsi province, on the Peiho River, which here flows from north to south. It is thus about 65 miles across country south of the Yangtzŭ River.

Everything in the city belongs to, or depends upon, the porcelain industry. Even the houses are built of fragments of fire clay and broken porcelain. The river bank for miles is covered with a stratum of broken chinaware and waste from the kilns, which a Japanese company building an electric plant there recently reported to have found sixteen feet thick at the point where their work was being carried on. As one has observed, an industry employing hundreds of thousands of hands in a single city for 900 years does not remain localized without giving the vicinity a character of its own.

At present there are more than one hundred pottery kilns in the city, of which about thirty work the year around and the others a few months during the summer. During the busy season, when each kiln is employing from 100 to 200 men, and others are engaged in hauling, etc., the population of Ching-tê Chên rises to about 400,000, of which perhaps half are laborers who come in and live in rows of barrack-like sheds. Some years ago a British Consular officer, Mr. W. J. Clennell, wrote a description of the city which is as true to-day as when he visited it. He wrote:

"One passes along street after street where every shop is occupied by men, women, and children all engaged in the designing, moulding, painting, or distributing of pottery. Potters' sheds where the clay is mixed and moulded on the wheel, seem innumerable. The river bank is crowded for three miles by junks either landing material and fuel or shipping the finished product. Shops for the retail sale of the ware, though numerous, are less in evidence than might have been expected, and the wholesale trade, which in the hands of guilds, makes little display. Apart from the meeting halls of these guilds there are scarcely any buildings with any architectural pretension, but the guild halls are rich and elaborate structures.

"The kilns are fed exclusively with wood fuel. The transport of wood, about 2,000 tons a day, is a large industry in itself. For each firing the kilns are kept alight and fed with fuel for about 36 hours, when the fact that a sufficient heat has been attained is made known by the color of the smoke that issues from the chimney, changing from black to a bluish white. The kiln is then allowed to cool, and after another 36 hours or so the contents can be removed. All the kilns appear to be of much the same construction. They are built in an oval shape with thick walls, a clay or common brick outside and fireclay within, and are surmounted by chimneys of some 30 to 40 feet in height, 8 feet wide at the base, and tapering to 4 or 5 feet at the top.

"The bricks at the top of the chimneys are never laid to an even height. The roofs and chimneys of the kilns seemed to be flimsily constructed. They are pulled down and rebuilt at frequent intervals, generally, it would seem, every year. The furnace is fed through a door in front about 6 or 7 feet above the ground, and three men are kept occupied in throwing in the wood, which seems to be consumed at the rate of about 60 to 100 pounds a minute. Under this aperture is a draught for removal of ash. A little above the stokehole are two eyes, round panels of fireclay, which become white hot and apparently transparent, and from the condition and appearance of this the workmen are able to judge the temperature of the kiln.

"The porcelain and pottery made at Ching-tê Chên is composed of a mixture, in different proportions according to the quality or nature of the article desired, of two minerals, called respectively 'kaolintu' (kaolin) and 'paituntzŭ' (petuntse), with a small proportion—about one in a thousand—of 'shihkao' (gypsum) added. Kaolin is the hydrated silicate alumina decomposed, pounded in a mill, precipitated in a series of water-troughs, then dried and moulded in bricks. It is the necessary base of all their pottery. Petuntse is unhydrated silicate of alumina, also pulverized and pressed into bricks. It is fusible in the heat of the kiln, and when used in a sufficient proportion, its vitrification causes the resultant porcelain to be translucent.

"The higher the proportion of petuntse, the nearer is the porcelain to transparency, but a limit is fixed to the quantity that is possible to use by the fact that a vessel deficient in kaolin would lose its form. Much work, especially in the higher grades of ware, is, in fact, spoilt and wasted through this cause. Perfectly formed pieces are placed in the kiln, and then overheated, with the result that they come out damaged and partly melted out of shape.

"After being dried, and before firing, the pottery is washed over with a coating, more or less thick, of a glazing material formed of the powder of a third mineral, called 'yukuo'—also a silicate—mixed with the ashes of a ferm called 'lanchihui,' the vitrification in the heat of the furnace of this 'yukuo' gives the polished surface.

"Articles for which only or a few colors are required are painted before firing, as, for instance, the common blue and blue-and-white ware. This blue is obtained with mineral pig ment made from a greyish, almost black, substance, which seemed to be an ore of cobalt. Before firing it does not appear as a blue tint at all, but as a grey, the blue being due to a chemical change under the influence of heat. Several other colors also result from chemical action during firing. In some cases, as in the real and imitation 'sangdebœuf' ware, the coloring matter is mixed with the glaze, or is itself more or less fusible. The greater or less melting of the glaze or the color in these cases gives rise to a great variety of effects—or defects—some of them very beautiful, and all of them quite incalculable beforehand. Besides local and other Chinese colors, many are imported from Japan and some from Europe. Most of the colors are simply mixed with water, for instance, the common blue, and laid on with a brush, but some of the reds and a few others are mixed in the resin of a tree called 'fêngshu,' a name that seems to cover several varieties of maple.

"For polychrome work some or all of the coloring has to be deferred until after the piece has been fired. It is then laid on over the glaze, and, to judge from a sample, the colors are mixed with 'yukuo.' When the painting is complete, it is then refired, but not in a kiln. For this second firing a much smaller furnace is sufficient.

"Although stencil plates are in use for some of the coarser work and simpler patterns, all the painting and drawing of any delicacy is done by hand. The ware with transparent interstices, known in Kiukiang as 'rice pattern,' is made by cutting little holes in the unbaked paste and leaving them to be filled in the firing by the fusing and running of the glaze. The transparent parts are, in fact, pure 'yukuo.' Some of the stippling effects are the result of blowing the color upon the surface of the porcelain through a tube.

"The potter's wheel as seen at Ching-tê Chên, is an extremely simple and primitive arrangement. Under a low shed half-a-dozen workmen will be seen each seated by a plain round table that revolves on a rude wooden socket by means of the impulse that he gives it with a piece of stick or a simple treadle-and-rope arrangement. Taking a lump of clay in his hand, he places it on the middle of the table, and, with a few deft touches of the hand, moulds it as required. Simple bowls are made entirely at one table. More complicated pieces are made in parts, which are then carried in a tray to another shed, where a second workman finishes and fixes them together by the simple process of wetting their edges, superimposing them, giving them a few more turns of the wheel, paring off whatever clay may be in excess. Then they go a bit further along the line of sheds to the artists, who paint the pattern. Simple patterns are painted in the moulding shed, but much, and apparently all, the more delicate work is done in shops along the street, much of it by women.

"Besides several private establishments, the former Imperial kilns were visited. They are approached by a wide street or elongated square, called Yü-yao Ch'ang, with pottery shops on either side, and imposing 'pailous,' or tall arches, at both ends. At the northern end of this street is the entrance to the State establishment and the official residence of the superintendents. Behind this are the modelling sheds, differing in no important respect from others in the town. This is backed by a large mound or small hill, an accumulation of debris, overgrown by many large trees—in fact, quite a picturesque bit of garden in the midst of this rather murky town. Just beyond this hill are the kilns, two in number. They were not working—in fact, not entirely rebuilt so that the interior arrangement of the furnaces could be examined.

"Ching-tê Chên, though the second town of Kiangsi at all times, and the first when the kilns are busy, is not the capital of any administrative district. Two or three miles outside Ching-tê Chên, and hidden by some hills, is a large town of 20,000 or 30,000 people, called Litsun. This place also contains pottery kilns, the smoke of which was visible from the hill at the back of the Catholic Mission. That hill, by the way, commands an excellent general panorama of the whole town.

"The kaolin, petuntse, and yukuo used in the pottery works are obtained from a great number of districts in addition to the immediate neighborhood (Fouliang Hsien). Some come from over the Anhwei border, from Chimen, by road, and from Tungliu by junk via the Pangtzŭ and P'oyang Lake. Much more is quarried on the foot-hills of the Lushan near Nanking, where a large new quarry was started last year. Yet more comes from two places called Meichiang and Huangchinpu in the valley of the Kuanghsin River, a few miles below Anjen, and there may be other sources as well. At all or most of these places the pulverized rock is precipitated in troughs, and made into bricks for transport to Ching-tê Chên.

"It is not easy to form an estimate of the average output of the potteries. The chinaware that passes out through the Customs at Kiukiang for export by steamer, either to foreign countries or to Chinese ports, is but a small fraction, probably not above a sixth of the whole. Probably as much more goes out through Kiukiang, but not in the way of commerce through the Customs. Formerly the tribute porcelain which was forwarded to the Court by the Taotai, who was ex-officio head superintendent of the Imperial kilns, amounted to 800 tubs, each containing, perhaps, a hundredweight of fine porcelain. There are also the many articles bought retail and taken away as personal effects of travellers. In this way perhaps a third of the output leaves the province through Kiukiang. At least as much goes south by junk through Nanch'ang and up the Kan River. Canton being generally the ultimate destination. A great deal more goes by road to Chimên, 60 miles, and to Wuyüan, 45 miles, whence it is passed on to Hangchow, Soochow, Shanghai, etc., and some goes overland to Hukou, Pêntzŭ, or Tungliu for shipment by junk on the Yangtzŭ. People have the impression that Kiukiang is the port of shipment of Ching-tê Chên pottery, and are apt to infer from the figures in the Kiukiang trade returns that the business cannot be a very big one. But if the Kiukiang trade returns figures are multiplied, at least by six, and perhaps by seven or eight, so that the total is about £50,000 a year, the dimensions of the industry are seen to be more respectable. Even so, it is difficult to see how a population of several hundred thousand, with many more employed in carriage and distribution all over the Empire, live on the profits."

Examples of chinaware which have been preserved show that between pieces produced in the Ming dynasty, for instance, and those of recent generations the chief distinctions are in shape, color and design rather than in any great difference in quality of the material itself. During the latter part of the Manchu dynasty there was talk of the deterioration of the once exquisite art in China. The result of several recent exhibitions in which goods from China took part seems to disprove the idea.

Of modern manufactures, Chinese porcelains were awarded first places among many competitors at Brussels in 1910, at Toulon, France, in 1911, at Taisho, Japan, in 1914 and at the Panama-Pacific Exposition at San Francisco in 1915. This would seem to show that Chinese workmen turn out as high a grade of ceramic ware as is produced in any country, and thus about as good as any in the history of the world.

The domestic demand at the present, however, is mostly for cheaper grades for everyday use. The more elaborate varieties are seldom marketed or produced. The designs now being sold have undergone considerable change lately. The growing popularity of imported chinaware, especially that from Japan, has prompted factories in Kiangsi and Kuangtung provinces to turn out simple dinner sets and household utensils with stamped figures after the modern style. The hand-painted old fashion wares are becoming comparatively rare on the home market. For export, however, the old-styled wares still are in good demand, since they are usually more painstakingly made.

The 1922 exports of chinaware, not including pottery and earthenware, from this country was given by the Chinese Maritime Customs as 218,930 piculs of 133 1/3 pounds, valued at 3,000,730 Haikwan Taels. Approximately two-thirds of these shipments went to Hongkong, thence to be reshipped. Singapore, including the Straits Settlements, and Siam each took shipments valued at just under Taels 400,000. The United States, including Hawaii, purchased goods to the value of Taels 45,029.

Pottery and earthenware exports in 1922 totaled 182,568 piculs, the value of which was Taels 648,045. Approximately two-thirds of this, or Taels 420,819, went to Hongkong. Japan took goods to the value of Taels 123,646. Shipments to the United States totaled Taels 1,760 and those to Great Britain Taels 183.

Nearly ninety per cent. of the porcelain exported is produced in Kiangsi and Kuangtung provinces, and passes through the ports of Kiukiang, Kowloon, Swatow and Canton (Kuangchow). Earthenware is exported mostly from Shanghai. In recent years a limited amount of porcelain clay, or kaolin, has been exported to Japan. There are deposits of this in many parts of China, but those of the best quality are south of the Yangtzŭ River. The Ching-tê Chên potters secure their raw material from Kimen, Anhwei, and from the vicinity of P'oyang Lake, as at Nankang and Yükan, Kiangsi.'

The earliest extant specimens are productions of the Sung dynasty (A.D. 960-1280). These are extremely scarce. All colouring up to a century after the Sung period was in the glaze, but a century after its fall painted decoration is found. During the Ming dynasty (A.D. 1368-1644) the decoration was nearly always by coloured glazes or by painting under the glaze, but enamels over the glaze were introduced. From the end of the Ming to the present time over-glaze enamel decoration has been most used, and has been brought to something like perfection.

References.—Hirth, *Ancient Porcelain: A Study in Chinese Mediæval Industry and Trade;* Paléologue, *L'Art Chinois;* Bushell, *Chinese Porcelain before the Present Dynasty;* Gulland, *Chinese Porcelain;* Prang and Bushell, *Oriental Ceramic Art;* Bushell, *Chinese Art; Chinese Pottery and Porcelain;* Dillon, *Porcelain;* Monkhouse, *Chinese Porcelain;* Hobson, *Chinese Pottery and Porcelain;* Julien, *Histoire et Fabrication de la Porcelain chinoise;* Gorer and Blacker, *Chinese Porcelain and Hard Stones;* Laufer, *The Beginnings of Porcelain in China;* Hodgson, *How to Identify Old Chinese Porcelain;* Hetherington, *The Early Ceramic Wares of China;* Hobson and Hetherington, *The Art of the Chinese Potter from the Han Dynasty to the End of the Ming.*

POSTS.—There was no Post Office department in the Chinese Government similar to our General Post Office and its branches. The Government sent its despatches by means of couriers, who were under a department of the Board of War, and for whom relays of horses were provided; the greatest speed attained by these Government couriers was 200 miles a day. This courier service was simply for governmental purposes; the common people did not share in its advantages and convenience. Commercial enterprise provided for the general community a system of local posts 'entirely independent of the State.' In most places, of any importance, letters were received by certain shops or agencies (private postal agencies), and on payment of a sum, its amount being contingent on the distance the letter, or parcel of silver, had to be carried, it would probably have a good chance of reaching its destination. Better to secure this result, it was sometimes customary to write on the envelope that a certain further sum would be paid to the postman on delivery, who had thus an incentive to try and find the addressee. The postage from Hongkong to Canton was twenty cash (2 cents), but from Hongkong to Fatshan, which is about twelve miles further than Canton, it was double that amount, viz., forty cash; this was one of the advantages—a cheapening of the postal rates—which would have resulted from foreigners being allowed to run steamers on all the inner waters of the Chinese Empire; for there are regular lines of American river steamers running between Hongkong and Canton. There are also steamers of the same kind running on the Yangtsz between Shanghai and the Riverine Ports.

Sir Robert Hart, the Inspector-General of the Imperial Maritime Customs, established a postal system between Peking and Shanghai, etc., which was of great benefit, not only to the Custom service, but to the foreign mercantile community. When the northern ports were ice-bound, a courier carried the letters; and a series of postage stamps were in use, of different denominations, such as one, two, and five candarins, having a dragon in the centre. We wrote some few years since that 'it is to be hoped that this will be the nucleus from which shall expand a general postage system for the whole of China.'

This has fortunately now been taken in hand, and a Postal Service instituted in imitation of European systems with Europeans at its head, which is being extended to the whole of China, even to its remotest corners. 'The Chinese Imperial Post Office was opened on 2nd February, 1897.' It is, however, not paying its way, but is carried on at a loss. The rates of postage with the Chinese Post Office are remarkably low, viz. at Swatow '1 cent per ½ oz. on letters to and from places in China,' and local letters ½ cent per ½ oz., and to Hongkong 4 cents per ½ oz. Four cents are taken for postal purposes, as the equivalent of an English penny, therefore 1 cent is a farthing, and ½ cent is a half farthing. Different issues of postage stamps, etc., have appeared during the last few years, some of which are now rare and consequently expensive, and the ardent philatelist has all the varieties of surcharges, etc., to delight himself with.

Under the present system each of the twenty-two districts is administered by a Postal Commissioner stationed at the District Head Office. These are under the control of the Directorate General of Posts in the Ministry of Communications in Peking. The postal establishments are classified into First, Second, and Third Class Offices, Sub-offices, Agencies and Box-office Agencies, the last two being merely shops where stamps are sold and letters posted. The total number of employees on December 31, 1916, was:

Foreign staff	122
Chinese „	4,714
Agents	7,185
Postmen	5,075
Couriers	6,807
Miscellaneous	1,097
	25,000

The Shanghai General Post Office is equipped to handle one thousand million letters a year.

The foreign post offices, numbering in all one hundred and seventy-eight, of which one hundred and twenty-five were Japanese, were closed in November, 1922 (as on January 1, 1923, the date agreed upon between the Chinese and foreign governments). These had been opened at several Treaty Ports soon after the signing of the first treaties on account of the uncertainty of safe transmission by the then-existing native agencies. Immediately on the withdrawal of these agencies the Chinese rate of postage was increased, but the former rate was reverted to on protest by the representatives of the foreign governments.

PO-TSZ, AND OTHER GAMES OF CHANCE.—Pò-tsz is only one of the many games of chance with which the Chinese are familiar: it is more a Hakka game than Cantonese, though Cantonese play it. For this game cards and dominoes are used like checks for umbrellas at public places of entertainment in England, one being handed to the gambler and one being kept by the holder of the gambling stall. These are placed with the gamblers' counters and serve to identify them as theirs; for counters are also used, viz., a large cash, a white, and a black, porcelain counter or bead, draftsmen (like Chinese chessmen) with the amounts they stand for cut in them. The amounts represented by these may, for example, be as follows—the cash =ten cents, white bead=$1, black do.=$5, and the rest=$10 and so on, and stakes are made. The materials for playing pò-tsz consist of two hollow cubes of brass, the one smaller than the other, and fitting one into the other, and a cube of black wood, which fits into the smaller brass cube, but does not quite reach up to the open top of it, so that often a piece of metal is placed below it to raise it, though this is not always done. On each surface of the cube of wood are two characters, cut into the wood and coloured white and red respectively, the characters are generally t'ung and pò, which are two of the characters on a Chinese cash, as these coins were first used to play pò-tsz. The first character (t'ung) is white, and the second (pò) red; white wins, and red loses. There is a board or table with one, two, three, and four written on each side, or they are often not written on the board, as one is always near the holder of the stall, two at his right hand, three opposite him, and four at his left hand. The cube of wood is put in the smaller hollow cube of brass which is open at one side for this reason, and then the smaller brass cube has the larger cube put over it as a cover, one side of this larger cube being also left open for that purpose. The owner of the gambling stall puts all these things together unseen by the players, and then spins them round. Any of the players is also at liberty to do the same after he has done so. The cube must stop plumb square with the sides of the board or table, and must be spun until it has done so. Then the cube is lifted off, and whatever number on the board the white character is next wins, red loses. The cube of wood is occasionally turned round inside the smaller brass cube for luck, and after the holder of the stall has done so, the others may look at it and change it themselves as well. False cubes with loadstone in the wood, and iron in the larger cube are made, and a confederate, when lifting the cover off after the spin, is able to attract the wood in the small cube round to a more favourable side, the crowd being hoodwinked, or prevented from seeing what is going on, by the confederates. The stakes on the white side of the metal, of course, win.

Fán-t'án is more widely known by the European resident in China. Stakes are laid on the number of cash that will be left, whether one, two, or three, after raking out, four at a time, a number of cash from under and round an upturned bowl.

The Waí Sing [*Wei Hsing*] *Lottery.*—Another well-known form of gambling is the Waí Sing Lottery, which was based on the Government Civil Service Examinations. Some time before the examination, the monopolist, who runs the lottery, finds out the surnames of the candidates of a certain district, and the players select twenty names on which to stake, having previously endeavoured to find out for their own guidance the capabilities of the candidates. Having made their selection, they send in the names and receive a receipt or ticket. These tickets are differently priced, but a book with half-dollar tickets amounts to $500, as each book contains a thousand tickets. Of this money, $50 goes to the monopolist for expenses, leaving three prizes of $300, $100, and $50 respectively, subject to be reduced by a ten per cent. commission and a further deduction of a considerable amount for the expenses of printing the books and distributing the prizes. The winners are, of course, those who have the highest number of names of successful candidates on their tickets. A perusal of the article on Examinations (p. 226) will show that, from the limited number allowed to pass at an examination, the element of chance must enter very largely into this lottery, and this, notwithstanding the efforts to obtain some idea of the attainments and capabilities of the candidates.

Pák Kòp Píú [*Pa Ko Piao*] is the name of another well-known lottery. Eighty characters (words) at the beginning of 'The Thousand Character Classic' are printed on a flyleaf—the characters in this book are largely used by the Chinese as numbers, or as we might use the letters of the alphabet in English to distinguish objects. No two characters in the book are alike—and twenty of them are winning numbers. A ticket to cover ten characters may cost four cash, and, if less than five characters are winning numbers, the gambler loses his four cash, while, if he has five winning characters, he makes a profit of a cash or so; each additional winning character adds immensely to his gains till they culminate in ten taels, should all his characters be winning numbers.

The Tsz-fá [*Tzŭ Hua*] *Lottery* has, in place of numbers, the names of thirty-six ancient Chinese celebrities; the prices for a name running from one cash upwards. The prizes of the winning names amount to thirty times the prices paid for them. Rhyming themes are issued which disclose in an enigmatical manner, to those who may be able to make a lucky guess, the winning name. Women, however, trust often to dreams to guide them in their selection; but the men rely on their knowledge of history and the incidents in the life of the celebrities, to make a good selection.

Another very common gambling amusement, and one often seen on the streets, is staking on the number of seeds in an orange. If a number of Chinese are seen surrounding a fruit hawker's stock of oranges in Hongkong, it will generally be found that this form of gambling is the attraction. Each player has a good look at the orange, a loose-skinned one, and makes a guess at the number of seeds in it, staking his money accordingly. After all have staked, the fruit-dealer skins the orange and opens each division, so as to count the pips carefully. The one that guesses right wins treble the amount of his stakes, whilst the two nearest in their guesses to him each win double theirs.

But time would fail to enumerate and describe all the different modes of gambling resorted to on street stalls; some known in the West, and some entirely Chinese or Oriental. The Chinese is deeply imbued with the spirit of gambling. He is brought up to it from his earliest youth, by first venturing a cash or two when buying a 'sweety,' a cake, or fruit; the women spend much of their ignorant leisure in games spiced by the naughtiness of bets and stakes; while the coolies amuse their unemployed moments by winning or losing their hard-earned cash on a game of chance; the gambling sheds in the purlieus of the cities are always swarming with votaries, and at New Year time a saturnalia of gambling is indulged in by all, even by those who religiously abstain from it at other times.

Of games of dice, the Chinese have several, played with different numbers of dice of different sizes. The spots on them range from one to six, and are arranged in the same way as on European dice and those of ancient Greece and Rome, but the four and the one are red on the Chinese and the other numbers black. The dice are thrown generally into a bowl, which is sometimes set into a casing of chunam, inside a tin box, to deaden the sound.

Kòn Mín Yöng [*Kan Mien Yang*], 'driving or pursuing sheep,' is played with six dice and by any number of players. Single and double stakes are deposited on the table, and up to any amount, the different throws of the dice deciding whether the players shall win or lose singles or doubles.

Haú Luk [*Hou Liu*] is played with three dice, the principle of this game and the last being much the same otherwise.

Chák T'ín Kaú [*Chih T'ien Chiu*] is played with two dice. 'In this game the twenty-one throws that can be made with two dice receive different names, and are divided into two series or suits, called man (mun) [wên] "civil" and mò [wu], "military."

Chong Yün Ch'aú [*Chuang Yüan Ch'ou*].—Little bundles of bamboo tallies with Chinese characters on them are found for sale in certain shops, and these are employed in playing this game. The world ch'aú means a tally and Chong-yün is the Optimus at the Han-lin Examination. (See EXAMINATIONS.) 'Two or more persons may play, using six dice and sixty-three bamboo tallies,' each drawing the tally, or tallies, he is entitled to from his throw of the dice, 'the one who counts highest becomes the winner.'

The *Shing Kwún T'ò* [*Shêng Kuan T'ai*], the celebrated game of 'The Table of the Promotion of Officials' is another famous game which 'is played by two or more persons upon a large paper diagram, on which are printed the titles of the different officials and dignitaries of the Chinese Government.

The moves are made by throwing dice, and the players, whose positions upon the diagram are indicated by notched or coloured splints, are advanced or set back, according to their throws.'

Chinese Dominoes.—There are thirty-two dominoes in a set, there are duplicates of each domino, and no blanks. Several games are played with dominoes and dice; they seem rather complicated. Shap-tsaí [*Shih Tsai*], P'áí-Kaú [*P'ai Chiu*], and T'in Kaú [*T'ien Chiu*], are names of such games.

Chinese Cards.—The cards used for playing the game of Ch'á-kam [*Ch'a t'an*] have the same names as dominoes, and have the same number of spots on them. They are long narrow bits of pasteboard about the size of a small finger. The pack contains thirty-two cards. In the game of Ngaú-p'áí [*Niu P'ai*] the pack contains thirty-six cards, and the cards are 'about two inches in length and half an inch wide.' It is said to be a very ancient game, and was first played by cowherds, hence its name 'cow-cards'; such, at least, is the Chinese account of the orgin of the name.

References.—Culin, *Chinese Games with Dice; The Gambling Games of the Chinese in America;* Ng Kwai-shang, *A Book on Chinese Games of Chance.*

POTATO.—Our common Irish potato was introduced into China by the Dutch, whence its name of the 'Holland potato' (Ho-lan shu) in Chinese. It is also called the 'little Potato' and *shan-yuo tou'rh,* lit., 'hill-herb beans.' It is largely cultivated in the neighbourhood of Macao for the consumption of foreigners, and, as a consequence of planting them, they are eaten also by the natives themselves. Before their cultivation there, the staple of food in that locality was half and half of rice and sweet potatoes.

Sweet potatoes, as their name in Chinese shows, are also a foreign introduction. The sweet potato (*pai shu*) is quite different from our potato. It is longer in shape, sweeter, and rather pleasant in flavour. It is said to be mealy when new. It is not grown from seed, but a cutting of the creeper is stuck into the ground two or three inches deep, covered up with earth for a foot of its length, the rest being allowing to trail over the ridge which these shoots soon cover with their leaves. When ripe, one or two are dug up and the rest of the tubers again covered up till ripe and wanted later on. A sandy soil appears to suit them well.

PRIMITIVE MAN.—It is impossible in our present state of knowledge to make final statements on this subject. The whole matter is at present being more thoroughly investigated as regards China than it has been hitherto. One or two discoveries have been made which show undoubtedly that relics of man in his earlier stages of semi-civilisation are to be found in China. There may be some faint attempts in the earlier records of the Chinese to describe man in his original condition, but it is impossible to separate any grains of wheat from all the chaff of myth and fable of these early stories. The Chinese are very fond of collecting antiquities—ancient bricks even claim their attention, and when once they are put on the right course by Western scientists—as they are now being put—they will no doubt be able to add to our knowledge of early man, and even some skull to rival the Neanderthal may yet be found in China or rudimentary attempts at drawing be discovered. Mr. Baber obtained a polished stone axehead of serpentine and a good specimen of one of polished flint in his journey of exploration in Western Szchuan ([Ssŭch'uan]. Yünnan is another province where celts may be found. A writer in 'Notes and Queries on China and Japan,' also mentions having had a bronze celt brought to him.

Within the last few years some palæolithic and neolithic implements and some fossilized skulls have been discovered. The precise ethnological and historical conclusions to be deduced from these discoveries have still to be determined.

PRINTING.—The Chinese Classics, which form the foundation of a great portion of Chinese literature, also gave the first hint to the Chinese for printing. They were engraved on stone, A.D. 177, and impressions (or possibly rubbings) taken from them. Printing from wooden blocks, the system in general use throughout country until within recent years, was known as early as A.D. 581-618, being practised during the course of the next three hundred years in the T'ang dynasty; and was adopted by Imperial order in reproducing the Classics in A.D. 952, thus anticipating Gutenberg and Caxton's discovery and work in Europe by five centuries. The wood used for the 'blocks,' as they are technically called, is generally that of the pear or plum. It is cut into small slabs about the size of a foolscap sheet of paper and about the thickness of an inch or less. These are soaked for some time in water. The book to be printed is written out most carefully by a good writer in the square form of the character employed in printing, and then pasted face downwards on the block; the block-cutter with his wetted finger rubs off the paper, leaving the impression; he then, with different graving instruments, and a piece of wood to act as a mallet, cuts away, to the depth of a quarter of an inch or so, all the surface of the wood which is not covered by the writing, thus leaving the writing in relief; the block is often cut on the under surface as well, and can thus be used to print on both sides. Each surface of the block generally contains two pages of the Chinese book to be printed. This done, the block is delivered to the printer who, adjusting it on a table in front of him with nails and pads of paper, prepares to print. Sitting down in front of the block, at his right hand is a board with a curiously shaped circular brush on it, the handle being also round, and thick enough to be grasped comfortably by the hand. The whole brush looks something like a bouquet of flowers turned upside down. An earthen crock with liquid ink is next to the ink-board, and a small brush, something like a diminutive circular carpet broom, with a long handle, lies in it. Beyond the block is a pile of paper cut into the right shape, that is, a little larger than the block. Within convenient reach is a pad made of coir, perfectly smooth on the surface; the brushes are likewise made of the same fibre. These then are the printer's primitive materials. Ready to begin work he takes up a quantity of ink on to the ink-board with the small brush; after which he works this ink into the large circular brush, and then rubs it all over the surface of the block; putting down the brush, he adroitly takes hold of the two nearest corners of the topmost sheet of paper, lifting it by the thumb and forefinger of each hand, giving it a jerk at the same time in order to keep it from falling limp; judging by his eye how much margin to leave, he lays it neatly on the surface of the block, and lifting the pad or pressing brush, he passes it deftly and lightly over the paper, exerting sufficient pressure for an impression to be taken. Printers get to be very quick at this work; it is easily learned. A good block-cutter gets a dollar per thousand characters cut. After about sixteen thousand impressions are taken off, the blocks get somewhat worn, but they can be retouched, when another ten thousand can be printed from them. It is a cheaper mode of printing a few small books than by metallic type, as the initial expense is slight compared with that of providing founts of type and expensive presses; the blocks for a large book take up a great deal of room and are very cumbersome and easily destroyed by insects. There is a softness and mellowness about the character which is wanting in the clear-cut metallic type.

References.—Julien, *Industries de l'Empire chinois;* Williams, *Middle Kingdom,* i. 600; *Chinese Recorder,* 1875.

PROVERBS.—It has been said that 'a Chinese proverb is something almost, if not utterly, indefinable. Of course it bears, in several features, a strong likeness to other branches of the family in various countries; but of "that sententious brevity," which is said to "constitute the principal beauty of a proverb"—of that brevity, without obscurity, which is said to be the very soul of a proverb, it is often totally lacking. Other features it has which are peculiarly its own, and which impart to it a terseness, beauty, and symmetry, inimitable, at least in the English language.'

Proverbs are very numerous in China. We give the few following samples:—

'To make a man of yourself you must toil; if you don't, you won't.'
'Strike a flint, and you'll get fire; strike it not, and you'll not get even smoke.'
'No pains no gains' is represented by 'never was a good work done without much trouble.'
'If an ox won't drink, you can't make him bend down his head.'
'Done leisurely, done well.'
'It is easier to know how to do a thing than to do it.'
'Cheap things are not good; good things are not cheap.'
'Better take eight hundred than give credit for a thousand cash.'
'All unskilful fools
'Quarrel with their tools.'
'Two of a trade hate one another.'
'There is dew for every blade of grass.'
'A stick's a stick whether short or tall.'
'A man's a man whether great or small.'
'As the twig is bent the mulberry grows.'
'There are pictures in poems, and poems in pictures.
'Learning is far more precious than gold.'
'You cannot open a book without learning something.'
'You may study to old age yet have things to learn.'
'No pleasure equals the pleasure of study.'
'Some study shows the need of more.'
'Strike while the iron's hot.'
'To persuade gentlemen not to gamble is to win for them.'
'The two words pure and leisure no money can buy.'
'Man's life is truly a performance.'
'Wine is a discoverer of secrets.'
'Speak carefully and be slow to speak.'
'He who talks much must err; he excels who says nothing.'
'True gold fears no fire.'
'He has the mouth of a Buddha, the heart of a snake.'

References.—Smith, *Chinese Proverbs;* Scarborough, *A Collection of Chinese Proverbs; China Review*, xv. 298; xvi; xvii; xx. 156-66 (Hakka and Swatow proverbs).

PUNKAH.—The word punkah is derived from India.

It is 'the Hindoostani name of a large palm-leaf fan, the stalk of which is rested on the ground, while the leaf itself is waved behind the party to be fanned. The word is now applied throughout the East to the swinging frames with cloth vallances fitted in European houses.'

The Chinese have not adopted the punkah, though a solitary instance of its use is occasionally seen. The reason seems to be that the draught of air caused by it gives them a headache.

RACE.—The Chinese as a nation are not of pure blood—what nation is? Doubtless, when the present inhabitants of China poured into the land they absorbed some at least of the original inhabitants, the Miao and the Man, while later, in historic times, 'large immigrations or bands of captives consisting of Tibetans, Huns, and the Mongolic Hienbi,' have each furnished their quota towards the amalgam, to say nothing of Manchu Tartars and others. These and climatic conditions have probably had something to do in differentiating the Southern Chinaman from the Northern, the former being well described by Ross as 'short, small, cute,' and the latter as 'tall, stout, stolid, and slow.'

This amalgamation of aborigines and Chinese goes on slightly still on the borders of the habitats of the former, as a few Chinese are to be found who have married wives from the different tribes. (See CHINESE, PHYSICAL CHARACTERISTICS OF.)

RADIO.—

'Many who do not know the situation are asking why Radio does not seem to take hold and develop more rapidly in China, in view of the enormous popularity which it has gained in America and England.

Due to an old clause in the Customs Regulations drawn up by the Chinese Government some years ago before Radio as it is now known came into existence, all wireless material was classified as Munitions of War. This is explained doubtless by the fact that at the time the regulation was drawn up wireless was only in the experimental stage and was considered useful only in great emergencies such as in time of war.

As everyone knows the confusion of wireless as known in those days and the Popular Radio of to-day is possible only through ignorance or a deliberate desire to delay its introduction. However, we understand new regulations are being drawn up in Peking that will make it possible to import material for small Radiophone Receiving Outfits, and we can only hope with the many enthusiasts already in this country that the day may not be far off when opportunity will be given for the proper development of one of the most wonderful inventions ever made. Radio could be made to mean more to China than to almost any other nation in the world due to poor existing means of communication. It could do more in the shortest space of time to bring the different parts of the country together than any other means, and there is no doubt that this is what this country needs more than anything else.' Since this was written the restriction on import has been withdrawn.

RAILWAYS.—China would seem to be an ideal land for a gigantic system of railways, for it is a 'land of magnificent distances'; but it is also a land of 'stupendous prejudices'; it is therefore not surprising that the railway is in its infancy in China. 'Europe has a mile of railway for every 2,400 inhabitants; China has, perhaps, about a mile or more for every million of her inhabitants.' It was stated in 1900 that there were 30,000 miles of railway in Asia, two-thirds of which belonged to British India. The Trans-Caspian and Trans-Siberian Railway accounted then in its unfinished state for 3,200 miles, Japan had 3,200 miles, French Indo-China 120 miles, but in Cochin-China, Annam, and Tonkin they were soon to have 2,400 miles. Java had 1,000 miles, Turkey-in-Asia 1,500 miles finished and 600 projected or under construction, and Russia was to join Astrakhan to the general Russian Railway system, while China at that time had only 300 miles completed and owned by the Government, which it was stated were 'very remunerative, and European syndicates' had 'obtained concessions for 3,600 miles of railway in China, the construction of which is already well advanced. These will traverse regions rich in minerals and agricultural products.' The splendid waterways afford great facilities for transit, and 'China is better supplied with waterways, both natural and artificial, than any other country in the world, except, perhaps, Holland'; but away from them carriage by land is often expensive. It sometimes costs two shillings per ton per mile to take coal by land in China, while in Great Britain the cost is a halfpenny to one penny a mile a ton, and in the United States a farthing for the same amount for the same distance. The coalfields in China have been laid down on a grand scale. To instance only one, that of Shansi, which has a continuous field 13,500 miles in area, of anthracite, equal to the best Pennsylvanian, with from 15 to 40 feet seams. There is also a rich bituminous deposit in the same province: so that in the mere carriage of coal there should be a fine future for railways in China; added to which there would be the passenger traffic, the goods trains, and those laden with market produce, etc.

About sixty years ago Sir R. Stephenson came out in the hope of being able to inaugurate a general railway system. All the foreign communities in China were naturally in favour of such a scheme; one or two individuals pointed out that the Chinese were not ready for it, and would not be for a long time to come, and, such being really the case, of course nothing could be done.

In 1876, a short line of railway, about 12 miles long, was constructed under the auspices of an English firm, and ran between Shanghai and Woosung at the mouth of the Shanghai River. There was considerable traffic, but the Chinese Government objected to its being in the hands of foreigners; they therefore bought and closed it in 1877; further they took it up, and transferred rails and rolling stock to the Island of Formosa, where they lay rusting for some years. A railway was constructed in Formosa by the Chinese; and this material and rolling stock found use in this then outlying island of the Chinese empire, where the harm it might do would be too far off to affect the stability of the mighty dominions of the Son of Heaven; the Chinese also thus having the control of it in their own hands. (A history of the Woosung Railway appears in the *Hongkong Daily Press*, of the 27th September, 1892.) This line between Shanghai and Woosung was afterwards reconstructed by the Chinese Government, and opened in 1898. It has since been incorporated as part of the Shanghai-Soochow system.

The next line, after this first Woosung Railway, was from the coal mines at K'ai-p'ing to the sea coast, whence it was carried on to the forts at Taku. It was first opened for carrying coals to the canal bank, but has now developed into a very large concern, and it may almost be said the whole welfare of the adjacent country depends on it. The investment has turned out to be very profitable. This railway was of invaluable use to the Chinese for the movement of troops during the Japanese war, but its construction had to be stopped during the conflict between the two nations. Trains 1,000 feet long have not been an uncommon sight on it.

The following was written some time before 1903:—

For some time past the construction has been going on (and it will show a few of the difficulties that stand in the way of the development of railways in China) of 'an Imperial railway, which is intended eventually to connect Tientsin with Kirin in Manchuria. Ninety-four miles (from Tientsin to Kuyeh) have been in working order since 1891, and during 1892 carried 488,300 passengers.' The line has 'been extended at the rate of fifty miles per annum.'

At the principal terminus, Tientsin, about a 100 Chinese clerks are employed, of whom about one-half are alleged to be totally unnecessary, 'being friends and hangers on.' At other stations the same condition of affairs obtains. 'The first-class fares are a little over one halfpenny a mile, and the second a decimal over a farthing. The third-class fares are even cheaper still. The fares for the entire year (1892) from all classes, over the ninety-four miles above mentioned, were only £10,000, taking the tael at its par value of 6s. 8d. The receipts, according to Consul Brenan's interesting report, from all sources, were only about 226,000 taels, or £75,500, and even these figures are, at the current rate of exchange, too high.'

'It is astonishing to see the use the Chinese are making . . . of the railway from K'aip'ing to Tientsin. The farmers bring their market produce along with them to Tientsin and other places on the line where they find a ready sale for their wares, and, instead of a curse, as the people too often consider it in places where they still stick to their antediluvian carts, wheelbarrows, and other clumsy modes of conveyance, the railway is beginning to be recognised as a blessing to rich and poor alike.'

'Native capitalists have but little confidence in the "Imperial line" as an investment. Moreover, no accounts are issued to show how money is expended. A Government grant of about £600,000 a year maintains the construction of the line, which is being completed for strategical reasons only, although the original idea was to treat it solely as a commercial undertaking. What with corruption, bad management, and a virtual boycott on the part of capitalists, the prospects of success do not seem very promising.' 'It is the intention of the Railway Administration to build a subsidiary line to Moukden, while the main line north will be continued on to Kirin. . . . From Lanchow, another line westwards is contemplated to north of T'ungchow (near Peking) and thence to Paoting-fu, the capital of Chihli province.'

'The K'aip'ing Coal Co's. line, at first intended only to carry coal to the canal bank, has been extended to Tientsin, and is open to passenger traffic.' An extension of the Tientsin line to Shanhaikwan, 'where the great wall reaches the sea,' has been completed, and 'a line from Linsi to Newchwang and then to Kirin has been sanctioned [see below]. A line from Tientsin to Peking was opened in 1897, which now, by the addition of an electric tram, takes one up to the very gates of Peking, in fact to the Yung Ting Gate.' (See below.)

With the Chinese Government, considerations of defence would have proved more effective in causing the construction of railways than anything else. Even the short line in existence in the North proved useful in a small rebellion that took place lately.

'The great object of the Chinese Government in making railways is to secure facilities for moving troops and munitions of war, not to promote trade or encourage industries.' 'So long as this is the case, the railways most needed are not likely to be constructed in a hurry.'

Every new railway project in China appears to have had a hard tussle at its inception. There was a progressive party in favour of the iron road; there was another party opposed to progress, conservative officials who deprecated the introduction of all foreign inventions. Both parties were united apparently in the idea of preventing all foreign intervention. The Chinese, fearful of foreign influence in their country, would not brook any interference in the way of any development of railway schemes for China, until compelled to permit them. 'China for the Chinese' was their motto; and for fear that an alien authority might be set up in their midst, they turned a deaf ear to all entreaties for permission to construct lines. So far did they carry these precautions, that they resolved to smelt their own ore and make their own rails, buying as little as possible in the foreign market. If this resolution had been adhered to, it would probably have been many years before railway lines of any great magnitude were in running order. Extensive iron-works were set up in the neighbourhood of Hankow, with this end in view, and a small line for the transportation of iron ore was laid at Hankow: it was called the Ta-ye Railway, and ran to Huang-si-kan—a distance of 60 *li* (20 miles). Looming up in the far distant future there was the Grand Trunk line from Peking viâ Wuch'ang to Canton. Whether this railway would really be commenced last century or this, or indefinitely postponed, was doubtful. The Viceroy, who had the undertaking in hand, having spent enormous sums of money on the initial stages of the work as outlined above, was getting into serious financial difficulties, and it was very questionable whether he would be able to proceed much further, for there was no capital for building railways in China: the Government had not the money available; would not borrow it from foreigners; nor allow private enterprise. Another proposal some years ago was for a line to be constructed from Canton to Shamshuípò, near the Cosmopolitan Docks in British territory, on the mainland opposite Hongkong. Surveys were made, and permission granted for its construction, but the project fell into abeyance. It was to have passed through the important town of Sheklung, as well as other places, running a total length of 380 *li*, or about 127 miles. But, like the other railways, no foreigners were to hold shares in it. Twice have surveys been made now for such a line, but it is not yet *un fait accompli;* when the Grand Hankow-Canton Trunk line is finished this will follow as a matter of course. (It has since been built.) Later, a railway was projected between Swatow and the prefectorial city of Ch'aochow-fú. Hopes were entertained that this line, of some 30 miles, more or less, would be the precursor of other short lines in the South of China, but they have been doomed to disappointment.

The last paragraph shows one stage (the second, the first being the strongest opposition to them, as shown above) in the history of railway enterprise in China. Since then great changes have taken place, and for some time little has been heard in connection with China but spheres of influence and railways, mining and other concessions: Russia, France, Germany, America, Belgium, Italy, Portugal, and England, all knocking at China's doors.

The Russian system of railways and those of China are joined together. France appears desirous of penetrating China with her railways from her Indo-Chinese empire next Yünnan, while many English are desirous that British lines shall develop the West of China in connection with our Asiatic Empire.

The whole history of the different railway concessions is thus described in the report of the China Association for 1898-1899:—

'Having selected their respective spheres [of influence] the Powers proceeded as it were by tacit consent to mark them off by Railway and Mining Concessions. Russia had set the example in an Agreement (dated September, 1896) for the construction of an "Eastern Chinese Railway" system of Manchuria.

'France had followed by requesting the Tsung-li-Yamên, in June, 1897, to promise that the Chinese Government would address itself to the Fives-Lille Company for prolongations of the Langson-Lungchow line toward Nanning and Pese, and would invite the aid of French Engineers for the opening of mines in Kwangtung, Kwangsi, and Yünnan.

'Pursuing this assertion of interest in the provinces bordering on Tongking, she exacted, in May, 1898, the concession of a railway from Pakhoi to a point on the West River, with the ulterior right of making any future lines radiating from Pakhoi.—The occasion was taken by the Association to emphasize the protest which had been made in April against this assertion of French influence in a province which constitutes, commercially, as well as geographically, the hinterland of Hongkong.

'An American Syndicate has obtained a concession for the Southern extension of the Great Trunk line—from the banks of the Yangtsze opposite Hankow to Canton; and Sir Claude MacDonald has obtained, finally, the concession of a right to make a railway from Canton to the coast (Kowloong) opposite Hongkong.

'Various other concessions of less political, but of considerable financial importance, have been made. The Russo-Chinese bank has undertaken to make a branch from Chêngting (a city on the Lu-Han line, in Pechili) [Chihli] to T'aiyuen, the capital of Shansi.

'A Syndicate combining British and Italian interests has obtained extensive mining rights in Shansi, coupled with the right of railway outlet to the Han river at Siang-yang.

'A British subject, Mr. Pritchard Morgan, has entered into an agreement having for its object the development of mines and concomitant railways in Szechuen [Ssŭch'uan]. France is understood to have protested that this arrangement is inconsistent with the undertaking not to seek exclusive privileges in South-West China, concluded between the two Governments . . . but the protest appears strained. . . .

'Broadly speaking, therefore, China has been partitioned into spheres of industrial interest that may become spheres of political influence in certain eventualities which the presnet *régime* appears not unlikely to precipitate.

'An Anglo-Italian syndicate has obtained a right to construct the line from Joyau in Hupeh to Taochau in Shansi, and Messrs. Jardine, Matheson & Co., have secured rights over the line from Sinyan in Honan to Nanking *viâ* Luchau in Anhui.

'Rivalry with England for the trade of Yünnan is being pursued actively in other respects, the Chamber having guaranteed a loan of 70,000,000 frs., to be employed in making a railway up the valley of the Red River, to Yünnanfu.

'Great Britain, on the other hand, has obtained permission to extend the Kunlon Ferry line into Yünnan.

'Germany gave it to be understood from the first, that she intended to keep in German hands the construction and management of railways in Shantung.

'In an agreement (dated 2nd September 1898) between English and German capitalists for the construction of a line between Tientsin and Chinkiang, the sphere of German interests is defined as the region watered by affluents of the Hwang-ho, and the English sphere as that watered by affluents of the Yangtsze. From Tientsin to the southern border of Shantung, therefore, the line will be controlled by German, and the continuation across Kiangpeh by British subjects. It followed, equally, that the British and Chinese Corporation obtained without further competition a concession for the construction of lines between Shanghai, Soochow, and Nanking.

'Negotiations were concluded by the British and Chinese Corporation, about the same time, with the aid of H.M. Government, for the proportioning of the Tientsin-Shanhaikwan line up the west coast of the Liao-tung Gulf to Sin-min-ting on the upper waters of the Liao, and to Newchwang.

'More important than all, in the eyes of the Chinese, is the great trunk line which is to connect Peking with Hankow. [*v. infra*]. Granted originally to a Belgian syndicate in 1897, after some ineffectual negotiations with American and British financiers this concession had lapsed and been revived more than once before a substantial contract was signed, in June, with a titular Belgian Syndicate supported by Russo-French diplomacy.

'Both these contracts have been the subject, since, of keen controversy, on the ground, broadly, that they constitute an intrusion, in either case, into alien spheres. A protest by the Russian Minister against the Newchwang agreement was met by surrendering all rights of mortage over the section of the line outside the Great Wall. A protest by the British Minister against the signature of the Lu-Han contract was disregarded by the Tsungli-Yamên, and the Chinese Government was punished for its disregard and bad faith by the exaction of certain other railway concessions. As the contract gives a Franco-Russo-Belgian combination full right of mortage and foreclosure over a line penetrating the heart of the Yangtsze

Valley, it needs to be revised, obviously, on a similar principle, if it is carried out.'

The following items contain further particulars as to some of the concessions mentioned above:—

'The negotiations concerning the construction of the Tsin-Chin (Tientsin-Chinkiang) Railway, have been successfully concluded between England, Germany, and China. It has been arranged that the sections between Tientsin and Tsinan, and Tsinan and Ichau, shall be placed under the control of Germany, and the section between Ichau and Chinkiang under British control.' The railway is to be completed within five years.

The loan is £7,400,000 gold, which is to be repaid in fifty years to the Hongkong and Shanghai Banking Corporation and the German Bank. 'The security is the guarrantee of the Chinese Government plus the railway itself.' Three Europeans and two Chinese are to have the mangement of it; from Tientsin to the Southern boundaries of Shantung, it is to be under German control and the rest is to be under British control.

There is a line between Tiehsanpu, in Hupeh, to a spot on the Yangtsze, 70 miles below Hankow, for conveying the iron ore from Hupeh to the ironworks at Hanyang.

The line from Peking to Tientsin is 86⅗ miles long.

There are further railway developments projected in Shantung, thanks to the advent of the Germans in the province.

'A German railway is to be constructed from Tapadurh, near Kiaochow, to Weihsien, and then to join the Tientsin-Chinkiang main line. A line is also to be built from Tapadurh to Tsintao. Both lines will take two years in construction. They have been secured by a German syndicate [and have since been built]. . . . The Weihsien branch will tap the rich coal district which is expected to be the mineral mainstay of the German sphere of interest in Shantung. Another line is to be constructed from Kiaochau (Tapadurh) to Ichow, and thence to the Tientsin-Chinkiang main line. Work on the Weihsien line commenced on Friday, 2nd June.' [1899].

The railway from Peking to Hankow, 'about 813 miles long, will pass through the three important provinces of Chihli, Honan, and Hupeh' ['from Peking to Hankow, about 650 miles, and from Hankow to Canton, about 500 miles, or about 1,150 miles in all.' Another writer says:—'The total length of line will be about 800 English miles, and the capital of the syndicate four and a half millions sterling, represented by 225,000 shares of £20 each], and it "will serve the rich basins of the Yangtsze-kiang and of the Hwangho."'

It was expected that in 1902 the railway from Hankow to Peking would reach 346 miles from the former place: it is progressing at the rate of ½ kilomètre per working day. [For completion and statistics *v. infra*].

'With reference to the proposed Hankow-Canton railway, the Chief Director, Chang Taotai, formerly Consul-General at Singapore,' we read, 'has informed his friends that the line will begin at Canton, pass Fatshan to the city of Samshui, on the West River. From this place the trunk line will go across and enter Hunan, joining at Hankow the Lū-Han Railway. From Samshui again there will be constructed branch lines; namely, one to Kueilin, the capital of Kwangsi province, which will be called the Western Branch line; while from Canton there will be an Eastern Branch line connecting that city with Huichow, thence to Swatow and northward into Fukien province. The Viceroy T'an has already detailed one Battalion of 500 men of the Chien Regiment to act as a guard to the workers on the new railway which it is intended to begin early in May next.' [1899].

'The party of engineers and experts of the Canton-Hankow Railway Syndicate have completed their survey up to Kupong in Punyu district, and are buying land from the owners holding titledeeds.' This line is now progressing from both ends.

A survey of a projected line from Soochow to Ningpo *viâ* Hangchow has been made, and the Hongkong and Shanghai Bank are to finance it.

The following was written a few years before 1903:—

'When the line of the Siberian Railway approaches the eastern shore of the Russian Empire, it is suddenly stopped by a long and broad wedge of land running from south to north. This is part of the Chinese territory of Manchuria, probably the richest portion of the Chinese Empire. In the centre of it is the important fortified town of Kirin, the capital of the province of that name. The province of Kirin is prolonged to the south-west by the province of Shinking, the capital of which is Moukden. and which ends in the long peninsula having the great naval base of Port Arthur for its most south-westerly point. The Siberian railway has to make a long detour to the north round this wedge, and the present treaty [1896] is intended first of all to enable it to avoid this by taking the chord instead of the arc. Thus the first advantage of Russia is to prolong its line from some point in Siberia; probably Nertchinsk, *viâ* Kirin, straight to Vladivostock. Besides this, however, Russia is now authorised to build a railway to join the main line at Kirin and run south-westwards, first to Port Arthur, and second to Shanhaikwan, which is the terminus of the present short railway to Tientsin. The Convention gives to Russia the right to carry her Trans-Siberian Railway to Kirin, the Chinese town of Central Manchuria, from two directions—first, some point in Siberia; and second, Vladivostock. Next, Russia obtains the right to build a railway from Kirin to Port Arthur should China fail to do so.'

'These three lines of railway are to be built with Russian money, and are to be defended by posts of Russian Cossacks; they will also be built to the Russian gauge. Russia is to work mines in Manchuria, and Russian officers are to drill the Chinese troops in Manchuria.'

With regard to the railway operations in the neighbourhood of Kirin, Mukden, and Port Arthur, an opinion has been expressed lately that the line cannot be finished in less than five years, on account of the scarcity of timber, and of workmen and labour. American pine is used, and has to be brought by sea, the supply of it being very limited. Wood is also brought from the Korean frontier, and the winter is likewise so severe that the Chinese labourers cannot stand it, and have to stop work for five months in the year.

The following extract, though the Trans-Siberian Railway is now finished, is still interesting in this connection:—

'The programme of Russian railway extension in Asia has lately undergone considerable revision. The original scheme of the Trans-Siberian Railway has been greatly modified, and it is probable that a portion of the proposed route through Eastern Siberia will be abandoned. When the line was originally authorised, the work of construction was commenced at both ends simultaneously, and the work at the Pacific terminus was inaugurated by the present Tsar, who cut the first sod of earth at Vladivostock on 29th March, 1891. The work at this end of the line has been completed as far as Khabarovka—a distance of 481 miles, and here the terminus is likely to remain for some years to come. The alternative route authorised by the Manchurian Railway Agreement of 1896 will start from Vladivostock and will pass by way of Nicolsk and Ninguta to Tsitsihar, and thence across the Siberian frontier to Nerchinsk, where it will join the railway now under construction. The energy with which the work of railway development is being pushed forward in Russian Manchuria is impressed on the visitor to Vladivostock, from the moment he lands: the country for miles round swarms with parties of labourers engaged in the construction of earthworks, the erection of bridges and the general work necessary to the the construction of a railway. The labourers are convicts who have been sent to Siberia for various offences. They work under a Cossack guard, and are paid for their labour at the rate of one-tenth of the value of the work they do. There are probably from 15,000 to 20,000 of these convict labourers at work in Manchuria at the present time.'

'Russia has demanded the right to carry a totally new branch of the Trans-Siberian line, or rather a feeder, from somewhere near the junction of the Shilka with the Amur, south to Kalgan, . . . No doubt, the line to Kalgan, whether constructed from Aigun or Maimatchin (Kiatkha) will take off a tremendously troublesome section of the Trans-Siberian line, and moreover it will most certainly be constructed, and it will as certainly be extended to connect with the Russian system in Shansi, which is expected she will begin to construct next year [1900].'

Railway concessions North of the Great Wall are to be left to Russian enterprise, and those in the basin of the Yangtzŭ to the British, but this agreement made between the two nations is not to infringe in any way on the rights acquired with regard to the Shanhaikuan-Newchuang line, though the line is to remain a Chinese line. The Peking-Tientsin-Shanhaikuan Railway has been handed over to the Chinese.

'Ten or twelve millions sterling' would be needed for a Burmo-China Railway from Kunlon Ferry, the proposed terminus of the Mandalay-Salween Railway to the Yangtsze Valley.' It would 'reach the Yangtsze at Luchow, about a hundred miles higher up the river than Chinkiang. . . . The length . . . would be about 1,000 miles.' It 'is not only not impracticable, but its construction would present no very extraordinary difficulties.

The following published in 1897 is of interest:—

'A light railway' is to be built 'between Peking and the Imperial mausolea.' 'Every time a member of the Imperial family or the harem dies it costs some Tls. 300,000 to Tls. 400,000 to transport the remains to the mausolea, whilst in the case of a deceased Emperor or Empress-Dowager, no less than two million taels are usually expended for transport expenses, etc. Hence the idea of a railway is to save such exorbitant expenses.'

At the end of 1900 the following railways were completed: Shantung Railway, nearly 100 miles (in Dec., 1901, 160 kilometres. In three years it will reach Chinan-fu, the main section toward which was finished in June, 1920); Imperial Railways of North China, 540 miles (now 901 kilometres or more); Shanghai-Woosung Railway, 11 miles; Lu-Han Railway, from Peking to Chêngtingfu about 160 miles, and northward from Hankow, about 105 miles. It is now (1903) making steady progress.

The Ministry of Communications is now in charge of railways, posts, telegraphs, telephones, and merchant vessels. In China there are (1924) about 8,000 miles of railway under Government control. The Ministry regulates railway freights, makes rules for safety and sanitation, authorizes through communication between different lines, and supervises traffic management. It appoints and dismisses all railway officials, including foreign engineers and accountants. It audits railway accounts and controls railway finance. Its more important function is, however, that of planning further railway extensions to be carried out either by the Government or by private enterprise or by foreign capitalists. Railway nationalization has been largely effected, and lines privately owned are also controlled by the Government. The construction of several important lines has been much delayed owing to mismanagement or to the difficulty of getting materials from abroad during the world war of 1914-8.

'The working of the railway closely follows what is commonly called the departmental system. At the head of each administration is the Managing Director, who is immediately responsible to the Central Government. Usually there is an Associate Director, whose duty it is to assist the Managing Director in the administration of the railway. During the absence of the Director, the Associate Director takes charge.

Sometimes a General Manager is also appointed to assist the Directors. Immediately reporting to the Directors are the departmental chiefs. As a rule, each railway has the following departments:

The General Department.
The Traffic Department.
The Engineering Department.
The Locomotive Department (also in charge of Workshops).
The Accounts Department.

For operating and engineering purposes each line is divided into a number of sections according to the length of line and density of traffic, and each section is placed under a district engineering or traffic inspector, as the case may be. Below the district engineers are the section foremen and gangers, who look after the maintenance and repairs of the line, while below the traffic inspectors are the station masters, train conductors, guards, etc. The Locomotive Department also divides the line into running sections, each of which is placed under a locomotive inspector, who supervises the locomotive staff and controls the engines. As each administration has only some 600 to 800 miles of line, this department system has proved quite suitable.

There is no distinct department for developing new business, such as exists in many countries. Questions of rates, fares and adaptation to commercial needs are in the charge of the same department which supervises transportation, *i.e.*, the Traffic Department.

'Methods of railway operation in China are not unlike those of other countries, although there are some distinctive features. For example, two firemen are commonly placed on each road locomotive in addition to the engine-driver. Train control is by the staff system. Manual block signals are installed at important stations. Operating forces are composed almost entirely of Chinese. On one line there are no foreign officers or employees. On other lines technical officers, a few technical inspectors, and a few passenger conductors are foreigners. Railway schools, which are a part of the railway programme in China, are designed to prepare Chinese young men to work on railways.'

'Passengers are divided into three main classes, First, Second, and Third. On the lines between Ningpo and Tientsin a fourth class, coolie, is also carried and amounts to nearly one-fourth of the total number of passengers these trains carry. Excursion rates are offered at times under all these classes, but the amount of business of this character so far is negligible. Third class passengers comprise over 87% of the total; first class less than one per cent. Rates vary considerably on the different lines, but, for the system, the average in 1915 was—

Total business	1.06 cents per kilometre.
First class	3.12
Second ,,	1.72
Third ,,	1.06
Coolie ,,	.49

For statistical purposes, goods traffic is divided into seven classes,—Products of Agriculture, Animals, Mines, Forests, Manufactures, Materials for other Railways, and Service Stores. On a tonnage basis mineral products are by far the most important, constituting over one half of the total. The great bulk of this is coal. The only lines on which minerals are not a leading class are those parallel to the coast south of Tientsin.

From a revenue standpoint, however, agricultural products take the lead with over a third of the total. Mining products come second with over a quarter of the total. Under this head salt is a very important commodity, although the revenue from that source is only about one-third that from coal. Revenue from manufactures has risen to about one-fourth of the total.

Rates vary widely not only as between classes of commodities, but also as between different lines. The average rate on all business on all lines of the government system is about one and a half cents per ton kilometre. . . . Taking the system as a whole, the lowest average commercial rate is on mineral products, and the highest on animal products; the first being about one cent and the latter two and three-quarter cents per ton kilometre.'

The Chinese Eastern Railway runs from Chita through the Chinese province of Manchuria to Vladivostock and connects the terminus of the Trans-Siberian Railway with the Russian Pacific port. Its length in Chinese territory is about 980 miles, and its total cost of construction 350,000,000 roubles. The management of the railway is entrusted to a Committee elected by shareholders, and its Chairman must be Chinese. But events have proved that, to all intents and purposes, the Chairman is only a figure-head elected to "save the face" of the Chinese Government. The full power of control rests with the Russian Minister of Finance, who guarantees the railway revenue for working expenses and amortization of bonds, which can only be issued with his consent. Moreover, he has the power to accept or reject nominations made by the Committee of Engineers and other officials.

The South Manchurian Railway now owned and controlled by Japan was originally the southern extension of the Chinese Eastern Railway. It was transferred to her after the Russo-Japanese War. The South Manchurian Railway Syndicate, the capital of which is almost entirely supplied by the Japanese Government (the authorized capital is 150,000,000 yen and the subscribed 120,000,000, of which the Japanese Government takes 100,000,000 yen) has now acquired the additional concession of the Antung-Mukden line and has built several branch lines, making a length, with the main line included, of 680 miles.

Under the contract between Russia and China, the latter has the right to redeem the lines thirty-six years from the date of their opening to traffic. This remains true, so far as the portion retained by Russia is concerned. For the portion transferred to Japan, the term of redemption has been extended from thirty-six to ninety-nine years and the earliest possible date of redemption has been fixed at 2002. "The term of the Antung-Mukden line shall expire in 2007."

The following extracts give a succinct account of the Kiaochow–Tsinan Railway in 1923:

'Goods traffic on the Kiaochow–Tsinan Railway is about three times as much as passenger traffic. The average daily receipts from passenger traffic is about $7,000 and from goods $21,000. The gross operating revenue of the line in 1923 was over $9,800,000 and expenditure $8,700,000, the latter being divided roughly into the following items: salaries, $2,600,000; pay and travelling allowance for discharged Japanese employees, $520,000; purchase of railway materials, $2,000,000; coal, $1,000,000; interest on treasury notes secured on the railway property, Yen $2,400,000 ($2,200,000); repayment of a loan for the Directorate-General of the Shantung Rehabilitation Affairs, $340,000. The net profit for the year amounted to about $1,000,000.

The length of trunk line is 400 kilometers, and there is a feeder line of 17 kilometers. The latter runs from Poshan to Shouchang through certain coal mining districts and brings in a yearly gross revenue of about $3,000,000, almost a third of the total operating revenue of the line. The railway has 102 locomotives, 196 passenger cars and 1,637 goods vans. Of this rolling stock about 15 per cent. is more or less in a state of disrepair. There are about 1,000 bridges on the whole line. Owing to the use of new American locomotives which carry a heavy dead weight, some of the bridges have been damaged. The railway authorities expect to build a sinking fund of $3,000,000 within the next three years to repair and replace 96 damaged bridges.

Hitherto the freight rate on coal has not been uniform. High discounts are granted to mining companies by special contract. The railway authorities have decided to do away with such irregularities and a uniform rate of 1.2 cents per ton-kilometer will be charged for coal. This will be put into effect as soon as certain negotiations with the coal companies are satisfactorily settled. The present number of railway officials is 1,480, showing an increase of 512 over the number employed when the line was under Japanese control. There is a similar increase in the number of railway workers. There were 4,944 people employed on the line under the Japanese administration. The present number is 5,923.'

In the province of Yünnan, France has extended her railway system from Indo-China. A syndicate with a capital of 12,500,000 francs, together with a subvention of 12,500,000 francs from the Government of Indo-China was entrusted with the construction of the line from Haiphong to Laokay on French territory, and from Loakay to Yünnanfu on Chinese territory. The total cost of construction is 165,000,000 francs and the mileage is 533.77, of which 288.94 miles are on Chinese soil. Under the agreement signed with France in 1903, China has the right on the expiry of twenty years from that date, " to get back the land granted and to repurchase the line from the French Government after the payment of all expenses put into the railway, including stocks, interest and principal of bonds, and all properties in connection with the line."

The following list shows the railway contracts entered into between 1912 and 1920:

1913.—Tatung–Chêngtu Railway.
—Sinyang–Pukou Railway.
—Shasi–Singyi Railway.
—Kaomi–Hanchuang Railway.
—Tsinan–Shuntê Railway.
—Yamchow (near Pakhoi)-Yünnan–Chungking.
1914.—Nanking–Hunan Railway.
—Shanghai Junction Line.
1915.—Japanese railways in Manchuria.
1916.—Harbin–Aigun and Mergen to Tsitsihar and Tsitsihar–Bodune–Harbin.
—Hêngchow (Hunan)-Chinchow (Yamchow), on Gulf of Tongking.
—Choukiakow (Honan)-Siangyang (Hupei).
—Sinyangchow (Honan)-Yünyang (Hupei).
—Yünyang (Hupei)-Hanchung (Shansi).
1917.—(Revised Changchun–Kirin Loan Agreement concluded).
1918.—Lines in Manchuria and Mongolia.
—Two lines in Shantung and Kiangsu.
1919.—Taokow Chinghua extension to Mênghsien.
1920.—Lung-Hai extensions.
—Mênghsien extension (Chinghua to Mênghsien).
—Peking–Kalgan extension to Kueihuat'ing and Paotow.
—Peking–Mukden developments.

The *Chinese Economic Monthly*, the official organ of the Chinese Government Bureau of Economic Information, contains, in its issue for February, 1924, a detailed statement regarding the Chinese Government Railways in 1922. From it we take the following extracts:

'China's railway system is located principally north of the Yangtze River. The Shanghai–Nanking, the Shanghai–Hangchow–Ningpo and the Hupeh–Hunan lines extend the contiguous system into south China. Plans for future construction promise to connect up other short lines in the south so as to duplicate ultimately the facilities now serving the north. Excluding the dependencies, Mongolia, Turkestan and Thibet, from consideration, China has approximately 172 square miles of territory and

33,700 population for each kilometer of railway. Per mile of railway, China has approximately 276 square miles of territory and 54,000 population. Korea has 71 square miles of territory and 13,000 population per mile of railway, India has 40 square miles and 8,600 population, Japan has 20 square miles and 8,800 population, and the United States has 12 square miles and 3,800 population per mile of railway. The extent of waterways in China will always serve to keep the average for China higher than in countries not so favored.

The total number of kilometers of railway owned by the Government in 1922 was 6,279.28 which is an increase of more than 250 kilometers over 1921. The railways now employ 91,356 persons in all departments; this is an increase of more than 2,000 over 1921. Less than seven per cent. of the total length of line consists of branches, and nearly 74 per cent. is found in main line. The railways are essentially through lines connecting strategic points, commercially and politically speaking, the hub of the system as it exists to-day being Peking.

The report of the Chinese Government Railways for 1922, which gives the above facts, includes the following summary of operations for the year:

	1922	1921	Increase	Decrease.
Operating Revenues	$99,556,229.22	$96,450.836.14	$3,105,393.08	—
Operating Expenses	56,659,483.79	53,967,045.49	2,692,438.30	—
Net Operating Revenues	42,896,745.43	42,483,790.65	412,954.78	—
Income Debits ..	18,560,445.51	16,268,129.27	2,292,316.24	—
Income Credits ..	1,680,402.17	2,485,404.58	—	$805,002.41
Net Income Debits .	6,880,043.34	13,782,724.69	3,097,318.65	—
Surplus for the year	26,016,702.09	28,701,065.96	—	2,684,363.87
Less :—				
Lung Hai Net Operating Revenue ..	1,779,440.35		1,779,440.35	
(Credited to Construction) ..				
True Surplus ..	$24,237,261.74	$28,701,065.96	—	$4,463,804.22

These returns are the least satisfactory of any since uniform statistics have been compiled in that they indicate a retrograde movement in revenues for the first time. In order to appraise this condition to better advantage, Revenues are restated together with certain non-cash items which they contained in 1922 and in 1921.

Total Revenues	1922 $99,556,229.22	1921 $96,450,836.14	Increase $3,105,393.08
Government Service :—			
Passenger	4,389,828.72	3,642,311.14	747,517.58
Goods	2,319,671.33	2,175,569.12	144,102.21
Material for other Railways ..	261,100.24	620,978.73	(d) 359,878.49
Service Stores	1,525,335.85	675,791.00	(d) 150,455.15
Interchange of Rolling Stock ..	4,114,278.25	1,185,846.50	2,928,431.75
Total Non-Commercial	12,610,214.39	9,280,496.49	3,329,717.90
Net Commercial revenue	$86,946,014.83	$87,170,339.65	(d) $244,324.82

(d) indicates decrease.

The revenues given above for 1922 include those for the Lung Hai line and the Suiyüan extension of the Peking–Suiyüan not included in the revenues for 1921. The revenues of 1922 do not contain those earned by the Peking–Mukden line north of the Great Wall after May 1 while those for 1921 do. Lung Hai revenue amounted to $3,163,000, in round numbers, and the Peking–Suiyüan reported an increase of $1,084,000. The Peking–Mukden decrease was $4,794,000, but probably not all of this was due to the loss of the section north of the Wall.

A certain decrease in revenue from the transport of agricultural products was to be expected because of the high earnings from that source in 1921 as a result of shortage in the Chihli plain, but the principal cause for the disappointing revenue results is undoubtedly the military use of the lines in April and May of 1922.

It should be noted also that after fluctuations in revenue from Interchange of Rolling Stock have been eliminated only three lines show decreases, the Peking–Mukden, the Tientsin–Pukow and the Peking–Hankow. These are the lines which were principally involved in the civil war during 1922. And as these are the three longest lines in the Government system, their combined decreases have been sufficient to overbalance increases in every other section.

Operating Expenses increased by about 5 per cent. The loss of revenues from the part of the Peking–Mukden railway lying beyond Shanhaikuan did not result in a corresponding decrease in Expenses. Sleepers and rail distributed along the line and under process of application were debited to Expense during the remainder of the year. Locomotives used on that section of the line during preceding months were in the Tongshan shops for repair, which necessarily involved the same expense as if the whole line had remained untouched. If the increase due to Interchange of Rolling Stock and that due to the inclusion of the Lung Hai line be allowed for, it will be found that there was a decrease in Operating Expenses equivalent to about 3 per cent. In addition, expenses for Maintenance of Equipment contain $3,333,876.15 for Depreciation of Rolling Stock, which is an increase of $719,839.06 after Lung Hai figures are excluded, thus making the decrease for actual operation and maintenance approximately 10 per cent.

While there was a reported Net Revenue over $412,000 greater than that in 1921, it must be remembered that $1,779,000 of this was reported by the Lung Hai and was credited by that line to Construction costs, so that the system had $1,367,000 less than it did in 1921 with which to meet Interest and other Income obligations.

The combined lines were compelled to pay out over $2,292,000 more under Income Obligations than in 1921 and received less by over $800,000 from interest on Government bonds and on current deposits, rents and from similar sources. The large increase in Income Debits is due but little to less favorable rates of exchange for the repayment of interest. Over a third of it is due to interest on short term bank loans and on bills due suppliers, large losses on exchange and discount on depreciated currency. Unfortunately, it must be confessed that the statement given is not fully correct. On the Peking–Suiyüan line the financial affairs are in such a condition that a considerable amount of accrued interest is unpaid. As much of this is payable in foreign currencies and certain accounts bear penalty clauses which render the rate of interest to be paid rather dependent upon future negotiations, the actual amount of interest accrued is problematical. Hence that line has accounted for payments rather than for accruals. This condition also impairs the integrity of the Balance Sheet of that line. It should be noted in passing that most of these short term loans bear interest ranging from 8 to 20 per cent. upon the funds actually received, compared with 3.88 paid upon the long term mortgage bonds and other secured indebtedness.

Only one line, the Changchow–Amoy, (28 kilometers long) reported Revenues lower than Expenses. But in addition, the Ssŭ-Tao, a new line, the Hupeh–Hunan, Canton–Kowloon and the Shanghai–Hangchow–Ningpo were not able, unaided, to meet all interest charges. The latter line, however, came so close to meeting its obligations that there is reason to believe that it will soon be in that desirable condition. After meeting the needs of the lines just mentioned, a Surplus of $24,237,000 remains. This is a decrease of nearly $4,500,000 compared with 1921 and of $16,600,000 compared with 1920. However, the 1922 Surplus represents a return of nearly 10 per cent. upon the equity of the Government represented by Additions to Property and Repayments of Funded Debt made out of Surplus included with Permanent Government Investment. The sources and destinations of all income funds accruing to the railways during the year may be recapitulated on the basis of a typical dollar of income as follows:—

	1922	1921	1920
SOURCES:—			
Operating Revenues ..	$0.98	$0.97½	$0.97
Income Credits	.02	.02½	.03
Income for the Year ..	$1.00	$1.00	$1.00
DESTINATIONS:—			
Operating Expenses ..	.56	.54½	.41
Income Debits (interest, rent, etc.)	.18	.16½	.11
Credited to Lung Hai Construction Cost ..	.02	—	—
Surplus for the Year:			
Government Transportation	.06	.06	.05¼
Interest on Goverment Investment @ 5 per ct.	.12¼	.11½	.10¾
Profits	.05¾	.11½	.32
	$1.00	$1.00	$1.00

For every eighteen cents of Interest charges and other Income Debits to pay, there were thirty-five and a half cents with which to pay, after allowing for Government Transportation, or at the rate of $1.97 to pay each $1.00 of obligation.

It may not be out of place to indicate at this point the relative financial results of the railway operations during the past five years.

Surplus for the Year Government Transportation Collectible Net Surplus

	Surplus for the Year	Government Transportation	Collectible Net Surplus
1922	$24,237,261.74	$6,709,500.05	$17,527,761.69
1921	28,701,065.96	5,797,880.26	23,003,185.70
1920	40,814,447.94	5,021,467.58	35,792,980.36
1919	36,449,392.34	4,932,666.48	32,516,725.86
1918	33,505,119.57	5,961,241.73	27,543,977.84

The tendencies during the past five years may be epitomized as follows: In 1919 and 1920 the per cent. increase in Expenses was greater than that in Revenues, in 1921 the actual increase in Expenses was greater than that in Revenues and in 1922 Revenues themselves no longer increased.

If the investment return upon the different Government lines be stated in terms of an average per kilometer of line, the relative profitableness of the various lines will be more clearly perceived. In the following summary the lines are listed in order of the profit per kilometer of line, after interest reckoned at the rate of five per cent. upon the total Government Investment in each line has been deducted from the Surplus for the year. By "Total Government Investment" is meant Permanent Government Investment plus Additions to Property through Surplus and Funded Dept Retired through Surplus.

Final Profit per Kilometer of Line

1. Peking-Hankow	$6,085	$4,956
2. K'aifeng-Honan	5,319	3,638
3. Chêng Tai..	4,512	4,201
4. Kirin-Ch'angch'un	4,195	5,831
5. Shanghai-Nanking..	3,680	4,149
6. Peking-Mukden	2,860	9,151
7. Tientsin-Pu'kow	1,008	2,512
8. Taokow-Chinghua..	729	772
9. Peking-Suiyüan	(less) 812	(less) 243
10. Ssŭ-Tao	" 1,440	" 1,933
11. Shanghai-H-Ningpo	" 2,273	" 2,497
12. Canton-Kowloon	" 2,273	" 2,518
13. Hupeh-Hunan..	" 4,601	" 5,360
14. Changchow-Amoy	" 6,938	" 8,523
15. Lung-Hai..	(Under construction)	—
Chinese Government Railways ..	$1,791	$2,785

"Less" indicates deficit per kilometer of line if interest on Government Investment at 5 per cent. were to be paid.

It will be noted that the profit over interest upon Government Investment is not two-thirds as great as in 1921 and barely one-third what it was in 1920. However ten out of the fourteen lines report larger figures, and the profitable lines comprise 4,093 kilometers of operated line compared with 2,186 on the other side.

In addition to the profits accruing from the use of the railway property and funds during the year, there are other transactions which add about $2,700,000 to the financial position of the combined lines. These items are recorded in the Profit and Loss accounts and consist of various sorts of items. The principal factor is the gain from exchange in connection with the repayment of Funded Debt. Funded Debt repaid during the year stood on the books at $9,279,323.19. This is the amount in silver dollars realized at the time the retired bonds, which bear denominations expressed in terms of pounds and francs, were issued. But in 1922 a pound or a franc could be purchased for much less than the silver value that prevailed when these bonds were issued. Hence the actual cash paid out in retiring the $9,279,000 odd of bonds probably cost some $3,000,000 less than that amount. This is credited to Profit and Loss as a gain from exchange, and is more than enough to offset the combined deficits on the four lines which reported deficits.

In addition to the amount expended in retiring the bonds just mentioned, approximately $21,000,000 was expended in addition to the property. Lines with surpluses met over $10,600,000 out of that source, while the remainder was met partially out of the surplus of the same lines, through the Ministry of Communications.

On December 31, 1922, the combined lines showed an Accumulated Surplus of $113,539,357.27—an increase of $14,108,325.79. The Accumulated Surplus consisted of Additions to Property approximating $79,700,000, Funded Debt Retired through Surplus, $42,200,000, Free Surplus amounting to nearly $7,700,000 and Funded Reserves of over $2,700,000. The aggregate of these items is offset by some $18,800,000 of Accumulated Deficits on other lines.

The change of the Government's equity in the ownership of the combined railway proporties is shown by the following statement.

Liability	Amount	Increase	Decrease
Government:—			
Permanent Government Investment	$ 125,545,094.20	—	$ 547,125.60
Additions to Property through Surplus	79,701,149,29	$ 9,757,645.76	—
FundedDebtRetired through Surplus	42,267,524,90	7,634,017.68	—
Total Government Equity..	$ 247,513,768.39	16,844,537.84	
Non-Government:—			
Shares (Canton-Samshui excluded)	$ 2,547,015.00	—	—
Mortgages Bonds..	301,679,491.95	2,137,343.48	—
Other Secured Indebtedness	29,011,777.05	—	$ 7,830,191.74
Total Non-Government Equity..	$ 333,238,284.00	—	$ 5,692,848.26

The increase in Stores is again one of the most important fluctuations. The total is now over $47,000,000.

The Cash situation appears to have been somewhat easier in 1922 than in 1921, since there was an increase at the end of the year of nearly $2,000,000. But this increase was enjoyed principally by the Shanghai–Nanking line, which is normally in a sound financial position. Loans and Bills of Exchange increased by over $5,000,000 and Sundry Creditors nearly $20,000,000. Although this is offset somewhat by a decrease of over $8,000,000 in Miscellaneous Deferred credits, the strained financial position of the combined lines is sufficiently indicated. An increase of over $10,000,000 in Temporary Advances to Government, which figure stood at over $31,000,000 at the end of the year, is sufficient explanation.

As would be expected from the conditions, physical performance of equipment was under that reported for 1921. Road locomotives ran an average of only 36,381 kilometers compared with 43,840 in 1921. Passenger cars carried an average of 116 passenger kilometers per carriage seat each day of 1922 compared with 118 in 1921. Goods Wagons hauled an average of 38.1 ton kilometers per ton of capacity each running day in 1922 compared with 58.8 in 1921.

A decrease in Cash amounting to $8,000,000 and an increase $11,000,000 in Loans and Bills of Exchange outstanding against the several lines indicates the increasing financial difficulties of the system as a whole. An increase in Accounts Payable of $2,350,000 is evidence in the same direction. Total Cash resources of only $7,800,000 against Matured Liabilities Unpaid in excess of $5,250,000 and Other Accounts Payable in excess of $13,200,000 indicate a serious condition. Besides there were $29,200,000 of Depreciation Reserves and $35,200,000 Miscellaneous Deferred Creditors which also constitute a contingent claim against Cash. The volume of Miscellaneous Deferred items, both Debits and Credits seriously impairs the meaning of the combined Balance Sheet, being nearly $34,000,000 in the case of Debits and over $35,000,000 in the case of Credits. The analysis of the Detailed Balance Sheet will indicate that the Peking–Suiyüan is principally responsible.

The more significant performances, compared with the same item for the preceding year, are as follows:—

Item	1922	1921	Per cent.	
			Increase	Decrease
Kilometers of Railway Operated	1) 6,279,282	6,013,997	4	
Operating Revenues	$99,556,229.22	$96,450,836.14	3	
Operating Expenses	$56,659,483.79	$53,967,045.49	5	
Net Operating Revenue	$42,896,745.43	$42,483,790.65	1	
Surplus for the year	2)$24,237,261.74	$28,701,065.96	3	
Number of Passengers carried..	35,600,834½	32,909,230	8	
Number of Passenger Kilometers	3,320,897,452	3,162,234,998	5	
Average Number of Passenger Kilometers per Km. of Line ..	528,865	525,812	1	
Average Number of Passenger Kilometers per Train Km. ..	262	257	2	
Average Journey per Passenger (kilometers)	93	96		3
Number of Tons carried.. ..	21,550,570	24,996,131		14
Number of Ton Kilometers ..	3,981,534,813	4,709,939,148		17
Average Number of Ton Kilometers Per Kilometer of Line	634,075	783,162		19
Average Number of Ton Kilometers per Train Kilometer ..	259	274		5
Average Haul per ton (kilometers)	185	188		2
Average Passenger Revenue per Passenger Kilometers	(cents) 1.09	(cents) 1.10		1
Average Goods Revenue per Ton (kilometers)	1.35	1.18	14	
Passenger Train Kilometers ..	12,684,447	12,286,954	3	10
Goods Train Kilometers	15,337,797	17,170,623		4
Locomotive Kilometers	42,356,077	44,124,098		
Number of Employees	91,356	3) 89,043	3	

1) Mean average reported.
2) Lung Hai excluded.
3) Chuchow Pinghsiang included.

Another section of the Government report deals with the statistics of railways which are not the property of the Chinese Government but which are situated within the territorial boundaries of China. These statistics are presented for the first time in the history of these reports and have been compiled from brief reports furnished to the Ministry by courtesy of the managements of the reporting lines. For the time being this tabulation is experimental and incomplete. The accounts of the various reporting railways are not kept in such a manner as to make comparative statement possible. While it would not be a difficult matter to adjust the accounts and statistics of any one railway to agree with another, it would be a more difficult task to adjust all to a common basis. Hence for the time being at least it is not possible to present statistics with any degree of detail. It is hoped that during future years such a degree of co-operation will be tendered by the several lines that more complete presentation will be given in subsequent reports.

Kilometers of Railway Owned

Name of Line	Main line	Branch lines	Other track	Total track
Chinese Government Railways	6,186.5	434.5	1,743.5	8,364.8
Chinese Eastern Railway	1,726.5	(a) 458.1	736.1	2,920.7
South Manchurian Railway	969.8	134.2	1,333.0	2,437.0
Kiaochow-Tsinan Railway (Shantung)	394.1	52.0	165.4	621.5
Yünnan Railway	464.0	—	—	—
Kowloon-Canton Railway (British section)	46.7	—	—	—
Total reported	9,787.6	—	—	—

(a) includes line into timber concession.

NOT OFFICIALLY REPORTED:

Kwangtung Provincial line	225
Sunning Railway	171
Kiukiang–Nanch'ang Railway	136
Tai-Tsao Railway (Chung Hsing Mining Co.)	52
Swatow–Ch'aochowfu Railway	42
Tayeh Mines Railway	30
Taiyaokou Mines Railway	29
Tsitsihar Narrow Gauge Railway	29
K'ailan Mining Administration Railway	16
Ching Hsing Mining Company Railway	15
Liu Chang Coal Mines Railway	12
Nanking City Railway	11
Total not officially reported	768

In order to present a complete statement of kilometers of railway in China it is necessary to go beyond reports rendered by the various lines for information. Railway Line in China may be summarized as follows:—

	Main Line	Branch Line	Total
Government Railway:			
In operation Reported	6,185.5	434.5	6,620.0
In operation, Not reported .	139.4	—	139.4
Under construction forces .	223.0	—	223.0
Other Railways, reporting	3,601.1	644.3	4,245.4
„ „ Not „	772.0	—	772.0
Total kilometers of railway in China	10,921.0	1,078.8	11,999.8

It is rather difficult to make a distinction between "line" and "track" in several instances. It is possible that some of the railways serving some of the mining companies carry no goods or passengers for hire. In such cases kilometers of such railways should be listed under industrial track rather than as railway line. Also in the case of the branch line on the Chinese Eastern Railway, much of the length consists of track into timber concessions. Most of the traffic over such track is for the purpose of hauling out fuel for the railway, but it is reported that charges are collected for haul of supplies to contractors, and hence the classification has placed such track under "Branch Line" rather than under "Other Track."

In computing the tons capacity of rolling stock, poods on the Chinese Eastern have been converted into metric tons by dividing the number of poods by 16.38. Short tons used on the South Manchurian and the Kiaochow–Tsinan (Shantung) railways have been converted into metric tons by using .90718 as a multiplier. English tons used on the Kowloon–Canton railway have not been converted since there is barely 1 per cent. difference in the two units.

Rolling Stock Owned

Name of Line	Locomotives Number	Carriages		Wagons	
		Number	Seating Capacity	Number	Tons Capacity
Chinese Government Railways	992	1,395	78,033	14,401	392,603
Chinese Eastern Railway	536	810	23,789	11,509	224,607
South Manchurian Railway	367	373	24,842	5,960	(1) 183,513
Kiaochow-Tsinan Railway	99	145	11,127	1,639	28,755
Yünnan Railway	Not Reported	—	—	—	—10
Kowloon-Canton Railway	15	36	3,392	79	1.8

(1) Includes 106 wagons, capacity 2,722 tons leased to Ssŭ-Tao Line.

The gold rouble was the unit of money on the Chinese Eastern, the gold yen was the unit of the South Manchurian and the Kiaochow–Tsinan (Shantung) railways, and some form of

Chinese dollar was the unit on the other lines from which reports have been received. Due to differences of metal prices the Chinese dollar was worth slightly more than the rouble or the yen during 1922, but the difference is too small to impair general comparisons.

Name of Line	Operating Revenues	Operating Expenses	Net Operating Revenues	Operating Percentage
Chinese Government Railways	1) $99,556,229.22	2) $56,659,483.79	$42,896,745.43	(3) 56.9
Chinese Eastern Railway	Rs. 33,333,779.00	27,577,675.00	5,756,095.00	82.6
South Manchurian Railway	Y 89,622,013.00	34,099,801.00	53,562,212.00	39.0
Kiaochow-Tsinan Railway	Y 8,455,683.00	4,411,618.00	4,044,065.00	52.3
Yünnan Railway	$2,658,661.00	Not reported	—	—
Kowloon-Canton Railway	710,295.00	562,144.00	148,151.00	78.1

(1) Includes $1,525,335.85 revenue from haul of Service Stores for which other lines do not have an equivalent.

(2) Includes debits $1,356,519.33 Carriage of Stores and $3,333,876.15 for which other lines do not have an equivalent.

(3) Excluding Carriage of Stores, Depreciation and Interchange of Rolling Stock, percentage would be 50.8.

Traffic Density

Name of Line	Average per Kilometer of Line					
	Passenger Traffic			Goods Traffic		
	No. Carried	Kilometers	Revenue	Tons Carried	Ton Kilometers	Revenue
Chinese Government Railways	6,022	528,866	$5,464.10	3,432	634,075	$8,535.16
Chinese Eastern Railway.. ..	1,402	253,432	R 4,614.38	1,482	502,038	R 12,953.26
South Manchurian Railway.	6,925	663,161	Y 11,222.34	9,897	3,666,515	Y 62,969.30
Kiaochow - Tsinan Railway .	8,215	488,455	Y 4,735.29	4,764	989,598	Y 13,393.74
Yünnan Railway	2,987	162,867	$1,830.54	282	not reported	$3,326.66
Kowloon - Canton Railway .	37,283	not reported	$13,190.63		not reported	$1,430.97

Train and Locomotive Kilometers and Employees

Name of Line	Train Kilometers			Locomotive Kilometers	Number of Employees
	Passenger	Goods	Total		
Chinese Government Railways	12,684,447	15,337,797	28,022,247	42,356,067	91,356
Chinese Eastern Railway	2,061,996	3,248,788	5,310,784	7,903,568	18,362
South Manchurian Railway..	3,367,930	9,404,122	12,772,052	14,759,425	18,267
Kiaochow - Tsinan Railway..	1,014,550	1,743,287	2,757,837	3,303,048	5,988
Yünnan Railway	544,620	660,883	1,205,503	not reported	not reported
Kowloon-Canton Railway	191,627	6,588	198,215	359,921	not reported

PASSENGER TRAFFIC.

Name of Line	Number of		Revenue	Average			
	Passengers Carried	Passengers Kilometers		Journey (Kms)	Rate per Pass. Km	Revenue per passenger	Passengers per train
Chinese Government Rlys	35,600,833	3,320,897,452	$34,310,622.30	93	c 1.09	$ .90	262
Chinese Eastern Railways	2,421,434	437,551,000	Rs. 7,966,727.92	181	k 1.82	Rs. 3.29	212
South Manchurian Rlys ..	7,645,068	732,130,142	Y. 12,389,465.00	96	s 1.69	Y. 1.62	243
Kiaochow-Tsinan Railway	3,664,666	217,899,672	Y. 2,112,415.44	60	s .97	Y. .58	215
Yünnan Railway	1,386,006	75,570,429	(1) 849,371.14	54	c .61	$1.52	139
Kowloon-Canton (British section)	1,741,160	Not reported	616,002.82	Not reported		—	—

(1) Collected by stations in Yünnan.
c indicates cents. k indicates kopecs. s indicates sen.

GOODS TRAFFIC.

Name of Line	Number of		Goods Revenue	Average			
	Tons Carried	Ton Kilometers		Haul	Rate per ton Km.	Revenue per ton	Tons per train
Chinese Government Rlys	21,550,600	3,981,534,813	$53,594,700.00	185	c 1.35	$ 2.49	274
Chinese Eastern Railway	2,559,448	866,768,570	Rs.22,363,815.09	339	k 2.58	Rs. 8.74	257
South Manchurian Railway	10,926,127	4,047,832,577	Y. 69,518,111.00	349	s 1.73	$ 6.36	430
Kiaochow-Tsinan Railway	2,125,147	441,459,453	5,974,951.19	207	s 1.35	$ 2.81	253
Yünan Railway	130,811	Not reported	(1)$1,543,572.50	185	c 5.07	$11.38	61
Kowloon-Canton Railway	Not reported	——	66,826.56	—	—	—	—

(1) Collected by stations in Yünnan.

CHINESE GOVERNMENT RAILWAYS

Total Kilometers of Main and Branch Lines

Name of Railway in full	Abbreviated Name	Starting at	Terminating at	Length in Kilometers		
				Main Line	Branch Line	Total
Canton-Hankow-Szech'uan (1)	Han-yüe-ch'uan	Wuchang	Chuchow	417.623	5.021	422.644
Canton-Kowloon	Kwang-Kiu	Tasaton, Canton	Kowloon	143.300	—	143.300
Canton-Samshui	Kwang-San	Canton	Shanghai	71.000	—	71.000
Changchow-Amoy (Lines in Operation)	Chang-Sia	Suengyuien, Amoy	Kiangtungch'iao, Changchow	28.000	—	28.000
Chefoo-Weihsien (2)	Yen-Wei	Chefoo	Weihsien	228.980	—	228.900
Chêngting-T'aiyüan	Chêng-T'ai	Shihchiachwang	Taiyüan	243.000	—	243.000
Chuchow-Pinghsiang	Chu-Ping	Anyuan, Chuchow	Hsinho, Pinghsiang	90.500	—	90.500
Kiaochow-Tsinan	Kiao-Tsi	Tsingtao	Tsinan	451.000	—	451.000
Kirin-Ch'angch'un	Ki-Ch'ang	Toutaokou, Changchun	Kirin	127.700	—	127.700
Lanchow-Haichow (3)	Lung-Tsing-Yü-Hai	Kaifeng	Kwanyintang	442.000	—	442.000
Peking-Hankow	Kin-Han	Peking	Hankow	1,214.174	106.826	1,321.000
Peking-Mukden	Kin-Fêng	Peking	Mukden	870.000	92.000	962.000
Peking-Suiyüan	King-Sui	Peking	Suiyüan	667.737	70.101	737.838
Honan-K'aifêng	Pien-Lo	Kaifeng	Loyang	185.000	—	185.000
Shanghai-Hangchow-Ningpo	Hu-Han-Yung	Shanghai	Ningpo	281.112	5.888	287.000
Shanghai-Nanking	Hu-Ning	Shanghai	Nanking	310.910	16.090	327.000
Ssŭp'ingkai-Taonan	Ssŭ-Tao	Ssŭp'ingchieh	Taonan	202.000	—	202.000
Taokow-Chinghua	Tao-Ching	Chinghua	Sanlinwan, Taokow	150.000	2.440	152.440
Tientsin-P'uk'ow	Tsin-P'u	Tientsin	P'uk'ow	1,009.130	96.580	1,105.710
			TOTAL KILOMETERS	7,133.166	394.946	7,528.032
Changchow-Shihchiachwang	Chang-Shih	Changchow	Shihchiachwang	225.000	—	225.000
Chinghsien-Ch'ungking	Ching-Yui	Chinghsien	Ch'ungking	1,130.000	—	1,130.000
Chuchow-Chinghsien	Chu-Ching-Chow-Hsiang	Chuchow	Chinghsien	1,327.000	—	1,327.000
Nanking-Hsiangtan (Lines Surveyed)	Ning-Hsiang	Nanking	Hsiangtan	992.000	—	992.000
P'uk'ow-Singyang	P'u-Sing	Woo-i, Pukow	Sinyang, Honan	437.000	—	437.000
Tat'ung-Chêngtu	T'ung-Chang	Tat'ung	Chêngtu	1,600.000	—	1,600.000
			TOTAL KILOMETERS	5,711.000	—	5,711.000

Description Name of Railway in full	Abbreviated Name	Starting at	Terminating at	Length in Kilometers		
				Main Line	Branch Line	Total
Harbin-Heilungkiang	Ping Hei	Harbin	Heilungkiang	Length not yet decided		
Kirin-Huei-ning	Ki-Huei	Kirin	Hueining			
Kaomi-Hsüchow	Kao-Hsü	Kaomi	Hsüchow			
Shêngtêh-Tsinan (Lines not yet surveyed)	Shêng-Tsi	Shêngtêh	Tsinan			
Four Railways of Manchuria and Mongolia	Ki-Yüan	Kirin	Kaiyüan			
	Jêh-Tao	Jêhol	Taonan			
	Ch'ang-Tao	Ch'ang-ch'un	Taonan			
	Jêh-Kong	Jêhol	Seaport			

NOTE: (1) This main trunk line comprises two railways, the Canton–Hankow and the Hankow–Szech'uan. The section completed and in operation is from Wuch'ang to Chuchow, passing through the provinces of Hupeh, Honan and Kwangsi, a distance of 417,623 kilometers. Work on the extension to Canton is suspended.

(2) Earth work and culverts of this line were constructed out of famine relief surtaxes collected on railway revenue in 1921. An automobile service has been opened on the road, and is under the supervision of the Ministry of Communications. Lack of funds has prevented the line from being railed.

(3) The Lanchow–Haichow Railway Line commences in Kansu province, passes through Shensi and Honan provinces, and terminates at Haichow in Kiangsu. The section opened to traffic is from K'aifeng to Kwanyingtang, beyond which work is still in progress.'

Suggestions and plans for the unification of the Chinese railways have been made by experts and Technical Boards, but the matter is extremely complicated and they have not as yet materialized.

References.—A leader in the *Hongkong Daily Press* of 9th September, 1891, gives an interesting account of the development of the Tientsin Railway from a seven-miles tram-line to the present dimensions. An interesting article has appeared in *The Engineer*, giving an account of the history and construction of the railway in Formosa. It was republished in the *London and China Express* and copied in the *Hongkong Telegraph* of the 10th of August, 1892. A perusal of this article will show the great difficulties encountered from Chinese ignorance, prejudice, and bribery in such works. 'Railway Enterprise in China,' an article in *Chambers's Journal* for May, 1899, by B. Taylor; Herstlet, *China Treaties; Reports of Chinese Government Railways* (Ministry of Communications); Chêng, *Modern China; Chinese Economic Monthly* (Chinese Government Bureau of Economic Information).

RATS.—The rat is as common a creature in China as elsewhere. In fact, scientists trace the brown, or Norway, rat back to Western China as its ancient home. From this, its original habitat, it journeyed westward to Europe, and reached England by the aid of ships arriving in the latter country in A.D. 1730, having crossed the Volga in 1727. They marched in large troops, appearing in 'Paris about the middle of the eighteenth century.'

'The rat, especially the Asiatic rat, is more susceptible to plague than any other animal, the guinea-pig coming next, and, as rats have a habit of joining ships at one port and leaving them at another, they become a menace, as they may form the the medium of conveying the plague infection round the world.'

To prevent this, tin shields are put on ships' cables to keep them from landing. (See also PLAGUE.)

It is a mistake to suppose that Chinese live on rats, etc. They are eaten occasionally by the very poor: in the country, some four or five out of a hundred have doubtless tasted them. These people, if they come across a large, fat one may cook it. Dried rats are to be seen hung up for sale in dried meat shops. The wealthy do not eat them, as a rule, though there is a notion that rat's flesh will produce the growth of hair: so some, though feeling squeamish about such meat, will force themselves to eat a little in order that their hair may grow again.

The Chinese appear to be very cruel occasionally when a rat is caught: sometimes the offending creature is nailed alive to a board; at other times it is dipped in kerosene and set fire to while its tormentors gloat over its agony. Doubtless there is a feeling that the thief and destroyer of their property is suffering a just reward for its depredations.

The family of rats, mice, hamsters and voles includes thirty-three species in North China and neighbourhood. Swinhoe names a dozen species of the *Mus* genus as found south of the Yangtzŭ, some probably included in the list of those found in the North. Of the *Spalacidæ,* a Family of the *Rodentia,* consisting of the Molerats, six species are known in North China; and of the *Dipodidæ,* or jumping rats and mice, six species are named.

References.—Journal, N.C.B.R.A.S., N.S. vol. xlvii; Swinhoe, *Catalogue of the Mammals of China.*

RELIGION.—In this ancient nation are to be found many persistent survivals of old-world religions and myths handed down from generation to generation through the long ages past. Faint traces of such beliefs and modes of worship are to be found by the diligent enquirer in our Western lands; but in China they form in many cases not only the basis on which have been super-imposed the more modern systems of religion; but they permeate the whole present amalgam of credulity, superstition, forms and ritual, which go to make up the average Chinaman's religion. The worship of Heaven and Earth, of mountains and rivers is still in existence, and traces of Sabianism are to be found; the adoration and planting of sacred trees near temples can be seen to this day; and a most common form of worship is the worship of stones, besides an ever present and most profound belief in evil spirits which cause disease, etc.

As Gibbon said of Rome, so it might almost be said of China to-day:—'To the common people all religions are equally true; to the philosopher all are equally false; to the magistrate all are equally useful.' To the superficial observer the Chinese appear a very religious people, and yet, an closer observation, it will be found that there is a great deal of formalism about their worship. They are very superstitious, and the whole land is full of idols. The women are most devout worshippers; many of the educated men profess scepticism, while giving an outward adhesion to the forms of worship. There are some earnest souls to be found among them who join different sects of Buddhism in order to find some satisfaction for the longings of their hearts; when the truths of Christianity are presented to such, they are sometimes received as a revelation from Heaven.

Briefly, the religion of the Chinese may be said to be Ancestor-worship and its derivatives (see Werner, *China of the Chinese*). (See also ANCESTOR-WORSHIP.)

References.—De Groot, *The Religious System of China.* See articles on Buddhism, Taoism, and Missions, and the books named at the end of those articles.

RICE.—The Chinese language has developed a number of names for rice in its different stages of growth, thus confirming what Archdeacon Trench pointed out—the tendency of a language to develop in any special direction. Rice being the main support of the inhabitants of the South of China, every stage of its growth is of the greatest interest to them; but to us, who never see it in our own land but in the hulled grain, it is simply rice whether in that state, or when the tender blade is just shooting out of the ground, or when nearly ripe; and we have to borrow from a foreign language the word paddy to represent it with the husk on—a word, by-the-bye, little used or known in England itself, as the necessity for its use there is but slight. For all of these different conditions of rice, the Chinese have names, and again, not only does one word do duty for cooked rice, but the soup-like drink made from boiling a small quantity of rice in a large quantity of water, has a distinctive name of its own, *chuk* (pronounced chook in Canton) [*chou*], for which Europeans in the East, being at a loss for a word to express it, have again had recourse to the borrowing of a Malay word to express it, *congee.* The ordinary name for uncooked rice is *mi* or *ta mi* (*Oryza sativa*). Glutinous rice (*O. glutinosa*), called *no mi,* is distinguished from this by its whiteness, opaqueness, and more globular shape. It is occasionally eaten as a change of diet, but is more usually baked and eaten as cakes between meals. There are also a few other kinds, such as water-grown rice (*shui mi*), upland rice (*han mi*), red rice (*O. sativa præcox*) (*hung-ku mi*), etc.

'To eat rice' is synonymous with taking a meal; and the equivalent of 'How do you do?' is 'Have you eaten your rice yet?' 'He cannot eat his rice' is tantamount to saying that a sick man is unable to take his food. Breakfast is *chíú* [*ch'ao* or *tsao*]-*fán*, 'morning rice,' and *ye* [*yeh*]-*fán*, or *mán* [*wan*]-*fán*, 'late rice,' or 'evening rice' stands for dinner. With regard to its use as food in the extreme South, see FOOD.

Rice is grown in all the provinces south of the Yellow River and to a small extent in South Manchuria (here by dry cultivation). The chief centres of production are the Yangtzŭ valley, especially the Anhui-Kiangsu belt, and the plains of Hunan and Kuangsi. The production of the former belt is estimated at from forty to forty-eight million piculs. In unusually productive years, as much as six million piculs may be available for exportation. The northern provinces draw their rice supplies from these regions. Japan, Tonking, Cochin-China, Siam, and Burma import rice to South China. The province of Kuangsi also sends some to other provinces in the south of China.

In South China two crops are obtained annually, in the north only one. The total production is given officially as three and three-quarter million tons per annum; but some estimates put it as high as thirty-seven and a half million tons.

The rice grows in small patches, scarcely entitled to be called fields. As the rice grows best in water, these are under a few inches of water the most of the time. There are no fences or walls between them, but the mud is piled up all round each little division of ground, and, drying in the sun, forms a narrow footpath only wide enough for one person to walk on. When the rice-plant, which has been thickly sown in one place, is 6 inches high, it is transplanted into the miniature fields by men and women wading through the mud, and five or six of these sprouts are stuck into one hole. In a very short time the fields present a beautiful sight, being converted from the muddy flats into masses of living, delicate green. Two, or sometimes even three, crops of rice, or other plants, succeed one another—a crop of fish is put into the field when they, the fish, are a few inches long, to fatten for the market while the rice is growing.

The Chinese prefer their own rice to that grown in foreign countries. There are several varieties of this useful grain, coarse and fine, white and red, glutinous and non-glutinous.

At New Year's time popped rice is largely used, and is carried about the streets in large baskets, looking like snow in its whiteness. It is prepared in the same way as the popped Indian corn, or maize, of the New England States, and is very much like it in appearance and taste.

About Swatow and Amoy more *congee* is eaten than at Canton and neighbourhood, while, up North, millet takes the place of rice; though rice is eaten at meals as supplementary to other food.

References.—For an interesting account of rice the world round, see Rhein's *Industries of Japan*, p. 37; King, *Farmers of Forty Centuries*; Hosie, *Ssŭch'uan*.

RIOTS.—Ever since the opening of China to foreign trade, there have been periodical riots directed against foreign residents at different treaty ports and cities. In their intensity and wild outburst they resemble the cyclonic disturbances, the typhoons, which carry death and destruction in their train. As before the typhoons premonitory symptoms are generally observable in a disturbed state of the atmosphere, so before these riots there is a heated state of opinion, which those who are in touch with the native mind may discover.

To those not intimately acquainted with the Chinese it may be supposed that as the proverbial Irishman is never happy unless he is in the midst of a row, so the Chinese are only in their native element when rushing in hordes against the defenceless European or American. To say that the Chinese are peaceful, law-abiding subjects seems preposterous when writing about Chinese riots, but such a statement, nevertheless, is the truth; for they are one of the most peaceful nations in the world. The Chinese, from a European standpoint, is made up of a mass of incongruities, the most opposite traits of character are to be found in juxtaposition; and this same quiet Chinaman is a perfect demon, a yelling, infuriated brute, a monster of destruction, in a riot; rapine, robbery, arson, and murder, all rapidly succeed each other at such a time, the howling mob ravening like wild beasts as they run wanton with life and property. 'There is no fear of Got in a riot,' so according to Shakespeare said Sir Hugh Evans.

What are the causes that transform the law-abiding Chinaman into a demon of destruction? We will mention what we consider to be some of them. It must first be taken into consideration that the Chinese as a mass are woefully ignorant of the commonest scientific facts which are taught to our children at school. When they find that we are able to rush along at the rate of 60 miles an hour in railways; when they see steamers go without wind and against the tide; when they hear some vague rumour of Westerners being able to see millions of miles into the sky, or on the other hand minutely examine some insect and make it as large as a buffalo; when they see tumours cut off and legs and arms amputated by the skilful surgeon; it is comparatively easy for them to believe that these magic-working foreigners can look several inches into the ground and discover precious metals, especially since their own geomancers pretend to the same power (foreigners in the interior, have been asked if they do not possess this power); and further, with such people, it does not require much stretch of the imagination to believe the story that foreigners, who are all blue-eyed, require the black eyes of Chinese children to compound their wonder-working medicines, or the eyes of dead Chinese to transform lead into silver. It will thus be seen that, owing to this dense ignorance, they are credulous to an extreme extent. They will believe almost any and everything. It must also be remembered that we are foreigners to them—enemies we have been at various times; and, unfortunately, in our relations with them, we have sometimes been overbearing; the nation looks upon us as the introducers of opium; the officials and *literati* fear (or did until recently) our science and civilisation will overturn theirs, and most of the mandarins were afraid that these would put an end to their corrupt system of government and their profits; some dreaded that we would eventually wrest their country from them. Besides, of late years, a knowledge of the shutting of foreign countries, such as America and Australia, against unrestricted Chinese immigration is becoming known; to which must be added the fact that the mass of foreigners do not understand the Chinese, at times fearing designs from them when they are to be trusted, and implicity trusting them when they are acting with duplicity; and we, unfortunately, do not always act with sufficient care in our intercourse with them, for our motives are often misunderstood and our actions misconstrued. We are strange, grotesque, bizarre objects in their eyes, our every action *outré*, and sinister motives are readily ascribed to such curious beings as we appear to them—devils as they call us. These ideas have as yet hardly been modified as regards the majority of the people. Given all this material, it needs but the dissemination of lying books against some foreigners, issued with the *imprimatur* of high officials; it requires but an incipient rebellion in the throes of its attempted birth; it wants but a few lewd fellows of the baser sort to start a riot; the apathetic, indifferent, and half-sympathising mandarins take care, as a rule, to keep out of the way until the mischief is done, while their soldiery, as often as not, lend a hand in the plundering of compounds, the dismantling of houses. And yet it is wonderful how an armed little force, consisting only of the mercantile residents, a dozen or a score of men, if resolutely facing the packed mass of the infuriated mob breathing out death and destruction, could, with scarcely firing a shot, disperse the armies of the aliens like smoke.

'The huge majority of Chinese, the peasants and traders, are eminently law-abiding folk, and would no more dream of sacking foreign chapels than they would dream of learning Euclid or of coming to help a foreigner who was being murdered.'

The following refers to pre-Republican times.

'Nine anti-foreign riots out of ten are directly fomented and instigated from the yamêns, possibly not by the mandarin himself, but at any rate by his *entourage*, or by the local *literati;* every yamên has a host of hangers on—lictors, squeezers, and their relations to the tenth degree. These people are invariably hand in glove with the loafers, gamblers, and opium-smokers who constitute the criminal classes of every Chinese town and who are ready for anything from the T'ái P'ing Rebellion to baiting a missionary, for they feel sure that their own skins will not suffer. The outrages on foreigners are rarely the result of a sudden outburst of passion; they are raked up by persons who are perfectly well known in the locality. When riots occur, the most innocent mandarin is invariably guilty of having lacked the courage to put his foot down and crush the movement before it had gathered force. . . . It should be made perfectly clear to the official classes of China that they will have to pay "through the nose" for allowing their underlings to indulge in the pastime of committing outrages on foreign subjects. The tariff for murdering a missionary should be made absolutely prohibitive. If every Vicerory felt convinced that he would have to pay a quarter of a million taels within three months for every missionary murdered within his jurisdiction, there can be little doubt that missionaries would be as safe in China as in Piccadilly. Under ordinary circumstances the people of China are totally indifferent to Christian or any other religious propaganda; they neither understand nor wish to understand nirvana, pure Tao, or justification by faith; they wish to pursue their ordinary avocations in peace, and would be quite willing to allow the missionary to do the same.'

We give a list of a few of the more notable riots:—

7th December, 1842.—European factories at Canton destroyed by a mob.

21st June, 1870.—Riot at Tientsin and massacre of R.C. nuns.

4th May, 1874.—Riot in French Concession, Shanghai.

10th September, 1883.—Riot by Chinese mob in Canton. Great destruction of foreign houses and property on Shameen.

3rd October, 1884.—Serious coolie riot in Hongkong.

4th October, 1884.—Attack on foreigners at Wenchow.

1st July, 1886.—Serious riot at Chungking.

5th February, 1889.—Anti-foreign riot at Chinkiang. Foreign houses burned and looted.

13th May, 1891.—Anti-foreign riot at Wuhu. Catholic mission premises, I.M. Custom House, and British Consulate burned and looted.

18th May, 1891.—Anti-foreign riot in the Hochow district. Anti-foreign riot at Ngankin.

25th May 1891. — Anti-foreign riot at Ngankin. Some foreign houses burned and looted.

1st June, 1891.—Anti-foreign riot at Tanyang, 20 miles from Chinkiang. Catholic property destroyed.

5th June, 1891.—Anti-foreign riot at Wusüeh, near Hankow. Foreign property destroyed, Rev. Mr. Argent, Wesleyan Missionary, and Mr. Green, of the Imperial Maritime Customs service, killed.

7th June, 1891.—Attempted anti-foreign riot at Kiukiang.

8th June 1891.—Destruction of French Missionaries' property at Woo-sih, near Foochow, by an anti-foreign mob.

9th June, 1891.—Attack on mission premises at Soochow. Rioters dispersed.

14th June, 1891.—Mission property burned down at Shasi.

20th June, 1891.—Riot at Ha-mien City on the Yangtzŭ. Catholic property destroyed.

25th and 26th June, 1891.—Riots attempted at Tsing-kiangpu and Hunan-fu on the Grand Canal, but suppressed.

30th June, 1891.—A mob loots and burns down Catholic chapel and schools at Yan-kao, near Tung-chow on the Yangtzŭ.

July, 1891.—Riot at Yü-yang-hsien, about half-way between Ichang and Ch'ung-king.

2nd September, 1891.—Riot at Ichang. Nearly all foreign property destroyed.

1st July, 1893.—Two Swedish Missionaries murdered at Sungpu, in Central China, by mob.

June, 1894.—Two medical missionary ladies attacked by a mob in Honam, Canton, because one of then rendered assistance to a plague patient, and on the 20th June, at Sheklung, Tung Kwún, the American Presbyterian Chapel demolished by a mob, and one man killed.

29th May, 1895.—Anti-foreign riots in Ssŭch'uan.

1st August, 1895.—At Kuch'êng (near Foochow) massacre, Rev. Mr. Stewart and ten helpless ladies and children murdered by a mob.

12th May, 1896.—Serious riot at Kiangyin. Mission property entirely destroyed.

1st November, 1897.—Murder of two German Catholic priests at Yenchow by a band of twenty men, which led up to the seizure of Kiaochow by the Germans.

16th March, 1898.—American Mission, in suburbs of Ch'ungking, sacked by mob, and Chinese medical assistants maltreated and one murdered.

9th April, 1898.—Riot in Shasi. Buildings on foreign bund destroyed.

8th July, 1898.—Protestant and Catholic Missions attacked by rioters at Shum-ching-fu [Shun-ch'ing Fu], in Ssŭch'uan. A French priest captured by brigands.

15th October, 1898.—Rioting at Ho Chou, 50 miles from Ch'ungking. American and French Mission places attacked and burned.

25th October, 1898.—Rioting at Shameen, Canton.

8th January, 1899.—Serious rioting at Sung-do, near Ningpo, over an attempt to work mines. $10,000 worth of mining property destroyed.

15th August, 1902.—Murder of two missionaries, Messrs. Bruce and Lowis, by mob, at Chengchow [Ch'ênchou], Hunan.

February, 1905.—Massacre of seven French and three British missionaries at Nanch'ang.

It is impossible to give an account of all the small unimportant riots or mob attacks. At times riots have been imminent but have not matured, while in a few cases they have actually taken place, but have been unattended with loss of life and with but little injury to property.

The terrible Boxer rising fostered by the Chinese Government, Chinese officials aiding and abetting the Boxers and Chinese soldiers fighting with them in a war of extermination against all Westerners, resulting in the dreadful siege of the legations in Peking, the fighting in Tientsin, the operations in North China and the taking of the Taku Forts, etc., scarcely comes under the category or Riots; but it may not be amiss to call attention to the number of murdered missionaries, many of them slaughtered in cold blood, some by order of officials with a slight semblance of legal procedure.

These massacres took place in 1899 and 1900. One Mission alone—the China Inland—lost 48 members and 21 children. The total Protestant loss, however, was 135 adults and 53 children. Of these, nearly 100 were British, more than 50 Swedish, and over 30 Americans. If the Roman Catholic losses are added and the martyred native Christians, it will be one of the greatest persecutions in history. Even the Diocletian persecution was less, according to Gibbon. See also SOCIETIES, SECRET.

References.—The Anti-Foreign Riots in China in 1891; Reid, *The Sources of the Anti-Foreign Disturbances in China; Hongkong Daily Press,* Feb. 21, 1894 (Swedish Missionary riot) ; *Fortnightly Review,* August, 1896. Innumerable books have been written about the Boxer rebellion. The principal ones are named in *Encyclopædia Sinica,* where a full account of the rebellion is given.

ROADS.—In the south of China the rivers are the natural roads, and in some places, especially in the delta of the Canton river, the country is reticulated with rivers, streams, cross canals, etc., which bring every few miles of country within easy reach of water communication. Back from the network of rivers, paths connect the market-towns and villages. In some places these paths are paved with granite slabs. It is considered a meritorious act to repair or construct roads.

The country near Swatow is well provided with water communication; some of the rivers have numerous boats of many descriptions. The public roads in this neighbourhood are good, as a rule, though but paths. They are often formed of a kind of cement in large slabs about a yard or so wide, occasionally square stones are let into this cement, while at other times, squares of a slightly different structure from the rest of the road, and looking like conglomerate, are so let in, while again at other times the stone is used. The roads in this locality are not straight, but ramble through the rice-fields with a very meandering course.

In the neighbourhood of Amoy there does not seem to be such a traffic on the rivers; and the same is said to hold good with regard to the great Yangtzŭ Kiang in the centre of China.

In the north of China, where carts are used, the roads are worn below the surface of the surrounding land, and in the heavy rains form water-courses for the deluges that pour from the skies to escape by: when in this state they have occasionally to be swum by travellers, and instances of wayfarers being drowned in the road are not unknown.

In some places, roads made five hundred or even thousands of years ago are in existence.

It would greatly develop trade and facilitate intercommunication were a Chinese MacAdam to arise or were the Chinese Government, instead of buying foreign war material, to devote its energy to the construction of these arteries of trade. With the curious topsyturvy way in which the Chinese do everything, it is not at all unlikely that the iron road will run its spider-like lines through the length and breadth of the empire before a system of properly constructed roads becomes *un fait accompli* in this land. In fact, the spread of railways and motor vehicles will necessitate improvement in roads.

SCHOOLS, STUDENTS AT.—

The following are the latest and most accurate figures very recently issued by the National Association for the Advancement of Education relative to the exact number of students in each province throughout the country:—

Provinces	*In Primary Schools*	*In Middle Schools*	*In College Schools*	*Total*
Peking	85,020	7,641	13,671	106,332
(Including the Meropolitan Area)				
Chihli	555,127	12,437	2,169	569,769
Fêngt'ien . . .	326,010	9,401	659	336,070
Kirin	68,785	2,283	102	71,170
Heilungkiang . .	51,463	1,804	75	53,342
Shantung . . .	777,771	11,066	787	789,624
Shansi	800,827	11,857	863	813,547
Honan	282,589	8,362	426	291,377
Kiangsu . . .	394,037	17,226	4,611	415,874
Anhui	95,979	8,268	171	104,778
Kiangsi	225,478	7,297	907	233,692
Fukien	150,817	6,260	843	157,920
Chêkiang . . .	416,202	11,513	1,041	428,756

Provinces	In Primary Schools	In Middle Schools	In College Schools	Total
Hupei	236,789	8,411	2,577	247,777
Hunan	324,451	14,698	1,799	340,948
Shensi	217,654	3,620	224	221,498
Kansu	122,018	1,600	190	123,808
Hsinkiang . . .	5,757	85	—	5,842
Ssŭch'uan . . .	375,636	12,174	1,428	589,238
Canton	376,799	11,914	1,716	390,429
Kuangsi	201,526	6,683	276	208,485
Yünnan	203,172	4,697	115	207,984
Kueichou . . .	66,855	2,273	230	69,358
Ad. Areas . . .	40,790	838	—	41,588
Grand Total . .	6,601,512	182,804	24,880	6,809,196

(See also EDUCATION.)

SHOOTING.—The Chinese are not sufficiently civilised to take delight in killing birds and other game for pleasure! A small amount of shooting goes on for food purposes. To those who glory in such pursuits there is no better book than Lieutenant Craddock's 'Sporting Notes in the Far East.' He seems to have had a varied experience, and gives it for the benefit of others, detailing the game to be found at the different ports, the seasons for them, and rules of procedure. Snipe, pheasants, woodcock, quail, and many other birds, as well as deer, etc., are to be found at different places. It would be a good day for the inhabitants of certain districts of China if sportsmen would follow the example of a few of their number and go tiger shooting. This is to be found in the neighbourhood of Amoy and Foochow, in some parts of the Canton province, and doubtless in many other places in China. The tigers are a regular pest, carrying off young children at times even from the doors of their houses, as well as dogs and other small animals. In two years, foreign sportsmen from Amoy 'have killed no fewer than twenty-five' of them.

SHUTTLECOCK.—The usual *reversé* occurs in China with regard to some of the games that happens with many other things in this land of contrarieties. Instead of shuttlecock being more especially a game for girls, it is more especially a game for boys, lads, and men. No girls ever play it. It may almost be said to be the national game of China, and kite-flying the national pastime. The latter is indulged in in autumn; the former in winter, though it is played at other times as well. What seems curious about the two is, that, though children find an amusement in them, they are largely enjoyed and indulged in by those who can scarcely be described as children, except with the qualifying phrase 'of an older growth' appended.

Things Chinese

There is no battledore used by the Chinese, but the shuttlecock is kept up in the air by the foot, the broad white sole of the Chinese shoe acting admirably for the purpose. Two, three, four, or more players get together; and, if two, stand opposite each other, if three or more, they form an irregular ring and kick the shuttlecock up into the air in such a manner that it may fall near another player, so that there is no violent exercise except what is necessary for the kicking. If a foot stroke is impossible, when the shuttlecock is falling near one, then it is allowable to keep it up by hitting it with the hand and thus send it to another player, or to bang it into the air in such a way that it may return in a position to be easily hit by the foot. There are several foot-strokes—the most common being with the inner side of the sole of the right shoe. A hit is sometimes made with the outer side of the sole of this shoe. Another hit that must require some dexterity (if we may be allowed to use such a word in connection with the foot) is given with the right foot—with the inner side of the sole of the right shoe—from under the calf of the left leg. The most usual form of this stroke is as follows: the left leg is doubled round so that the foot is in front of the body and about ten or twelve inches from the ground: this is done while the shuttlecock is descending: and, when it is almost near enough to hit, a spring is taken off the ground with the right foot last, and the shuttlecock is immediately hit by the inner side of the sole of the right shoe from under the left calf. Another variety of this stroke is to stretch the leg out in a sloping direction downwards from the body with the foot a few inches above the ground, and then a similar stroke is made as described above. Another stroke is made with the sole of the right foot from behind the body, the foot in delivering it being kicked backwards and upwards. With many of the strokes delivered from the feet, the shuttlecock is sent up some ten, twenty, or thirty feet into the air, though occasionally a forward kick is given which directs it towards another player, with perhaps a slightly rising direction. The play often begins by one player tossing the shuttlecock with his hand up in the air toward another player opposite him. The object of the play is, of course, to keep the shuttlecok up as long as possible. The shuttlecock itself is rather different in construction from that in use in the West, no cork being used; but a number of layers of skin are employed, the two outer being snake's skin and the inner ones are said to be shark's skin, there being from eight or ten to twenty layers. The feathers used are duck's feathers and three in number.

SILK.—Notwithstanding the disparagement of early Chinese inventions by some, no one has yet been found bold enough to try and wrest the palm from them for the three discoveries of porcelain, lacquer-ware, and the manufacture of silk. 'The cultivation of silk, as of tea, had its origin in China,' and 'China still stands first amongst the silk-producing countries of the earth, and the amount exported annually from it to Europe, North America, and Bombay, is between 52,000 and 85,000 bales.' The total annual production of silk in China is now estimated at more than 120,000,000 lbs. The value of exports abroad in 1916 was 111,000,000 Hk. taels.

Silk culture is of very ancient origin; from references in the *Shu ching* to it, it is evident that it was well known when that work was written. Silkworms are said to have been first reared by Hsi Ling Shih (or Lei Tsu), the Empress of Huang Ti (2698-2598 B.C.), who was deified and worshipped, under the name of Yüan Fei, as the Goddess of Silk. Offerings are made to her annually, in April, by the Empress, at a temple in the palace grounds at Peking. Again, however, it is stated, that 'the raising of silkworms (at first upon the mulberry boughs—as now in some parts of Honan and Ssŭch'uan) is traced to the Emperor Huang Ti himself. The great Yü is credited by the Chinese 'as the most prominent promoter' of the cultivation of silk, and he is likewise said to 'have planted the hill country of Shansi with mulberries.' The Chinese Government has followed the good example of this semi-mythical monarch, by giving encouragement to the people and endeavouring to incite them to engage in this industrial occupation. In fact it has bestowed unremitting attention on this important branch of industry.

'The silk weaving industry in China flourished as early as the Chow Dynasty (1122-220 B.C.), although Hwangti, about 2700 B.C., was the first emperor to teach the people to raise silk worms. A fabric of raw silk known as "chüan" was at first the popular material for clothing, but now it is only used for painting, as Western artists use canvas. It is stiff and does not have a flossy surface. It is the simplest kind of silk fabric, and came into use first. Later three kinds of silk were manufactured: silk, gauze, and crepe. The plain, like that now produced in Hangchow and known as China silk, is only a step advanced from raw silk, or "chüan." It is known as "ch'ou," and Hangchow silk is known as "fang ch'ou," or "Hang fang" meaning Hangchow silk.

In the Han dynasty (206 B.C.-A.D. 211), a finer grade called "ling" resembling damask, was made. According to a book of anecdotes written in that dynasty, the first manufacturer of this goods was named Ch'ên Pao-kuang and he spent sixty days in producing a single piece. His product came to the knowledge of an influential nobleman after his death and as his wife had learned his methods, she was summoned to the nobleman's mansion to manufacture the silk for the rich man's private use. Gradually others learned to make the same thing, and in the T'ang dynasty (A.D. 618-906) nine different varieties of "ling" were mentioned in historical records. The "ling" is still manufactured to some extent, but it is not so popular as satin, silk, gauze, crepe, or brocade.

Gauze came into popularity during the Six Dynasties (265-617 B.C.), when it was worn in all seasons of the year. Officials were required to wear black or red gauze robes in their offices, and black shiny gauze hats, such as are now often seen on the stage. Later it was only used as summer wear, and many different designs were woven into the gauze. There have been such names as "shan-yi-sha," or "cicada wing," characterizing the thinness and transparency; "hsiang-yün-sha,' or "perfumed cloud," suggesting the draperies of the fairies living in the clouds; etc., etc. A variety of plain gauze without designs is still known as official gauze, a name which probably had its origin in the official robes worn during the Six Dynasties.

Another kind of silk fabric resembling grenadine is known in China as "lo." It has alternating knots and interstices. In a way, it also resembles mosquito netting, permitting freer circulation of air than ordinary silk. It is therefore particularly for summer wear. But the threads in "lo" are much closer than in mosquito netting, and the material is thicker. This material was generally manufactured plain, but in the T'ang (A.D. 618-906), and Sung dynasties (A.D. 960-1280) many varieties of "lo" with different designs were produced, such as the peacock, the magpie and the dragon. They were used for curtains, gowns, skirts, handkerchiefs, fans, and many other articles. At present Hangchow is still well known for its "lo." The material is used there mainly for clothing and bed curtains.'

In the 13th century the introduction of cotton from India caused silk production to decline, until in the 17th century it was only produced in Honan, Chêkiang, Ssŭch'uan, and Kuangtung, and then only for local consumption and the supply of the Government looms. With the advent of foreigners the industry revived, both as regards export and local consumption.

As the mulberry leaf is the chief food of the silkworm, much labour and the greatest care is expended on the cultivation of the mulberry tree. In the neighbourhood of Chinkiang there are two kinds of mulberries—a wild and a domestic—the domestic is grafted on the wild. The young mulberry trees are transplanted in December, and are placed at regular distances of five or six feet from one another; they are then cut down to one foot six inches in height, and two shoots are allowed to grow; with the systematic pruning carried on each year, after five or six years there are only sixteen branches left; the continual cutting off of all but two fresh twigs on each branch produces a knobbed appearance of the tree; and finally, from these knobbed-like fists, about fifty to eighty branches are preserved. The trees live more than fifty years; but are not allowed to grow higher than five or six feet. The wild mulberry, which grows to a height of fifty or sixty feet, is also used, and there is a smaller kind as well.

The silkworm undergoes several changes; but different species would appear to differ in this respect, for it seems that the 'southern silkworm' has four periods for moulting, as a rule, while the 'northern silkworm' generally casts its skin three times.

The greatest care is taken to keep the silkworms from noise, which they dislike; so far indeed do the silkworm carers carry their precautions that they become superstitious, the silkworms at certain places being informed by their keepers of the arrival of travellers, and, if this is omitted, any luckless wight, chancing on a village unannounced, will receive but scant courtesy, and be driven away with curses, if nothing worse.

There are ten rules laid down for breeding silkworms:—

'The eggs when on paper must be kept cool; after having been hatched they require to be kept warm; during their period of moulting they must be kept hungry; in the intervals between their sleeps they must be well supplied with food; they should not be placed too close together nor too far apart; during their sleeps they should be kept dark and warm; after they have cast their skins, cool, and allowed plenty of light; for a little time after moulting they should be sparsely fed; and when they are full grown ought never to be without food; their eggs should be laid close together, but not heaped upon each other.' Wet, withered, or dusty leaves are not given to them. Rather less than two ozs. in weight of young worms will eat 1 ton and 420 lbs. weight of leaves.

'While the worms are growing, care is taken to keep them' from 'bright light; they are often changed from one hurdle to another that they may have roomy and clean places; the utmost attention is paid to their condition and feeding, and noting the right time for preparing them for spinning cocoons. Three days are required for this, and in six it is time to stifle the larvæ and reel the silk from the cocoons; this being usually done by other workmen. Those who rear the worms enclose the cocoons in a jar buried in the ground and lined with mats and leaves, interlaying them with salt, which kills the pupæ but keeps the silk supple, strong, and lustrous; preserved in this manner, they can be transported to anv distance, or the reeling of the silk can be delayed until convenient. Another mode destroying the cocoons is to spread them on trays and expose them by twos to the steam of boiling water, putting the upper in the place of the lower one according to the degree of heat they are in, taking care that the chrysalides are killed and the silk not injured. After exposure to steam the silk can be reeled off immediately, but if placed in the jars they must be put into warm water to dissolve the glue before the floss can be unwound.'

Silk from wild worms of different species (chiefly the larvæ of *Antherœa pernyi*) is also used in some of the provinces (chiefly Shantung).

In Shêngking in Manchuria, silk is produced from a species of silkworm, *Bombyx Pernyi*, or *Bombyx Fantoni*, of Italy, which feeds on the leaves of a species of oak, *Quercus Mongolica*, or *Quercus robur*. Other species are *Q. dentata*, *Q. aliena*, and *Q. serrata*. A small quantity is also produced from the *Bombyx Cynthia*. The chrysalides are an article of diet with the Chinese. The spinning wheel is similar to that in the West. It requires from 4,000 to 5,000 cocoons for a piece of silk, and it takes a man two days to weave it. There were no large manufactories for its production, but 'each one spins, weaves, and dyes his own material' in Manchuria, and this was also largely the case throughout China, though not entirely, but steam filatures have now been introduced in many places (*v. infra*). A black silk is produced from the *Bombyx Pernyi* due to the worm eating the whole of the leaf and stalk.

Wusieh, in Kiangsu, is said to produce the finest white silk in the world.

In the district about Chefoo there are two kinds of silk produced: 'wild silk,' spun from the cocoons of the *Bombyx Pernyi*, the wild silkworm mentioned above, but of late years Shantung has drawn its supplies from Fêngt'ien; and 'yellow silk,' spun from the cocoons of the *Bombyx Mori*, or silkworm proper. Most of the yellow silk comes from Ssŭch'uan, Shantung, and Hupei, these being the only provinces where it is cultivated on a large scale.

The women in some places keep the eggs on their persons to hatch them by the warmth of their bodies, while in other places they are put under the blankets in the bed.

'A newly hatched silkworm is as fine as a hair. Immediately under its head there are four legs, a little beyond on the body there are six more, and again six more near the end at the tail; their whole length is about one-tenth of an inch, and their colour is black.' The greatest care is taken in supplying them with leaves, the men actually washing their hands before touching the leaves. They are fed five or six times a day for three days, but after that constantly. After one or two days, the worms become brown and, after five days more, a yellowish white. The fifth days seem memorable ones with the silkworm, for on the fifth day they stop feeding and 'undergo their first moult,' and at intervals of about five days after each waking they again cast their skins, ceasing eating for periods varying from a day and night to the 'long repose,' the fourth one of, if the weather is cold, two or three days, their colour changing at these different periods from yellow or a yellowish-white from before the stupors to a slight yellowish tint or a white colour after. After these moults they will, if in good condition, eat twenty times their weight in leaves. After another five days they attain maturity and are about two inches in length. What look like sheaves of straw are used for the silkworms to construct their cocoons on, each sheaf or bundle being tied round the middle and spread out at the top and bottom; sixty or seventy worms are put on each bundle, care being taken not to crowd them too much together. They then proceed to spin their cocoons amongst the stalks of straw by first attaching themselves with some looser threads, after which they spin the compact 'oblong case,' as the dictionary terms it, but beautifully rounded, working of course from the outside in. They finish spinning in five days, and, if the silk is not spun off, they pierce their yellow shrouds in ten days.

'From two catties of good cocoons, nine catties of silk are reeled off. . . . A quick hand with a double reeling machine reels about 1½ catties of silk per day, thus 100 catties of cocoons are about six days' work.' A certain number of cocoons are kept for breeding purposes. The female moths die in five days after laying their eggs, which they do within a day or so of coming out.

In Kuangtung there are six, and occasionally seven, crops annually. In Shuntak, the leading district, more than two hundred steam filatures have been opened since 1874.

In this province the two principal qualities of silk are Tai-tsam and Lun-yut: the eggs of the worm producing silk for the former are hatched once or twice a year; those for the latter seven times.

In Swatow, some curious, large, wild caterpillars, brightly coloured, spin a species of silk used in making lanterns.

In Kiangsu, the leading districts are Soochow, Wusieh, Shêng-tzu, Pin-niu, and Liyang. There are twenty-five or more steam filatures at Shanghai, employing 20,000 hands. Soochow has three filatures, and Chinkiang two.

In Chêkiang, the chief centres are Hangchow, Huchow, Kash-ing, Haining, and Shaoshing. Hangchow, Dongsi, and Siaoshan have steam filatures. The industry declined after the Revolution of 1911, but has since been stimulated by the provincial authorit-ies.

In Ssŭch'uan, silk is produced throughout the central and eastern portions of the province, but especially in the Ch'êngtu plain, at Kiating, Paoning, and Shunching. There have of recent years been many reforms in sericulture, including schools in every prefecture. There are some thirty steam filatures in the province.

In Shantung, silk is the chief industry, but the product is inferior to that of Kiangsu and Chêkiang. The chief districts are Ichow, Tsingchow, and Tsinan. There are steam filatures at the two latter towns.

In Hupei, there is a steam filature at Hangchow. Tangyang and Hojung are noted for their yellow silk.

Other provinces have made attempts to produce silk, but without success, though the Ch'angsha district in Hunan has a promising industry, chiefly in embroideries. Further information regarding the products of the "silk towns" will be found in the extracts at the end of this article.

Generally the silk trade with the West has grown from its beginning in the eighteenth century to the present time, the main set-backs being political disturbances, such as the T'aip'ing rebellion, periodical insufficiency of skilled labour, adulteration of better-class silk with poorer thread, economy or over-speculation in Europe, the introduction of Government protected Japanese silk, and disease among the silkworms. In spite of all this, however, China silk remains intrinsically the best in the world.

Wild silkworms in the north of China are fed on different kinds of oak, and they supply two crops of cocoons annually. The natives hatch them, and, after feeding them themselves, place them on the branches, when the leaves of the trees are fully out, and transfer them to other trees as they eat the leaves of one. They spin their cocoons on the trees, whence they are gathered. After the female moths have come out, and are ready to lay their eggs, the natives tie them by one leg with fine threads to the branches of the tree, when they lay their eggs on the leaves. These wild silkworms are 'smaller than the domestic ones and of a greyish black colour.' The silk filaments of the domestic silkworm cocoons are wound into thread by the aid of a primitive reeling machine.

For reeling the silk filament off the cocoons, they are placed in hot water to loosen the ends of the silk, the rough parts are cleared away, and the clean filament taken with the hand and then passed over, or through, the different parts of the reeling machine. As soon as the cocoon gets thin and the chrysalis is visible, a new filament is taken in its place. The best threads are made with six or seven cocoons, ranging from this number to twenty or more for the coarsest. 'A quick hand can reel in one day . . . about 20 taels weight fine or 30 taels coarse silk.' The wild worm cocoons are treated in a different manner.

As an example of the work done by Chinese weavers, in 1880 there were in Chinkiang 1,000 looms employing 4,000 labourers. In one day, three men could turn out about 12 feet to 16 feet of silk; for plain goods, two men only were required at each loom; and only one man for weaving gauze, there being 200 looms for this with 300 men at work, of which 14,000 to 15,000 pieces were annually produced for local consumption within the province of Kiangsu. Besides this, there were 50 or 60 looms 'engaged in weaving silk ribbons, each attended to by one man; a second is required only in weaving the broader kinds. . . . On an average, one man can weave about 40 feet per day. There are about 100 men engaged in this branch of the business; and there are about 30 or 40 looms for weaving red plain satin.'

For making sewing silk 'two filaments are twisted together into threads.' For crape manufacture there are about 200 looms and 800 men employed.'

'The greatest silk-producing province in China is Chêkiang, and Kiangsu comes second,' while 'Hu-chow holds the first place among the departments of the whole empire of China for the production of silk' (*v.* also *infra*). It may, therefore, be interesting to note the production of this one department. The production then for 1878 was 2,925,232 catties (1,755,139 kilos.), and for 1879, 3,304,196 catties (1,982,517 kilos.). There were 4,000 looms, each loom producing about 100 pieces a year.

Hangchow produces the best kinds of silk piece goods.

There is a complaint of the defective reeling and adulteration of silk from North China, which, unless checked, is bound to do injury to the silk trade of China.

There are silk filature establishments in China where foreign machinery is employed in reeling and weaving the silk (*v. infra*).

'Filatures produce silk realising Tls. 200 a picul more than will that spun from the same cocoons by the old primitive method.'

'The steps initiated by the Inspector-General [of Imperial Maritime Customs] to implant in China the Pasteur system of detecting and eradicating disease in silkworms have succeeded in the Kuangtung province.' Some time ago it was stated that, in Kiangsu and Chêkiang they 'are considering the establishment of silkworm nurseries for the selection of eggs on the Pasteur system,' these steps being necessary to cope with the silkworm disease.

'Sericulture is now [1895] the leading industry in China, since tea has gradually receded to a subordinate position.'

The export of China silk is increasing, but not at a rapid rate. The following extract from a consular report may prove of interest:—

'China silk is intrinsically the best silk in the world, but from ignorance or lack of energy on the part of the producers, it continues from year to year to be prepared in the old faulty method, while Japan silk, by nature much inferior, is beating it in the market, simply by the care and attention bestowed on its preparation, and by the fostering provision of the Japanese government, who provide the means of educating their people in the most approved methods in vogue in Europe.'

Enormous quantities of silk are not only sent abroad, but even larger quantities are used by the Chinese themselves. Silk is a common article of attire and is not confined to the gentler sex, who delight to array themselves in bright and soft fabrics in the West; in the gorgeous East, men are clothed in as brilliant robes as women (with the exception of those who have adopted Western costumes). It is utterly impossible to say exactly how much silk is used in China, but the Chinese consider that their consumption is more than double the amount exported to foreign countries (*cf. supra*). In 1890 the amount exported was 158,427 piculs; in the previous year, 1889, it was 182,939 piculs, doubling these sums would give 316,854 piculs and 365,878 piculs respectively; and no one who has seen the quantity of silk used by Chinese would doubt that these amounts must be well within the mark of their actual consumption of that useful commodity. (See also *infra.*)

The following extracts from the valuable *Chinese Economic Monthly* give full information regarding the development of the silk weaving industry in recent times.

'Huchow, Chêkiang province, is a most important silk producing center of China. It is best known for its silk and crepe. When they are woven with designs, both silk and crepe are known to the people in the industry as "san-chih" or "three weaving." Under that generic name are included all the following varieties: Chu-chien, Kwang-yi, Chin-chang, Chien-liu-chiu, Kia-kwo, Chin-hsien, Shun-shu, Er-chih-hwa-chien-liao and Tu-hwa-chien-liao. They may be explained as follows:—

Chu[tsu]-chien or "complete tip," is the ordinary grade of silk, and is woven with a fine grade of silk fiber. Hang-yi is a superior grade of silk especially manufactured for consumption in Hangchow, which, being itself a silk-producing district, can produce enough silk of the ordinary kind to supply itself. Kwangyi is midway between Hang-yi and Chu-chien in fineness, and is intended for consumption is Kwangtung, Kwangsi, Yünnan and Kweichow provinces. It is almost as closely woven as Hang-yi, but is a little heavier, and therefore inferior. Yi means clothing, Hang means Hangchow, and Kwang means Kwangchow, the Chinese name for Canton.

Chin-chang [ch'ing-ch'ang] or "light and long," is not much in demand in the south. It was originally intended to supply the imperial family in Peking, and therefore was also known as Pei-kung or "for Imperial consumption." It was chiefly sold in the six Peking silk stores, each having the word "Hsiang" in its name: for instance, Chien Hsiang, Cnin [Ch'ing] Hsiang, Lung Hsiang, Jui Fu Hsiang, the last named being still the largest silk store in the Capital. These stores, on account of the similarity in their names, formed what was called the Hsiang group, and they supplied the imperial family with southern silk when the latter did not buy through its regular silk purchasing agents in the south. This grade of silk is said to be the highest of all manufactured in Huchow.

Between the Hang-yi and the Chu-chien in quality and intended for general consumption are Hang-liu-chiu, Yi-chien-liu-chiu, and Chien-liu-chiu, in the order of their fineness. The Kia-Kwo [k'uo] is of three varieties, the widths being 1.9 feet, 2 feet and 2.2 feet, Chinese measure where 1 foot is made up of 10 inches and is equivalent to about 1 foot and 1/3 of an incn in English measure. The first variety is about as good as Kwang-yi and is sold in Kwangtung and the south-western provinces. The second variety sells chiefly along the Yangtzŭ Valley. The third is comparatively rare. Kia-kwo means "additional width."

Chin-hsien and Shun-shu are what foreigners call crepe. Chin-hsien means "tightened thread," and Shun-shu means "along the shuttle," both indicating that one group of threads is tighter than another, and produces wrinkles on the surface of the fabric. Er-chih-hwa-chien-liao and Tu-hwa-chien-liao are both manufactured to order only, as they are fabrics with patterns to suit the exact size of the coat or robe, and cannot be easily sold to the public. The difference between the two is that the former has many designs on all parts of the clothing, while the latter has just one pattern which covers the whole piece.

Plain silk of the best quality is known in Huchow as Yi-chih[ch'ih]-pa-su, a kind of crepe lighter than Chih-hsien and Shun-shu. Next to it is Liu-chi-chih[ch'i-ch'ih]-pa-su, which is mostly exported to foreign countries, because it is even lighter than the first named. Shun-shu-su corresponds to Shun-shu of the former group, the only difference being explained by the word " su," which means plain (no flowery designs). Hwa-chi-su is not crepe, but ordinary silk, and is also lower in quality than the other kinds of plain silk. The lowest grade is Er-i-wu-sen[shêng]-su which is almost like raw silk, although a little heavier than it.

The above names are all used by men in the trade. To customers such classification is unknown, but the difference is reflected in the prices. There are also two grades of silk especially manufactured for sashes; namely Ping[p'ing]-chin and Lion-ping [lien-p'ing], the latter being slightly wider.

The importation of the so-called Ye-chi-ko from Japan, a kind of flowery Japanese silk, suggested to the Huchow merchants the manufacture of a new variety of silk called Hwa-ssŭ-ko, meaning Chinese silk "ko." The word "ko" originally stood for ramie textile and the Japanese fabric is called Ye-chi-ko because it contains a mixture of silk and remie fibers. Ye-chi means not of standard quality. Hwa-ssu-ko on the other hand, contains no ramie at all, but the designs have a flossy appearance like the Japanese material, different from other kinds of Chinese silk, and so it is also called "ko." In fact, it is brocaded silk, because the background is silk, while the designs are like brocade, though usually of the same color as the background. It is woven on modern Jacquard looms.

Varieties of Hwa-ssu-ko are known as Su-chih-lo, Hwa-chih-lo, Shwang-ssu-ko and Wu-hwa-ko. Su-chih-lo is silk that looks more or less like "lo," mentioned in a former paragraph, and Hwa-chih-lo has more flowery patterns. Both are of the same grade. Shwang-ssu-ko is heavier than Hwa-ssu-ko or Su-chih-lo, and usually also wider. It was most popular in China last year. This year [1924] the latest fashion is Wu-hwa-ko meaning "ko" manufactured by the Wu-hwa Silk Mill. The patterns are newer and more shiny.

Pu-yüan, a small town in the district of T'unghiang, Chêkiang, produces also San-chih, but it is inferior to the silk of Huchow, and is mainly sold to the people of Shensi, Shansi, Shantung and Chihli. In the south the only use made of it is by the clothing stores for ready made clothing, because it is cheap. These stores also use a very low grade of Huchow silk known as Chih[ch'ih]-wu-wu-hwa-chow [ch'ou], for the same reason. A higher grade manufactured at Pu-yüan is Kia-kwo[k'uo]-sze-chih, but even that is inferior to ordinary Huchow silk.

The laborers in the modern silk mills of Huchow are mostly natives of Tanyang, Kiangsu (near Chinkiang). More than fifteen years ago, this city also produced a kind of San-chih (i.e. silk and crepe) which, however, was of an inferior quality. But the people there are accustomed to silk weaving, and hence many of them work in the Huchow mills. Five years ago, however, Tanyang began to produce a fine grade of San-chih, with many new designs, and it became a strong competitor of Huchow as a silk-manufacturing center. To show this spirit of competition, the Tanyang merchants called their best silk "Kwan-hu," meaning "better than Huchow."

Another rival was the city of Nanyang, Honan. It is a wild silk producing center. Pongee silk was manufactured there as early as the beginning of the nineteenth century. Around 1860, however, a native of Tientsin named Yin Ju-pi, became the city magistrate. Yin came from a family which had long been in the silk business, and he taught the people to improve their silk fabrics. In a few years, the business flourished, and large quantities of Nanyang silk began to be sold in other provinces. Hence Nanyang silk is sometimes also called Yin silk.

Nanyang also produces a kind of silk similar to the China silk of Hangchow, known as Pa-ssu-chow or silk of eight threads. Its width is from 1.4 to 1.6 feet Chinese measure, and its length from 60 to 90 feet. Its color is white, blue, or gray, but never bright red or green. There were at one time over 700 families in Nanyang weaving this kind of silk, employing over 3,000 looms and producing about 1,000 pieces daily.

Since the wild silk produced in the district is not fine enough for high grade fabrics, the Nanyang weavers combine it with silk imported from other cities, of which that of ᴦuan and Yangcheng, Shansi province, is the best, that of Tsaohsien, Shantung, and Teian, Hupeh province, is of the second grade, while that of Chechwan and Mihsien Honan, is the lowest. The large weavers usually have sales managers in the different provinces, but the fabrics are sold in Mongolia, Japan and other places through purchasing agents and exporters of other provinces.

Chênp'inghsien, 70 *li* west of Nanyang, produces similar fabrics, but of a lower grade. About 120 li north of Nanyang, Nanshao produces Chu-ssu-chow, which is a kind of pongee, and is sometimes more popular than Nanyang silk. K'aifeng is known for the so-called Honan silk, but it is of a very inferior quality from the Chinese point of view, although, like Shantung pongee, it is widely used in making foreign style shirts and suits.

Shantung pongee is woven from wild silk from the cocoon of the tussock moth. Its width was originally only 1.4 feet, but has been increased to a maximum of 2.2 feet. It is lighter than Honan pongee, and has a better market. The first process in manufacturing pongee is to strengthen the silk thread, which is done with tu-feng [t'u-fên] a kind of white powder found extensively in Mongolia and north China, and bean curd. These remove the soda substance from the silk, and make it cleaner, stronger and more flossy. The weight is, however, increased by 10 or 20 per cent. through strengthening. As the original silk is grayish yellow in color, it is often bleached, yielding a very light yellowish-white fabric.

Chefoo is the principal market for this pongee. The silk was originally produced in Shantung, but now the tussock moth is extensively raised in South Manchuria, through immigration of Shantung people into those provinces, and Manchuria supplies Shantung witn a large proportion of the raw material. As early as the first part of the reign of T'ung-chih, Manchu dynasty (A.D. 1862-1874), Shantung pongee began to be exported to Europe and America, but the business received a strong impetus in 1885, when Shantung manufacturers established special exporting agents in Hongkong and other treaty ports. After another decade, direct exportation through Chefoo and Tsingtao became the rule. According to a statement of the Shantung and Honan Pongee Silk Association, the trade in 1885 was valued at only half a million dollars, but the Customs Reports show that it had grown to more than 13,000,000 Haikwan taels in 1921, although it dropped again to 8,700,000 taels in 1922. One Haikwan tael is equivalent to about U.S. $0.75 or 3 to 4 shillings sterling.

Chowts'un in Shantung has 15 silk weaving mills with 85 modern looms and 360 to 370 workmen. Small workshops number over 100, having about 500 looms among them. The principal product is Hwa-ssŭ-ko, similar to that manufactured in Huchow, Chekiang. The silk fiber usually comes from Ishui or Mongyin, but sometimes finer silk from Sint'ai is also used. All three cities are in Shantung. The weavers are generally paid by the piece, being about 150 coppers each piece and as one man can weave one piece in two days, he can earn 2,250 coppers or about $10 to $12 in a month.

Hangchow is best known for its China silk. The most popular variety is known to the traders as Sze-ch'wan-kia-chung, *i.e.*, extra heavy No. 4. A slightly inferior grade is called Liu-ch'wan, or No. 6. Kia-k'wo-fang or "extra wide silk," 1.8 feet in width, is not very common, and it needs special looms in weaving. Shao-hing, Chekiang, now competes with Hangchow in the production of such silks, and the village of Pan-kiao in that district produces a very high grade, known as Pan-fang.

Lo, a kind of grenadine, is another important product of Hangchow. At first an interstice was made between every five threads in the woof; later, between every seven or nine threads; but recently thirteen threads are woven in the woof before an interstice is made. It is all plain, except for the interstices, while formerly patterns were also woven into the fabric. An extra wide variety of "lo" is not very popular.

Hsien-tsun [ch'un] is a fabric of raw silk. It is very strong and can stand much wearing, but not very flossy and both color and patterns are not attractive. It is now seldom worn outside, but may be used for underwear. Another kind of raw silk fabric is called the "iron loom silk," sometimes "brocaded silk," and it resembles "Hwa-ssŭ-ko" described some paragraphs back. Hsien-tsow, Ning-ch'ow and Kung-ch'ow are manufactured from "boiled off" silk, some with patterns and some not. Ning-ch'ow has a larger variety than Hsien-tsow, and Kung-ch'ow is similar to the former, but a little inferior.

Of the different kinds of gauze manufactured in Hangchow. Tsun[ch'un]-sha, "spring gauze," T'ieh-chi-sha, "iron loom gauze," Hang-kwan-sha, "Hangchow official gauze," Hwa-kwan-sha, "flowery official gauze," and Chan[shan]-yi-sha, "cicada wing gauze," are all made from raw silk. Tsun-sha is of two varieties; one plain and the other having a large number of knots which resemble linseeds, and is known as "linseed finish." Hwa-kwan-sha has two similar varieties, and although it has patterns besides, they do not stand out prominently and are called An-hwa or "hidden pattern." The designs on Chan-yi-sha are also hidden, but the background is very flossy and bright, and offers a beautiful contrast.

From prepared silk five kinds of gauze are manufactured; namely, Shih-ti-hwa-sha, Tze[chih]-ti-hwa sha, Hwai-ti-hwa sha, Shih-ti-su-sha, and Hwai-ti-su-sha. Shih-ti means plain background. Tze-ti is linseed finish, and it may have patterns (hwa-sha) and may have none (su-sha). Hwai-ti is another kind of background where the knots are bigger than in Tze-ti, and this kind of gauze may be either hwa-sha (with designs) or su-sha (without designs). Shih-ti-hwa-sha is sometimes also known as P'ing-sha. Gauze from "boiled off" silk is sometimes also woven on modern looms, and is then called "iron loom gauze."

Shêngtsechêng in the district of Wukiang, Kiangsu province, produces even a larger variety of silks than Hangchow, though it may not be so well-known to foreigners. "Four-eight-fang" is woven after a Japanese model, known in China as Tung-ch'ow, but it is done on modern looms, while the Japanese Tung-ch'ow is manufactured with wooden ones. There are two grades of "four-eight-fang," and below them is Siao-fang, or small China silk, manufactured on wooden looms, and used only for summer underwear. When "four-eight-fang" has patterns, it is known as Sze-pa-hwa-fang, and is classified into Kwang-chwang for consumption in Kwangtung and other southern provinces, T'i-chien best grade, and other grades.

Lo-fang is a combination of "lo" and "fang," or China silk. Many varieties of it are manufactured in Shêngtsechêng. Hsien-lo-fang is a silk and cotton union where the cotton threads stand out in the fabric and make it look like "lo." It is very popular as material for summer wear, because it is soft, yet will not fall flat on the skin as pure silk does. The color may be white, blue or variegated. When the cotton threads run horizontally instead of lengthwise, it is known as Heng-t'iao-hsien-lo-fang or horizontal threads "lo fang." In Ssŭ-hsien-lo-fang, the horizontal threads consist alternately of one silk and one cotton thread, and the fabric is of white, light blue, and other light colors Ssŭ-lo-fang and Ke-fang are two other varieties of cotton and silk unions.

When the silk has a satin finish, it is called Hwa-twan-t'iao-fang (with flowery patterns) or Su-twan-t'iao fang (plain) by the people in the trade, but to the customers it is known as Yi-hsia-ch'ow or "sunset silk." A new variety, known to the trade as new Hwa-twan-t'iao-fang, is called by outsiders Pao-kwang-fang (sparkling silk). The background sometimes contains round spots, and the silk is then known as Tien-tze-twan-t'iao-fang. If there are slant lines on the fabric, the natives of Shêngtsechêng call it Hsia-wên-twan-fang while the Shanghai people call it Ssŭ-chang[ch'iang]-ch'ow.

Shêngtsechêng also produces gauze of the Kwangtung type, known as "fragrant cloud." It produces a kind of Hwa-P'uyüan, similar to the silks of P'uyüan mentioned under Huchow, and is usually for linings. Hwa-chieh-ch'ow is used for the same purpose. Su-ch'ow, which was formerly occasionally used for gowns and robes, is now not even used for lining, because it is too plain. A variety of it, called Ch'ih-sze-su is mostly sold in Manchuria. Su-ling is of an even lower grade, some of which is manufactured especially for dressing the dead. Lo manufactured from raw silk is of many kinds, of which Ch'iu-lo and Hwa-ch'iu are intended for consumption in Kwangtung and other southern provinces, while Ch'ih-sze-lo and Wu-êr are for use as lining. On the whole, the raw silk fabrics of Shêngtsechêng are inferior to its "boiled off" silks, as well as to the raw silk fabrics of Hangchow.

Soochow is better known for its embroidery than for its silk, but of the latter it also produces a considerable quantity. There are Soochow crepe and Soochow silk, but both are now rather unpopular, because they are inferior to similar Hangchow goods. Its gauze was once an important item of trade and a special kind was manufactured for summer underwear, known by the beautiful name of Fu-yung gauze, Fu-yung means the Hibiscus flower, a very beautiful blossom of China often mentioned in poetry.

Chinkiang has also silk and crepe, which are used in place of Soochow silk and crepe, but in fact they are inferior to the latter. Ningpo produces Wên-chow similar to the Hwa-fang of Shêngtsechêng. Much improvement has been made in the manufacture of this product, and two varieties, woven with stripes and squares, are very popular with the Ningpo people.

Kasing, in Chêkiang, produces Hsing-sha sometimes known as "treading gauze." It is used mainly in making women's skirts. However, since the "iron loom" gauze of Hangchow and Shêngtsechêng came in vogue, the Kasing gauze has been practically driven out of the field. Many other cities in Kiangsu and Chêkiang manufacture silk fabrics, but few except Nanking, which will be referred to later, can compare with those already mentioned. In fact, even among those above mentioned, the silk business chiefly centers around Huchow, Hangchow and Shêngtsechêng, the rest being of minor importance.

Satin was first manufactured in the Han Dynasty (206 B.C.-A.D. 219). Mention was first made of it in the Four Poems of Sorrow, by Chang Hêng, a well known poet of that dynasty. In the T'ang Dynasty, the government weaving mills did not include satin among its record of products, but private manufacturers of certain districts were supposed to supply the imperial family with this material. The greatest popularity was gained by satin during and since the Ming and the Manchu Dynasties (A.D. 1368-1912). Nanking, Soochow, and Hangchow then became the centers of this industry. The satin of Nanking was originally manufactured for consumption by the imperial house, and was therefore known as Kung-twan or "tribute satin." Soochow followed the example of Nanking and produced a heavier variety, called Lei-twan, Hangchow again improved on the product of Soochow, weaving beautiful designs into the fabric, and called it Hwa-twan. Changchow, Fukien, produced a kind of satin after Japanese pattern, and it was known as Chang-twan. It was something like a brocade, but the background was shiny while the designs had a velvet finish. It was very popular some twenty years ago, but is now seldom seen on the market.

As to brocade, it had an early origin, too. It was first produced in the Hsia Dynasty (B.C. 2205-1766), when three kinds were distinguished: those with a plain background called plain brocade, those with a red background called red brocade, and those completely covered with patterns called Chih-chên [ch'êng]. During the Ch'in (221-206 B.C.) and Han dynasties, the officials were distinguished as to their ranks by the patterns they wore on their brocaded coats. Later, Szechwan became well known for its brocade, but the industry lost its foothold there since the Yüan dynasty (A.D. 1280-1368). In the Sung dynasty (A.D. 960-1280) the weavers of brocade were able to weave landscapes into the fabrics, and the work was so exquisite that it looked more like natural landscapes than similar embroidered designs. With the use of Jacquard looms, hand made brocade lost its popularity, and the center of production of brocaded silks and satins was shifted to Hangchow.

Similar to brocade is tapestry. It had a very early origin in China, but did not become well known until the Sung dynasty. There are still many specimens of the tapestry of that period, while modern ones can be made at Soochow even at the present time. The following is an account of satin manufacture during recent years.

The satin for which Nanking is famous is Kung-twan, or "tribute satin." It is plain and dyed black, and is used for making formal dresses. Similar material is manufactured elsewhere, yet the color of the Nanking Kung-twan is the best, for it does not turn yellow with wearing, but on the contrary, gains in lustre. This is supposed to be due to the water of the poetic

Ch'in-hwai River, which seems to be a good fixer when used in making dyes. The warp usually consists of silk from Siasl ih or T'angki, Chêkiang, while for the woof local silk is used. The market of the satin is mainly in the northern provinces, where dark colors are generally preferred, but in the last few years the demand slackened a good deal, because other material, such as black brocaded Hangchow satin or imported henrietta, is used in its place in making formal dresses. The largest manufacturers now seldom have more than 100 looms. The different varieties of Kung-twan, the number of threads in the warp and the width of the pieces are as follow:—

Variety	Threads	Width of Piece
K'u-twan	18,000-22,000	2.9-3.1 feet Chinese measure
Ching-su or Ta-ching	15,000-18,000	3.2 feet
Hsüeh su	15,000-16,000	2.7 feet
Hung-shu-t'ang	9,000-13,000	2.7-2.9 feet

Besides Kung-twan, Nanking also produces Hwa-twan, i.e., satin in colors and with designs. During 1914 and 1915, a variety of Nanking Hwa-twan, known as "three color Hwa-twan," was very popular. Sometimes, the background was blue, and the patterns were white, with light blue shading around. Sometimes a different combination of three colors was used. But the material was not as strong as Kung-twan and the designs were not as beautiful as those of Hangchow satin, and consequently it could not compete with either. At present very little Nanking Hwa-twan is sold in such fashionable cities as Peking, Tientsin, or Shanghai.

Changchow satin, mentioned in a foregoing paragraph, had its counterpart in Nanking. In fact, after the Changchow people had forgotten how to manufacture that kind of satin, Nanking produced large quantities of it and became well-known for this product. At the same time, Changchow velvet was also manufactured in Nanking, as well as ordinary velvet. The best grade of the latter is "goose velvet," which is very flossy and soft. Changchow velvet is heavier and stiffer, while Changchow satin has a velvet appearance only in its patterns.

The best grade of Soochow satin is Lei-twan, either plain or with design, but best plain. Lei-twan is only equivalent to the second grade Nanking Kungtwan. T'ieh-chi-twan, woven on modern looms in Soochow, is generally inferior to Hangchow satin. It may be pure silk or silk and cotton union; it may be regular or iridescent. The names of the different varieties are very beautiful, but do not tell anything about the quality of the product. For instance, they are called by such fancy names as Yi-hsa[hsia]-twan (sunset satin), Yün-kwang-twan (bright cloud satin), and Yüeh-hwa-twan (moon light satin).

Soochow also produces single piece bed-spreads with special patterns to fit the sizes. It makes satin trimmings, interwoven with imitation gold and silver threads. Many kinds of velvet, including Changchow velvet and Changchow satin, are also manufactured. A particular variety, with white spots on a black background, has been very popular as lining for Chinese collars. Other colors are also used for such collar velvet to match the colors of the robes. A special kind of satin with a silk or gauze finish is intended for consumption in Korea, and it is known under such names as Shih-ti-su-k'u-twan, Chih[shih]-ti-hwa-k'u-twan, etc. It appears as if the Koreans, whose costume resembles that of the Chinese many centuries ago, and who were in fact in close relation to China at that time, had taken a special liking to gauze which was very popular in China during the Six Dynasties, and that taste has survived to the present time.

The Jacquard loom was first used in this country by Sze[Shih] Ho-ch'u of Hupeh, who started in 1908 or 1909 a silk weaving mill in Hankow, called the Chao-sing[hsin] Mill. In 1911 and 1912, similar mills began to spring up in Hangchow, where the silk supply is abundant, and Wei-chên [ch'ên], Hu-lin, Chin-chên [Ch'ing-ch'êng]. Jih-sin, Cheng[ch'ên]-sin and many other modern mills came into existence. According to some silk merchants, there are now over 4,000 Jacquard looms in Hangchow, and about 3,000 in Huchow, which are used in manufacturing brocaded silk and satin. The old Hangchow satin (Hang-twan) and "flowery satin" (Hwa-twan) have now been entirely replaced by the new varieties woven on the new looms, and in the manufacture of satin, as of silk, Hangchow stands first among all the producing centers.

In regard to the widths given in this article, it must be remembered that different measures are used in different localities. In the silk trade, one Shanghai foot is about 9.8 inches of the so-called standard foot, Hangchow, 9.7 inches, and Soochow, 9.5 inches. One foot is equivalent to ten inches in Chinese measure. The Kwangtung foot is half an inch longer than the standard, and therefore from 0.7 to 1 inch longer than that of the other cities. The tailor's footstick again differs from that of the silk merchants, hence no accurate comparison can be made between the widths and lengths of silk piece goods of different localities, and it is therefore not attempted in this account.

The grading of silk is made by Chinese merchants according to the fineness of the silk fiber and the weight and strength of the fabric. Hence, what is considered as inferior silk by them may not be inferior in the eyes of foreign consumers. In fact, foreigners buy more of Shantung pongee and thin Hangchow and Huchow silk, both of which are not supposed to be high grade in China, while high grade Chinese silk and satin are often useless in making foreign dresses. With all these facts in mind, the meaning of the above article will be better understood.

Another remark must be made concerning this. Although under each city a number of silk fabrics are mentioned, it does not mean that these alone are produced in that city. They are given special mention because the city is known for these products or because in the mind of the Chinese silk merchants its name is usually associated with their production. Some fabrics are mentioned merely on account of their historical interest, and they are now no more manufactured. Some of the names have changed too; consequently comprehensiveness cannot be claimed. The following are perhaps the principal silk dealers in Shanghai:

Laou Kai Fook, 23 Honan Road.
Laou Kiu Chwang Co., P. 128 Nanking Road.
Laou Kiu Woo Silk Co., 9 Honan Road.
Laou Kiu Luen Co., P. 424 Nanking Road.
Dah Luen, 404 Honan Road.
Dah Zung and Co., P. 505 Nanking Road.
Dah Chen, 11 Pao-tai Road, Siao Tung-men.
Dah Chong, Ming Kuo Road (Republic Road).
Ho Heng Chang, 10 Pao-tai Road, Siao Tung-men (Little East Gate)

Export of Chinese Silk Goods

Year	Silk Piece Goods		Shantung Pongee	
	Quantity (Piculs)	Value (Hk. Tls.)	Quantity (Piculs)	Value Hk. Tls.
1913	17,751	14,235,709	16,749	6,638,069
1914	13,571	10,841,472	13,150	4,720,914
1915	16,382	12,850,970	24,776	8,707,103
1916	14,855	12,206,588	24,266	7,813,378
1917	12,981	10,904,546	17,228	6,325,220
1918	14,787	12,761,809	19,772	6,149,438
1919	17,719	15,744,583	21,745	7,515,645
1920	16,851	15 801,813	20,602	8,515.664
1921	16,108	17,079,435	26,716	13,177,217
1922	13,270	14,904,418	17,976	8,726,866

Export of Silk Piece Goods and Pongee in 1922

	Silk Piece Goods		Silk Pongee	
	Quantity (Piculs)	Value (Hk. Tls.)	Quantity (Piculs)	Value (Hk. Tls.)
Hongkong	11,151	12,758,772	3,618	1,963,137
Singapore, Straits, etc.	476	523,495	(insignificant)	(insignificant)
British India	382	411,480	1,114	496,290
Turkey, Persia, Egypt, etc.	(insignificant)	(insignificant)	1,989	820,813
Korea	880	797,890	(insignificant)	(insignificant)
France	(insignificant)	(insignificant)	1,540	732,983
U.S. of America	59	64,847	3,278	1,553,142
Great Britain	60	63,790	3,267	1,619,892
Japan	61	67,234	341	153,116
Australia, New Zealand, etc.	(insignificant)	(insignificant)	1,907	1,087,635

The picul is one of 133 1/3 pounds. The Haikwan Tael, the term in which the Chinese Maritime Customs renders returns, had the average value of U.S. $1.39 in 1919; $1.24 in 1920; $0.76 in 1921; $0.83 in 1922.'

'The efforts of the government to induce the Chihli farmers to cultivate the mulberry and the silk worm are indicated in the figures which have just been published. Agents of the government purchased 280,000 trees from other provinces in 1923 and sold them in certain districts of Chihli, while thus far this year [June, 1924], the figure has reached 190,000 trees imported into this province. The purchases are made mostly in Kiangsu and Chêkiang.'

References.—The Chinese Economic Monthly, 1924; *Chinese Maritime Customs Special Series,* Nos. 3 & 12.

SLAVERY.—China, in common with most Asiatic countries where the liberty of the subject is unknown, has the institution of slavery; but slavery, as a general rule, is milder in the despotic East than where, in direct contravention of all the free instincts of the West, it has been found nestling under the flag of liberty. One would expect the contrary to be the rule, but it is not. Where the right of the individual was generally respected, as in America, if equal justice was not meted out to every man as man, but on the contrary the fundamental principles at the foundation of society were not only ignored but persistently transgressed with respect to one section of the community, it needed but little more, all barriers of law and morality as regards one branch of the human family being swept away, to transform the otherwise mild master into a cruel one, and a few generations, or even less, to develop tyranny which knew no law but that of interest and the almighty dollar.

In the East, the individual knows no rights, as an individual, as we understand such rights in the West. He is but a member of the family; the family is the unit of society: the members of the family are but fractions of the whole; the slave owes his existence as a slave to this patriarchal rule; and ejected from one family, generally by circumstances over which he has no control, he is engulfed in another.

Slavery then appears almost to be the normal condition of part of the inhabitants in a country where the rights of the individual, *qua* individual, are unknown, and where the conservation, preservation, and perpetuation of the family are the aims of human society, and every means has to be employed with these ends in view. To this is due some of the buying and selling of human beings as chattels; for should no son be born to a man be often purchases one from poor parents and adopts him as his own. Girls are also bought to become daughters; but these can scarcely be looked upon as slaves, as they become the children of the family into which they are adopted, and are in no more bondage than the children born in the family itself.

A species of debt-slavery exists to some extent in China, where a man will give his son to his creditor either to adopt or to be his slave, or his daughter for either a slave or a domestic slave (see below) in full settlement of the debt; and in some provinces (but not in Kwangtung) a wife is even given to be a concubine for the same purpose.

Slaves in China are (1) prisoners of war (now rare); (2) people sold or self-sold into slavery (common); and (3) born slaves (these supply recruits to theatres and brothels). The old class of State slaves (criminals, rebels, etc.) is now obsolete.

A species of domestic slavery exists to a very large extent: there is scarcely a family of good means in Hongkong, Canton, or Macao but what possesses one or often several slave-girls. It must, in all fairness to the Chinese, be said that this domestic slave-girl system is a very mild form of slavery, as we understand that word. This is perhaps due to the fact that slaves in China are not of an alien race. The girls are as a rule purchased from their parents, who probably sell them on account of poverty; they are sold when they are young, at any age, some as young as three years, and from that up to fifteen; but seven, eight, or ten, is a common age. It is better to buy them young, as they might otherwise run home. The prices range from ten or twenty to a hundred dollars, the larger amounts being given for good-looking ones, as they will bring in a larger number of presents (at their marriage) to the family, and thus possibly recoup the owner with a two or three-fold amount of money on their purchase price, besides the owner having the use of them as domestic servants for ten or more years without wages, food and clothing being the only outlay on them. As to lodging, it is not worth while taking account of that, for Chinese servants, like dogs or cats, can sleep almost anywhere.

These transactions often take place through go-betweens. It is somewhat safer, in such cases, to have a broker of human flesh, as a charge of kidnapping might be more difficult to bring; for when there is a go-between the rule is that a deed of sale is drawn up, which is held by the purchaser. It sometimes happens, but not often, that the parents stipulate that they shall be at liberty to come and see the girl; but this stipulation, if made, is not reduced to writing, as it would obviously clash with the interests of the purchaser to have the mother coming about interviewing the girl and hearing her complaints.

Should such a verbal agreement as the above have been come to, the girl's parents are consulted about her marriage, otherwise, for the ten or fifteen years, the girl is virtually and actually the property of her master or mistress, and is an asset not realised, under the ordinary circumstances of life, until her marriage, though realisable, and should reverses in business reduce the family, it would be in the power of its head to sell her just as her parents originally sold her. At the same time this is not often done. A clause is often inserted in the agreement, that the girl is not to be sold into prostitution; but, should this clause have been omitted, the parents are powerless to prevent it in practice.

Arrived at marriageable age, the girl is married, and thus ends her domestic servitude.

If chance has thrown her into the hands of a fairly kind mistress her lot may not be such a dreadful one, but instances occur of brutal mistresses half murdering their poor little slave-girls, even in the British Colony of Hongkong. Theoretically, of course, there are no slaves in Hongkong, as it is British territory, but practically there are thousands of them. All the young maid-servants that follow their mistresses' sedan chairs, and that go about with little children, belong to this class. No young unmarried free women go out into service, though old women do.

These little slave-girls are the most numerous class of slaves in China. While mentioning the female sex, it may be remarked, in passing, that nearly all prostitutes are slaves, the property of their mistresses, the keepers of the houses of ill-fame in which they reside, having often been kidnapped, or deceived by promises of work being found for them as seamstresses, and thus inveigled into the clutches of the old harridans who run these establishments. So completely do they come under the power of these pests of society, and so cowed and frightened are they by the threats and intimidations of their mistresses, that even in Hongkong, where notices were put up in all the registered houses of that character that all were free—yet, notwithstanding this, and the fact that they are theoretically free to go and see the Registrar-General and Protector of Chinese, whose duty it is, once knowing their wrongs, to have them righted, they but seldom, in proportion to their numbers, avail themselves of their rights, and when brought up before him, almost invariably say they enter on such a life freely. (Before being allowed to enter as inmates of these houses, all appear before this official, or his assistant, in order to have a chance, if they will avail themselves of it, of stating their unwillingness to be coerced into a life of shame.) And though every Chinese woman that goes abroad, as a common emigrant, is questioned and examined as to her willingness to go, yet but few, who are being taken against their will, avail themselves of the chance of recovering their freedom.

The cases of little boys sold to be servants is even worse than that of the servant-girls, as they do not have marriage to look forward to, to set them free and end their life of servitude. They are slaves for ever, unless they purchase their freedom.

'The Manchu code does not recognise the right of the slave to free himself by his labour, nor punish the master who refuses affranchisement. There is, in short, no regulation on the subject (in practice the slave frequently purchases his body with his *peculium*, which is usually, though not legally, held to be the slave's own property). . . . Many Chinese allow their slaves to embark in trade, and ransom themselves with the profits.'

In ancient times, in China, there were State slaves, but banishment now [under the Manchu monarchy] takes the place of the Government slavery to a large extent. Priestesses, however, who found a new nunnery without the sanction of Government, become the slaves of Government.

'The wives, children, and relatives in the first degree of rebels are given as slaves to Government officers. . . . Slaves are composed of (1) prisoners of war; (2) those who sell themselves or are sold; (3) the children of slaves.' The first are now rare. We have spoken of some already who come under the second heading. 'Though the penal code forbids the sale of free persons, even by a husband, a father, or a grandfather, the number of persons whom misery forces to sell themselves or be sold is considerable. The punishment varies from 84 to 90 blows, and banishment for 2½ years, according to the relation existing between seller and sold. The punishment is one degree less when the person sold consents, but young children are exempt from all punishment, though they may have consented, on account of the obedience due to their older relations, and must be returned to their families. . . . Though to keep a free man or lost child as a slave, or to give or take in hire a wife or daughter, are severely punishable, the adoption of stolen or lost children and the sale of free children and inferior wives are daily transactions in China. Inundations and famines are the chief cause. Every slave born in a house belongs to his master or his heir; to detain a runaway slave is punishable. Players and brothel-keepers recruit their numbers from this class, as they are forbidden by the code to purchase free men or women for their professions. . . . The inferior wife ranks above a slave; she is married with fewer formalities than the first wife under whose orders she is put. The husband can only dismiss her for certain specified reasons; but in practice inferior wives are frequently sold.'

No property is divisible during the period of mourning, but after that is over, if the different sons of the deceased wish to separate, they are at liberty to do so, and the eldest son then divides the property amongst them equally, whether they be sons of the first wife or of inferior wives or of slaves. 'We may add that such slaves by the birth of children become in China *ipso facto* inferior wives.'

Slaves are not allowed to be married to free girls. In a general way it may be said that slaves convicted of crime are punished more severely than if they were free, while crimes committed against slaves meet with a lighter punishment than if committed against free men. 'Masters may beat their slaves or hired servants at pleasure.'

It is interesting to note that during the fifteenth and sixteenth centuries large numbers of black slaves of both sexes from the East Indian Archipelago 'were purchased by the great houses of Canton, to serve as gate-keepers.' They were called 'devil slaves' and it is not improbable that the term 'foreign devil,' so freely used by the Chinese for foreigners, may have had this origin. In the T'ang dynasty even, it is said that they were kept in large numbers by the Chinese. Three pages in a Chinese work, 'The Kwangtung San Yü,' are taken up with an account of them, and other Chinese books notice them as well.

There is a curious slang phrase in use for slaves; it is 'two candarins and two lis,' used for example in this way:—'they were two candarins and two lis,' equivalent to saying 'They were slaves.' This strange term is said to have arisen toward the close of the Ming dynasty, during the troublous times, when a Chinese took advantage of his opportunity, and, representing himself as a General of the Manchus, levied an impost on each inhabitant of the villages of three candarins, but, finding that the slaves in these warlike times were mostly poor and neglected, he reduced the amount to be paid by them to two candarins and two lis, hence the name.

References.—Chinese Repository, July 1849; Biot, *Memoir on the Condition of Slaves in China;* Parker, *Comparative Chinese Family Law,* Excursus No. 6—Slaves; Werner, *Descriptive Sociology—Chinese.*

SNAKES.—The ophidians of China are worthy of a treatise to themselves. They abound, though we question whether the mortality from snake-bites is as fearfully great as in India. Not that there are no poisonous ones to be found, for there are many of them as well as of harmless ones.

There are many species of the harmless Colubrine snakes, from *Zamenis mucosus* (seven feet) to the little worm-like *Calamaria septentrionalis.* Some species, such as *Coluber tœniurus* and *Lycodon rufozonatus* are found practically all over China. *Zaocys dhumnades*, an active, tree-climbing snake, also has a wide distribution. Not many of the Blind snakes (*Typhlopidæ*) are found. *Typhlops braminus* is found as far north as Fukien province. Two big Pythons (*reticulatus* and *molurus*), twenty feet long, are found in the southernmost part of China. Snakes with posterior poison fangs (*Opisthoglypha*), which are not dangerous to mankind, are well represented. The venomous *Proteroglypha* (with anterior poison fangs) are represented by terrestrial forms (*Elapinæ*) and marine forms (sea-snakes).

All the Vipers of China are Pit-vipers (so-called from the curious little pit between the nose and the eye). This dangerous Chinese species does not possess rattles (as in the American Rattlesnakes), but belongs to the genera *Ancistrodon* and *Trimeresurus*. *Ancistrodon blomhoffii* is the only poisonous snake found in North China, but at least six other species of these genera are found south of the 30th parallel of latitude, one of which, *Ancistrodon acutus*, grows to six feet in length and is called by the Chinese 'five pace snake,' its bite being said to be rapidly fatal.

There are several varieties of cobras. The common cobra (*Naja tripudians*) is found in Hongkong; its bite is fatal; and it grows to 6 feet 4 inches or more in length. It was thought at one time that the cobra was not a native of China, but had been simply introduced in some cargo brought by a ship from some foreign port; but this is a mistake, as they are to be found in the country as well as in Hongkong. Even the rare black variety has been killed in Hongkong.

Another snake whose bite is usually fatal is what is known as the *Bungarus fasciatus*. It grows in length to 8 feet 6 inches, and appears to be common in Hongkong and neighbourhood. It has been described as 'handsomely marked with alternate rings of bright yellow and black,' though to the casual observer alternate rings of white and black would seem to be a more accurate description. The ring of white is about half an inch wide on the top of its back, while the black is about an inch and a half wide. It is said to frequent swampy ground.

Another species of the *Bungarus* is also found in Hongkong, the *B. semifasciatus*, whose bite is also fatal. It is a smaller snake than the last, only growing to about 4 feet in length; it also has alternate rings of the same colours as the larger snake.

The *Hamadryad*, or king cobra, or snake-eating cobra, the *Naja bungarus vel ophiophagus elaps*, is rarer than any of the above snakes in Hongkong, we are thankful to say; for its bite is as deadly as that of the cobra; and it frequently attacks man when disturbed; a case is even recorded of its following a man in South America, if we remember rightly, for the considerable distance of a mile or two. It is the largest known poisonous snake in the world. A young specimen is in the City Hall Museum, Hongkong, and some years ago two fairly large ones were killed in the New Territory of that colony.

One of the prettiest snakes, and very common, is the beautiful, bright-green bamboo-snake, or green pit viper, *Trimeresurus gramineus*. The shape of its head shows it to be poisonous; but it is stated that its bite is not usually fatal to a healthy adult, though producing serious symptoms. It is common in Burma as well. The largest known specimen recorded is 3 feet 8 inches, though it is seldom seen in Hongkong more than a foot or 18 inches in length. The *Gardins* is a snake not often seen; but it is found in Hongkong and elsewhere in the Kwongtung Province. It is said by the Chinese to be the most deadly of all snakes, no cure being possible for its bite. It is even found on the house-tops, or roofs, rather. Its name in Chinese is *t'eet seen she* [*t'ieh hsien shê*], or iron-wire snake; it is generally black in colour; but is also seen of a sort of rusty brown shade, is about 7 or 8 inches in length, and of the size of a thick piece of iron wire.

The *Python, Python reticulatus*, or diamond-marked *Python*, is also found in Hongkong in the jungle, or woods, growing in the Happy Valley, or near Stanley. Two specimens are to be seen in the Museum, 12 and 14 feet in length, as well as one, bottled and preserved in spirits. As the City of Hongkong grows in size, the snakes are driven back from the roads and adjacent hill-sides. Snakes, which used to be occasionally seen in the Bonham and Kennedy Roads, scarcely ever appear now; more especially is this the case on the Mount Kellett Road, in the Peak District where a few years ago it was a most common sight to find a snake; whereas now it is very rarely indeed that one sets eyes on one on that road, or to find them, as one occasionally used to, in the basement of one's house at the Peak.

Specimens of the following snakes found in Hongkong are to be seen in the City Hall Museum:—

Naja tripudians.
Ptyas mucosus.
Bungarus fasciatus.
B. semifasciatus.
Python reticulatus.
Pelamis bicolor.
Compoossomia radiatum.
Trimeresus erythrurus.
T. gramineus.
Ophiophagus elaps.
Tropidonotus stolatus.
T. subminatus.
Homalopsis buccata.
Dipsas multimaculata.
Cyclophis major.
Fareas lœvis.
Hydrus major.
Gardins.
Typhlops braminus.

Captain Wall, I.M.S., mentions other snakes, 'the *Callophis macclellandi*, a small and very beautiful little snake—bite not likely to be fatal . . . the *Ancistrodon blomhoffi vel Halys blomhoffi* [see above], a pit viper, found in Japan, Formosa, and China.' The following cutting also mentions yet another kind:—

'A poisonous snake was killed by a Goorkha in a field behind the camp at Shanghai, last week. It was a specimen of the *Daboia elegans* (Russell's viper), and its bite is one of the most rapidly fatal to man and the lower animals. A suggestion is made that this viper came from India in the fodder brought for the use of the horses, but the species is said not to be rare in Mid-China.'

Snakes form an article of diet in some parts of the country. (See FOOD.)

References.—Journal N.C.B.R.A.S., N.S. xlv. 22; xlvii. 83; *Proceedings of the Zoological Society of London*, 1903, i. 84; Boettger, *Mat. herp. Faun. von China;* Boulenger, *Catalogue of Snakes in the British Museum.*

SNIPE.—Snipe are common in some parts of China. The following is an account of them from the pen of a naturalist who resided for many years in the East:—

'Six species of true snipe are to be met with in this part of China [Hongkong], but the sportsman rarely comes across more than the following three varieties: Winter, Swinhoe, Pintailed.

'1st.—The Common or Winter Snipe.—Is generally to be found on marsh or wet land, from November to March. Length, bill to tail, 10½ inches. Weight, 4 to 4½ ounces. Feathers, 14 in tail, all ordinary full-sized.

'2nd.—Swinhoe's Snipe.—Is one of the two migratory (spring and autumn) species; is to be found on grass land, in bean fields, etc. Spring, 15th April to 12th May. Autumn, August and September. Length, bill to tail, 11½ to 12 inches. Weight, 6 to 8¼ ounces. Feathers, 20 tail feathers, of which 8 central are ordinary or winter, 12 (6 on each side) are stiff and narrow.

'3rd.—Pintailed Snipe.—Is the second of the two migratory species; is to be found frequenting the same haunts as the Swinhoe's, and in their company, and migrates practically at the same seasons, that is to say, that in a day's bag both species will probably be found. Length, bill to tail, 10½ to 11 inches. Weight, 5 ounces and up. Feathers, 26 tail feathers, 10 central are ordinary or winter, 16 (8 on each side) are very short, narrow and stiff; *with scarcely any web.* These webless feathers are *pins,* from which the bird is named.

'Winter birds have more white on the breast than, and are not so much barred under the wings as, the more popular immigrants. *But the great point of distinction, always reliable, lies in the tail feathers.* Roughly speaking, a *Pintail* is an ounce heavier than the Winter, and an ounce less than the Swinhoe.'

The great and common snipe is termed *Gallinago megala* (Swinhoe) and *G. scolopacina* (Bp.) and *Totanus calidres.* Others are the Jack Snipe (*Gallinago gallinula;* Fukien, Lower

Yangtzŭ, Chihli), the Painted Snipe (*Rostratula capensis;* resident in S. China, but as far north as Chihli in summer), the Red-necked Snipe (*Lobipes hyper-boreus;* winter visitor), the Himalayan Solitary Snipe (*G. solitaria;* Mongolia, Chihli, Lower Yangtzŭ, Shensi, and Mu-p'in).

References.—David et Oustalet, *Les Oiseaux de la Chine.*

SOCIETIES.—The Chinese are fully aware of the force of the adage that 'union is strength,' and have not a few different forms of associations, societies, and guilds. One of the most common, at all events in the South, is the Money Loan Association. Foreigners have considerable difficulty in understanding this form of Association, as the arrangements connected with it seem complicated; but, when once understood, are simple enough. There are several kinds of Money Loan Associations, but the most common is the Yí-wúí [*I-hui*] (pronounced Ye-wooee). These Associations form a ready and convenient means for Chinese to obtain, what is to them, a large sum of money when the exigencies of business or their social customs, such as those connected with marriage, make it necessary for them to procure a larger sum of ready cash for use than can easily be obtained in any other way.

Supposing then, by way of example, that A requires a sum of money, say $100, he or she then (for women engage more largely in these Associations even than men) invites a number of friends or acquaintances to join with him or her in forming a Money Loan Association, they becoming members or shareholders while A is the Head of the Association. Should the sum fixed upon as the amount of the periodical contribution or share be $5, then A, having invited twenty others to join as members, will get the sum of money he requires, for twenty times $5 is $100 A enrols the names of all in a book, with amounts and dates of payments, totals, and particulars of the Association. Sometimes a page of this book is devoted to each meeting of the Association and the accounts connected therewith. Each member has likewise a small book, a pass-book, supplied by A, who fills it up. Each member is expected to bring his little book with him to each meeting so that the necessary particulars may be entered in it, in the event of his obtaining the money. The date is written in the centre of the yellow cover of the book, or at least the year and month, and the words 'started on a lucky day' below the last, while at the left-hand end of the cover is put the name of the person to whom the book belongs. The Head has a similar book. These books have printed forms at the beginning, containing a preamble, giving, in rather a vague manner, the origin of these Associations, followed, for the guidance of those entering into them, by the rules, with blanks for the insertion of the amount of the contribution or share, and any other matters incident to each particular Association. At all events, whatever else may be omitted, a list of members appears in the book, a name being allotted to each column and placed at the top of the column. A number of blank pages follow for the entries of dates and contributions, or subscriptions, as they might be termed, or payments. In well-kept books, by careful persons for instance, the drawing is sometimes put just below the name of the person who draws, at times, in the following manner: 'Second drawing, interest money 80 cents. Received small shares (that is payments from persons who have not yet drawn), twelve shares (besides the drawer's own share), and one large share' (that is a payment from some one who has already drawn).

One of the most common times for the periods of payments is by the month, though fortnightly Associations are not uncommon: quarterly ones are known, and even annual ones are formed by wealthy men for large sums of money.

Let it be supposed that the one which A forms is a monthly one. A certain day of the month is fixed upon for the future meetings, and no alteration is allowed subsequently, 'no matter how unfavourable the weather may be,' as the Chinese rule puts it. Intercalary months are not counted, though sometimes an exception is made to the rule. In that case the rule should be expunged from the book. The members are apprised by notice being sent to them by the Head, requesting them to prepare their share and take it to the meeting for collection. The money is examined in the presence of the members. No set-off of private debts is allowed or anything in the nature of a pledge, but the money must be actually paid. 'Should any of the members be kept back by any important business, he must send one of his friends to represent him and pay his share of the money.' Each of the members then pays to A the sum of $5, the nominal amount of their monthly contribution, and for the first month the actual amount. On the first occasion A keeps the money, viz. $100, as that is the reason he has formed the Association, and it is the prerogative of the Head of the Association, to have the use of the first monthly amount of money subscribed, or paid in. Also by virtue of his being the Head, he gets this money without needing to pay any interest on it—in short, he gets the full amount of $5 from each of the twenty members. What follows will explain more fully what is meant here. This privilege is accorded to him as a set-off for the work to be done, and trouble to be taken, by him, on behalf of the Association. The money is his for any use to which he likes to apply it. In fact, it is a loan made to him by all of the twenty members, each contributing his share ($5) to it; but having thus secured the loan, he commences the very next month to repay it, in monthly instalments of $5. He does not, however, hand this $5 separately to a separate creditor each month until he has paid the whole twenty; but he does what is tantamount to the same thing, he pays in $5 each month into the funds of the Association—the funds are, of course, the aggregate of the monthly payments in by the Head and members of the Association, which A as Head is responsible for, and holds in trust for the members. It is equivalent to a personal payment of his debt to each member, because each member obtains the loan of all the monthly contributions of that month in which he, the member, draws the money, consequently this $5 goes each month to liquidate in rotation every member for the $5 originally paid in to A, and which A drew out for his own use; for each member, as has already been said, draws out in rotation the monthly sum made up of all the payments in. In other words, when B draws out the amount of money in the second month, in that sum, made up of the payments in by the other members, is also the sum of $5 paid in by the Head, which item of $5 is in repayment of the $5 he, B, paid in the first month to A, the Head, which, as we have already seen, A drew out for his own use along with all the other items of $5 paid in by the other members. A and B are therefore quits—his, B's, loan, has been refunded to him; and the same thing happens with C the next month, that is the third month, and the same with D the month after, and so on with all the members, till all are repaid; and, in fact, at the end of twenty months A has repaid the whole of the $100.

But what makes the matter appear complicated is that B, C, and D, and all the rest, get loans, and on their part repay—in reality each one, except the Head, lends to everyone else, and each one, including the head, borrows from everyone else, and as soon as each one borrows, each one, except the last then begins to repay everyone else. This seems confusion worst confounded, and the maze appears too intricate to the European observer, as he sees in his mind's eye each member transformed, after the first month, one by one, from a lender into a receiver, a borrower, and a payer-back. It is, however, simple enough; and the clue to the maze is to be found in fixing on one member at a time, as we have done with the Head, and following this one member through all the intricacies until, with the close of the Association, his accounts are all settled, at the same time resolutely closing our eyes to the action of the Head and other members, except inasmuch as they affect the actions and money of the one member we are following.

Let us then take B. How does he get his loan? He is not the Head: he cannot draw the money as the Head would at the very start without paying any interest for it, but, by virtue of being a member, be is entitled to the loan. All the members are, however, equally entitled. What shall decide the respective times at which they are permitted to draw? The rule is, after the Head has had his, that the drawings of loans every month shall be by tender, and the highest bidder shall get it. This seems a very fair rule, as the man or woman most in want of money is likely to offer the most for it. These tenders are then put in at every meeting by the members desirous of drawing the money, except at the first and last meetings. At the first, as has already been seen, the Head has it by right, at the last it devolves, as a matter of course, to the residuary member, as all the rest have drawn. The tenders for the loan are written on any kind of paper. If sent by another's hand they are enclosed in an envelope, and the name should be written on the paper as well as the price tendered. If the member is present in person he may write it at the time of handing it in, but in that case he need only write the amount on it without his name, and no envelope is required. The Head of the Association opens the tenders, which are placed on the table before him, in the presence of the members, who see them. The highest tender is taken, and should two be equal in amount the first opened is considered as the successful one. It is not compulsory on all the members to tender each time, but the tendency is for most to do so, as, if there is a demand for the money, one who is in actual want of it, seeing so many present, will, though he may not know what the others have offered, make a big bid in order to overtop theirs, and thus, though the others may not have cared for the money, yet, by their presence and tendering, they have raised the interest which they will each obtain for that loan. In short, a monthly loan is given by the Association in rotation to each of its members, and this rotation is conditioned by the highest bid offered on each occasion, as explained above. In the second month we will suppose then that B writes on a piece of paper—'Offers interest, 50 cents,' and hands this in; we will further suppose that this is the highest amount offered, consequently B obtains the loan. Sometimes three days of grace are allowed for payment in of the money after the tenders have been opened, but it often happens that the contributions have to be paid in immediately after the tendering is over. In this case then B pays nothing in, as he is obtaining a loan: the Head pays his $5, as he does every month after; but all the other members pay, not $5, the nominal amount of their contributions, but $4.50, that is to say, they each deduct the fifty cents offered as interest. (Looking at it in one way, they thus get their interest in advance, as it were, and, should the Association come to grief, their loss, if they do not recover their money, is not quite so great, though, as will be seen from what is said further on, it would be better to say they each only lend $4.50, the borrower having to pay $5 for each of these sums of $4.50, thus repaying principal and interest.) These amounts are handed to the Head, who, after collecting them, pays them over to B along with his, the Head's own $5, making a total of $4.50 × 19 + $5 = $90.50. This then is the loan that B draws. On each occasion after this B pays the full amount of the contribution, $5. It will thus be seen that by doing so he pays the interest on his loan; for every subsequent drawing by a member contains, of course, amongst the different items of which it is made up, one of $5 from B; and as the subsequent drawer, however, only paid into the Association $4.50 on the occasion that B drew, he the subsequent drawer, consequently has got paid back to him $5 for the $4.50, *i.e.*, the 50 cents for interest that B offered, and which was accepted, as his, B's, tender was the highest on that occasion. It will be remembered though that B originally paid $5 to A on the first drawing when A took the drawing by right of being the Head. As we have already said, A pays $5 every time after the first, consequently B has got his $5 back from A, the exact sum he, as one of the members, had loaned to him through the Association, for, as we have already said, A, being the Head, pays no interest, so it will be seen A's and B's accounts are settled as regards each other. B, again, by paying in $5 every month, subsequent to to the one in which he got the loan, virtually pays the other members back the amounts due to them with interest as above, viz., nineteen monthly instalments of $5; counting in that he has already paid $5 to A, as we have just pointed out, his whole payments therefore are $5 × 19 + $5 = $100, that is for the $90.50, and its use, he has paid $100, *i.e.*, $9.50 of interest, which is a very cheap rate of interest for China.

With regard to C. Let us suppose that C offers 25 cents interest, and his tender, being the highest in the third month, is necessarily accepted. He will receive A's $5, and he receives from B $5, as B commences this month (see above) to pay $5;

for after each loan obtained each member pays the full amount of the subscription. From the others, eighteen in number, C receives $4.75 × 18 + $85.50; add to this the $10 above and it makes $95.50, the whole amount which the Head of the Association hands to him. His payments are as follows:—

1st month to A	. . . . .	$ 5.00
2nd month to B	. . . . .	4.50
3rd month nothing	. . . . .	..
4th to 21st month, 18 months @ $5	=	90.00
Total	. . . . .	$99.50

He thus pays $99.50 for the use of $95.50, *i.e.*, $4 of interest.

Let us now take T's case, the twentieth man: to use an Irishism he repays his loan before obtaining it, or, in other words, he pays in a varying sum each month, after the first month, dependent, as has already been shown in the cases of B and C, upon the amount of interest offered. Of course, the higher the interest has been the better for T, as well as for all the other members in a varying degree. Suppose the interest deducted averaged 25 cents. a month, T's payments would then be $5 to A the first month, and nineteen payments of $4.75 = $90.25, add to this the $5 to A = $95.25. He pays that amount and gets $100 for it. In short, the other members have been using his money and he gets paid interest, $4.75, for its use. He does not need to tender for the $100, but gets it, as no one else is entitled to it but him, all having previously drawn. The Association ends with him, for it only runs as long as there are members, as soon as these have each had their turn at a loan the Association is finished. The Society has thus a twofold character: that of a borrowing club; and that of a lending club: for there is a regular succession of borrowers, beginning with A, and a body of lenders, decreasing in number with each meeting. It will thus be seen that this Mutual Loan Benefit Association is most ingeniously arranged, and that it affords exceptional facilities for obtaining a loan on easy terms, with the chances to the members of good interest and easy payments, in small sums distributed over a long period. It needs only to be added that, should a member delay his payment, the Head of the Association may pay it for him, if he likes, or it may stand over if the members are friendly with the defaulting member; should any member die before drawing his loan, his wife or children, or in default of them, nearest of kin, may continue to go on with the Association in the place of the deceased, on condition that the Head of the Association approves of them doing so; but if the Head is unwilling, then the heirs must wait till the winding up of the whole affair, when, on the accounts being made up, it will be seen how many payments the dead man had made, and a sum equivalent to an equal number of $5 payments will be made to them: should he already have obtained his drawing before his death, his heirs are required to make the usual monthly payments of $5 to repay the Association; if they are not able to do so, it is accepted as as a misfortune, the Head is not considered liable, as a Head of the Association, and the members only suffer. Should it be written on the top margin of the book that 'should any member abscond, the principal is to be refunded but not the interest, any accidents, etc., are to be taken as the will of God,' then the Head of the Association has to conform to this rule, but otherwise a principle of practical equity, much practised by the Chinese, when circumstances over which they have no control occur, is brought into play, and the Head of the Association makes good one-half of what the absconding member ought to have paid; or, rather, he makes good half of the principal, the other half being a loss to the members, and this holds good in both the Yí-wúí [I-hui], now written about, and the Téí-p'ò-wúí (pronounced Tay p'o wooee) [Ti-p'u Hui] to be mentioned later on.

Whether the above words are written or not, the Head is not responsible for the subscriptions of a dead member.

With regard to the subscriptions to the Association, it may be remarked that, in practice, it seems often to be considered sufficient if the money is paid into the hands of the Head of the Association at any place somewhere near the time that it should be paid, *i.e.*, it is not necessary that the money should be paid absolutely punctually.

The members have no redress when the Head of the Association absconds while the Association is in progress. Those who have had their drawing are content, of course, to let the matter rest, as they have had all their benefit and cannot be called upon by the other members who have not had the loan to continue their payments, as the contract is not between member and member, but is a contract between each separate member of the Association and the Head. On the latter absconding, the Association is broken up. This can be seen by the fact that in the poorer Associations—where the contributions are confined to a few dollars, and where the members do not meet for dinners—the members may not even see each other or know anything at all about each other. (This view of the matter has been held in the Hongkong Courts in an appeal case. See report of Judgment by the Full Court in *The Hongkong Daily Press*, of the 19th March, 1892.) The Head in some of such Associations sometimes goes round to each of the members at their own houses, etc., with an earthenware money-box, and the members drop their tenders into it. After the collection of tenders is thus made, the crock is broken and the tenders taken out.

In the more important Associations, when the amount of the subscription is $100 or so, the Head of the Association, having asked his friends to join, and got their consent, follows it up in the course of a few days with invitation cards to a dinner or wine-party at some eating-house, and they are asked to bring their subscriptions with them. All who respond to the invitations become members; from five to ten days after, their names are all entered by the Head in the books, with rules, amount of subscription, etc., and one is given to each member. The expenses of the first dinner are paid by the Head; and the same individual, on behalf of the members, provides a dinner again, issuing invitation cards the previous day, as before, but on each occasion subsequent to the first it is the member who obtains the loan who pays the expenses of the dinner; the money (a certain sum at very first being fixed for its cost) for it being deducted out of his loan; the dinner, however, is ordered by the previous drawer. One who does not attend the dinner, or dinners, is not exempted thereby from his share of the expenses, and one who wishes to enjoy the feast must come to it, as no portion will be sent to the absentee. When the dinners are given in connection with these Associations, the business is attended to first, and after that the members have their feasting: business first and pleasure afterwards. This feasting, however, does not take place in the smaller Associations where the shares are only a few dollars each. A member in an Association is not confined to one share, but may have two or more if he chooses.

There is another kind of these associations called the Téí-p'ò-wúí [Ti-p'u Hui], 'Spread on the Ground Association,' so called because it is said the original starter was too poor to have any place to receive his friends, and had to spread a mat on the ground to collect the amounts subscribed. The Téí-p'ò are slightly different from the Yí-úí, though in many of the details they are the same, the differences being so slight that the same book is used. The chief point of difference is that the Head of the Association, as Head, is out of it altogether, that is to say, he or she does not obtain a loan. At the same time, in the Téí-p'ò-wúí, the Head may be a member of the Association or not as he (or she, as it is very often a woman who is Head in these societies) chooses. If the latter, he then has no share in the matter at all. He is in fact a paid servant of the members, that is to say, he does all the work that the ordinary Head does and gets half the value of one share paid to him by the successful drawer. Under these circumstances the Head does not get the first drawing as in the Yí-wúí, but the first drawing is balloted for as well as the others. All his other duties are just the same as the others. All his other duties are just the same as those assigned to the Head of the Yí-wúí, and he is responsible for the money. The position occupied by the Head is more analogous to that of a paid servant, though no salary is his reward; but he gets a commission, as it were, to recoup him for his trouble, the amount of the commission being fixed at one-half of the subscription, *i.e.*, if the periodical subscription paid were $5, the Head would get $2.50; and this is paid to him by the person who obtains the drawing on each occasion. In the Téí-p'ò-wúí no dinners or wine parties are given. The Head goes round personally and informs the members of the meetings, which are held in his house. Some bring written tenders, but the majority, being women and unable to write, being sticks of bamboo of different lengths with them, to represent the amounts they are willing to offer as interest. These sticks of bamboo are unburnt ends of incense-sticks, and the women break them into the right lengths, perhaps in a corner of the room where no one can see them, the owner telling the Head what each bamboo stick stands for: the longer ones, say one dollar, the shorter ones may be fifty cents, and the still shorter ones, perhaps, ten cents. After all are laid down, and before opening, sometimes the tenderer may say, 'I add verbally so many cents to my tender.'

Claims in connection with these Associations have been ruled out of Court in Hongkong, should the numbers of those forming them exceed twenty, as, by the laws of the colony, every company, if twenty in number, must be registered as a public company, if less in number, they have been tried upon their merits. In the case of an Association, not completed, Sir James Russell ruled that the Head of the Association could be sued for the money had. As in the Téí-p'ò the Trustee (or Head) gets a commission on each drawing, but in the Yí-wúí he gets the first drawing, it was held by one of the Hongkong Judges (the Hon. F. Snowden) that in the latter case the Trustee is responsible for the future payments, but not in the Téí-p'ò-wúí, as in that the Head only puts himself, or herself, to the trouble of collecting, and does not make himself, or herself, responsible for the members paying it, merely drawing a commission for the trouble of collecting.

It seems strange to find what one thought was an entirely Chinese institution in use amongst factory girls in England, as the following extract will show. Has someone from China introduced it into the West, or can it be one of those old-world customs handed down through the ages? This is an account of one:—

'While we stand watching, I am struck by a knot of girls who are in hot dispute or discussion over some point. "Oh, it's only 'Liz,' says my guide, 'holding a club. Her mother's in a bit of trouble about the rent, and so she's getting the money this way. . . . " The girls all do it, and photograph clubs, clothing clubs, money clubs, abound on every side. This special one held by "Liz" happens to be a guinea club. . . . "Liz" and twenty other girls have joined together for twenty-one weeks, each girl subscribing one shilling per week. Their names are written on papers, and then drawn in rotation. The girl who draws out No. 1 is entitled to her guinea at once, and in this case, as "Liz," for holding the club, is entitled to be No. 1, she has her money wherewith to pay off the rent. No. 2 gets her guinea in two weeks, No. 3 in three weeks, and so on till No. 21 gets hers, after the twenty-one weeks. All pay their shilling per week, whether they receive their guinea first or later, so that the only advantage of the club is that a girl may draw an early number, and have a sum of money at once.'

It will be noticed that this is a simpler form of the Money Loan Association than that found in China, as no interest is paid and the rather complicated system of the Chinese form does not come into play.

'China is a land of associations which are as numerous and the objects of which are as varied as the needs of man. Their formation is simple and easy. Certain villagers, whatever their object may be, meet in a temple, ancestral hall, or private house, to deliberate over some scheme. If it is approved, a fund is raised, to which the members contribute equally, their contributions being devoted to the purchase of a piece of land, landed property in China being considered the safest investment. The rent derived from this land may be used for the burial of a member of the association when he dies, or may be let out on interest, or may be used to assist members to emigrate to California and Australia, or for any other enterprise or good object that may be desired.'

References.—Records of 1890 Missionary Conference; Hastings, *Encyclopædia of Religions;* De Groot, *Sectarianism and Religious Persecution in China.*

SOCIETIES, SECRET.—A book dealing with 'Things Chinese' would scarcely be complete without some reference to secret societies, as these combinations are so common, not only in their own native land, but they often obtain a more powerful position and even exert at times a greater influence when transplanted to foreign soil.

There seems to be a world-wide similarity between secret societies, in many respects. In their fundamental principles there is a wonderful likeness, as well as in many points of practice, ceremonial, and ritual. When we come, however, to examine into them, it seems, as a general rule, to be a family likeness, perhaps the result of heredity, and not a servile imitation of one another during recent times.

Especially is this true of some of the Chinese secret societies. Of them it may be said that they are founded upon a spirit of fraternity, devotion, filial piety, and religion. At least this is the case with the most famous, the Sám Hòp Wúí [San-ho Hui], or Triad Society, though it has shown itself in the terrible rebellion that was carried on for many years under its banners in opposite aspects to these. In its 'Words of Exhortation' we find it written, 'If people insult you, injure you, revile you, abuse you,—how ought you to take it? You ought to bear it, suffer it, endure it, and forgive it.' How then, it may be asked, is revolt and rebellion against the Government compatible with such principles? They are quite in harmony according to the Chinese idea; for it is the duty of the good to upset the government of the bad. In such a case it is not rebellion, but the raising of the standard of righteousness against tyranny and oppression. We must give the leaders of the great T'áí-p'ing rebellion credit for motives of this character at their inception of the rebellion, though some of them may have had their heads turned eventually by lust of power, while the rag-tag and bobtail which followed in their train had no higher motives than plunder and loot.

The origin of the Hung league, one of the names of the Triad Brotherhood, is shrouded in the mists of uncertainty. They claim, like the Freemasons, a high antiquity, but it is impossible, as far as researches have been carried at present, to say with any certainty whence they sprang. There would appear to be some slight indications or possibilities of the existence of this society in some form or another in previous times, but it was only during the rule of China by the Tartars that it appeared as a regular political body. The two provinces of Canton and Fukien, which most energetically resisted the Tartar sway, were the cradles of the Triad Society. In course of time the Triads awoke the displeasure of the Government. Unfortunately, the followers of the Society 'degenerated into a band of rebels and robbers, that seemed to have lost every notion of the proper spirit of its association.' But a change came over them, for one of their members, Hung Saú-ts'ün [Hsiu-ch'üan], had obtained some knowledge of Christianity, which he engrafted on the old stock; and it is a matter of recent history, how, the standard of rebellion raised, the forces of the insurgents were increased by ever swelling bands of recruits, while many were forced to join their ranks in the hopes of escaping immediate death; all hopes of desertion were denied them in some cases by the words T'áí P'ing being branded on their cheeks, a positive proof, if found by the Imperialists, that they were rebels. Their leader took the title of 'King of the Heavenly Realm of Universal Peace,' and he had associated with him several co-kings. Under their leadership many of the finest provinces were overrun; death and destruction dealt out to the inhabitants; the idol temples demolished, and the idols mutilated; the fair land turned into a desert; Nanking, the ancient capital of China, captured, and the new dynasty started its reign within the old walls of the 'Southern Capital,' for that is the meaning of the name. In fact it looked much as if the Manchu Tartars were doomed, and doubtless they might have been, had not foreign aid come chiefly in the person of General Gordon, and the 'Ever Victorious Army,' which so effectually assisted the Imperial forces that they gained the day, and, after many a hard-fought battle, the rebellion was quelled and the then effete Manchu dynasty bolstered up on the throne. At the same time there was so much of corruption and evil in the ranks of the rebels that it is questionable, had they succeeded, whether their rule would have been any better, or even as good, as that of those they endeavoured to overthrow; for, with the great mass of their followers, murder, rapine, and plunder were the aims, while the leader developed into a visionary of a curious type; he was possessed by a most extraordinary craze, giving out that he was the younger brother of Jesus Christ, and a number of other blasphemies. These were published in books and pamphlets issued from the press. These books, are most wonderful productions. The diplomas, or certificates, are curious documents; they are written on white linen. There is much paraphernalia connected with the Lodges, such as numerous flags, banners, state umbrellas, warrants, working tools, etc.

Each Lodge in the Society—how many there are we are unable to say—is governed by a President, two Vice-Presidents, one Master, two Introducers, one Fiscal, who is styled 'The Red Stick' from the red staff with which he punishes offenders; thirteen Councillors, amongst whom are a Treasurer, a Receiver, and an Acting Treasurer; there are also Agents and minor officials who wear flowers in their hair. Some of the brethren, who are styled Horse-leaders, are appointed to act as recruiters of new members. Besides these, four brethren summon the others to the meetings. The officials are appointed by the vote of the whole Lodge. After one year, a brother can be promoted to be an Introducer; after two, to be a Vanguard; after three, to be a Master, if a vacancy occurs. The Meetings are generally held on the 25th day of the Chinese month. (Ten days' notice has to be given, by summons, of each Meeting of Lodge.) One of these calls to Lodge used in Hongkong consists of a slip of bamboo on which is written the name of the Lodge, and the other particulars requisite. Contributions, varying in amount, are made at the usual Chinese festivals, etc. Recruits for the society are got by persuasion, but, failing that, notices are put into the houses of those they wish to have join them, instructing them to go to a certain spot at a given time, and threats are held out that, if the authorities are informed, destruction will overtake them and their relations and property. Arrived at the *rendezvous* they are conducted to the Lodge; at other times they are assaulted and decoyed on till, overpowered by numbers, they are put into a sack and carried there. The candidates for initiation present themselves barefooted with dishevelled hair and with the lappels of their coats hanging open. Five incense-sticks are taken in their hands and four quatrians repeated by them, after which they swear to their certificates of birth, while the Introducer, acting as Herald, gives their names, so that all the brethren may hear them. Having arrived at the gate an incense-stick is taken in both hands and the candidates salute the two Generals. On entering the first gate of the camp their names, surnames, ages, and times of birth are all carefully entered in a book by the Vanguard. An arch of steel is then formed—one-half of the swords being of copper, however—and the candidates are led under it; sometimes a red cloth does duty for the arch of steel. The candidates, holding three red stones in their hands, have to pay, after passing, twenty-one cash as first entry money, and find themselves before the Hung Gate, which is guarded by two Generals; here they kneel thrice. Their names are demanded from the Vanguard, who gives them; the Generals then go in to obtain the Master's permission for them to enter, after which they are allowed to pass 'and are brought to the Hall of Fidelity and Loyalty,' where two more Generals are on guard, who also ask their names, and the candidates kneel four times. There, at last, they are instructed, in the objects of the Society; and 'are exhorted to be faithful and loyal to the league to which they are about to be affiliated.' The grievances 'against the Tartar dominion are enumerated, and promises' made to 'those who shall accomplish their duties faithfully; whilst fearful threats are pronounced against those who should dare to refuse to enter the league.' 'The last enclosure before the Lodge' is the Heaven and Earth Circle, which is again guarded by two Generals. 'After having passed through, and gone across the surrounding moat or ditch, they reach the East Gate of the City of Willows, guarded by *Han-p'ang*.' The candidates here kneel twice. They are led to the Council Room, called 'The Lodge of Universal Peace,' where the whole of the council is assembled. 'Two Generals keep guard at the door of this room.' The Vanguard speaks to them and requests permission for *T'ien-yu-hung* (the candidates are supposed to personate him) to enter, which the Master grants. The Vanguard then enters the Council Room, after which a number of questions are asked, which are answered, a quatrain or some verses being repeated after each statement as a proof. Next to each candidate stands a member who answers for him. There are 333 questions, and they refer to the objects of the Society, its different working tools, banners, parts of the Lodge, historical and legendary history, etc.

After the examination is through, the Master is satisfied, and those who wish to proceed with their Initiation have further ceremonies to go through, while those who refuse to join the brotherhood are taken to the West Gate and have their heads cut off. The next thing, for those who are proceeding with the ceremony, is the cutting off of the queue, the queue being a sign of subjection to the Manchu rule; but this cannot always be carried out, as it would be a sign of rebellion to be seen without one, though it is sometimes done and a false queue braided on again. The candidates are shaved and their hair done up as under the Ming dynasty, and they would appear to be clothed in sackcloth and mourning. The next ceremony is that of washing the faces of the candidates, emblematical of cleansing traitorous hearts, after which the outer garments are taken off, as they are cut after the Manchu style. This ceremony of 'undressing' having been gone through, they are clothed in long white robes and a red handkerchief wrapped round the head, and later on a pair of straw mourning shoes, in place of the ordinary shoes, is put on; during the course of all these ceremonies numerous quatrains are recited bearing on them. These preliminaries being ended, the candidates are led before the altar, on which is a censer of white porcelain. The whole of the brethren present take nine blades of grass in their hands to pledge fidelity, in commemoration, it is said, of the plan employed by the original founders; two quatrains are repeated, the oath, written on large sheets of yellow paper, is next laid on the censer, and incense-sticks taken in the hands of all present, verses again being recited; the incense is offered and a blade of grass is put by each member into the ashes of the censer, and a verse repeated; a second and third are placed in, in the same way. After this, three sticks of fine incense are stuck into the censer, one by one, a verse being repeated with each; 'two candles of dry wood are now lighted,'—and another quatrain recited, followed by the lighting of a red candle in the same manner. All this being through, a silver wine-jug and three jade stone wine-cups are brought in, and the brethren worship Heaven and Earth 'by pledging three cups of wine,' with the usual accompaniment of verses. After the wine has been offered, the Seven Starred Lamp is lit, followed by the lighting of the 'Lamp of the Gemmeous Ruler' and the Hung Light, all accompanied by verses. All the lamps being thus lit and the incense giving forth its fragrant odours, a solemn prayer, read slowly and reverentially, is offered to the gods—Buddhist, and Taoist, as well as to the deified Spirits of Nature and of Heroes. After rising from this prayer, eight salutations on bended knee are made, to Heaven, Earth, the Sun, the Moon, 'the Five Founders, Wan-yün-lung, the Brethren, and the renowned amongst their companions,' a verse again being recited. One of the members then takes the oath, which has been lying on the censer all this time, and reads it to the candidates 'who remain kneeling during the reading.' It is in thirty-six articles, and enjoins the practice of equity and justice amongst the members; the shielding of the brethren in times of trouble; the chastity of a brother's wife or concubine, and of his child, are to be strictly respected; and, besides, the members are told 'you must consider the father of a brother as your own father, his mother as your mother, his sister as your sister, and his wife as your sister-in-law.'

After reading the oath, the brethren rise from their knees and proceed to the ceremony of confirming it by shedding blood, first making and drinking tea to cleanse the mouth, with the usual recitations. A large bowl is next filled with wine, and another quatrain repeated. The brethren prick themselves in the middle finger and thus mingle some of their own blood with the wine, all drinking of it, several quatrains bearing on the subject being recited at the time. Sometimes a cock's blood is used instead. 'The Drinking of the Bloody Wine' being over, a white cock's head is chopped off, to the usual accompaniment, followed by an execration, solemnly pronounced, beginning:—'The white cock is the token, and we have shed its blood and taken an oath. The unfaithful and disloyal shall perish like this cock.'

'The new members are now led without the West Gate where a furnace is burning'; there the oath is burned, thus being sent into the spirit world and coming to the knowledge of the gods, who will punish any perjurers.

The President then presents the new members with their certificates, on the back of which their names are written in a secret manner. 'The book, containing the oath, laws, regulations, secret signs, etc., is also given to them,' and sometimes a pair of daggers. Besides keeping their certificates on their persons, they also keep three of the T'ái-p'ing coins, as signs of recognition; for all of these things they pay fees.

They are next led round the building, to have the flags and working tools shown to them, to the accompaniment of quatrains.

The banners are then consecrated, three cups of wine being poured on the ground at the same time, as a libation to the gods, a prayer is offered, and another quatrain recited. After this prayer, the spear-heads are dipped in the blood of a white horse and a black ox, which are slaughtered as offerings to the solar and telluric principles respectively; they are then cooked and a supper eaten, during, and after, which theatricals take place. As dawn approaches the members reclothe themselves in their present, everyday attire, and return home.

There is a code of laws and statutes, the articles of law being seventy-two in number, and the regulations twenty-one; besides these there are ten prohibitory Bye-laws relating to Meetings of Lodge. All these laws and regulations inculcate brotherly kindness, assisting of brethren in time of need, shielding them from the authorities, and abstaining from giving evidence against them in the Courts of Law; the trial of all cases in which brethren alone are concerned is to be held before the Lodge, and not to be brought before the magistrates; letters are to be carried from foreign countries for the brethren, and any brother found purloining money entrusted to him by a brother is severely punished. The infraction of each of the regulations is followed by imprecations or threatened punishments, among which may be noted those of having the head cut off, an ear chopped off, etc. We cannot, however, give even a short *résumé* of all the offences provided for; but amongst these laws, as can well be imagined, the divulgence of the secrets in any way is a most serious offence.

The brethren have besides a perfect system of secret signs adapted for all times and seasons and conditions. We will just instance a few of them:—'If people ask you on the road,

"Whence come you?" Answer, "I come from the East." If they ask you, "Whither are you going?" Answer, "I want to go to the place where I can join the myriads of brethren."' In entering the house of a brother, one is directed to stop for a moment and enter with the left foot first. In sitting down, the points of the grass shoes are turned towards each other, while the heels are separate: this is a sign that one is a brother. The queue so done up as to have the end hanging down behind the left ear denotes business. Another sign in use is the tucking up the right leg of the trousers while the left leg is allowed to hang down. The brethren have different signs, passwords, and quatrains for use if attacked by robbers and pirates who may chance to be Triad men; and though they are not allowed to divulge the secrets to outsiders, yet they are permitted to teach their sisters and wives certain verses for their protection under similar circumstances. All contingencies appear to be provided for, amongst others, directions are given how to put up a secret sign over one's door in case of a revolt. This is not a part of a mere system, but is of practical use, as, for instance, houses in Chinese cities were thus protected, when it was feared that the T'ái-p'ing rebels would attack the place. Numerous signs and counter-signs, forms of recognition, and wishes expressed secretly, are all revealed by the manipulation of tea-pots, tea-cups, wine-cups, tobacco and opium pipes, chop-sticks, white fans, and betel nuts, by placing them in different positions, holding them in different ways, and presenting them to one another.

The Triad Society has brought itself prominently into notice in the English and Dutch colonial possessions, where its members have exerted a great influence, and almost absolute power at times, over their fellow-countrymen. Their membership in some places is enormous: in the Straits Settlements it would appear, if we are to judge by the figures, that at one time, at all events, their number was equal to that of the Chinese population; for in 1887 the census returns the Chinese population as less than the Triad members, which were 156,440.

The Ghee Hin, a Hokkien, or Fukien, Society, had a membership in the year 1889, in Singapore, of 18,973 members with 478 office-bearers; the total membership of the ten Societies registered in 1889 was 68,316, an increase of 5,000 on the previous year, making a total since 1877 of 68,316, while there was an approximate increase of 9,000 in Penang, the total number of 113,300 being the approximate membership. One Society, named the Ghi Hing, had an approximate membership of 75,000.

A new Societies Ordinance came into force in 1890, in the Straits Settlements. Its chief object was to abolish the Triad Society, as well as other Dangerous Societies, 'some of which have existed in Singapore since 1821, and in Penang for a much longer period'; one or two of the Penang Societies are very wealthy, but the Singapore ones only own the *Kong-si* [*Kung-ssŭ*], or Club-houses. The Singapore and Penang Societies delivered up their chops and books, and the diplomas of the six Triad branches were formally renounced and burnt in the presence of two English officials. Chinese Advisory Boards have been instituted to assist the officials.

There would seem to be no Grand Master of the whole Triad body; but a central government is in existence, composed of the five Grand Masters of the five Grand Lodges of Fukien, Kuangtung, Yünnan, Hunan, and Chêkiang. This governing body then has some sort of control over millions of Chinese, not only in China itself, but throughout the world.

One writer says of this organisation:—'These principles, the repudiation of all jurisdiction, and the assumption of their power by an irresponsible tribunal, constitute an *imperium in imperio*, the foulest, the bloodiest, the most oppressive of which there is record on such a scale.' Another says:—'The Hung League has carried civil war and murder wherever it has gone.' Yet another says:—'They engage to defend each other against the police, to hide each other's crimes, to assist detected members in making their escape from justice.' And yet again another says:—That it is a 'combination to carry out private quarrels, and to uphold the interests of the members in spite of law, and lastly, to raise money by subscription or by levying fees on brothels or gaming-houses.'

Born in bloodshed when the famous Wu San-kuei lived (who, as has happened before now in the West, lost the empire to a foreign prince, invited to aid in driving out some unwelcome aspirant to the throne), the Triad Society was almost extinguished in blood in our own day. But though not only scotched but receiving terrible punishment, the Association has not lost its vitality. Unable to snatch the sceptre even from the weak and nerveless hands that hold it, though its aspirations are as high as ever and its watchwords ring with the cry of battle as grandly as of yore, it perforce has to content itself, instead of being the wholesale conqueror and marauder, the inspiriting force that has carried on the hosts of rebels, grand robbers, to victory against the erstwhile bordes of imperial and provincial troops—instead of this it has had to descend to the rôle of being the nexus which has bound together the 'little robbers' who prey on the home and cottage for the paltry sums which the night thief may find when he has overcome a few startled women, old men, and children: it only breaks out into spasmodic eruptions of political, or rather military, energy, when a fitting opportunity presents itself.

Here then is sufficient reason for their suppression; and, owing to the misuse of their power, and the rioting and murders committed by them in the Straits Settlements, they have been forbidden there as secret unregistered Associations. The principal recent legislative enactment against them in Hongkong is Ordinance No. 8 of 1887, by which the Triad Society is declared to be unlawful, and the managers and office-bearers are liable to a fine of a thousand dollars and to imprisonment for one year; the former Ordinances which related to them were Nos. 1 and 12 of 1845, which meted out more drastic punishment than the last one mentioned above. Some of the prominent members of the Society have been deported by the Hongkong Government, when necessity arose for it, for unfortunately in this colony, they have degenerated into nests of thieves and bands of robbers.

In the United States they have done great injury to the well-being of those who did not belong to their societies.

This account of the Triad Society will show what Chinese secret societies are capable of both in China and abroad. There are hundreds of these secret societies in China itself, but they are not all political in their aim; some are merely sects of Buddhists; one in the North, 'The T'sai Li,' or Temperance Society, forbids the use of tobacco, wine and spirits, amongst its other tenets and prohibitions, and has a large membership, there being nearly 50,000 in the province of Chihli and in Peking. Its doings were exposed some years ago 'by certain members of the society, by which' it was hoped that 'a serious outbreak in the capital might possibly be averted.' The Government tried to keep matters secret. It is said that 80,000 members of it were to be found under Li Hung-chang's rule a few years ago.

An association which attracted much attention in the eighties, nineties, and later especially in 1911, is the Kò-lò-wúí [*Ko-lao Hui*], which had its headquarters in the province of Hunan, the army being quite honeycombed by this political Association which, like the Triad, had for its object the overthrow of the Manchu dynasty. It is said to have its emissaries in every province, who travel under the assumed character of doctors, disseminating news and gathering in members as they go. It was believed by some to be answerable for the riots in 1891 directed against foreigners in Central China, with the òbject of embroiling them with the Manchu Government. (See RIOTS.) Its organisation is in all probability on somewhat similar lines to that of the Triad Society, for there are five Heads, Certificates printed on linen (a fac-simile of one is given in the *China Review*, vol. xv. p. 129), etc., and an elaborate initiation ceremony is said to be employed. It is described as resembling Freemasonry, and not essentially seditious; but opportunities for a thorough study of it have not yet been afforded to those interested in such subjects. It took its rise at the time of the T'ái-p'ing rebellion, General Tsêng Kuo-fan himself, so it is reported, having established it at the siege of Nanking; but this body, instead of seeking to a re-establish the Ming dynasty, would appear to look further back, even as far as to the T'ang dynasty, and, probably, if their chance ever comes, some one will be put forward as of reputed Imperial descent from rulers of that dynasty, though the house of T'ang is supposed to be extinct long since. [' T'ang,' however, is used as meaning ' Chinese,' as opposed to Manchu, etc.]

' The Kolao-hwei Society is known to have been in existence for the past twenty years, and there are great numbers of men connected with it, distributed over the provinces of Kiangsu, Anhui, Hunan, Hupeh, Kiangsi, and Kuangtung.'

This was written before 1903; but the Society, though founded in early times in Ssŭch'uan, in its present form dates from the beginning of the Manchu dynasty. It was then anti-dynastic, but not necessarily pro-Ming.

A secret society which committed the massacres on the missionaries at Kuch'êng in 1895, styled itself vegetarian. One of the members appears to have cured eight opium smokers. The Vegetarians were divided into nine companies. As to their worship, they say:—

' When worshipping we present the following eight kinds of things:—melon seeds, candy, red dates, black dates, pea-nuts,' oranges, dried melons, and dried lengkeng [*lung-yen*], or dragons' eyes. (The lengkeng is the symbol of the vegetarians.) The ceremony of saluting the flag is as follows:—' We bring our palms together, and kneel down five times before it, to worship Heaven, Earth, the Emperor, our parents, and teachers, after which we kneel three times, to salute our brothers, other relatives and friends.'

The dreadful Boxers which created such disturbances in the North, and were encouraged by the Chinese officials, were also a secret society, based to some extent on the same principles and ceremonials as the Triads. They believed largely in hypnotism, and one of their tenets was that they could render themselves invulnerable in fight. They imposed on numbers of people, who joined them in crowds.

' The Boxers include not only boys of from 12 to 15, but girls of the same age, and they form different branches. The branch to which the girls belong is known as the Hing Tong Chin [*Hung-têng K'an*], or Red Lantern Shrines; they carry about with them red lanterns, and they profess that they have only to throw the lanterns up into the air and they will alight on any house, whether near or far, which they wish to set on fire. The boys' branch is called the I Wo Tun [*I-ho T'uan*]. On a man joining the Boxers he commences to bow to the south-east, and says a prayer daily. When he has done this about a hundred times he becomes possessed of the power to hypnotise himself at the right moment, any time he likes. He makes a bow to the south-east, says a prayer, and next begins to shiver, and he can then take up a sword and play with it. It is usual for them to hypnotise themselves before commencing to fight. . . . Most of them are between 12 and 16 or 18 years of age, and are farmers and farmers' children. . . . When anyone joins the Boxers he puts pieces of red cloth round his head, stomach, and legs, and dons two shoulder-straps, on which are characters which mean, "Protect China and kill the foreigners."'

Secret societies originally were either (1) political, such as the *Ch'ih Mei*, or Red Eyebrow, Sect; (2) religions, such as the Vegetarian Sect; (3) politico-religious, such as the Triad Society; or (4) personal, such as the Golden Orchid Society, a girl's Anti-Marriage Society. In 1896, the members of secret sects were said to average from 20,000 to 200,000 members per province.

A vivid light is thrown on the spread of banditry in recent years by the following extracts on 'Chinese Bandit Guilds.'

'That there are beggars' guilds, thieves' guilds, and kidnappers' guilds in Hongkong, as in other cities in China, is commonly accepted. Naturally little is known of their organizations, but that they are complete and extensive goes without saying; the guild system is deeply rooted in Chinese life.

Some particulars that have been revealed of the *modus operandi* of kidnappers indicate a surprisingly well-co-ordinated business. There is a trade in captives, reminding one of the slave markets, in which the unfortunates figure as less than cattle.

Sum is the Chinese slang term for a prisoner held for ransom. The word means literally heart, but expresses body and soul. *Lai sum* (to lead the body away) is to kidnap. Those who in their time have been *sums* must number thousands; abduction is rife in China, and has been rife since ordered government ceased to exist. Every piracy, every raid by bandits has yielded a batch of *sum* to be carried away against redemption. Moreover, there are always the more subtle members of the kidnapping profession who work quietly in the cities, enticing away sons and heirs, or women and girls if there seems to be a market for them. Some have been rescued; some have been recovered with horrible memories of torture seen and experienced; some have been duly murdered; and others have merely languished and died.

Not many weeks ago a sorter employed in the Canton Post Office brought his stamp down on a small parcel that seemed to contain a fragment of leather. Curious, he decided to deliver it himself, and watched while the addressee opened it. It was a human ear for the father of a boy who had been abducted, just to remind him that the gang meant business. Sometimes it is a finger that is received. In extreme case roasted bodies have been delivered to difficult parents, in trays such as are used for cooking pigs. In ways that are dark the Chinese kidnapper is devilishly ingenious with his tortures. It is rare to hear of a *sum* returning without some mark of his captivity, for all are ill-treated on general principle and are thus inspired to write really appealing letters to anxious relatives and speed up the negotiations.

Cannibalism is alleged, as the result of discoveries of portions of children's bodies in bandit caves, but the proof is not definite. But all is grist that comes to the kidnapper's mill. Not far from Hongkong recently an old woman was captured. She pleaded her poverty, her age, and her general worthlessness; but the bandit chief had a fine sense of humour. "A skinny old pig," be said in effect, "and they shall ransom you as pork." So he had her weighed and demanded for her the market price of meat.

Negotiations for the release of a *sum* are always a protracted business. Bargaining enters here, as in all business in China. There comes to the distressed relatives a message from a wretched middleman fixing a secret appointment and naming a sum. The relatives must first sweeten this parasite with gifts and a negotiation fee. The family appoints an agent, since either side wishes to appear in the open, and the barter then proceeds. The middleman, called a *ha'an yan* (outside man), rakes in as much as possible by way of commission.

As long as negotiations continue the captive is safe from death, if not from occasional torture. When the relatives, miserly or impatient, break off relations, however, a crisis arises. It is then that the captive's ear or finger or toe may come along. Before conversations can be resumed the middleman must be sweetened again, so the expenditure may be unending. A Canton family, bargaining for the release of a member, a well-known schoolmaster, found a very helpful go-between; he promised much and they hoped and were grateful. Mysteriously, on conveying the money to the meeting-place, the family deputation was itself captured and the ransom lost. They escaped eventually and with more money ventured again. This time, by the middleman's good offices, the matter was satisfactorily arranged, whereafter it was revealed that their guide, philosopher, and friend was none other than the bandit chief himself.

Negotiation is rendered more difficult by the existence of a market in which unhappy *sums* are bought, speculatively, from one bandit gang by another. Bandits with small organization and insecure hiding-places dispose of their prisoners to more firmly established concerns. There are bandit capitalists and *sum* dealers in a wholesale way of trade. One captive in his time may travel far and change prisons frequently, and if his immediate owner decides to sell on the eve of conclusion of negotiations, the disappointed relatives have to go through the sorry business all over again, a higher price being demanded. Cash before delivery is the rule, and the bearer of the silver is known by the fanciful title of "Man who Shoulders the Silver Pole."

In spite of police vigilance isolated cases of abduction still occur in Hongkong and occasionally figure in criminal proceedings. In not a few instances on the rivers foreigners have been taken; but they are comparatively fortunate. Where only Chinese are concerned no official outcry is raised; with no Government to help them, they ransom themselves as best they can. Knowing the risks, those who have come to Hongkong to live venture out of the colony again with the greatest caution. Some of the younger Hongkong Chinese generation have never seen their fathers' villages. For them, *Ch'ing Ming*, the Feast of Pure Brightness (April 5 this year), when every good Chinese must worship at his ancestors' tombs, means nothing.'

References.—The Thian Ti Hwui [*T'ien-ti Hui*], by G. Schlegel, contains the fullest account of the Triad Society that has yet been published, and is recommended to the student who wishes to enter into a knowledge of its mysteries. It is illustrated with diagrams of diplomas and flags, etc. For the general reader, a short article in *Harper's Magazine* for September, 1891, entitled, 'Chinese Secret Societies,' by F. Boyle, will be found interesting. A paper in the transactions of the Missionary Conference, held at Shanghai in 1890, contains a list of a good many of these societies, in the province of Shantung, with some little account of them. In that province alone it is stated that there are over a hundred secret societies. An account of the workings of these Secret Societies in the United States amongst the Chinese, appears in the *California Illustrated Magazine*. See also references at end of article SOCIETIES.

STAMPS.—Owing to the want of a general postal system in China under the auspices of the Government (such as that since introduced), there has been a great variety of stamps in use in the country. In fact the want of this general governmental system of posts in the past has given rise to rather an anomalous condition of things with regard to the use of postage stamps, that is, until the unification of the postal administration at the end of 1922. In Shanghai, letters might be posted at the French Consulate for conveyence to Hongkong or foreign countries, by the Messageries Maritimes (the French Mail) steamers, French postage stamps being used, at first unsurcharged, but afterwards with the word 'Chine' on them. In the same way letters were posted at Shanghai at the German consulate, for conveyance by German mail steamers to similar destinations, German stamps, latterly surcharged 'China,' being affixed on the envelopes. If we are not mistaken, American as well as Japanese stamps were used in a similar way in Shanghai, and this obtained to a more or less degree at a few of the other Treaty Ports. The Russian, French, and German Governments, as well as the British, and the Customs, all had Post Offices at Tientsin.

The first issue of stamps in China was, in Hongkong, by the British Colonial Government of the Colony. These stamps are not, however, confined in their use to the small, but important island of Hongkong; but the British Government, for the convenience of its own and other foreign residents in China, was compelled, no other facilities existing, to establish Branch Post Offices of its own (under the control of the Hongkong General Post Office) at each of the treaty ports—in fact wherever there was a British Consulate—and the Hongkong postage stamps were employed for many years in paying the postages between the different treaty ports, and between them and foreign countries. These British Branch Post Offices had under their control only the mails conveyed in foreign-built ships running between the places mentioned above. For all letters into the interior, the foreign resident, if he wished to send any, a very rare occurrence usually, had to depend upon the private, local, native posts, until the establishment in 1896 of the Imperial Chinese Postal Service. Though these stamps were British colonial stamps, they have been more used in China, as above, than any other postage stamps. There have been numbers of different issues and surcharges, the first being in 1862.

The Hongkong Jubilee stamp was only issued for three days, on the anniversary of the jubilee of the colony, 22nd to 24th January, 1891; it was a two-cents rose-coloured stamp, surcharged with the words (in four lines, over the face of the stamp) '1841—Hongkong—Jubilee—1891.' There have been several mistakes made by the Chinese printer in printing this surcharge, such as a small J, etc.; so that there are about four or five of these varieties, and they are highly priced. Two other rare stamps are a twelve-cents surcharged on a ten-dollars revenue stamp, and a two-cents revenue stamp. They appear to have been used but a short time for purposes of postage. Embossed envelope stamps of different denominations, as well as embossed registered envelope stamps, have been added; and there have been a number of different issues of post-cards.

In connection with the Imperial Maritime Customs Post Office mentioned in our article on Posts, a series of stamps was issued in 1878. The stamps were rather large, the centre contained a dragon; 'China' was the device at the top, flanked in the top corners by the two Chinese characters T'ái Ts'ing [*Ta Ch'ing*], meaning 'Great Pure,' that being the name taken by the Manchu dynasty. The word 'Candarin,' or 'Candarins,' appeared at the bottom of the stamp, and in the two lower corners were the Arabic figures giving the number of candarins the stamp stood for. A candarin is a tenth of a mace, a mace being worth about fourteen cents, say nearly threepence halfpenny; ten mace make one tael. On the right-hand side (on the left of the dragon) and running down the stamp are the three Chinese characters, Yaú Ching Kúk [*Yu Chêng Chü*], standing for Official Post

Office, while the opposite column of Chinese (Chinese printing or writing is in vertical columns, not in horizontal lines like ours) were composed of the three Chinese characters representing the value of the stamp, viz., Yat (*or* Yat *or* Sám [*san*], as the case was) Fun Ngan [*fên yin*], one candarin (*or* three *or* five, as the case was) for the denominations were one, three, and five candarins. The colours were green, lilac, and yellow respectively.

The 1878 issue also contained the same denominations of stamps, but they were somewhat smaller, being about the size of the British stamps, the colours being green, rose, and yellow respectively. In other respects the stamps are very similar, the general features of the two issues being the same. There seemed to be some slight difference in the shades of colour of some of the stamps, but whether it was due to fading, or a different ink being used, we cannot say.

Out of this Customs Post has developed a Chinese Imperial Postal Service. Several issues of stamps, and surcharges and post-cards as well, were provided for this department. They are distinguished by the Chinese dragon, and have their denominations on them in English and Chinese.

Some years ago (in 1889) postage stamps were prepared for use in Formosa. They were rather large, had a dragon and a horse on them and the word 'Formosa.' There were two issues, twenty cash rose, and twenty cash green (say about the value of one penny, English money). They do not seem to have been much used for postage purposes; but were made to do service at one time as railway tickets—being surcharged—on the short line of rail in Formosa. They are now of great value, and collectors consider them great rarities. We have heard thirty dollars mentioned as a price asked for two.

There is a Municipal Council in Shanghai which had a local Post Office. In 1865, a series of five stamps was issued with a dragon in the centre, and 'Shanghai' at the top, in English and Chinese. On the right-hand side the words in Chinese, Shü Sun Kwún, [*Shu-hsin Kuan*], Post Office, and on the other side the denomination, in some cases in cash, in others in candarins. There have been a number of issues since, and of surcharges, the devices in their general features being very similar.

With regard to this Local Post Office, the following statement may be of interest:—

'The Shanghai Local Post Office was taken over by the Imperial Post in November, 1897, and thoroughly reorganised, but Local Postage rates have been maintained.'

Stamps

Many years after the Shanghai Local Post issued its first stamps, a number of the small foreign municipalities at some of the other treaty ports followed the example of Shanghai, and started Local Post Offices and issued sets of stamps. Hankow seems to have led the way amongst the riverine ports, Kiukiang following at a little distance, after which Chinkiang and Wuhu followed suit, and finally, Ichang and Chungking and Nanking. The coast ports have also not been behindhand with regard to these local issues, Chefoo, Foochow, and Amoy all having sets of stamps. Post-cards were also prepared and used in some of these places, and in one or two ports taxed stamps appeared. Different issues also succeeded one another from more than one of these local post offices. These ventures in many cases proved pecuniarily successful, and the money thus earned was applied to the necessary works in connection with the different municipalities; unfortunately the chief authority in England for philatelists frowned on such means for turning an honest penny (as many of the issues simply were), and they were soon considered as outside the pale of legitimate stamp collecting in that country. Many of the stamps were quite unique, pretty, and interesting—some being finely executed, though others were rather rude attempts.

The latest was the issue of two stamps at Weihaiwei, where, there being no post office, 'a private firm started a courier post at irregular intervals.' They are very rare, and command a high price, as only 4,000 were printed.

In the Portuguese settlement of Macao, there have been several issues of stamps by the Portuguese Colonial Government, beginning in 1878. The old issues command a good price. A number of surcharges have been used at different times; and there is a set of very neat postcards, in more than one issue. The denominations are in *reis*. The Timour stamps were at first Macao stamps surcharged. A Vasco da Gama Tricentenary set of stamps was issued a few years since in Macao.

We have already noted the French stamps in use in the French post office at Shanghai; but later they established post offices in Canton—on Shamien, and in the native city as well—and issued a complete set of stamps, surcharged 'Canton.' The Germans have also had stamps for their post offices in China, and until recently a regular issue for Kiautschau [Kiaochow].

At the present time, the Chinese Post Office is the only recognized post office in China. It has about 9,000 offices and agencies, handles about 300,000,000 articles of mail matter and about 3,000,000 parcels, issues about $20,000,000 worth of money orders, and has a staff of about 26,000, of whom about 150 are foreigners. The postage stamps no longer bear the dragon design, but pictures of boats, birds, etc.

SUICIDE.—We have already remarked that China has the unenviable notoriety of having more suicides than any other country, though those who know anything about the Chinese will not be surprised when we state that it is impossible to adduce absolute proof of such a statement. That there are many suicides cannot for a moment be doubted by those who have paid any attention to this gruesome subject.

The causes which lead to such a rash, foolish, and wicked act in the West are not absent in China; and besides those common to all states of civilisation and to all countries must be added some which are unknown to our modern conditions of life. Many suicides in China have their *fons et origo* in the peculiar marriage relationships of the Chinese; for a very fruitful source of marital trouble in China is the much married state of many of its people—the polygamy sanctioned by the all-powerful 'olo custom' has to answer for not a few suicides of women. Slighted by her husband for some new favourite, jealous of the influence of another concubine, the Chinese wife flees from ills which appear to have no redress. Again, an inferior wife, oppressed and ill-treated by a superior wife, has also, at times, recourse to such a misguided act. In some districts the young girls so dread the matrimonial state that they band together against being compelled to enter it, and take the extreme measure of remonstrating against it by going hand in hand into some pond and drowning themselves. (See MARRIAGE.) Again, in some districts near Foochow a species of suttee takes place, and is considered to be a highly meritorious act, having even a *quasi* sanction of Government. A widow in other parts of China, who refuses to live after the death of her husband, also receives a meed of praise, not only from officials, but from friends as well.

So common were suicides from the Bridge at Foochow that a society was formed some years since to maintain four boats to be continually on the watch for the prevention of it—two to be in attendance above the bridge, and two below. To one unacquainted with Chinese life it may seem strange that Buddhists, as so many of the Chinese are, should go in direct contravention of one of the express commandments of Buddhism—not to take life; and yet it is possibly due, in some measure, to the system of Buddhism that prevails in China that some of the suicides take place, for the doctrines of metempsychosis is one of the prominent tenets of Buddhism in China. Belief in a religion that in its popular aspects gives a leading position to the idea of the transmigration of souls, and holds out the hope that the ill deeds of this life and its good actions are punished or rewarded by future avatars, cannot act effectively as a deterrent against self-murder; such a religion cannot thunder out as strong anathemas against, or denounce with as equal force, the crime of suicide, as a religion that is based on a different and more rational system of future rewards and punishments. With such a creed, some Chinese suicides may therefore hope to return to this mundane sphere of existence again.

Added to all this is the slight esteem in which human life is held, as for instance, with regard to infanticide, the neglect of beggars, and in the matter of the death penalty so freely exacted, as in our own countries fifty or a hundred years ago, for offences so trivial when weighed against the sacredness of human life. With such a low estimate of the worth of human existence, it would appear to take but little more to neglect the fostering of one's own existence when a sea of troubles overwhelms one—but a step further to shuffle off this mortal coil one's self—to act with an assumption of power unwarranted by the facts, and to usurp the right of life and death over one's own mortal being. But, as tending often to the comparatively light heart with which many a Chinaman, of his own accord, leaves this sub-lunary stage of existence, must be noted the curious feelings about revenge that they hold. One of the most dreadful things that can happen to a Chinese is to have a death take place on his premises or at his door. No enemy thirsting for an adequate *quid pro quo*, to balance up the account of injury done him in the past, can hope, or desire, to have his enemy brought to book in a more effectual manner than by such an untoward event happening to his adversary. Here, then, is the chance long looked for and almost despaired of; here is an opportunity too good to let slip of doing a mortal injury to the hated one; for a trumped-up charge of murder or ill-treatment can easily be laid at the yamên, and all the minions of the law—the hosts of harpies of the unjust mandarin with all the ungovernable rapacity that they are infamous for will be let loose on the unfortunate householder. Even without a formal charge being laid against him, the ordinary course of procedure must be followed by the great annoyance of a visit from the equivalent of our Coroner, and the grand chances for all his underlings of having squeezes, pressure being brought to bear on him in an infinitude of ways never dreamed of in our favoured lands of the West. If the dead body of a poor, helpless, unknown, and unbefriended beggar will start the whole machinery of oppression and injustice, and bring untold miseries upon an unfortunate householder at whose door the corpse has been found, to the delight of his malicious enemy—if all this is the resultant of such a simple and not uncommon accident—it is but a step further for the quick-witted enemy, or man who has been injured and who has no other means, either on account of poverty or insignificance, of avenging himself on his foe, it is then but a step further for such an one to hit upon the expedient of forcing circumstances in his own favour, and, as even dead beggars are not procurable at a moment's notice, or, if procurable, the difficulties of transportation offer insuperable obstacles in the way of their employment—it is but a step further for such a man to offer himself as a substitute for the dead beggar, a sacrifice on the altar of wounded feelings or outraged justice. In China, this is one of the most telling modes of wiping out one's injuries, for besides the troubles that would result from any dead body being found in such a position, they are intensified by the knowledge that the dead body is that of one injured and so outraged that his feelings could brook no revenge short of that awful act that his silent body testifies to, the dead and solemn witness of the victim of injustice or oppression. There seems nothing incongruous to the Chinese mind in such an action. The only drawback is that the act once committed cannot be repeated; and a case is actually known of a man on the point of thus committing suicide bewailing the inexorable circumstance and the hard fact which would prevent him immolating himself in the houses of two enemies instead of in that of one alone. Ghosts to annoy the man; the necessity of purchasing a coffin at least, and trying to hush up the matter with the relatives by money freely given, the dangers of squeezes from official underlings and of the interference of the officials themselves, as stated above; and lastly, the trouble which may be brought on his enemy in a future state of existence—these all render such a mode of revenge one of the most effective that can be taken. The chance, or almost certainty, of trouble with the officials has also given rise to the custom or necessity, of generally providing a coffin for any poor beggar who may have chanced to crawl to one's door when *in extremis* and expired there. At the very least one may only hope to escape by being a subscriber to a list, should the people of the neighbourhood be willing to form a fund for the burial of this particular case.

The European, therefore, who may live amongst the Chinese, may thus find himself called upon to pay for a coffin.

High officials who were condemned to death had sometimes, as an act of Imperial clemency, a silken cord sent to them by the Emperor to strangle themselves with, instead of having the indignity offered them of suffering at the hands of the common executioner.

The most common modes of suicide were by opium-taking and drowning. With the Chinese superstition as to the consequences of going into the next world with a multilated body (for they believe the same mutilation will be permanent, in a future state of existence, and it is for this reason that decapitation is the general mode of capital punishment, as, once beheaded, the ghost would be a headless one), they do not inflict on themselves bodily injury or wounds such as would result from the use of razor or fire-arms for the purpose of suicide. But suicide by cutting the throat with a knife or pieces of broken glass or porcelain is not unknown. Since the prohibition of the use of opium, the poorer people often poison themselves with arsenic, phosphorus, mercury, or kerosene. Drowning and hanging are still much in vogue.

The 'swallowing of gold' is the term sometimes employed for suicide amongst wealthy Chinese. It has been the universal belief that gold leaf, or gold, was actually swallowed and suffocated the victim, and such, possibly, or even probably, does happen in some cases, but doubt has been thrown on the whole subject of late. It would be satisfactory before deciding against the belief of both foreigners and Chinese, and the circumstantial statements of the latter, to have convincing proofs from many sources that 'swallowing gold' is only another of those euphemistic phrases the Chinese are so fond of.

The following attempt, made by one resident in Chaotong [Chao-t'ung] in the West of China, is interesting as an attempt to arrive at the number of suicides in the whole of China, and we therefore give it *in extenso*. It was published in 1898:—

THE LAND OF SUICIDES: 500,000 CASES A YEAR.

'The fourth Chinese moon of the present year contained thirty days, and ended on June 18. In those thirty days, persons came to our home seeking help in nineteen cases of opium suicide, and one of opium poisoning. China may truly be called the land of suicides. I have gathered statistics from five cities in four different provinces. These were given me by missionaries working in these cities, who came in contact with the cases recorded.

'The first city is in the Province of Yünnan, and has a population of 100,000. The cases of opium suicide in which the missionary's help was solicited amounted to an average for twelve months of one a day. I have known four cases in one day.

'The second city in the same province has a population of about 50,000, and in one year the missionaries were called to seventy-two cases.

'The third city is in the Province of Kueichou, and has about 80,000 people. In one year three hundred cases occurred in which the missionaries' help was sought. Once, eight cases of suicide happened in one day.

'The fourth city is in the great Province of Szchuan [Ssŭch'uan]. and has a population of 300,000. When the statistics were taken there were two missions working in the city. In one year the missionaries of one of these missions were asked to save life in four hundred cases of opium suicide. I have no record of what the other mission did.

'The fifth city is in the Province of Anhwei, the home of the notorious Li Hung-chang. The city has a population of 50,000, and in one year eighty cases were brought to the missionary's notice.

'Thus, in a population of 580,000 more than 1,200 cases of opium suicide occurred in twelve months in which the help of missionaries was sought. It is rather uncertain work to argue from these figures to the whole of China. Most of these statistics refer to the West of China, which is pre-eminently the opium-growing district of China. The drug is cheap and easily obtained. On the other hand, such vast quantities are exported from these provinces that in many other parts more than 80 per cent. of the adult males are users of the drug. In nearly the whole of China opium can be readily and cheaply obtained.

'I have only recorded the cases in which the help of the missionary was requested. There are many cases where native remedies are successfully used, and the aid of the hated foreigner is not called in. We have noticed on many occasions that the missionary is not sent for till all other help has failed. Taking these figures and facts into account, I do not think any one who understands the case will say I exaggerate when I reach the conclusion that in China every year half a million people attempt suicide by opium. If the average of the figures above held true for the whole of China, then the number would be one million of attempted suicides every year. Surely China may be termed the Land of Suicides! The majority of these cases are women, who, having no appeal in law against the tyranny and cruelty of husbands, mothers-in-law, or brothers-in-law make their appeal through suicide to the god of Hades. In many a case a woman can only escape from a cruel fate by death. A young girl of about seventeen summers lived three doors from the first house occupied by the missionaries in this city. Her parents sold her to a man nearly three times her age. The night before he came to take her away she swallowed opium, and before morning had escaped his lustful clutches.

'Quite a number are double suicides. Two persons quarrel. One carries the case into Hades by suicide, hoping both to get the first chance there and to involve the surviving one in trouble, knowing he will be accused of so persecuting the first one that there was no help for it but suicide. The second resolves to stop this by following the first, and removing the whole theatre of war to the Land of Shades. In one such case in this city one of the patients was too far gone to be saved, whereas the other could easily be restored. The friends, seeing how matters stood, said: "If one dies, let both die," and refused absolutely to render any help. I have before now saved the husband in one room and the wife in another.

'We are successful in about 80 per cent. of the cases. Sometimes the suicides struggle like demons before they will be saved. A friend of mine was called to a strong man who resisted all efforts to make him take an emetic. At last, with the aid of some of the friends, he was pinioned on a table and held there by the weight of a big door placed on him. This was indeed dragging a man by force from the jaws of death. After the paroxysm is over the patient is usually amenable to all reasoning.

'On one occasion I was alone with a strong young fellow who resisted all my efforts to do what his mother begged me to do. He dashed my medicine away in a furious rage and refused to be saved. Not feeling equal to tying him up and saving him by force, I appealed to his superstitions by opening my eyes wide and roaring at him as a "foreign devil" is supposed to be able to roar. The result was a quiet, easy cure. Later on the victim thanked me heartily.

Sometimes we are not called in till the patient is dead, and even then we are expected to succeed. One strong man, the only son of his mother, lost all his money in a gambling bout. He came home and swallowed opium. When too late his mother asked our help. On seeing the case we told the poor woman her son was dead and beyond our assistance. Thereupon her tears fell like the rain, and she dashed her head furiously against the wall again and again, crying in agony, "My son! My only son."

'What a sarcastic misnomer to term this land of suicides the Celestial Land!'

This would make, with the round figures, a population of 400,000,000, one in every 400 of the people. When any opportunity for an attempt at statistics presents itself, the results are most appalling, but it will be many years before a certainty on the subject can be attained.

References.—Medhurst, *Foreigner in Far Cathay* (sutteeism); Matignon, *Superstition, Crime, et Misére en Chine;* Alabaster, *Notes and Commentaries on Chinese Criminal Law* (law regarding suicide).

SUN, MOON, AND STARS.—The sun, moon, and stars, with that fondness for numerical categories which possesses the Chinese, are classed together as 'The Three Lights.' The first is supposed to be four thousand miles distant from the earth, and the heavens, by one writer, to be seventy-three thousand miles off. After this it would be superfluous to adduce any more instances of the knowledge, or rather want of knowledge, of the Chinese of the heavenly bodies. A raven in a circle represents the sun.

The Chinese are more gallant than we are with regard to the moon. They do not see any man in the moon, but their legend, instead of being that of a man gathering sticks on the Sabbath, and being sent to the moon as a punishment, is of a female beauty, Chang-ngo by name, who drank the elixir of immortality and went to the moon, where she was transformed into a toad, which Chinese eyes still trace in the shadows visible on that luminary's surface. One of the most popular festivals is that of the moon, which is worshipped in autumn, and moon-cakes are made and exposed for sale everywhere. These are circular indigestible cakes, elaborately decorated in the more expensive varieties, and enclosed in circular pasteboard boxes with a piece of netting over the top. The children go wild about them, and each little youngster is provided with one to admire to his heart's content and gloat over.

The stars are arranged in constellations which would quite puzzle the Western astronomer, though we question if their combinations into nominal clusters are any more arbitrary than our system of grouping them.

The five planets, according to the Chinese system, are Mercury, Mars, Jupiter, Venus, and Saturn. A most wonderful system is evolved from the elementary correspondences of these planets with water (Mercury), fire (Mars), wood (Jupiter), metal (Venus), and earth (Saturn): the combinations and permutations of which are the cause of the different effects produced in the visible universe. The above are supposed to be intimately connected with the five colours, black, carnation, azure, white, and yellow; with the five human viscera; and with the five tastes, etc. To descend from the wild visionary ideas of this scheme of philosophy, we next find ourselves in the mazes of superstition as regards the stars; for not a few of them are objects of worship, some of the most popular being the Seven Sisters, for the Chinese, in common with the ancient Greeks, represent the Pleiades as such. At their festival a paper tray filled with seven imitation mirrors, and other objects in sets of seven, are burned as offerings to these star spirits.

Eclipses are a source of terror to the mass of the Chinese, who believe that a celestial dog has the sun or moon in its jaws and is about to swallow it. Gongs are beaten to frighten away the monster: even the Government used to lend its sanction to this absurd superstition, and the high officials offered worship and added their official gongs to the general din of the ignorant populace. This has been generally abandoned in recent years, though still observed in some places.

References.—Werner, *Myths and Legends of China;* Doré, *Superstitions.*

TAOISM AND ITS FOUNDER.—

'Taoism embraces the primeval religion of China and all the intellectual tendencies which did not find satisfaction in Confucianism. To these belong the various experiments in natural philosophy, and in connection with them the belief in the possibility of overcoming death by means of the elixir of immortality. By this, man enters the everlasting life, leads a higher existence above the range of material laws, in beautiful grottoes, on the sacred mountains, or on the islands of the blessed, and so on. It is worthy of note that such a belief, which bears some faint resemblance to the Christian belief of the Resurrection, should have found acceptance from the earliest to most recent times among the sober Chinese. There is a record of the names of thousands of people who are supposed to have reached this condition of immortality, and the life history of many of these is preserved. It has even been asserted that more than 100,000 had reached this goal.'

Thus wrote Dr. Faber about this religion, which influences the lives of almost all of the Chinese people to a greater or lesser extent.

At about the same time that Confucius, the great Sage of China, was endeavouring to get his principles adopted, there lived another of China's great men whose views were diametrically opposed to those of Confucius, and whose opinions, or whose reputed opinions, formed the foundations of a system as powerful over masses of the Chinese as Confucianism itself. Of Lao-tzŭ our ignorance is profound: his birth is mystified with legend; of his life, little is known; and his death is hidden in obscurity. Amongst all the uncertainty and doubt is found a short treatise, his one work, 'The Tao Teh King' [*Tao-tê Ching*]; its translation has taxed the best endeavours of several eminent sinologists. Amidst its short, terse, ringing sentences, flash jewels of the first water, set in much that is obscure to the foreign reader, who longs to know what this ancient worthy, China's Grand Old Man, really meant. In this Lao tzŭ the founder of Taoism, we have one of those men whose writings, life, and reputed actions, have exerted an untold influence on the course of human life in this world, but of whom the world, during his lifetime, took so little account that all that is authentically known about him may be summed up in a few lines: 'Even his parentage is surrounded with uncertainty, of his life we know nothing except one or two facts, and we are ignorant of the manner of his death and of the place of his burial. And yet he was one of the deepest thinkers China has produced.' This much appears to be certain, that he held some Government appointment, Keeper of the Archives, or Treasury Keeper, or Keeper of the Imperial Museum, as it has been variously rendered into English. This was in the state of Chou, and, foreseeing its inevitable downfall, he 'resigned his office and went into retirement, cultivating *Tao* and virtue.' The disorders increased in the state of Chou, and, though living 'a life of retirement and oblivion,' his place of retreat was not secure from violence. So he started on that mysterious journey of which we have no record, to some bourne whence the old traveller never returned; lost to mortal ken, he left behind him (with the Keeper of the Pass, with whom he stopped some time before disappearing into obscurity) the small book mentioned above, the only literary remains we have of one who has exerted such an influence on the Chinese nation.

Besides these facts, we are told that Confucius met him; and a son of the philosopher is mentioned who became a General in the state of Wei, but in a few generations, as far as we are aware, the line seems to have gone out in obscure darkness.

Legend has gathered round the few facts until quite a halo has surrounded the old philosopher: myth and fable have crystallised round the short and simple story of his life till his whole being and actions are glorified; they gleam and glitter with the splendour of the marvellous, and are magnified to the wonderful and miraculous; added glories are borrowed from the meretricious charms of a debased and idolatrous Buddhism until the whole system is transformed, aided by the vagaries of its own professors, into a monstrous mass of charlatanism and thaumaturgic mysteries which would shock Lao-tzŭ himself were another avatar granted him; for different incarnations are ascribed to him in the past, and attributes pertaining to the Deity are freely given to him to raise him in popular estimation. Being thus metamorphosed into one amongst hosts of the demigods of China's pantheon, his birth is made to take place amidst the marvellous—the sight of a falling star caused his conception, but he appears to have experienced reluctance in entering into the world, for he was 81 years of age when he was born, being an old grey-beard, hence the names, or titles, by which he is known, Lao-tzŭ, 'The Old Boy,' or 'The Ancient Philosopher,' and 'The Venerable Prince.'

The Chinese always give their sages most extraordinary characteristics. As a sample of them we will give those which Lao-tzŭ was said to possess:—

'His complexion was white and yellow; his ears were of an extraordinary size, and were each pierced with three passages. He had handsome eyebrows, large eyes, ragged teeth, a double-ridged nose, and a square mouth; on each foot he had ten toes, and each hand was ornamented with ten lines.'

The small book which Lao-tzŭ left behind him contains only 5,000 words. It has been well said of it:—

'Probably no widely-spread religion was ever founded on so small a base. Like an inverted pyramid the ever-increasing growth of Taoist literature and superstitious doctrines, which make the sum of modern Taoism, rests on this small volume as its ultimate support. We say "ultimate" advisedly, for other works have long surpassed it in popularity. Its philosophical speculations are far beyond the reach of the ordinary reader, and even scholars are obliged to confess that they have but a general idea of the meaning of the old recluse. "It is not easy," says one of the best-known commentators, "to explain clearly the more profound passages of Lao-tzŭ; all that science is able to do is to give the general sense." To European scholars the difficulty is even greater. As Rémusat remarks in his *Mémoire de Lao-tseu*: "The text is so full of obscurity, we have so few means of acquiring a perfect understanding of it, so little knowledge of the circumstances to which the author makes allusion; we are, in a word, so distant in all respects from the ideas under the influence to which he writes, that it would be temerity to pretend to reproduce exactly the sense which he had in view, when that sense is beyond our grasp." It is, however, always easy to affix a plausible interpretation to that which is not susceptible of any definite explanation, and consequently a host of commentators and translators have arisen, who find in the *Tao Teh King* confirmation of their preconceived theories of his meaning and of their preconceived wishes on his behalf.'

The Jesuit missionaries found in these mystical utterances of the first Taoist philosopher a knowledge of the Triune God, revealed five centuries before Christ, and the mystic name of Jehovah. These fanciful speculations, based probably on a misapprehension of a book most difficult of comprehension, are not now received with seriousness.

'In the Tao Teh King, Lao-tzŭ has elaborated his idea of the relations existing between the Universe and that which he calls Taou.' 'The primary meaning of this name of a thing, which he declares to be "without name," is "The Way," hence it has acquired the symbolic meanings of "the right course of conduct," "reason," and it also signifies "the word" (Logos). By all these meanings it has been severally rendered by the translators of Lao-tzŭ's celebrated work. In support of each rendering it is possible to adduce quotations from the text, but none is the equivalent of Lao-tzŭ's *Tao*. The word *Tao* is not the invention of Lao-tzŭ. It was constantly in the mouth of Confucius, and with him it meant the "Way." The Buddhists also used it in the sense of "Intelligence," and called their co-religionists Tao-jin, or "Men of Intelligence." If we were compelled to adopt a single word to represent the *Tao* of Lao-tzŭ, we should prefer the sense in which it is used by Confucius, "The Way," that is μέθοδος. "If I were endowed with prudence, I should walk in the great *Tao*. . . . The great *Tao* is exceeding plain, but the people like the footpaths," said *Lao-tzŭ* (chapter 53). But it is more than the way. It is the way and the way-goer. It is an eternal road; along it all beings and things walk, but no being made it, for it is Being itself; it is everything and nothing, and the cause and effect of all. All originate from *Tao*, conform to *Tao*, and to *Tao* they at last return.

'*Tao* is impalpable. You look at it and you cannot see it. You listen and you cannot hear it. You try to touch it and you cannot reach it. You use it and cannot exhaust it. It is not to be expressed in words. It is still and void; it stands alone, and changes not; it circulates everywhere, and is not endangered.

It is ever inactive, and yet leaves nothing undone. From it phenomena appear, through it they change, in it they disappear. Formless, it is the cause of form. Nameless, it is the origin of heaven and earth; with a name it is the mother of all things. It is the ethical nature of the good man and the principles of his action. If we had then to express the meaning of *Tao*, we should describe is as (1) the Absolute, the totality of Being and Things; (2) the phenomenal world and its order; and (3) the ethical nature of the good man and the principle of his action.'

To the English reader this book is one of the most delightful of Chinese books of that class.—'The deepest thought is to be found in the Taoist classical works.'—It seems to approach nearer to the grand truths so magnificently expressed in parts of our own incomparable Bible. Its diction is simple; its sentences terse; but its style enigmatic; the Westerner feels, though unable to put himself in complete *rapport* with the grand old philosopher, more in sympathy with him than with the more highly lauded Confucius. In the words of one writer: 'In such utterances as these Lao-tzŭ showed himself to be as superior to Confucius as the Christian dispensation is to the Mosaic law.'

As the first purity of Christianity was sullied by the superstitions and idolatry of the mediæval times, so a system of charms, idolatry, exorcism, elixirs of immortality, masses of superstition, *et hoc genus omne*, has gathered round the original Taoism. This growth of centuries forms what is now known as Taoism, and, in common with Buddhism and an adhesion to Confucianism, stands for religion to the average Chinaman. It is believed in, in moments of danger and death, but laughed at in their sceptical hours by the better educated, who then profess themselves Confucianists alone; it, however, receives only formal acknowledgment from many, though its thaumaturgic priests, in harmony with those of the Buddhists, are relied on by all to rescue the souls of their relatives from the punishments of Hades by the performance of masses.

Earlier Taoism boasts of two philosophers, Lieh-tzŭ and Chuang-tzŭ who have been latinised as Licius and Chancius. We have not the space to go into a dissertation on all their opinions.

Suffice it to say of Licius that 'the belief in the identity of existence and non-existence, and the constant alternations from the one to the other observable in all nature, assumed in his eyes a warrant for the old doctrine, "Let us eat and drink, for tomorrow we die."'

'The vanity of human effort' was Chancius's 'main theme, and the Confucianists were the principal objects of his denunciations.' 'The fussy politician who boasts of having governed the empire is given to understand that the empire would have been very much better governed if it had been left alone, and the man who seeks to establish a reputation is told that reputation is but "the guest of reality." He was at one with the code of Menu, and pronounced the waking state one of deceptive appearances, . . . but though there was this unreality in existence, life was yet a thing to be cared for. . . . This care for life was quite compatible . . . with an indifference for death.' Of his own funeral, he said:—'I will have heaven and earth for my sarcophagus, the sun and moon shall be the insignia when I lie in state, and all creation shall be the mourners at my funeral.'

The mass of Chinese have cast aside the philosophical and metaphysical speculations of the old philosopher and his immediate followers, and on the small foundations of the Tao Teh King a superstructure of hay, stubble, rubbish, and rottenness has been raised. They appear to have started off at a tangent from his ideas,and evolved some elaborate systems, wandering off into empty space. The craving of man for immortality degenerated into a fruitless search for plants, which, when eaten, would confer it; for charms which would bestow it; for elixirs, the quaffing of which would send it coursing through one's veins. So strong were these beliefs that Taoist books were spared in the general destruction by the hated Ts'in [Ch'in] Shih Huang-ti (221-209 B.C.); and the same monarch, who was a Taoist himself, dispatched a naval expedition to discover the 'golden isles of the blest, where dwelt genii, whose business and delight it was to dispense to all visitors to their shores a draught of immortality, compounded of the fragrant herbs which grew in profusion around them.

Magicians arose under the ægis of Taoism who 'professed to have mastered the powers of nature. They threw themselves into fire without being burned, and into water without being drowned. They held the secret of the philosopher's stone, and raised tempests at their will.'

So soon was the original Taoism of Lao-tzŭ forgotten, that all the vagaries of these mystic jugglers were believed in, and the attention of all his professed followers was directed to obtaining the elixir of immortality and the philosopher's stone. . . . The mania for these magical arts among the Chinese during the Ts'in and Western Han dynasties seems to have been as general and as acute as the South Sea Scheme madness among our forefathers. From the emperors downwards, the people devoted their lives to seeking immunity from death and poverty. Business of every kind was neglected, fields were left untilled, the markets were deserted, and the only people who gained any share of the promised benefits were the professors of Taoism who trafficked with the follies of their countrymen, and who fattened on the wealth of the credulous.'

One of the votaries is said to have been the Emperor Woo. '"I know," said Le Shaou-keun [Li Shao-chün] to the Emperor, "how to harden snow and to change it into white silver; I know how cinnabar transforms its nature and passes into yellow gold. I can rein the flying dragon and visit the extremities of the earth; I can bestride the hoary crane and soar above the nine degrees of heaven," and in return for these imaginary powers he became the chosen adviser of the Emperor, and received the most exalted honours.' After this reign, however, the Taoism of this character lost favour and 'the ethics of Confucius and the mysticism of Lao-tzŭ' grew in estimation.

Later on, Imperial sacrifices were ordained to the philosopher; and Buddhism exerted its influence on Taoism. With regard to the latter it is almost amusing to notice the plagiarism of the writers of Taoist books in adopting into, and adapting to, their religion the legends and tales of the idols of Buddhism; for in modern Chinese thought and practice the saints and the deified dogmas of Buddhism really form a pantheon of that religion.

Taoism not only basked in Imperial favour at times, but also suffered the withering scorn of those rulers who pinned their faith exclusively to the tenets of the politico-ethical Confucianism. 'Asceticism and public worship soon became engrafted on the doctrine of Lao-tzŭ'; the Buddhists and Taoists, however, were sworn enemies, the one party taunting the other with being jugglers, while the other retorted that the Buddhists were strangers in the land. With the accession of the T'ang dynasty the delusions of the elixir of immortality and the philosopher's stone began to exercise their influence over the minds of men. Lao-tzŭ was canonised, and one of the Emperors actually went so far as to introduce his writings into the syllabus for literary competitive examinations. The Taoists flourished and suffered alternately under different sovereigns and dynasties, until the time of the Sung dynasty. In A.D. 859, one of the Emperors found his death instead of eternal life in the elixir of immortality. Two of the sovereigns had already succumbed to it in A.D. 824 and 846. Shortly after that, in another 150 years, Taoism lost its hold in the Imperial Court. A Chinese poem sums up this phase of Taoism and 'gives a concise view of the craze which seized on Chinese alchemists two thousand years ago, of which the search for the elixir of life and the philosopher's stone in Europe was a mere echo.' Dr. Martin thus puts it into English:—

'A prince the draught immortal went to seek;
And finding it he soared above the spheres.
In mountain caverns he had dwelt a week;
Of earthly time it was a thousand years.'

The priests of Lao-tzŭ married, and were like the common people in all points but in the matter of paying taxes, from which they were exempt, though by their law or custom, in imitation of Buddhism, they were supposed to be celibates; but 'under the first Emperor of the Sung dynasty (A.D. 960-76), however, a return to a stricter system was enforced, and they were forbidden to marry.' At the present day the Taoist priests, who have become such since their marriage, retain their wives, nor are those who have not hitherto been married prevented from marrying, thus presenting a striking contrast to the Buddhist priests.

One of the books which exerts the greatest influence over the mass of the Chinese people is the 'Book of Rewards and Punishments,' which is based upon Taoism; it leaves untouched the abstruse philosophy of Lao-tzŭ, but elaborates a system of morality for everyday life upon the foundation of his sayings. Amidst much chaff and modern superstition there are many grains of truth and good advice, enforced by the promises of rewards for good, virtuous actions, and the threatening of evildoers with present and future punishment.

Another book must be mentioned in this connection as exerting an influence in the Chinese mind: it is 'The Book of Secret Blessings,' which has been described as having 'no reference whatever to the doctrines of Taoism, but only a number of moral injunctions of great ethical purity.' 'These two works may fairly be taken to represent the moral side of modern Taoism. Few professing Taoists trouble themselves at the present day about the musings of Lao-tzŭ or the dreamy imaginings of his early followers. They pursue only their own good, mainly temporal, but also moral. To secure the former they have recourse to the magical works of the sect, and to the expounders of these, the Taoist priests. They buy charms and practise exorcisms, at the bidding and for the profit of these needy charlatans, and they study with never-failing interest the advice and receipts contained in the numberless books and pamphlets published for their benefit. Into some of these, Buddhist ideas are largely imported, and the doctrine of the existence of hell, which finds no kind of canonical sanction, is commonly preached. Liturgies, also framed on Buddhist models, abound, and in some cases not only the form, but even the phraseology, of Hindoo works is incorporated into these prayer-books.'

At the head of the Taoist pantheon stands a trinity, in imitation of the Buddhist trinity—that of the 'Three Pure Ones'—and though Taoism originally was not an idolatrous system, the baneful influence of latter-day Buddhism on the Chinese mind has induced the votaries of the Chinese system (for, as has already been seen, Taoism is of native origin) to pander to the material instincts of the idolatrous mind, and a whole host of superior and inferior deities—gods, genii, heroes, good men, and virtuous women, the spirits of stars and the visible manifestations of nature and of the elements, such as thunder and lightning, as well as dragons—have all been classed together as objects of worship, while the God of Literature, and Gods and Goddesses of Smallpox, Measles, etc., all receive their share of attention. Below the trinity of Three Pure Ones, and above the others, presides the Gemmeous Supreme Ruler, and one of the strongest objections to the use of the words Shangti (Supreme Ruler) as the equivalent in Chinese for the Christian God is that this title is by common usage that *par excellence* of that idol, and the common people instinctively think of the Taoist Shangti when the words are used, though it is employed in the ancient Chinese classics in a different sense. After these hierarchical deities come hosts of other gods:—

'Star gods, the 28 constellations, the 60 cycle-stars, the 129 lucky or unlucky stars; then the gods of the five elements, of natural phenomena, of sickness and of medicine; the animal gods, such as the fox, tiger, dragon, etc. ; the gods of literature, specially the innumerable local divinities, at the head of which stand the city gods.'

The Pope of Taoism, who lives in the 'Dragon and Tiger Mountains' in the province of Kiangsi, is styled 'Heavenly Teacher,' a title bestowed on his first predecessor by one of the Chinese Emperors in A.D. 423. Since then this dignity has been hereditary in the family.

'The Chinese believe that this pope is head over the gods and spirits which are worshipped throughout the realm, that he instals or suspends, exalts or degrades them according to imperial—not divine!—command. He grants an audience to the gods on the first of every month, and all attend, those of the heavens, the nether world, the ocean, etc. He has possession of the magic sword with which he controls the demons and shuts them up in earthen pitchers. He rules as the representative on earth of the Jasper-god [the Gemmeous Ruler mentioned above] and grants the Taoist monasteries their licence.' 'Although popes have existed, for nearly 1,500 years, there is no record in Chinese history of any one of them opposing an imperial libertine or of causing any wild rebel to relinquish his cause and settle down peacefully.'

Another writer thus sums up Taoism:—describing its position in the Chinese eclecticism which stands for religion amongst this curious people:—

'In early Chinese records we find many references to the worship of Supernatural Beings; the Emperor worships Heaven, the people worship the gods of each particular spot of land; Mountains and Streams are worshipped, and the Spirits of Departed Men. In fact they seem always to have been free—they now are—to picture in their minds and worship just what Supernatural Beings they chose. There was then in the Chinese mind, as there is now, a vague image of a Supernatural World consisting of countless Beings who were behind and controlled phenomena. The chief of these Beings was called Shangti, the Supreme God, who seems to have been pictured as ruling the Supernatural World, much as the Feudal Lord or Emperor ruled the Kingdoms of which China then consisted. To this state of things came Confucius who summed up the practical philosophy and ethics of the day and occupied with his teaching the sphere of human relations—man's duty to his neighbour—but left the rest much as he found it. Then followed Buddhism from India, and occupied the sphere of man's relations to a future life, with fixed tenets and teaching, in fact a Religion—and the first China had heard of. That she had no religion of her own is proved by the fact that she has no word with that meaning, *kiao*, the word in use, meaning no more than "doctrine." *Taoism was the attempt of the native scholars to make out of the heterogeneous materials of Nature Worship a religion after the model of, and to serve as a rival to, Buddhism.* . . . But to the above a correction must be applied, tending, however, to make the subject matter of Taoism more mixed still. There is (1) Lao Tzŭ's teaching about *Tao, the way;* and there is (2) the Black Art, the search for the elixir of life and the philosopher's stone—these two have both been important elements in Taoism and cannot be disregarded: the second requires no explanation. Chinese alchemy seems to have followed much the same course as in the West. In regard to *Tao*, we will venture a word of explanation, for it is far the most important term in Chinese philosophy and seems to embrace a valuable idea. What does it mean? *The way or right course.* But whither? Suppose the universe of mind and matter to be subject to immutable forces and laws from the effects of which man has absolutely no hope of escape; and suppose a man contemplated doing something, whether with hands or with his brain, there is one best way to effect his object and that *best way is Tao.* It is true that the word is often very vaguely used, but in its abstract sense it usually means either (1) the immutable laws of the universe themselves when it corresponds to *natura*, of the Stoics (See Watters' learned disquisition on this word "Essays on the Chinese Language," page 229), or (2) the right way to act with regard to those laws as explained above.

'Clearly this idea of *Tao* is for the learned, and alchemy being long ago dead, there remains only Nature-worship—and that is what Taoism is for the mass of the people,' combined with the worship of a host of idols. (See also PHILOSOPHY.)

References.—Watters, *Lao-tzŭ, a Study in Chinese Philosophy;* Parker, *China and Religion; Studies in Chinese Religion;* Balfour, *Taoist Texts;* Douglas, *Confucianism and Taoism; China Review*, Vols. ix; xi; xii; xiii; xxiii; xxiv; *Chinese Recorder*, xxvii. 387-90; *Faber, The Historical Basis of Taoism.*

TEA.—The names for tea in the West are amongst the few words derived from Chinese, and were introduced with the leaf into Europe. These names, though they seem dissimilar in some languages, are all originally from the same words, the differences being due to the particular Chinese speech (or so-called dialect) from which they have been borrowed. In the Fuhkienese type of languages, tea is known by the word *te* (pronounced *teh*), and it is from this source that the French word *thé*, the Italian *tè*, the Spanish *té*, German *thee*, Dutch *thee*, Danish *the*, Gaelic *té* (pronounced tay), and Malay *teh*, are all derived, as well as our English word *tea*. In the greater part of the Chinese empire the word for 'the cup that cheers but not inebriates' is *ch'á* (pronounced ch'ah), and it is from this pronunciation of it that the names used in Russia (*tshai*), in Portugal (*chá*), and in Italy (*cià*) are derived. Strange to say, the Italians, however, have two names for tea, *cià* and *tè*, the latter, of course, is from the Chinese word *te*, noticed above, while the former is derived from the word *ch'á*. It is curious to note in this connection that an early mention, if not the first notice, of the word in English is under the form *cha* (in an English Glossary of A.D. 1671): we are also told that it was once spelt *tcha*—both evidently derived from the Cantonese form of the word; but thirteen years later we have the word derived from the Fokienese *te*, but borrowed through the French and spelt as in the latter language *thé*; the next change in the word is early in the following century, when it drops the French spelling and adopts the present form of *tea*, though the Fokienese pronunciation, which the French still retain, is not dropped for the modern pronunciation of the now wholly Anglicised word *tea* till comparatively lately. It will thus be seen that we, like the Italians, might have had two forms of the word, had we not discarded the first, which seemed to have made but little lodgment with us, for the second.

The tea-bush belongs to the botanical family of the *Ternstroemiaceæ*, to which the camellia likewise belongs. It is an evergreen, and 'has come lately to be looked upon by many as only a particular species of the genus camellia, since there are no generic differences (*e.g.*, in Bentham and Hooper's "Genera Plantarum").' It does not grow in the northern provinces of China, but ranges between the twenty-third and thirty-fifth degrees of latitude. Though tea will grow on poor soil, it has been proved, by experiments in India, that the best soil for it is a friable, light-coloured, porous one with a fair proportion of sand and a superabundance of decaying vegetable matter on the surface. To produce good tea, high cultivation is necessary: a small plantation with such cultivation will pay better than one twice the size with low cultivation. Tea, especially the China variety, will grow in varying climates and soils, but it will not flourish in all of them. 'The rainfall should not be less than 80 to 100 inches per annum.' It can grow where the thermometer falls below freezing-point, but it 'cannot be too hot for tea if the heat is accompanied with moisture.' The yield is double in a hot and moist climate from what it is in a comparatively dry and temperate one, for it yields most abundantly with hot sunshine and showers and with the rain equally diffused. Fogs, in the early part of the year, in the morning, and a considerable amount of rain in February, March, and

April, benefit the plant. Hot winds combined with a dry temperature do not suit it. These observations on the right climate for tea are the results of experiments in India; and any one knowing that of Southern China will see that these are just the climatic conditions of that part of the world.

Some Botanists seem to be in doubt as to 'whether China, the land where it has been so long cultivated, is its original home, and, if so, which part of China.' 'No accounts have come to us of the tea-shrub being cultivated for its infusion till A.D. 350.' The tea-plant in China is the common tea-bush. In Assam, where it was discovered fifty years ago, it has been looked upon as an indigenous plant.

'The home of the China tea-plant is now [1900] believed to have been Upper Assam, although its existence in this region was not generally known until 1834. Professor A. Kratsnow of Kharkoff, Russia, decides further that the tea-plant must be indigenous to the whole monsoon region of Eastern Asia, as he has found it growing wild in dense uncultivated forests as far north as the island of Southern Japan. He believes that it existed in China and Japan long before the cultivated form was introduced from the south-west. The period of cultivation having been too short to produce the modification existing, he concludes that the peculiar properties of the Chinese plant have resulted from changes of climate in Eastern Asia since the Tertiary Epoch, instead of from cultivation in a colder climate or from exhausted soil. He traces the two varieties—Assam and Chinese—to remote times, finding the first still growing wild in India and the other occurring still wild in Southern Japan.'

The China plant grows to be six or seven feet in height in India, while the Assam plant becomes a little tree (but it is said if the China tea-plant is allowed to grow it also attains considerable size) and grows to the height of fifteen or eighteen feet. In China, the tea-plants seldom exceed three feet, 'most of them are half that height, straggling, and full of twigs, often covered with lichens,' but the ground round them is well hoed and clean. Unlike the large tea-gardens in India, the Chinese plantations are simply little patches, often on the slopes, or at the foot of hills, where both drainage and moisture are easily provided. The tea-growers either pick the leaves themselves or sell them to middle-men. The leaf of the China tea-plant is four inches long at the most, and of a dull dark-green colour, while the lowest branches grow out close to the ground. 'The tea flower is small, single, and white, has no smell, and soon falls. . . . The seeds are three small nuts, like filberts in colour, in a triangular shell which splits open when ripe, with valves between the seeds.' All the varieties of the Chinese tea-plant have probably arisen from culture. When ripe, in October, the nuts are put in a mixture of damp sand and earth; they are thus preserved fresh till spring, when, in March, they are sown in a nursery; a year after, the shoots are transplanted, being put in rows about four feet apart. The leaf is first plucked when the shrub is three years old, and the picking is continued till the eighth year, on an average.

The first picking of the tea leaf is that over which the most pains is taken, and consists of the young leaves, a great many of which are not fully grown. There is a whitish down on these leaves, and from this circumstance comes the name *pecoe* [*pai hao*], the words in Chinese from which it has been derived meaning 'white down.' In this connection it may be interesting to give the derivation of some of the other names of tea. *Hyson*, so we are told, is a corruption of two Chinese words, *yü-ts'ín* [*yü ch'ien*], 'before the rain,' the young hyson being half-opened leaves plucked in April before the spring rains; but with regard to this explanation it may be said that the Chinese have a variety of teas known as *yü-ts'ín*, so named for the reason given above. We also read that hyson is derived from the name Hí-chun [Hsi-ch'un]. Hí-chun, so the story goes, was a maiden living about two hundred years ago, who introduced a better method of sorting her father's tea, which so increased his business that the tea was named after her. Of this pretty story it may be remarked, *se non è vero è ben trovato*. The meaning of the Chinese characters used, viz.: *hí-ch'un* 'felicitious spring,' though perhaps more prosaic than the above explanations of the derivation of the name, is still sufficiently poetical to satisfy one without searching further. *Sou-chong* [*hsiao chung*] means *small*, or *rare variety*. *Congou* [*kung fu*] means *work* or *worked*, from being well worked, while *Bohea* is the name of the hills in the Fukien province where that variety of tea is grown. The same province also gives the well-known tea name, *oo-long* [*wu lung*], i.e., *black dragon*. Here we have another story to account for the origin of this name:—A black snake (and snakes are sometimes looked upon as dragons in China) was coiled round a plant of this tea, and hence the name.

Chinese teas may be divided into the following main classes; (1) Black teas, (a) Northern, such as Keemun, Ningchow, Oopacks, Oonahms; (b) Southern, such as Congon, Oolong, Scented Orange Pekoe, etc., (2) Green teas, Moyune, Pingsuey, etc., (3) Blends, Sownee, Gunpowder, Imperial, Hyson, etc.

But to return to the tea-pickings: care has to be exercised in plucking so as not to injure the plant and prevent a supply of future 'flushes,' as they are technically called. After the spring rains the second plucking is made; this takes place in different latitudes at different times, say from 15th May to June: it is then that the tea-plant is in full leaf. Women and children strip the twigs, and fifteen pounds picked in a day by one person is considered good work, but the pay is only six or eight cents. One tea-tree will yield from eight or ten to sixteen or twenty-two ounces of leaf. This second picking only lasts ten or twelve days. The curing is done as follows:—

> The leaves are first 'thinly spread on shallow trays to dry off all moisture by two or three hours' exposure' to the air by day, or they are left out over-night. 'They are thrown into the air and tossed about and patted till they become soft; a heap is made of these wilted leaves and left to lie for an hour or more, when they become moist and dark in colour. They are then thrown on the hot pans for five minutes and rolled on the rattan table, previous to exposure out-of-doors for three or four hours on sieves, during which time they are turned over and opened out. After this they get a second roasting and rolling to give them their final curl. When the charcoal fire is ready, a basket, shaped something like an hour-glass,' but about three feet high, 'is placed endwise over it, having a sieve in the middle, on which the leaves are thinly spread. When dried five minutes in this way they undergo another rolling, and are then thrown into a heap, until all the lot has passed over the fire. When this firing is finished, the leaves are opened out, and are again thinly spread on the sieve in the basket for a few minutes, which finishes the drying and rolling for most of the heap, and makes the leaves a uniform black. They are now replaced in the basket in greater mass, and pushed against its sides by the hands in order to allow the heat to come up through the sieve and the vapour to escape; a basket over all retains the heat, but the contents are turned over until perfectly dry and the leaves become uniformly dark.'

The green tea is subjected to somewhat similar operations, with the exception of the fermentation process. 'While the leaves of each species of the shrub can be cured into either green or black tea, the workmen in one district are able by practice to produce one kind in a superior style and quality; those in another region will do better with another kind.' 'The colour of the green tea, as well as its quality, depends very much on rapid and expert drying.' The sea air is a sworn enemy to all delicately fired leaves, and tea, to be perfect, requires to be lightly fired. The caravan teas, so called from being transported overland through cold, dry countries, were able to dispense with 'the final thorough heating in the drying establishments of the ports,' accorded to that shipped, and the aroma was consequently not dissipated, but such a long land journey is expensive.

Brick tea used to be sent overland to Siberia; but an experiment which was attended with success was tried in 1897, the tea being shipped from Hankow to London, and thence transhipped by steamers to the mouth of the Yenisei River, and, after a further water journey, finally reaching the Siberian Railway.

But comparatively few foreigners, even in China itself, drink anything but the excessively fired teas; for having been used to them from infancy in England and other countries, they do not appreciate the lightly fired kinds, and often are not even aware of their existence, while the Chinese, believing foreigners like the exported varieties, supply them with it. Good tea should be of a light brown; the water, to pour on the leaves, should be quite boiling, and only just boiling; and the tea should not be allowed to draw for half an hour or more, as the theine is thus drawn out of the leaves. Far better a fresh infusion, if required, some time after the first drawing, thus following the Chinese fashion of making a fresh brew for each visitor that calls.

Another excellent plan of the Chinese, with regard to tea, is that of sometimes using large cups containing almost as much as a large breakfast coffee-cup. Leaves, sufficient for a cup of tea, are thrown into the bottom of this, and the boiling water poured on. The cup has a lid which covers it up for the first few minutes that it is drawing, and the tea is handed piping hot and freshly made to each one; the lid also serves to saucer a few sips of it at a time and cool it when drinking, while at the bottom of the cup, covered by the delicate almost amber-coloured fluid, lie the leaves, uncurled by the heat of the water.

In Swatow and neighbourhood, tiny, toy tea-cups and tea-pots are used, the cups containing scarcely more than two or three sips of tea. It looks very ridiculous to see grown-up people produce a small tray with this lilliputian ware on it. The ordinary tea-cups used by the Cantonese are small enough, but they are much larger than these Swatow ones.

Though green tea, *i.e.*, natural green tea, may be, and is, produced, the danger of fermentation on the voyage, and its unmarketable state, if fired sufficiently to stand the sea air, has probably given rise to the practice of colouring tea to cause it to retain its green colour; there is no necessity for doing so with tea for home consumption in China, the Chinese are not so foolish as to drink an infusion of Prussian blue, for this is the substance that is used, mixed with gypsum, to colour, or face, the green tea.

The well-known character of the Chinese for temperance has been ascribed to their universal use of tea, and it would be well for many in Western lands if, instead of soaking themselves with beer, they would copy the example of the abstemious Chinese in this respect.

Different kinds of flowers are used to scent tea, such as roses, tuberoses, oranges, jasmines, gardenias, azaleas, as well as the *olea fragrans;* only the petals are used for the purpose. Some choice brands of tea are grown on small plots of ground, and command almost a fabulous price: such as in some of the gardens near monasteries, owned by the priests and attended to by their inferior followers.

Tea for many years furnished the greatest article of commerce in China.

'China has been the fountain-head whence the tea culture has spread to other countries.' It is only within recent years that tea cultivation has been undertaken in other lands, where it 'is assuming large proportions. . . . The Spanish authorities have tried to raise it in the Philippines; the Dutch in Sumatra, Java, and Borneo; the English in the Straits Settlements; and the French in Cochin China. Nearly all these experiments have been failures, the only successes reported being from mountainous countries, where there was moisture, good soil, and not an excess of warmth. The Dutch have turned this discovery to account, and now confine their efforts to the high mountainous districts with which their colonial possessions abound; good tea has been produced in a number of places under these conditions, but the quality has been very inferior to the fine growths of Formosa and Foochow.'

The above quotation does not mention, however, all the places where tea is cultivated, or where attempts have been made to do so; we may add to the list the well-known names of Ceylon, India, Assam, Japan, and the lesser known experiments in Johore, the United States, Natal, Fiji, Borneo, Servia, Mexico, and South Carolina; doubtless, in other places as well, trial has been made of the cultivation of this useful shrub. The troops in Java are supplied with local tea. The attempts to grow it in the Trans-Caucasian territory have turned out a success, flourishing plantations are in the neighbourhood of Batoum, and during the last few years Natal has developed into a tea-producing country, the output in 1898 amounting to over 1,000,000 lbs., one estate alone producing more than one half of this.

'Successful attempts have been made this year [1901] to grow tea in America. Experts declare it to be equal in flavour and aroma to the best imported product.'

Machinery would appear to have been largely used of late years in the manufacture of Indian teas; electricity has even been yoked in the service of man for the preparation of tea; but the Chinese still retain their old style, and object, probably from prejudice, to any innovations, and as long as their tea sells they are content, though attempts have been made to influence them in the favour of machinery.

'Whether China tea, if and when it is prepared by machinery, will retain its present advantage in the time that it will last in comparison with the short period that Indian and Ceylon teas keep, is a question that can only be answered when we have had actual experience. It is notorious at present that Indian and Ceylon teas go off a few months after arrival in this country (England), whilst China tea, as hitherto prepared, could be kept for considerable periods of time without showing any decided signs of having "gone off."'

A trial of preparation of tea by machinery has been made by the 'Foochow Tea Improvement Company,' and some parcels of this tea were put on the London market, and all concerned were very sanguine of success, but the venture has not been able to make its way.

This experiment has unfortunately proved a failure on account, so we are told, of the difficulty of procuring a sufficiency of tea to keep the machinery going.

In fact, machine rolling has been tried in several places—two at least, and it is to be hoped that it, or something else to be discovered, will resuscitate the dying China tea trade. One of the difficulties in the way will be shown by the following:—

'It is the custom in this country [this is written at Hankow in 1897] often to keep the newly picked leaf for a day or so, in hopes of obtaining a higher price for it, or it is passed on in bags from one district to another where a better sale is looked for. This of course entirely spoils it for the London taste of the present day—that is, strength and rankness, which is obtained only through immediate firing. So long as quotations of taels 50 or so continue for fine teas suitable for Russia, it is hardly to be expected a change will be made. The old fashion pays well enough.'

That this should be so seems unfortunate, as it is stated that:—

'Machine-rolling gives the leaf a more even twist and causes less breakage than by hand; but, more important still, the even regulated pressure of the machine keeps the sap of the green leaf working among the rolling leaf, and it is not expressed, as is the case with teas prepared by the Chinese method. The use of the roller, too, brings out the small Pekoe leaves with a bright golden appearance, whereas the Chinese method of preparation causes the leaves to turn black.' . . . The first small shipment of these teas to Melbourne gave a result of some Taels 7 per picul more than was obtained by native-made tea selling side by side with it; such teas 'received most favourable notice in the London reports,' and 'some "Golden Pekoe" sold at 10¾d.'

To those who like a good article, the 'darker liquor which brews out from Indian and Ceylon tea' with its greater pungency will be no recommendation in its favour; for softness of flavour is to be found in China teas; but cost seems to be the point round which the struggle will be maintained; and if China will only listen to the suggestions of those who are able to advise her, and send home as good an article as she used to ship so largely, the victory may yet be hers.

The Indian and Ceylon teas are offering a serious competition to China, the original tea-producing country. The trade is declining, and some vigorous efforts will have to be made to retain what they already possess; but, unfortunately, the Chinese do not appear to be alive to the importance of taking steps to hold their own in the world's market against the stronger article produced in India, neither have they yet learned the wisdom of putting up smaller 'chops' (brands) of tea, as is the practice in India, nor have they entered into the combinations which the Indian planters have formed to push their productions into notice wherever a chance of doing so presents itself.

'Americans having acquired a taste for green tea which is now chiefly supplied by China, and the crusade to push Indian and Ceylon black teas in the United States not having met with the success anticipated, a few Indian planters have turned their attention to the manufacture of green tea for the American market. The first consignment of this tea has now arrived in Calcutta.'

There is necessity for improvement, at some places in China, in the manufacture of tea prepared for the foreign market; and some endeavours have been made to meet the competition of Indian and other teas, and the heavy burden of Chinese taxation, by lessening the costs of production. Both Foochow and Shanghai foreign merchants have recommended more careful cultivation and packing.

'If China were to remove the export duty on tea and sweep away the various local burdens that hamper the planter, then indeed Chinese tea might be regarded as a formidable competitor with the product of India and Ceylon, but so long as it is weighted with a burden of taxation that leaves no reasonable margin of profit, the tea trade of China will continue on the down grade.'

Were it not for the heavy taxation on the China leaf by the Chinese Government, in the way of likin and export duties, Chinese tea, when carefully manufactured and cultivated, could easily stand the competition of India, Ceylon and other countries, and 'would be always able to command a good market.'

'"I fear that unless the Chinese can produce stronger and more Indian and Ceylon-like tea, it is only a question of time to see their total exclusion from foreign markets; and the only chance for China now is, in my opinion, to produce a good, wholesome, sweet article at a low price—something that can be mixed with Indian and Ceylon teas."'

'These remarks, confirmed as they are by all our local [Kiukiang] experts, make it appear that two requirements are specially wanted to retrieve the fortunes of the China tea trade —improved cultivation and manipulation (so as to produce "a good, wholesome article ") and a reduction in the cost of production. So long, however, as the present heavy taxation exists in China all along the route from the place of origin to the point of shipment—a taxation amounting to about 25 per cent. of the cost—whilst the teas of other countries (India, Ceylon, etc.) are free of duty, neither the improvement of the leaf nor the reduction of the original cost can be reckoned as prime factors in the question. The wonder is that an article so heavily handicapped as China tea is in the matter of duty and taxes should still hold a respectable place in the world's markets and still retain such a large share of foreign patronage. It would almost seem as if, even without any other alteration in the present state of affairs, China tea, with a wise removal of, say, half its fiscal burdens, could hold its own with its modern rivals, to the immense benefit of the Chinese Government and people.'

'The China tea is undoubtedly the best tea in the world naturally, but no pains are taken to maintain the stock, and the lower qualities exported were so mixed with dust and rubbish that much harm was done and the way effectually prepared for the competition of the Indian leaf.'

In this connection it may be interesting to give the results of the analyses of different teas.

'The following table, taken from a number of analyses recently made by the late Professor Dittmar, shows clearly the effect of allowing the water to stand on the tea leaves 5 minutes and 10 minutes respectively, and the varying amount of theine and tannin given off by China, Ceylon, and Indian teas:—

Five Minutes Infusion.			Ten Minutes Infusion.		
	Theine.	*Tannin.*		*Theine.*	*Tannin.*
China . .	2.58	3.06	China . .	2.79	3.78
Ceylon . .	3.15	5.87	Ceylon . .	3.29	7.30
Indian . .	3.63	6.77	Indian . .	3.73	8.09

'From this it will be seen that though Indian tea contains 25 per cent. more theine than China tea, it also contains 100 per cent. more tannin. Indian teas are much more widely used in England than China teas, and the "strong syrupy teas" advertised as of good value, and so largely consumed by the working classes, are, as a rule, blends of various Indian teas rich in tannin and astringent matters.'

It is thought that if the nearly contiguous towns of Lung-sing, Wong-sa-ping and Kie-kow in the turbulent province of Hunan were only opened to foreign trade, the English merchants resident at the centres of the Onfa tea trade could then compete with better success with the Indian tea merchants as the laid down cost on the spot is so low. At present these are taken to Hankow.

The following extracts will show how China tea has been ousted out of the English market:—

'In tea the most observable phenomenon of the twelvemonth has been the rapid rise in the imports from Ceylon. It is 48 per cent., the increase being gained at the expense alike of Indian tea and of Chinese. For the first time Ceylon tea has exceeded China tea in quantity. Year by year China tea declines, and it is impossible to say where the decadence will stop. To a certain extent, China planters and merchants might arrest the tendency by more care in cultivation, preparation of the leaf, and attention to European tastes. In general, though the best Chinese will please delicate palates, the Indian and Ceylon kinds are certain to predominate popularly on account of their strength.' —[1892].

'It is noteworthy that while we took 93 per cent. of our tea from China in 1865, and only 2 per cent. from India, and not so much as 1 per cent. from Ceylon, in 1895, we took 46 per cent. from India, 32 per cent. from Ceylon, and only 16 per cent. from China. The importations from China have steadily dwindled.'

In 1890 there were 101,000,000 lbs. tea imported from India into Great Britain, 74,000,000 from China, and over 42,000,000 from Ceylon, Ceylon was expected to export 70,000,000 lbs. of tea in 1892; there being then 230,000 acres of land planted with tea in that colony, an increase of nearly 40,000 acres during two years. Japan and China still retain the two largest markets for tea which are those of America and Australia. The trade in tea with Russia is increasing.

In four months, in 1894, the consumption of Indian tea in England had increased by about 11,000,000 lbs. and that of China had decreased 5,000,000.

The following figures will show how the China tea trade with England is being eclipsed by the Indian:—

In 1859 there was no Indian tea trade, and China sent 70,303,664 lbs. to England; ten years after the Chinese export of tea to England had increased to 101,080,491 lbs., and there was an Indian trade of 10,716,000 lbs. In 1879 the export of the two countries to England was, China, 126,340,000 lbs., India, 34,092,000 lbs., which shows both China and India with a material increase, and China with still a long lead ahead of India. The tables, however, were turned in the next decade, for China's export to England had fallen to 61,000,000 lbs., while India's had risen to 124,500,000, and in 1899 China had fallen to the figure of 16,677,835 lbs., and India had risen to the enormous figure —a figure never attained by China—of 219,136,185 lbs. Ceylon began the export of tea in 1884, and in five years sent 28,500,000 lbs. In 1889 Ceylon sent five times what China sent to England.

Amoy, some 30 years ago, exported as much as 65,800 piculs; in 1898 the amount was 10,528 piculs, for the tea trade of Amoy has gone down hill rapidly. 'At one time the Amoy teas were excellent and tea districts correspondingly prosperous'; but both quality and quantity fell off with the natural consequences in trade.

As an illustration of how the decline in the tea trade has affected the Chinese cultivator, the following statement in the report on Amoy, in the Customs' Annual Returns for 1896, is not devoid of interest:—

'The annual value of the trade has fallen from Hk. Taels 2,000,000 a quarter of a century ago to less than Hk. Taels 100,000 to-day, and the cultivator, whose plantation formerly supplied him with a comfortable income, is now compelled to plant rows of sweet potatoes between the tea-bushes to keep body and soul together.'

The report by the Commissioner of Customs for Amoy in 1897 showed to what a low state the tea trade in China had arrived.

'In all probability this trade report will be the last in which reference will be made to Amoy tea as an important factor in our trade. Twenty-five years ago, 65,800 piculs were exported; this year the total is 12,127 piculs. . . . The extinction of the Amoy tea trade has been predicted in previous trade reports. The export and likin duty are factors which militate against the hopes of the most sanguine. It is now too late to propose remedial measures which would resuscitate the already moribund leaf, formerly the leading article of export. The native growers are not entirely free from blame; of late years they have been content to produce any article which would sell, but the new United States law establishing standards has practically shut out the article as now produced.'

Tea has now disappeared from Amoy. (See TRADE.) There were no shipments to London direct from Hankow in 1900, for the first time on record.

The total annual average amount of tea exported from China in the years 1888-92 was 242,213,000 lbs., in 1893-7, 234,507,000 lbs., in 1898-1902, 192,427,000 lbs., and in 1903-7, 200,320,000 lbs., a steady decline corresponding to a rapid increase in the exports from India and Ceylon.

The following is from the Report on the Foreign Trade of China for the year 1897, by F. E. Taylor, of the I.M. Customs' Service:—

'I am one of those who believe in the possibility of reviving this trade. It may not be generally known that the most delicate and highly prized teas from India and Ceylon are grown on the higher altitudes and are produced from plants of Chinese origin. The bulk of the tea exported from India comes from the plains, and is the product of the indigenous plant which grows as a forest tree in Manipur—attaining in its wild state a height of thirty feet—and which will not flourish except at low elevations. The teas made from these plants yield a strong liquor, and they are consequently economical in use; but they are certainly unwholesome, and they lack altogether the delicious aroma of the teas grown at higher altitudes from Chinese plants. They can be placed on the market at low prices because the tea-estates are so large that the quantity of leaf to be dealt with makes the use of machinery profitable and even necessary. The essential difference between the process of manufacture in India and Ceylon and in China is that the teas are packed within 24 hours of the leaves having been plucked, which would seem to be impossible in this country under present conditions. It has been stated recently that the peculiar excellence of fine China teas would be ruined by the adoption of Indian methods. This may be true of fancy teas for exhibition, but is certainly not true if applied to ordinary fine teas. Not being an expert, my opinion is of little value, but I may be permitted to say that I have been unable to procure, in China, tea of such delightful fragrance and digestibility as some I have tasted from Darjeeling and the Kangra Valley—grown from Chinese plants, but manufactured by machinery.'

The following extracts show pretty much how matters stood about twenty years ago:—

'Experts in tea are agreed that the *desiderata* to retrieve the fortunes of the China tea trade, are improved cultivation and manipulation, and a reduction in the cost of production.'

'The 25 per cent. mentioned by Mr. Hughes as the amount of taxation to which Kiuking tea is subjected is somewhat less than the amount given by competent authorities at other ports. Mr. Brenan, in the Canton Consular Report for 1897, placed the figure at 35 per cent., while Mr. Cass, of Amoy, in a review of the tea trade supplied by him to the Consul and incorporated in the 1896 report, said the reason for the decline was not far to seek; the entire crop realised $136,000 while the likin paid amounted to $20,000 and the export duty to $35,000, or a total of $55,000, considerably more than one-third of the value of the tea. The result is that at Amoy the tea trade has practically ceased to exist.'

Notwithstanding the above, it is interesting to find the following statement made in 1901:—

'It is generally supposed that China tea trade has been beaten out of field by the more potent brands of British India and Ceylon. That is not entirely the case. China's exports dropped in the earlier years of the decade; but since the year of Jubilee they have risen from 204,000,000 to 217,000,000. This, however, is a serious decrease from 282,000,000 lbs., fifteen years ago.'

This is doubtless the result of the reaction which it was reported two years before had set in, in favour of China tea in England. China tea was about a third dearer than the Indian and Ceylon article. It was said that in the best hotels and best houses in London, China tea was generally used, and medical men more and more advised their patients to give it the preference. It remains to be seen whether the new regulations as to likin being abolished and a new incident of taxation imposed will have any appreciable effect upon lowering the charges on tea which at present so handicap and form one of the important factors in the decline of the China tea trade.

Some idea of the immense consumption of tea in the world, and the quantities that the most successful tea-producing countries might put on the market may be gathered from the calculation that the whole number of cups of tea taken a day in the United Kingdom 'will probably be not less on the average than 100,000,000.' The British people drank 184,000,000 lbs. per annum a few years since, being at the rate of 5 lbs. per head. In England the consumption is rapidly increasing, so that it is a pound or two higher now. The Dutch are the greatest tea and coffee drinkers, the quantity consumed by each being 240 ozs., or 15 lbs., a year. We are unable to say how much of this is tea and how much coffee. 'The French only consume half an ounce in the same period, whilst the Australians, the greatest tea drinkers in the world, consume 7½ lbs. of tea per head every year.' Even the Maoris drink tea; their consumption is very small though, not having been more than 1 lb. per head per annum in 1889, and the people of Tunis 'consume a certain amount of green tea.' It was stated in 1892 that the Kamchatkans are beginning to use tea. The largest annual consumption [of tea] per head was in Western Australia 10.70 lbs.; 'Great Britain figures at 4.70; the United States at 1.40' [there were 83,494,956 lbs. of tea imported into the United States in 1890, an increase over the previous decade, and amounting to 1½ lbs. for each inhabitant]; 'Germany stood at .07, and France at .03; the 'continental nations, even including Russia,' came 'a long way behind the United Kingdom.' The large consumption of wine in France and Germany unfortunately retards the more healthy consumption of tea. It is calculated that 500,000,000 people drink Chinese and Indian tea; and all over the world there would appear to be a constant increase to their number, for nations which never drunk it before are being taught its use, while amongst those people who know it, larger numbers are gradually imbibing more and more of it.

TELEGRAPHS.—An abortive attempt to introduce telegraphs into China was made in 1865 by an Englishman named Reynolds. He began to erect a line between Shanghai and the mouth of the Huang-p'u, but the poles and wire were destroyed by the people with the connivance of the Chinese officials.

In 1869 a short line was erected by the firm of Russell & Co. in Shanghai to connect their office with the Shanghai Steam Navigation Co's wharf.

Telegraphs

In 1871 the Great Northern Telegraph Co. laid a cable from Hongkong to Shanghai. Land lines were sanctioned in 1881 (the earliest being from Shanghai to Tientsin, extended to Peking three years later), and of recent years the Chinese Government finding the necessity, by the Franco-Chinese war, of having rapid communication with the centres of its numerous provinces, has established telegraph lines at other places.

' " The telegraph is the only institution of modern science which has obtained any considerable foothold in China," say Messrs. Fearon and Allen in an article in *The Engineering Magazine* [writing in the early eighties]. " Peking is connected by wire with Tientsin and with Manchurian points up to the Russian frontier, whence connection is continued by Russian Siberian lines to Europe. The capital is also connected with all the treaty ports, and principal cities in China proper, and these again with each other. Canton has connection also through Yünnan with Burma. China learned the value of the telegraph in the war with France, and it has long since been admitted to have become indispensable. The telegraph, however, is under imperial control, and there is probably little opportunity for its extension as a private enterprise. Chinese writing being not alphabetic, but syllabic, and there being as many characters as there are words in use, the telegraphic messages are sent in a number cypher. For transcribing messages received, a double-ended type is used; on one end is the character, and on the other the corresponding number. When a message is received, it is set up by the numbers, and then printed from the reverse, or character, end." '

Speaking in a general way, the system may be described as consisting, in the main, of a line, starting from the northern part of China's colonial possessions, lying to the north of China proper, and running down not far from the coast to the south; in the southern portion there is another line as well, forming a loop further inland, while from this northern and southern main line spring three large lines running in a westerly direction, the northernmost one through the northern provinces, the southern one through the southern provinces, and a central one along the Yangtzŭ valley. Besides these grand lines there are short branch lines connecting different places with the main lines. By means of all these, telegraphic communication is maintained with every province. The province of Hunan even has it now; the people of the frontier town of Lichow rose *en masse* in 1891 to prevent its introduction into their province, but five years later the introduction of it excited no opposition.

Extensions are being still made every little while to the system, and it is being rapidly extended over the empire. In 1908 the Ministry of Communications took control of all the land lines.

The work of putting up the lines in China was entrusted to the Danish Great Northern Telegraph Company. Compared with the numerous important centres of trade, the stations are but few in number; and the rate for messages is not sufficiently low to bring them within the reach of the multitudes that avail themselves of such conveniences in the West. Looked at from a foreign point of view, it is unsatisfactory to find that these native lines are not available to Europeans if a riot occurs. The following was written about Chinese telegraphs in 1892, and is still of interest, though the lines have extended considerably since:—

'The Chinese telegraph system already comprises about 42,000 li [say 14,000 miles] of line, carrying 58,000 li of wire; stations have been established in 171 different towns; and Formosa, the Pescadores, and Hainan have been connected by submarine cable with the mainland. From Hehlungkiang to Hainan and from Corea to the Burma frontier of Yünnan, the Chinese telegraph lines stretch over greater distances than from Norway to Sicily and from Lisbon to the Caucasus.'

'The telegraph lines [in China] have a length [in 1901] of nearly 14,000 miles, with 250 telegraph offices.' By 1924 the total length of the telegraph lines was more than 40,000 miles, with more than six hundred telegraph stations.

Amongst the wonders of the Chinese telegraphs may be mentioned the line across the Gobi desert, 3,000 miles long.

References.—Reid, *Peeps into China; Chinese Economic Bulletin.*

TENURE OF LAND.—All land was held direct from the crown in China, there being no allodial property; and no law of entail. As has been so often stated, the family being the unit of society in China, it is natural to find that a large amount of land is held by the family or by the clan, though individuals as well often invest their savings in the South of China in paddy fields.

'The conditions of common tenure are the payment of an annual tax, the fee for alienation with a money composition for personal service to the Government, a charge generally incorporated into the direct tax as a kind of scutage.'

The land tax varied from 1½ to 10 cents a mao [mu], or Chinese acre, which is equivalent to from 10 to 66 cents an acre, the amount being dependent on 'the quality of the land and the difficulty of tillage,' its fertility, situation, or the use to which it is put (see also below). Reckoning this tax at an average of 25 cents an acre, the income to the Government from this source ought to have been about $150,000,000, had it all gone into the Imperial coffers without paying tribute to the host of rapacious underlings, clerks, and constables, and the hundred and one people who all put in for a share of the plunder.

'Although land taxes are high in China . . . it is not infrequent for the same tax to be levied twice and even three times in one year. Inquiries regarding the land taxes among farmers in different parts of China showed rates running from three cents to a dollar and a half Mexican, per mow; or from about eight cents to $3.87 gold, per acre. At these rates a forty acre farm would pay from $3.20 to $154.80, and a quarter section four times these amounts. . . . In Shantung the land tax is about one dollar per acre, and in Chihli, twenty cents. In Kiangsi province the rate is 200 to 300 cash per mow, and in Kiangsu, from 500 to 600 cash per mow, or . . . . [at the rate of 1,500 to 2,000 cash to the United States dollar] from 60 to 80 cents, or 90 cents to $1.20 per acre in Kiangsi; and $1.50 to $2.00 or $1.80 to $2.40 in Kiangsu province. The lowest of these rates would make the land tax on 160 acres, $96, and the highest would place it at $384, gold.'

'As the exactions for alienation on sale of lands are high, amounting to as much as one-third of the sale price sometimes, the people accept white deeds from each other as proofs of ownership and responsibility for taxes. As many as twenty or thirty such deeds of sale occasionally accompany the original *hung k'aí* [*hung ch'i*], without which they are suspicious, if not valueless. In order to keep the knowledge of the alienations of land in Government offices, so that the taxes can be assured, it is customary to furnish a *k'aí méí* [*ch'i wei*], or "deed-end," containing a note of the terms of sale and amount of tax liable on the property. There is no other proof of ownership required; and the simplicity and efficiency of this mode of transfer offer a striking contrast to the cumbrous rules enforced in Western Kingdoms.'

The eldest son inherits his father's property, but, from the customs of the people, it appears more as if it devolved upon him as a trust administered by him for the good of the family, for all the members of the family are allowed to reside on and live upon the property, generation after generation, if they so choose, or an 'amicable composition can be made.'

A mortgagee enters into possession of the property and 'makes himself responsible for the payment of the taxes'; the land may be redeemed at any time on the payment of the sum advanced, if the payment be made within thirty years.

The Chinese Government is liberal in its treatment of those who reclaim waste hill-sides, and poor soil; or who first cultivate newly-formed alluvial strips of land: in the former cases sufficient time is allowed for the cultivator to recoup himself for the outlay incurred before his land is assessed; and in the latter case the authorities have to be informed.

'All buildings pay a ground rent to the Government, but no data are available for comparing this tax with that levied in Western cities. The Government furnishes the owner of the ground with a *hung k'aí*, or "red deed," in testimony of his right to occupancy, which puts him in possession as long as he pays the taxes [ground rent]. There is a record office in the local magistracy of such documents.'

Most explicit rules are laid down for the registration of land in China, and theoretically everything should be clear and plain as possible; but if we may be excused the apparently contradictory statement, we should describe, like many things in China, the system of land registration in this land as normally in what should be an abnormal condition. It is often difficult to get such a good insight into a state of affairs such as the acquisition of the New Territory in Hongkong has revealed. Those who know the Chinese in their transactions with their officials will have little difficulty in reasoning from the small to the great, or drawing inferences concerning the unknown from what is known. True, there are certain reasons assigned for what, viewed from the standpoint of the laws and regulations, appear an anomalous state; but those who know China, the invasions of its coasts in the past, its almost chronic rebellions, the waves of immigration that have swept down from the North to the South bringing sometimes civil war and internecine struggles in their train—those who know their China thoroughly will have but little difficulty in believing that similar anomalous conditions prevail largely in this land where morals, ethics, laws and regulations are of a very high order, but where practice differs so widely from precept. As showing in a general way what may be expected to be found in other parts of China we shall enlarge on the conditions prevalent in the neighbourhood of Hongkong.

Different clans, who were the first settlers in the neighbourhood of the Canton Delta, collected land-tax for which they never accounted to the Chinese Government, though paying Crown Rent on a small area, which was but a small fraction of the whole land they claimed. Unrest and disorders have prevailed for generations in this part of China. About two centuries and a half ago the coast and some distance inland was laid waste to prevent Koxinga (see HISTORY) from being able to carry on his operations in favour of the late Ming dynasty. Supposing now, on resettlement, a family should have a certain number of Chinese acres on which they paid Crown Rent, doubtless a certain latitude would be allowed, and the family might cultivate, as the years went on, though still confined to the same number of acres, different plots of land in the same upland valley or sea-coast. As the years then went on it would be essentially Chinese-like for this family to claim the whole district of land over which they had cultivated plots here and there at different times; and further, it would be essentially Chinese-like for other new settlers, as they arrived in the depopulated districts, to acknowledge the assumption of the family; especially would they have no disposition to dispute such a claim when told that such was the case, as it would be more to their interests to keep quiet, pay some yearly sum to them and thus avoid the expenses, squeezes, and troubles incident to litigation in this land of squeezes and official corruption. Besides, by so doing, they would not incur the enmity of the family, who would feel incensed should the facts of the case come to light, and they be required to pay full taxation on the land thus occupied instead of only on a moiety of it. These sums would be paid as taxes (though they never reached the Government) to the family by these subsequent settlers as they arrived and the wasted lands were thus repopulated. Any trouble with the Mandarin, or his subordinates, could be easily hushed up by the family by the judicious use of bribes which they could pay out of the monies received from these curiously obtained tenants of theirs.

Another reason for the registration laws not being complied with is the excessive cost of registration, the original cost was $100 for a heading in the Register, and this was necessary, if a man's own name or that of his ancestors had not already appeared. After this initial expense, other expenses, legal and illegal, were incurred, and there was the trouble of going to the Land Registry in the District City. All these things combined, along with what has been already stated, to lead in the New Territory to what Mr. Gompertz, the President of the Land Court, estimates as 'four-fifths of the land-tax passing through the hands of intermediaries before reaching the Government.'

The result of all this is natural, and it can be stated in a few words: 'few sales of land were registered.'

What resulted from these sales not being registered is not confined to the immediate vicinity of Hongkong, but prevails elsewhere as well, and it is as follows. A 'red deed,' or registered deed as it is called, is necessary; this is granted on registration by the proprietors; but in lieu of the handing over of this 'red deed' on alienation of property, one which is styled a 'white deed,' is generally given. This 'unregistered deed containing a Covenant by the purchaser to pay the vendor a yearly sum to meet the tax which the vendor continued to pay as before.' The purchaser occasionally got the 'red deed' as well as a 'white deed,' even if he bought the whole parcel of land set forth in the former. This he kept as security against the vendor trying to sell the land again to some one else. 'Thus the taxes were still paid in the old name though the land had passed into other hands.'

It can thus easily be imagined what confusion arises from land matters in China. The modes of acquiring ownership of property was by grant from the Crown and by purchase; but the most common way of dealing with land is by perpetual lease from the Government, and even between private individuals this was carried out, and most often in the latter case it was simply a verbal agreement, and at times, without even this, it was taken an agreement was implied. Another common mode of acquiring property was by mortgage.

This Chinese mortgage is tantamount to a conditional sale; in this respect being like 'the Welsh mortgage of the text-books.' It is either in writing or orally, more often the latter; it is hardly ever registered.

What is known as a Welsh mortgage is thus described in the English law-books, and the same account might have been written of the Chinese.

'What is known as a Welsh mortgage is a Transaction whereby the estate is conveyed to the mortgagee, who is to go into possession and take the rents and profits as an equivalent for his interest, the principal remaining undiminished. In such a Transaction there is no contract, express or implied, between the parties, for the repayment of the debt at a given time, and though the mortgagee has no remedy by action to enforce payment of his money, yet the mortgagor or his heirs may redeem at any time.'

These mortgages when oral give occasion to many disputes and much litigation, as the mortgagor wishes to redeem if the value of the land appreciates; and the difficulties are increased when, as is often the case, 'mortgages are frequently assigned three or four times over.'

Daughters never inherit land in China.

References.—Williams, *Middle Kingdom; Transactions N.C.B.R.A.S.*, Vol. i; *Hongkong Government Gazette Supplement*, April 28, 1900, Appendix III; *ditto.* 1901 ('Report on the Land Court for 1900:' 'Some Notes on Land Tenure in the New Territory'); Werner, *Descriptive Sociology—Chinese*.

THEATRE.—Theatrical exhibitions (which were introduced by the Mongols in the Yüan dynasty, though some sinologists place their origin in the T'ang dynasty and traces of the drama in the form of ceremonial dancing, etc., are found as early as the Chou dynasty) in China are often connected with religion, as mystery plays were in the mediæval times in the West, for in China they are often held in honour of a god's birthday. Subscriptions in these cases are obtained from the residents of the locality, and a large stage of bamboo and matting covered in, is put up. No nails are used in its construction, but the bamboos are securely tied together with strips of rattan. The putting up of matsheds is a trade by itself; they are quickly run up, a few days' time suffices for erecting one large enough for holding two thousand people. They are taken down even quicker, as sharp hook-knives cut through the rattan strips, and these latter are the only materials which cannot be used again, the same bamboo poles and oblongs of matted leaves bound together, doing duty scores, if not hundreds, of times. One large shed may serve for the performers, while smaller ones accommodate those who pay for seats; the pit is the paved square, and standing room is all that the rabble, who are packed as thick as herrings in a barrel, are allowed.

Players stroll in companies from place to place, open to engagements as above, or are hired by wealthy families to perform their plays in their private dwellings, where all the inconveniences of the female members of the family appearing in public are avoided. In Hongkong there are two substantial buildings used for native theatres, and the Chinese appear to be copying this example at Canton and elsewhere.

What would we think in the West of performances [made up, however, of a succession of short plays, not of one long one, as is commonly supposed by foreigners] lasting three days instead of three hours, and only rests for sleeping and eating? Smoking and refreshments are allowed in the theatre itself, and the splitting and munching of dried melon seeds which is carried on must be immense, while play follows play without any interval.

The stage is simplicity itself, with two entrances from the back where the 'green-room' is placed; and a few tables, chairs, and stools, are about all that are used, and they do duty for any and every thing. A frail structure, composed of tables and chairs piled up in the middle of the stage, is used to represent lofty crags and precipitous mountains, over which the heroine of the play, accompanied and assisted by a trusty family retainer, clambers up, clutching imaginary projecting points, trees, bushes, or grass, to help her in her dangerous climb. Some of the actors display considerable talent, most realistic effects being produced at times.

The assistants come in and remove different articles when done with, or bring them as required, going out and in among the actors with perfect *nonchalance*, as no curtain falls between the different acts. Considerable force of imagination is required to add all the accessories so vividly pictured on the modern stage in the West; but perhaps their absence is not an entire defect, as more attention can be bestowed, without their distraction, on the acting itself. Young men dressed as women, take the female parts, and the others are so represented as to be known at once, the villain, for instance, being painted with a white nose.

Historical plays are often performed, the dresses being those of the Chinese when under native rule, between two and three centuries ago, and most gorgeous they are, making up for all the lack of scenic effect; robes of rich hues, glittering with gold; long feathers, several feet in length, falling in graceful curves from the caps of the performers, and swaying with every motion of the actors. The spectacular effect of all this glitter and sheen proves a strange contrast to the poverty of the building and the bare appearance of the stage. Marches past of soldiers; the exaggerated stride of the hero; the prancing of the warriors as they enter into mimic contests where lunges and feints, *à la Chinois,* are indulged in to an extravagant extent; all present a *coup d'œil,* weird and fantastic, grotesque at times, but so full of life and vigour that for some time one enjoys the kaleidoscopic scene to be witnessed nowhere else in the world: and were it not for the clash of the cymbals which emphasise different passages, the scrapings of the fiddles, and the indescribable effect of the Chinese music, added to the heat of the crowded building and the disagreeable odour from the perspiring and unwashed masses, one would enjoy it more, but a headache is the Westerner's reward for the patient sitting out of a Chinese play.

'The efforts of certain actors are worthy of the highest commendation from the naturalness of their actions and the vivid portrayal of the incidents of the play. There is, however, much of conventionality reminding one of the Italian opera among us.' 'The performances' are 'largely of the character of pantomime and more largely perhaps . . . opera.'

Though we have particularised the historic play, it must not be supposed that the 'Brethren of the Pear Orchard,' as Thespians are called in China, confine their attention to that branch of the histrionic art. Plays of various kinds, comedies, tragedies, and farces, all find acceptance from a Chinese audience.

'While it is true that the Chinese themselves make no distinction between comedy and tragedy, a translator from their language is still at liberty to apply these terms, according to the serious and dignified, or comic and familiar character, of the composition which he selects.' Sir John Davis, from whom we quote, says further, of a tragedy which he translated from Chinese into English:—'In the unity of the plot, the dignity of the personages, the grandeur and importance of the events, the strict award of what is called poetical justice—nay, in the division into five principal portions or acts, it might satisfy the most fastidious and strait-laced of the old European critics. Love and war, too, constitute its whole action, and the language of the imperial lover is frequently passionate to a degree one is not prepared for in such a country as China.'

'The stage, and everything pertaining to it, enjoys a lower estimation than in any part of Europe.' It is not considered proper for respectable Chinese ladies to go frequently to the theatre. 'The Chinese cannot strictly be said to possess *dramatic* poetry.' 'No Shakespeare has . . . yet arisen in China; no analyst of motives either amongst novelists or playwrights.' 'The dialogue of their stage pieces is composed in ordinary *prose;* while the principal performer now and then chaunts forth, in unison with music, a species of song or "vaudeville"; and the name of the tune or air is always inserted at the top of the passage to be sung.' 'A considerable portion of the plays of the Chinese consists of a sort of irregular verse, which is sung or chanted with music. This is often very obscure in its import; and as, according to the Chinese themselves, the gratification of the ear is its main object, sense itself appears sometimes to be neglected for the sake of a pleasing sound.' 'The Chinese are enthusiastic theatre-goers, and sit for hours enthralled by the performance, bereft as it necessarily is of much of the scenic effects of the Western stage.'

'The Chinese drama . . . was marked out into three distinct epochs—The T'ang Dynasty (A.D. 720-905), the Sung Dynasty (A.D. 960-1119), the Kin and Yüan Dynasty (A.D. 1123-1341).'

'The character of the plays represented was at first religious, but subsequently was more devoted to historical subjects, and also represented the occupations of the people in times of peace as well as the exploits of their heroes in war.'

'The Chinese drama sprang up no earlier than the time of the caliphate and subsequent ages. The Greek drama was already transplanted and had grown luxuriantly in India. The Mohammedans naturally derived pure ideas from it in their religious shows, and the miracle-plays of Europe show how the same principle of dramatic imitation was working there also. So it was in China. The whole idea of the Chinese play is Greek. The mask, the chorus, the music, the colloquy, the scene and the act, are Greek. The difference between Chinese plays, and those of Terence and Plautus is simply that the Roman dramatists translated a good deal. The Chinese took the idea and worked up the play from their own history and their own social life. The Chinese drama is based on music just as the Greek play was, and the whole conception of the play is foreign, while the details and the language are Chinese. But for the arrival of Western musicians in the Sung and Yüan dynasties, pleasing the people's ear with more lively and stirring strains than they had ever heard in the old music of China, the modern dramatic music would not have been developed. The spread of education and the love of poetry in the T'ang dynasty constituted a training for dramatic authorship. The Sung dynasty influence in this direction is vouched for by Su Tung-p'o. After such men had appeared it was easy for the drama and romance to be originated, but it was the increasing inflow of foreign actors and musicians all through the age of the Golden Tartars which gave direction and shape to the new power. Every attempt to explain the Chinese drama as purely native must therefore fail.'

The social position the actor holds in China is low; he is considered on a par with the barber, and was debarred from entering the examinations; and this, though the Chinese play has a moral tendency, the villain getting his deserts, and the virtuous hero and heroine coming off with flying colours.

A movement for dramatic reform was begun after the establishment of the Republic. For a time the plays of many western dramatists were translated and performed, but this phase soon passed, yet though the modernizing of the Chinese drama (whose aim is entirely different from that of Western drama) has failed, a change has been effected in the status of the actor, in his education, and consequently in the quality and presentation of the dramas on the stage.

An enormous number of cinemas have been opened within recent years. At first, and in some still, separate portions of the auditorium were reserved for male and female spectators respectively, but this system has now been abandoned in most of these establishments.

References.—Stanton, *The Chinese Drama;* Williams, *Middle Kingdom;* Douglas, *Chinese Stories,* Introd., pp. xxiii-vi; Johnson, *The Chinese Drama.*

TIGERS.—In the earlier days of European residence in the East, and even until a recent date, most foreigners were very sceptical of the tiger stories of the Chinese; but of recent years it has been well established that in some parts of China the tiger (*Felis tigris*; in Chinese, *lao hu*) is a common beast of prey and a source of constant danger, especially to the juvenile members of the community. There have been numerous cases of children being seized and carried off from the very doors of their homes, nor has the abduction of a child from the very gates of a city been unknown. The tiger appears to be widely spread over the country, but it is mostly found in Manchuria, and in the provinces of Fukien, Kiangsi, Kuangtung, and Kuangsi. They even come, at times, within the New Territory on the mainland opposite Hongkong. In 1685, K'ang Hsi is said to have killed sixty in one day in Liaotung. They frequent, amongst other spots, the neighbourhood of Swatow, Amoy, and Foochow, and a few days' journey from Canton up the North, East, or West Rivers would bring one to tiger districts. Tigers are also found in Manchuria. One foreign resident 'in Amoy has shot 19 tigers to his own rifle, and has been present at the death of 40.' Foreign sportsmen, however, with but few exceptions, have not gone tiger shooting. The average length of those that have fallen to their guns has been for males 9 feet and females 8 feet. 'Immensely long tigers are not always proportionately large; they are mostly thin and low animals; the heaviest and most muscular tigers average about 9 feet 6 inches. The longest tiger shot in India measured 12 feet 2 inches. . . . In China there are several good records; one of 10 feet 6 inches, and another of 11 feet 2 inches.'

The writer, from whom we quote above, states that he has measured tanned skins in Shanghai and found some of them as long as 12 feet 9 inches 'and they were not "faked" in any way.' The tiger is supposed to attain maturity in the course of four years, and only those full grown could be of large size.

As compared with his Indian brother, the Chinese tiger—being a very well-fed animal which generally inhabits the hills, while the Indian tiger being a jungle animal has his hair and skin much damaged by friction against the undergrowth—is better marked, and the skin naturally commands a higher price in Europe, for, while a 'full-grown Chinese tiger will fetch a price of £100 in some of the large zoological gardens in Europe,' the highest amount given for an Indian tiger is £70. The Chinese tiger is said not to be so aggressive as the Indian tiger, though its ferocity 'when aroused and put to bay' is equal: 'the tiger living in the jungle [the Indian] has less supply of food and will attack more instantaneously and with less provocation.' The Chinese dig a pit and cover it with poles or branches, the tiger's weight carries him through, and a common way of killing him then is to run a red-hot iron down his throat, though he often escapes from these pits.

A tiger shot by trap-gun at Kuliang, and measuring 7½ feet and weighing 210 lbs., was sold in Foochow for $80—in 1898. They are shot with poisoned arrows, probably from cross-bows in that neighbourhood, and the poison is said to do its work in two or three minutes.

The 'white tiger' is an important element in the pseudo-science of *fêng-shui*: it represents one of the 'two supposed currents running through the earth,' the other being the 'green dragon.' These are believed to be situated on the right and left respectively of propitious sites and graves. 'A skilful observer can detect and describe them, with the help of the [geomantic] compass, direction of the water-courses, shapes of the male and female ground, and their proportions, colour of the soil, and the permutations of the elements.'

See also GEOMANCY.

References.—Proceedings of the Zoological Society of London, 1870, p. 626; *Hongkong Weekly Press,* May 27, 1896.

TIME.—At the Treaty Ports and in their neighbourhood, as well as at Hongkong and Macao, clocks are found in almost every shop, and watches abound, but in many places there is no standard of correct time, and, in places where there is, it is ignored extensively. Life is not such a mad rush as with us in our feverish pursuit of wealth, a livelihood, or learning. Fix a time for an engagement with a Chinese, and he comes in half-an-hour late, or even two or three hours after, occasionally a few days later than the day fixed upon, with no idea that he has done anything out of the way. Hire a coolie or a street vehicle or a boat, and what the man employed bases his calculation on, as to payment, is more the distance traversed than the time spent over it; and, compared with his fraternity in the West, he patiently waits your return, while the minutes and hours that fly are almost next to nothing to him. This disregard of time is seen in the language, where vagueness takes the place of our precision. When a man says 'to-morrow' he does not necessarily mean the next day, but some indefinite time in the future which sometimes never comes, like St. Patrick's 'to-morrow,' for the saint when exterminating the snakes in Ireland put the last one in a box, and flung it to the bottom of a lake, promising to let it out 'to-morrow,' and as each new day began, the snake asked to be let out, but the saint always replied that this was to-day and not to-morrow.

The Chinese employ two methods in reckoning time: one, the cycle of sixty years (see CYCLE); but this way of counting time is an uncertain one, for, unless it is distinctly stated, one is at a loss to know whether, say, a certain book was copied or printed some score or two years ago, or fourscore or more years ago. Another better method, one of the most common—and one used by us to a small extent, notably in the headings of Acts of Parliament—is that of employing the years of the reign; but with the Chinese it is not the sovereign's name that is used, that is too sacred to be so debased, but some high-sounding combination of words is employed, and this designates the reign, or a part of it, as has often happened in ancient Chinese history, when the reign-name was changed several times in the life-time of one monarch. The last but one occupant of the imperial throne had selected for him for his 'year-style' the words Kuang-Hsü, which may be rendered into English as 'Illustrious Succession'; so the year, for example, which we date from the birth of Christ as A.D. 1903, is known to the Chinese as parts of the Jên-yin and Kuei-mao years of the cycle and parts of the 28th and 29th years of the 'Illustrious Succession' period. The Chinese year is a lunar one 'but its commencement is regulated by the sun.' To those who are astronomically inclined, it may be interesting to know that 'New Year falls on the first new moon after the sun enters Aquarius, which makes it come not before January 21st nor after February 19th.' In 1899 it happened on the 10th of February. It is therefore unlike the Mohammedan year which now has its new year in summer and now in winter; the Chinese feasts are almost as certain as our European movable ones, for by the addition of an intercalary month every three years or so the differences are roughly adjusted; this extra month is, however, not the thirteenth and added on at the end of the year, but it is inserted at different times in different years, and takes its name from the month it immediately follows; for instance, one year it may be the intercalary second month, on another occasion it may be the intercalary seventh month, and so on. 'An intercalary moon must lie completely within one sign of the zodiac; *i.e.*, the sun must not pass from one sign to another.' The Quakers would not be a singular people in China as far as their nomenclature of time was concerned; for instead (in common parlance) of the months having names as we, who are outside the pale of Quakerism in the West, employ, the Chinese know them as the first, the second, the third months, and so on. The close connection between the month and the moon is more noticeable in Chinese even than with us, for the same word does duty for both. Again, the indefiniteness of the Chinese as regards time is seen in the days, for though they are known as the first, second, etc., yet they are further divided into three decades as regards their position in the month, so a Chinese can fix a matter as having occurred in the first decade, or the second, or the third, as the case may be, and delight his unprecise nature by a margin of ten days.

There is no week, amongst the Chinese, in our acceptation of the term, but multitudes of them have learned what a week is, and have terms to express it and its days, and it is well known wherever foreigners have stayed or travelled much.

The Chinese hour is twice the length of ours, but again, in the neighbourhood of the Treaty Ports, where clocks and watches are common, the more convenient foreign system, as shown by the faces of those important and useful horological instruments, is largely used, and is probably increasing in use every year; and we may say in passing that it is in this way that progress is accomplished in China, by the adoption of some foreign invention which gradually extends from the sphere of foreign influence or introduction further into the country. There is no rapid, wholesale sweeping away of former things, and the importation, *en bloc*, of new ideas, as has frequently happened with Japan—in her case often to be followed by a revulsion, or the acceptance of something else, and a discarding of the former inventions adopted so hastily. China's progress, being slower, is steadier, and will be none the less sure in the long run.

'The Chinese calendar, more or less in its present form, is of very old origin. Errors crept in naturally in the course of time, as they did into the Julian Calendar, and the first Jesuit missionaries turned to good account their mathematical skill by proving the inaccuracy of the native calendar upon occasions of eclipses. Fr. Schall was the first to introduce corrections, and Fr. Verbiest, in the time of the Emperor K'ang Hsi, drew up the calendar in its present form, carrying his calculations as far as the year 2020. His calendar has been faithfully followed ever since, with some rare exceptions, as when the year 1894 or rather the twentieth year of Kuang Hsü was curtailed of a day on account of the disastrous war with the Japanese.'

The Chinese watch at night is like the Western dog-watch, only two hours in length. The first watch lasts from 7 P.M. to 9 P.M. and is shown by one beat on the revenue-cutter's drum or one blow on the street-watchman's hollow bamboo tube; the second watch is from 9 P.M. to 11 P.M. and is signalled by two beats, etc.; the third, fourth, and fifth are of equal duration, and shown in a corresponding manner. Each of these watches is divided into five lesser divisions, which are distinguished on the revenue-cutters by their numbers from one to five strokes on a small gong, the stroke on the gong immediately following the drum beat. The watch is set and called off both afloat and ashore by a tattoo on the drum or bamboo, commencing with slow and measured beat, gradually increasing in time until it ends in a regular rattle; this is repeated several times.

The peculiar phrases that one comes across, in use by the common people, for the expression of short periods of time strike one as very odd. The following are examples of such phrases:—

The time it would take to drink a cup of tea.
The time it would take to drink a cup of hot tea.
The time it would take to eat a meal.
The time it would take to eat a bowl of rice.
The time it would take to smoke a cigarette.
The time it would take for an incense-stick to burn.

The Western system of chronology has now been largely adopted; some calendars print the old and new systems side by side. The general unpunctuality above referred to is now diminishing.

TOBACCO AND PIPES.—Tobacco (*nicotiana tabacum*, in Chinese *yen*) was introduced into China from Luzon about A.D. 1530 'and smoking spread among all classes of the people, and both sexes, with incredible rapidity.' Some say it was introduced via Japan. Decrees were issued against its use by some of the Ming dynasty rulers, but proved as ineffectual as those of James I. against it in England, for everyone smokes in China. There are two kinds of pipe in use, the dry pipe, and the water-pipe: the latter is a copy of the Indian hookah; it consists of a receptacle for the water into which a tube-like piece, about the size of a small finger, is inserted; the upper end of this tube contains a small cavity into which the tobacco is put. The smoke is inhaled through the water up the pipe part, which is a tube about a foot long, gradually narrowing and bending over at the mouth-piece. These pipes are made of copper and argentan (an alloy of copper, zinc, nickel, iron, and sometimes a little silver), and are used by ladies and gentlemen. The common coolies have a primitive style of water-pipe which consists of a length of bamboo about the size of a man's arm, and, part of the way up, a little tube of bamboo, the size of a finger, is inserted for the tobacco.

The other pipes are often made of bamboo, as far as the stems are concerned, and vary in length from a few feet to a few inches, though short pipes are not very common. The bowls, of metal, are small, holding scarcely more than a thimbleful of tobacco; a few whiffs exhaust them; and with the gentleman or lady a servant is ready who steps up, takes the pipe, empties out the ashes, refills it, sticks it into the mouth of his master or mistress, and lights it with a paper spill.

The tobacco is prepared for smoking by drying the leaves and cutting them into shreds; it is milder than that used in the West, and is of different preparations. It is used in several ways, such as in pipes, in paper cigarettes, and in snuff, but not in cigars: when used as snuff, it is put into snuff-bottles, over the purchase of which the man of means spends money lavishly, and the patient toiler also lavishly spends weeks, or sometimes even months, in the production of one. They are often cut out of 'stone, amber, agate, and other rare minerals, with most exquisite taste.' They are carved at times like cameos; a little bone spoon is attached to the stopper, and a pinch of snuff is taken out by it and put on the thumb-nail, from which it is drawn up into the nose.

Considerable quantities of tobacco are exported to the East Indian Islands; and an attempt was made to introduce it on the Western markets. 'Japanese tobacco is already largely consumed in Europe, but the bulk of it goes to Antwerp, Amsterdam, and Hamburg, where, with the addition of the Sumatra or Havana leaf, it is made into cigars.'

On the other hand, the Chinese have developed a liking for Manila cigars, and many of them may be seen smoking them. The street coolies in Hongkong, whose stock of cash is too small to invest in such luxuries, keep an eye open for the discarded ends tossed away by the extravagant foreigner, and, picking them up, enjoy a few whiffs. Nor is the manufacture of these cigar ends into new cigars unknown to the ingenious Chinaman.

Things Chinese

It is curious to notice how very similar pipes that were used in England on the first introduction of tobacco smoking are to the small Chinese pipes in use in China at present. If the general opinion that the Portuguese spread the knowledge of tobacco smoking into Asia soon after its introduction be accepted (the Chinese, it is stated, learned it from the Philippine Islands), then this similarity in the pipes is easily accounted for. A writer in *Macmillan's Magazine* for August, 1896, throws out the suggestion that, as with so many other things, the Chinese were the introducers of tobacco smoking into America and the West. If this be true, the similarity in pipes is also accounted for.

In this connection it may be interesting to note the following account of tobacco cultivation in the Szchuan [Ssŭch'uan] Province, as reported on by Mr. Smithers, the United States Consul at Chungking.

'The tobacco plant (*nicotiana rustica*) is grown all over the provinces of Szechuan [Ssŭch'uan], but more abundantly in the districts of Pe-shan Hsien, which is about 150 li (60 miles) north-east of this city, and Kin-t'ang [Chin-t'ang] Hsien, about 100 li (40 miles) east of Ch'êngtu, the provincial capital.

'The plant grows to the height of about 2½ to 3 feet from the ground, and the usual time for planting the seed is during the tenth or eleventh moon (November or December). The method, before putting the seed into the ground, is to sift out a quantity of soil and manure it. When dry, the seed is wrapped with this soil and put into the ground at intervals of a foot and a half. The soil must not be rich, and ground where cereals have not been already planted is generally chosen.

'During the year, there are three crops—the first is cut six months after it has been planted, the second twenty days afterwards, and the third crop twenty days after the second crop.

'So soon as it is cut, it is hung up to dry for about a fortnight, in a sheltered place with a good draught, so that it may dry quickly. When ready for sale, it is done up in bundles weighing 70 to 80 catties (93.3 to 106.6 pounds) a piece.

'The Kin-t'ang tobacco leaf receives a little more care. After it is dried, it is put into a press, to enable some of the juice to be pressed out and the leaf made much milder than the other leaves that are sold in the market. It is done up in bundles of 40 to 50 catties (53.3 to 66.6 pounds) each. The seed is sown under shelter. When the leaves are ready, they are picked, and exposed to the dew for several nights; they are then dipped in a dye, and hung up to dry again before being taken to the markets for sale.'

The article goes on to say that a Chinese is making cigars, but they are not equal to Manila cigars; but with proper curing they would be probably improved. The Chinese in that neighbourhood are said to take off a piece of leaf, roll it into a sort of cheroot, and smoke it in their pipes, consisting of a small brass bowl and long bamboo or cane stem.

'Tobacco leaf was shipped away [from Shanghai in 1898] to the extent of 210,000 piculs, of which 94 per cent. went to Japan, or say, 197,000 piculs, as against 13,000 piculs in 1897.'

'Tobacco of excellent quality is produced in China, and at one time it looked as though this was a promising trade, 371,137 piculs having been exported in 1898; but fraudulent packing has spoiled these prospects and the export has fallen off, although the export of 158,383 piculs was an improvement on the figures for the previous year.'

TOMBS.—A book might be written on the subject of tombs in China, so important are they considered in this land; they are frequently to be found scattered over the hill-sides everywhere, or forming a compact mass of whited sepulchres, as at Amoy; or occupying a place of honour in the middle of a rice-field, as in the neighbourhood of Swatow. Different chapters in such a book might be filled with accounts of the graves themselves; their construction; the different styles used in different dynasties; the different styles used in different parts of the country at the present day; the different styles used by high officials, lower officials, and the common people; the inscriptions on the tomb-stones differing at different periods of history and even in different parts of the country at the present day; the different superstitions connected with the graves, the folklore, the worship paid at the tombs to the spirits of the deceased; the wonderful geomantic superstition which centres round the tomb of the deceased ancestor as the hope and dread of future generations (see FUNG SHUI [FENG SHUI]). Not a few chapters might be occupied with descriptions of the coffin to be put in the tomb, accounts of the procession to the tomb, and the funeral with all the varying customs for different parts of the country; while interesting pages might contain investigations as to how much of all the ceremonial has come down from a high antiquity and how much has grown on to the original system in the course of ages—how much is original ancestor-worship and how much is due to Buddhism and Taoism; all these would require a full treatment to do justice to the subject, and even then much of interest would have been left out. We cannot, therefore, in this article do more than thus point to some of the various aspects that the tomb presents itself to the Chinese in, and refer our readers to our articles on Ancestral Worship, Fung Shui, and Mourning, for a notice of one or two of the aspects mentioned above.

The best-known surviving imperial tombs are the mausolea of the Ming emperors at Nanking and to the north-west of Peking, and those of the Manchu (Ch'ing) rulers in Manchuria and Chihli province. Tomb-mounds and monuments of earlier dynasties also exist in some provinces, but they probably are the outer shells only, the interior of the tombs having been rifled, as far as is known, in all, or nearly all, cases.

References.—De Groot, *The Religious System of China;* Gray, *China,* i. 308-25; Williams, *Middle Kingdom,* ii. 246, 252; *Journ. N.C.B.R.A.S.*, N.S., vol. for 1925. Most books on China contain chapters or sections on this subject.

TOPSYTURVYDOM.—It is the unexpected that one must expect, especially in this land of topsyturvydom. The Chinese are not only remote from us with regard to position on the globe, but they are our opposites in almost every action and thought. It never does to judge how a Chinese would act under certain circumstances from what we ourselves would do if placed in similar conditions: the chances are that he would do the very actions we would never think of performing; think the very thoughts that would never occur to us; and say what no foreigner would ever think of uttering. He laughs when he tells you his father or mother, brother or sister, is dead; a bride that did not wail as if for the dead would be a fraud. He asks you if you have eaten your rice, instead of saying 'How do you do?' and locates his intellect in his stomach. For 'goodbye' he says 'walk slowly.' Instead of telling you to take heart and be brave when any danger threatens, he tells you to lessen your heart; he makes the most earnest enquiries, not only as to your health, but asks your age, and compliments you if you are old; he wishes to know what your salary or income is, what your rent is, and numberless other polite questions which we think impertinent. On the other hand, let no enquiry cross your lips as to the welfare of his wife; nor had you better ask after his daughters—his sons he will be glad to parade before you; but do not compliment him on the chubby cheeks and healthy looks of his baby boy, as any accident or disease happening to the youngster will be laid to your account. While you have doffed your hat on entering his house, he has put his on before receiving you. He shakes his own hands instead of clasping yours; he places you on his left as the seat of honour; and if he hands you anything he does so with two hands. He, perhaps, shows you with pride the set of coffin boards which his dutiful son has presented to him.

If we look at Chinese books, here again everything seems different: the end is the beginning and the beginning is the end; the lines of printing are vertical and not horizontal, as with us; the title is often written on the outside bottom edges of the books, as they are not stood up in rows in book-cases, but laid on the shelves one above the other; while the reader puts in his marker at the bottom of the page and not at the top; footnotes are on the top margin or occur in the body of the text, the title is on the edge, where the headings of the pages also appear, as well as their numbers; the edges are uncut and are intended to remain so, as the paper is only printed on one side, and the interior pages are blank. Sometimes two books are bound in one, but then the upper half of the page is taken up with one, and the lower half with the other, all the way through the book, Somewhat like the French *feuilleton* printed at the bottom of the newspaper in France. It is in the same way that he keeps his debit and credit accounts in his office or shop books, one on the upper half of the page and the other on the lower.

His classical works of poetry of ancient times, as well as of the great T'ang and Sung dynasties, are printed like prose, just as German hymn-books are.

In his dictionaries he uses no alphabet, but laying hold of 214 key words, he arranges his tens of thousands of words under these. At other times he arranges them by the termination of their sounds, so that *ling, ming, ting, sing,* would all come under one heading, just as if we were to class all our words ending in *er* together in one part of our dictionary, like a rhyming dictionary, or a terminal index to a telegraph code.

In the matter of dress we come again across curious examples of doing things in a different way from ours. The Chinese official rank was shown by different coloured buttons of various materials stuck on the top of the official hat; the mandarin's clothes were embroidered with animals and birds, front and back, for the same reason, and a peacock's and other feathers showed his honours—all these instead of epaulettes, gold-lace, and decorations—while a string of beads round his neck completed the 'great man's' effeminate appearance. The wearing of bracelets is not confined to women, men often have expensive jadestone ones on. Neither men nor women wear gloves, but their sleeves are so long, falling over their hands, as to be used as muffs in cold weather; these capacious sleeves also serve as pockets.

A Chinaman wore his hair on the back of his head as long as a woman's, but on the front it was all shaven off. By the hair on his face you may approximately judge his age; before forty-five or thereabouts he is clean shaved, after that he cultivates his moustache, and later in life he grows all he can, which is not much. The women, as well as the men, wear jackets and trousers, and the men long robes. As a general rule, the women wear socks, and the men often wear stockings. The men go with comparatively thin soles, and the large-footed women often with thick ones. Some of our ladies are (or were) foolish enough to tight-lace; the Chinese ladies bind (or bound) their feet. We blacken our shoes; the Chinese whiten the sides of their soles. We use our hands to play at battledore and shuttlecock; the Chinese have no battledore and kick the shuttlecock with their feet. Boys fly kits with us; they do also in China, but the finest kites are the property of grown-up men, who enjoy the flying of them as much as boys, if not more.

Black is mourning with us; white (or rather undyed material), grey, and blue, with the Chinese, and the shoes, as well as cap, hair, and clothes, all show it. Red is the sign of rejoicing, and is consequently used at marriages.

Babies are habitually carried on the back, nor does a gentleman or lady hesitate to accept a similar position when being landed from a boat through the mud. Most of the small boats are 'manned' by woman. Ladies smoke as well as gentlemen, and gentlemen fan themselves as well as the ladies.

The Chinese compass points to the south, not to the north, as with us, nor do they say north-west, north-east, south-east, and south-west; but, on the contrary, west-north, east-north, east-south, and west-south. On Chinese boats the cooking is done at the stern and not in a galley forward. They often haul their boats up on the shore stern foremost; their oars, instead of being in one piece, are in two, joined in the middle, a short end piece being put on at the handle, and, in contravention of our rules of rowing, one hand often caps it. They, as often as not, do not keep stroke in rowing, but each one pulls his own time; nor does a Chinaman ever think of walking in step, they follow each other, one after the other, like a flock of geese. The stone coolies, carrying heavy slabs of granite, persistently keep out of step, if we may be allowed the Irishism.

We have read of an exhibition in Western lands where a house was built upside down, and the attic built on the ground and the cellar up in the air. The Chinaman, however, does not do this, but he puts his ridge pole up first, suspended in the air and then he builds his house up to it.

But there seems to be no limit to the contrariety of the Chinese. He turns his names backforwards, as we do in our directories: the surnames first and the other names afterwards; and in the same way he transposes (according to our ideas) his titles of respect and relationship; for instead of saying His Lordship the Chief Justice, the Chinese he uses, if literally translated, would be Chief Justice His Lordship. Uncle Sam would be Sam Uncle, and Mr. Brown would be Brown Mr. There is one occasion when we put an official's titles after his name, and that is in a proclamation issued by him; here again the Chinese reverses his usual method and put all the titles first. and the official's name last. 'As regards their order of nobility, the Chinese offer another instance of their contrariness; not only . . . do a son's deeds ennoble his ancestors, but heredity is the exception, and extinction the rule.' He arranges his dates just the opposite to what we do ours, for he puts the year first, the month next, and the day last. He sometimes buys a little girl and brings her up in the house as a future bride for his son, who, in any case, has not the trouble of searching one out, for his father and mother will do that for him, sometimes even arranging a matrimonial alliance before he is born, on the contingency that he will prove to be a boy and that the other family will chance to have a girl. When a servant wishes to leave your employ, instead of telling you so, it often happens that he asks leave to return to the country, puts in a substitute, and never returns. When a Chinese wishes to consult you about any matter he generally sends a friend, and either does not come at all, or waits downstairs, to be ready if it is imperatively necessary for him to appear; and in the same way nearly everything is done through a friend, or go-between, or middle-man.

He turns his fractions upside down and, instead of saying four-sixths, says sixths-four.

Man is the beast of burden in a great part of China, and not only does he carry his fellow-man, but pigs are even carried by the coolies.

The blade of the saw is set at right angles to the frame, and the Chinese carpenter sits to his work, using his feet to hold the wood firm; he sticks his footrule in his stocking or down his back.

TORTURE.—Torture was divided in China into two classes: legal and illegal; what is permitted, and what is supposed not to be allowed. The rules are stated in the Penal Code of the late Manchu dynasty.

'The clauses under Section 1 of the Code describe the legal instruments of torture; they consist of three boards with proper grooves for compressing the ankles, and five round sticks for squeezing the fingers, to which may be added the bamboo; besides these, no instruments of torture are legally allowed, though other ways of putting the question are so common as to give the impression that some of them at least are sanctioned. Pulling or twisting the ears with roughened fingers, and keeping them in a bent position while making the prisoner kneel on chains, or making him kneel for a long time, are among the illegal modes. Striking the lips with sticks until they are nearly jellied, putting the hands in stocks before or behind the back, wrapping the fingers in oiled cloth to burn them, suspending the body by the thumbs and fingers, tying the hands to a bar under the knees, so as to bend the body double, and chaining by the neck close to a stone, are resorted to when the prisoner is contumacious. One magistrate is accused of having fastened up two criminals to boards by nails driven through their palms; one of them tore his hands loose and was nailed up again, which caused his death; using beds of iron, boiling water, red-hot spikes, and cutting the tendon Achilles are also charged against him, but the Emperor exonerated him on account of the atrocious character of the criminals. Compelling them to kneel upon pounded glass, sand, and salt mixed together, until the knees become excoriated, or simply kneeling upon chains is a lighter mode of the same infliction. . . Flogging is one of the five authorised punishments, but it is used more than any other means to elicit confession; the bamboo, rattan, cudgel, and whip are all employed. When death ensues, the magistrate reports that the criminal died of sickness, or hushes it up by bribing his friends, few of whom are ever allowed access within the walls of the prison to see and comfort the sufferers. From the manner in which such a result is spoken of it may be inferred that immediate death does not often take place from torture.'

It was not only the prisoner who was tortured; but the witnesses were also liable to be so treated; the prisoner to make him confess, without which he could not be punished; the witnesses to make them divulge what they were supposed to know, and were holding back. The fear that the lower officials were in of being reported by their superiors acted as a deterrent in some cases; but, notwithstanding this check, there was undoubtedly an immense amount of torture inflicted on poor humanity in China, when once within the clutches of the law. No wonder the Chinese dreaded the law and its minions: they had reason to do so. The mere incarceration in the loathsome cells attached to the yamêns was torture itself; and how much more this was aggravated by the racks and bambooings and hangings up by thumbs and big toes can be better imagined than described.

Torture was legally abolished after the establishment of the Republic, having been ameliorated by an Imperial edict in 1905, but is still at times resorted to by judges and magistrates.

References.—Williams, *Middle Kingdom*, i. 507-8; Gray, *China*, i. 32-8.

TRADE.—The Chinese are pre-eminently a trading race; 'their merchants are acute, methodical, sagacious, and enterprising, not over-scrupulous as to their mercantile honesty in small transactions, but in large dealings exhibiting that regard for character in the fulfilment of their obligations which extensive commercial engagements usually produce.'

In dealing with the trade of China, it may conveniently be divided into internal, or domestic, and foreign. Trade may be compared to the breath of prosperity. A nation that has little trade is in a backward state of development, and those nations which place few or no restrictions on the interchange of commodities, occupy a foremost place in the world's march of progress.

The volume of the internal trade of China is of course enormous. When one travels into the interior, especially in the vicinity of some large distributing centre like Canton, one is surprised at the constant succession of craft, sailing swiftly to remote towns and villages, laden with goods for local consumption. The natural facilities in the way of broad rivers have been fully availed of and added to by numerous canals, while footpaths connect all the inland towns and villages, and are traversed by carriers bearing loads of merchandise slung to poles thrown across their shoulders. In the North of China animals are used as beasts of burden, but, in the South, man fulfils that function.

Nor has the trade of China been simply a modern affair. From remote antiquity the Chinese have been true to their commercial instincts, and have not only been the civilisers of Eastern Asia, supplying them with their letters and literature; but they have also provided for their more material wants, and received in exchange the commodities which they required from the neighbouring nations. Nor did their trading voyages go no further than to their immediate neighbours; as they extended to India and even beyond (see CHINESE ABROAD). This trade with foreign lands was continued through successive dynasties, and to it has been added, during the last two or three centuries, the maritime trade with European countries, which has risen from small beginnings, till it has now attained vast proportions. A most interesting chapter in the world's history will be revealed when future investigations have added sufficient to the material, already gathered and published by patient scholars, to form a comprehensive survey of the commercial relations of this vast country, not only with her immediate neighbours, but with distant countries in Asia, and even with the Roman empire, while its more modern developments with Europe and America will not be found devoid of interest.

The Foreign Trade of China 'has been gradually growing since the days, when, in the forties, a few ships made one voyage each year to China in order to barter their cargoes, and has now become positively enormous. Moreover, it involves so many interests, and touches so many people, that those who have not studied the matter can form' no idea of its varied character and vastness.

When thus 'refreshing our memories, and informing our minds, of the tremendous volume of trade done with China by foreign countries, of which Great Britain is responsible for considerably more than one-half, we are, after all, only looking at the branches of the tree, with its rich foliage of leaves and burden of fruit. We have not yet looked, so to speak, at the soil and the roots which have produced the tree. Yet these must not be forgotten. In other words, we must not overlook the sources whence this enormous mass of cargo comes. We must look upon the almost countless number of human beings who are employed in the production thereof. Without noticing, for the moment, the destination of the exports, though this is really as important as the other, let us call to mind the many sources whence China's imports come. We shall only refer to a few specimens, but by so doing, when we multiply the number by ten, we shall see how many people are involved in the China trade and how important it is that in the arrangements about to be made, not only should every care be taken to protect it, but every facility be insisted on for its further development. The thousands of lamps, of which China now uses so many, are made in America, whilst most of the lamp glasses are made in Germany. Shirtings, calicoes and woollens are made in England, whilst cotton yarns come from India. Kerosene comes from America, Dutch East Indies, and Russia. In these two or three brief references almost all the civilised world is involved. Moreover, the different classes of persons, whose living, more or less, depends on China trade, will appear evident, when we recall the fact that during 1899 no less than 2,566 musical boxes were imported into Shanghai alone. Indeed, the Customs report will show that the number and different classes of workers interested in the making and the receiving of goods from China, were almost uncountable.

'Much might be added, pointing out the possibility of gradually introducing new industries into China, which in course of time would benefit all parties. We need only point to the large area of practically valueless land in the North of Kwangtung province. Huge flocks of sheep could, without doubt, be reared thereon, which would supply the people with much acceptable food and necessary clothing.'

Doubtless, in years to come, this or similar projects will be tried.

There was a great expansion in the Foreign Trade of China in 1899 and the first half of 1900, but the Boxer disturbances and the resultant hostilities with the Foreign Powers acted not only as an estoppel on all trade at the two Northern Ports but affected, more or less seriously, other of the Treaty Ports, as well; but the recuperative energy of the Foreign Trade of China is great, and the unrest and uncertainty, incident to the war in the North, over its vitality was quickly shown.

[The following paragraphs, referring to the trade during the last decade of the nineteenth century, are of interest in comparison with the later developments described below.]

With the end of 1900 another decade in the modern compilation of statistics under the cognisance of the Imperial Maritime

Customs is available, and the following points are worthy of attention.

The importation of cotton piece goods has remained practically stationary, though some items shown total up a smaller figure than before, and others have advanced. The advance of American Trade is evinced in drills, jeans, shirtings and cotton, flannel and lastings; the class of English goods of this nature generally have shown no advance. Japanese cotton goods are in favour, Indian and Japanese yarns have made rapid headway. Woollen goods and metals are stationary, candles, cement, clocks and watches, aniline dyes, windowglass, paints, and perfumery are rising in demand, by gradual steps. Flour, kerosene, matches, and soap arrive in much larger quantities every year.

Not only will the future development of railways afford a better means of communication and bring distant parts of the country within easy reach of the ports where cargo is landed from foreign parts, and which are now almost inaccessible to goods on account of the difficulty and cost of transit and the dangers from robbers and pirates *in transitu*, but the capital employed for their construction will afford the means to purchase the foreign goods ardently desired by the native.

In 1890 the Foreign Goods imported into China were valued at Hk. Tls. 134,640,288 (£34,922,320). In 1899 they were 223,791,888 (£34,734,365). They rose to 280,907,296 (£42,282,402) in 1900; to 462,964,894 (£44,608,075) in 1910; to 762,250,230 (£296,959,985) in 1920; and to 906,122,439 (£179,100,763) in 1921; the sterling values varying with the sterling quotation for the Haekuan tael.

As to exports, nearly every year shows a large increase in nearly every article. Bristles, fans, feathers, hemp, hides, mats and matting, oils, rhubarb, sesamum seed, skins, tobacco, and wool, all are increasing in the quantity sent out of the country. Silk, excepting steam-filature silk, is not doing well, the disease amongst the worms being against it.

Black tea is in a bad way, green tea holds its own, and brick is doing better than it did. The statistics published by the I.M. Customs do not, however, include the considerable trade across the Russian frontier, and they take no cognisance of the trade with Tibet. The Export Trade was valued at Hk. Tls. 100,947,849 (£24,816,346) in 1891 and in 1900 it was 158,996,752 (£24,677,621). In 1913 it was 25,278,000 (£3,370,400); in 1920, 8,548,000 (£2,813,716); and in 1921, 12,227,000 (£2,139,725).

The record of the Trade for 1901 is a very good one indeed, the total revenue being Hk. Tls. 25,537,574, the only year previously exceeding it being 1899, with 26,661,460. The Statistical Secretary writes:—

'It was to be expected that the figures would compare favourably with those for 1900, but even when compared with 1899 we find increases under Import Duties, Coast Trade Duty, Tonnage Dues, and Transit Dues. There was a falling off in Export Duty and in Opium Duty and Likin; the former is of no significance, as it was due to exceptional circumstances. . . . From the 11th November the Import Duties were under the provisions of the Peace Protocol, calculated on an effective 5 per cent. basis, but there was no time for the adjustment to add much to the year's collection. With the additional Import Duties, and the opening up of so much country by railways, it seems not unreasonable to hope that the collection during 1902 may not fall far short of thirty millions of taels.

'In spite of the adverse circumstances alluded to above, the year was a good one for Foreign Trade, especially as regards Imports, and the total estimated value of Imports and Exports was Hk. Tls. 437,959,675, higher than any other year except 1899. The northern ports showed a satisfactory recovery, although Tientsin did not altogether regain its former position. There was no rush of Imports to escape the increased Duty, except at one or two of the southern ports, and the trade was thoroughly healthy. The future depends very much on an increase in the trade and the course of exchange. Heavy taxation to pay indemnities will to that extent diminish the purchasing power of the people, and unless Exports are stimulated, silver must be exported or Imports must decline. . . . The value of Imports exceeded the value of Exports by Hk. Tls. 49,916,706 and for first time for many years, there was a net export of silver to the value of Hk. Tls. 6,097,802. The explanation why more silver was not exported to pay for the difference between Imports and Exports is that an unusually large proportion of Imports came in during the last three months and were not paid for when the year closed, and also that China never has to pay for part of the goods received. Remittances from Chinese emigrants abroad, contributions to missionary societies, expenditure on Foreign troops and officials, expenses of exploitation by sundry syndicates, and of railway construction with Foreign capital, as well as value in China's favour of the frontier trade across the Russian border and into Thibet, would probably be found to cover the difference as well as providing for other obligations. The net value of gold exported amounting to Hk. Tls. 6,635,313, must also be taken into consideration. The principal fact to bear in mind, however, would seem to be that the Chinese, in spite of their difficulties, were able to spend twice as much silver on Foreign goods as they did in 1891.'

As to foreign shipping entering Chinese ports (in the decade above-mentioned), the British, notwithstanding the then keen competition of the Germans, still held a preponderating enormous advantage both as regards entries and tonnage, and largely increased it during the decade.

As far as entries into port are concerned, the British shipping in 1890 figured to the extent of 1,836 in 1890, and in 1900 the numbers were 3,335. The tonnage was 2,031,608 and 3,239,924, for the two periods respectively. The German entries were in 1890, 393, in 1900, 433; tonnage, 262,480 in 1890, and 637,653 in 1900. It will be seen from these figures how rapidly the Germans had advanced in these respects. Next after Germans came the Chinese, who, though making an immense number more of entries, had not proportionately increased the tonnage—entries in 1890, 382, in 1900 1,485; tonnage in 1890, 205,667, in 1900, 223,255.

The Japanese came fourth, with also a very large advance in the decennial period, viz., 1890, entries 267, in 1900, 751; tonnage in 1890, 219,263; in 1900, 774,481. With the coastwise trade in foreign bottoms, the British again led well, the figures in 1890 being for entries 6,632, and in 1900, 8,080; and for tonnage, 6,025,347 in 1890, and 8,303,336 in 1900. In entries in the same trade the Germans are again rapidly pulling up, as in 1890 they were 677, and in 1900, 1,334, while the tonnage in 1890 was 410,940 and in 1900, 1,381,467. The Chinese also made 15,331 entries in 1900, as against 4,689 in 1890; and the tonnage in 1900 was 3,674,917, as against 2,944,033 in 1890. In 1917 the entries (not including junks) were 46,422 (tonnage 18,517,957); in 1920 the figures were 50,791 (tonnage 23,632,198); and in 1921, 54,817 (tonnage 27,063,389). The Japanese increase in this branch of the carrying trade is very large; for whereas in 1890 there were only 46 entries put down to their credit, they had increased to the comparatively enormous number of 1,712; and the tonnage, of course, also shows a large increase, for in 1890 it was 33,225 and in 1900, 1,165,879. In 1917 the figures were 22,454 (tonnage 24,581,647); in 1920, 25,152 (tonnage 28,191,592); and in 1921, 25,385 (tonnage 31,738,783). The total tonnage employed in the foreign trade entries and clearances, was 48,416,000 tons, Great Britain contributing 54 per cent., Germany 16, China 13, Japan 11, America 2, Russia 1, and all other countries 1 per cent.

The increase under the German flag, as well as that to be noted in the case of the British and American, is further accounted for by the disappearance in June. . . . 'of the Chinese ensign from all steamers on the coast.' This was on account of the war. In 1917 the total tonnage entered and cleared was 86,907,049; in 1920, 104,266,695; and in 1921, 114,619,544.

The French also have shared in a large increase in both the foreign carrying trade and the coastwise carrying trade. Foreign trade entries for 1890, were 63, ten years after, 376;

tonnage 114,479 at the beginning of the decade and at the end 280,539. In 1917 the figures were 328 (tonnage 584,891); in 1920, 603 (tonnage, 852,979); and in 1921, 1,240 (tonnage 1,221,758). In the coastwise trade the figures (for 1890 and 1900) were 24 and 115, and 4,500 and 50,923 respectively. In 1921 they were 765 and 474,007 respectively.

The Danish and Spanish ships would appear from the statistics to be either run off the China coast through competition, or nearly so; for though there was a slight rise in the tonnage trade as regards the Danish, yet the other figures all showed a large fall; the Spanish had none of the foreign carrying trade in 1900, as against 14 entries in 1890, though on the other hand they had 6 entries and 269 tons in 1900, as against none in 1890. There were no Spanish entries registered in 1917-21. In 1917, 83 Danish vessels, with tonnage of 142,238 entered and cleared; in 1920, 78 (tonnage 184,164); and in 1921, 84 (tonnage 235,342)

All the other figures pertaining to other nationalities show an increase in the period (1890-1900), the totals for all nations in 1890 being entries under the heading of Foreign Trade 3,114; in 1900, 6,948; tonnage 2,944,092 and 5,539,404; while in the Coastwise Trade the figures are — entries 12,243 in 1890, and in 1900, 27,431; the tonnage in 1890 being 9,490,316 and in 1900, 14,850,166. In 1920 there were 82,171 entries (tonnage 57,579,184); in 1921 the figures were 68,890 (tonnage 39,794,890).

We will now proceed to take the Treaty Ports seriatim, making a few remarks on the trade of each in 1900, commencing with Newchwang, the most northerly. The total Exports added to the total net Foreign and Chinese Imports for the years 1920-1 for the ports mentioned are given at the end of this article for the sake of comparison.

The year started with brilliant prospects 'Wonderful as had been the progress during the preceding year, there was every indication that it was to be exceeded,' both exports and imports arriving and departing in large quantities. Over 2,000,000 piculs of bean cake were exported, and melon seeds and medicines were in excess of previous years; the season was favourable, bubonic plague was absent; but suddenly the Boxer troubles arose, and trade virtually stopped.

Chefoo is again another port which the Boxer troubles affected seriously. Chinese merchants and labourers left the port, the Boxers threatening to kill all connected with Foreigners, and a coolie riot occurred, fortunately quelled before ill results ensued. 'Inland waters steam traffic has doubled,' and 'silk filatures are increasing in number.' What Chefoo requires is a railway to connect it with the capital of the province.

At Kiaochow, the German port, the unsettled state of the country, due to rumours of war from the North, was a disturbing element and prevented the possibility of a bumper years being reported. But on the resumption of trade there was a sharp demand for cottons, yarn, and kerosene, while a new line was opened in exports in straw braid at the expense of Chefoo. A famine season affected the supply of salted pigs, as the peasants not having sufficient for themselves were not able to rear their pigs.

Chungking, in the heart of the Szchuan Province, was seriously affected by the war in the North, and business went to the dogs.

Ichang did better, all things considered, while Shashi's trade was almost double of any year, due to the drought and shipping facilities offered, when native boats were not available for the traffic.

Yochow's first year of being open to foreign trade is not an encouraging one. Its selection as a Treaty Port appears an unfortunate one, for one thing, and the hampering restrictions of the Inland Waters Rules are another factor telling against it. In Hankow again, the uprecedented prosperity with which the year commenced in all branches of trade was checked by the Boxer war, and almost paralysed. Some 70,000 piculs of antimony were exported to Europe. Only a third of the brick tea sent to Kalgan reached its destination, and no trace of it is discoverable.

In Kewkiang the same old story is told of the disastrous consequences resulting from the war in the North—'a considerable falling-off as compared with the splendid figures of the two preceding years. A few items are reported as showing an increase,' notably beans and peas, which show an extraordinary advance of 108,669 piculs, due to the stoppage of trade at Newchwang, and the consequent enhanced demand in the southern ports.

Almost a standstill of trade, owing to the troubles in the North, in the summer in Wuhu; the revenue from this port would have been as great if not greater than in 1899, but for the above cause.

1900 was the first complete year of Nanking as a Treaty Port. There was a panic amongst the merchants, owing to the same causes that affected the trade at the other Treaty Ports. There was consequently 'an utter stagnation throughout all branches of the silk industry. 77 per cent. of the Exports here are silk products of one sort or another.'

In Chinkiang the loss was 2½ million taels for the year 1900, as compared with 1899; but this port did not suffer as much as might have been expected. Strange to say, the Mexican dollar appreciated in value, as every one wished to realise owing to the general uneasiness disorganising trade, and the native banks would not part with their money. 1901, however, showed, a reassuring buoyancy in trade.

In Shanghai, on the whole, the storm was weathered remarkably well, all things considered, merchants and traders adapting themselves to the altered circumstances of the case. Cotton mills did badly, having abnormally adverse circumstances to contend with. Were 'lighter taxation afforded, these Chinese mills could easily compete with their Indian and Japanese rivals.' The Commissioner of Customs in his report calls attention to a circumstance which shows what a necessity kerosene has become to the Chinese; for, 'notwithstanding the loss of the northern trade [due to the war], deliveries were only about 10 per cent. short of those of 1899.' The Russian product maintains its popularity; American oil dropped from 26,438,138 to 19 million odd gallons, while the Sumatra article showed an increase of a million odd gallons. Kerosene is such a bright light compared with pea-nut oil and the tiny wick formerly used so largely. Notwithstanding the general business integrity of the Chinese mercantile class, which compares favourably with that of the Japanese, the Chinese trader is not above resorting at times, like his Western contemporary in Europe, to tricks of trade. The practice of putting inferior quality of goods in the middle of straw bundles, tends to drive this branch of trade to Japan, where the Japanese turn out, it appears, a reliable article. What a disquieting effect the war caused, may be gathered from the wholesale departure of natives from this large Treaty Port; for, though far distant from the seat of operations, 'it is estimated that something like 80,000 persons left the port.' In 1901 the trade improved by 20 per cent.

An upheaval of business and a panic is reported from Soochow, while Ningpo reports a certain depression in trade, and Hangchow, that the trade suffered, though the Customs Revenue only declined 10 per cent., and in Wenchow the trade 'was influenced to a great extent by the troubles in the north of China'; 'from July onwards, there was very little demand for the principal Exports.'

In Santuao, the year was 'an unventful one, from a commercial point of view.'

In Foochow the year 1900 was a disastrous one, the outbreak in the North being one of the factors, and a flood which paralysed trade another. The Swedish matches, which poured into China a few years ago, gave way to the Japanese article, and the latest development in Foochow and other parts of China has been the ousting of the last by the native manufacture. 'The great increase in the production of both Indian and Ceylon Tea has seriously interfered with the China Tea Trade.' In the season 1899-1900, Foochow exported 16 million lbs. odd of tea to Europe, and 6 million odd to the Colonies. In the next season this small amount had still fallen to 11 million odd and 6 million odd. Shanghai and Hankow sent in 1900-1901, 14 million lbs. odd of tea, a falling-off of well on for 1½ millions on the previous year. Canton and Macao in 1900-1901, sent 3,818,000 a falling-off of more than 2 million lbs. on 1899. There was a total of 52,486,000 lbs. for the season 1900-01 from Shanghai, Foochow, and Amoy (Formosan Tea) to Canada and America, being an increase of 7,495,000 lbs. Such enormous quantities of tea were in stock in London, Hamburg, Melbourne, and Sydney, the chief distributing markets, that the lowest prices for tea ever known were reached. In Australia, tea selling in China at 7d. a lb. was sold for 5¼d. to 5½d. a lb. Something similar happened in America, but from a different cause, as the following extract from the Customs Report will show:—

'From China last season there was an increase of 5,381,000 lbs. to America, brought about by international complications. American importers were under the impression that the unrest prevailing would stop the Tea trade, so they made haste to buy all they could in advance. The result is that the market is now overstocked, and that great losses have resulted in consequence. New York circulars quote Congou at 7¾ cents. per lb., which costs 9 to 10 cents. out here.'

Locally-grown opium has increased enormously:—

'As the Native looks to the profit to be reaped from his land, he, in many cases, turns to the poppy, which yields him 300 or 400 per cent. more than wheat would. The cheapness of the Native drug, as compared with the Foreign, commends its use to the Native, who either uses it pure or mixed with the Foreign drug.'

In 1901 the Foochow Customs Revenue was the smallest for ten years.

In Amoy the trade in 1900 'was unremunerative and unsatisfactory all round.' The kerosene oil trade continued to expand. For the first time since Amoy has been a Treaty Port, nearly sixty years, 'no Amoy-grown Tea was purchased by foreign buyers for the home markets, and thus an important commodity, the export of which 25 years ago, amounted to upwards of 9 million pounds, finally disappears.' The Reports call attention to the continuous demand for morphia, which has increased thirty-five times what it was ten years ago, reaching for the year 1900 the total of 16,776 ounces. The native-grown opium is also increasing in quantity, the local production being estimated at 8,000 piculs, being over 30 per cent. more than in the previous year. Both cultivation of the poppy and the yield of opium are on the increase rapidly, and there appears to be very little doubt will continue to increase in the future, and before long it is expected that the province of Fukien will be independent of all other sources for opium. It may be here remarked that the people of Amoy are great opium smokers. Besides the 8,000 piculs already mentioned, about 4,000 piculs were brought by land from Ssŭch'uan, and 241 by steamer, 1,250 piculs from Yünnan, and some further amount by junk from Wênchow. In 1901 the Revenue showed a slight improvement.

In Swatow, strange to say, the year's figures compare satisfactorily with those of the year before, for not only was there the war in the North, but an incipient rebellion in the South. With all this the Customs Revenue suffered only a fall of rather less than 10 per cent. The Commissioner makes the following remarks:—

'Woollen goods nowhere appeal to the Chinese. . . . Nor do the people seem to need metals, three-quarters of a million taels only being paid for them. Old iron (*i.e.*, worn-out cart-tires horseshoes, and such things) supplies the small needs of local blacksmiths. Tin is used in making the well-known Swatow pewterware.' 'Though [American flour is] nearly 10 per cent. dearer than the native product, it is preferred, as superior in colour and fineness and for its freedom from grit.' 'The export of fresh eggs grows steadily, and the value for 1900 reached Hk. Tls. 128,000, representing 18 million eggs.'

The trade improved in 1901.

At Wuchow 'a wave of restlessness, succeeded by nervousness, swept along trade routes from Wuchow north to the capital, and west to Nanning. Trade was affected between June and September, particularly in July and August, when business was almost at a standstill.' 'The check in the Kerosene Oil business is reported to be due to the wide distribution of an anti-Foreign placard which appeared in July. This placard deprecated the use of [Kerosene] Oil as being made from human bone ashes, and harmful to the eyes. The use of Ground-nut Oil, on which the prosperity of the people largely depended, was urged, and a good harvest with higher prices promised. Strangely enough the autumn crop was good, and prices rose; many "stupid people" threw away their Kerosene Oil, others hid lamps and stock, and importers say they must take steps to counteract the harm thus done to the trade. But

Kerosene will doubtless win its own battle, on account of its convenience and cheapness.'

There was a large export of mouse deer-skins, 63,000 pieces; there is a large demand for star aniseed; and a company has been formed to cultivate the castor-oil plant.

Under the Report on Samshui are included Kongmun, Shiuhing, and Takhing. The trade was less by two-thirds of a million of taels. But in 1901 trade was prosperous, and the figures of the Customs' Revenue amounted to a million taels more than in 1900.

Canton does not seem to have been so largely affected by the unrest and disturbances as might have been supposed. The exports are silk, tea, cassia, matting, sugar, chinaware, fresh eggs, fruit, vegetables, black-wood furniture, human hair, medicines, prepared tobacco, etc. In 1901, the I.M. Customs having taken over the Native Customs Department, the Revenue was well on for 61 million Hk. Tls.

At the Kowloon Customs the value of the trade was less by 9½ million taels than in the record year 1899.

'Troubles in the North, and local troubles in the Province have caused a feeling of uncertainty in the minds of the Commercial class, and made it very cautious in business transactions,' was the Report from Lappa; but 1901 appears to have been a record year.

Kiungchow suffered severely from the plague, 5,000 dying in the city. This, with small-pox and the dislocation of trade from the troubles in the North, all had a disastrous effect. As in other parts of China, ground-nut oil is being superseded by kerosene.

At Pakhoi the same reiterated story of disturbances in the North affecting the trade.

In Lungchow, notwithstanding all the disturbing elements, the year 1900 was a good one from a Customs point of view. In Mengtsz the year's transactions were, on the whole, satisfactory, while in Szemao it had been a gloomy year, and in Yatung trade 'experienced a "setback,"' unsettled times and disease being responsible for this.

Tientsin is 'the second largest port in China whose trade has doubled itself during the last ten years [this was written in 1900], and is capable of enormous development. No port in China has increased in trade in the same ratio in the corresponding time.' The Returns for the first half of 1902 showed that the trade had progressed, the totals being Hk. Tls. 7,992,394. In 1901 the total for the same half year was Hk. Tls. 6,440,160, and in 1900 Hk. Tls. 6,385,596.

What has been written above deals mainly with the foreign exports and the import trade of China, though goods sent from one treaty port of China to another, etc., are included in the Returns, as such goods are carried in foreign bottoms and have to pass the Maritime Customs.

The value of the whole trade (*i.e.* Net Foreign and Chinese Imports and Exports) of the above-mentioned ports, etc., for the years 1920-1 is shown in the subjoined table:—

PORT, etc.	1920. *Hk. Tls.*	1921. *Hk. Tls.*
Newchuang	46,129,768	57,364,464
Tientsin	173,482,542	224,779,202
Chefoo	37,838,877	55,575,867
Kiaochou	67,584,110	81,962,027
Chungking	35,429,409	52,115,511
Ichang	9,154,066	4,341,809
Shasi	7,567,551	7,780,037
Yochow	11,556,101	13,449,540
Ch'angsha	32,973,476	29,545,544
Hankow	169,951,530	173,546,774
Kiukiang	48,416,293	43,457,565
Wuhu	40,144,619	32,992,971
Nanking	53,323,696	45,134,492
Chinkiang	28,836,607	27,507,564
Shanghai	511,915,033	511,774,463
Soochow	18,314,722	19,376,987
Ningpo	28,407,884	34,416,836
Wenchow	4,860,246	8,859,854
Hangchow	19,968,643	22,216,913
Santuao	2,238,403	1,985,869
Foochow	25,612,810	33,020,688
Amoy	22,299,335	30,970,060
Swatow	63,853,119	82,121,489
Wuchow	19,175,716	15,531,140
Samshui	4,900,593	5,965,028
Kongmoon	6,588,479	8,236,251
Canton	140,814,317	165,232,378
Kowloon	41,222,995	72,711,446
Lappa	17,983,235	30,854,147
Kiungchow	5,822,072	7,491,672
Pakhoi	4,123,314	4,819,656
Lungchow	88,722	85,552
Mêngtzŭ	22,226,143	18,321,246
Ssŭmao	346,970	301,322
Ch'inwangtao	17,180,516	22,447,055
Lungk'ou	3,968,089	5,871,878
Wanhsien	3,875,695	7,683,776
Nanning	7,985,856	4,903,334
T'êngyüeh	5,647,850	4,946,784
Aigun	2,476,825	4,545,353
Sansing	4,916,614	6,445,813
Manchouli	4,264,440	3,521,612
Harbin	11,368,888	18,343,395

PORT, etc	1920.	1921.
	Hk. Tls.	*Hk. Tls.*
Suifênho	10,057,815	20,704,036
Hunchun	779,283	1,446,886
Lungchingtsun . . .	2,233,651	3,056,037
Antung	63,071,523	63,304,457
Tatungk'ou	46,652	55,007

The value of goods imported by China during 1923 was Hk. Tls. 948,633,920. The following table summarises the value of exports of China's produce during the years 1914 to 1923.

Year.	*Hk. Tls.*
1914	356,226,629
1915	418,861,164
1916	481,797,366
1917	462,931,630
1918	485,883,031
1919	630,809,411
1920	541,631,300
1921	601,255,537
1922	654,891,933
1923	752,917,416

References.—The history of the foreign trade with China will be found in Williams's *Middle Kingdom*, and interesting accounts of this branch of the subject will be found in different books on China as well as in papers scattered through the *China Review*. See Articles in this book on Chinese Abroad, Tea, Silk, Opium, etc. For an account of ancient trade, see *China and the Roman Orient; Researches into their Ancient and Mediæval Relations as represented in Old Chinese Record*, by F. Hirth, Ph.D.

TREATY PORTS.—The Treaty Ports in China are so called from having been designated by treaties, entered into between England and other Foreign Powers on the one part, and China on the other, as places where foreign merchants shall be allowed to reside and trade. The first of these treaties was that of 1842, signed at Nanking, and consequently known as the Nanking Treaty. By it, the five cities of Canton, Amoy, Foochow, Ningpo, and Shanghai, were declared to be treaty ports. By the Treaty of Tientsin, so called owing to its having been signed there in 1858 (though ratified at Peking in 1860), the additional ports of Newchwang, Têngchow (Chefoo), T'aiwan (Formosa), Ch'ao-chow (Swatow), and Kiungchow, were opened to foreign trade. By the Chefoo Convention, signed at that port in 1876, though not ratified till 1886 in London, 'Ich'ang in the province of Hupeh, Wuhu in Anhui, Wênchôw, in Chêkiang, and Pei-hai' (Pakhoi in the local pronunication) in Kuangtung, were opened to trade and made Consular stations. By the Chungking Commercial Convention, concluded in February, 1890, it was arranged that Chungking in Ssŭch'uan should be a Treaty Port, but cargoes have to go in native boats, owned by natives or foreigners, until Chinese-owned steamers ply as far up the

Yangtzŭ as that city, when British steamers may do likewise (which they have since done—in 1898). By the Chefoo Convention Tat'ung and Nganching [Anking or Anch'ing], in the province of Anhui, Hukau, in Kiangsi, Wusüeh, Luch'ikou, and Shashih, in Hukuang, all on the Yangtzŭ, though not considered treaty ports, were allowed to be used as stopping places by steamers on that river, but native boats are employed to land and ship the cargo and passengers. By the Burma Frontier Treaty the West River was what is styled 'opened to trade' on the 4th of June, 1897, and two ports on it made treaty ports, Samshui and Wuchou-fu, and four ports of call established, viz., the towns of Kongmoon and Kamchuk, and the cities of Shiuhing and Takhing. In 1899 Santuao also came into the list of treaty ports. By the Commercial Treaty of the 5th Sept., 1902, four new ports—Ch'angsha, in Hunan, Ngankin [Anking], in Anhuei, Wanhsien, in Ssŭch'uan, and Waichou, in Kuangtung, are named as treaty ports, to be opened in 1904, and also Kongmoon. The first and last have since been made Treaty ports.

The above is what the English Government has done. The French, by their Treaty of 1858 (ratified in 1860), mention, in addition to some of the ports in the English treaties, Nanking as an open port, and it was supposed to 'enjoy the same privileges as Canton, Shanghai, Ningpo, and Foochow.' However, Nanking was not an open port until the 1st of May, 1899, although specified as such, though formal opening could doubtless have been claimed at pleasure by the French Government. By the Convention of Peace between France and China, signed in 1860, Tientsin, in the province of Chihli, is made a treaty port.

Again, by the Treaty between France and China, signed 9th June, 1885, provision was made for two more places to possess similar privileges to the Treaty Ports, though situated inland near the French possessions in Tongking; and by the Subsequent Trade Regulations for the Annam frontier, jointly determined on by France and China, signed in 1886, it was agreed that two places should be so opened; these two places are named in the Additional Convention between France and China of 1887, they are Lungchou in Kuangsi, Mêngtzŭ in Yünnan, and another place, Manghao, is also put in the same category.

'Under the provisions of the Convention between France and China signed at Peking on the 20th June, 1895, a Vice-Consulate was established on the 29th October, 1895, at Tunghsing, a port on the coast and Chinese frontier, some 80 miles west of Pakhoi and opposite the village of Moncay in Tonkin, the French Consul at Pakhoi representing his country at Tunghsiang as well.

'In accordance with the stipulations contained in the third paragraph of the "Gérard Supplementary Frontier Convention of 1895" Szemao was opened to the frontier trade on the 2nd January, 1897.'

'Under the provisions of the [same] Supplementary Convention between China and France . . . a French Consulate was opened at Szemao early in August, 1890, and a Vice-Consulate subordinate to the Mêngtsz Consulate, was established on the 22nd August at Hokau, a small village opposite Laokai on the left bank of the Red River, at its junction with the Nan-hsi River.'

We next come to the part taken by Germany in extorting concessions from China: in the Treaty between Prussia and China, signed in 1861 (ratified in 1863), the names of Treaty Ports are set out in Article 6, and the riverine ports of Chinkiang, Kiukiang, and Hankow appear in addition to those already at that time granted to England and France. By the Supplementary Convention between Germany and China, signed in 1860 (ratified the following year), German ships are allowed to touch at Woosung, in the province of Kiangsu, to take in or discharge merchandise intended for, or coming from, Shanghai.

Besides all these must be mentioned Whampoa (locally pronounced Wong-po), the port of Canton, now shorn of all its ancient glory.

'By a new convention with China,' it is stated that 'Russia is to be allowed to establish consulates in Central China, Mongolia, and Manchuria. The main purpose of these consulates is believed to be the prosecution of Russian trade in these regions.'

Japan, profiting by her war with China, amongst other matters, procured the opening of several other treaty ports to trade. By the Treaty between China and Japan, signed on 17th April, 1895, at Shimonoseki, and ratified at Chefoo on 8th May, 1895, by Article 6, the following places were opened to 'trade, residence, industries, and manufactures,' viz. Shashih, in Hupei; Chungking, in Ssŭch'uan; Suchow, in Kiangsu; and Hangchow, in Chêkiang (port opened in 1896); and by the same Article 'steam navigation for vessels under Japanese flag on the Upper Yangtzŭ River from Ichang to Chungking,' and 'on the Woosung River and the Canal, from Shanghai to Suchow and Hangchow.' In the Protocol made at Peking 19th October, 1896, to the Treaty of Commerce and Navigation between China and Japan (made at Peking on the 21st July, 1896), sites for special Japanese settlements at Shanghai, Tientsin, Amoy, and Hankow, are provided for, in addition to special Japanese settlements to be formed at the places newly opened to commerce, as stated above. China announced, on the 5th April, 1898, the opening to trade of three ports, viz., Funing (opened 8th May, 1899), in Fukien, Yochow on the Tungt'ing Lake, and Chinwangtao, [properly, Ch'inhuang Tao], near Shanhaikuan. These were opened in 1899, Santu being a treaty port in the Bay of Samsah in the Fukien province, was opened in 1899. Woosung has also been made a treaty port. Szemao was opened to the frontier trade in 1897, in accordance with the Gérard General Supplementary Frontier Convention of 1895.

The Chinese Government opened the West River and several ports to trade, on the 3rd June, 1897, under the Special Article of the British Treaty of 4th February, 1897. These ports are four in number, viz., Kongmoon and Kamchuk, Shiuhing and Takhing. The two treaty ports opened on the West River under the same Article are Samshui and Wuchow.

The ratification of the Burma Agreement, exchanged on the 5th June, 1897, allows the settlement of British subjects at Szŭmao and Momein or Shunning-fu.

Nanning, in the Kuangsi province, with a population of 120,000, was made a treaty port by the treaty with Great Britain of 1897.

A writer thus sums up the incidents that led to the acquisition of the rights to use the Treaty Ports, etc.:—

'Outrages on subjects of powerful states . . . led to the first war of 1842, and the opening of the five ports. A renewal of these outrages led to the second and third wars, and the opening of the northern and Yangtsze ports. The massacres in Szchuen and Fukien led to still further demands, and the attempts to oust the Japanese from Korea only ended in the loss of Formosa and Shingking. Outrages in Shantung led to the establishment of Germany in Shantung, and this to a military occupation by Russia of Manchuria and Liaotung, the cession of Weihaiwei to England, and, as a counterpoise, of Kwongchaú to France.'

We have prepared the following table showing the position and other particulars about the different treaty ports, ports of call, etc., trusting that it may prove of interest to our readers. It must be remembered that the attempt to give the population of a Chinese city or town is often a mere guess on the part of those who state it, and, at the very best, rather uncertain; also that the actual opening of the ports often took place from one to forty or more years later than the date of the agreements between the Governments concerned or the issue of the decrees by which the opening was sanctioned.

TREATY PORTS.

Province.	Port.	Date of Opening by Treaty or Decree.	Population.	Remarks.
Shêngking	Newchuang	1858	60,000	On River Liao, 13 miles from mouth. The port is Yingk'ou.
	Antung	1903	90,000	Near Japanese (Corean)
	Tatungk'ou	,,	4,200	,, ,, [frontier.
	Mukden	,,	178,000	
	Fênghuang	1905	....	
	Liaoyang	1915	....	
	Hsinmênfu	1905	....	
	T'iehling	,,	....	
	T'ungkiang-tzŭ	,,	....	
	Fak'umên	,,	....	
Kirin	Kirin	1915	....	
	Ch'ang-ch'un (K'uanchêng tzŭ)	,,	....	
	Harbin	1905	150,400	
	Ninguta	1909	....	
	Hunchun	1905	3,800	Near Russian frontier.
	Sansing	,,	1,400	
	Suifênho	1895	4,300	Near Russian frontier.
	Lungching-tsun	1905	3,200	
	Chützŭchieh	1909	....	
	Toutaokou	,,	....	
	Paitsaokou	,,	....	
Heilung-kiang	Tsitsihar	1905	....	
	Hailar	,,	....	
	Aigun	,,	15,000	Near Russian frontier.
	Manchouli	,,	11,000	On ,, ,,
Sinkiang	Kashgar	1860	70,000	
Tibet	Yatung (Darjiling)	1893	—	
	Gartok	1904	....	Source of the Indus
	Gyangtzŭ	,,	....	
Chihli	Ch'inwang-tao	1898	3,000	Ice-free port, 10 miles west of Shanhaikuan.
	Tientsin	1860	100,000	On Peiho.
Shantung	Chefoo	1858	54,000	Chinese name Yent'ai.
	Kiaochou		....	
	Chinan		....	
	Chouts'un		....	
	Weihsien		....	
	Lungk'ou		....	
Kiangsu	Shanghai	1842	1,500,000	At junction of Hwangpo and Woosung Rivers, 24 miles from sea.
	Woosung	1898	35,000	12 miles from sea, on Woosung River. Was made a port of call in 1861.
	Soochow	1895	500,000	60 miles west of Shanghai.
	Chinkiang	1858	128,000	On Yangtzŭ, 150 miles from mouth, at junction of Grand Canal.
	Nanking	1858	392,000	On S. bank of Yangtzû, 45 miles beyond Chinkiang.
Anhuei	Wuhu	1870	126,000	282 miles from sea, on Yangtzŭ.
Kiangsi	Kiukiang	1858	70,000	On Yangtzŭ, 466 miles from esa, near outlet of P'oyang Lake.

TREATY PORTS.—*Continued.*

Province.	Port.	Date of Opening by Treaty or Decree	Population.	Remarks.
Hupei	Hankow	1858	1,000,000	River Han, at its junction with the Yangtzŭ 600 miles from Shanghai.
	Shasi	1895	105,000	836 miles from sea, on Yangtzŭ and 85 miles below Ichang.
	Ichang	1876	55,000	On Yangtzŭ, 393 miles above Hankow and 966 from sea.
Hunan	Yochou	1898	20,000	On Yangtzŭ, 722 miles from sea.
	Ch'angsha	1903	536,000	Capital of the Province. On right bank of Hsiang Kiang, 190 miles S.S.E. of Ichang.
Ssŭch'uan	Chungking	1890	500,000	On Yangtzŭ, 1,400 miles from sea.
Chêkiang	Hangchow	1895	592,000	150 miles S.W. of Shanghai. On Ch'ien-t'ang R.
	Ningpo	1842	400,000	On River Yung.
	Wênchow	1858	200,000	On River Ou 20 miles from mouth.
Fukien	Foochow	1842	650,000	On River Min, 34 miles from sea.
	Amoy	1842	114,000	At mouth of Lung Chiang, on Hai-mên (or A. mên, locally A. mun) Is.
	Santuao	1898	....	Near Samsha Bay, the port is Funing, 70 M. South of Foochow.
Kuangtung	Swatow	1858	85,000	On Han River. Ch'aochow, 35 miles distant, is really the treaty port.
	Canton	1842	1,000,000	On Pearl River, 50 miles from mouth.
	Pakhoi	1876	20,000	On N. of Gulf of Tongking.
	Samhsui	1897	6,000	Near junction of North, West and Canton Rivers, 2 miles from the bank. Hok'ou is the port.
	Hoihow	1858	30,000	Kiungchow—50,000— the capital, is really the treaty port, Hoihow being the actual port, from which it is distant 3½ miles.
	Kongmoon	1902	73,000	On W. River, in Delta of Canton River. Was made a port of call in 1898.
Kuangsi	Wuchow	1897	50,000	West River, at junction with Cassia River, 220 miles from Canton.
	Nanning	1897	50,000	
	Lungchow	1886	22,000	At junction of Sungchi and Kaoping Rivers.
Yünnan	Mêngtzŭ	1886	12,000	Was opened with Manghao, latter being on left bank of Red River.
	T'êngyüeh (Momein)	1897	10,000	5,500 feet above sea-level.
	Szemao	1895	15,000	On a plain, 4,600 feet above sea-level.
	Hokow	1896	4,000	At junction of Man-hsi and Red Rivers.
Tibet	Yatung	1893	..	250 miles from Lhassa.

PORTS OF CALL, &c.

PROVINCE.	PORT.	DATE OF OPENING BY TREATY OR DECREE.	POPULATION.	REMARKS.
Chihli	Taku	..	....	At the mouth of the Peiho; is the port of Tientsin, and 67 miles distant from it.
Anhui	Anking	1876	....	
„	Tat'ung	1876	....	
Kiangsi	Huk'ow	..	....	
Hupei	Wusüeh	1887	....	
	Luchikou	1887	....	
	Huangchih-kang	..	....	
	Huangchou			
Kiangsu	Kiangyin	..	....	
	Ichêng			
Kuangtung	Hok'ou	1897	....	Harbour of Samshui.
	Kamchuk	1897	....	Delta of Canton River. Passengers and cargo.
	Shiuhing	1897	80,000	On West River. Passengers and cargo.
	Takhing	1897	6,000	On West River. Passengers and cargo.
	Loting	1902	....	
	Tunghsing	1895	....	80 miles West of Pakhoi. French Consulate established. Passengers and cargo.
	Paktau	1902	....	Passengers and cargo.
	Dosing	1902	....	Passengers and cargo.
	Fêngtsun	1902	....	Passengers and cargo.
	Yüethsing	1902	....	Passengers and cargo.
	Lukpo	1902	....	Passengers and cargo.
	Lutu	1902	....	Passengers and cargo.
	Howlik	1902	....	Passengers and cargo.
	Kaukong	1902	....	Passengers and cargo.
	Mahning	1902	....	Passengers and cargo.
	Jungki	1902	....	Passengers and cargo.
	Kulo	1902	....	Passengers and cargo.
	Yungan	1902	....	Passengers and cargo.

Foreign subjects are allowed to travel for five days within 100 li, about thirty-three miles, of the treaty ports; but for longer distances or time, passports, obtained from their respective consuls, are required.

At the treaty ports there are certain spots reserved for the use of the foreign residents, foreign concessions they are often called, though at the same time foreigners are allowed to reside amongst the Chinese as well. These have generally been common to all nationalities, the Americans having Hongkew, and the French also having a separate one at Shanghai. Of late years a strong tendency has developed toward the securing of concessions by different nationalities for themselves, instead of joining together as has hitherto been done to a great extent, and there are now a number of such concessions at various treaty ports. A part of Shamien in Canton was set apart for the French. At Tientsin there are concessions for British, French, German, Italian, Russian, and Japanese, and at Hankow for Japanese, German, British, French, and Russian. At Newchwang the Japanese have acquired a slice of land for a concession, and the British also a piece for the same purpose. The Japanese have also a settlement at Shasi, and at Hangchow, Soochow, and at Chungking. There are constantly new developments on these lines.

There are said to be about 50,000 European residents at the treaty ports—over 10,000 being British. To the total of European residents must be added a very large number since the revolution in Russia.

'The Authorities at Amoy have consented to the Island of Kulangsu becoming a foreign settlement entirely under international control,' 'under the pattern of Shanghai.'

Besides these treaty ports there are the different ports or portions of land belonging, or leased, to foreign nations.

There is Port Arthur at the point of the Regent's Sword, guarding the Northern entrance of the Gulf of Pechili with Talienwan (which Russia declared to be a free port), and the Russian zone of influence. 'By Agreement with the Chinese Government, dated 27th March, 1898, Russia is in possession of Port Arthur, and Talienwan and their adjacent territories and waters, on lease for the term of 25 years, which may be extended by agreement.' These were taken by Japan in the Russo-Japanese War. Then there is Weihaiwei, held by the British since the 24th May, 1898 (and to be held 'for such period as Russia may hold Port Arthur.' Negotiations are now—1924—proceeding for its return to China. The agreement is dated 2nd April, 1898), close to the Shantung province and guarding the southern entrance of the gulf mentioned above, which gives access to Tientsin and Peking, with a portion of land on the map described as the British zone of influence. The territory of Weihaiwei is 300 sq. miles in area, with an estimated population of 80,000, while the 'sphere of influence' is very much more extensive, with a population of 900,000. A few miles further south, down the coast, we come to the late German port at Kiauchau, and their zone of influence. Kiauchau was declared a free port on 2nd September, 1898. It was seized by the Germans in November, 1897, and a 99 years' lease of the town, harbour, and district, was obtained in January, 1898. It is situated on the east coast of Shantung. It was taken by the Japanese and British forces in the world war of 1914-8 and has since (1922) been returned to China. While in the south we have the important British Colony of Hongkong which has twice enlarged its boundaries on the mainland opposite. Forty miles off is the ancient Portuguese settlement (and colony now) of Macao, some 300 years old. Further south, 'on the coast of the Lien-Chau peninsula, opposite the Island of Hainan,' is Kuangchouwan, with some adjacent land where the Frnech have established themselves, hauling up the tricolour on the 2nd April, 1898. The French hold it by lease, dated 2nd April, 1898, for 99 years. 'In November, 1899, China conceded to France the possession of the two islands commanding the entrance to the bay.'

It must be remembered by strangers that Hongkong and Kowloon (British), Macao (Portuguese), Port Arthur (Russian), Kiaochau (late German), Weihaiwei (British), and Kuangchouwan (French), are not treaty ports, but colonies or settlements, belonging to the different nationalities mentioned above.

References.—Mayers, Dennys, and King, *The Treaty Ports of China and Japan; The China and Hongkong Directory;* Smith, *European Settlements in the Far East: China, Japan, Corea, Indo-China, Straits Settlements, Malay States, Siam, Netherlands India, Borneo, The Philippines, etc.*

TYPHOONS.—The similarity of this word to the Greek word τυφῶν, a whirlwind, has attracted the attention of scholars; but it is thought that the Chinese word *tai-fêng* [*ta fêng*], used in Formosa, is the origin of the term, for, strange to say, the Chinese themselves, in the South of China, at all events, do not call these cyclonic disturbances *táí-fung*, which simply means a big wind, but they speak of them as *fung-kaú* [*fêng chü* or *chü fêng*], storms, or they say *tá-fung-kaú*, a storm is blowing *ta*[3] *chü*[4] *fêng*[1], being to meet a typhoon. In Amoy the term *hang-t'ai* [*fêng-t'ai*] 'storm's womb,' is used.

Much has been done of late years in studying the 'grand but perplexing laws which regulate the formations and movements of typhoons'; but still much remains to be done, and when stations for their observation shall have been established at elevated heights, such as at the Peak in Hongkong, and Táí Mò Shán in the New Territory, much more in all probability will be known, and complete mastery of the difficult subject may be hoped for; as yet the upper strata of the air, as regards typhoons, is almost unexplored. Col. Palmer writes of these storms:—

'The theory of rotatory storms (whether called cyclones, typhoons, or hurricanes) . . . may be popularly stated thus. If from any initial cause, interchanging motions are set up between the air in a certain district and another surrounding it, the air in the first, or inner district, tends, in consequence of the earth's rotation, to gyrate round its centre, in a direction contrary to that of watch-hands in the Northern hemisphere, and with watch-hands in the Southern hemisphere. In the outer district these movements are reversed, by the principle of the preservation of areas (or moments). These two systems of contrary gyrations, especially in the upper strata of the atmosphere, where they are less influenced by friction with the earth's surface, and therefore more circular, than those below, tend to draw the air from the centre of the inner district and from the exterior part of the outer district, and heap it up along the zone dividing the two. On this zone accordingly, which is the annular region where the gyratory velocity in one direction dies out and that in the other direction begins, the atmospheric pressure is greatest, while it is least at the centre and at the outermost limit; and the pressure from this accumulation tends to force the air near the earth's surface out from beneath it, on the one side towards the centre of the cyclone, and on the other towards the exterior limit of the outer district, or " anti-cyclone."

'The gyrations once set up, two other forces come into play—centrifugal force, and friction of the moving air with the earth's surface, the former tending to drive the air still more from the centre of the inner district and so increase the barometric pressure there.

'To be brief, the result of all the conditions which affect the case is that, on and near the earth's surface, the air of the inner district, instead of preserving a circular movement, converges somewhat to the centre, flowing round and round in a spiral directed inward from the zone of maximum pressure. Under ordinary circumstances, this inclination diminishes with the altitude, and it diminishes as the velocity of the wind increases, so that it is least near the centre of the storm, where, indeed, the winds, being of intense violence, are circular, or very nearly so. It is greatest on the periphery of the typhoon, where, at great distances, the convergence is often nearly directly towards the centre. It is greater also on land than on the sea, owing to the increased friction with the rugged surface of the land; and it is greater in low than in high latitudes. The air of the outer district, on the other hand, describes a spiral directed outwards from the centre. In the middle regions of the atmosphere, the air above the cyclone inclines outwards from the centre, and at a great distance flows nearly directly away from it.'

The causes of typhoons, though they are not quite understood yet, appear to be 'differences of temperature; pressure, and humidity, the last named being less conspicuous as a primary cause than as a means of maintaining the cyclonic action after it has once been started. The typhoon, once being evolved from 'the manifold and highly complicated operations' of the causes stated above, having begun its life in the Pacific, starts on its travels, at first slowly, and then more rapidly. The tendency of typhoons is to seek the north, but, influenced by the currents of air, they are deflected westwards towards the continent of Asia, and the consequence is they generally take a north-westerly direction. They are more at home on the sea, as, when they go inland, mountain ranges block their progress and they lose much of their energy, and finally, after proceeding northwards, they seek the sea again, ending their course in the Yellow Sea, Corea, or Japan. 'As a broad definition then, applicable to the normal typhoon, it may be stated that its path is approximately a parabola, the vertex of the curve being turned westward and situated not far from the boundary of the tropic, while its two branches pass respectively over the archipelago of the Philippines and that of Japan.'

The following interesting account may serve to make plainer this difficult subject to the reader. It is from the pen of a former Harbour Master at Kobe:—

'The body of wind of which a typhoon consists is in shape nearly circular. . . . The diameter of this circle has been found to vary from about fifty to several hundred miles in length, and the height of this body of wind is estimated to be from one to ten miles in perpendicular height. This mass of wind, or typhoon, has two different motions, one being progressive and the other circular. When a typhoon forms near the Equator its progressive motion is first towards the westward, but its course thereafter changes gradually northward of this, and by the time it reaches Japan its course has thus been changed to some direction between north and east. This progressive motion may be taken to be from 7 to 24 miles per hour. While the typhoon is thus moving onward, the whole body of wind within its circumference is whirling round its centre at a velocity of from 50 to perhaps 100 miles per hour. An observer standing at the centre of a typhoon would most likely be surrounded by a calm, extending probably to a distance of from one to ten miles; but if he moved towards the circumference of the typhoon he would, upon coming within the wind circles, find the direction of the wind to be from his right towards his left, or in other words, the wind would have a rotary movement in a direction opposite to that of the hands of a watch. Consequently the wind must be east at the most northern margin of a typhoon and west at its southern margin. In like manner it must be south at the most eastern margin and north at the western, and it follows that the wind on every part of any straight line drawn from any part of the margin to the storm's centre must be from the same direction as it is at the point where such line cuts the margin. It also follows that the direction of wind on opposite semi-diameters must blow from opposite directions. The winds outside the limits of typhoons often blow in a direction pointing more or less towards the typhoon's centre; this is mostly the case in front and rear of such storms. As has been stated, the motion of the wind within the body of a typhoon is circular, and it must therefore blow from every point of the compass during its circuit; and in order to more fully explain from which direction the wind blows at different places, the body of the storm may be divided into sections by imaginary diameters. First by drawing two diameters through the body of the storm, one in a direction from north to south and the other from west to east, the storm is divided into four quadrants, called the N.E., S.E., S.W., and N.W.

quadrants; and, bearing in mind the explanation already given, it will be found that the wind in the N.E. quadrant must always be from between east and south, in the S.E. quadrant between south and west, in the S.W. quadrant between west and north, and in the N.W. quadrant between north and east. Another division of the typhoon is made by drawing a line (called the axis line) through its centre representing the latter's path, or in other words, its progressive motion; this divides the storm into two semicircles, named the right-hand and left-hand semicircles, according as they are to the right or left hand of the said line. To distinguish one from the other the reader should imagine himself placed on this axis line at the rear of the typhoon, looking at it in the direction it is travelling. As the path of typhoons do not always lie in the same direction, it becomes evident that the axis line does not always cut off semicircles containing the same winds. For instance, in the right-hand semicircle of a typhoon travelling to the north-east, the winds would be from S.E. to N.W., round by way of S., S.W., and W., while in the left-hand semicircle the winds would be from S.E. to N.W., round by way of E., N.E., and N. On the other hand, in a typhoon travelling due north, the winds in the right-hand semicircle would be from E. to W., by way of S., and in the left-hand semicircle from E. to W., by way of N. In the latter case the wind on the axis line would be E. on the northern side of the centre, and W. on the southern side thereof. The number of compass points through which the wind veers at any place depends therefore upon how near the centre passes to such a place. The veering of the wind indicates at once whether the right or left-hand semicircle is passing over a place, for if it veers from its initial direction towards the right, say from S.S.E. to S., then the right-hand semicircle is passing over the place, but should the wind veer to the left, or say from S.S.E. to S.E. then the left-hand semicircle is passing over. The Barometer falls as long as the centre of a typhoon is getting nearer, and *vice versâ*.

'. . . . According to the above explanation, the wind strikes all straight lines, joining the centre and circumference of a typhoon at right angles.

. . . .

'With the given explanation, the reader will find no difficulty in making other interesting deductions, by comparing the two observations. To aid him in this, I suggest that he supply himself with a circular piece of cardboard, make a small hole in its centre, and draw through this two diameters at right angles to each other. Mark the ends of the diameters N., E., S., and W. respectively. Placing this card before him on a table, with that part of its diameter marked N. pointing towards the north, and imagining a body of wind to be whirling round the centre, but limited by the circumference of the card, he will then have a very good illustration of a typhoon, and one which will make the meaning of quadrants, semicircles, circular motion, etc., easily understood. To further represent the progressive motion of a typhoon, the card requires to be moved in the direction towards which the storm is travelling, still keeping the N. point of the card pointing towards the north, and still supposing the wind to be whirling round the centre of the card.'

Typhoons

September is the month *par excellence*, for typhoons, but the typhoon months are generally considered to be those of July, August, September, and part of October, though they are not confined to those months.

Until late years the advent of typhoons had to be judged by the intense heat which prevailed for several days, the fall of the barometer, and other signs, but, with the extension of the telegraph to this part of the world, timely warning of their probable arrival or vicinity is telegraphed from Manila, and many lives have been thus preserved. Fortunately for Hongkong, the course of these dreadful storms is often deflected by one cause or another before they reach this 'dot in the ocean [Hongkong],' and they generally strike the land further North, up the coast of China, or further South, down in the neighbourhood of Hainan or Annam. Occasionally, in the course of many years, some of most dreadful intensity occur; such especially was the awful one of the 27th of July, 1862, the terrific force of which expended itself in wrecking the whole river frontage of Canton, so that scarcely a house on the river escaped more or less damage, in fact the place looked as if it had suffered from a bombardment, while thousands of the boat people were drowned before the eyes of the spectators on shore, who were powerless to render them any assistance. The loss of life in the city and neighbourhood was estimated at 40,000. The wind blew with titanic force in great bursts which shook the buildings, the air was darkened with leaves and bits of debris, the raging of the usually calm river, the cries of the drowning, the consciousness that any moment might be one's last, the passing of the centre of the storm when a lull occurred, giving one hopes that the worst was past, to be followed by a recurrence of all its force and danger; the flooded houses, streets like rivers—all combined to form a lurid picture, which, once seen, one never cares to see again. Such an indelible impression did this great typhoon make on the Chinese of that city that for many years they dated occurrences from that event.

Fortunately, such terrific typhoons occur but seldom. The places in their vicinity, however, participate in the disturbances which they cause around them, having blows of more or less intensity, or high winds and downfalls of rain, lasting for several days, which serve to cool the atmosphere. The minimum velocity of the wind entitled to be called typhoon force is 80 miles an hour. It is interesting in a slight typhoon, when one feels tolerably safe, to watch the needle of the barometer fall slightly with each gust of the wind, and rise slightly again as it dies down. In a typhoon the barometer falls from 28.80 to 28.50, and even lower readings are seen. In 1880 there were fourteen recorded typhoons; in 1881, twenty; but the average is more than fifteen a year.

References.—Palmer, *The Typhoons of the Eastern Seas;* Doberck, *The Law of Storms in the Eastern Seas;* Dechevrens, *The Typhoons of the Chinese Seas in the year* 1880 (1881, 1882, *et seq.*) ; *Hongkong Government Gazette* (annual reports) ; *T'oung Pao*, 1896, p. 581.

VACCINATION AND INOCULATION.—From the reports of the European doctors in China in the earlier years of the century, there is no doubt that smallpox used to be a common disease, not only in the south of China, in the neighbourhood of Hongkong, Canton, and Macao, but also in the north in Peking, in the metropolis of the empire, where it was epidemic in spring, and much mortality resulted from the visitations, not only to children, but also amongst the grown-up population. In the neighbourhood of Canton, or in a portion of the province of Kuangtung, it is also stated to have been an invariable annual epidemic, lasting from February to June, amongst the crowded native population in boats and elsewhere. In the province of Shansi, the mortality from it was very great, not even inoculation, much less vaccination, being known there in the first half of this century. In the western provinces of China, the ravages must have been great in those days, as also there inoculation was said not to be practised.

These instances are sufficient to show that smallpox was a dreadful and dreaded visitant in China, the means for coping with it, or stopping its spread, being either entirely wanting or inadequate.

Before the introduction of vaccination, the Chinese were acquainted with, and employed, inoculation, which is said to have been introduced by a philosopher of Go-mei Shan in the province of Szchuen [Ssŭch'uan]. This knowledge was handed down to posterity from the time of Chên Tsung of the Sung dynasty (A.D. 1014).

Another account states that:—

'It is not to be wondered at that in China they have tried some means to check the virulence of smallpox which has repeatedly produced terrible havoc amongst its inhabitants. Chinese practitioners describe various methods of inoculation which, it is said, was discovered at the latter end of the second century for protecting a grandson of Prince Tchiu-Siang (P. Dabry's 'La Médecine chez les Chinois'). They have also learned by experience the dangers of inoculation.'

Different methods were employed; one plan was to insert in the nose a pledget (a piece of cotton-wool, in most cases probably), impregnated with the virus; another plan was to take the lymph itself, or the crust rubbed down with water, and introduce into the sore; while another mode was to dry the crusts, reduce them to powder, and blow this powder up the nose—this being called dry inoculation; yet another and more loathsome way was to dress the child with clothes that had been worn by some one with smallpox. Inoculation would appear to have been largely practised by the Chinese. It was stated that in Shanghai the greatest number of the children were thus treated. One Chinese writer, the author of a treatise entitled, 'The Preservation of Infants by Inoculation,' supposed that smallpox arose from poison introduced into the system from the mother's womb, and he believed this to be proved since smallpox only occurs once in a life-time. All diseases amongst the Chinese are associated with, or are the result of, the principles of heat or cold. Smallpox is due to the heat principle. It remains latent, or concealed, in the human system 'till it is developed through the agency of some external, exciting cause.' Hence, as it might break out at any time, they thought it advisable to use some means to modify its virulence: they believed that, by inoculation, when the patient's system was in a healthy condition, and at times and seasons which appeared most advantageous, this might be accomplished. The Chinese writer mentioned above says:—

> 'The disease when it breaks out spontaneously is very severe, and often fatal; whereas, when it is introduced by inoculation, it is generally mild, and casualties do not occur oftener than once in ten thousand cases. . . . To discard this excellent plan and sit waiting for the calamity, is much to be deprecated.'

This author has evidently been carried away with enthusiasm for his subject, as foreign writers speak of the dangers attendant on inoculation as compared with vaccination. The fatality is described as being very great, by one in Soochow, and when the doctor comes to 'plant the smallpox,' as it is described, 'the family go through extensive religious ceremonies, the god being worshipped with a feast, incense, and firecrackers.' Another, a doctor, writes:

> 'A child generally thus takes the smallpox mildly, but the children thus treated sometimes take the confluent form of the disease, by which sight and even life is lost.
>
> 'It is true that the disease taken by inoculation is generally milder than when it is taken spontaneously, but the great objection to inoculation is, that the disease itself is thus maintained among the community, and every case is a focus of infection; whereas in vaccination the tendency is to get rid of smallpox altogether, serious accidents do not occur from it, and there is no liability to take on a fatal form of disease.' In the report of the hospital at Ningpo published in 1851, it is stated that, 'inoculation at one time proved frequently fatal.'

However, in lieu of a more excellent way, the Chinese put their confidence in inoculation.

It was stated that without inoculation the mortality from smallpox in Shansi under the most favourable circumstances was 20 to 30 per cent. of deaths, while in worse cases it rose to 50 or 60 per cent.; but 'after inoculation only one per cent. proved fatal.'

It is curious that, like several other things, inoculation appears to have been introduced into the West from China.

'It has been known and practised in China since the time of the Sung dynasty, about 800 years ago. It was first introduced into England by Lady Montague, the wife of the British Ambassador at Constantinople in 1721, and doubtless had found its way to Turkey across the centre of Asia from China. The Turks who lived on the Chinese frontier must have carried the knowledge of it when they moved westward.'

There are ten rules with regard to inoculation compiled by a retired scholar of the name of Lew Lan in obedience to an Imperial Decree, and these were inserted in the 'Golden Mirror of the Medical Practice.' They have in latter times been discoursed upon by celebrated physicians who have 'revised them with much care and attention.'

The rules are as follows:—

'1st. Regarding variolous lymph:—This is the fluid that comes from the smallpox pustules, and must be taken from a child which has a mild form of the disease; whether arising spontaneously or from inoculation, the pustules ought to be round or pointed, and of a clear red colour, the fluid abundant and the crust which comes away clear and consistent like wax.

'. . . After [inoculation] seven days, fever appears; three days afterwards the spots show themselves; three days after this the spots become pustular; in three days more the crusts form, when the whole is completed. If the inoculation does not take effect it may be repeated in fourteen days.

'2nd. Seasons:—The Spring and Autumn are the most favourable seasons for inoculation, or any time when the weather is moderate; during the very hot, or cold months, it ought not to be done.

'3rd. Choice of Lucky Days:—A lucky day ought always to be chosen; the 11th and 13th days of the moon must always be avoided.

'4th. Management of the Patients:—During the process of inoculation it is of great importance that strict rules of management be adopted in respect to heat and cold, with attention to diet and the avoidance of any cause of alarm or fright.

'5th. At the time for inoculation the child must be examined and the state of its health ascertained; strict attention must also be paid to the state of the family, and if the child be sick, the operation must not be performed. All children ought to be inoculated when they are one year old; if the health be good, this ought by no means to be neglected.

'6th. Restricting:—The room of the inoculated child ought to be clean and airy, and well lighted; all excitement must be avoided, and the child kept quiet and placid.

'7th. Promise of the Eruption:—After the inoculation and before the fever appears, there suddenly arise on the child's face several pustules like smallpox; these are called the "sin miaŭ," promise, or belief of emption; it is the forerunner of the disease, and the evidence of the poison having taken effect.

'8th. Repetition of the Inoculation:—If after waiting fourteen days, the fever does not appear, should the season still be favourable, the inoculation may be repeated.

'9th. Mode of Action:—The inoculation must affect the viscera, and the fever commences. The nose is the external orifice of the lungs; when the variolous lymph is placed in the nose, its influence is first communicated to the lungs; the lungs govern the hair and the skin; the lungs transfer the poison to the heart; the heart governs the pulse, and transfers the poison to the spleen; the spleen governs the flesh, and transfers the poison to the liver; the liver governs the tendons, and transfers the poison to the kidneys; the kidneys govern the bones, the poison of the smallpox lies hid originally in the marrow of the bones; but when it receives the impression from the inoculation, it manifests itself and breaks out externally.

'10th. General Rules:—Inoculation is to be performed when there is no disease present in the system; good lymph must be selected, a proper time chosen, and good management adopted, and then all will go on well.'

As to the introduction of vaccination.

'Many attempts were made to introduce the practice of vaccination into China during the early period when commercial relations were in existence between the East India Company and the Chinese. In 1805 a Portuguese subject, a merchant in Macao of the name of Hewit, brought vaccine over "upon live subjects from Manila," the King having had vaccine conveyed to the Philippines by suitable means and professional men across the South American continent. It was extensively practised by Portuguese practitioners in Macao as well as by Dr. Pearson upon the inhabitants of that ancient city, as well as amongst the Chinese.'

Dr. Pearson, a surgeon of the East India Company in China, carried on the work of its introduction to the natives with great vigour and perseverance.

'Stated periods were fixed at which the Chinese received the benefits of vaccination from the doctor's hands, nor was the experiment unattended with success. It soon sprang into favour amongst the Chinese, who, though very conservative in their feelings, when once convinced of the benefit of any new method, take it up very readily, and great numbers were brought to be operated on during the period of the raging of smallpox in the course of the winter and spring months of 1805-6.'

Thousands were vaccinated in the course of twelve months, and the Chinese who had been instructed by Dr. Pearson, practised it extensively, not only under his immediate inspection but at a distance as well. When the immediate need for this protective influence against the fell and foul disease was gone—when in short, smallpox ceased to be epidemic, 'the evil and the remedy against it were equally forgotten,' and Dr. Pearson 'found great difficulty in procuring a sufficient number of subjects by means of which, merely to preserve the vaccine.' Twice was it necessary to have it reintroduced from the 'islands of Lucona,' and twice it was found to have been kept up at country districts. In his report for 1816, Dr. Pearson speaks about its spreading greatly 'from among the lower classes of society, so as to have become general among the middling ranks, and to be frequently resorted to by those of the higher conditions.'

The Chinese native doctors had strenuously opposed it, and still at that period it met with but little acceptation by them, and alarms of failures had occasionally been spread; there was also a prejudice against submitting children to vaccination in the summer and autumnal months, doubtless owing to the fact that in the time of such great heats it had been observed 'that all diseases attacking or brought on at that season are more than usually dangerous or severe.'

The principal members of the 'Chinese commercial corporation, in whom was vested the exclusive privilege of dealing with Europeans,' established a fund for the gratuitous vaccination of the poor at all times, offering a small premium to those who brought their children for that purpose; and from fifteen to forty were vaccinated every ninth day by a Chinese vaccinator, while Dr. Pearson inspected the pustules from which the lymph was taken, and this simply to put an end to a malicious rumour that the Chinese vaccinators had not been circumspect in the choice of the matter they used.

The medical servants of the East India Company were always ready to vaccinate gratuitously all persons who wished it; though the taking of it thus up by the Chinese themselves conduced to the spread of the practice; and it became a source of reputation and emolument to the Chinese who were employed for the purpose.

Great numbers must have been vaccinated at this early stage, and it was believed that the greater mildness of the epidemics of smallpox which followed were due to the Chinese acceptance to such an extent of this protective against the disease.

A report on the subject was again made in 1821. This states that 'the practice of vaccination had been uninterruptedly continued' and had 'received a steady and great extension with increased confidence in its efficacy.' Smallpox had in the preceding and that season 'prevailed in an unusual degree of severity and attended with mortality'; but the results of the investigations that were instituted proved that vaccination was satisfactory, though every endeavour was made to discover whether certain complaints were well founded. These complaints had divided themselves into two heads: viz., vaccination with spurious matter, or imperfectly, or unskilfully conducted; and the other, the following of the vaccination by a modified smallpox. Under the first heading none presented themselves who had been vaccinated under inspection, or at the Canton Institute; under the other heading the number was few. The general reliance of the Chinese was not shaken.

Vaccination had by this time extended to the neighbouring province of Kuangtung, but had met with a check from the hostility of the priesthood, and had been dropped. This opposition was due to two circumstances; for the priests had been used to inoculate after the Chinese methods, and their deities had been resorted to in times of visitation of this plague. Unfortunately scarlet-fever also broke out, and the blame of this was laid on vaccination, which it was said 'retained the poison in the system, to appear at a future time in still worse shapes.'

Between 1821 and 1833 two reports were made, and from them it is learned that the practice extended itself largely amongst all sorts and conditions of Chinese in the Canton province. It was also conveyed to the Kiangsi, Kiangnan, and Fukien provinces, and even reached Peking, but was lost there.

'Its anti-variolous efficacy' was 'universally known and confided in; . . . its preservation during the period specified had greatly, almost exclusively, resulted from the well-adapted system pursued at the institution, and the agency of the Chinese vaccinators; the principal of whom A-he-qua (who' had 'been engaged in the practice since 1805') was 'a man remarkably qualified for the business, by his cast of judgment, method, and perseverance. He had been encouraged in his laudable exertions by the favourable opinion of his countrymen and by marks of distinction or consideration which' had 'been conferred upon him by the higher functionaries of the local government.'

A further mention is made of the same man at a later date in the same magazine for the year 1842, when it was stated that some cases of smallpox prevailed, and it goes on to add that 'vaccination for the prevention of this disease had been regularly and successfully practised every eighth day during many years by He-qua at the Public Hall of the Hong merchants.' Dr. Pearson, at the same time as he started vaccination, caused a tract to be printed on it in Chinese, Sir George Staunton translating it: this was in A.D. 1805. It set forth the advantages and benefits to be derived from vaccination, and was of great use, being republished at Shanghai subsequently, with some corrections and slight additions; part of this same tract of Dr. Pearson's was incorporated into a native tract also republished in Peking in 1828, this latter having been originally published at Canton in 1817.

The Russians introduced vaccination into Peking before 1828 'as early as 1820, the medical gentlemen attached to the Legation . . . practised vaccination among the Albasines—now Chinese naturalised subjects.'

'Vaccination among the Mongols was attempted before it was introduced at Canton by Dr. Pearson, but excepting the following notice, we do not know whether it has since been practised. "Mr. Rehmann, physician to his S.H. Prince of Fürstenberg, has lately received a letter from his son, physician to the Russian embassy in China. This letter is dated from Kiakhta on the frontiers of China, 14th October, 1805. Mr. Rehmann, Junr., writes that he has vaccinated a great number of the children of the Mongols. . . . He assures his father, that in consequence of the measures he has employed, vaccination is now propagated from Jekutzh, as far as Jakutsh and Ochotzk, and consequently from England to the remotest extremity of the northern part of the globe."'

We have seen how it was introduced into Canton and some of the other provinces. Its utility soon became known, 'and the practice quickly spread over the empire.'

Vaccination was introduced into Peking 'by the Prefect Tsêng who had formerly been a mandarin in the South' in 1828. In 1864 there were three vaccination establishments in the city, one having a branch in Tientsin. It was stated then concerning Peking:—

'Smallpox is still a great scourge, owing chiefly to the carelessness of the people in not availing themselves of it [vaccination] in time. It is said to be endemic—all children, they assert, take it by the will of Heaven; there is no escape—*sic volvere Parcas.*' This report goes on to say 'the vaccine establishments here are well conducted. Attendance is given every eighth day, or oftener, if the weather be very dry, and the lymph operates rapidly. Tickets of admission are granted, the name, address, age, and sex are carefully noted down in a register kept for the purpose. A note is taken of the number of vaccination days each year; the number of children vaccinated, those in which it succeeds amongst those who return. The statistics for 1893, of the oldest and principal establishment here I subjoin, as given by the vaccinator:—

'Number of vaccination days, 61; number vaccinated, 2227; children, of those who returned, 1229; of successful vaccination, each child being vaccinated in six places, 6080; vaccination days during 37 years, 811.

'The establishments are not only gratuitous, but a gratuity is given to the parents to bring the children back. In Spring, when the cases are numerous, they receive, on their second visit, about 2d.; in the Autumn and Winter, when the cases are few, they receive about 2d. on their first visit, and on their return, about 9d. When there is the least danger of the lymph becoming exhausted, beggar children are hired to be vaccinated, who live in the Hospital.

'When called upon to vaccinate the nobility, these children are taken in a cart to the residences of the aristocracy, in order to have the lymph, in the recent state, transferred from their arms to those of more fortunately-situated children. This method, which could not always have been of the most agreeable description, has been superseded by tubes from this Hospital [London Mission Hospital]. When it was first proposed to introduce vaccination into the metropolis, it was arranged to have a relay of boys upon the road to be vaccinated in succession every eighth day, but this plan was abandoned when the means of conveying scabs was found out. The dried scabs on reaching Peking were mixed with Mother's milk. . . . The tracts and sheets printed and distributed on the subject display a great ignorance of the true principles of physiology. They suppose the poison of the smallpox to be located about the insertion of the *deltoid* muscle, and hence direct the lymph to be introduced at three distinct places in each arm, the upper one to be four inches from the shoulder, and the lower one two inches from the elbow. They give drawings of the position and of the lancets which, by-the-bye, are all of foreign manufacture. They are very particular regarding the diet, warning most carefully to avoid the smells of whisky, opium, heated *kangs,* and dirty or decaying matter.

'For at least 100 days after vaccination, cocks, certain kinds of fish, beef, eggs, beans, and bean flour are to be avoided. For three years after vaccination, buckwheat, and cherries are to be shunned. The things enjoined are vegetables, pork, and salted ham. Three days after vaccination, they are allowed to eat shrimps, with rice spirit, Mongolian mushrooms, and mutton; and only in Winter must birds' nests, steamed with sugar-candy, be eaten.'

The medical missionary hospitals have had a large share in both carrying on the work of vaccination when once started and in introducing it into parts of the country where it was unknown before. In this way it was first brought into Shanghai in 1861, and at other times into various other places.

By all these different ways, included in which, of course, is the use of it by the Chinese themselves, the employment of vaccination has pretty well spread through the empire; not only have individual Chinese taken it up as a means of earning their living; but charitable institutions have employed men to go about the country and vaccinate, as well as at the institutions themselves.

The following extract from a Customs' Medical Report for 1877-8, by Dr. Wong Fung, a Chinese, but an M.D. of Edinburgh University, the doctor for some years of the Foreign Community in Canton, and of the Imperial Maritime Customs, will be of interest here:

'To Dr. Alexander Pearson of the East India Company is due the great credit of first establishing by a long course of labour extending from 1805 to 1820, the practice of vaccination among the natives of Canton. But although this practice was introduced so early and has been kept up, more or less, among the population ever since, it appears that the people have been rather careless to avail themselves of it; and it is only of late, perhaps within the last 15 years, that it has obtained extension to all classes and conditions of men from the highest to the lowest, whether living on land or on water, so that at present it may be estimated that, at least 95 per cent. of the children of the city receive the benefits of vaccination. The general age at which children are vaccinated is about the second year, and the earliest about the fourth or fifth month. There are in the city many men engaged in the practice, some of whom receive pay from benevolent individuals to open dispensaries for free attendance on the poor on stated days. In the country, vaccination has also made great progress in the confidence of the people, and professional men are found in villages, either practising on their own account, or hired by the gentry for the purpose. The two most noted vaccinators of the city are Yan Hee and Tan Yih-sing. The grandfather of the former was instructed in the art by Dr. Pearson in 1806, and carried it on with such success and became so widely known that his family' received 'marks of recognition from the Government in the shape of some official title, and also, I believe, a grant of Tls. 100 per annum for the preservation of lymph. Tan Yih-sing has also a large practice, some say on account of the confidence placed in him as one skilful in the diagnosis of leprosy, and likely to be circumspect in the selection of lymph. It was always the custom to vaccinate direct from the arm, but of late years many Chinese, including the individuals above mentioned, have been taught by Dr. Kerr to preserve lymph in glass tubes. Chinese mothers strongly object to have lymph taken from their children, under the idea that it weakens their constitution, and would not part with it but for money, so that vaccinators have to secure their supply of lymph by paying children successfully vaccinated to come to their houses. When a doctor is called to a family to perform vaccination he takes a child with him to furnish the vaccine, for which he generally gets 50 cents or $1, as a fee, and the child 25 cents for the lymph. Poor people may be vaccinated for 10 or 25 cents.'

Again as to its present practice. In the Report on Ningpo, in the Customs' Annual Trade Report for 1896, appears this:—

'Among the local developments of the year may be noticed a free vaccination institution supported by contributions from the Customs' banker, Yen Taot'ai.'

Vaccination is carried on at the Tung Wa Hospital in Hongkong, free to all comers; the subjects are nearly all children, but there are some grown-up people as well. This hospital does not send out doctors into the country to vaccinate; but some hospitals in Canton do. These doctors go to some principal city and stay there for some time and vaccinate. At these benevolent hospitals there is no charge; but the private practitioners charge a small fee, and only have occasional patients. The Chinese within the last ten years are beginning to see the good of it more and more every day. In the country they vaccinate from child to child without procuring fresh lymph. This is done amongst the poor and even amongst the rich, unless they understand about it; there is, of course, a chance of getting it from a poor subject; they take precautions to inoculate only from the healthy, though the possibility exists of getting it from an unhealthy child. In one case the lymph was taken from a leper's child, who appeared to be free from the disease, and the vaccinated child took it. The general run of doctors take their lymph from the arm; but rich people, who can afford it, do not. The Chinese are not aware of the necessity of re-vaccination. They think they are not so liable to smallpox as Europeans, for they do not eat roasted and broiled meats, as they (the Europeans) do.

The Chinese doctors vaccinate very carefully three spots on each arm, that is six spots, with an English lancet, and cutting very deep.

The lymph now used in Hongkong, Canton, and neighbourhood, is procured from the Government Vaccine Institute in this Colony.

Except in the neighbourhood of treaty ports or where European influence prevails, as at all mission stations, it may be said that practically vaccination, as at present performed by the Chinese themselves, is from arm to arm, lymph being now used is hundreds of generations from the original arms; but where, as above, European influence prevails, calf lymph is being introduced, but the style of vaccination from arm to arm prevails. Re-vaccination is not practised.

'When vaccinating, the child is first given a bath and its head shaved, either of which performances is not repeated until ten days have passed. The boys, of course, being more valuable than the girls, the doctor charges 50 per cent. more for them, the price being generally $1.00 for a boy, and 50 cents for a girl.'

Special attention is given to vaccination at the Mission Hospital in Canton, 'and the work begun by the hospital has been taken up and pushed vigorously forward by native associations, as many as five hundred specialists being despatched in one season to interior districts, in the interests of this work.'

References.—Chinese Repository, passim; Chinese and Japanese Repository. The Annual Reports of the numerous missionary hospitals throughout China also contain, very often, accounts of what is being done not only in the hospitals themselves, but, sometimes, of what is being done by the Chinese in their neighbourhood with regard to vaccination.

WAGES.—Some idea of the rates of wages paid in China may be gathered from the following figures referring to some of the trades. They represent the daily wages with board obtaining in 1919. If board is excluded an "e" is affixed to the money rate.

		Farmers		Filature Workers	
		Men	Women	Men	Women
Metropolitan Area	Highest	$0.50	$0.30	$0.24	$0.17
	Ordinary	0.20	0.15	0.14	0.10
	Lowest	0.08	0.06	0.07	0.05
Chihli	Highest	0,29	0.20	0.55	0.31
	Ordinary	0.15	0.08	0.25	0.16
	Lowest	0.06	0.03	0.14	0.09
Kirin	Highest	0.39	0.16		
	Ordinary	0.27	0.12		
	Lowest	0.21	0.10		
Shantung	Highest	0.28	0.16	0.31	0.22
	Ordinary	0.22	0.12	0.25	0.17
	Lowest	0.16	0.09	0.20	0.12
Honan	Highest	0.14	0.34	0.30	0.17
	Ordinary	0.10	0.21	0.23	0.13
	Lowest	0.06	0.04	0.16	0.07
Shansi	Highest	0.28	0.13	0.57	0.29
	Ordinary	0.20	0.09	0.32	0.21
	Lowest	0.09	0.06	0.18	0.14
Kiangsu	Highest	0.34	0.29	0.58	0.48
	Ordinary	0.25	0.21	0.36	0.25
	Lowest	0.14	0.09	0.19	0.14
Anhwei	Highest	0.30		0.28	0.25
	Ordinary	0.24		0.20	0.16
	Lowest	0.20		0.10	0.10
Fukien	Highest	0.46	0.40	0.90	0.80
	Ordinary	0.35	0.32	0.58	0.48
	Lowest	0.21	0.17	0.35	0.30
Chêkiang	Highest	0.35	0.18	0.46	0·38
	Ordinary	0.19	0.10	0.29	0.25
	Lowest	0.10	0.06	0.14	0.12

		Weavers		Tailors
		Men	Women	
Metropolitan Area	Highest	$0.20	$0.20	$0.35
	Ordinary	0.16	0.16	0.25
	Lowest	0.08	0.08	0.12
		0.32 (e)	0.32 (e)	
		0.21 (e)	0.21 (e)	
		0.12 (e)	0.12 (e)	
Chihli	Highest	0.31	0.23	0.32
	Ordinary	0 16	0.11	0.17
	Lowest	0. 8	0.06	0.08
		0.43 (e)	0.35 (e)	
		0.27 (e)	0.22 (e)	
		0.19 (e)	0.14 (e)	
Kirin	Highest	0.45	0.58	0.32
	Ordinary	0.38	0.49	0.86
	Lowest	0.30	0.40	0.69
		0.23 (e)	0.23 (e)	
		0.16 (e)	0.18 (e)	
		0.11 (e)	0.12 (e)	
Shantung	Highest	0.25	0.18	0.28
	Ordinary	0.22	0.15	0.25
	Lowest	0.19	0.12	0.22
		0.38 (e)	0.32 (e)	
		0.34 (e)	0.27 (e)	
		0.31 (e)	0.23 (e)	
Honan	Highest	0.28	0.16	0.29
	Ordinary	0.19	0.11	0.20
	Lowest	0.13	0.08	0.17
		0.41 (e)	0.27 (e)	
		0.30 (e)	0 22 (e)	
		0.26 (e)	0.20 (e)	
Shansi	Highest	0.26	0.22	0.25
	Ordinary	0.19	0.19	0.19
	Lowest	0.14	0.12	0.15
		0.35 (e)	0.28 (e)	
		0.27 (e)	0.22 (e)	
		0.20 (e)	0.18 (e)	
Kiangsu	Highest	0.43	0.33	0.55
	Ordinary	0.28	0.22	0.30
	Lowest	0.15	0.12	0.18
		0.60 (e)	0.46 (e)	
		0.41 (e)	0.36 (e)	
		0.34 (e)	0.22 (e)	
Anhwei	Highest	0.22	0.18	0.25
	Ordinary	0.16	0.12	0.20
	Lowest	0.12	0.10	0.15
		0.32 (e)	0.26 (e)	
		0.26 (e)	0.22 (e)	
		0.22 (e)	0.15 (e)	
Fukien	Highest	0.51	0.48	0.44
	Ordinary	0.33	0.29	0.31
	Lowest	0.21	0.19	0.19
		0.68 (e)	0.65 (e)	
		0.47 (e)	0.34 (e)	
		0.33 (e)	0.32 (e)	
Chêkiang	Highest	0.44	0.25	0.25
	Ordinary	0.25	0.16	0.17
	Lowest	0 14	0.09	0.11
		0.56 (e)	0.34 (e)	
		0.34 (e)	0.26 (e)	
		0.24 (e)	0.17 (e)	

		Boot Makers
Metropolitan Area	Highest	$0.34
	Ordinary	0.22
	Lowest	0.10
Chihli	Highest	0.36
	Ordinary	0.17
	Lowest	0.08
Kirin	Highest	0.57
	Ordinary	0.46
	Lowest	0.37
Shantung	Highest	0.25
	Ordinary	0.22
	Lowest	0.18
Honan	Highest	0.27
	Ordinary	0.20
	Lowest	0.15
Shansi	Highest	0.17
	Ordinary	0.14
	Lowest	0.11
Kiangsu	Highest	0.45
	Ordinary	0.29
	Lowest	0.18
Anhwei	Highest	0.16
	Ordinary	0.19
	Lowest	0.10
Fukien	Highest	0.49
	Ordinary	0.34
	Lowest	0.20
Chêkiang	Highest	0.28
	Ordinary	0.21
	Lowest	0.14

		Tea Curers	Carpenters	Bricklayers
Metropolitan Area	Highest	$0.30	$0.40	$0.40
	Ordinary	0.20	0.28	0.28
	Lowest	0.10	0.10	0.10
		0.40 (e)	0.50 (e)	0.50 (e)
		0.26 (e)	0.36 (e)	0.36 (e)
		0.18 (e)	0.20 (e)	0.20 (e)
Chihli	Highest	0.32	0.29	0.28
	Ordinary	0.17	0.17	0.15
	Lowest	0.08	0.08	0.08
		0.44 (e)	0.42 (e)	0.42 (e)
		0.28 (e)	0.28 (e)	0.26 (e)
		0.15 (e)	0.20 (e)	0.19 (e)
Kirin	Highest		0.58	0.53
	Ordinary		0.44	0.36
	Lowest		0.35	0.28
			0.84 (e)	0.79 (e)
			0.68 (e)	0.65 (e)
			0.60 (e)	0.58 (e)
Shantung	Highest	0.24	0.25	0.24
	Ordinary	0.19	0.26	0.19
	Lowest	0.14	0.16	0.15
		0.36 (e)	0.32 (e)	0.33 (e)
		0.29 (e)	0.27 (e)	0.30 (e)
		0.24 (e)	0.21 (e)	0.25 (e)
Honan	Highest	0.32	0.24	0.23
	Ordinary	0.20	0.18	0.15
	Lowest	0.14	0.13	0.12
		0.44 (e)	0.39 (e)	0.33 (e)
		0.32 (e)	0.30 (e)	0.26 (e)
		0.25 (e)	0.26 (e)	0.25 (e)
Shansi	Highest		0.21	0.24
	Ordinary		0.16	0.20
	Lowest		0.12	0.14
			0.28 (e)	0.32 (e)
			0.23 (e)	0.26 (e)
			0.17 (e)	0.20 (e)
Kiangsu	Highest	0.29	0.39	0.31
	Ordinary	0.18	0.26	0.24
	Lowest	0.11	0.15	0.11
		0.43 (e)	0.54 (e)	0.43 (e)
		0.32 (e)	0.37 (e)	0.36 (e)
		0.21 (e)	0.23 (e)	0.18 (e)
Anhwei	Highest	0.30	0.20	0.20
	Ordinary	0.21	0.15	0.16
	Lowest	0.15	0.10	0.10
		0.40 (e)	0.30 (e)	0.30 (e)
		0.30 (e)	0.22 (e)	0.22 (e)
		0.20 (e)	0.18 (e)	0.18 (e)
Fukien	Highest	0.50	0.48	0.53
	Ordinary	0.38	0.33	0.38
	Lowest	0.25	0.21	0.26
		0.63 (e)	0.60 (e)	0.70 (e)
		0.50 (e)	0.43 (e)	0.53 (e)
		0.36 (e)	0.33 (e)	0.38 (e)
Chêkiang	Highest	0.37	0.27	0.28
	Ordinary	0.25	0.20	0.20
	Lowest	0.16	0.14	0.14
		0.47 (e)	0.39 (e)	0.38 (e)
		0.34 (e)	0.29 (e)	0.26 (e)
		0.25 (e)	0.23 (e)	0.20 (e)

		Gold & Silver Smiths	Copper and Tin Smiths
Metropolitan Area	Highest	$0.40	$0.38
	Ordinary	0.26	0.25
	Lowest	0.11	0.12
Chihli	Highest	0.36	0.36
	Ordinary	0.21	0.19
	Lowest	0.10	0.10
Kirin	Highest	0.56	0.54
	Ordinary	0.43	0.36
	Lowest	0.25	0.26
Shantung	Highest	0.50	0.35
	Ordinary	0.41	0.27
	Lowest	0.30	0.23
Honan	Highest	0.39	0.32
	Ordinary	0.26	0.22
	Lowest	0.21	0.18
Shansi	Highest	0.25	0.33
	Ordinary	0.18	0.25
	Lowest	0.12	0.18
Kiangsu	Highest	0.63	0.42
	Ordinary	0.37	0.30
	Lowest	0.20	0.16
Anhwei	Highest	0.37	0.30
	Ordinary	0.27	0.20
	Lowest	0.18	0.15
Fukien	Highest	0.64	0.55
	Ordinary	0.44	0.40
	Lowest	0.29	0.29
Chêkiang	Highest	0.41	0.34
	Ordinary	0.27	0.26
	Lowest	0.19	0.15

		Painters	Carvers & Engravers	Leather Tanners
Metropolitan Area	Highest	$0.40	$0.42	$0.30
	Ordinary	0.26	0.30	0.24
	Lowest	0.12	0.14	0.11
		0.50 (e)	0.50 (e)	0.40 (e)
		0.34 (e)	0.40 (e)	0.34 (e)
		0.24 (e)	0.28 (e)	0.22 (e)
Chihli	Highest	0.29	0.31	0.32
	Ordinary	0.17	0.17	0.18
	Lowest	0.03	0.08	0.09
		0.42 (e)	0.47 (e)	0.45 (e)
		0.26 (e)	0.27 (e)	0.19 (e)
		0.18 (e)	0.19 (e)	0.19 (e)
Kirin	Highest	0.58	0.71	0.80
	Ordinarg	0.56	0.56	0.76
	Lowest	0.31	0.44	0.47
		0.82 (e)	0.05 (e)	0.98 (e)
		0.68 (e)	0.92 (e)	0.90 (e)
		0.50 (e)	0.85 (e)	0.82 (e)
Shantung	Highest	0.24	0.21	0.27
	Ordinary	0.20	0.26	0.22
	Lowest	0.16	0.20	0.18
		0.34 (e)	0.42 (e)	0.37 (e)
		0.31 (e)	0.33 (e)	0.32 (e)
		0.26 (e)	0.28 (e)	0.23 (e)
Honan	Highest	0.24	0.30	0.26
	Ordinary	0.18	0.28	0.19
	Lowest	0.14	0.18	0.13
		0.36 (e)	0.42 (e)	0.38 (e)
		0.30 (e)	0.35 (e)	0.32 (e)
		0.26 (e)	0.30 (e)	0.25 (e)
Shansi	Highest	0.22	0.28	0.18
	Ordinary	0.17	0.18	0.12
	Lowest	0.13	0.13	0.07
		0.35 (e)	0.41 (e)	0.26 (e)
		0.28 (e)	0.29 (e)	0.21 (e)
		0.21 (e)	0.22 (e)	0.16 (e)
Kiangsu	Highest	0.38	0.51	0.45
	Ordinary	0.23	0.33	0.28
	Lowest	0.11	0.16	0.18
		0.54 (e)	0.61 (e)	0.80 (e)
		0.38 (e)	0.50 (e)	0.36 (e)
		0.21 (e)	0.31 (e)	0.30 (e)
Anhwei	Highest	0.30	0.32	0.30
	Ordinary	0.22	0.21	0.20
	Lowest	0.18	0.10	0.14
		0.40 (e)	0.42 (e)	0.40 (e)
		0.32 (e)	0.29 (e)	0.32 (e)
		0.20 (e)	0.21 (e)	0.20 (e)
Fukien	Highest	0.55	0.60	0.53
	Ordinary	0.41	6.40	0.41
	Lowest	0.25	0.25	0.25
		0.67 (e)	0.80 (e)	0.68 (e)
		0.52 (e)	0.53 (e)	0.55 (e)
		0.35 (e)	0.37 (e)	0.38 (e)
Chêkiang	Highest	0.27	0.36	0.24
	Ordinary	0.20	0.27	0.16
	Lowest	0.14	0.17	0.12
		0.38 (e)	0.44 (e)	0.33 (e)
		0.29 (e)	0.35 (e)	0.26 (e)
		0.24 (e)	0.27 (e)	0.22 (e)

		Matting Weavers	Servants		Coolies	Printers
			Boys	Maids		
Metropolitan Area	Highest	$0.24	$5.00	$4.00	$0.30	$0.30
	Ordinary	0.12	3.00	2.00	0.20	0.25
	Lowest	0.10	2.00	1.00	0.10	0.13
		0.30 (e)				0.40 (e)
		0.24 (e)				0.35 (e)
		0.20 (e)				0.26 (e)
Chihli	Highest	0.21	4.90	3.03	0.32	0.32
	Ordinary	0.13	2.52	1.78	0.23	0.17
	Lowest	0.09	1.48	0.88	0.14	0.09
		0.32 (e)				0.46 (e)
		0.20 (e)				0.29 (e)
		0.20 (e)				0.19 (e)
Kirin	Highest	0.62	6.32	3.30	0.70	0.59
	Ordinary	0.48	5.05	2.55	0.45	0.47
	Lowest	0.28	3.10	1.70	0.35	0.29
		0.88 (e)				0.90 (e)
		0.75 (e)				0.80 (e)
		0.65 (e)				0.70 (e)
Shantung	Highest	0.19	2.35	1.50	0.26	0.25
	Ordinary	0.14	1.82	1.00	0.21	0.18
	Lowest	0.10	1.20	0.70	0.17	0.13
		0.28 (e)				0.35 (e)
		0.24 (e)				0.29 (e)
		0.18 (e)				0.25 (e)
Honan	Highest	0.20	4.60	2.55	0.30	0.24
	Ordinary	0.14	2.28	1.52	0.21	0.17
	Lowest	0.10	1.30	0.94	0.17	0.13
		0.32 (e)				0.36 (e)
		0.25 (e)				0.29 (e)
		0.21 (e)				0.25 (e)
Shansi	Highest	0.18	3.10	2.67	0.29	0.23
	Ordinary	0.14	2.20	2.10	0.23	0.13
	Lowest	0.09	1.00	1.43	0.16	0.07
		0.24 (e)				0.41 (e)
		0.19 (e)				0.23 (e)
		0.13 (e)				0.16 (e)
Kiangsu	Highest	0.48	5.20	3.30	0.48	0.45
	Ordinary	0.30	2.90	1.80	0.30	0.28
	Lowest	0.16	1.50	1.00	0.17	0.15
		0.34 (e)				0.57 (e)
		0.32 (e)				0.37 (e)
		0.22 (e)				0.24 (e)
Anhwei	Highest	0.20	4.33	2.00	0.28	0.30
	Ordinary	0.15	2.33	0.80	0.20	0.20
	Lowest	0.10	1.00	0.50	0.14	0.13
		0.30 (e)				0.40 (e)
		0.24 (e)				0.30 (e)
		0.18 (e)				9.22 (e)
Fukien	Highest	0.41	5.63	4.13	0.54	0.55
	Ordinary	0.29	4.25	3.00	0.39	0.39
	Lowest	0.18	2.38	1.50	0.25	0.24
		0.52 (e)				0.70 (e)
		0.37 (e)				0.52 (e)
		0.27 (e)				0.35 (e)
Chêkiang	Highest	0.25	4.50	2.80	0.48	0.25
	Ordinary	0.19	2.80	1.80	0.34	0.20
	Lowest	0.12	1.50	1.00	0.21	0.14
		0.32 (e)				0.35 (e)
		0.28 (e)				0.29 (e)
		0.20 (e)				0.22 (e)

Reference.—Chinese Economic Monthly, February, 1924.

WOMAN, THE STATUS OF.—Woman, in China, occupies a totally different sphere from that of man; a sphere which, though it must of necessity touch that of man at certain points, should be kept as separate as possible. At the early age of seven, according to the practice of the ancients, 'boys and girls did not occupy the same mat nor eat together'; and this is still carried to such an extent that a woman's clothes should not hang on the same peg as a man's nor should she use the same place to bathe in. The finical nonsense that all this engenders is something absurd; it is not even proper for a woman to eat with her husband. Amongst the lower classes, fortunately, the proprieties in this respect are more honoured in the breach than in the observance, and it is a pleasant sight to see a labourer and his wife partaking together of their frugal meal; common-sense and the exigencies of common life getting the better of over-strict orthodox regulations.

Woman is made to serve in China, and the bondage is often a long and bitter one: a life of servitude to her parents; a life of submission to her parents-in-law at marriage; and the looking forward to a life of bondage to her husband in the next world, for she belongs to the same husband there, and is not allowed, by the sentiment of the people, to be properly married to another after his death. The birth of a son frees her to a certain extent from the degradation of her position, for it promotes her to some degree, within the house only, of equality with her husband. All these restrictive customs are based on the idea that woman occupies a lower plane than man: he is the superior, she the inferior; as heaven is to earth, so is man to woman. All her bringing up is with the aim of teaching her perfect submission to the paramount authority of man; for she ought to have no will of her own: her will must be in complete subjection to his. Does her husband have friends at his house? She is invisible, a nameless thing, for it would be an insult for a visitor to enquire after his host's wife. Do the gentlemen require female society? The absurd seclusion of respectable women drives them to seek it in the company of the courtesans, who, in order to fit them for their life, are educated in music, and taught such accomplishments as will render their society more acceptable; reminding one of the position held by the Grecian *hetæræ*.

Of so little account is woman in China, that a father, if asked the number of his children, will probably leave out the girls in reckoning; or, if he has no boys, his reply will be 'only one girl,' said in such a tone of voice, as to call forth the sympathy of his listener for his unfortunate position.

In the very great majority of cases the girls are not taught to read or write; not, as was the case with some of our great-grandmothers, for fear they should learn how to write love-letters (for the *billet-doux* does not flourish in China), but for the simple reason that it is useless for girls to learn to read (see EDUCATION). Embroidery, plain sewing, the manufacture of tiny shoes for her cramped-up feet, 'golden lilies,' as they are euphemistically termed, and interminable gossip, fill up the lady's uneventful life, not even broken by the pleasure of a daily walk, for she must be closely shut up in her sedan if she ventures out on a call. The chivalry of the West, with its modern Christianised crystallisation of *place aux dames* and other mottoes of polite conduct where the weaker sex is concerned, is utterly unknown, as witness the brutal chaff, descending sometimes even to obscenity, whenever a young girl or lady is seen in the street: every man makes a point of turning round and staring at her; no matter how respectable she may be, some boisterous fun is made of her pretty face; she has to run the gauntlet of jeers from a crowd of rough men, all the worse to bear on account of her usual seclusion from all out-door life, and as her small feet handicap her pace, her rude reception is reduced to a slow torture.

No fashionable mother in England, lost to all the instincts of natural affection, who sacrifices her daughter in marriage to position or wealth, but will find a counterpart in nearly every Chinese mother and father, who no more think of taking their daughter's feelings into consideration than they would think of asking her to fly. Shut up in the 'inner apartment,'—the Chinese equivalent of the Indian zenana, though not such a horrible imprisonment as the latter—the young maiden, as she blossoms into womanhood, has but little chance of seeing her future husband.

As the Chinese poet sings:—

'A mien severe and eyes that freeze,
Become the future bride;
No whispering underneath the trees,
Ere yet the knot be tied.'

But it would not be human nature were such stolen pleasures not to be found sometimes amongst the sweets of life for a Chinese girl; and if she chance to have picked up a little knowledge of the Chinese printed character, her novel reading will occasionally give her natural feelings such a fillip as to develop the latent instincts of affection and enable her to burst through some of the prudery of the unnatural system of Confucianism.

Woman, The Status of

Human nature is the same the wide world over, and Chinese boys' and girls' hearts are cast in the same mould as those of the West; but, unfortunately, girls' hearts here, like their feet, are cramped and distorted out of all shape and recognition. Every tendency towards love between man and woman is immoral, and to be repressed, and, being repressed in its natural and pure direction, takes an unnatural one; for many a Chinese girl or woman has to be content with the position of a secondary wife; her husband having married his first—legitimate one—from family policy, may select his secondary or subsequently-taken wives, from pure affection. Women are sometimes thus rescued from an immoral life and brought into a home; but a dwelling where several wives usurp the place which ought to be reserved for one, falls far short of the English conception of the word home. Sometimes the husband distributes his 'weaker vessels' into as many different houses as there are wives, in order to minimise or prevent altogether the jealousies or bickerings which often ensue when all live in one house. In the latter case they are sometimes distributed through the house, which must be a large one. Apropos of this is the Chinese proverb, 'one key makes no noise, but two keys create a jingling.'

Notwithstanding all the disadvantages under which women labour in China, they at times rise superior to them, and, pushing past all the obstacles in their path, take a foremost position, not only in the state, but in the humbler sphere of the family, as well as in the more difficult one of letters and literature.

In some Chinese works, passages are found which show that the respective authors look upon marriage, occasionally at all events, as we in the West do, for instance:—

'They ate together of the same animal and joined in supping from cups made of the same gourd; thus showing that they now formed one body, were of equal rank, and pledged to mutual affection.'

'The ceremony of marriage was intended to be a bond of love between two of different surnames'—after which this passage goes on to speak of ancestor-worship, etc.

Whatever affection a girl may feel for her own family must receive a wrench on her marriage, for she is after that important event almost entirely lost to her own kin and transferred to that of her husband. In fact, so far is this carried that, should her intended die, it is an act of virtue for the girl to leave her own people, and embosom herself in the bereaved household, there to live in subjection to the deceased's mother till death joins the couple whom the fates kept separate on earth.

A woman can never marry twice,—legitimately, that is to say —a man falling in love with a widow, may take her as a concubine. A woman only once rides in a red sedan, and only then if she is being married as a legal, that is a first, wife.

A high type of virtue for a woman, in some parts of China, is to commit suicide on the death of her husband or intended; in some cases the relatives force her to do it, in hopes of the *éclat* and the erection of a stone portal, which a representation of the case will probably cause the Government to sanction. Remaining a perpetual so-called widow without ever being married (in the event of her intended dying), is another strong recommendation for these monuments to virtue! What wonder that in some places the girls band themselves together never to marry, and, to prevent being forced into matrimony, commit suicide!

The lower classes have more freedom of action in some respects; that is to say, they are not confined to the house, but, as the exigencies of their life demand it, they go about in public to perform their duties: seamstresses sit at the street corners, repairing clothes; farmers' wives assist in field operations; servants go about the streets and make purchases; domestic slave-girls run errands; grass-cutters ramble up the hill-sides to cut the grass for fodder or fuel; villagers go from house to house of the big cities to gather pig's wash for food for these unsavoury quadrupeds; scavengers busy themselves in the narrow streets and crowded thoroughfares, to the discomfort of the foot passengers; tea-girls pick tea, seated at the doors of the tea hongs; beggars go in troops, or singly through the crowds; while the blind singing-girls, with their duennas, seek for hire; and the little sampans are manned by women and girls.

But the employment of women in outdoor pursuits differs in different parts of the country; in some places they are conspicuous by their absence, whilst in other places their engaging in labour, for which they are not so well fitted as man, renders their presence even more conspicuous. To one accustomed in Canton and neighbourhood to the constant presence of women in the fields and streets and on the river and sea, busy with various kinds of manual labour, it is strange to note their entire absence, with but trifling exceptions, in the country round Swatow.

The above paragraphs describe the conditions which obtained until recent years. Nowadays, women have much more freedom, may go out of doors, even unattended, go to school, or to theatres, etc., and may even have a voice in the choosing of their husbands.

References.—Faber, *The Status of Women in China; The Famous Women of China;* Safford, *Typical Women of China* (an abridgment of the Chinese work, *Records of Virtuous Women of Ancient and Modern Times*) ; *Chinese Recorder*, xxviii. 10-8.

WRITING.—As to the introduction of writing amongst the Chinese, it has been stated that:—

'Chinese writers, unable to trace the gradual formation of their characters (for, of course, there could be no intelligible historical data until long after their formation), have ascribed them to Huang Ti, one of their primitive monarchs, or, even earlier, to Fu-hsi. A mythical personage, Tsang-kieh, who flourished about B.C. 2700, is credited with the invention of symbols to represent ideas, from noticing the markings on tortoise-shell, and thence imitating common objects in nature.'

If the study of the origin of English words is interesting, that of Chinese, is, if anything, even more so. The mode of writing the character presents facilities for this study which are wanting in English. Here are hundreds and thousands of word pictures, some of them patent to the most casual glance, requiring scarcely a thought to elucidate them.

The Chinese divide their language into six classes; the first class, 'imitative symbols,' includes 608 characters, amongst them some of the first characters invented, but they have been modified by the exigencies of time and convenience in writing, the metal stylus having been replaced by the modern pencil, or brush, so that angular strokes have given place to curves, and circles to squares and oblongs, while parts of the original character have dropped out as the writing became more contracted. As a specimen of this class of character is the word for child, the rude picture having given way to the modern character 子 where the head, arms, and legs, in profile, are still visible. Again, the outline of three peaks, which was used to represent the idea of a hill, has been modified into the present form, 山. Yet again, the rude picture of an eye has changed into an upright oblong with two strokes in the middle, viz., 目, and so we might go on at great length.

The second class, which only contains 107 characters, is called 'symbols indicating thought.' These characters are formed by the combination of those of the previous class, for instance, the sun appearing above a line indicates the morning, as 旦.

The third class contains 740 characters, called 'combined ideas.' These ideographs are built up of two or three of the other symbols: for instance, 'sun' and 'moon' are put in juxtaposition to represent brightness, as 明; a boy and a girl together represent the idea good, 好: it is not good for man to be alone.

The fifth class is called 'uniting sound symbols,' containing 21,810 characters; nearly all words, it will thus be seen, belong to this class. They are formed of two distinct parts: one called the phonetic, giving the sound to the complex character thus formed, while the other component part of the character is 'formed of an imitative symbol,' as, for example, 鯉, a carp.

The sixth class contains 598 characters, and is styled 'borrowed uses,' including 'metaphoric symbols and combinations, in which the meaning is deducted by a fanciful accommodation.' As an example of this class there is the word for character, word, or letters (literature), 字, a child under a shelter—'characters being considered as the well-nurtured offspring of hieroglyphics.'

Besides this sixfold division there is likewise another sixfold division of Chinese characters, with respect not to their original formation but to their form, which may be compared to Roman, italic, or writing, German, Arabesque, and other forms used in English; for, though the correct form of writing Chinese approaches very nearly to the printed form, more so than in English, yet there are, besides this somewhat easy style of writing, a flowing hand, which requires special study, and a still more running hand, which is undecipherable to those unfamiliar with it. These two latter styles allow latitude, as in English writing, for the idiosyncrasies of the individual writer. In them, more especially in the latter of the two, contractions are largely availed of, the brush (Chinese pen) flies over the paper linking word to word somewhat in the style of shorthand writers in English. In short this running or 'grass writing' may be likened in some degree to shorthand, though many of the Chinese characters, even in it, are too complicated to permit of a rapid enough writing to constitute it shorthand. Neither of these styles is allowed to be employed in the Government examinations, where every character must be well formed, and no contractions used; but they are found necessary for business purposes. The books of large firms are kept most beautifully, very few contractions being used, but the ordinary business firms intersperse the more correct and formal characters with running forms to a greater or lesser extent. Scarcely any Europeans trouble themselves to learn thoroughly more than one style, if they even go as far as that.

Chinese writing is largely employed for ornamental purposes. The caligraphy of masters of the art, for it is an art in China, is highly prized, and commands a high price. Even the prosaic shop is ornamented with numerous scrolls, bearing poetical phrases, antithetical sentences, sometimes of high moral import, and even single words, beautifully engrossed, which line the bare brick walls, and are hung here and there. Fans are inscribed with poetic effusions and presented to friends, who treasure them as autographs. Some fine specimens of a fluent writer's skill are carved into the semicylindrical surface of a pair of nicely varnished split bamboos, and these form another embellishment for the mansions of the wealthy Chinese. The backs of combs, the end pieces of folding fans, porcelain vases, and numerous other objects, are all adorned with specimens of caligraphic skill, and most effective this ornamentation is; at times, the stiff, rigid forms of the seal character are employed; and at other times the rambling style of the rapid writer, with its bold dashes, firm curves, slender, spider-like threads connecting distant parts, thick down-strokes, and all the other elegancies, which constitute the beauty of Chinese writing, so highly appreciated by Chinese connoisseurs.

Chinese writing, when written carefully, is slow work at the best: its speed is comparable to the engrossing of a legal document by a lawyer's clerk with us; or again, one may liken the slow, laborious writing of the careful scribe to an attempt in English to write in print, while the rapid-running hand approaches nearer to our writing.

Although Chinese is not an alphabetical language, the Chinese writing is composed of simple strokes and dots, perpendiculars and horizontals, modified according to certain rules, conditioned by the position in which they are to appear; further, the more complex characters are built up of the simpler ones, some of the compound characters being formed of a combination of only two or three, while others may be the result of a union of half a dozen or more. A page of writing would present an unsymmetrical appearance were the original size of the component parts of the characters to be preserved. They are modified to suit their position—lengthened, shortened, compressed, enlarged, or diminished as necessary—the idea being that each character shall only occupy a given space.

'The Chinese have the greatest respect for any writing, and it no doubt enhances their contempt for us by noticing how we fail to reverence the written character, and, no doubt, they also fancy that we must indeed be barbarians and our writing not "that fairest jewel in heaven above or earth beneath" which theirs is, or we would doubtless take the greatest care that not a scrap of it should fall to the ground and be trodden under foot, or torn, or destroyed in any way but by fire, when the extremely punctilious will also go as far as to bury them deep in the earth in a sealed earthen vessel, or sink them to the bottom of the river.' Men go about the streets gathering up every scrap of paper on which there is the least bit of writing or printing, so that they may be destroyed by fire at certain places prepared for that purpose. These *chiffoniers* are paid by rich men. Little boxes will also be seen here and there along the streets, not only in Chinese cities but in Hongkong itself, with the four characters King sik tsz chí [*Ching hsi tzŭ chih*], 'Reverence printed (or written) paper' on them. These boxes serve as receptacles into which the passers-by, or neighbours, may stuff their refuse paper.

References.—Hopkins, *The Six Scripts;* Dyer Ball, *How to Write Chinese.*

ZOOLOGY.—Though China is a well-settled country, there are still vast tracts sparsely inhabited, and sufficiently different species of animals are found to make the study of zoology a pleasure, and the discovery every now and then of some new species lends a zest to its pursuit.

The Fauna in the South, in the Island of Hainan and a portion of the mainland, is tropical to some extent; but North China and Manchuria resemble, in their zoology, Corea and Japan.

Of monkeys, there are several varieties, some of most remarkable appearance; the Chinese train a few to perform tricks. Of bats, one list gives twenty species, belonging to nine genera. There are black and brown bears, as well as other varieties. The carnivora, though not such a pest as in India, are still common enough in some parts, and, in certain thickly-populated places, they are a cause of considerable apprehension to the natives. Amongst them may be mentioned the tiger (see TIGERS) ranging over large districts in the southern provinces; panthers, leopards, and tiger-cats are also not unknown. Wild cats are occasionally seen in Hongkong; civet cats, tree-civets, and martens, are found in China. The domestic cat is very common, a species of Angora cat being a pet in Peking. As to the dog, a glance at it reminds one of the pictures of Esquimaux dogs. These are known as 'chow' dogs, or 'wonks,' amongst foreigners, looking very pretty when pups, with their fluffy, yellow, black, or reddish hair, but they often deteriorate in appearance as they grow older, though this does not appear to be a general opinion, as they are sometimes made pets of by foreigners. The tongues and mouths of dogs and cats are often black or blue-black (see DOGS). Wolves, foxes, and racoon-dogs are common. The Chinese horses are ponies, and the cattle are also small; some of the latter have a hump. The water-buffalo is an uncouth, large, clumsy-looking animal, and is used for drawing the plough, as well as for other agricultural purposes; the milk supplied by the buffalo cow is richer than common cow's milk. The black tongue and mouth are also found in buffaloes (see BUFFALO). Yaks are found in Tibet and Kokonor. Sheep abound in the North, and goats all over China. Antelopes and deer of eleven varieties are known—deer are kept in gentlemen's grounds in China as well as in England—and many other genera of ruminants are included in China's fauna. Three varieties of the musk-deer may be mentioned. Mules and donkeys are largely used in the North as beasts of burden, and the wild ass, or onager, is to be found in Kokonor. The elephant, rhinoceros, and tapir, are to be met with in the forests of Yünnan; the wild boar in the North and in Chêkiang. Different varieties of pigs abound in the North and South, and pork is largely consumed by the Chinese. The camel is also a beast of burden in Manchuria, Mongolia, and Northern China. Among smaller animals may be mentioned weasels, otters (used for fishing, for which purpose they are trained), badgers, sable-ermine, pole-cats, stoats, sea-otters, moles, musk-rats, shrew mice, hedgehogs, marmots, and mole-rats.

There are many kinds of rodents. Hares and rabbits abound in some places, but are almost, if not entirely, unknown in others. There are ten or twelve kinds of squirrels known, as well as two genera of flying squirrels. Twenty-five species of rats (see RATS), and mice are known as existing in China, and all but three are peculiar to the country. One species has been named after Confucius (*mus Confucianus*), an honour which probably the sage would not appreciate were he aware of it, while another has been named after Koxinga, the conqueror of Formosa. The porcupine is supposed by the Chinese to use its quills as javelins to fling at its enemies, while the scaly ant-eater, or pangolin, is thus described by one sapient(!) Chinese writer:—

'Its shape resembles a crocodile; it can go in dry paths as well as in the water; it has four legs. In the day time it ascends the banks of streams, and, lying down, opens its scales wide, putting on the appearance of death, which induces the ants to enter between them; as soon as they are in, the animal closes its scales and returns to the water to open them: the ants float out dead, and he devours them at leisure.'

The great, white porpoise (*Delphinus chinensis*) is found in the estuary of the Canton river, and at Swatow, as well as in the Yangtzŭ. It is an amusing sight to watch one or two of them swimming for an hour or more just in front of a steamer. A species of fin-whale is found between Formosa and Hainan. Seals disport themselves on the coast of Liang-tung.

The lists of Swinhoe and David contain 200 species of mammalia; many more have been discovered since these lists were drawn up.

Of birds there have already been over 700 species described. ('The avifauna of the Yangtzŭ Valley comprises, at least . . . 359 species, of which 97 species are known to be migrant.') Vultures, eagles, and ernes are widespread; the golden eagle is trained by the Mongols for the chase; falcons are common in the streets of Peking, where they act as scavengers. Bustards, gledes, sparrow-hawks, night-hawks, and swallows, are all to be seen; of the latter bird there are 15 species. The feathers of kingfishers are used for decorative purposes (see KINGFISHER). The hoopoe, bee-eater, and cuckoo are all known, as well as 11 species of shrikes and many other birds, such as nut-hatches, tree-creepers, wall-creepers, wrens, chats, willow-wrens, and redstarts. There are great varieties of song-birds, such as the thrush and lark, of which the Chinese are very fond; for a Mongolian lark $25 will be given (see LARKS AND OTHER SONGSTERS). Amongst other birds may be named wagtails, orioles, jays (a most beautiful blue jay is found in Hongkong), magpies, choughs, crows, blackbirds, owls, mainahs (see LARKS AND OTHER SONGSTERS), robins, ouzels, tailor-birds, woodpeckers, parrots, 14 species of pigeons, gold and silver pheasants, and others; and poultry, of which the common fowl, the Shanghai and the diminutive white bantam are the best known. Some of the Chinese fowls appear to have black bones, owing to a thin membrane of that colour surrounding the bones. Besides these, are grouse, quails, francolins, partridges, snipe, cranes, plovers, curlews, herons, egrets, ibis, spoonbills, crackes, and rails. 'The Chinese ring-necked species of pheasant has been successfully introduced' into England (see PHEASANTS). Sixty-five species of webfooted birds are known as existing in China, amongst which are ten species of duck. The whole seacoast is alive with gulls, terns, and grebes; and swans, geese, and mallards are found in the inland waters. The mandarin duck, a native of the central provinces, is a beautiful object, having as brilliant a plumage as a parrot (see MANDARIN).

Alligators, though rare, are to be found in one or two spots, and probably they, or crocodiles, were more numerous formerly than now. Snakes abound, many of which are deadly (see SNAKES). Frogs are most abundant, and are eaten (see FROGS). Tortoises and turtles are plentiful. 'The ichthyology of China is one of the richest in the world, though it may be so more from the greater proportion of food furnished by the waters than from any real super-abundance of the finny tribes.' By this time about a thousand different kinds are known as being found in China. It is said that in Macao one may have a different kind of fish for breakfast every morning in the year if one will eat every sort which the Chinese use as food. Amongst Chinese fish may be mentioned mackerel, goby, herrings, sharks, rays, saw-fish, sturgeon, huge skates, garoupa, sole, mullet, the white rice-fish (or silver-fish as it is called in some of the languages of China), shad, and carp (52 species of the last). The gold-fish is a most grotesque specimen of nature's caricatures, imitated or fostered by artifice and selection, the eyes are like goggles, sticking out of its head, and tail and fins are tufted and lobed to a most extraordinary extent. 'Gold-fish were first known in China'; they were 'brought to Europe in the seventeenth century.' The Chinese say their original habitat was Lake Tsau in the province of Ngan-hwui (see GOLD-FISH). Another variety is the silver-fish. We cannot complete the list of Chinese fish, but we may mention pipe-fish, of a red colour, gar-pike with green bones, beautiful parrot-fish, sun-fish, eels, file-fish, bream, gudgeon, anchovies, perch, and gurnard. There are great varieties of shellfish; oysters are common, so are prawns, shrimps, crabs, craw-fish, and kingcrabs, the last strange-looking objects. Amongst curiosities, may be mentioned the hammer oyster (*Avicula* [*malleus*] *vulgaris*), found at Swatow. (See also CORMORANT FISHING.) 'Chinese ichthyology is still almost unknown.'

'The insects of China are almost unknown to the naturalist.' There are hundreds of different kinds of spiders, some with bodies as large as small birds, which spin their webs from tree to tree, high up in the air. Locusts, centipedes, scorpions, silkworms, fireflies, glow-worms, and beetles; and many other numerous species of insects have their home in China (see INSECTS).

References.—Williams, *Middle Kingdom*, i. 313-54; *Proceedings of the Zoological Society*, May, 1871; Oustalet et David, *Les Oiseaux de la Chine*; *Report of the British Association for the Advancement of Science*, 1845 (fishes); Donovan, *Natural History of the Insects of China*. Also see articles on 'Silk' in this book, and *Encyclopædia Sinica* under the various sections on Zoology.

GLOSSARY

Attap. A Malay word signifying the kind of mats, or leaves made into these mats, used to cover a house, or even for the walls of a house.

Bogue. The mouth of the Canton River. The word is derived from the Portuguese Bocca. Bocca Tigris is a translation of the Chinese Fú-mún [Hu-mên], 'The Tiger's Mouth.'

Candarin is the $\frac{1}{10}$ of a mace, worth 1⅗ cents silver, or nearly a farthing and a half.

Cash was the current coin of the Chinese, ten or more of which were worth a cent silver, and forty a penny English. The old monetary unit of China.

Catty $= 1\frac{1}{3}$ lbs. avoirdupois. Plural—catties.

Cent $= \frac{1}{100}$ of a dollar (silver) worth ¼*d.* (but varies with the rate of exchange).

Chang = chöng is ten Chinese feet (ch'ek or ch'ik), the latter being approximately 14 English inches (but varies for different kinds of measures).

Character. A Chinese written or printed word, or a syllable in a compound word.

Chow has a number of meanings as used by foreigners in China. It is not a Chinese word. Amongst its meanings is that of 'food,' or 'to eat.'

Chunam. A mixture of lime and earth beaten into a hard substance, and used in place of cement and concrete.

Coir is the external husk of the cocoa-nut palm which is made into ropes, cordage, brooms, brushes, etc.

Colloquial is the language as spoken, differing in different parts of China. In character colloquial the Chinese characters are employed, or adaptations of them. In romanised colloquial the sound of the Chinese is represented by an English spelling, *i.e.* by the letters of our (or Roman) alphabet.

Concubine. A secondary wife not holding legally the status of the chief or fully legitimate wife, but whose children are legitimate and who shares as a widow in her husband's estate. Socially she is looked on as a wife, and there is no stigma attached to her position, though subordinate and inferior to the first wife, and a position not desired by well-to-do people for their daughters.

District is a division of country, geographical and political, somewhat equivalent to an English county, and occasionally so styled. A district city is the capital city of a district where the district magistrate (the ruler of the district) resides. Its analogue in our country is a county town.

Dollar always means a silver dollar in the East, constantly fluctuating in value, but varying in the course of years between extremes of, *e.g.* 7*s.* 1⅝*d.* (just after the war of 1914-8) and 1*s.* 6*d.* (just before the war). The normal value is reckoned at 2*s.* 0*d.* A cent is $\frac{1}{100}$ part of this.

Dutch-wife is a kind of pillow or frame-work, made of bamboo, and used to rest the legs on in bed in hot weather to keep them cool.

Fish-maws are the stomachs of certain kinds of fish used as food.

Fú means a city of the second order, *i.e.* a prefectorial one. This class of city has now been included in that of the *Hsien*, or District Magistracy.

Go-between is a broker, or brokeress in betrothals, marriages, business transactions, the sale and purchase of slave-girls, and of women and boys, etc.

Governor. Each province has a Governor.

Hong is a mercantile firm.

Hsiu-ts'ai=síú-ts'ai=saú ts'oí was the Chinese B.A. under the monarchical system.

Joss-paper is paper stamped with holes to represent money, or folded into the shape of sycee and scattered on the roadside at funerals especially, or burned in worship at the temples, or at the front doors of shops or houses, the incineration, according to the Chinese idea, transmuting it into real money in the spirit world, to which it is wafted by the flames. Joss is from Deos, the Portuguese for God.

Joss-sticks=incense-sticks. The various substances used for the manufacture of incense are made into a paste and rolled round the upper part of a tiny stick of bamboo. The lower part of this, being uncovered, serves to support it upright in a censer full of ashes or in any hole, while the upper part burns slowly, giving out a fragrant smell.

Kam-kwat (or kumquat) is a fruit of the orange or citron tribe, of a golden-reddish colour, and about the size of half a finger.

Kowtow. The nine knockings of the forehead on the ground distributed equally over three kneelings on both knees, which is an act of worship or reverence before the Gods of heaven and earth, and an act of reverence or respect accorded to the sovereign officers of Government. It is also rendered to parents on their birthdays, and to superiors in age or station by their inferiors or by those younger in years. It was officially abolished on the establishment of the Republic.

Kung-héí-fát-ts'oí [*kung ho fa ts'ai*]=' Congratulations: may you gather wealth.'

Li has two meanings as thus spelled in English: first, a Chinese mile= $\frac{1}{3}$ English mile; and second, $\frac{1}{10}$ of a candarin. Lis, candarins, mace, and taels are used in expressing the weights of medicine as well as of silver.

Lictors. See Yamên lictors.

Mace, $\frac{1}{10}$ of a tael, in money worth 14 cents silver, or 3½*d*. As a measure of weight a trifle less than $\frac{1}{7}$ of an ounce avoirdupois.

Meiling. A range of mountains at the north of the Canton province.

Moon=Month. The same word is used in Chinese for both moon and month, being also employed very generally by the foreign resident in China to designate the Chinese month, which is a lunar one, to differentiate it, without the need of any explanation, from the foreign month.

New Dominion=Turkestan.

New Territory=The latest addition of land to the Colony of Hongkong, leased from the Chinese Government.

Pei Yang Squadron is the Northern Squadron.

Provincial Governor. Every province has a Governor. Some are at present under military Governors.

Riverine ports. Usually applied to the treaty ports, on the Yangtzŭ, such as Chinkiang, Kiukiang, etc.

Runners. See Yamên.

Sampan. A small boat.

Sên, or rather Shên, or Shêng, means city, a provincial city.

Shan-sz [*Shên shih*] are the gentry and elders and literary graduates of a village, or of a locality in a city. They are invested by custom, etc., with a quasi-authority over their fellow-villagers and neighbours.

Shên-nung. A mythical (?) emperor of China, deified as the God of Agriculture.

Soy. A sauce made from beans, largely used by the Chinese.

Sycee. Lumps of silver cast into a curious shape said to be like a shoe, but requiring a strong imagination to see the likeness. These were, and are used instead of coins, as the Chinese till recently have had no silver coins in general use.

Tanka. The boat population, descendants of aborigines, despised by the landsmen, and with customs and habits of their own, scarcely ever intermarrying with the dwellers on shore.

Taotai. An Intendant of Circuit under the Manchu régime.

Tartar-General. Generals who had the banner-men (see Army), etc., under their command at certain important cities, such as Canton, Foochow, and Hangchow, in the monarchical administrative system abolished in 1912.

Tiao. A string of cash=1000 (but usually 960 to 990 only), worth about $1 silver (see Dollar).

Yamên. An official residence, comprising within its boundaries prisons, court-houses, offices, gardens, etc., etc.

Yamên lictors. A species of police attached to a yamên.

Yamên Runners. A species of process-servers or bailiffs, etc., attached to a yamên.

Yen is the Japanese pronunciation for yüan or yün, which is used as a name for the dollar by the Chinese.

Yin and **Yang**=Yum and yöng in Cantonese. The two principles of Nature from which everything is derived.

Viceroy, or Governor-General, had rule over one or two provinces usually. This was one of the offices abolished on the establishment of the Republic.

Wán means a bay. Kuangchouwan=Kuangchou Bay.

INDEX

Index

B

Index

C

Index

Index

Index

D

E

G

H

Index

Index

L

Index

N

O

P

Index

S

T

Index

U